MANAGING
SERVICES

MANAGING SERVICES

Marketing, Operations, and Human Resources

Second Edition

CHRISTOPHER H. LOVELOCK

*International Institute
For Management Development
(IMD)*

 Prentice-Hall International, Inc.

© 1992 by Prentice-Hall, Inc.
A Simon & Schuster Company
Englewood Cliffs, New Jersey 07632

Printed in the United States of America

10 9 8 7 6

ISBN 0-13-561572-0

Prentice-Hall International (UK) Limited, *London*
Prentice-Hall of Australia Pty. Limited, *Sydney*
Prentice-Hall Canada Inc., *Toronto*
Prentice-Hall Hispanoamericana, S.A., *Mexico*
Prentice-Hall of India Private Limited, *New Delhi*
Prentice-Hall of Japan, Inc., *Tokyo*
Simon & Schuster Asia Pte. Ltd., *Singapore*
Editora Prentice-Hall do Brasil, Ltda., *Rio de Janeiro*
Prentice-Hall, Inc., *Englewood Cliffs, New Jersey*

To the memory of
Daryl Wyckoff

Contents

II   UNDERSTANDING SERVICES: BREAKING FREE FROM INDUSTRY TUNNEL VISION

III   DESIGNING AND DELIVERING SERVICES

IV   MANAGING CAPACITY AND MANAGING DEMAND

VIII   STRATEGY AND INTEGRATION

PREFACE

The field of service management has been evolving rapidly in recent years. Both managers and academics are waking up to the fact that better management of service businesses — and of the service divisions of manufacturing firms — is vital to competitive success and, indeed, to economic development. It is not only customers who benefit from dealing with well-managed service organizations but also employees. The satisfaction they derive from their jobs is closely related to the quality of management and the way in which those jobs are defined.

In developing the second edition of *Managing Services: Marketing, Operations, and Human Resources,* I have been able to introduce new thinking, new examples, and the findings of recent research projects to complement some classic conceptual articles and cases. Among the 26 readings in this book, 17 are new to this edition, 4 have been substantially revised, and 5 are carried over from the first edition. Of the 15 cases, 7 are new, 2 have been revised, and 6 have been retained unchanged.

SCOPE OF THE BOOK

The value of a book of readings and cases lies not only in bringing together an array of materials previously published over several years in a variety of locations, but also in grouping them in meaningful clusters and in structuring the sequence in which they appear. The framework of this book reflects my experience in teaching courses in service management — initially at the Harvard Business School, subsequently in Harvard University Extension, and more recently at IMD during two years as a visiting professor.

As the title of this book suggests, effective management of service businesses requires the integration of three key functions — marketing, operations, and human resources. Each function can be examined independently, of course, but effective implementation requires ongoing coordination between them. In manufacturing firms, by contrast, marketing tends to be most heavily involved only after the product leaves the factory gates and it's the rare organization where production and operations personnel have direct contact with customers.

Managing Services is divided into eight parts:

- Part I — The Challenge of Services
- Part II — Understanding Services: Breaking Free from Industry Tunnel Vision
- Part III — Designing and Delivering Services
- Part IV — Managing Capacity and Managing Demand
- Part V — The Search for Service Quality
- Part VI — Adding Value Through Customer Service
- Part VII — The Human Dimension in Services Management
- Part VIII — Strategy and Integration

The early parts of the book provide an understanding of the service sector and a framework for analyzing service organizations. Later parts address specific management issues. Finally, Part VIII focuses on organizational issues and on how to integrate marketing, operations, and human resources.

With the exception of Part I, which is composed of readings only, the several readings in each part are followed by two or three cases. Brief synopses in front of each reading and case are designed to orient readers and help them to identify materials of particular interest. An index at the end of the book provides useful reference to key topics in both readings and cases.

ACKNOWLEDGEMENTS

By definition, a book of readings and cases is a collaborative effort. I'm very appreciative of the contributions made by each of the authors and co-authors of the materials in this book. Their names and affiliations will be found in the following section, "About the Contributors." I'm grateful, too, to the copyright holders for granting permission to reproduce previously published articles and cases.

Thanks are also due to the following reviewers: Cleveland Gilcrest, formerly of Merrimac College; Peter McClure, University of Massachusetts — Boston; Curtis McLaughlin, University of North Carolina; Mike Myers, DePaul University; and James Fitzsimmons, University of Texas — Austin, who provided valuable suggestions for enhancing the second edition. I'm grateful, too, to my secretary at IMD, Josiane Cosendai, and to Joanne Palmer at Prentice Hall for their help in bringing the volume to publication.

Over the years, many people have helped me in my teaching activities on services and have contributed helpful comments on my own cases and research output. My thanks are especially due to Gabriel R. Bitran, James L. Heskett, Theodore Levitt, David H. Maister, Christopher W. L. Hart, John A. Quelch, W. Earl Sasser, Sandra Vandermerwe, and Charles B. Weinberg. Earlier, I also benefitted significantly from collaborative work with John E. G. Bateson, Pierre Eiglier, and Eric Langeard. I have learned much, too, from discussions with my own students and with participants in IMD's executive programs.

My thinking has also been influenced in useful ways by the Marketing Science Institute and the American Marketing Association. MSI, initially under the leadership of Alden Clayton and Diane Schmalensee, has played a key role in facilitating research in services. And AMA, particularly under the presidencies of Stephen Brown and Leonard Berry, has helped to bring together academics and managers from different fields to discuss how marketing management in service businesses can be better integrated with other management functions.

Finally, I would like to pay special tribute to the late D. Daryl Wyckoff, a friend and colleague at the Harvard Business School, who died in 1985 at the age of 47. Daryl, who held the James J. Hill Chair of Transportation, was one of several Harvard faculty members who helped to pioneer the application of production and operations management techniques to service businesses. Having earlier taught Management of Service Operations at Harvard, Daryl was scheduled to take over the Service Management course from me in January 1985. My last memory of him is at a meeting we had in his office the previous December to discuss his plans for the course.

No one who had ever been in Daryl's office at Harvard could easily forget it. It epitomized his zest for life — which he knew might be cut short early — and his enthusiasm for his field. Glowering at the visitor from the opposite wall was a gold-framed oil portrait of James J. Hill, founder of the Great Northern Railroad. Decorative Chinese artifacts in red and gold, souvenirs of his visits to the Far East, hung from the high ceiling. A large poster advertised the Twentieth Century Limited as it was in the heyday of US rail travel. There were model trains and model aircraft, two of the latter bearing the colors of Midway Airlines of which he was a director. Linking his interest in both railroading and restaurants was a collection of British railway memorabilia, presumably acquired through his association with the Victoria Station restaurant chain, on whose board he also served.

Although visibly ailing on this occasion, Daryl spoke with enthusiasm about some innovations he planned for the course, including several sessions on service quality based on his own work in this field. His article, "New Tools for Service Quality," (reproduced in Part V of this book) had just been published and the two of us had used some of the concepts and tools it presented when teaching together in a corporate seminar some months earlier. Sadly, health problems prevented Daryl from teaching the course, and less than two months later he was gone. Had he lived, he would surely have had a major impact on how managers approach the task of improving service quality. The second edition of this book, like the first, is dedicated to his memory.

Christopher H. Lovelock
Lausanne, Switzerland

ABOUT THE CONTRIBUTORS

AUTHOR AND EDITOR

- **Christopher H. Lovelock** is visiting professor at the International Institute for Management Development (IMD) in Lausanne, Switzerland. He has had extensive experience working with service organizations. For 11 years, he was on the faculty of the Harvard Business School, where he developed courses in both Marketing of Services and Service Management. Dr. Lovelock has also held visiting appointments at MIT's Sloan School of Management, Stanford University, and the University of California at Berkeley. A native of Great Britain, he graduated with an MA in economics and a BCom degree from the University of Edinburgh, later obtaining an MBA from Harvard and a PhD from Stanford. He has written or co-authored twelve books and numerous articles and cases, including 7 of the readings and 11 of the cases reproduced in this second edition of *Managing Services: Marketing, Operations, and Human Resources.*

CONTRIBUTING AUTHORS

- **George R. Beam** was formerly a casewriter at the Colgate Darden Graduate School, University of Virginia.

- **Leonard L. Berry** holds the J.C. Penney Chair of Retailing Studies and is Director of the Center for Retailing Studies at Texas A&M University.

- **Gabriel R. Bitran** is Professor of Management at the Sloan School of Management.

- **Richard B. Chase** is professor of operations management and director of the Center for Operations Management, Education, and Research at the University of Southern California.

- **Sydney Coffey** was formerly a graduate student at the University of North Carolina.

- **Linda R. Cooper** is vice president and director of Consumer Affairs at The First National Bank Chicago.

- **Shauna Doyle** was formerly a research assistant at the Harvard Business School.
- **Peter F. Drucker** is Clarke Professor of Social Sciences at the Claremont Graduate School in California.
- **Susan C. Faludi** is a staff reporter at *The Wall Street Journal.*
- **Sula Fiszman** was formerly a research assistant at the Harvard Law School.
- **James R. Freeland** is a professor of business administration at the Colgate Darden Graduate School, University of Virginia.
- **Paul E. Green** is S. S. Kresge Professor of Marketing at the Wharton School, University of Pennsylvania.
- **Christian Grönroos** is a professor at the Swedish School of Economics in Helsinki, Finland.
- **James. L. Heskett** is UPS Foundation Professor of Business Logistics at the Harvard Business School.
- **Johannes Hoech** is a consultant with McKinsey & Co.'s office in San Jose, California.
- **Michael Kelly** is a writer and journalist in Chicago.
- **Karen L. Katz** is a consultant at Index Group, Inc., Cambridge, Massachusetts.
- **Sheryl E. Kimes** is assistant professor at the School of Hotel and Restaurant Administration, Cornell University.
- **Jane Kingman-Brundage** is president of Kingman-Brundage, Inc., a consulting firm based in North Salem, N Y.
- **Robert J. Kopp** is associate professor at Babson College.
- **Blaire M. Larson** is a consultant at Index Group, Inc., Cambridge, Massachusetts.
- **Richard C. Larson** is professor of electrical engineering and computer science at the Massachusetts Institute of Technology.
- **David H. Maister** is president of Maister Associates, a Boston consulting firm specializing in management of professional service firms.

- **Curtis R. McLaughlin** is professor of business administration at the University of North Carolina.
- **A. Parasuraman** is Federated Professor of Marketing at Texas A&M University.
- **Rocco Pigneri** was formerly a research assistant at the Harvard Business School.
- **Frederick F. Reicheld** is a vice president in the Boston office of Bain & Company and leads the firm's customer retention practice.
- **Tom Richman** writes for *Inc.* magazine.
- **Stephen S. Roach** is principal and senior economist at Morgan Stanley & Co. in New York.
- **W. Earl Sasser, Jr.** is professor of business administration at the Harvard Business School.
- **Marsha Scarbrough** is director of product development for Courtyard by Marriot.
- **Daniel Schechter** is in the Department of Psychology at the University of Maryland.
- **Leonard A. Schlesinger** is associate professor of business administration at the Harvard Business School.
- **Roger W. Schmenner** is visiting professor at the International Institute for Management Development (IMD), on leave from the School of Business at Indiana University.
- **Douglas Shifflet** is president of D. K. Shifflet & Associates, a marketing consulting firm.
- **Sandra Vandermerwe** is professor of marketing and service management at the International Institute for Management Development (IMD).
- **Jerry Wind** is Lauder Professor of Marketing at the Wharton School, University of Pennsylvania.
- The late **D. Daryl Wyckoff** was James J. Hill Professor of Transportation at the Harvard Business School at the time of his death in 1985.
- **Valarie A. Zeithaml** is associate professor at the Fuqua School of Business Administration, Duke University.

MANAGING
SERVICES

PART I
The Challenge of Services

Are Services Really Different?

CHRISTOPHER H. LOVELOCK

The service sector is in a state of rapid change, reflecting a variety of factors from regulatory changes to globalization and use of new technologies. The net effect is increased competition. A clear understanding of the distinctive characteristics of service management, free of traditional misconceptions, is needed if service businesses are to succeed in the future.

"Stop the World, I Want to Get Off!" was a popular British song in the 1960s. Service managers of all nationalities in the 1990s can be forgiven if they sometimes feel the same way. Old ways of doing things have ceased to be either effective or profitable, reflecting the fast-changing shape and composition of service industries and radical changes in the ways in which they do business.

Consider some of the indicators:

- New airlines come and go while some long-established carriers adopt major changes in route structure and operational strategy, are merged out of existence, or are liquidated.

- Financial service firms expand into banking, brokerage, and insurance activities that were previously denied them, as brokers and insurance companies muscle in on the bankers' turf.

- Realty firms and restaurants, once the epitome of local "mom-and-pop" operations, go nationwide.

- Large manufacturing firms derive a third or more of their revenues from the service businesses that they operate.

- The old healthcare system of hospitals and doctors' offices is augmented—and in part displaced—by a complex array of delivery systems that now embraces health maintenance organizations, out-patient surgicenters, chains of small walk-in medical centers, and expensive diagnostic equipment that travels by truck from one location to another.

- A tiny island nation, Singapore, creates one of the world's largest and most successful airlines as well as a world-class telecommunications service.

- Service organizations once owned by governments are transformed into private enterprises, not only in Europe but around the world.

- Customers everywhere decry an alleged decline in service quality across a broad cross section of industries, lamenting loss of the personal touch, frequent failures, and uncaring employees.
- Acting without the assistance of service personnel, consumers use modern technology to conduct financial or other information-based transactions across thousands of miles, accurately and almost instantaneously.

FORCES FOR CHANGE

Why is the service sector in such a state of flux? What are the forces for change and the ingredients for success? Many factors underlie the ongoing transformation of service management that is taking place in both developed and developing nations. They include changes in both government regulations and professional standards, privatization, technological innovation, the growth of franchising, expansion of leasing and rental businesses, a growing focus on services within manufacturing firms, pressures on public and nonprofit organizations to act in more businesslike ways, and globalization of service firms.

Like the factors underlying any revolution, some of the origins of today's service sector revolution go back a number of years, whereas others reflect a chain of relatively recent events that continues to unfold. Let's look at each of these dynamics in turn.

Changing Patterns of Government Regulation

Many service industries have traditionally been highly regulated. Regulatory agencies have mandated price levels, constrained distribution strategies by limiting transportation route structures and banking service areas, and, in some instances, prescribed product attributes.

Since the late 1970s there has been a trend in the United States toward complete or partial federal deregulation in several major service industries. Changes in the regulatory environment are taking place at the state level, too.

Reduced government regulation, especially in the United States, has already eliminated or minimized many constraints on competitive activity in such industries as airfreight, airlines, railroads, and trucking; banking, securities, and insurance; and telecommunications. Barriers to entry by new firms have been dropped in many instances, geographic restrictions on service delivery have been reduced, there is more freedom to compete on price, and existing firms often find themselves able to expand into new markets or new lines of business. Fears have been expressed, however, that if successful firms become too large — through a combination of internal growth and acquisitions — then there may eventually be a decline in the level of competition.

Other nations have been watching the American experience with interest and making changes of their own. Substantial relaxations of regulations on trade in services between the 12 member nations of the European Community are anticipated after 1992.

But not all changes represent relaxations of government regulations. Many steps continue to be taken to strengthen consumer protection laws, to improve safety and public security, and to protect both workers and the physical environment.

Relaxation of Professional Association Standards

Another American initiative, also copied elsewhere, has been government or legal pressure to force professional associations to remove or relax bans on advertising and promotional activities. Among the types of professionals affected by such rulings are accountants, architects, doctors, lawyers, and optometrists, whose firms or practices now engage in much more vigorous competitive activity than previously. The freedom to engage in advertising, promotion, and overt selling activities is, after all, essential in bringing innovative services, price cuts, and new delivery systems to the attention of prospective customers.

Privatization

The term "privatization" was coined in Great Britain to describe the policy of returning nationalized industries to private ownership. Led by Britain, privatization of public corporations has been moving ahead at speed in a number of countries. The transformation of such service operations as national airlines, telecommunication services, and natural gas utilities into private enterprise services has led to restructuring, cost cutting, and a more market-focused posture.

Similar results have been achieved by government agencies — often at the local level — which have subcontracted certain services (such as trash removal) to private firms. Another form of privatization occurs when nonprofit organizations, notably hospitals in the United States, convert to for-profit status.

Computerization and Technological Innovation

New technologies are radically impacting service operations and altering the ways in which many services do business with their customers — as well as what goes on behind the scenes. Data-based services, such as information and financial service firms, are seeing the nature and scope of their businesses totally transformed by the advent of national (or even global) electronic delivery systems. But technological change affects many other types of services — from airfreight to hotels to retail stores. Technology facilitates creation of new or improved services, ability to maintain more consistent standards through centralized customer service departments, replacement of personnel by machines for repetitive tasks, and greater involvement of customers in operations through self-service.

Growth of Franchising

Franchising has become a very popular method of financing the expansion of multisite service chains that deliver a consistent service concept. The growth of franchising is seeing large franchise chains replace or absorb a vast array of atomistic service businesses in fields as diverse as bookkeeping, car rentals, haircutting, muffler repair, photocopying, plumbing, quick service restaurants, and real estate brokerage. Among the requirements for success are creation of

mass media advertising campaigns to promote brand names nationwide (and even worldwide), standardization of service operations, formalized training programs, an ongoing search for new products, continued emphasis on improving efficiency, and dual marketing programs directed at customers and prospective franchisees, respectively.

Expansion of Leasing and Rental Businesses

Leasing and rental businesses represent a marriage between service and manufacturing businesses. To an increasing degree, both corporate and individual customers find that they can enjoy use of a physical product without actually owning it. Fixed costs may be transformed into semivariable costs, and there may be tax benefits, too.

Long-term leases may involve use of the product alone — such as a truck — or provision of a host of related services at the same time. In trucking, for instance, full-service leasing provides almost everything but the driver, including painting, washing, maintenance, tires, fuel, license fees, road service, substitute trucks, and driver safety programs. Personnel, too, can be rented rather than employed full time, as evidenced by the growth of temporary personnel services.

Manufacturers as Service Providers

Service profit centers within manufacturing firms are transforming many well-known companies in fields such as computers, automobiles, and electrical and mechanical equipment. Ancillary services once designed to help sell equipment — including consultation, credit, transportation and delivery, installation, training, and maintenance — are now offered as profit-seeking services in their own right, even to customers who have chosen to purchase competing equipment.

Many large manufacturers have become important players in the financial services industry as a result of developing credit financing and leasing divisions. Service profit centers often contribute a third or more of the revenues earned by such well-known "manufacturers" as IBM and General Electric.

Businesslike Behavior by Nonbusiness Organizations

Financial pressures facing public and non-profit organizations are forcing such organizations to cut costs, develop more efficient operations, and pay more attention to customer needs and competitive activities. Faced, in many instances, with declining sources of free or inexpensive labor (such as that provided by volunteers or members of religious orders), many nonprofit agencies are having to take a more businesslike approach to recruitment, training, and motivation of managers and staff members.

Nonbusiness organizations are also rethinking their product lines, adding profit-seeking services such as museum shops, retail catalogs, restaurants, and consultancy; being more selective about the market segments they target; and adopting more market-oriented pricing policies.[1]

Globalization

The internationalization of service companies is readily apparent to any tourist or business executive traveling abroad. Airlines and airfreight companies that were formerly just domestic in scope now have foreign route networks. Numerous financial service firms, advertising agencies, hotel chains, fast-food restaurants, car rental agencies, and even hospital groups now operate on several continents. This strategy — which has not always been successful — may reflect a desire to serve existing customers better, to penetrate new markets, or both.

Many well-known service companies in the United States are owned by foreign investors, but American service businesses have also been expanding abroad. Franchising, of course, allows a service concept developed in one nation to be delivered around the world through distribution systems owned by local investors.

Internationalization of service businesses is being facilitated by free-trade agreements (such as those between Canada, Mexico, and the United States, and between the member nations of the European Community), but there are fears lest barriers be erected to impede trade in services between free-trade blocs and other nations, as well as between the blocs themselves.

DO SERVICES REALLY MATTER?

"What a silly question!" you may say. After all, more than two-thirds of the gross national product in many industrialized nations is now devoted to service industries (including the activities of government and nonprofit organizations). And yet some commentators still seem to hold the view that services that do not add value to a physical product (such as freight transportation) neither contribute to wealth nor create value.

This view of services as parasitical was shared by two writers at opposite ends of the political spectrum, Adam Smith and Karl Marx. Today, many people still seem to have a "macho" view of manufacturing as a symbol of strength and see services as a symbol of lost focus and industrial decline. Depending on one's values, some services may seem frivolous or a wasteful use of resources, but the same is also true of many manufactured products.

As late as the American presidential election of 1988, some candidates were still trotting out the tired old canard that a service economy is one in which we all take in each other's laundry.

Myths and Misconceptions

A number of erroneous myths continue to circulate about the service sector and it is worth demolishing them.[2]

Myth No. 1: A Service Economy Produces Services At the Expense of Other Sectors. What is sold reflects what customers (of all types) wish to buy. A more salient issue is whether the goods and services purchased were created domestically or by foreign suppliers. Many service industries are, in fact, major purchasers of manufactured products — consider airlines, hospitals, car rental firms, hotels, and the back offices of financial service firms.

Myth No. 2: Service Jobs Are Low-Paying and Menial. This view reflects headlines like the one in *The New York Times* that announced,

"Big Mac Supplants Big Steel." It implied that as high-paying manufacturing jobs declined, new employment opportunities were most likely to be found in low-paying, menial service positions. In fact, both sectors of the economy offer high wage and low wage positions, and some of the highest earnings today are to be found in skilled white-collar service occupations.

Myth No. 3: Service Production Is Primarily Labor Intensive and Low in Productivity. The service sector is at least as capital intensive as the manufacturing sector and many service industries are highly technological. Further, many service industries lend themselves to productivity increases great enough to fuel continuing real growth in per capita income.

Myth No. 4: The Growth of Government Is the Main Reason that the Service Sector Is Dominant. Since 1980, more than 50% of Americans have been working in private service industries. In many other countries with a larger public sector than the US, government agencies run service businesses — ranging from telephone service to airlines to healthcare — which are already in private hands (or in the process of being privatized) elsewhere.

Myth No. 5: Services Are Responses to Marginal Demands that People Satisfy Only After They Meet Their Product Needs. Research shows that people value services at least as much as manufactured products and that they buy them in much less cyclical patterns.

Myth No. 6: Service Businesses Are Composed Primarily of Cottage Industries and Mom & Pop Operations. A comparison of the Fortune Service 500 against the Fortune Industrial 500 quickly dispels that myth, since the two groups are very closely matched in terms of assets, employees, and operating revenues.[3]

Importance of Both Sectors

In truth, a modern economy should be based upon a healthy balance between manufacturing and services industries — reflecting the needs and comparative advantages of the nation in question. The fact is that many services are more than just useful facilitating ac-

tivities for manufactured products: They may spell the difference between success and failure in a marketplace where demanding customers expect services along with their goods. Other services add enormously to the quality of modern life, including health care, passenger transportation, lodging, telecommunications, the arts and entertainment and, of course, education.

Speaking of education, business educators must take some of the blame for the lack of understanding of service industries. Until the early 1980s, business school curricula paid little or no attention to service management. Few textbook examples and few case studies highlighted service firms — the focus was consistently on manufacturing businesses and their products. Today, the situation is changing (perhaps you are reading this book as part of a course on service management), but there is still a way to go before the majority service sector is placed on an equal basis with its smaller cousin, manufacturing.

Perhaps part of the explanation for the historic lack of interest in services management among business school professors may have reflected a lack of understanding of the differences involved in managing service and manufacturing organizations. In fact, the differences are significant — and they are as important for managers as they are for educators and students.

KEY DIFFERENCES BETWEEN MANUFACTURING AND SERVICE ORGANIZATIONS

Service industries have dominated most Western industrialized economies for more than a quarter of a century. Yet policy makers, economists, and management educators have tended to focus on manufacturing, agriculture, and natural resources. It's only recently that the challenging task of how to manage service organizations more effectively has finally begun to attract the attention that it deserves.

Are the management skills developed in manufacturing organizations *directly* transferable to service organizations? I think not. Although there are some generalizable principles, it's my belief— and that of many other researchers and practitioners — that management tasks in the service sector differ from those in manufacturing industries in several important respects.[4] As we shall see later in some of the readings, the differences are most marked in what might be termed the "front office," where customers interface with the service operation. "Back office" operations, by contrast, may be sealed off from the customer and managed in ways that are often not unlike a manufacturing plant. The major focus of this book will be on managing the front-office aspects of service businesses.

Among the characteristics distinguishing services management from manufacturing management are the nature of the product, the involvement of customers in the production process, greater importance of the time factor, difficulties in achieving and maintaining quality standards, the absence of inventories, and the structure of distribution channels. Let's look briefly at each, while recognizing that not all of these generalizations apply with equal force to all services.

Nature of the Product

Leonard Berry captures the distinction well when he describes a good as "an object, a device, a thing," in contrast to a service which is "a deed, a performance, an effort."[5] Marketing a performance (which in the case of rental services may involve an object like a power tool or a car) is very different from attempting to market the physical object itself. For instance, in car rentals, customers usually reserve a particular category of vehicle rather than a specific model, paying more attention to such elements as location and appearance of pickup and delivery facilities; availability of inclusive insurance, cleaning, and maintenance; provision of free shuttle buses at airports; availability of 24-hour reservations service; hours when rental locations are staffed; and quality of service provided by customer-contact personnel.

Although services often include tangible actions — such as sitting in an airline seat, eating a meal, or getting damaged equipment repaired — the service performance itself is basically an *intangible*. Like all performances, services are timebound and experiential, even though they may have lasting consequences.

Customer Involvement in Production

Performing a service involves assembling and delivering the output of a mix of physical facilities and mental or physical labor. Often customers are actively involved in helping to create the service product — either by serving themselves (as in a fast-food restaurant or laundromat) or by cooperating with service personnel in settings such as hair salons, hotels, colleges, or hospitals.

As we shall see, services can be categorized according to the degree of contact that the customer has with the service organization.

People as Part of the Product

In high-contact services, customers not only come into contact with service personnel, they may also rub shoulders with other customers (literally so, if they ride a bus or subway during the rush hour). The difference between two service businesses often lies in the quality of employees who deliver the service. Similarly, the type of customers who patronize a particular service business helps to define the nature of the service experience. As such, people become part of the product in many services.

Quality Control Problems

Manufactured goods can be checked for conformance with quality standards long before they reach the customer. But when services are consumed as they are produced, final "assembly" must take place under real-time conditions. As a result, mistakes and shortcomings are harder to conceal. Further variability is introduced by the presence of service personnel and other customers. These factors make it hard for service organizations to control quality and offer a consistent product.

No Inventories for Services

Because a service is a deed or performance rather than a tangible item that the customer keeps, it cannot be inventoried. Of course, the necessary equipment, facilities, and labor can be held in readiness to create the service, but these simply represent productive capacity, not the product itself. Unused capacity in a service business is rather like having a running tap in a sink with no plug: the flow is wasted unless customers (or possessions of theirs requiring servicing) are present to receive it. And when demand exceeds capacity, customers are likely to be sent away disappointed, since no inventory is available for backup. An important task for service managers, therefore, is to find ways of smoothing demand levels to match capacity.

Importance of the Time Factor

Many services are delivered in real time. Customers have to be present to receive service from airlines, hospitals, haircutters, restaurants, and many other types of organizations. There are limits as to how long customers are willing to be kept waiting for service to be provided; further, that service must be delivered expeditiously so that customers do not spend longer receiving service than appears reasonable to them. Even when the service operation takes place in the back office, customers have expectations about how long it should take to complete the task — whether it be repairing a machine, completing a research report, cleaning a suit, or preparing a legal document.

Different Distribution Channels

Unlike manufacturing firms, which require physical distribution channels for moving goods from factory to customers, service businesses either use electronic channels (as in broadcasting or electronic funds transfer) or else combine the service factory, retail outlet, and point of consumption into one. In the latter instance, service firms often find themselves responsible for managing customer-contact personnel (rather than contracting out the retailing task to intermediaries). They may also have to manage the consumption behavior of cusomters who enter the service factory to ensure that the operation runs smoothly and that one person's

behavior doesn't irritate other customers who are present at the same time.

IMPLICATIONS FOR MANAGEMENT

Although no service organization is affected by all of these factors, few are untouched by any of them — and none will remain untouched. There's an old Chinese curse that wishes its recipient, "May you live in a time of change." Caught up in the turmoil of change, many managers must yearn for the good old days, when the behavior of competitors was more predictable — even implicitly agreed upon, when customers or clients were less demanding and more loyal, when employees could be relied on to spend their entire careers within the same organization (or at least the same industry), when government regulations and professional standards discouraged both new market entrants and service innovations, and when established ways of creating and delivering services remained just that: established.

Many of the factors described above have served to stimulate competition, which, in turn, places a premium on encouraging innovation and improving cost efficiency. New technologies often provide solutions to both problems. But technology may require heavy capital investments, redefinition of jobs, and hiring or retraining of workers to ensure that the necessary human resources are available to operate and manage the new technical resources.

To recover these upfront investments, the service firm needs higher profits. Some profit improvement may come from cutting operating costs, but revenues also need to be increased. Effective marketing may enable the firm to grow by improving and expanding its product line, targeting new market segments, seeking new distribution and delivery systems, and employing both pricing and advertising strategies to expand its market share.

Increased size of operations — whether through internal growth, franchising, or mergers — allows service suppliers to achieve economies of scale. Capital expenditures can then be spread over a larger base of market transactions. At the same time, the firm can hire staff specialists to provide a long-term, strategic perspective and expert assistance to operating managers whose principal focus is on solving day-to-day problems.

Not every service organization is growing: Some have cut back their operations in order to focus on the needs of specific types of customers, to specialize in certain types of services, and/or to reduce costs. Yet the survivors in most service industries will have to transform themselves in order to remain competitive and to incorporate modern technology.

The service organization that emerges from this transformation will require a different and more sophisticated approach to management than its predecessor.

NOTES

[1]For indepth coverage of this topic, see CHRISTOPHER H. LOVELOCK and CHARLES B. WEINBERG, *Public and Nonprofit Marketing,* 2nd edition. South San Francisco: The Scientific Press, 1989.

[2]Four of the myths in this section are drawn from RONALD K. SHELP, "The Service Economy Gets No Respect," *Across The Board,* February 1984.

[3]CHRISTOPHER H. LOVELOCK, "Biz Schools Owe Students Better Service," *Wall Street Journal,* February 10, 1984.

[4]For additional viewpoints, see CHRISTIAN GRONROOS, *Service Management and Marketing: Moments of Truth in Service Competition.* Lexington, Mass.: D.C. Heath/Lexington Books, 1990; and Leonard L. Berry and A. Parasuraman, *Marketing Services: The Quality Imperative.* New York: The Free Press, 1991.

[5]LEONARD L. BERRY, "Service Marketing is Different," *Business,* May–June, 1980.

Service Management: A Management Focus for Service Competition

CHRISTIAN GRÖNROOS

Effective service management requires a change in focus — from creating product quality and utitlity to creating total quality and utility across every aspect of the customer relationship. It also requires a shift in thinking from short-term transactions to long-term relationships. Managers need to understand six principles that depart from the approaches traditionally found in manufacturing.

UNDERSTANDING SERVICES AND SERVICE MANAGEMENT BECOMES IMPERATIVE TO SUCCESS

Services have rapidly grown in importance in the USA as well as in most western societies. From half to over two-thirds of the economic activity in these economies take place in the service sector. Moreover, a constantly growing percentage of the active workforce is employed within the service sector (see Table I). However, today it is not only so-called service firms which need to understand the nature and the management of services. Services go far beyond what is traditionally called the "service sector." For many manufacturers of goods, it has become difficult to find a basis for a competitive advantage which distin-

guishes a given firm from the competition. "Everyone can produce the goods" is a saying which makes more and more sense. Therefore, some other means of differentiating the offerings have to be found or developed; otherwise there is nothing other than price to turn to. And a low price strategy works only for a firm which consistently over time can maintain a cost advantage over the competition. Hence, the figures in Table I, as in any statistical measure of the size and importance of services to economies, is a huge understatement of reality.

Pursuing a service strategy can be a way of differentiating the offering and creating a competitive advantage. This, however, demands a thorough understanding on the part of management of the characteristics of ser-

Reprinted with permission from the International Journal of Service Industry Management.

TABLE I
Employment within the Service Sector —
Percentage of the Total Workforce

	1970 %	1980 %	1986 %
OECD Total	49.4	56.4	60.9
OECD Europe	42.9	50.1	55.4
Canada	61.4	66.0	69.6
USA	61.1	65.9	69.3
UK	52.0	59.7	66.6
Norway	53.6	62.5	66.1
Denmark	50.7	62.4	65.9
Sweden	53.5	62.2	65.5
France	47.2	55.4	61.3
Finland	42.8	51.8	57.0
Italy	40.3	47.8	56.0
West Germany	42.9	50.3	53.7
Spain	37.4	44.7	51.8
Japan	46.9	54.5	57.1

SOURCE: [1]

vices and the nature of service competition, i.e., management must understand that traditional management methods and common wisdom from manufacturing may often be a trap in service contexts. In this article, some unique principles of managing in service competition will be put forward, so that managers in service firms and manufacturers of goods alike can avoid falling into a management trap and focus their interest on the right issues. This new focus we call service management [cf. 2-14]. We offer the following definition of service management [14]. Service management is to:

1. understand the utility of value customers receive by consuming or using the offerings of the organization and how services alone or together with physical goods or other kinds of tangibles contribute to this utility, that is, to understand how total quality is perceived in customer relationships and how it changes over time;

2. understand how the organization (personnel, technology and physical resources, systems and customers) will be able to produce and deliver this utility or quality;

3. understand how the organization should be developed and managed so that the intended utility or quality is achieved; and

4. make the organization function so that this utility or quality is achieved and the objectives of the parties involved (the organization, the customers, other partners, the society, etc.) are met.

This is a fairly exhaustive way of describing what service management is. A shorter definition may be more selling, but it is less complete. Albrecht offers the following definition: "Service management is a total organizational approach that makes quality of service, as perceived by the customer, the number one driving force for the operation of the business" [10, p. 20]. It can be said with even fewer words, as Schneider and Rentsch [15] do. They argue that firms that apply service management principles consider "service as *the* organizational imperative."

A CHANGE OF FOCUS

A service management perspective changes the general focus of management in service firms as well as in manufacturing firms [16]:

1. from the product-based utility to total utility in the customer relationship [17];

2. from short-term transactions to long-term relationships;

3. from core product (goods or services) quality (the technical quality of the outcome) to total customer perceived quality [18] in enduring customer relationships, and

4. from production of the technical solution as the key process in the organization to developing total utility and total quality as the key process.

Two major basic shifts in management thinking are implicit in the service management principles as compared to a traditional management approach from manufacturing. These are (1) a shift from an interest in internal consequences of performance to an interest in the external consequences, and (2) a shift from a focus on structure to a focus on process. These two shifts are of paramount importance. A service strategy requires both to be successfully implemented.

Service management as a management philosophy is predominantly related to managing processes where the underlying structures are of less importance, but of course are not unimportant. If the structures take over, flexibility of operations and handling customer contacts suffer, and frequently the flow of information from customers, suppliers, distributors and other stakeholders through the front line to top management and back suffers [cf. 19]. Moreover, if structure is expected to govern behavior, managers and supervisors frequently do not fully appreciate their responsibility for continuously encouraging their subordinates, and the motivation of the employees suffers. The perceived service quality deteriorates, and customers are probably lost.

Traditionally, in mainstream management thinking from the industrial era economies of scale and productivity of capital and labor are considered the driving forces behind a profitable business. Hence, the internal efficiency of the business is the main focus of management. In managing service competition, the complicated characteristics of services and the nature of service production and consumption (e.g., the inseparability of production from consumption and the role of customers as co-producers, as well as the broad interface between the service provider and the customers) make the external efficiency of the business, i.e., customer satisfaction with the operations of the organization, the focal·point of management [3, 4, 6, 11, 13, 14]. The internal efficiency and cost considerations are still of great importance, of course, but customer satisfaction and external efficiency come first. The concepts of "internal efficiency" and "external efficiency" used in this sense were introduced by Ekholm [20].

SIX PRINCIPLES OF SERVICE MANAGEMENT

The focus on process and external consequences leads to some more or less unique principles of service management, which change the traditional approaches to (1) the business logic and what drives profit, (2) decision-making authority, (3) organizational structure, (4) supervisory control, and (5) reward systems; and when there is a shift in the focus of reward systems different tasks and types of achievements than traditionally have to be (6) monitored and measured. These six principles of service management are summarised in Table II.

The Business Logic

As has been discussed in some detail in the present chapter, the general economic focus or the business logic is shifted from managing internal efficiency of the productivity of capital and labor to managing total efficiency based on a notion that customer perceived quality drives profit. Scale economies may or may not be a strategically reasonable objective; but it is never sound, and it is always dangerous, automatically to consider economies of scale a source of profitability. Rather, an uncritical pursuit of large-scale production and of potential benefits of scale economies easily turns an operation into disaster. Frequently, the opportunities of developing "market economies" [cf. 21] can be used to create a solid competitive advantage and a basis for profitable operations. And because of the nature of services and service competition, some sort of pursuit of "market economies" should always be incorporated in the strategic approach.

Service management appreciates the critical importance to success of managing customer relationships and customer perceived quality. The internal efficiency needed to function profitably is an inevitable issue, but it is not a prime issue. It must be totally integrated with external efficiency issues and geared to managing customer perceived quality. As soon as the internal perspective starts to dominate, interests in costs and managing productivity without a simultaneous consideration of the quality implications will take over; and issues related to creating and maintaining excellence and revenue generation become secondary and get less or no management attention.

TABLE II
Principles of Service Management

Principle		Remark
(1) The profit equation and business logic	Customer perceived service quality drives profit	Decisions on external efficiency and internal effiency (cost control and productivity of capital and labor) have to be carefully integrated
(2) Decision-making authority	Decision making has to be decentralized as close as possible to the organization-customer interface	Some strategically important decisions have to be made centrally
(3) Organizational focus	The organization has to be structured and functioning so that its main goal is the mobilization of resources to support the front-line operations	This may often require a flat organization without unnecessary layers
(4) Supervisory control	Managers and supervisors have to focus on the encouragement and support of employees	As little legislative control procedures as possible, although some may be required
(5) Reward systems	Production of customer perceived quality has to be the focus of reward systems	All relevant facets of service quality should be considered, although all cannot always be built into a reward system
(6) Measurement focus	Customer satisfaction with service quality has to be the focus of measurement of achievements	To monitor productivity and internal efficiency, internal measurement criteria may have to be used as well; the focus on customer satisfaction is, however, dominating

SOURCE: [14]

Decision-making Authority

Because of the characteristics of services, e.g., the inseparability of critical parts of production and consumption, and the facets of customer perceived service quality, e.g., the demand for flexibility and recovery capabilities, decisions concerning how a service operation is supposed to function have to be made as close as possible to the interface between the organization and its customers. Ideally, the front-line employees involved in the moments of truth (to use a concept introduced in the service management literature by Normann [4, 10]) of the interactions of

this interface should have the authority to make prompt decisions. Otherwise sales opportunities and opportunities to correct quality mistakes and avoid quality problems in these moments of truth are not used intelligently, and become truly wasted moments of opportunity to correct mistakes, recover critical situations and achieve re-sales and cross-sales. If these moments go totally unmanaged, service quality deteriorates quickly and becomes mediocre [6]. Of course, a front line contact employee, e.g., a bank clerk, cannot always have the professional knowledge required if a customer wants, for example, a sophisticated financial solution for an international business. However, he or she should nevertheless keep the decision-making authority, for example, to ask for assistance of back office or staff professionals.

However, if the employees in customer contacts (and support employees serving the front line) are not given authority to think and make decisions for themselves, they become victims of a rigid system. As Gummesson [22] says in a straightforward manner: "You can *stupify* your front line service personnel by making them robots with discretion to handle only a limited number of standard operations. Or you can *empower* them to handle also deviations...thus being more efficient"(pg. 85). "Empowering" the personnel is a powerful way of mobilizing the energy which human beings have. It means that the employees are encouraged, and trained, to recognize the diversity of customer contact situations and to use their judgment to take care of the situations and solve problems following from deviations from standard procedures so that customer satisfaction is created. Thus, the continuously occurring moments of truth become well-utilized "moments of opportunity."

Thus, operational decision making needs to be decentralized as much as possible; normally more than one first considers possible. However, as Ivar Samrén, CEO of SAS Service Partners, points out, not all decision making can and should be decentralized. According to him, chaos may follow in an organization if strategic decisions, for example, concerning overall strategies, business missions and service concepts, are not made centrally [23]. The unique knowledge among front-line personnel of important aspects of the business which is vital to making such strategic decisions should, however, always be used in centrally occurring decision making. First of all, this improves the decisions, and second, it creates a better commitment to these decisions among those who in the final analysis will have to live with them and execute them.

The "local" manager, be it the head of a branch in a network organization, such as a bank or hotel chain, or the head of a department in a manufacturer of goods which produces services, such as technical service, deliveries, claims handling or customer training, has of course the overall responsibility for his or her subordinates. He/she is also responsible for the total operation of the "local" organization. Hence, these people have dual responsibilities, one towards the customers, one towards the corporation: the "local" manager is responsible for perceived service quality towards the customers and for profitability towards the corporation [24].

Organizational Focus

Traditionally, the organizational focus is to build up and maintain a structure where management is executed through processes involving legislative control. This often creates a lack of flexibility, fuels centralization tendencies throughout and is easily a hindrance to the vertical flow of information in the organization. In the final analysis, it urges people not to think for themselves, especially not to make decisions which are not endorsed by rules and regulations formulated by management. Organizationally, service management shifts the focus away from structure and control procedures to process and how improved external efficiency and customer perceived quality, with acceptable internal efficiency, are achieved. This, in turn, requires a more flexible organizational solution, where mobilization of resources — management, staff, back office, etc. — to support customer contact activities is imperative. The organizational structure which suits this requirement may differ from situation to situation, but some common principles can be identified. For example, the organization has to be much flatter than traditionally [e.g., 10].

Supervisory Control

(Or rather supervisory support.) In traditional management approaches supervisory systems are very much related to monitoring how the organization, and its various parts, is capable of performing its tasks according to predetermined standards (legislative control). If such standards are met, the employee or group of employees has performed satisfactorily, and is perhaps rewarded for this.

However, such a supervisory control system does not fit the nature of services and service production very well. By their very nature, services most often cannot be completely standardized. Moreover, if employees are to deliver quality services, guidelines and visions and a substantial degree of flexibility to meet the special wishes of customers or successfully to recover negative situations in the buyer-seller interactions, a looser structure is preferable to rigidly defined standards. Only the technical quality aspects of services can be well monitored by standards. The functional quality aspects related to how the service process and the service encounter are perceived, which from a competitive edge standpoint is so important, are not very well suited to traditional standards. Functional quality-creating performance cannot easily, if at all, be monitored by comparing it to predetermined standards. Instead, service management requires that the supervisory focus has to be on the encouragement of employees and on their support. This may require new management methods. In order to make this approach to supervisor control, or rather supervisory support, work, the previously mentioned concept of "empowering" the employees is essential. However, empowering by providing front-line employees with adequate skills and decision-making authority to perform well is not always enough. Davis argues that in addition to being empowered, the employees have to be "enabled" to produce quality services: "Customer satisfaction depends upon the *enabling* tools provided the customer service representatives" [25, p. 13]. And in the final analysis, a supportive service culture [e.g., 14, 15, 26] guides the employees so that they make correct decisions on their own without interference by supervisors. Management by service culture replaces supervision by legislative control and direct interference by managers and supervisors in organizations where the personnel are empowered and enabled to think for themselves and make decisions of their own for the benefit of the organization's customers.

Reward Systems

Normally, reward systems are geared to the focus of supervisory control. What is monitored can be measured, although naturally not all, if any, of the tasks and factors that are controlled are geared to reward systems. And the other way round, what is measured can most easily be controlled and rewarded. However, as well as a shift in supervisory focus, a corresponding shift of focus of rewarding is called for. Generally speaking, service management requires that producing perceived service quality at some level — excellent or otherwise acceptable — should be rewarded, rather than mere compliance with predetermined standards. All too frequently, service firms make their employees do stupid things by rewarding the wrong actions: e.g., number of meals served in a restaurant or the cost of food (internal efficiency) instead of the satisfaction of patrons (external efficiency). By such reward systems, management and front-line employees alike are forced to shift their interest from customer satisfaction to internal issues. Customer perceived quality most certainly suffers.

Measurement Focus

What is controlled and perhaps rewarded has first to be measured, one way or the other. The focus here has, of course, also to be shifted, or at least expanded. The ultimate signs of success are customer satisfaction with total perceived quality and the bottom line. Thus, according to service management principles, in order to enable management to establish service-oriented supervisory approaches and reward systems, customer satisfaction with service quality, as well as tasks which boost satisfaction, have to be measured. Just measuring how standards are met and the bottom line is not enough, although internal efficiency criteria may have to be used as well, so that the productivity of capital and labor is kept under control. The external efficiency criteria always dominate, however, and monitoring customer satisfaction must never be surpassed, only supported by other measures.

CONCLUSIONS

The customer relationships of service organizations have special features which easily make well-known management methods less effective, sometimes even dangerous. The business logic is different in service. If this is not taken into consideration, mistakes are easily made. Some distinct service management principles have to be understood and applied. A failure to do this may result in mediocre service quality as perceived by the customers, a weaker competitive position, less motivation for service among the personnel and, finally, lost customers.

NOTES AND REFERENCES

[1]OECD, *Labour Force Statistics,* 1988.

[2]LUND, K. and KNUDSEN, K., *Introduktion til Service Management* (Introduction to Service Management), Civilokonomernes Forlag, Copenhagen, 1982.

[3]GRÖNROOS, C., *Strategic Management and Marketing in the Service Sector,* Marketing Science Institute, Cambridge, Mass., 1983.

[4]NORMANN, R., *Service Management,* Wiley, New York, 1984.

[5]CLEMENT, J., *Ledelse af Servicevirksomheder* (Management of Service Firms), Civilokonomernes Forlag, Copenhagen, 1985.

[6]ALBRECHT, K. and ZEMKE, R., *Service America!,* Dow Jones-Irwin, Homewood, Ill., 1986.

[7]HESKETT, J. L., *Managing in the Service Economy,* Harvard Business School Press, Cambridge, Mass., 1986.

[8]LEHTINEN, J. and STORBACKA, K., *Palvelujohtaminen* Service Management), Jarmo R. Lehtinen, Veikkola, Finland, 1986.

[9]MILLS, P. K., *Managing Service Indutries: Organizational Practices in a Post-industrial Economy,* Ballinger, New York, 1986.

[10]CARLZON, J., *Moments of Truth,* Ballinger, New York, 1987.

[11]ALBRECHT, K., *At Amercia's Service,* Dow Jones-Irwin, Homewood, Ill., 1988.

[12]BOWEN, D. E. and SCHNEIDER, B., "Service Marketing and Management: Implications for Organizational Behavior," *Research in Organizational Behavior,* Vol. 10, 1988.

[13]ZEMKE, R., *The Service Edge,* NAL Books, New York, 1989.

[14]GRÖNROSS, C., *Service Management and Marketing: Managing the Moments of Truth in Service Competition,* Lexington Books, Lexington, Mass., 1990.

[15]SCHNEIDER, B. and RENTSCH, J., "The Management of Climate and Culture: A Future Perspective," in Hage, J. (Ed.), *Futures of Organizations,* Lexington Books, Lexington, Mass., 1987.

[16]This change of focus and the corresponding service management principles, as well as many other related issues, such as marketing, developing service offerings, internal marketing and creating a service culture are described in depth in [14].

[17]Focusing on the total utility instead of more narrowly on the product-based utility means that the value added for the customers following from other elements of the customer relationships is, from a strategic and operational point of view, considered equally important as the value, or utility, inherent in the product (a good or a service) itself.

[18]Service quality research has demonstrated that total service quality as perceived by customers has two dimensions, namely the quality of the outcome of the service production process (*what* the customer perceives he or she has received from having used the service) and the quality of the process (*how* the customer perceives the buyer-seller interaction or the service encounter). Grönross [e.g. 3, 14] calls the former quality dimension technical quality of the outcome and the latter functional quality of the process.

[19]PETERS, T., "Restoring American Competitiveness: Looking for New Models of Organizations," *The Academy of Management Executive,* No.2, 1988.

[20]EKHOLM, B-G., *The Business Idea and its Life Path,* research report, Fourth Annual Strategic Management Society Conference, Philadephia, Penn., October 1984.

[21]HESKETT, J. L., "Lessons in the Service Sector," *Harvard Business Review,* March-April, 1987.

[22]GUMMESSON, E., "Nine Lessons on Service Quality," *Total Quality Management,* February, 1989.

[23]SAMRÉN, I., "Service Strategies in Practice," *European Research,* ESOMAR, February, 1988.

[24]This thesis has been formulated in this form as an internal service management rule by another highly successful Scandinavian service firm, Svenska Handelsbanken, one of the consistently most service-oriented and customer-oriented, and most profitable, banks operating nationwide in Sweden. In this corporation the phrase, "moment of opportunity", as it has been used here was coined.

[25]DAVIS, F. W. JR., "Enabling Is as Important as Empowering: A Case for Extended Service Blueprinting," in *Service Excellence: Marketing's Impact on Performance,* papers from the Eighth Annual Services Marketing Conference, American Marketing Association, Chicago, Ill., October, 1989.

[26]SCHNEIDER, B., "Notes on Climate and Culture," in Venkatesan, M., Schmalensee, D. M. and Marshall, C. E., (Eds.), *Creativity in Services Marketing: What's New, What Works, What's Developing,* American Marketing Association, Chicago, Ill., 1986.

A Basic Toolkit for Service Managers

CHRISTOPHER H. LOVELOCK

Service management involves integration of three functional perspectives — marketing, operations, and human resources. Key tools for examining service situations from this multifunctional perspective include: identifying different types of service processes; analysis of service systems; breaking down service products into core and supplementary elements; and flowcharting service delivery to establish linkages between front stage and backstage activities.

"Where should we start?" asks a manager faced with a complex situation. Trying to get a handle on service management situations requires clear thinking, which puts a premium on finding useful frameworks for analysis and practical tools for crafting strategy. In services, no single management function can be effective if it operates in isolation, so the relevant tools and concepts have to be meaningful to managers from different functional backgrounds.

Three management functions should be involved in nearly all facets of creating and delivering services — marketing, operations, and human resources. This is not to suggest that other functions, such as accounting and finance, are unimportant. Indeed, they play vital roles monitoring the financial health of the business, ensuring that both capital and daily operational activities are properly funded, and documenting day-to-day transactions. But except for billing, payment, and credit activities, these other functions involve little customer contact.

Since the output of a service business tends to be intangible and ephemeral, managers can't inventory raw ingredients and components as they are processed, assembled into finished products, packaged, shipped through distribution channels, purchased by customers, and then put to use. Services deal with processes rather than things, with performances more than physical objects.[1] In many

---

[1]See, for example, G. Lynn Shostack, "Breaking Free from Product Marketing," *Journal of Marketing,* 41 (April 1977), 73-80.

17

services, the "product" is experienced rather than consumed.

THE SERVICE MANAGEMENT TRINITY

As emphasized throughout this book, three management functions are actively involved in creating and delivering services: marketing, operations, and human resources. The customer should always be the center of their focus — after all, serving customers is the reason that the organization is in business. Unfortunately, managers sometimes forget that fact and see customers as a nuisance, getting in the way of a smoothly functioning operation! Information technology plays an increasingly important role in linking the three functions to each other and to customers.

In a well-managed service business, each function will have a clear concept that defines its contribution to the overall mission. Part of the challenge of service management is to ensure that each of these three functional concepts is compatible with the others and that all are mutually reinforcing.

One of the three — usually marketing or operations — will usually provide the initial thrust: It may be a marketing concept which presents excellent sales possibilities if operations and human resources can meet the required service levels and delivery standards (within the cost constraints imposed by the price that target customers are willing to pay). Alternatively, it could be an operations concept that is capable of producing and delivering a certain type of service at a given price if customers can be found who are interested in buying it and the necessary employees found to run the operations and delivery systems.

Figure 1 outlines a generic framework for creating each of these three functional concepts and seeking to integrate them.

The Marketing Function

Production and consumption tend to be clearly separated in manufacturing firms. In

FIGURE 1
Integrating Three Functional Concepts

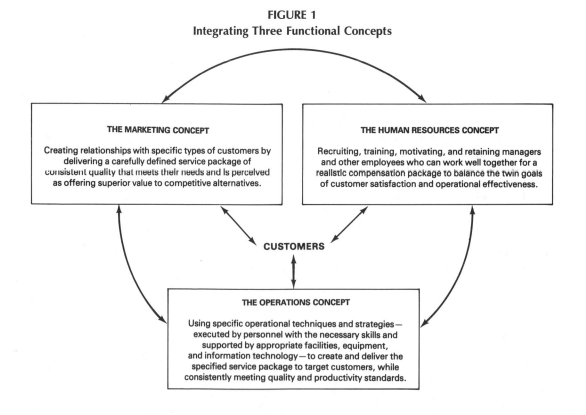

THE MARKETING CONCEPT

Creating relationships with specific types of customers by delivering a carefully defined service package of consistent quality that meets their needs and is perceived as offering superior value to competitive alternatives.

THE HUMAN RESOURCES CONCEPT

Recruiting, training, motivating, and retaining managers and other employees who can work well together for a realistic compensation package to balance the twin goals of customer satisfaction and operational effectiveness.

CUSTOMERS

THE OPERATIONS CONCEPT

Using specific operational techniques and strategies — executed by personnel with the necessary skills and supported by appropriate facilities, equipment, and information technology — to create and deliver the specified service package to target customers, while consistently meeting quality and productivity standards.

most instances, a physical good is produced in a factory in one geographic location, shipped to a retailer or other intermediary for sale in a different location, and consumed or used by the customer in a third location. As a result, it is not usually necessary for production personnel to have any direct involvement with customers, especially where consumer goods are concerned. In such firms, marketing acts to link producers and consumers, providing the manufacturing division with guidelines for product specifications that reflect consumer needs, as well as projections of market demand, information on competitive activity, and feedback on performance in the marketplace. In this linking role, marketing also works with logistics and transportation specialists to develop strategies for distributing the product to prospective purchasers.

In service firms, things are different. Many service operations are literally "factories in the field," which customers enter when they need the service. Since the completed service is often consumed as it is produced, there may be direct contact between production (operations) and customers.

How should marketing relate to operations when production and consumption take place simultaneously? In manufacturing firms, marketers assume full responsibility for the product once it leaves the production line. But in services, contact between operations personnel and customers is the rule rather than the exception — although the extent of this contact varies according to the nature of the service. In many instances, operations management is responsible for running service distribution systems, including retail outlets. Yet none of this reduces the need for a strong, efficient marketing organization to perform the following tasks:

- Evaluate and select the market segments to be served.
- Select service attributes that are tailored to the needs of the target market segments and equal or superior to those of competitive offerings.
- Set prices that reflect costs, competitive strategies, and consumer sensitivity to different price levels.
- Tailor location and timing of service availability to consumer needs and preferences.

- Develop communication programs to inform prospective customers about the service and promote its use.

The net result is that the marketing function in service businesses finds itself closely interrelated with — and dependent upon — the procedures, personnel, and facilities managed by the operations function. To a greater degree than in manufacturing, marketing and operations managers must work together on a day-to-day basis. As we shall see, both find themselves increasingly dependent on human resource managers to help them find and retain appropriate employees, and to advise them on how to create a satisfactory working environment.

The Operations Function

Although marketing has assumed greater importance to service organizations in recent years, the operations function still tends to dominate line management. This is hardly surprising, since operations has traditionally been the central function and effective management of the operation remains a key requirement for success in any service business.

Operations is typically the largest department. Operations managers are responsible not only for operating equipment and procedures behind the scenes, but also for retail outlets and other facilities used by customers. In labor-intensive services, operations managers are likely to supervise the work of large numbers of employees, including many who serve customers directly. Human resource managers may be responsible for such tasks as recruitment, compensation, and training of personnel, but the fact is that in most service businesses the majority of employees report to operations.

Operations managers like to point out that it is their department, not marketing, that has direct contact with customers. These managers are also likely to have been with the organization longer than their marketing colleagues and to understand it better. Yet there is growing recognition of the contributions that marketers can make in terms of understanding customer motivations and habits, identifying opportunities, and telling customers about the product. Marketing is moving up the learning curve and acquiring more management clout in many service organizations.

The Human Resource Function

Few service organizations are so technologically advanced that they can operate without employees. Indeed, many service industries remain highly labor intensive. People are needed for operational tasks (either front stage or backstage), to perform a wide array of marketing tasks, and for administrative support.

Human resources emerged as a coherent management function during the 1980s. Historically, responsibility for matters relating to employees was often divided among a number of different departments, such as personnel, compensation, labor relations, and organization development (or training). As defined by academic specialists in this field, "Human resource management (HRM) involves all managerial decisions and actions that affect the nature of the relationship between the organization and its employees — its human resources."[2]

Just as some forward-looking service businesses have developed a much expanded vision of marketing, viewing it from a strategic perspective rather than a narrow functional and tactical one, so is HRM coming to be seen as a key element in business strategy. Personnel-related activities in a modern service corporation can be subsumed under four broad policy areas.[3]

- *Human resource flow* is concerned with ensuring that the right number of people and mix of competencies is available to meet the firm's long-term strategic requirements. Issues include recruitment, training, career development, and promotions.
- *Work systems* involve all tasks associated with arranging people, information, facilities, and technology to create (or support) the services produced by the organization.

- *Reward systems* send powerful messages to all employees as to what kind of organization management seeks to create and maintain, especially as to desired attitudes and behavior.
- *Employee influence* relates to the inputs that employees should have with respect to business goals, pay, working conditions, career progression, employment security, and the design and implementation of work tasks.

In many service businesses, both the quality of the labor force and its commitment to the tasks at hand have become a major source of competitive advantage — especially when there is a high degree of contact between employees and customers. A strong commitment by top management to effective human resource management is a feature of most successful service firms. To the extent that employees understand and support the goals of their organization, have the skills needed to succeed in their jobs, and recognize the importance of enhancing customer satisfaction, the marketing and operational functions will be much easier to manage.

Interfunctional Conflict

As service organizations change and devote more emphasis to proactive marketing efforts, there is increased potential for conflict between the three functions, especially between marketing and operations functions.[4] Marketing managers are likely to see the operations perspective as narrow and one-sided; even if they recognize the dominance of operations, they may not accept it. Alternatively (and representing the opposite extreme), marketing may be content to accept a passive staff role in which it assumes no initiative whatsoever.

Revenue versus Cost Orientation. Because of the ways in which they are evaluated, operations managers tend to be concerned with improving efficiency and keeping down costs, whereas marketers look for opportunities to increase sales. Although a marketing idea may

---

[2]M. Beer, B. Spector, P. R. Lawrence, D. Q. Mills, and R. E. Walton, *Human Resources Management: A General Manager's Perspective* (New York: The Free Press, 1985).

[3]Ibid.

[4]For a more detailed discussion of interfunctional conflict, see E. Langeard, J. E. G. Bateson, C. H. Lovelock, and P. Eiglier, *Services Marketing: New Insights from Customers and Managers* (Cambridge, Mass.: Marketing Science Institute, 1981).

have the potential to attract customers and offer the likelihood of increased sales, the financial and opportunity costs may sometimes be too high. One pitfall for marketers is failure to understand the cost implications for the operation of changes in volume. As a result, they may design a service or promotion that boosts sales but not net revenues.

Different Time Horizons. Marketing and operations often have different viewpoints on the need to expedite a new service. For instance, marketers may be oriented to current customer concerns and anxious to achieve an early competitive advantage (or to regain competitive parity) by introducing a new product. The operations division may prefer to adopt a longer time horizon in order to develop a new technology or to refine new operating procedures.

Perceived Fit of New Products with Existing Operations. Another problem relates to compatibility: How well does a new product, which may be very appealing to existing and prospective customers, fit into the operation? If a new product is incompatible with existing production facilities, expertise, and employee skills, good-quality execution may be infeasible. There is, of course, a difference between a permanently bad fit and short-term start-up problems. Resistance by operating personnel is one such start-up problem. There's often a natural tendency to want to make the job as easy as possible. Supervisors may be reluctant to disturb existing patterns by imposing new procedures on employees. This mindset can be summed up as "Somebody 'up there' has come up with a new-fangled operation, which they expect me to learn. But it's going to complicate my life, so I'm opposed to it."

As service firms develop a stronger marketing orientation, the need for coordination across functions will increase. But so, too, will the risk of conflict between marketing, operations, and human resources. The challenge for top management is to develop organizational structures and procedures that harness the energy of managers in different departments, rather than allowing it to be dissipated in interfunctional disputes or permitting one department to dominate (and thereby frus-

trate) the ot) are seeking tions mor transfers. cross tr?

A

The Challenge of Se

22

improving, repa
care of physi
inanimate —
group of ser
ing posse
informa
nipula
tion
bri

UND'
PRO

Earlier we emp. rather than just a "u. is required to provide go to ask ourselves a couple of key q *what sorts of processes* are involved in services? And second, *where does the custom.* *fit* in a service organization? After identifying three broad categories of service process, we'll look at service as a system, examining how services are created, how they're delivered, and how the customer is involved in this process. Later, we'll consider how service products can be defined from a marketing rather than an operations perspective, and then introduce the notion of flowcharting to study the sequence of steps that customers must go through in order to receive service.[5]

Service as a Process

If service is a process, then what is being processed? A process implies input and output. Writing from an operations perspective, Morris and Johnson suggest that three types of inputs can be processed: customers themselves, materials, and information.[6]

When the process is directed at the customer, then the system is processing people. Processing of materials suggests a manufacturing operation, but many services are, in fact, quasimanufacturing operations working to tight deadlines to restore customers' possessions to good working order. Such activities may involve cleaning, maintaining, storing,

---

[5]Although some writers use the term "product" to refer to just manufactured goods, we use it in its generic sense to refer to the output of both service and goods producing organizations.

[6]Barbara Morris and Robert Johnston, "Dealing with Inherent Variability: The Difference Between Manufacturing and Service?" *International Journal of Production Management,* vol. 7, no. 4 (1987), pp. 13–22.

...ring, or otherwise taking ...cal objects — both live and ...that belong to the customer; this ...vices can be described as process-...sions. Finally, there's processing of ...ion, which includes not just data ma-...ion but also collection and interpreta-...f facts, ideas, and opinions. Let's take a ...f look at each.

Processing people takes place when customers seek some service directed at themselves. They may wish (or need) to be transported, entertained, fed, lodged, barbered, made more healthy, or educated. To receive such a service the customer must enter the service system — usually physically but sometimes at a distance through the medium of telecommunication links. The nature of the treatment or process will involve the cooperation of the customer, entailing anything from boarding a subway car for a 5-minute ride to spending long periods of time participating in classroom discussions and working in libraries. The output (after a period of time that may vary from minutes to years) may be a customer who is now in a different location; or one who feels amused or thrilled or stimulated; or one who has had a meal, been lodged for one or more nights, had a haircut, feels or may come to feel more healthy; or one who is more knowledgeable.

Processing possessions occurs when customers ask a service organization to provide treatment not to themselves but rather to some possession — which could be anything from a house to a hedge, from a car to a computer, or from a dress to a dog. Customer involvement tends to be much lower than for processing people. Other than requesting the service, customers need not get directly involved in service delivery (although some prefer to do so). Sometimes customers drop off their possessions (if portable) at the service factory. Alternatively, service personnel may come to the customer's location.

The actual service process might involve exterminating a house to get rid of termites, trimming a hedge, repairing a car, installing software in a computer, cleaning a dress, or neutering a dog. The output in each instance (if the work has been done properly) should be a satisfactory solution to a problem or some other enhancement to the item in question.

Processing information has been revolutionized by computers. But not all information is processed by computers — professionals in a wide variety of fields use their brains, too. Information is the most intangible form of service output and may be presented to the customer either face to face or through telecommunications. The output of information processing may also be transformed into physical form through letters, reports, books, or tapes. Among the services that are highly dependent on effective collection and processing of information are financial services, accounting, law, education, marketing research, management consulting, news dissemination, weather forecasting, medical diagnosis, and a variety of other professional services.

Many service products consist of a core activity, augmented by several supplementary elements. The latter may involve all three of the process categories. These three basic ways of categorizing services are useful in helping us understand how customers' experiences and involvement differ among various types of services. Later, in Part II, we'll look at a variety of more detailed approaches to classifying services.

SERVICE AS A SYSTEM

Any service business can be thought of as a *system* comprising service operations, where inputs are processed and the elements of the service product are created, and service delivery, where final "assembly" of these elements takes place and the product is delivered to the customer. Parts of this system are visible (or otherwise apparent) to customers; other parts are hidden from view in what is sometimes referred to as the technical core,[7] and the customer may not even know of their existence. Some writers use the terms "front office" and "back office" in referring to the visible and invisible parts of the operation. Others talk

---

[7]Richard B. Chase, "Where Does the Customer Fit in a Service Organization?" *Harvard Business Review* (November–December 1978).

about "front stage" and "backstage," using the analogy of theater to dramatize the notion that service is a performance.[8]

Service Operations System

As in a play, the visible components of the service operations system can be divided into those relating to the actors (or service personnel) and those relating to the stage set (or physical facilities and equipment). What goes on backstage is of little interest to customers. Like any audience, they evaluate the production with reference to those elements that they actually experience in the course of service delivery and — of course — on the perceived service outcome. Naturally, if the folks backstage fail to perform their support tasks properly, the impact will be apparent to customers. For instance, restaurant patrons may find that menu items are not available, because someone forgot to go to the fish market that morning, or that their food is overcooked because the ovens were not adjusted properly.

The proportion of the overall service operation that is visible to customers varies according to the nature of the service. People-processing services, such as airline travel, hairdressing, and hospitals, directly involve the physical person of the customer. They require customers to enter the "factory," although there may still be some backstage activities that customers don't see. Possession-processing services, such as repair and maintenance, may require the customer to drop off the item at the "factory door" and then pick it up once the work has been completed. Alternatively, some services provide pickup and delivery service at the customer's own home, office, or plant. For service to large or immovable items, such as a house, the service personnel may perform the work on site — essentially bringing portions of their factory with them. Because the customer is less involved in service delivery, the visible component of the service operations system tends to be proportionately smaller than for people-processing services.

[8]Stephen Grove and Raymon Fisk, "The Dramaturgy of Service Exchange: An Analytical Framework for Services Marketing," in L. L. Berry, G. L. Shostack, and G. D. Upah, *Emerging Perspectives in Services Marketing* (Chicago: American Marketing Association, 1983).

Information-processing services, such as broadcasting, insurance, information, and legal services, do not require the customer's physical presence from an operational standpoint. Interactions between customer and service provider can often be conducted at arm's length by mail, telephone, or other electronic media. That's because there may be no operational reason at all for the customer to see the "factory" where the work is performed — although some people feel more confident, especially in the case of financial and professional services, if they can meet the service provider in person at least once.

Service Delivery System

Service delivery is concerned with where, when, and how the service product is delivered to the customer. As can be seen in Figure 2, this system embraces not only the visible elements of the service operating system — physical support and personnel — but may also entail exposure to other customers. Traditionally, the interaction between service providers and their customers has been a close one. But for reasons of both operational efficiency and customer convenience, people seeking services that don't require their *physical* presence are finding that the amount of direct contact with the service organization is being reduced nowadays. In short, the visible component of the service operations system is shrinking as the delivery system changes to emphasize more self-service and arm's length transactions.

Electronic delivery often offers greater convenience than face-to-face contact. Self-service equipment, such as automatic teller machines, is available in numerous locations and is accessible 24 hours a day, 7 days a week. But there are potential disadvantages, too. Customers sometimes find the shift from personal service to self-service disconcerting. So implementing this type of change in the delivery system may require an information campaign to educate customers, a responsive attitude toward consumer concerns, and even some initial promotional incentives.

Responsibility for designing and managing the service delivery system has traditionally

FIGURE 2
Three Overlapping Service Marketing Systems

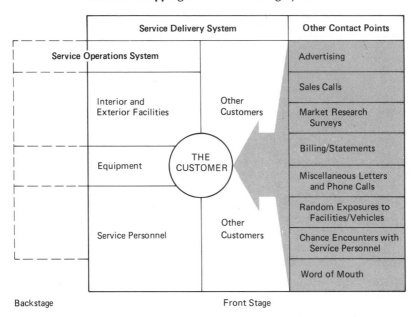

Backstage   Front Stage

fallen to operations managers. But marketing needs to be involved, too, since a good understanding of customer needs and concerns is important if the system is to work well. What's more, if we're dealing with a service facility where customers may interact with each other — such as a hotel or post office — people's behavior has to be managed discreetly so that customers will act in ways that are consistent with the organization's strategy.

A key challenge for designers of new services is to match the nature of the delivery system to the needs and preferences of the target customer groups. When the two do not match well, customers are likely to be turned off. Either the operation has to be redesigned to better match the preferences of the chosen market segment, or the firm will have to target those market segments that are looking for the benefits offered by the planned delivery system.

Service Marketing System

Other elements beyond the service delivery system may contribute to the customer's overall view of the service organization. These include the communication efforts of the advertising and sales departments, telephone calls and letters from service personnel, billings from the accounting department, random exposures to service personnel and facilities, news stories and editorials in the mass media, word-of-mouth comments from current or former customers, and even participation in market research studies.

Collectively, the components just cited — plus those in the service delivery system — add up to what may be called the *service marketing system* (see Figure 2). In essence, this represents all the different ways in which the customer may encounter or learn about the service organization in question. Since services are experiential, each of these elements offers clues about the nature and quality of the service product. Inconsistency between different elements may weaken the organization's credibility in the customers' eyes.

All these components are categorized and summarized in Table 1, which can serve as a checklist to help an organization identify the nature of the service marketing system for a particular type of customer.

TABLE 1
Components of the Service Marketing System

1. *Service personnel.* Contacts with customers may be face-to-face, by telecommunications (telephone, fax, telegram, telex, electronic mail) or by mail and express delivery services.
   These personnel may include:
   - Sales representatives
   - Customer service staff
   - Accounting/billing staff
   - Operations staff who do not normally provide direct service to customers (e.g., engineers, janitors)
   - Designated intermediaries whom customers perceive as directly representing the service firm
2. *Service facilities and equipment*
   - Building exteriors, parking areas, landscaping
   - Building interiors and furnishings
   - Self-service equipment operated by customers
   - Vehicles and other equipment
3. *Nonpersonal communications*
   - Form letters
   - Brochures/catalogs/instruction manuals
   - Advertising
   - Signage
   - News stories/editorials in the mass media
4. *Other people*
   - Fellow customers encountered during service delivery
   - Word-of-mouth comments from friends, acquaintances, or even strangers.

The significance of this approach is that it represents a customer's view of the service organization, looking at it from the outside, as opposed to an internally focused operations perspective. Managers should remember that it is how customers *perceive* the organization that determines their decisions to select one service rather than another.

The scope and structure of the service marketing system may vary sharply for different types of organizations. Try using the list in Table 1 to develop a profile of the service marketing system for a variety of services — a hospital, an airline, a college, a hotel, a dry cleaners, a bank, an automobile service shop, and the postal service. Recognize, though, that interactions with many of the components listed may be random rather than planned. For instance, what impression does it create for a prospective customer to see a truck belonging to an express delivery service broken down by the side of the road? Or to be buying stamps at the post office and observe a uniformed employee (say a doorman) from a nearby hotel shouting rudely at the postal clerk at the adjacent window?

Although it's clearly the function of operations to manage the service operations system — and of human resources to ensure that this system is staffed with trained and motivated personnel — it's the marketer's task to ensure that the overall service marketing system runs in ways that balance customer satisfaction against operational concerns with efficiency and cost control.

Much operations work is done behind the scenes and is only relevant to customers to the extent that it results in the creation and delivery of a good product. But the visible elements of the operation, where service delivery takes place, must be seen in the context of the broader service marketing system. In short, there's an overlap between the marketing and operations spheres of influence. All managers must try to understand both perspectives, and then to think about how service employees can be managed to achieve optimum results.

Service employees often find themselves in what are termed "boundary spanning roles" where they are expected to be responsive to the concerns of different departments.[9] Customer contact employees, in particular, may find themselves evaluated on both operational efficiency and customer satisfaction. Often, it is left to them to decide how to resolve conflicts between these two goals. Human resource managers need to clarify responsibilities and priorities when preparing job descriptions. They can also help by recruiting employees who are comfortable in making judgments when presented with ambiguous situations, and in training them through scenario building and role playing to resolve conflicting priorities.

[9]See, for example, David E. Bowen and Benjamin Schneider, "Boundary-Spanning Employees and the Service Encounter: Some Guidelines for Management and Research," in J. A. Czepiel, M. R. Solomon, and C. F. Surprenant, *The Service Encounter.* Lexington, Mass.: D. C. Heath and Company, 1985.

CORE PRODUCTS AND SUPPLEMENTARY SERVICES

One of the simplest, yet most comprehensive, definitions of service that I know comes from Federal Express. Some years ago, they redefined service as "All actions and reactions that customers perceive they have purchased."[10]

This statement clarifies that the service product is essentially a bundle of activities, consisting of the *core product* — which in Federal's case consists of transporting packages overnight, and delivering them the next morning to the addressee — *plus* a cluster of supplementary services. An important question for any service manager to ask is: "What actions and reactions do our customers expect as part of the overall package?" This question needs to be asked of each different market segment

[10]Christopher H. Lovelock, "Federal Express: Quality Improvement Program" (Lausanne, Switzerland: International Institute for Management Development — IMD, 1990). Case GM-456 (reproduced on pages 270-284 of this book).

and each different product offered by the firm. Figure 3 shows the core service and supplementary services offered to business travelers by a good hotel.

Although the core product differs from industry to industry, many supplementary service elements are essentially generic, being found across a broad cross section of industries, in both service and manufacturing firms. These generic supplementary elements — which are all information based — include:

- Offering advice and information
- Taking orders or reservations
- Providing documentation of activities performed
- Sending accurate, intelligible billing statements
- Resolving problems promptly

A second set of supplementary elements tend to be limited to people processing services. They include:

- Hospitality (for example, offering customers food or beverages, comfortable waiting areas,

FIGURE 3
Core and Supplementary Services at a Hotel for Business Travelers

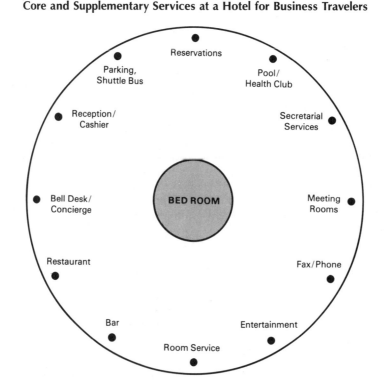

reading materials or other entertainment to pass the time, washroom facilities, and so forth)

- Care of physical possessions, such as cars or coats, that customers may bring with them.

Lastly comes a group of supplementary services that can add value to processing of possessions. These may include:

- Pick up and delivery
- Storage
- Installation
- Warranties for work performed

In summary, all service firms must learn to think in terms of performing well on each of the actions and reactions that their customers perceive themselves to be purchasing. Managers must group these various interactions into core and supplementary service elements and determine how well their organization is performing on each one — if indeed their firm even responds to each of the customer's requirements.

Supplementary Services as the Competitive Edge

The concept of the augmented product is well established in the marketing literature — the marketer's task is to implement that concept. As Theodore Levitt observed almost two decades ago:

> We live in an age in which our thinking about what a product or a service is must be quite different from what it ever was before. It is not so much the basic, generic central thing we are selling that counts, but the whole cluster of satisfactions with which we surround it.[11]

Among both service and manufacturing industries, the *core product* sooner or later becomes a commodity as competition increases and the industry matures. As a result, competitive advantage usually emphasizes performance on the *supplementary service elements*. After all, if a firm can't do a decent job on the core elements, it's eventually going to go out of business.

Consider the car rental industry. The core product of a firm in this industry is providing customers with safe and well-functioning vehicles for personal transportation on business or pleasure trips. A failure of that core product would be represented by the inability to deliver a car at the promised time and place, or a car that breaks down on the road. But if a car rental firm gets a reputation for performing (or rather, misperforming) in that way, it will soon be unable to attract any customers and will eventually go bankrupt.

In industrialized countries with well-developed car rental industries, the real choice criteria for car renters selecting a between competing firms don't usually center on whether they will get a car at all or drive a car that runs properly. That's normally taken for granted. Instead customers are more likely to evaluate competitors against such criteria as special benefits for frequent renters, ease of getting through to reservations, speedy check-in at the airport or other rental location, assurance in getting the class of car and features they requested (or failing that, an upgrade to a better car at the same price), receiving a clean vehicle with a full tank, availability of maps and instruction manuals, adequate insurance coverage at reasonable rates, rapid return procedures at the end of the trip, and fast accurate billing without hidden extras.

FLOWCHARTING THE SERVICE EXPERIENCE

Customers usually expect firms that provide service to understand the full extent of the relationship they have with that provider. But service operating and delivery processes are often highly compartmentalized, composed of a series of discrete activities performed by numerous different players. As a result, it's easy for customers to get "lost" in the system and to feel that nobody knows who they are or what they need. For a service firm to understand the nature of the process, and in particular the nature of the customer's personal experience, it's necessary to flowchart the constituent processes step by step.

Flowcharting can usefully be applied to any type of service where management needs to gain a better understanding of how the service

---

[11]Theodore Levitt, "What's Your Product and What's Your Business?" Chapter 2 in *Marketing for Business Growth.* (New York: McGraw-Hill, 1973), p. 7.

is created and delivered. Developing a flow-chart begins by identifying each interaction that a particular type of customer has when using a specific service. Managers need to distinguish between the core product and the supplementary service elements — in fact, flowcharting is a very useful way of figuring out what the supplementary elements actually are!

The next step is to put all these interactions linearly into the sequence in which they occur. The service delivery process is like a river — some activities take place upstream, others downstream. At each step, management needs to ask: What does the customer really want? Where is the potential for failure at this step?

Let's illustrate flowcharting with a simplified model of a widely used service: renting a car. As with many services, the customer's first encounter with a car-rental firm involves a supplementary service rather than a core product. Renting a car is usually a planned purchase, so the initial step involves making an advance reservation. On the day of rental, the customer needs to check in so that the agent can verify the driver's license, insurance requirements, credit card (or other payment mechanism) and personal details — which for regular customers may already be on file. A customer may also request other needs such as maps or a baby seat. He or she will then sign and receive the contract. If the cars are parked some distance from the check-in site — as is common at airports — the firm may offer bus transport to this location. At the car lot, the customer will be shown the vehicle — which should be fully fueled, in good working order, and clean inside and out — and given the keys. When requested, the agent should demonstrate features of the car and provide local driving directions.

If the car should break down during the period of the rental, the customer should be able to obtain roadside assistance. Although many car rental firms tell the customer to find a local breakdown service and claim reimbursement later, some have contracts with automobile associations to assist any renter experiencing car problems. On returning the car, the renter will receive a bill, computed on duration of rental plus (sometimes) mile-age and the amount of gasoline needed to fill the tank. Many firms encourage customers to refuel the car before returning it by charging premium prices for gas. At the return site, speed is often of the essence in completing billing formalities. Finally, the renter may expect transport from the car return facility to an airport terminal, hotel, or other location.

Figure 4 depicts the customer's experience, in simplified form, as a series of boxes on the *front stage* portion of the flowchart. But a variety of *backstage* activities are taking place, behind the scenes, to ensure that the process works smoothly. We've captured a few of these backstage steps on the chart for illustrative purposes (to show every detail of the backstage service processes would require a substantially larger page format than used in this book!). In fact, each step in the front stage process is supported by a series of backstage activities, including assignment of staff, maintenance of facilities and equipment, and storage and transfer of data — depicted here by the big arrows at the bottom.

Although the operations function is responsible for backstage activities (such as car maintenance, preparation, cleaning, and so forth) and for implementing many of the front stage elements, marketing plays a vital role in determining customer needs and in helping design front stage activities and facilities. Similarly, marketing managers need to work with their colleagues in both human resources and operations to ensure that customer service personnel possess not only the necessary technical skills for the job but can also relate well to customers at a human level.

Another important role for marketing is to monitor customer satisfaction, evaluate competitive activities, and identify market trends and opportunities. By providing feedback to operations and human resource managers on current performance and by identifying new opportunities, marketing can play a key role in promoting improved performance, advocating changes in service standards, and helping to design service enhancements that will improve the firm's competitive posture. Recognizing that service personnel are also "internal customers" of the organization, marketers and human resource managers

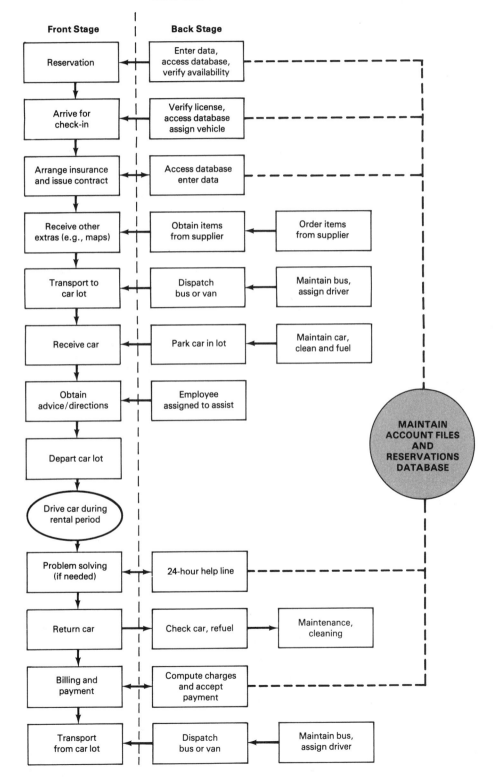

FIGURE 4
Flow Chart of Car Rental Process

Front Stage | Back Stage

Reservation → Enter data, access database, verify availability

Arrive for check-in → Verify license, access database assign vehicle

Arrange insurance and issue contract ↔ Access database enter data

Receive other extras (e.g., maps) → Obtain items from supplier → Order items from supplier

Transport to car lot → Dispatch bus or van → Maintain bus, assign driver

Receive car → Park car in lot → Maintain car, clean and fuel

Obtain advice/directions → Employee assigned to assist

Depart car lot

Drive car during rental period

Problem solving (if needed) ↔ 24-hour help line

Return car → Check car, refuel → Maintenance, cleaning

Billing and payment ↔ Compute charges and accept payment

Transport from car lot → Dispatch bus or van → Maintain bus, assign driver

MAINTAIN ACCOUNT FILES AND RESERVATIONS DATABASE

29

should work together to identify employee needs and concerns. Improving the working environment and increasing employee job satisfaction are often key steps in improving service for "external customers."

CONCLUSION

Although the operations function has long been the kingpin in service businesses, success in an increasingly competitive environment requires that operations managers work closely with their counterparts in marketing and human resources. Ideally, line managers should be trained in all three functions so that they recognize the constraints faced by each functional area and can understand (and resolve) their sometimes conflicting objectives.

A first step in understanding service organizations involves clarifying what is being processed: is it people, is it physical possessions, or is it information? The type of processing that takes place affects how closely customers need to interact with the service operation. Customers tend to see more of the service factory front stage when they themselves are being processed.

From a customer perspective, services are often described as intangible, ephemeral, and experiential. This is true inasmuch as one cannot buy all the elements of a service, wrap them up, and take them home for later consumption. But a whole host of features in a service business are quite evident to one or more of a customer's senses. Collectively, these front stage elements represent all the ways in which the service organization — or information about it — touches current and prospective customers.

Service businesses can be divided into three overlapping systems. The operations system consists of the personnel, facilities, and equipment required to run the service operation and create the service product; only the front stage elements of this system are visible to the customer, the rest are hidden "backstage." The delivery system unites these front-stage operations elements with the customers, who may themselves take an active role in helping create the service product, as opposed to being passively waited upon. The marketing system includes not only the delivery system, but also additional components such as billing and payment systems, exposure to advertising and sales personnel, and word-of-mouth comments from other people.

Service managers should recognize that a customer's evaluation of a service usually reflects performance on supplementary services as well as on the core service. An important task for designing and managing service businesses is to understand how specific types of customers actually experience the different service elements. Flowcharting service delivery is a very useful approach to understanding how all the pieces fit together.

PART II
Understanding Services: Breaking Free from Industry Tunnel Vision

How Can Service Businesses Survive and Prosper?

ROGER W. SCHMENNER

Through the use of a service matrix, the author shows how service businesses can broaden their professional relationships with other services that have similar operations and managerial challenges, and in so doing, gain the economic foothold needed to survive and prosper.

Presently the service sector of our economy is characterized by both profusion and confusion. By profusion, I mean that it has done wonderfully well at generating jobs, for new kinds of services are sprouting continually. By confusion, I mean that service businesses seem to rise and fall from Wall Street grace with regularity. Moreover, as many are markedly entrepreneurial in spirit, they all claim to have idiosyncratic operations. For example, while manufacturing management enjoys the benefits of various professional societies (i.e., those for materials management, manufacturing engineering, industrial engineering, and quality control) whose roles are to find management principles that apply across many different kinds of manufacturing enterprises, service business management does not enjoy such cooperation. All too often, service companies view themselves as unique, and consequently they do not promote service operation management techniques with the same vigor as does the manufacturing sector.

Some manufacturers, of course, also claim that they are unique. However, over the years, manufacturers have been unified by their acceptance of certain terminology to describe generic production processes—job shop, batch flow, assembly line, continuous flow process. This not only helps to solidify manufacturers of sometimes widely divergent product lines, but it also helps to reveal the challenges manufacturers face.

THE CHARACTERISTICS OF A SERVICE BUSINESS

The confusion surrounding service operations can be lessened in part by looking at key aspects of service businesses that significantly affect the character of the service delivery process. Specifically, there are two elements that can be used to classify different kinds of service businesses. These elements will serve later as a springboard for investigating the strategic changes of service operations and the challenges that lie ahead for managers.

Labor Intensity

The first key element is the labor intensity of the service business process. Labor intensity is defined as the ratio of the labor cost incurred to the value of the plant and equipment. (Note that the value of inventories is excluded because the concept seems "cleaner" without taking inventories into account.) A high labor-intensive business involves relatively little plant and equipment and considerable worker time, effort, and cost. For example, professional services are typically a high labor-intensive business. A low labor-intensive business, on the other hand, is characterized by relatively low levels of labor cost compared to plant and equipment. Trucking firms with their breakbulks and other kinds of terminals, trailers, and tractors are an example. It is important to think of labor intensity as a ratio. Many, for example, think of hospitals as labor intensive—after all, hospitals are filled with nurses, technicians, orderlies, and doctors. Nevertheless, despite employing large numbers of people, a hospital has a comparatively low labor intensity because of the very expensive plant and equipment it must have. Table 1 documents the labor intensity of some broad service industries.

Consumer Interaction and Service Customization

The other key element of a service business is somewhat more confusing because it combines two similar but distinct concepts: (1) the degree to which the consumer interacts with the service process; and (2) the degree to which the service is customized for the consumer. This joint measure has a high value when a service evidences both a high level of interaction and a high level of customization for the customer. Similarly, when both individual measures are low, the joint measure has a low value. Where there is a mix of high interaction with low customization (or the other way around), the joint measure falls somewhere in between.

What exactly do these measures mean? A service with a high level of interaction is one where the consumer can actively intervene in the service process, at will, often to demand additional service of a particular kind or to request that some aspects of the service be deleted. However, high visibility or duration of contact with the process is not enough to indicate high interaction. College teaching, for example, is a highly visible service activity in that students are in class for long periods of time. However, seldom do student consumers actively intervene in the process. Thus college teaching has a comparatively low level of interaction.

A service with high service customization will work to satisfy an individual's particular, and perhaps full range, of preferences. A physician typically gives very individual, customized service. Furthermore, good physicians are always open to feedback from their patients and willing to rethink and modify the service they provide. College teachers, on the other hand, are reluctant to throw out the syllabus to accommodate student desires: they "teach what they know."

To clarify further this joint measure, consider the restaurant industry. At the low end of the spectrum are McDonald's and Kentucky Fried Chicken. Here, the consumer's

TABLE 1
Labor Intensity of Some Broad Service Groups

Low Labor-Intensive Services	Capital-Labor Ratio
Electric Utilities, Gas, Sanitation Services	14.21
Communications	5.31
Amusement & Recreation	2.49
Hospitals:	
—Teaching	1.59
—For-Profit	1.63
—All Other (e.g., community)	1.75
Auto & Other Repair	1.60
Transportation	1.27
Banking	1.20
Hotels, etc.	1.01

High Labor-Intensive Services	Capital-Labor Ratio
Security, Commodity Brokers	0.15
Insurance Agents & Service	0.18
Business Services (e.g., advertising, credit reporting, mailing & reproduction, building services, personnel supply, computer & data processing, management consulting & public relations)	0.42
Personal Services (e.g., laundry, photo, beauty/barber shops, funeral services)	0.53
Wholesale Trade	0.54
Retail Trade	0.62

Notes:

The labor intensities of specific types of service businesses are not routinely calculated. Most of the following estimates are based on 1980 data on depreciable assets (from the 1980 Statistics of Income, Corporation Income Tax Returns, Internal Revenue Service) and compensation to employees (from the Revised Estimates of the National Income and Product Accounts, Survey of Current Business, Bureau of Economic Analysis, U.S. Department of Commerce). The hospital estimates are based on data compiled by the American Hospital Association for 1981.

The calculations shown are capital-to-labor ratios (gross depreciable assets divided by compensation to employees) for very broad groups of service businesses. Services with capital-labor ratios greater than about 1 could be viewed as having "low labor intensity," while services with ratios less than 1 could be viewed as having "high labor intensity." By contrast, the average capital-labor ratio by this measure for manufacturing in 1980 was 1.90.

The service industry classifications are broad ones as a result of the Standard Industrial Classification codes.

interaction with the process is typically brief and controlled (i.e., order, payment, and pickup), and customization does not prevail. The service is prompt and courteous, but everybody is treated the same. At Burger King and Wendy's consumer interaction is similarly brief and controlled. However, these fast-food chains offer measurably more customization for the consumer—you can have a burger "your way." This process permits some customization.

Cafeterias provide even more customization for the consumer (i.e., the opportunity to choose from a wide range of foods) and a modest increase in interaction (e.g., as one proceeds down the line, one can often request the staff to replenish an item or to serve a rarer cut of roast beef). Next in line are restaurants with salad bars that have some waiter assistance. Such restaurants offer customization similar to that of a cafeteria but there is more customer interaction: the waiter can be called on, at will.

Finally, there are restaurants with extensive waiter services. Such restaurants typically permit a high degree of customization and interaction: the customer decides what he or she wants to eat and when he or she wants to be served (e.g., "We'd like to enjoy our cocktail now and order later"; "Coffee later, thank you"), and the waiter is on call, at will, to fill any particular desires. However, it should be noted that the haute-cuisine restaurant is not necessarily at the highest end of the customization/interaction spectrum, as some of them offer limited menus and many even decide the particular seating time. In this case, consumers are willing to trust the chef because of the food's known quality and the restaurant's ambience.

For many services, customization and interaction go hand in hand: if one is high, the other is high; if one is low, the other is low. There are services, however, where they differ. Insurance underwriting, especially at Lloyd's of London, offers considerable customization but a low degree of interaction with the client. On the other hand, an advertising agency typically is high on both customization and interaction. A travel agency provides a different example. The typical business traveler service is fairly standard and often involves merely presenting the schedule options to the traveler and issuing the ticket. Here, the degree of customization is not nearly as great as it is for planning a pleasure trip. On the other hand, business travel often demands rescheduling and a good deal of tinkering with timetables. Thus, business travel agency work often involves more interaction than customization.

OTHER SERVICE CLASSIFICATION SCHEMES

Other observers have sought to classify service operations, notably Richard Chase, David Maister, and Christopher Lovelock. Chase arrays various services along a continuum from high to low "contact."[1] For Chase, contact refers to the duration of a customer's presence in the service system. According to this scheme, hotels are high contact, "pure" services, while the postal service is low contact. Repair shops are medium contact services, lying in between the prior extremes.

Although Chase makes a useful distinction, his distinction is not as helpful as it could be. A number of services can be judged high contact even though they only "shelter the customer" and in the process have very little interaction with the client. To use Chase's example, a hotel is a high-contact service, but, to me, hotels are vastly less demanding than are hospitals, primarily because hotels interact with customers in limited and very structured ways, whereas hospitals must interact with patients in irregular and frequently sustained ways. Hospital management is much more demanding, and is, therefore, worthy of classification apart from that of hotel management.

Chase's classification scheme becomes even more problematic when he turns to examining potential operating efficiency.[2] Here, Chase asserts that

$$\text{potential facility efficiency} = f \left(1 - \frac{\text{customer contact time}}{\text{service creation time}} \right).$$

By this mode of thinking, the greater the ratio of customer contact time to service creation time (a somewhat nebulous term that refers to the work process involved in providing the service itself), the lower is the potential efficiency of the service facility. If this is so, hotels have lower potential efficiencies than do either the postal service or repair shops. If I am not misinterpreting Chase, the implication of his assertion is curious. For many people, hotels are often viewed as considerably more efficient, and certainly more profitable, than the postal service or many repair shops. As far as I am concerned, contact time simply does not capture completely what is challenging about service sector management.

Maister and Lovelock come closer to the mark.[3] They use both the extent of client contact and the extent of customization to dimension a two-by-two matrix that distinguishes among the factory, the job shop, mass service, and professional service. Unfortunately, Maister and Lovelock do not spend much time either describing or pursuing this characterization. They do not identify particular services as belonging to one or the other of their matrix quadrants, and, therefore, it is difficult to take them to task. However, they do use client contact, and, as was discussed above, the notion of client contact may be fraught with more ambiguity than is necessary.

Here, I argue that services are better classified by using both the degree of labor intensity and the degree to which (1) the consumer interacts with the service and (2) the service is customized for the consumer. By expanding the two-by-two matrix, it is possible to analyze the challenges service managements face and the dynamics of operation changes in their businesses.

THE SERVICE PROCESS MATRIX

I have characterized services as being either "high" or "low" in terms of client interaction and customization. Naturally, not all service businesses fit cleanly into these extremes: there are many shades of gray. Nevertheless, these extremes are helpful in developing a two-by-two matrix that can categorize a whole host of diverse service businesses. Figure 1 displays a service matrix and indicates some of the classic service businesses that fit neatly in one of the four quadrants. As this figure shows, service businesses that have a relatively low labor intensity and a low degree of customer interaction and customization are labeled "service factories": airlines, trucking, hotels, and resorts are classic ex-

amples. As the degree of interaction or customization for the consumer increases, however, the service factory gives way to the "service shop," much as the line flow operation gives way to a job shop operation when customization is required in manufacturing. Service shops still have a high degree of plant and equipment relative to labor, but they offer more interaction and customization. Hospitals, auto repair garages, and most restaurants are examples of service shops.

"Mass service" businesses have a high degree of labor intensity but a rather low degree of interaction and customization. Many traditional kinds of services can be found in this category, such as retailing, wholesaling, schools of all types, and many services like laundry, cleaning, and many routine computer software and data-processing functions. If the degree of interaction with the consumer increases and/or customization of this service becomes the watchword, mass service gives way to "professional service": doctors, lawyers, accountants, architects, investment bankers, and the like are the archetypal examples.

CHALLENGES FOR SERVICE MANAGERS

Variations in the managerial challenges of different services stem from the high and low distinctions made of labor intensity and interaction/customization. For example, in the case of low labor intensity (e.g., hospitals, airlines, hotels), the choice of plant and equipment is heightened. Monitoring and implementing any technological advantages are also critical. In such low labor-intensive services, capacity cannot be augmented easily and so demand must be managed to smooth out any peaks and to promote off-peak times. The inflexibility of capacity also implies that scheduling service delivery is relatively more important for these low labor-intensive businesses than it is for others.

As for services with high labor intensity (e.g., stores, professional associations), managing and controlling the workforce becomes paramount. Hiring, training, de-

FIGURE 1
The Service Process Matrix

Degree of Interaction and Customization

		Low	High
Degree of Labor Intensity	Low	**Service Factory:** —Airlines —Trucking —Hotels —Resorts and recreation	**Service Shop:** —Hospitals —Auto repair —Other repair services
	High	**Mass Service:** —Retailing —Wholesaling —Schools —Retail aspects of commercial banking	**Professional Service:** —Doctors —Lawyers —Accountants —Architects

veloping methods and controls, employee welfare, scheduling the workforce, and controlling work for any far-flung geographic locations are critical elements. If new units of operation are contemplated, startup may become a problem and managing the growth of such units can often be difficult.

Different managerial challenges also surface when we consider the distinction made between high and low levels of consumer interaction and customization. When the degree of interaction and customization is low (i.e., airlines, retail stores, commercial banks), the service business faces a stiff marketing challenge. Such a business must try to make the service it provides warm, even though it does not give all the personal attention that a customer might want. This means that attention to physical surroundings becomes important. In addition, with a low degree of interaction and with little customization, standard operating procedures can be instituted safely. In this type of service, the hierarchy of the operation itself tends to be the classic pyramid with a broad base of workers and many layers of management. Furthermore, the relationships between levels in the pyramid tend to be fairly rigid.

As the service takes on a higher degree of interaction and customization (i.e., professional associations, hospitals, repair

FIGURE 2
Challenges for Service Managers

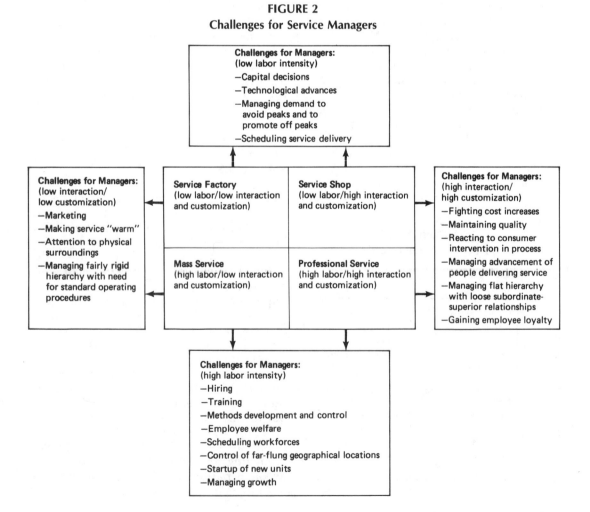

services), management must deal with higher costs and more talented labor. Managing costs effectively—either by keeping them down or by passing them on to consumers—becomes a significant challenge. Maintaining quality and responding to consumer intervention are also important. In addition, talented employees demand attention and expect advancement in the organization. In effect, what this all means for many service businesses with high interaction and customization is that the hierarchy of control tends to be flat and unlike the classic pyramid. As the relationship between superiors and subordinates tends to be much less rigid, management must continually strive to keep workers "attached" to the firm by offering innovative pay and benefits packages and by paying close attention to quality of worklife issues.

As Figure 2 demonstrates, the high versus low differentiation made for labor intensity and the degree of consumer interaction and customization yield distinct combinations of management challenges for the four service types identified. Typically, well-run service factories, service shops, mass-service firms, or professional firms pay close attention to all of the managerial challenges that apply to their quadrant of the matrix.

INNOVATIONS AND STRATEGIC CHANGES

Categorizing service businesses into quadrants can be used to investigate the strategic changes of service operations over time. At least some of the current confusion has occurred because service industries are changing rapidly. The most salient development in the service sector is vast segmentation and diversification. Services that were once clearly service shops or mass service firms are no longer clearly labeled as such. Service firms are spreading themselves out across the service matrix. Below are examples illustrating this trend.

Fast-Food Restaurants. A classic strategic change involved the development and evolution of fast-food restaurants. The traditional restaurant could be positioned as a service shop with relatively high customization and interaction for the consumer and a middling labor intensity. The elegant gourmet restaurant may even be classified as a professional service. On the other hand, with the advent of fast foods, interaction and customization for the consumer have been lowered dramatically, as has labor intensity. As a result, the restaurant industry today encompasses a wide diversity of operations.

Hospitals. Another interesting innovation within the service shop quadrant involved hospitals. The new kinds of hospitals developed by Humana, Hospital Corporation of America, and others are different from the traditional community hospital or university medical center. Whereas the traditional hospital (especially the university medical center) is set up to diagnose and treat any disease by investing in all of the latest equipment and technology, this new breed of hospital customarily deals with the more routine kinds of medical treatment: intensive care units and other high expense units for very sick or dying patients are often not a part of these hospitals. Very ill patients are referred to larger, and better-equipped hospitals. For its part, the new type of hospital offers a much lower cost service that is convenient for the consumer. In this respect, this new breed of hospital offers less customization but, at the same time, demands a higher degree of labor intensity. As Table 1 shows, there is a lower capital-to-labor ratio for "for-profit" hospitals than there is for traditional community hospitals. For-profit hospitals are not burdened with all the capital expenditures that are part of the traditional hospital. Table 1 also shows that teaching hospitals, perhaps for understandable reasons, are more labor intensive than are community hospitals.

Mass Services. Another series of changes occurred in some of the mass service operations. Retailing offers some interesting examples. The expansion of catalog stores (e.g., Best's), warehouse stores (e.g., Toys R Us), mail-order sales (e.g., L. L. Bean), and brand-name discounters (e.g., Loehmann's) has shifted the emphasis of traditional retailing operation toward a lower degree of labor intensity. This was made possible because such services provide less than department store-type "full service." On the other hand, the proliferation of boutiques and specialty operations within stores like Bloomingdale's is evidence of a different kind of change, one where interaction and customization are stressed. This often demands higher labor intensity (more than "full service"). By being more "professional"—frequently by putting salespeople on commission—such stores hope to convert more "browsers" into "buyers."

The deregulation of commercial banking and financial services also created some intriguing strategic operation changes within the mass service quadrant. Automation in commercial banking (i.e., automatic teller machines, electronic transfers, and other new technological advances) has made commercial banking less labor intensive. Indeed, credit-card operations and check clearing are now placed in their own facilities (often at quite a distance from the commercial banks themselves), and they do essentially the kind of work that one would expect in a service factory. A similar change is evident in some other financial service companies. One of the justifications given for the acquisition of Lehman Brothers Kuhn Loeb by Shearson/American Express was the fact that the trading operations of Lehman Brothers could be absorbed easily by slack capacity in the backroom operations at Shearson.

However, even though technological advances have made it possible for some aspects of commercial banking to become less labor intensive, there is still a move to customize other services even more. Customization in this business grew out of the removal of interest rate ceilings on certificates of deposit, the cessation of fixed brokerage commissions, the demise of Regulation Q, which affects interest rates on bank accounts, and the initial steps toward interstate banking. Moreover, many of the services that have been acquired by the "financial supermarket" companies are essentially services that will give those companies greater interaction and customization. Consequently, the increasing menu of services provided by the traditional brokerage houses may cause the old-time broker, who tried to be all things

to his client, to become an anachronism. Merrill Lynch, for example, is promoting both greater automation and increasing customization of its services.

CHOOSING APPROPRIATE OPERATIONS

Service-business innovations, which have resulted in increasing segmentation and diversification of this sector, point up the need to assess the industry's operational choices. The insights of Wickham Skinner are as relevant to service businesses as they are to manufacturing organizations.[4] Service operations, like factories, have to be tailored to do certain things well at the expense of doing other things well. Moreover, one cannot assume that the "formula" that has been so successful in one service business will necessarily carry over to another service business, even if that business is merely a segmentation of the old one. Thus, the more explicit a service business can be about the demands of the business in light of its operations choices, the more appropriate those choices are likely to be.

McDonald's, for example, has been adamant in maintaining its focus on the fast-food business and has resisted diversifying into other types of fast-food chains or service businesses. On the other hand, Toys R Us has moved away from the warehouse-type store operation and has ventured into children's clothing, Kids R Us. Recognizing that children's clothes cannot be sold like toys, the company has altered its operations to provide more interaction and customization. At Kids R Us, the store sizes and layouts are different, the workers (clerk-counselors and clothes "runners") that are hired and trained to provide a more personalized service are different, and the inventory control systems are different.

MOVING TOWARD THE DIAGONAL

Given the quickening pace of segmentation and diversification of service businesses, several observations concerning the dynamics of service processes bear mentioning. First, many of the segmentation steps that service businesses have taken have been *toward* the diagonal that runs from the service factory to the professional service firm. Figure 3 illustrates this move. Still, one may ask, What makes the diagonal so attractive to existing services? The answer seems to be better control. However, it should be noted that the kinds of controls needed for mass services are different from those needed for service shops.

On one side of the diagonal, mass service controls often relate to labor costs and efficiency, for these services are trying constantly to get a grip on labor scheduling and productivity. Here, plant and equipment are rarely constraints. For example, in retailing, labor is a critical variable cost, and, therefore, scheduling labor is an important ac-

FIGURE 3
Strategic Operation Changes within the Service Process Matrix

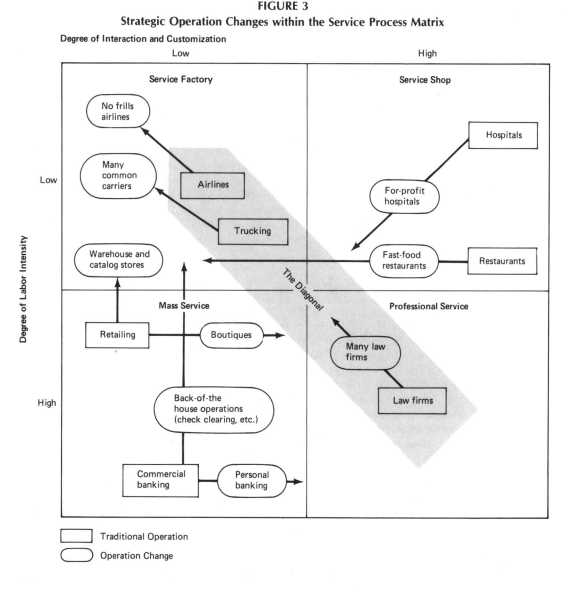

tivity. The increased use of point-of-sale terminals has permitted the tracking of sales of different items by 15-minute intervals throughout the day. Such information, in combination with sales per salesperson per hour (a productivity measure), is tremendously useful to inventory control, not to mention workforce scheduling. Moves toward more customization (e.g., the department store boutique and its commissioned salespeople) can also be understood as a move to increase control of the selling situation, with higher revenues, profits, and productivity as the end result.

On the other side of the diagonal, the service shop frets about control of the service itself. With this kind of service, plant and equipment are constant constraints. Therefore, there are concerns for how frequently unpredictable jobs (e.g., auto repairs, patients) can be scheduled through expensive capital equipment. Control is also affected by the uncertainty over when and how people can tell when a service is rendered satisfactorily. Hospitals, for example, have a high proportion of fixed costs and thus worry a great deal about capacity utilization. Current debates about who should dictate the utilization of hospital resources—administrative staffs or medical staffs—are, at the core, debates about resource control. In this context, one can understand pressures to provide less customized and/or interactive service (e.g., fewer tests, more ambulatory care).

The service factory and the professional service firm, on the other hand, suffer less from loss of control. Although control is still an issue for both kinds of services, for the professional service firm, control is more of an individual concern, relatively free of constraints of plant and equipment. The high degree of interaction and customization required of such firms is at least matched with a high degree of training and skill in the workforce.

The service factory can develop its "production process" to foster more control. The process that defines the service and the flow of information and materials is relatively smooth. In this regard, the service factory shares many of the benefits that manufac-turing operations enjoy. The labor needed is well known for given levels of demand, and scheduling of labor, plant, and equipment is fairly straightforward.

Even though there are pressures for *existing* operations to move toward the diagonal, there is no reason to think that all service shops or mass service operations will become extinct. Many operations will be able to adhere to their traditional operations. Moreover, marketing pressures for increased customization and generation of completely new services are likely to replenish the supply of service shops or mass service operations. Witness, for example, the demand for luxury airplane travel or luxury hotel accommodation. These are new services that are rendered to particular market niches. Note too the recent change in how computers are sold—that is, through mass outlets as opposed to individual salespeople. The recent shift by J. C. Penney toward more "full service" is yet another example.

MOVING UP THE DIAGONAL

Another observation centers on some of the service businesses already located on the diagonal. The professional service firm and the service factory are not immune to strategic changes. Of those services that have changed their positions within the service process matrix, most have moved up the diagonal. Consider, for example, the changes that have occurred within many law firms over the last decades. The institution of paralegals and other lower cost labor and the increasing specialization of many law firms have driven many firms within that industry toward lower labor intensity and less customization (i.e., less full service). Similarly, other professional service firms have invested in equipment, much of it for word processing or data processing.

Commercial banking in California is an example of a service business in the throes of change. Given its faltering economic position, the state is currently applying pressure on bank loan portfolios. Deregulation has also pressed heavily on the industry. Banks have been forced to seek lower costs to compensate for the increased rates they have had to pay to attract funds. In addition, deregulation has permitted banks to explore new lines of business. Given these pressures, it is understandable that BankAmerica, for instance, closed 132 branches in 1984 and reduced its workforce by 4 percent. Such decisions reflect a move up the diagonal, away from the old "formula." Furthermore, the bank scouted out the insurance industry as a potential source of earnings.

In a similar vein, the deregulation of trucking and air travel has meant significant change for the service factories. Trucking deregulation has forced many of the old-line common carriers to invest dramatically in breakbulks and additional freight terminals for less-than-truckload shipments. While such capital investments have meant increased barriers to entry for trucking firms, these firms can no longer afford to offer as customized a service as they used to for their clients. Today, their services are more specialized. In addition, their pricing structures have been changed to encourage the clients to ship in particular ways. Consequently, common carriers are moving up the diagonal.

A similar story can be told of the airlines. Deregulation encouraged major airlines to shift to hub-and-spoke systems, which means that a number of "pushes" can be made from their major airport hubs during any day. Where once competition focused on time of day and elegant service, competition these days centers more on price and less on the number of flights and the optimum time of day. The result for most airlines has been both less customization and lower labor intensity, given the significant investments that have been made at the hubs.

But just as movement toward the diagonal does not necessarily mean that service shops and mass service firms will cease to exist, the move up the diagonal does not necessarily mean that professional service firms will become small service factories. There will always be some firms that will be able to maintain successfully a high labor intensity

and high interaction and customization. Furthermore, new professional services will spring up that will demand, at least initially, a combination of high labor intensity and high interaction and customization.

CONCLUSION

For many existing services, the pressures for control and lower costs will tend to drive them toward the diagonal and/or up it. For many service firms, such positions will be the most profitable ones. Understanding such pressures on a service operation is well advised because it can help existing service businesses anticipate the nature of competitors' changes as well as many of the management challenges they will face over time (see Figure 2). In fact, what will be demanded of many newly created service businesses will be very different from what was demanded of their predecessors. Therefore, companies that appreciate and anticipate these differences will be at a strategic advantage. Those businesses that are diversifying or segmenting will know that the old "formula" may have to be changed for the new business, and they will have more than an inkling about how such operations should change. Competing service businesses that understand these changes will have a better appreciation for competitor moves and will also better understand relative strengths and weaknesses of their own operations.

Service managers who continue to claim that their operations are unique may be left in the dust by those who see their operations as more generic. When service firms begin to appraise themselves as service factories, service shops, mass service, or professional services—much as manufacturers see themselves as job shops, assembly lines, continuous flow processes, and the like—the service version of the not-invented-here syndrome will fade away and management minds will be more receptive to general, and generalizable, service management concepts.

Notes

[1] R. B. Chase, "The Customer Contact Approach to Services: Theoretical Bases and Practical Extensions," *Operations Research* **29** (1981): 698–706; R. B. Chase, "Where Does the Customer Fit in a Service Operation?" *Harvard Business Review*, November–December 1978, pp. 137–142; R. B. Chase and D. A. Tansik, "The Customer Contact Model for Organizational Design," *Management Science* **29** (1983): 1037–1050; R. B. Chase and N. Aquilano, *Production and Operations Management* (Homewood, IL: Richard D. Irwin, 1985), ch. 3.

[2] Chase (1981).

[3] D. H. Maister and C. H. Lovelock, "Managing Facilitator Services," *Sloan Management Review*, Summer 1982, pp. 19–31.

[4] W. Skinner, "The Focused Factory," *Harvard Business Review*, May–June 1974, pp. 113–121.

The Customer Contact
Approach to Services: Theoretical Bases
and Practical Extensions

RICHARD B. CHASE

This paper reviews the underlying theory of the customer contact approach to services and suggests specific applications to a wide range of service systems. The approach holds that the potential efficiency of a service system is a function of the degree of customer contact entailed in the creation of the service product. A number of propositions about high contact systems are identified and some simple heuristics for service system design and operation are proposed.

There is probably no area of operations management (OM) of greater current interest than services. Some of the reasons for this are (1) the rapid growth of services relative to manufacturing in the last decade, (2) the pressures on service operations to become cost efficient in their production processes, and (3) the (debatable) point that most of the intriguing OM problems in manufacturing have been dealt with so extensively that few new major breakthroughs appear likely, thus services provide a fresh target for applications of OM concepts. However, despite these compelling reasons for studying services, there is still a real question as to how services should be approached as a distinctive OM subfield for both research and teaching purposes. What seems to be called for is the development and dissemination of one or more theories of OM in services. One such theory is the "customer contact" approach, which is the focus of this paper.

Before explaining the customer contact approach, however, it is useful to discuss briefly some of the other efforts which have been undertaken to categorize services according to some specific managerially useful dimensions.

The literature on services is diffuse, but it appears that service marketing specialists have given the most attention to developing service taxonomies and generating prescriptions relative to each service system category. A common theme running through these efforts is the classification of services into tangible and intangible components in order to help determine how to choose an effective marketing strategy. [See, for example, Rathmell (1966) and Shostack (1977b).] Eiglier and Langeard (1977) have proposed a classification scheme which, in addition to tangibility/intangibility, considers the effect of the organization and client interface and user participation on the customer's perception of the product. Thomas (1978) dichotomizes service into equipment-based and people-based service as a means of developing strategy.

With respect to OM, writers in the field tend to model service systems by drawing structural analogies with manufacturing systems: e.g., intermittent, continuous, and project flows, in Buffa (1975); and input, transformation, and output, in Wild (1977). Though helpful in understanding flow properties of given services, these types of analogies cannot account directly for the presence or absence of behavioral and marketing elements which are embodied in the service product. In this sense, they suffer from the same limitations as process charts and operations charts of work design—they describe only the physical aspects of what takes place, not the psychosocial dynamics of the environment where they occur.

Approaches which address these more subjective aspects of service production to a greater extent are given in Sasser et al. (1978) and in Levitt (1972). Sasser et al. provide a descriptive model which they label as "operating characteristics in a service environment." This model postulates causal relationships among three elements: the service concept, the service delivery system, and service levels. In their view, the service concept (i.e., facilitating good, explicit intangibles and implicit intangibles) dictates, and is defined by, the service delivery system (i.e., performance characteristics of materials, atmosphere and image of facilities, attitudes of

employees). Both of these elements in turn are used by management to create service levels (in terms of materials, facilities, and personnel), which are then communicated to the consumer (via advertising) to determine "consumer perceived service levels." Levitt, in contrast, offers a normative view of services, advocating that service managers take a manufacturing approach to services by substituting "technology and systems for people." The prime example of this design philosophy is McDonald's Hamburgers, where, as Levitt notes, "Through painstaking attention to total design and facilities planning, everything is built integrally into the machine itself, into the technology of the system." Levitt (1972, 1976) provides a variety of other examples to buttress his contentions.

Both of these views have advantages and disadvantages relative to further development of service theory for OM. Sasser et al. provide a descriptively valid model of what takes place in a service operation but do not articulate what, if any, design or operation criteria derive directly from their model. Levitt's philosophy does have implications for design and operations but it does not develop specific criteria for the organization of services or for measuring the effectiveness of service performance. In fairness, neither approach was presented as an all-embracing theory, but by virtue of their general coverage of services they must be considered as yardsticks by which to measure subsequent approaches.

In addition to these two preceding approaches to services (which seem to emphasize what will be termed "high contact" services in this paper), there have been some interesting papers focusing on "low contact" or back office operations in banking. [See Matteis (1979), Shostack (1977a), and Reed (1971).] Also, there is a very extensive literature on services which bears tangentially on OM issues in economics (Gartner and Riesman 1974), public administration (Quinn 1978), and organization theory (Schneider 1973). Finally, there are some direct applications of quantitative techniques to such service OM problems as staff scheduling (Buffa et al. 1976), vehicle deployment (Kolesar and Walker 1974), and check processing (Boyd and Mabert 1977). Space does not permit a review of these efforts.

CUSTOMER CONTACT APPROACH

The customer contact approach holds that a service system's potential operating efficiency is a function of the degree to which the customer is in direct contact with the service facility relative to total service creation time for that customer:

potential facility efficiency

$$= f \left(1 - \frac{\text{customer contact time}}{\text{service creation time}} \right).$$

Efficiency is seen as the ratio of outputs to inputs for a given service facility; it does not account for customer utility functions or for organization-wide production or marketing performance. Service facilities characterized by high customer contact are perceived as being inherently limited in their production efficiency because of the uncertainty that people introduce into the service creation process. This uncertainty derives from individual differences in customers' attitudes and behaviors. Systems characterized by low customer contact are seen as being essentially free of this type of uncertainty and therefore are capable of operating at high levels of production efficiency, analogous to that achieved in well-run manufacturing organizations. (See Chase 1978 and Chase and Aquilano 1977.)

THE TECHNICAL CORE AND DECOUPLING

The contact approach was formulated partly in response to insights by several writers on two general concepts of organization design—protection of the technical core, and selective decoupling of organizational units. As can be seen from the following brief review, these concepts themselves are highly interrelated. Thompson (1967) proposed that organizational rationality logically leads designers to seal off the technical core (the production processes) of the organization from environmental influences. In Thompson's words, ". . . organizations seek to buffer environmental influences by surrounding their technical core with input and output components." The objective of this is to enable the core to produce ". . . at a continuous rate and with specified quality." Herbst (1974) defines the work domain of a team as consisting of a core region, a maintenance and service region, and an extra task region. He emphasizes that the mission of the last two regions is to facilitate performance of the core region. Miller (1959), in describing how systems can be differentiated, suggests that the management of operations is enhanced when homogeneous tasks are spatially and sequentially combined. Regarding decoupling, Simon (1969) has argued that complex systems can be disaggregated into stable subassemblies and that these are significant elements in any organization. Weick (1976) notes that "the coupling imagery gives researchers access to one of the more powerful ways of talking about complexity now available." Magee and Boodman (1967), in discussing the functions of inventory, emphasize its ability to decouple operations, making ". . . it unnecessary to gear production directly to consumption." (The implications of this observation relative to services are particularly intriguing.) Finally, there is Skinner's (1974) "plant-within-a-plant" concept (PWP) which makes operational both the technological core idea and decoupling, by advocating segmentation of a manufacturing facility "both organizationally and physically" into homogeneous units. "Each PWP has its own facilities in which it can concentrate on its particular manufacturing task using its own workforce management approaches, production control, organization structure, and so forth."

A CONTACT-BASED CLASSIFICATION SCHEME

In Chase and Chase and Aquilano it was proposed that common service systems could be grouped according to decreasing contact under three broad headings: pure services, mixed services, and quasi-manufacturing. Pure services include those organizations whose major production is carried on in the presence of the customers (medical care, restaurants, transportation, personal services); mixed services which commonly involve a mix of face-to-face contact and loosely coupled back office work (primarily branch offices); and quasi-manufacturing that entails virtually no face-to-face contact (home offices and distribution centers). Admittedly, pure services do have noncontact production, but their main business entails heavy customer involvement.

Following the basic premise of the approach, quasi-manufacturing service units are most amenable to a manufacturing rationale, mixed services are less so, and pure services hardly at all. Obviously, the classification scheme is highly simplified and at this time can be supported only on the basis of intuitive appeal and experience rather than directed research. However, for practical application specific cases can be incorporated readily within it and, perhaps most importantly, a working language and point of departure for service system study is available. (See Lovelock and Young 1979 for its use in a discussion of marketing strategy.)

DERIVATIVE PROPOSITIONS

One of the attributes of the contact view of services is that it leads fairly directly to some interesting propositions about the nature and limitations of high contact systems relative to low contact systems (and manufacturing systems). Table 1, containing a few representative propositions, is drawn from several sources (see Bessom and Jackson, Kolesar and Walker, Sasser 1976, and Chase and Aquilano) although only the latter identify them as propositions. (Some propositions taken from Chase and Aquilano have been modified in light of further examination.)

With reference to the propositions, it can be seen that each one has implications for one or more of the primary OM functions of planning, scheduling, and control. Also,

TABLE 1

OM Characteristics of High Contact Services— Some Propositions

1. The service product is multidimensional (time, place, atmosphere) and hence its quality is in the eye of the beholder.
2. The direct worker is part of the service product.
3. Demand for the service is often instantaneous and hence cannot be stored.
4. Because production is generally customer initiated, an optimal balance between service system demand and resources is difficult to achieve.
5. Changes in the capacity of the system affect the nature of the service product.
6. The production schedule has a direct, personal effect on the consumer.
7. Only part of the service can be kept in inventory.
8. Verbal skills and knowledge of policy are usually required of the service worker.
9. Wage payments must usually be related to labor hours spent rather than output.
10. It is assumed that service system capacity is at its long run level when the system first opens.
11. A service system malfunction will have an immediate, direct effect on the customer.
12. The location of the service system modifies its value to the customer.

they serve to illustrate some of the implicitly recognized but rarely articulated aspects of the marketing production interface.

APPLICATION OF THE CONCEPT

As mentioned earlier, typical service organizations have been placed under headings of pure service, mixed service, or quasi-manufacturing according to their dominant service product. However, since most service systems are really a mixture of high and low contact, the steps which follow are felt to be suitable for analyzing any service organization. The steps are:

1. Identify those points in the service system where decoupling is possible and desirable. (It will be necessary to trade off cost savings from operations improvement against marketing losses that result from changes in the nature of the services provided.)

TABLE 2
Contact Reduction and Improvement Strategies

Contact Reduction Strategies:

- Handle only exceptions on a face-to-face basis; all other transactions by phone, or better yet by mail.
- Use reservations or appointments-only systems.
- Decentralize using kiosks with one person for information handling (this takes pressure off the main facility).
- Use drop-off points such as automatic teller machines.
- Bring service to customer through postal rounds or mobile offices.
- Use a roving greeter or signs outside facility to act as buffers and information providers.

Contact Improvement Strategies:

- Take-a-number systems.
- Assign contact workers who are people-oriented and knowledgeable about service system processes and policies.
- Maintain consistent work hours.
- Partition back office from the public service counter; do not permit work breaks in front of the customer.
- Provide queueing patterns and signs to indicate standardized and customized service channels.

Low Contact Improvement Strategies (for back office or home office):

- Establish control points for items entering and leaving departments (log times and quantities to control work in process and provide a basis for capacity planning).
- Process standard items in an assembly line mode; customized items as whole tasks.
- Utilize manufacturing-based concepts such as standard times, cost centers, acceptance sampling techniques, and resource-oriented scheduling and dispatching criteria.

2. Employ contact reduction strategies where appropriate.
3. Employ contact enhancement strategies where appropriate.
4. Employ traditional efficiency improvement techniques (production control, industrial engineering, etc.) to improve low contact operations.

In carrying out Steps 2, 3, and 4, a number of widely used, common-sense heuristics come to mind (Table 2). The interesting thing about them is that a contact view of the world will lead the system designer or manager directly to them. On the other hand, without this perspective few organizations are likely to apply them all, or seek out others.

Of course, some companies have shown an understanding of the effects of customer contact and decoupling as illustrated by the following simple examples.

An international bank in Paris is in the process of physically relocating its back office (low contact) operations outside the city to take advantage of lower office space costs and to utilize a newly constructed building designed to handle paperwork in a factory-like way.

Benihana of Tokyo restaurants have flamboyant chefs cook all meals on a hibachi at the customer's table (thereby providing a "show"), while simultaneously eliminating the need for a large kitchen at their expensive downtown locations.

A local car wash, in response to declining business, shifted its high-seniority but less personable old-timers from customer contact points at the beginning and end of the process, to low contact points at intermediate stages. They were replaced by clean-cut college students who could relate well to the customers. (The sign on the car wash marquee subsequently read "Sudsiness with a Smile.")

FURTHER DEVELOPMENT OF THE CONTACT APPROACH

There are several aspects of the customer contact approach which need to be expanded and validated. One is the categorization itself. For instance, the distinction between pure service and mixed service is far from precise. How much back office work has to be done before a pure service becomes a mixed service, and vice versa? At what point along the contact continuum does the presence of the customer entail a shift in service policy? Likewise, what role does the extent of coordination required play in segmenting pure, mixed, and quasi-manufacturing services? That is, when does the need for tight coordination across the boundary between high and low contact operations change the nature of a given service (and hence its placement within the typology)? What is the effect on organization structure of decoupling by customer contact?

Regarding additional refinements, one possibility is the description of service systems using a taxonomical approach roughly similar to that used in job shop scheduling research. [See for example the four-parameter notation used in Conway et al. (1967).] Such a taxonomy might employ a set of descriptions such as: High (low) contact/ Standardized (customized) service/Tangible (intangible) product dominant/Automated (nonautomated) technology. Obviously, a tight taxonomy would be of immense value in focusing OM research efforts and synthesizing results.

Finally, there is the need to test the propositions and heuristics proposed here. Do they hold across the entire range of services? Are there other variables or contingencies not yet identified which ultimately determine their applicability? Can both be used in some way to develop "true" principles of services?

CONCLUSION

In addition to explicitly advocating the customer contact approach, this paper has implicitly supported the feasibility of developing a general theory of services for OM. Thus, if the ideas presented here stimulate others to join in the development of alternative general approaches and theories, the objective of this paper will be more than met. The study of services is a fascinating activity; indeed, by virtue of being constantly involved with them in our everyday lives we become "experts" on them to some degree. Certainly the time is ripe for OM specialists to begin to study them in earnest.*

---

*ACKNOWLEDGMENTS: The author thanks Nicholas Aquilano, Dwight Smith, and the anonymous referees for their helpful and thought-provoking comments on the manuscript.

REFERENCES

Bessom, R. M., and D. W. Jackson. 1975. Service Retailing: A Strategic Marketing Approach. *J. Retailing* **51,** 75–84.

Boyd, K., and V. Mabert. 1977. A Two Stage Forecasting Approach at Chemical Bank of New York for Check Processing. *J. Bank Res.* **8,** 101–107.

Buffa, E. 1975. *Operations Management: The Management of Productive Systems.* Wiley/Hamilton, New York.

Buffa, E., M. Cosgrove, and B. Luce. 1976. An Integrated Work Shift Scheduling System. *Decision Sci.* **7,** 620–630.

Chase, R. B. 1978. Where Does the Customer Fit in a Service Operation? *Harvard Bus. Rev.* **56,** 137–142.

Chase, R. B., and N. J. Aquilano. 1977. *Production and Operations Management: A Life Cycle Approach,* rev. ed. Richard D. Irwin, Homewood, Ill.

Conway, R., W. Maxwell, and L. Miller. 1967. *Theory of Scheduling.* Addison-Wesley, Reading, Mass.

Eiglier, P., and E. Langeard. 1977. A New Approach to Service Marketing. In *Marketing Consumer Services: New Insights, Report 77-115.* Marketing Science Institute, Boston.

Gartner, A., and F. Riesman. 1974. *The Service Society and the Consumer Vanguard.* Harper & Row, New York.

Herbst, P. G. 1974. *Socio-technical Design: Strategies in Multidisciplinary Research,* pp. 143–147. Tavistock Publications, London.

Kolesar, P., and W. Walker. 1974. An Algorithm for the Dynamic Relocation of Fire Companies. *Opns. Res.* **22,** 249–274.

Levitt, T. 1972. Production Line Approach to Service. *Harvard Bus. Rev.* **50,** 41–52.

Levitt, T. 1976. The Industrialization of Services. *Harvard Bus. Rev.* **54,** 41–52.

Lovelock, C. H., and R. F. Young. 1979. Look to Customers to Increase Productivity. *Harvard Bus. Rev.* **57,** 168–178.

Magee, J. F., and D. M. Boodman. 1967. *Production Planning and Inventory Control,* 2nd ed. pp. 20–21. McGraw-Hill, New York.

Matteis, R. J. 1979. The New Back Office Focuses on Customer Service. *Harvard Bus. Rev.* **57,** 146–159.

Miller, E. J. 1959. Technology, Territory and Time: The Internal Differentiation of Complex Production Systems. *Human Rel.* **12,** 243–272.

QUINN, R. 1978. Productivity and the Process of Organizational Improvement: Why We Cannot Talk to Each Other. *Pub. Admin. Rev.* **38,** 41–45.

RATHMELL, J. M. 1966. What Is Meant by Services? *J. Marktg.* **30,** 32–36.

REED, J. 1971. Sure It's a Bank but I Think of It as a Factory. *Innovation* **23,** 19–27.

SASSER, W. E. 1976. Match Supply and Demand in Service Industries. *Harvard Bus. Rev.* **54,** 61–65.

SASSER, W. E., R. P. OLSEN, AND D. D. WYCKOFF. 1978. *Management of Service Operations,* pp. 20–21. Allyn & Bacon, Boston.

SCHNEIDER, B. 1973. The Perceptions of Organizational Climate: The Customer's View. *J. Appl. Psychol.* **57,** 248–256.

SHOSTACK, G. L. 1977a. Banks Sell Services—Not Things. *Bankers Magazine,* Winter, pp. 40–45.

SHOSTACK, G. L. 1977b. Breaking Free from Product Marketing. *J. Marktg.* **41,** 73–80.

SIMON, H. A. 1969. The Architecture of Complexity. *Proc. Am. Phil. Soc.* **106,** 457–482.

SKINNER, W. 1974. The Focused Factory. *Harvard Bus. Rev.* **52,** 113–121.

THOMAS, D. 1978. Strategy Is Different in Service Businesses. *Harvard Bus. Rev.* **56,** 158–165.

THOMPSON, J. D. 1967. *Organizations in Action,* pp. 14–37. McGraw-Hill, New York.

WEICK, K. E. 1976. Educational Organizations as Loosely Coupled Systems. *Admin. Sci. Quart.* **21,** 1–19.

WILD, R. 1977. *Concepts for Operations Management.* John Wiley & Sons, London.

Classifying Services to Gain Strategic Marketing Insights

CHRISTOPHER H. LOVELOCK

The diversity of the service sector makes it difficult to come up with managerially useful generalizations concerning marketing practice in service organizations. This article argues for a focus on specific categories of services and proposes five schemes for classifying services in ways that transcend narrow industry boundaries. In each instance insights are offered into how the nature of the service might affect the marketing task.

Developing professional skills in marketing management requires the ability to look across a broad cross section of marketing situations, to understand their differences and commonalities, and to identify appropriate marketing strategies in each instance. In the manufacturing sector many experienced marketers have worked for a variety of companies in several different industries, often including both consumer goods and industrial firms. As a result, they have a perspective that transcends narrow industry boundaries.

But exposure to marketing problems and strategies in different industries is still quite rare among managers in the service sector. Not only is the concept of a formalized marketing function still relatively new to most service firms, but service industries have historically been somewhat inbred. The majority of railroad managers, for instance, have spent their entire working lives within the railroad industry—even within a single company. Most hoteliers have grown up in the hotel industry. And most hospital or college administrators have remained within the confines of health care or higher education, respectively. The net result of such narrow exposure is that it restricts a manager's ability to identify and learn from the experience

Reprinted from *Journal of Marketing*, Vol. 47 (Summer 1983), 9–20, published by The American Marketing Association.

of organizations facing parallel situations in other service industries—and, of course, from marketing experience in the manufacturing sector. Conversely, marketers from the manufacturing sector who take positions in service businesses often find that their past experience has not prepared them well for working on some of the problems that regularly challenge service marketers (Knisely 1979, Lovelock 1981, Shostack 1977).

This article argues that development of greater sophistication in services marketing will be aided if we can find new ways to group services other than by current industry classifications. A more useful approach may be to segment services into clusters that share certain relevant marketing characteristics—such as the nature of the relationship between the service organization and its customers or patterns of demand relative to supply—and then to examine the implications for marketing action.

After briefly reviewing the value of classification schemes in marketing, the article summarizes past proposals for classifying services. This is followed by presentation and discussion of five classification schemes based on past proposals or on clinical research. In each instance examples are given of how various services fall into similar or different categories, and an evaluation is made of the resulting marketing insights and what they imply for marketing strategy development.

THE VALUE OF CLASSIFICATION IN MARKETING

Hunt (1976) has emphasized the usefulness of classification schemes in marketing. Various attempts have been made in the past by marketing theorists to classify goods into different categories. One of the most famous and enduring is Copeland's (1923) classification of convenience, shopping and specialty goods. Not only did this help managers obtain a better understanding of consumer needs and behavior, it also provided insights into the management of retail distribution systems. Bucklin (1963) and others have re-

vised and refined Copeland's original classification and thereby been able to provide important strategic guidelines for retailers. Another major classification has been between durable and nondurable goods. Durability is closely associated with purchase frequency, which has important implications for development of both distribution and communications strategy. Yet another classification is consumer goods versus industrial goods; this classification relates both to the type of goods purchased (although there is some overlap) and to product evaluation, purchasing procedures and usage behavior. Recognition of these distinctions by marketers has led to different types of marketing strategy being directed at each of these groups. Through such classifications the application of marketing management tools and strategies in manufacturing has become a professional skill that transcends industry divisions.

By contrast, service industries remain dominated by an operations orientation that insists that each industry is different. This mind set is often manifested in managerial attitudes that suggest, for example, that the marketing of airlines has nothing at all in common with that of banks, insurance, motels, hospitals or household movers. But if it can be shown that some of these services do share certain relevant marketing characteristics, then the stage may be set for some useful cross-fertilization of concepts and strategies.

How Might Services Be Classified?

Various attempts have been proposed in the past for classifying services and are outlined, with brief commentaries, in Table 1. But developing classification schemes is not enough. If they are to have managerial value, they must offer strategic insights. That is why it is important to develop ways of analyzing services that highlight the characteristics they have in common, and then to examine the implications for marketing management.

This article builds on past research by ex-

TABLE 1

Summary of Previously Proposed Schemes for Classifying Services

Author	Proposed Classification Schemes	Comment
Judd (1964)	1. Rented goods services (right to own and use a good for a defined time period) 2. Owned goods services (custom creation, repair or improvement of goods owned by the customer) 3. Nongoods services (personal experiences or "experiential possession")	First two are fairly specific, but third category is very broad and ignores services such as insurance, banking, legal advice and accounting.
Rathmell (1974)	1. Type of seller 2. Type of buyer 3. Buying motives 4. Buying practice 5. Degree of regulation	No specific application to services—could apply equally well to goods.
Shostack (1977)[a] Sasser et al.[a] (1978)	Proportion of physical goods and intangible services contained within each product "package"	Offers opportunities for multiattribute modeling. Emphasizes that there are few pure goods or pure services.
Hill (1977)	1. Services affecting persons vs. those affecting goods 2. Permanent vs. temporary effects of the service 3. Reversibility vs. nonreversibility of these effects 4. Physical effects vs. mental effects 5. Individual vs. collective services	Emphasizes nature of service benefits and (in 5) variations in the service delivery/ consumption environment.
Thomas (1978)	1. Primarily equipment-based a. Automated (e.g., car wash) b. Monitored by unskilled operators (e.g., movie theater) c. Operated by skilled personnel (e.g., airline) 2. Primarily people-based a. Unskilled labor (e.g., lawn care) b. Skilled labor (e.g., repair work) c. Professional staff (e.g., lawyers, dentists)	Although operational rather than marketing in orientation, provides a useful way of understanding product attributes.
Chase (1978)	Extent of customer contact required in service delivery a. High contact (e.g., health care, hotels, restaurants) b. Low contact (e.g., postal service, wholesaling)	Recognizes that product variability is harder to control in high contact services because customers exert more influence on timing of demand and service features, due to their greater involvement in the service process.
Kotler (1980)	1. People-based vs. equipment-based 2. Extent to which client's presence is necessary 3. Meets personal needs vs. business needs 4. Public vs. private, for-profit vs. nonprofit	Synthesizes previous work, recognizes differences in purpose of service organization.
Lovelock (1980)	1. Basic demand characteristics —Object served (persons vs. property) —Extent of demand/supply imbalances —Discrete vs. continuous relationships between customers and providers 2. Service content and benefits —Extent of physical goods content —Extent of personal service content —Single service vs. bundle of services —Timing and duration of benefits 3. Service delivery procedures —Multisite vs. single site delivery —Allocation of capacity (reservations vs. first come, first served) —Independent vs. collective consumption —Time defined vs. task defined transactions —Extent to which customers must be present during service delivery	Synthesizes previous classifications and adds several new schemes. Proposes several categories within each classification. Concludes that defining object served is most fundamental classification scheme. Suggests that valuable marketing insights would come from combining two or more classification schemes in a matrix.

[a]These were two independent studies that drew broadly similar conclusions.

amining characteristics of services that transcend industry boundaries and are different in degree or kind from the categorization schemes traditionally applied to manufactured goods. Five classification schemes have been selected for presentation and discussion, reflecting their potential for affecting the way marketing management strategies are developed and implemented. Each represents an attempt to answer one of the following questions:

1. What is the nature of the service act?
2. What type of relationship does the service organization have with its customers?
3. How much room is there for customization and judgment on the part of the service provider?
4. What is the nature of demand and supply for the service?
5. How is the service delivered?

Each question will be examined on two dimensions, reflecting my conclusion in an earlier study (Lovelock 1980) that combining classification schemes in a matrix may yield better marketing insights than classifying service organizations on one variable at a time.

WHAT IS THE NATURE OF THE SERVICE ACT?

A service has been described as a "deed, act or performance" (Berry 1980). Two fundamental issues are at whom (or what) is the act directed, and is this act tangible or intangible in nature?

As shown in Figure 1, these two questions result in a four-way classification scheme involving (1) tangible actions to people's bodies, such as airline transportation, haircutting and surgery; (2) tangible actions to goods and other physical possessions, such as air freight, lawn mowing and janitorial services; (3) intangible actions directed at people's minds, such as broadcasting and education; and (4) intangible actions directed at people's intangible assets, such as insurance, investment banking and consulting.

Sometimes a service may seem to spill over into two or more categories. For instance, the delivery of educational, religious or entertainment services (directed primarily at the mind) often entails tangible actions such as being in a classroom, church or theater; the delivery of financial services may require a visit to a bank to transform intangible financial assets into hard cash; and the deliv-

FIGURE 1

Understanding the Nature of the Service Act

Who or What is the Direct Recipient of the Service?

	People	Things
Tangible Actions	Services directed at people's bodies: • Health care • Passenger transportation • Beauty salons • Exercise clinics • Restaurants • Haircutting	Services directed at goods and other physical possessions: • Freight transportation • Industrial equipment repair and maintenance • Janitorial services • Laundry and dry cleaning • Landscaping/lawn care • Veterinary care
Intangible Actions	Services directed at people's minds: • Education • Broadcasting • Information services • Theaters • Museums	Services directed at intangible assets: • Banking • Legal services • Accounting • Securities • Insurance

What is the Nature of the Service Act?

ery of airline services may affect some travelers' states of mind as well as physically moving their bodies from one airport to another. But in most instances the core service act is confined to one of the four categories, although there may be secondary acts in another category.

Insights and Implications

Why is this categorization scheme useful to service marketers? Basically it helps answer the following questions:

1. Does the customer need to be *physically* present:
   a. Throughout service delivery?
   b. Only to initiate or terminate the service transaction (e.g., dropping off a car for repair and picking it up again afterwards)?
   c. Not at all (the relationship with the service supplier can be at arm's length through the mails, telephone or other electronic media)?
2. Does the customer need to be *mentally* present during service delivery? Can mental presence be maintained across physical distances through mail or electronic communications?
3. In what ways is the target of the service act "modified" by receipt of the service? And how does the customer benefit from these "modifications"?

It's not always obvious what the service is and what it does for the customer because services are ephemeral. By identifying the target of the service and then examining how it is "modified" or changed by receipt of the service act, we can develop a better understanding of the nature of the service product and the core benefits that it offers. For instance, a haircut leaves the recipient with shorter and presumably more appealingly styled hair, air freight gets the customer's goods speedily and safely between two points, a news radio broadcast updates the listener's knowledge about recent events, and life insurance protects the future value of the insured person's assets.

If customers need to be physically present during service delivery, then they must enter the service "factory" (whether it be a train, a hairdressing salon, or a hospital at a particular location) and spend time there while the service is performed. Their satisfaction with the service will be influenced by the interactions they have with service personnel, the nature of the service facilities, and also perhaps by the characteristics of other customers using the same service. Questions of location and schedule convenience assume great importance when a customer has to be physically present or must appear in person to initiate and terminate the transaction.

Dealing with a service organization at arm's length, by contrast, may mean that a customer never sees the service facilities at all and may not even meet the service personnel face-to-face. In this sort of situation, the outcome of the service act remains very important, but the process of service delivery may be of little interest, since the customer never goes near the "factory." For instance, credit cards and many types of insurance can be obtained by mail or telephone.

For operational reasons it may be very desirable to get the customer out of the factory and to transform a "high-contact" service into a "low-contact" one (Chase 1978). The chances of success in such an endeavor will be enhanced when the new procedures also offer customers greater convenience. Many services directed at *things* rather than at people formerly required the customer's presence but are now delivered at arm's length. Certain financial services have long used the mails to save customers the inconvenience of personal visits to a specific office location. Today, new electronic distribution channels have made it possible to offer instantaneous delivery of financial services to a wide array of alternative locations. Retail banking provides a good example, with its growing use of such electronic delivery systems as automatic teller machines in airports or shopping centers, pay-by-phone bill paying, or on-line banking facilities in retail stores.

By thinking creatively about the nature of their services, managers of service organizations may be able to identify opportunities for alternative, more convenient forms of service delivery or even for transformation of the service into a manufactured good. For instance, services to the mind such as education do not necessarily require attendance in person since they can be delivered through the mails or electronic media (Britain's Open University, which makes extensive use of television and radio broadcasts, is a prime example). Two-way communication hook-ups can make it possible for a physically distant teacher and students to interact directly where this is necessary to the educational process (one recent Bell System advertisement featured a chamber music class in a small town being taught by an instructor several hundred miles away). Alternatively, lectures can be packaged and sold as books, records or videotapes. And programmed learning exercises can be developed in computerized form, with the terminal serving as a Socratic surrogate.

WHAT TYPE OF RELATIONSHIP DOES THE SERVICE ORGANIZATION HAVE WITH ITS CUSTOMERS?

With very few exceptions, consumers buy manufactured goods at discrete intervals, paying for each purchase separately and rarely entering into a formal relationship with the manufacturer. (Industrial purchasers, by contrast, often enter into long-term relationships with suppliers and sometimes receive almost continuous delivery of certain supplies.)

In the service sector both household and institutional purchasers may enter into on-going relationships with service suppliers and may receive service on a continuing basis. This offers a way of categorizing services. We can ask, does the service organization enter into a "membership" relationship with its customers—as in telephone subscriptions, banking and the family doctor—or is there no formal relationship? And is service delivered on a continuous basis—as in insurance, broadcasting and police protection —or is each transaction recorded and charged separately? Figure 2 shows the 2 × 2 matrix resulting from this categorization, with some additional examples in each category.

Insights and Implications

The advantage to the service organization of a membership relationship is that it knows who its current customers are and, usually, what use they make of the services offered. This can be valuable for segmentation purposes if good records are kept and the data are readily accessible in a format that lends itself to computerized analysis. Knowing the identities and addresses of current customers enables the organization to make effective use of direct mail, telephone selling and personal sales calls—all highly targeted marketing communication media.

The nature of service relationships also has important implications for pricing. In situations where service is offered on an ongoing basis, there is often just a single pe-

FIGURE 2
Relationships with Customers

	Type of Relationship between the Service Organization and Its Customers	
Nature of Service Delivery	"Membership" Relationship	No Formal Relationship
Continuous Delivery of Service	Insurance Telephone subscription College enrollment Banking American Automobile Association	Radio station Police protection Lighthouse Public highway
Discrete Transactions	Long-distance phone calls Theater series subscription Commuter ticket or transit pass	Car rental Mail service Toll highway Pay phone Movie theater Public transportation Restaurant

riodic charge covering all services contracted for. Most insurance policies fall in this category, as do tuition and board fees at a residential college. The big advantage of this package approach is its simplicity. Some memberships, however, entail a series of separate and identifiable transactions with the price paid being tied explicitly to the number and type of such transactions. While more complex to administer, such an approach is fairer to customers (whose usage patterns may vary widely) and may discourage wasteful use of what are perceived as "free" services. In such instances, members may be offered advantages over casual users, such as discounted rates (telephone subscribers pay less for long-distance calls made from their own phones than do pay-phone users) or advance notification and priority reservations (as in theater subscriptions). Some membership services offer certain services (such as rental of equipment or connection to a public utility system) for a base fee and then make incremental charges for each separate transaction above a defined minimum.

Profitability and customer convenience are central issues in deciding how to price membership services. Will the organization generate greater long-term profits by tying payment explicitly to consumption, by charging a flat rate regardless of consumption, or by unbundling the components of the service and charging a flat rate for some and an incremental rate for others? Telephone and electricity services, for instance, typically charge a base fee for connection to the system and rental of equipment, plus a variety of incremental charges for consumption above a defined minimum. On the other hand, Wide Area Telephone Service (WATS) offers the convenience of unlimited long-distance calling for a fixed fee. How important is it to customers to have the convenience of paying a single periodic fee that is known in advance? For instance, members of the American Automobile Association (AAA) can obtain information booklets, travel advice and certain types of emergency road services free of additional charges. Such a package offers elements of both insurance and convenience to customers who may not be able to predict their exact needs in advance.

Where no formal relationship exists between supplier and customer, continuous delivery of the product is normally found only among that class of services that economists term "public goods"—such as broadcasting, police and lighthouse services, and public highways—where no charge is made for use of a service that is continuously available and financed from tax revenues. Discrete transactions, where each usage involves a payment to the service supplier by an essentially "anonymous" consumer, are exemplified by many transportation services, restaurants, movie theaters, shoe repairs and so forth. The problem of such services is that marketers tend to be much less well-informed about who their customers are and what use each customer makes of the service than their counterparts in membership organizations.

Membership relationships usually result in customer loyalty to a particular service supplier (sometimes there is no choice because the supplier has a monopoly). As a marketing strategy, many service businesses seek ways to develop formal, ongoing relations with customers in order to ensure repeat business and/or ongoing financial support. Public radio and television broadcasters, for instance, develop membership clubs for donors and offer monthly program guides in return; performing arts organizations sell subscription series; transit agencies offer monthly passes; airlines create clubs for high mileage fliers; and hotels develop "executive service plans" offering priority reservations and upgraded rooms for frequent guests. The marketing task here is to determine how it might be possible to build sales and revenues through such memberships but to avoid requiring membership when this would result in freezing out a large volume of desirable casual business.

HOW MUCH ROOM IS THERE FOR CUSTOMIZATION AND JUDGMENT?

Relatively few consumer goods nowadays are built to special order; most are purchased "off the shelf." The same is true for a majority of industrial goods, although by permutating options it's possible to give the impression of customization. Once they've purchased their goods, of course, customers are usually free to use them as they see fit.

The situation in the service sector, by contrast, is sharply different. Because services are created as they are consumed, and because the customer is often actually involved in the production process, there is far more scope for tailoring the service to meet the needs of individual customers. As shown in Figure 3, customization can proceed along at least two dimensions. The first concerns the extent to which the characteristics of the service and its delivery system lend themselves to customization; the second relates to how much judgment customer contact personnel are able to exercise in defining the nature of the service received by individual customers.

Some service concepts are quite standardized. Public transportation, for instance, runs over fixed routes on predetermined schedules. Routine appliance repairs typically involve a fixed charge, and the customer is responsible for dropping off the item at a given retail location and picking it up again afterwards. Fast food restaurants have a small, set menu; few offer the customer much choice in how the food will be cooked and served. Movies, entertainment and spectator sports place the audience in a relatively passive role, albeit a sometimes noisy one.

Other services offer customers a wide choice of options. Each telephone subscriber enjoys an individual number and can use the phone to obtain a broad array of different services—from receiving personal calls from a next-door neighbor to calling a business associate on the other side of the world, and from data transmission to dial-a-prayer. Retail bank accounts are also customized, with each check or bank card carrying the customer's name and personal code. Within the constraints set down by the bank, the customer enjoys considerable latitude in how and when the account is used and receives a personalized monthly statement. Good hotels and restaurants usually offer their customers an array of service options from which to choose, as well as considerable flexibility in how the service product is delivered to them.

But in each of these instances, the role of the customer contact personnel (if there are any) is somewhat constrained. Other than

FIGURE 3
Customization and Judgment in Service Delivery

Extent to Which Service Characteristics Are Customized

	High	Low
High	Legal services Health care/surgery Architectural design Executive search firm Real Estate agency Taxi service Beautician Plumber Education (tutorials)	Education (large classes) Preventive health programs
Low	Telephone service Hotel services Retail banking (excl. major loans) Good restaurant	Public transportation Routine appliance repair Fast food restaurant Movie theater Spectator sports

Extent to Which Customer Contact Personnel Exercise Judgment in Meeting Individual Customer Needs tailoring their personal manner to the customer and answering straightforward questions, contact personnel have relatively little discretion in altering the characteristics of the service they deliver: their role is basically that of operator or order taker. Judgment and discretion in customer dealings is usually reserved for managers or supervisors who will not normally become involved in service delivery unless a problem arises.

A third category of services gives the customer contact personnel wide latitude in how they deliver the service, yet these individuals do not significantly differentiate the characteristics of their service between one customer and another. For instance, educators who teach courses by lectures and give multiple choice, computer scored exams expose each of their students to a potentially similar experience, yet one professor may elect to teach a specific course in a very different way from a colleague at the same institution.

However, there is a class of services that not only involves a high degree of customization but also requires customer contact personnel to exercise judgment concerning the characteristics of the service and how it is delivered to each customer. Far from being reactive in their dealings with customers, these service personnel are often prescriptive: users (or clients) look to them for advice as well as for customized execution. In this category the locus of control shifts from the user to the supplier—a situation that some customers may find disconcerting. Consumers of surgical services literally place their lives in the surgeon's hands (the same, unfortunately, is also true of taxi services in many cities). Professional services such as law, medicine, accounting and architecture fall within this category. They are all white collar "knowledge industries," requiring extensive training to develop the requisite skills and judgment needed for satisfactory service delivery. Deliverers of such services as taxi drivers, beauticians and plumbers are also found in this category. Their work is customized to the situation at hand and in each instance, the customer purchases the expertise required to devise a tailor-made solution.

Insights and Implications

To a much greater degree than in the manufacturing sector, service products are "custom-made." Yet customization has its costs. Service management often represents an ongoing struggle between the desires of marketing managers to add value and the goals of operations managers to reduce costs through standardization. Resolving such disputes, a task that may require arbitration by the general manager, requires a good understanding of consumer choice criteria, particularly as these relate to price/value trade-offs and competitive positioning strategy. At the present time, most senior managers in service businesses have come up through the operations route; hence, participation in executive education programs may be needed to give them the necessary perspective on marketing to make balanced decisions.

Customization is not necessarily important to success. As Levitt (1972, 1976) has pointed out, industrializing a service to take advantage of the economies of mass production may actually increase consumer satisfaction. Speed, consistency and price savings may be more important to many customers than customized service. In some instances, such as spectator sports and the performing arts, part of the product experience is sharing the service with many other people. In other instances the customer expects to share the service facilities with other consumers, as in hotels or airlines, yet still hopes for some individual recognition and custom treatment. Allowing customers to reserve specific rooms or seats in advance, having contact personnel address them by name (it's on their ticket or reservation slip), and providing some latitude for individual choice (room service and morning calls, drinks and meals) are all ways to create an image of customization.

Generally, customers like to know in advance what they are buying—what the product features are, what the service will do for them. Surprises and uncertainty are not normally popular. Yet when the nature of the service requires a judgment-based, customized solution, as in a professional service, it is not always clear to either the customer or the professional what the outcome will be. Frequently, an important dimension of the professional's role is diagnosing the nature of the situation, then designing a solution.

In such situations those responsible for developing marketing strategy would do well to recognize that customers may be uneasy concerning the prior lack of certainty about the outcome. Customer contact personnel in these instances are not only part of the product but also determine what that product should be.

One solution to this problem is to divide the product into two separate components, diagnosis and implementation of a solution, that are executed and paid for separately. The process of diagnosis can and should be explained to the customer in advance, since the outcome of the diagnosis cannot always be predicted accurately. However, once that diagnosis has been made, the customer need not proceed immediately with the proposed solution; indeed, there is always the option of seeking a second opinion. The solution "product," by contrast, can often be spelled out in detail beforehand, so that the customer has a reasonable idea of what to expect. Although there may still be some uncertainty, as in legal actions or medical treatment, the range of possibilities should be narrower by this point, and it may be feasible to assign probabilities to specified alternative outcomes.

Marketing efforts may need to focus on the process of client-provider interactions. It will help prospective clients make choices between alternative suppliers, especially where professionals are concerned, if they know something of the organization's (or individual's) approach to diagnosis and problem-solving, as well as client-relationship style. These are considerations that transcend mere statements of qualification in an advertisement or brochure. For instance, some pediatricians allow new parents time for a free interview before any commitments are made. Such a trial encounter has the advantage of allowing both parties to decide whether or not a good match exists.

WHAT IS THE NATURE OF DEMAND AND SUPPLY FOR THE SERVICE?

Manufacturing firms can inventory supplies of their products as a hedge against fluctuations in demand. This enables them to enjoy the economies derived from operating plants at a steady level of production. Service businesses can't do this because it's not possible to inventory the finished service. For instance, the potential income from an empty seat on an airline flight is lost forever once that flight takes off, and each hotel daily room vacancy is equally perishable. Likewise, the productive capacity of an auto repair shop is wasted if no one brings a car for servicing on a day when the shop is open. Conversely, if the demand for a service exceeds supply on a particular day, the excess business may be lost. Thus, if someone can't get a seat on one airline, another carrier gets the business or the trip is cancelled or postponed. If an accounting firm is too busy to accept tax and audit work from a prospective client, another firm will get the assignment.

But demand and supply imbalances are not found in all service situations. A useful way of categorizing services for this purpose is shown in Figure 4. The horizontal axis classifies organizations according to whether demand for the service fluctuates widely or narrowly over time; the vertical axis classifies them according to whether or not capacity is sufficient to meet peak demand.

Organizations in Box 1 could use increases in demand outside peak periods, those in Box 2 must decide whether to seek continued growth in demand and capacity or to continue the status quo, while those in Box 3 represent growing organizations that may need temporary demarketing until capacity can be increased to meet or exceed current demand levels. But service organizations in Box 4 face an ongoing problem of trying to smooth demand to match capacity, involving both stimulation and discouragement of demand.

Insights and Implications

Managing demand is a task faced by nearly all marketers, whether offering goods or ser-

FIGURE 4

What Is the Nature of Demand for the Service Relative to Supply?

Extent of Demand Fluctuations over Time

	Wide	Narrow
Peak Demand Can Usually Be Met without a Major Delay	1 Electricity Natural gas Telephone Hospital maternity unit Police and fire emergencies	2 Insurance Legal services Banking Laundry and dry cleaning
Peak Demand Regularly Exceeds Capacity	4 Accounting and tax preparation Passenger transportation Hotels and motels Restaurants Theaters	3 Services similar to those in 2 but which have insufficient capacity for their base level of business

Extent to Which Supply Is Constrained

vices. Even where the fluctuations are sharp, and inventories cannot be used to act as a buffer between supply and demand, it may still be possible to manage capacity in a service business—for instance, by hiring part-time employees or renting extra facilities at peak periods. But for a substantial group of service organizations, successfully managing demand fluctuations through marketing actions is the key to profitability.

To determine the most appropriate strategy in each instance, it's necessary to seek answers to some additional questions:

1. What is the typical cycle period of these demand fluctuations?
   - Predictable (i.e., demand varies by hour of the day, day of the week or month, season of the year).
   - Random (i.e., no apparent pattern to demand fluctuations).
2. What are the underlying causes of these demand fluctuations?
   - Customer habits or preferences (could marketing efforts change these)?
   - Actions by third parties (for instance, employers set working hours, hence marketing efforts might usefully be directed at those employers).
   - Nonforecastable events, such as health symptoms, weather conditions, acts of God

and so forth—marketing can do only a few things about these, such as offering priority services to members and disseminating information about alternative services to other people.

One way to smooth out the ups and downs of demand is through strategies that encourage customers to change their plans voluntarily, such as offering special discount prices or added product value during periods of low demand. Another approach is to ration demand through a reservation or queuing system (which basically inventories demand rather than supply). Alternatively, to generate demand in periods of excess capacity, new business development efforts might be targeted at prospective customers with a countercyclical demand pattern. For instance, an accounting firm with a surfeit of work at the end of each calendar year might seek new customers whose financial year ended on June 30 or September 30.

Determining what strategy is appropriate requires an understanding of who or what is the target of the service (as discussed in an earlier section of this article). If the service is delivered to customers in person, there are limits to how long a customer will wait in line; hence strategies to inventory or ration demand should focus on adoption of reservation systems (Sasser 1976). But if the service is delivered to goods or to intangible assets, then a strategy of inventorying demand should be more feasible (unless the good is a vital necessity such as a car, in which case reservations may be the best approach).

HOW IS THE SERVICE DELIVERED?

Understanding distribution issues in service marketing requires that two basic issues be addressed. The first relates to the method of delivery. Is it necessary for the customer to be in direct physical contact with the service organization (customers may have to go to the service organization, or the latter may come to the former), or can transactions be completed at arm's length? And does the service organization maintain just a single outlet or does it serve customers through multiple outlets at different sites? The outcome of this analysis can be seen in Figure 5, which consists of six different cells.

Insights and Implications

The convenience of receiving service is presumably lowest when a customer has to come to the service organization and must use a specific outlet. Offering service through several outlets increases the convenience of access for customers but may start to raise problems of quality control as convenience of access relates to the consistency of the service product delivered. For some types of services the organization will come to the customer. This is, of course, essential when the target of the service is some immovable physical item (such as a building that needs repairs or pest control treatment, or a garden that needs landscaping). But since it's usually more expensive to take service personnel and equipment to the customer than vice versa, the trend has been away from this approach to delivering consumer services (e.g., doctors no longer like to make house calls). In many instances, however, direct contact between customers and the service organization is not necessary; instead, transactions can be handled at arm's length by mail or electronic communications. Through the use of 800 numbers many service organizations have found that they can bring their services as close as the nearest telephone, yet obtain important economies from operating out of a single physical location.

Although not all services can be delivered through arm's length transactions, it may be possible to separate certain components of the service from the core product and to handle them separately. This suggests an additional classification scheme: categorizing services according to whether transactions such as obtaining information, making reservations and making payment can be broken out separately from delivery of the core service. If they can be separated, then the question is whether or not it is advantageous

FIGURE 5
Method of Service Delivery

	Availability of Service Outlets	
Nature of Interaction between Customer and Service Organization	Single Site	Multiple Sites
Customer Goes to Service Organization	Theater Barbershop	Bus service Fast food chain
Service Organization Comes to Customer	Lawn care service Pest control service Taxi	Mail delivery AAA emergency repairs
Customer and Service Organization Transact at Arm's Length (mail or electronic communications)	Credit card company Local TV station	Broadcast network Telephone co.

to the service firm to allow customers to make these peripheral transactions through an intermediary or broker.

For instance, information about airline flights, reservations for such flights and purchases of tickets can all be made through a travel agent as well as directly through the airline. For those who prefer to visit in person, rather than conduct business by telephoning, this greatly increases the geographic coverage of distribution, since there are usually several travel agencies located more conveniently than the nearest airline office. Added value from using a travel agent comes from the "one-stop shopping" aspect of travel agents; the customer can inquire about several airlines and make car rental and hotel reservations during the same call. Insurance brokers and theater ticket agencies are also examples of specialist intermediaries that represent a number of different service organizations. Consumers sometimes perceive such intermediaries as more objective and more knowledgeable about alternatives than the various service suppliers they represent. The risk to the service firm of working through specialist intermediaries is, of course, that they may recommend use of a competitor's product!

DISCUSSION

Widespread interest in the marketing of services among both academics and practitioners is a relatively recent phenomenon. Possibly this reflects the fact that marketing expertise in the service sector has significantly lagged behind that in the manufacturing sector. Up to now most academic research and discussion has centered on the issue, "How do services differ from goods?" A number of authors including Shostack (1977), Bateson (1979), and Berry (1980) have argued that there are significant distinctions between the two and have proposed several generalizations for management practice. But others such as Enis and Roering (1981) remain unconvinced that these differences have meaningful strategic implications.

Rather than continue to debate the existence of this broad dichotomy, it seems more useful to get on with the task of helping managers in service businesses do a better job of developing and marketing their products. We need to recognize that the service sector, particularly in the United States, is beoming increasingly competitive (Langeard et al., 1981), reflecting such developments as the partial or complete deregulation of several major service industries in recent years, the removal of professional association restrictions on using marketing techniques (particularly advertising), the replacement (or absorption) of independent service units by franchise chains, and the growth of new electronic delivery systems. As competition intensifies within the service sector, the development of more effective marketing efforts becomes essential to survival.

The classification schemes proposed in this article can contribute usefully to management practice in two ways. First, by addressing each of the five questions posed earlier, marketing managers can obtain a better understanding of the nature of their product, of the types of relationships their service organizations have with customers, of the factors underlying any sharp variations in demand, and of the characteristics of their service delivery systems. This understanding should help them identify how these factors shape marketing problems and opportunities and thereby affect the nature of the marketing task. Second, by recognizing which characteristics their own service shares with other services, often in seemingly unrelated industries, managers will learn to look beyond their immediate competitors for new ideas as to how to resolve marketing problems that they share in common with firms in other service industries.

Recognizing that the products of service organizations previously considered as "different" actually face similar problems or share certain characteristics in common can yield valuable managerial insights. Innovation in marketing, after all, often reflects a manager's ability to seek out and learn from analogous situations in other contexts. These classification schemes should also be of value to researchers to whom they offer an alternative to either broad-brush research into services or an industry-by-industry approach. Instead, they suggest a variety of new ways of looking at service businesses, each of which may offer opportunities for focused research efforts. Undoubtedly there is also room for further refinement of the schemes proposed.

REFERENCES

BATESON, JOHN E. G. (1979), "Why We Need Service Marketing," in *Conceptual and Theoretical Developments in Marketing*, O. C. Ferrell, S. W. Brown, and C. W. Lamb, eds. Chicago, American Marketing Association, 131–146.

BERRY, LEONARD L. (1980), "Services Marketing Is Different," *Business* (May–June), 24–29.

BUCKLIN, LOUIS (1963), "Retail Strategy and the Classification of Consumer Goods," *Journal of Marketing*, **27** (January), 50.

CHASE, RICHARD B. (1978), "Where Does the Customer Fit in a Service Operation?," *Harvard Business Review*, **56** (November–December), 137–142.

COPELAND, MELVIN T. (1923), "The Relation of Consumers' Buying Habits to Marketing Methods," *Harvard Business Review*, **1** (April), 282–289.

ENIS, BEN M., and KENNETH J. ROERING (1981), "Services Marketing: Different Products, Similar Strategies," in *Marketing of Services*, J. H. Donnelly and W. R. George, eds. Chicago: American Marketing Association.

HILL, T. P. (1977), "On Goods and Services," *Review of Income and Wealth*, **23** (December), 315–338.

HUNT, SHELBY D. (1976), *Marketing Theory*. Columbus, OH: Grid.

JUDD, ROBERT C. (1964), "The Case for Redefining Services," *Journal of Marketing*, **28** (January), 59.

KNISELY, GARY (1979), "Marketing and the Services Industry," *Advertising Age* (January 15), 47–50; (February 19), 54–60; (March 19), 58–62; (May 15), 57–58.

KOTLER, PHILIP (1980), *Principles of Marketing*. Englewood Cliffs, NJ: Prentice-Hall, Inc.

LANGEARD, ERIC, JOHN E. G. BATESON, CHRISTOPHER H. LOVELOCK, and PIERRE EIGLIER (1981), *Services Marketing: New Insights from Consumers and Managers*. Cambridge, MA: Marketing Science Institute.

LEVITT, THEODORE (1972), "Production Line Approach to Service," *Harvard Business Review*, **50** (September–October), 41.

———— (1976), "The Industrialization of Service," *Harvard Business Review*, **54** (September-October), 63–74.

LOVELOCK, CHRISTOPHER H. (1980), "Towards a Classification of Services," in *Theoretical Developments in Marketing*, C. W. Lamb and P. M. Dunne, eds. Chicago: American Marketing Association, 72–76.

———— (1981), "Why Marketing Management Needs to Be Different for Services," in *Marketing of Services*, J. H. Donnelly and W. R. George, eds. Chicago: American Marketing Association.

RATHMELL, JOHN M. (1974), *Marketing in the Service Sector*. Cambridge, MA: Winthrop.

SASSER, W. EARL, JR. (1976), "Match Supply and Demand in Service Industries," *Harvard Business Review*, **54** (November–December), 133.

————, R. PAUL OLSEN, and D. DARYL WYCKOFF (1978), *Management of Service Operations: Text and Cases*. Boston: Allyn & Bacon.

SHOSTACK, G. LYNN (1977), "Breaking Free from Product Marketing," *Journal of Marketing*, **41** (April), 73–80.

THOMAS, DAN R. E. (1978), "Strategy Is Different in Service Businesses," *Harvard Business Review*, **56** (July–August), 158–165.

Managing Facilitator Services

DAVID H. MAISTER
CHRISTOPHER H. LOVELOCK

This article examines a group of industries—including stock-brokerage operations, real estate, and travel agencies—that facilitate the buying and selling of goods and services. These facilitator industries exhibit many common features, such as the general types of services that they provide, their compensation structures, and the relationships found between the firms and their brokers and clients. By following developments in other facilitator services, managers of facilitator firms should be able to anticipate future trends in their own industries.

Part of the art of management is learning how to benefit from the experience of others: being able to recognize similarities in problems and situations that have been encountered before so that the lessons learned in those situations can be brought to bear on the problems at hand. Frequently, the search for common experiences reaches across industry boundaries. Consumer goods producers study each other's actions in the search for the common experiences of marketing such products. Manufacturers with assembly-line factories attempt to draw upon each other's experience with such operations. In each of these examples, the area of common ground that unifies the experiences is clear: consumer goods marketing in the former case, assembly-line operations in the latter.

The ability to classify industries in these ways is the result of many years of research. Over time we have learned that it is, indeed, a useful categorization to divide marketing into consumer marketing and industrial marketing; to divide operations into job shops, assembly lines, and continuous-flow types. However, much of what is known about such industry "types" has developed in the manufacturing sector. When we turn our attention to services, few such useful categorizations can be found.

Many authors have sought to develop useful generalizations about the entire service sector. Yet there is as much—or more—diversity among service businesses as there is among manufacturing firms, and few generalizations (whether about marketing, operations, or any other managerial topic) are likely to hold true for all services.

THE NATURE AND ROLE OF FACILITATOR FIRMS

This article examines a group of service industries that, we believe, have much in common with each other but are notably different from other types of services. They are what we term the facilitator service industries.

Who Are the Facilitators?

Facilitator services include those industries that are in the business of facilitating market transactions, the buying and selling of other goods or services. Prime examples of such industries are travel agencies, employment agencies, and real estate brokerage operations. The use of the word "broker" also suggests other types of facilitators, including stockbrokerage operations, insurance brokers, and even marriage brokerage and dating services.

Facilitators act as "experts for hire" in their respective markets, bringing buyers and sellers together and advising (perhaps at different times) both buyer and seller. Their fee, which is usually in the form of a commission, is earned when the buyer and the seller complete their transaction. This commission may be paid by the buyer, the seller, or both.

A distinction must be drawn between facilitator services and other intermediary functions, such as retail (or wholesale) merchandising. The latter involves taking possession of a physical product (on either a purchase or consignment basis) and then reselling it, thus serving as the distribution channel for some seller or group of sellers. Some brokerage operations may indeed engage in purchase and resale (travel agents

sometimes act in this way), but there is an important distinction between the two roles. The merchandiser is primarily a seller; the facilitator, primarily an *advisor*. In some industries these roles may sit happily together in one business; in others they are being forced apart.

The Facilitators' Role

Why do facilitators exist? Basically, the facilitators' services are required whenever there is some form of market "failure." In the economist's model, one of the preconditions for the successful functioning of a "free" market is perfect information. To make a wise purchase or sale decision, both buyer and seller need to be able to know who is in the market, what the range of offerings is, how the characteristics of different offerings compare, what their prices are, and so forth. When these conditions are absent, there is an opportunity for the facilitator, whose role is basically that of a market expert.

The facilitator's key stock in trade is *information*. A potential client who visits a real estate broker wants to know what houses or apartments are for sale, their condition, the current state of the market in terms of prices, and so forth. Similar types of informational services are provided by travel agents who assist customers in searching through alternative travel offerings, and by employment agencies which help job seekers uncover job opportunities. In providing these services, the facilitator adds value by assembling in one place a great deal of relevant information. Buyers (and sellers) *could* perform the "market search" for themselves, but the use of the agency or broker allows this search to be conducted much more efficiently.

However, this is only one component of facilitator services. In addition to simple information exchange, real estate agents, employment agents, and travel agents all offer *advice* (as, indeed, do stockbrokers and insurance brokers). Their clients seek assistance in evaluating alternative courses of action and the various factors that may influence the buying or selling decision. For instance, home sellers seek advice on current market values of homes in the area and the prices they should ask for their own homes. Meantime, home buyers seek advice on the quality of different neighborhoods and probable future trends in the values of different types of houses. The travel agent evaluates alternative vacation spots, the stockbroker advises on individual stocks and bonds, and the employment agency advises on the characteristics of individual companies.

The common thread running through these examples is that what is being sought in engaging the facilitator's services is not only efficient access to market information, but, more crucially, assistance in evaluating it. Whether the purchase (or sale) is a home, a vacation, a job, an insurance policy, or an investment, it involves a degree of risk for the client. In most cases, the client does not feel fully competent to appraise the available alternatives alone, and therefore seeks out expert assistance.

A third way in which facilitators add value to their clients is that they assist in *completion of the transaction*. Travel agents issue tickets and hotel vouchers; employment agencies forward resumes and employer information; stockbrokers handle the actual buying and selling of the securities. Increasingly, real estate agents are providing access to mortgage financing and assisting with (if not necessarily performing) the legal paperwork requirements necessary to complete the transaction.

PROBLEMS FOR FACILITATORS

It is important to stress the tripartite nature of the facilitator's services: information exchange, advice, and transaction processing. Many of the management problems (and opportunities) in facilitator industries derive from the interaction of these three elements and the attempt to balance them appropriately.

In most facilitator industries, commission or fee revenue is only obtained when the transaction is completed. The commission rate is usually standard across the industry, whether by legal fiat or entrenched industry practice. All employment agencies tend to charge the same commission; for professional positions, this is normally 1 percent for every $1,000 of starting salary, up to a limit such as $30,000. Real estate agents charge 5 to 6 percent of the sales price of the home, and travel agents receive 7 to 11 percent of the sales price of the airfare, depending on the nature of the travel. Fixed commissions existed, of course, in the stockbrokerage industry until "Mayday"—May 1, 1975; later we shall review the impact of the abolition of fixed commissions. It should be noted here that events in the brokerage industry may serve as a foretaste of what other facilitators can expect when and if fee competition develops in their own industries.

The circumstances of providing *three* types (or levels) of service while being compensated for only one (the completion of the transaction) creates significant problems for the facilitator firm. A large amount of effort and cost may be invested in the provision of the first two levels of service (information and advice) without generating any corresponding revenues. Indeed, the need for this investment is often given as a reason for preserving the fixed commission system. In most facilitator industries, the return on the investment, when it comes, can be substantial. An employment agency's fee for successfully placing a candidate may be as high as $5,000; selling a house may result in commissions in excess of $10,000. But a great deal of speculative effort on behalf of a number of *potential* clients is necessary to reap the rewards from a single completed transaction.

Historically, this risk to the facilitator firm has been reduced by sharing it with the frontline work force. Real estate brokers, stockbrokers, employment agents, and insurance agents (although not travel agents) usually receive a substantial component (if not the majority) of their compensation in the form of shared commissions. In employment agencies and real estate, the norm has been as much as 50 percent of the commission earned by the firm, although proportions in other industries have varied.

Because of this traditional compensation system, relations between the individual broker and the facilitator firm are unlike employee-employer relations in many other industries. In fact, the firm is more dependent upon the individual broker than vice versa. It is the broker who undertakes most of the interaction with the client and who develops the loyalty of the client. The client may have little involvement with the firm as such: in many clients' eyes the broker handling their transactions *is* the firm. A classic syndrome in all of these industries is the talented broker with a loyal customer base who leaves the firm, taking along a customer following. Competition in these industries may often be as much to attract (and retain) quality employees as it is to attract clients.

Client-Broker-Firm Relations

What are the causes (and results) of the tripartite relationship formed by the firm, its brokers, and its clients in Figure 1? As we have seen, the "bond" between the broker and the client is often stronger than the bond between the client and the firm or the bond between the broker and the firm. This reflects the fact that in many facilitator services it is individual brokers rather than the firm

FIGURE 1
A Tripartite Relationship

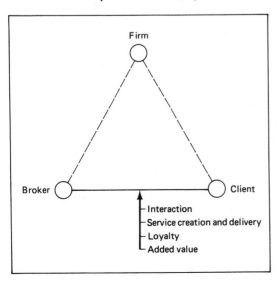

who add the most value in the delivery of the service. The broker is not only the salesperson, but also the producer of the service.

This is particularly true of those facilitator firms whose strategy is to place emphasis on the *advice* component of the facilitator's three services. A key characteristic of the advice function that distinguishes it from information exchange and transaction completion is that it is, by its very nature, a customizing process (if not necessarily a customized one). A crucial part of the interactive process necessary to delivery of the facilitator's services is a diagnostic stage in which the client's needs, wishes, and values (i.e., what constitutes a good home, vacation, job, investment goal, or insurance coverage?) are established. If this task is performed well, then succeeding tasks become much easier, if not routine. It is the ability and skill to diagnose and customize effectively that lie at the heart of the advice function; these activities have traditionally been assigned to frontline professionals in the typical facilitator service firm. Regardless of the firm's efficiency in assembling and disseminating relevant market information, or of its ability to establish routinized procedures to complete transactions, it is the interactive process termed "advice" that constitutes much of the added value of the firm. Providing this advice has traditionally been the function of the individual broker.

POSITIONING THE FACILITATOR FIRM

The relative emphasis given to information exchange, advice, and transaction processing is, of course, a strategic decision for the individual firm that serves to position itself in the marketplace. It is possible for the firm to specialize in one or more of these functions. The discount stockbrokerage operations that have spread since the ending of fixed commissions clearly are focused upon transaction processing, while "old-style" brokerage houses continue to emphasize their research and advice functions.

A policy of pursuing two strategies aimed

at different markets is exemplified by those travel agents that solicit both commercial (business travel) accounts and individual/ family vacationers. In fact, these two types of accounts are distinctly different and should probably be managed separately. Commercial account business is transacted largely by telephone and made up of reasonably routine activities. The traveler, typically an executive, wishes to get from point A to point B. The agent takes the order by telephone, checks the flight schedule, and issues the ticket. Little or no advice is given. By contrast, a vacation traveler may visit the office and remain seated with the agent while a large number of options are reviewed and an extended debate takes place. In the former case, the service is primarily one of transaction processing, while in the latter the service emphasizes advice. As might be expected, those firms following high-advice strategies have a greater need for a "professional" work force, and have the most firmly entrenched commission system (and tripartite relations problem). Later we shall explore the techniques used by the management of such firms to overcome this problem.

EXPANSION AND DIVERSIFICATION STRATEGIES

In positioning itself in the marketplace, the facilitator firm first must choose which of the three tasks (information, advice, and transaction) to emphasize. However, since a firm only receives revenue when a transaction is completed, it also has a vested interest in ensuring that no "roadblocks" exist, for either buyer or seller, that prevent completion of the deal. Anything that may prevent this threatens the revenue stream. This is an incentive for the facilitator to expand its activities to remove these roadblocks, taking on additional components of the transaction task in a form of horizontal integration.

Consider, for example, the real estate industry, where difficulty in obtaining a mortgage loan has prevented many otherwise satisfactory sales transactions from being completed. Now there is a growing trend for realtors to provide access to mortgage funds

as part of their service offerings. In recent years Merrill Lynch has entered the real estate brokerage market, with the announced strategy of offering a full line of all services (from brokerage to mortgage financing to insurance) that might be required during a residential real estate transaction. Also led by Merrill Lynch, the securities brokerage industry is similarly diversifying its services with such offerings as "Cash Management Accounts" which allow the customer to move funds in and out of the securities market with the minimum of friction. In the employment agency field, some firms assist applicants in the preparation of resumes, or they check references for employers. In the travel agency business, firms long ago expanded their basic business of travel bookings to include reservations for hotels, car rentals, and other adjuncts to travel.

When additional services are added to facilitate successful completion of the primary transaction, the facilitator firm has to choose between offering the additional services as *separate* services or as a "bundle." In its early stages, a new service is frequently introduced as an ancillary service at no charge to the client (effectively "bundling" the existing and new services). For example, arranging mortgage loans was introduced by some real estate brokers solely to ensure that the home sale went through. Subsequently, as the firm expands its activities in this new way, a charge may be imposed for each separate service. Now the key advantage is that of "one-stop shopping" for an array of services.

A final stage is for the firm to get involved not only in assembling the product or service bundle, but also in modifying the package and taking a "position" in the actual creation of the services being transacted. A prime example is when travel agents create their own charter tours and offer them for sale in the marketplace. Investment banking firms, which facilitate large financial transactions such as mergers and acquisitions, also engage in this activity.

The Facilitator Life Cycle

In this review of facilitator firm activities, we have seen that the firm must choose the

TABLE 1
Stages in the Development of Facilitator Organizations

Passive brokerage	Basic information exchange (simple listings of would-be buyers and sellers)
Active brokerage	Attempts to match buyer and seller needs, involving advice and counseling
Multiservice brokerage	Wide range of services related to completed transactions offered to provide "one-stop shopping"
Packaging brokerage	Services and products from various sellers are commissioned or modified by broker

level of its involvement in the transaction it is attempting to facilitate. The various levels are summarized in Table 1. They are presented in the form of an industry "life cycle," since this is the way that many such facilitator industries have evolved. It is, however, not necessary for firms to go through all of the stages. In emerging facilitator industries, different firms may attempt to enter the market at different stages.

Apart from the levels of service shown in Table 1, the facilitator firm must make choices along another dimension in positioning itself in its industry. It must decide whether to target the buyers or sellers (or both) of the product it is attempting to facilitate. While realtors and employment agencies, of necessity, attempt to serve both buyers and sellers, travel agents target their services primarily at buyers of travel services, acting as a form of distributor for a large number of firms in the transportation, travel, and hospitality industries, rather than seeking exclusive franchises.

Serving Both Buyers and Sellers

A facilitator industry can only exist when it provides advantages to both buyer and seller. If there is some form of market failure (for example, sellers find it difficult to communicate with buyers), it is in the ultimate interests of both buyers and sellers that the market friction or barriers be overcome. One side or the other may have the power

and resources to accomplish this for itself: for example, the airline or insurance industries might decide to invest the resources to reach their market directly through their own consumer outlets. The travel agency and insurance brokerage businesses can exist only to the extent that they add value to both sides of the transaction they are facilitating. The interests, resources, and capabilities of both sides must be considered in defining the nature of the facilitator business.

The difficulty posed by this "middleman" function is best seen in the real estate or employment agency fields, where it is conventional for firms to acknowledge both sides of the transaction as their potential clients. The problem is that the services desired from the facilitator by the buyers are not necessarily compatible with those desired by the sellers. For example, in serving a job hunter well, a firm may offer assistance in resume preparation, advice on how to behave in an interview, and so forth. However, these services may not be in the best interests of the potential employer who wishes to be able to evaluate the "real" candidate, rather than a carefully packaged one. Similarly, in a residential real estate transaction, the broker's advice to sellers on how to smarten up their homes for profitable resale may not be in the best interests of buyers. Attempting to design services that will attract both buyers and sellers may even represent a conflict of interest on the part of the facilitator. This problem is recognized by investment bankers who have addressed it by forming separate departments for dealing with buyers and sellers and maintaining a "Chinese Wall" between these departments.

While the potential for conflict of interest is not as great in other facilitator industries as it is in investment banking, the lesson that the different interests of the two parties to a transaction might best be served by different departments is one that other facilitators might usefully consider. In real estate brokerage, for example, it is generally the practice that the same individual broker (at different times) will be required to act on behalf of a seller and a buyer. However, the way in which good service is rendered to those two groups, and the personal talents and skills necessary to their delivery may be quite distinct. Sellers wish for advice on how to present their home, what price to ask, and assurances that their privacy will not be interrupted too much as buyers are shown around. Buyers want detailed information not only about individual homes, but also about communities and availability of financing; they want to be able to make a detailed inspection of any property they are seriously interested in buying, and to be reassured as to the value of their prospective purchases. Even if the expertise (or knowledge) required to serve both groups well is sometimes the same, the process (interactive) skills necessary to deal with each group are not, and there may be great benefits to specialization.

The relative emphasis given by the firm toward buyer or seller groups may change over time. Consider, for example, an employment agency. In booming times when employees of a particular profession are

scarce and job openings numerous, the firm needs to strengthen its ability to attract potential candidates. However, in recessionary periods when there is a glut of job seekers, the competitive position of the firm will be enhanced to the extent that it can provide superior service in meeting the needs of employers seeking to fill a position. Over time the firm must learn to balance its capabilities.

STEPS IN THE FACILITATING PROCESS

We have seen that the facilitator firm is defined by its ability to acquire market information and expertise (which are *not* the same), and to bring these to bear in matching the needs of buyers and sellers in order to complete a transaction. To review the management tasks this imposes on the firm, let us look at a conceptual model of the necessary steps in this process (see Figure 2).

FIGURE 2
The Facilitating Process

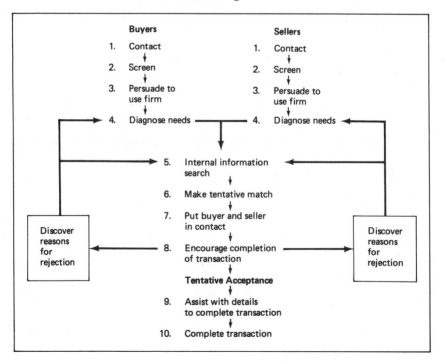

Encouraging Contact with the Firm

The first step, naturally, is to encourage both buyers and sellers to contact the firm: the primary marketing task. The approaches taken to accomplish this in various facilitator industries have varied widely, including reliance on personal contact and referral (widely encountered in old-style real estate and stockbrokerage firms), development of high-traffic retail office locations to attract walk-in clients (travel agencies), and use of mass-media advertising (which is increasingly common in all facilitator industries).

Screening Prospective Clients

The next step in the facilitating process should logically be one of screening. As noted earlier, facilitator firms can expend a great deal of time and effort on potential clients who do not ultimately complete a transaction. It is, therefore, crucial that the firm screen its potential clients so that this wasted effort is minimized. In some firms, a form of "coding" is employed that categorizes potential clients both by the probability of successfully helping them ("placeability" in employment agencies, available funds to spend or invest in real estate and stockbrokerage) and by the size of the resulting transaction. In old-style firms, this decision (on the amount of effort to expend, if any, on an individual potential client) is left up to the individual broker. At more "modern" (or "professional") firms, a formal system is employed. (If such a system is *not* used, then one of the crucial training tasks inside the firm is ensuring that new or junior brokers learn how to be selective in accepting or turning away prospective clients.)

Signing Up Clients

Just because a prospective client is attractive to the facilitator does not automatically mean that the reverse is true. The next task is to get the prospect to use the firm's services. Where personal referral is relied upon for developing contacts, the task of per-

suading the client to *use* the firm tends to be personal; however, there is an increasing trend to institutionalize this function through the means of giving away ancillary services and products. The task here is to get the client to "list" with the firm: to give the firm the opportunity to make a match. Many firms attempt to lock in clients with free services, such as securities research reports (stockbrokerage), home maintenance hints (real estate brokerage), free resume kits (employment agencies), and travel brochures (travel agencies).

In part, the function of these free products and services is to create an implicit sense of obligation in the potential client. They also serve to reinforce the facilitator firm's image of expertise, offering proof of the firm's knowledge of market dynamics. Some firms have taken this a step further by providing brief seminars: stockbrokers hold investment counseling evenings, real estate agents hold home improvement seminars, and one innovative employment firm (Scientific Placement) recently announced a seminar for corporations on how to improve their recruiting activities. By promoting the expertise of the firm, these activities strengthen the customer appeal of the firm as opposed to that of the broker.

Diagnosing Client Needs

The next step in the facilitating process is to diagnose the client's specific needs. It is at this stage that the crucial task of customization enters into the system. For most facilitator firms, this stage is the real test of the firm's effectiveness. Usually, good diagnosis directly affects the client's perception both of service quality ("That broker understood what we were looking for in a house"; "They didn't send me to any job interviews that weren't close to what I was looking for"), and of efficiency (no wasted effort in making matches that one or both of the parties would not realistically consider).

The diagnosis stage has a significant educational component. Clients often look to a facilitator firm for guidance in how to make a choice, advice on what to look for, and suggestions on how to appraise alternatives. Again this is not only an opportunity to provide service, but also an opportunity to improve the efficiency of the firm's performance. To the extent that clients' expectations as either buyers or sellers can be made more realistic, the probabilities of a successful match (and, hence, revenue to the firm) are enhanced.

Search for Potential Matches

The next step in the facilitating process is a search for potential matches. This is usually an *internal* process for the firm, as it "mines" its files for lists of buyers to offer sellers and lists of sellers to offer buyers. The computer revolution has the potential for greatly enhancing the efficiency of this process. Since the stock in trade of the facilitator firm is market information, the great advantage of the computer is that it allows firms to accumulate (and *access more efficiently*) larger quantities and types of information. Travel agencies are well along this road, thanks to the efforts of individual airlines in sharing access, through leased CRT units, to their schedule and seat availability information. (It is interesting to note, however, that as yet there is no *combined* data base for all airlines, so the full efficiencies in this regard have not yet been reaped.) The computer is also beginning to be used in real estate brokerage; there is much talk in that industry (and some progress) in computerizing the "multiple listing service" (homes available for sale) to which most agencies in a given locality usually subscribe. In the employment agency field, at least one agency has computerized its files on job openings and available candidates, leading to efficiencies in making "quality" matches.

Making a Tentative Match

The next stage in the facilitating process is making a "tentative" match and putting buyer and seller in touch with each other. In real estate and employment agencies, this is a physical phenomenon: the house buyer

must see the house and the job hunter must be interviewed by the potential employer. In a travel agency or stockbrokerage, this can be accomplished through paperwork: showing brochures of travel destinations and annual reports and research reports. It should be noted that, here too, the facilitator industries are learning from each other. Real estate agents and employment agencies are increasingly providing more information about specific homes and jobs in paper form. This enhances the service in the clients' eyes, saving travel time and providing more information to make a reasoned decision on whether to explore the match further. There is also speculation about—and some experimentation in—the use of video tapes or slide projection machines to show pictures of homes in the realtor's office. Once again, this represents an opportunity for the firm to provide service to its own brokers and add to value above that created by them. At the same time, it constitutes an additional fixed cost.

Encouraging Completion

The next step is to encourage the buyer and seller in a tentative match to complete the transaction (to buy *this* security, to accept *this* offer for the home, to go on *this* vacation, to hire *this* candidate). This stage of the process will never be completely institutionalized, since it involves skills in personal selling on the part of frontline personnel. Success comes in part from creating a feeling on the part of the buyer and seller that they cannot do better by continuing to search the market. The more the firm can subtly but effectively communicate its market expertise and the fact that it has done a complete market search on behalf of its clients, the easier it should be to convince the buyer and/or seller to close the deal.

Evaluating the Reasons for Failure

If the parties in a tentative match fail to "close," then it is important to learn why, so that the next attempted match (and future matches of a similar nature) can respond more closely to individual needs. This stage is difficult, but by no means impossible to institutionalize. If the firm is utilizing a computer data base, the relevant files can be updated so that the facts about what advantages and disadvantages are possessed by individual offerings (homes, jobs, stocks, travel destinations) can be disseminated through the firm. In the old-style firm, inefficiencies generally result as each of a number of brokers wastefully discovers independently how the market is reacting to a specific type of offering.

Assisting with Completion of a Match

The final stage in the facilitating process is to assist with the details of completion once a successful match has been accomplished. As noted already, firms are tending to become increasingly involved in this stage of the process through addition of ancillary services.

INSIGHTS AND TRENDS

What insights can be drawn from this analysis for managers of facilitator services? What trends can be anticipated in the future? A number of comments and caveats need to be made in the light of our review of the steps in the facilitating process. We recognize that not all steps will be of equal importance to all firms in all industries. In particular, as firms move through the life cycle referred to in Table 1, the relative importance of and the relative emphasis on different stages in the process will change. There is a trend towards significant changes in the way facilitator firms create and deliver their services, particularly as these relate to "deprofessionalizing" the frontline tasks and embodying more of the added value in the systems and in the firms themselves. The extent of this trend varies across industries but it is present in all. Greater sophistication has come to the real estate business through the growth of large franchise systems (Century 21, formed in 1972, had obtained over 5,000 franchises by the late 1970s and was

sold for $90 million in 1979). Franchise systems are also beginning to develop in the employment agency field. Travel agencies, while becoming increasingly sophisticated from a technological standpoint, are still characterized by small operations displaying the relatively low level of managerial sophistication encountered in most small businesses. Stockbrokerage operations have become increasingly sophisticated and larger in scale. In part, this reflects a firm's ability to back up its frontline personnel with back-room activities.

Moves to Standardization

The differentiation between "front-room" (high customer contact) and "back-room" (low customer contact) activities is a crucial one. Much of the success in transforming the facilitator industries comes from two directions: standardizing the customer-contact process, and learning how to take more steps in the process into the back room. There they can be treated as production-type operations (Figure 3), and the lessons of modern production-line management methods can be brought to bear. As long as the process involves a high degree of customer con-

FIGURE 3
Alternative Directions for Facilitators

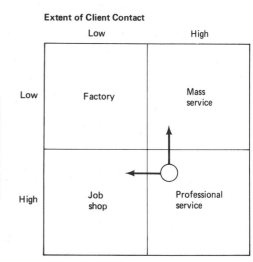

Extent of Client Contact

	Low	High
Low	Factory	Mass service
High	Job shop	Professional service

Extent of Customization

tact, there will be a premium on the process skills required by frontline personnel, and the firm's added value will be embedded mostly in its professionals.

Compensation Problems at the Management Level

One of the classic management problems inside facilitator firms derives from the high customer-contact nature of the businesses. There are a number of steps in the facilitating process where interactive skills between broker and client are critical. Such skills are not easily taught in schools; they are best learned from experience. A primary management task in facilitator firms is to coach new brokers, helping them to develop the key interactive skills necessary to the delivery of quality service. The reason that this has been a problem for many facilitator firms is that the compensation system has been based on commissions, even for managers. This raises a conflict for individual managers between allocating time on earning personal commissions, and allocating it to coaching, training, and managing.

Two steps are usually taken to address this problem. First, managers may be given an "override" commission based either on the sales commissions generated by the brokers working under their control, or on the profits (contribution to overhead) made by their office. This can be difficult to design and administer. Selecting the appropriate level to balance competing incentives may be problematic. Moreover, the appropriate override must reflect the training, coaching, and management needs of the specific office or group. The second approach to this problem is to "force" managers to give up their sales activities on being promoted, and to devote themselves exclusively to the managerial tasks. (This is, for example, how the problem is addressed at Merrill Lynch.) We predict that, as the shifts we have described take place and more of the firm's added value is embedded in its systems, the latter route will increasingly be the one that is taken.

Mass versus Professional Services

As Figure 3 suggests, the increasing application of hard and soft technologies in the facilitator industries will involve the firms in a shift in their target markets. Increasing standardization of procedure will involve less personalization, turning the firm into a mass service rather than a "professional" one. Consequently, there will still be a role for "old-style" firms at the upper end of the market. (This is the common view held about Century 21's success: that its methods of doing business appeal to the low- and mid-range home buyer, and that one way to compete against the firm is to preserve a people-intensive, nonstandardized approach in the premium market.)

Pricing Issues

The traditional pricing mechanism for facilitator firms has been the use of a commission structure that has tended to be standardized across all firms in each industry. This approach had the great advantage of simplicity but is now beginning to disintegrate. Deregulation of the airline industry is likely to result in a move away from the standard percentage commissions received by travel agents from the airlines (their biggest "selling" customers). In the stockbrokerage industry, discount brokers are now offering significant savings to customers who only want to buy and sell stocks and who have no interest in the ancillary services offered by most brokers.

As facilitators expand their range of services, there are likely to be moves to unbundle the services rendered and to start charging for each separately. Just as many stockbrokers now sell information and advice through the medium of "market letters" available only to subscribers, so other facilitators may start charging fees separately for the different components of their activities. However, for the information and advisory services to pay their own way, four criteria must be met. First, there must be no legal barriers to charging either prospective buyers or sellers for these services. Second, the facilitator firm that elects this strategy must be perceived as having a differential advantage over competing firms that choose not to charge for these services. Third, there should be a market demand for standardized information and advice of a more broadly defined nature than that required to complete a specific transaction. Finally, cost accounting procedures should be able to determine with a reasonable degree of accuracy what costs are associated with the provision of each service component.

Impact of the Computer

By accumulating market information and updating it rapidly and continually, the computer allows the firm to disseminate its market expertise rapidly throughout the firm; *all* frontline personnel can be made instant experts about the current state of the market. The expertise of the individual is converted into the expertise of the firm, improving its ability to deliver quality service consistently through *all* of its frontline personnel. With suitable software, the search activities themselves can be made more programmatic, by identifying key customizing variables that reflect the particular client's needs. For example, employment agencies try to identify for a job seeker openings offering the desired salary, location, type of work, level of responsibility, and so forth. Computer programs can be written to search the job-opening files and automatically generate a list of feasible matches. The same can be done in real estate brokerage.

If the most relevant "customizing variables" can be specified and programmed in advance, the firm becomes, less dependent upon its frontline personnel to perform the customizing tasks. Not only is the market knowledge institutionalized, but so is much of the necessary expertise, namely, the individual *judgment* that previously had to be exercised by the frontline personnel. Customization can still be delivered, but it is no longer entirely dependent on the discretion and professional expertise of the brokers.

One final way in which the computer may be employed is in the *generation* of market knowledge. Through its capturing of market transaction information, the facilitator firm is well positioned with a large data base which it can routinely analyze to uncover market trends, demographic detail, and other matters. The firm can obtain market expertise not only passively (by accumulation), but also *actively* (by processing its available information).

The impact of such changes on the internal structure of facilitator firms will be drastic. We have already said that the firm will become less dependent upon its brokers; we expect this to be reflected not only in lower turnover in the broker ranks, but also in dramatic changes in the compensation system. With these new systems, a fundamental shift will take place in where (and how) the firm "adds value." In the old-style firm, as we noted, much of the added value was provided by the individual broker, and this justified the high commission structure. Now the added value is built-in to the firm and its systems, and a significantly lower commission structure will be necessitated.

The introduction of computer-based systems will add significantly to the fixed costs of the firms, transforming them from the high-variable-cost systems that were implied by the commission compensation systems. This will force the firms into more active marketing efforts to generate the revenues (and smooth the fluctuations in demand) necessary to cover these fixed costs. In turn, the necessity for these fixed expenditures will provide a driving force toward the large multi-site firm. In the past, most facilitator firms have been characterized by large numbers of small, single outlets. (In 1968 there were 6,000 authorized travel agencies in the U.S.; by 1977 there were 13,500. In the late 1970s there were more than 10,000 employment agencies and 150,000 real estate firms, of which some 80 percent were single-office outlets.) The drive to cover increased fixed costs may also lead to increased price competition. (In the past, firms responded to downturns by laying off brokers and weathering the storm by keeping fixed costs low.)

More Emphasis on the Advisory Function

One final trend should be noted. The ultimate impact of the combined computer and communications revolution may be to enable buyers and sellers to search for each other by direct access to a computer-based market file. While it may be possible to make a business of this by owning the data bank and charging an access fee, this development will threaten existing facilitator businesses. To the extent that existing facilitator firms have relied upon the information-exchange (market *knowledge*) service they provide, they may be threatened. Survival will require expansion of their advisory functions.

This trend toward *expertise* as the added value is notable. New specialist firms are springing up in many industries. For example, an article in the *New York Times* on June 5, 1981, described a new firm specializing in booking top-of-the-line hotel reservations. It is attempting to compete against travel agents, it appears, because of the latter's "generality" and their inability to bring specialist. expertise to bear on advising the client well as to the quality of hotels in remote locations. Similarly, employment agencies are increasingly tending to specialize by type of job function, because such specialization gives them a greater ability to be expert advisors. In stockbrokerage, while specialization by firm is not necessarily taking place, there is a trend to specialization *within* the firm. Rather than the general broker handling all of the client's needs, market experts in each of the financial services are brought to bear on the client's specific problems, changing the relationship of client to broker and enhancing the bond linking client to firm and broker to firm. This will create new problems as the frontline broker is now required to cross-sell services and concentrate on process/interactive skills. As with the other changes outlined here, a fundamental realignment of relations (and compensation) between the firm and its personnel will be required.

CONCLUSION

In this article we have tried to demonstrate the commonality of tasks, problems, and opportunities faced by a group of industries engaged in facilitating market transactions. We have, of necessity, focused on what they have in common, rather than on what distinguishes them. Although the differences may be considerable, this article makes the case that managers in each of these facilitator industries should begin to watch each other more closely, and should reflect on how developments in the other industries might be relevant to their own.

Sullivan's Auto World

CHRISTOPHER H. LOVELOCK

A young health care manager unexpectedly finds herself responsible for running a family-owned car dealership that is in trouble. She is very concerned about the poor performance of the service department and wonders if a turnaround is possible.

Viewed from Wilson Avenue, the dealership presented a festive sight. Strings of triangular pennants in red, white, and blue fluttered gaily in the late afternoon breeze. Rows of new model cars gleamed and winked in the sunlight. Geraniums graced the flowerbeds outside the showroom entrance. A huge rotating sign at the corner of Wilson Avenue and Route 23 sported the Ford logo and identified the business as Sullivan's Auto World. Banners below urged "Let's Make a Deal!"

Inside the handsome, high ceilinged showroom, three of the new model Fords were on display—a dark-blue station wagon, a red convertible, and a white Thunderbird. Each car was polished to a high sheen. Two groups

of customers were chatting with salespeople, and a middle-aged man sat in the driver's seat of the convertible, studying the controls.

Upstairs in the comfortably furnished general manager's office, Carol Sullivan-Diaz finished running another spreadsheet analysis on the computer. She felt tired and depressed. Her father, Walter Sullivan, had died four weeks earlier at the age of 56 of a sudden heart attack. As executor of his estate, the bank had asked her to temporarily assume the position of general manager of the dealership. The only visible changes that she had made to her father's office were installing the computer and printer, but she had been very busy analyzing the current position of the business.

Sullivan-Diaz did not like the look of the numbers on the printout. Auto World's financial situation had been deteriorating for 18 months, and it had been running in the red for the first half of the current year. New car sales had declined, reflecting high interest rates and a turndown in the regional economy. Margins had been squeezed by promotions and other efforts to move new cars off the lot. Industry forecasts of future sales were discouraging, and so were her own financial projections for Auto World's sales department. Service revenues, which were below average for a dealership of this size, had also declined, although the service department still made a small surplus.

Had she had made a mistake last week, Carol wondered, in turning down Bill Froelich's offer to buy the business? It was true that the price offered had been substantially below the offer from Froelich that her father had rejected two years earlier, but the business had been more profitable then.

The Sullivan Family

Walter Sullivan had purchased a small Ford dealership in 1971, renamed it Sullivan Auto, and built it up to become one of the best known in the metro area. Six years back, he had borrowed heavily to purchase the current site at a major suburban intersection, in an area of town with many new housing developments.

There had been a dealership on the site, but the buildings were 30 years old. Sullivan had retained the service and repair bays, but torn down the showroom in front of them, and replaced it by an attractive modern facility. On moving to the new location, which was substantially larger than the old one, he had renamed his business Sullivan's Auto World.

Everybody had seemed to know Walt Sullivan. He had been a consummate showman and entrepreneur, appearing in his own radio and television commercials and active in community affairs. His approach to car sales had emphasized promotions, discounts, and deals in order to maintain volume. He was never happier than when making a sale.

Carol Sullivan-Diaz, aged 28, was the eldest of Walter and Carmen Sullivan's three daughters. After obtaining a bachelor's degree in economics, she had gone on to take an M.B.A.

degree and had then embarked on a career in health care management. She was married to Dr. Roberto Diaz, a surgeon at St. Luke's Hospital. Her 20-year old twin sisters, Gail and Joanne, who were college sophomores, lived with their mother.

As a college student, Sullivan-Diaz had worked part-time in her father's business on secretarial and bookkeeping tasks, and also as a service writer in the service department; so she was quite familiar with the operations of the dealership. At business school, she had decided on a career in health care management. After graduation, she had worked as an executive assistant to the president of St. Luke's, a large teaching hospital. Two years later, she joined Metropolitan Health Plan, a large health maintenance organization (HMO), as assistant director of marketing — a position she had now held for almost three years. Her responsibilities included attracting new members, complaint handling, market research, and member retention programs.

Carol's employer had given her a six-week leave of absence to put her father's affairs in order. She doubted that she could extend that leave much beyond the two weeks still remaining. Neither she nor other family members were interested in making a career of running the dealership. However, she was prepared to take time out from her health care career to work on a turnaround if that seemed a viable proposition. She had been successful in her present job and believed it would not be difficult to find another health management position in the future.

The Dealership

Like other car dealerships, Sullivan's Auto World operated both sales and service departments, often referred to in the trade as "front end" and "back end," respectively. However, Auto World did not have a body shop for repairing damaged bodywork. Both new and used vehicles were sold, since a high proportion of new car and van purchases involved trading in the purchaser's existing vehicle. Auto World would also buy low-mileage used cars at auction for resale. Purchasers who decided that they could not afford a new car would often buy a "preowned" vehicle instead, while shoppers who came in looking for a used car could sometimes be persuaded to buy a new one.

The front end of the dealership employed a sales manager, seven salespeople, an office manager, and a secretary. One of the salespeople had given notice and would be leaving at the end of the following week. The service department, when fully staffed, consisted of a service manager, a parts supervisor, nine mechanics, and two service writers. The Sullivan twins often worked part-time as service writers, filling in at busy periods, when one of the other writers was sick or on vacation, or when — as currently — there was an unfilled vacancy. The job entailed scheduling appointments for repairs and maintenance, writing up each work order, calling customers with repair estimates, and assisting customers when they returned to pick up the cars and pay for the work that had been done.

Sullivan-Diaz knew from her own experience as a service writer that it could be a stressful job. Few people liked to be without their car, even for a day. When a car broke down or was having problems, the owner was often nervous about how long it would take to get it fixed and, if the warranty had expired, how much the labor and parts would cost. Customers were quite unforgiving when a problem was not fixed completely on the first attempt and they had to return their vehicle for further work.

Major mechanical failures were not usually difficult to repair, although the parts replacement costs might be expensive. It was often the "little" things like water leaks and wiring problems that were the hardest to diagnose and correct, and it might be necessary for the customer to return two or three times before such a problem was resolved. In these situations, parts and materials costs were relatively low, but labor costs mounted up quickly, being charged out at $40 an hour. Customers could often be quite abusive, yelling at service writers over the phone or arguing with service writers, mechanics, and the service manager in person.

Turnover in the service writer job was high, which was one reason why Carol — and more

recently her sisters — had often been pressed into service by their father to "hold the fort" as he described it. More than once, she had seen an exasperated service writer snap back at a complaining customer or hang up on one who was being abusive over the telephone. Gail and Joanne were currently taking turns to cover the vacant position, but there were times when both of them had classes and the dealership had only one service writer on duty.

By national standards, Sullivan's Auto World was a medium-sized dealership, selling around 1,100 cars a year, equally divided between new and used vehicles. In the most recent year, its revenues totaled $23.1 million from new and used car sales and $2.51 million from service (including parts) — down from $26.5 million and $3.12 million, respectively, in the previous year. Although the unit value of car sales was high, the margins were quite low. The reverse was true for service. Industry guidelines suggested that the contribution margin (known as the departmental selling gross) from car sales should be about 5.5 percent of sales revenues, and from service, around 25 percent of revenues. In a typical dealership, 60 percent of the selling gross came from sales and 40 percent from service. The selling gross was then applied to fixed expenses, such as administrative salaries, rent or mortgage payments, and utilities.

For the most recent 12 months at Auto World, Sullivan-Diaz had determined that the selling gross figures were 4.6 percent and 24 percent, respectively, both of them lower than in the previous year and insufficient to cover the dealership's fixed expenses. Her father had made no mention of financial difficulties and she had been shocked to learn from the bank after his death that Auto World had been two months behind in mortgage payments on the property. Further analysis also showed that accounts payable had also risen sharply in the previous six months. Fortunately, the dealership held a large insurance policy on Sullivan's life, and the proceeds from this had been more than sufficient to bring mortgage payments up to date and pay down all overdue accounts.

The opportunities for expanding new car sales did not appear promising, given the state of the economy. However, recent promotional incentives had reduced the inventory to manageable levels. From discussions with Larry Winters, Auto World's sales manager, Sullivan-Diaz had concluded that costs could be reduced by not replacing the departing sales rep, maintaining inventory at somewhat lower levels, and trying to make more efficient use of advertising and promotion. Although Winters did not have Walter Sullivan's exuberant personality, he had been Auto World's leading sales rep before being promoted, and had shown strong managerial capabilities in his current position.

As she reviewed the figures for the service department, Sullivan-Diaz wondered what potential might exist for improving its sales volume and selling gross. Her father had never been very interested in the parts and service business, seeing it simply as a necessary adjunct of the dealership. "Customers always seem to be miserable back there," he had once remarked to her. "But here in the front end, everybody's happy when someone buys a new car." The service facility was not easily visible from the main highway, being hidden behind the showroom. The building was old and greasy, although the equipment was modern and well maintained.

Customers were required to bring cars in for servicing before 8:30 A.M. After parking their cars, customers entered the service building by a side door and waited their turn to see the service writers, who occupied a cramped room with peeling paint and an interior window overlooking the service bays. Customers stood while work orders for their cars were written up by hand on large sheets. Ringing telephones frequently interrupted the process. Filing cabinets containing customer records and other documents lined the far wall of the room.

If the work were of a routine nature, such as an oil change or tune up, the customer was given an estimate immediately. For more complex jobs, they would be called with an estimate later in the morning once the car had been examined. Customers were required to pick up their cars by 6:00 P.M. on the day the work was completed. On several occasions, Carol had urged her father to computerize the

service work order process, but he had never acted on her suggestions.

The service manager, Rick Obert, who was in his late forties, had held the position since Auto World had opened at its current location. The Sullivan family considered him to be technically skilled, and he managed the mechanics effectively. However, his manner with customers could be gruff and argumentative.

Customer Survey Results

Another set of data that Sullivan-Diaz had studied carefully were the results of the customer satisfaction surveys that were mailed to the dealership monthly by a research firm retained by the Ford Motor Company.

Purchasers of all new Ford cars were sent a questionnaire by mail within 30 days of making the purchase and asked to use a five-point scale to rate their satisfaction with the dealership sales department, vehicle preparation, and the characteristics of the vehicle itself. The questionnaire asked how likely the purchaser would be to recommend the dealership, the salesperson, and the manufacturer to someone else. Other questions asked if the customers had been introduced to the dealer's service department and been given explanations on what to do if their cars needed service. Finally, there were some classification questions relating to customer demographics.

A second survey was sent to new car purchasers nine months after they had bought their cars. This questionnaire began by asking about satisfaction with the vehicle and then asked customers if they had taken their vehicles to the selling dealer for service of any kind. If so, respondents were then asked to rate the service department on 14 different attributes — ranging from the attitudes of service personnel to the quality of the work performed — and then to rate their overall satisfaction with service from the dealer.

Customers were also asked about where they would go in the future for maintenance service, minor mechanical and electrical repairs, major repairs in those same categories, and bodywork. The options listed for service were selling dealer, another Ford dealer, "some other place," or "do-it-yourself." Finally, there were questions about overall satisfaction with the dealer sales department and the dealership in general, as well as the likelihood of their purchasing another Ford Motor Company product and buying it from the same dealership.

Dealers received monthly reports summarizing customer ratings of their dealership for the most recent month and for several previous months. To provide a comparison with how other Ford dealerships performed, the reports also included regional and national rating averages. After analysis, completed questionnaires were returned to the dealership; since these included each customer's name, a dealer could see which customers were satisfied and which were not.

In the 30-day survey of new purchasers, Auto World achieved better than average ratings on most dimensions. One finding which puzzled Carol was that almost 90 percent of respondents answered "yes" when asked if someone from Auto World had explained what to do if they needed service, but less than a third said that they had been introduced to someone in the service department. She resolved to ask Larry Winters about this discrepancy.

The nine-month survey findings disturbed her. Although vehicle ratings were in line with national averages, the overall level of satisfaction with service at Auto World was consistently low, placing it in the bottom 25 percent of all Ford dealerships.

The worst ratings for service concerned promptness of writing up orders, convenience of scheduling the work, convenience of service hours, and appearance of the service department. On length of time to complete the work, availability of needed parts, and quality of work done ("was it fixed right?"), Auto World's rating was close to the average. For interpersonal variables such as attitude of service department personnel, politeness, understanding of customer problems, and explanation of work performed, its ratings were relatively poor.

When Sullivan-Diaz reviewed the individual questionnaires, she found that there was a wide degree of variation between customers' responses on these interpersonal variables, ranging all the way across a 5-point scale from "completely satisfied" to "very dissatisfied."

Curious, she had gone to the service files and examined the records for several dozen customers who had recently completed the nine-month surveys. At least part of the ratings could be explained by which service writers the customer had dealt with. Those who had been served two or more times by her sisters, for instance, gave much better ratings than those who had dealt primarily with Jim Fiskell, the service writer who had recently quit.

Perhaps the most worrying responses were those relating to customers' likely use of Auto World's service department in the future. More than half indicated that they would use another Ford dealer or "some other place" for maintenance service (such as oil change, lube, or tuneup) or for minor mechanical and electrical repairs. About 30 per cent would use another source for major repairs. The rating for overall satisfaction with the selling dealer after nine months was below average and the customer's likelihood of purchasing from the same dealership again was a full point below that of buying another Ford product.

An Unwelcome Disturbance

Sullivan-Diaz pushed aside the spreadsheets she had printed out and turned off the computer. It was time to go home for dinner. She saw the options for the dealership as basically twofold: either prepare the business for an early sale at what would amount to a distress price, or take a year or two to try to turn it around financially. In the latter instance, if the turnaround succeeded, the business could subsequently be sold at a higher price than it presently commanded, or the family could install a general manager to run the dealership for them.

Bill Froelich, owner of a Lincoln-Mercury dealership about 2 miles away, had offered to buy Auto World for a price that represented a fair valuation of the net assets, according to Auto World's accountants, plus $125,000 in goodwill. However, the rule of thumb when the auto industry was enjoying good times was that goodwill should be valued at $1,000 per vehicle sold each year.

As Carol left her office, she spotted the sales manager coming up the stairs leading from the showroom floor. "Larry," she said, "I've got a question for you."

"Fire away!" replied the sales manager.

"I've been looking at the customer satisfaction surveys. Why aren't our sales reps introducing new customers to the folks in the Service Department? It's supposedly part of our sales protocol, but it only seems to be happening about one-third of the time!"

Larry Winters shuffled his feet. "Well, Carol, basically I leave it to their discretion. We tell them about service, of course, but some of the guys on the floor feel a bit uncomfortable taking folks over to the service bays after they've been in here. It's quite a contrast, if you know what I mean."

Suddenly, the sound of shouting arose from the floor below. A man of about 40, wearing a windbreaker and jeans, was standing in the doorway yelling at one of the salespeople. The two managers could catch snatches of what he was saying, in between various obscenities:

"...three visits...still not fixed right...service stinks...who's in charge here?" Everybody else in the showroom had stopped what they were doing and had turned to look at the newcomer.

Winters looked at his young employer and rolled his eyes. "If there was something your dad couldn't stand, it was guys like that, yelling and screaming in the showroom and asking for the boss. Walt would go hide out in his office! Don't worry, Tom'll take care of that fellow and get him out of here. What a jerk!"

"No," said Sullivan-Diaz, "I'll deal with him. One thing I learned when I worked at St. Luke's was that you don't let people yell about their problems in front of everybody else. You take them off somewhere, calm them down, and find out what's bugging them."

She stepped quickly down the stairs, wondering to herself, "What else have I learned in health care that I can apply to this business?"

The Law Offices of Lewin & Associates

SULA FISZMAN
CHRISTOPHER H. LOVELOCK

A chain of legal clinics is losing money at several of its 18 offices. The managing partner is reviewing office procedures and seeking to increase the number of legal cases handled.

Elizabeth Lewin, managing partner of The Law Offices of Lewin & Associates, was concerned. It was January 1983 and business was in a precarious state for one of the largest law clinics in the United States. Four of the firm's 17 offices in the large midwestern city of Lakeshore were losing money, and two more were financially marginal. Altogether, the firm was losing somewhere around $15,000 per month. Over the next two months, Lewin and her associates needed to agree on a plan to increase the number of cases per office and to improve office efficiency.

THE FIRM

The Law Offices of Lewin & Associates (L&A) was founded in 1978, growing out of a long-held concern of Elizabeth Lewin with the limited accessibility of legal services. Lewin, then aged 33, was a graduate of the Stanford Law School who had worked in government agencies as well as for a major law firm in downtown Lakeshore. She believed strongly in the need for a full-service law firm devoted to handling the legal problems of middle-income people at affordable prices. Other investors, including several lawyers, accepted her invitation to invest capital in the new firm that she decided to found. It was agreed that only Lewin, who was named managing partner, would be involved in the day-to-day administration of the firm.

The partners sought to achieve economies of scale by modeling the new organization after successful retail chains. They intended to achieve these economies by:

• Opening a significant number of small neighborhood offices, to increase clients' accessibility to the firm.

• Creating a system of standardized forms and procedures for handling personal legal problems to achieve more efficient processing of clients' cases.

• Delegating routine administrative tasks to secretaries so that the more highly paid lawyers would be available for client consultation and for handling those tasks which only they were qualified to perform.

• Centralizing and computerizing the administrative functions, such as accounts payable, purchasing, and personnel hiring.

• Concentrating the work of attorneys on a limited number of recurring legal needs to take advantage of economies of scale and learning curve effects.

• Utilizing specialists who served more than one office to enable the firm to offer a broad product line.

The firm sought to target two very large market segments: (1) middle-income people who patronized traditional law firms, but could be served equally well through the new firm's less costly system; (2) people who did not use legal services as often as they needed them because the services were too expensive or inaccessible.

Lewin selected a product line that was general in that it covered every kind of personal legal service and specialized in that not all L&A lawyers handled all types of legal cases. For complex problems ranging from bankruptcy to consumer law, the firm had specialists located in various offices to whom its other lawyers referred these problems. This system enabled L&A to serve all clients and yet achieve the learning curve effects which occurred when a lawyer handled many similar cases. As one of the firm's attorneys said: "We are in law what family practitioners are in medicine."

Lewin spent her first six months preparing for the simultaneous opening of nine offices in October 1978. She noted that there were economies of scale involved for furniture and equipment purchases. "More important, though," she added, "it was the only way to make advertising economical." The firm's rapid development precluded any formal planning. "In general," Lewin said, "our offices were located with a view both to the population and a sense of the neighborhood we'd be serving." Offices were established in commercial buildings, shopping centers, and malls in downtown Lakeshore and its suburbs. Five offices were on the ground floor of the buildings they occupied, but this location did not seem to bring in more clients than offices situated on higher floors.

By late 1981, the firm had expanded to 10 offices. Lewin then arranged to open seven offices in the Valu-Rite chain of discount retail stores, which sold household items and clothing. The firm needed more suburban offices in Bulbeck County, south and west of Lakeshore, to spread advertising costs and to maximize advertising potential. Valu-Rite customers were the group at which L&A was aiming. "Putting offices in a chain store has great potential," said Lewin. "It offers us a convenient location and a captured client." Some L&A employees thought that the Valu-Rite image was negative; they were also concerned that the new offices were too near several existing offices and competed directly with them. *Exhibit 1* summarizes information on each of the 17 offices operated by Lewin & Associates in January 1983.

THE CHANGING FACE OF THE LEGAL PROFESSION

According to a 1971 article in the *American Bar Association Journal*, approximately 70 percent of the U.S. population lacked access to needed legal services, because they had too little money to afford the services yet not so little that they qualified for free legal aid.

It was estimated that one-third of all adults had never consulted an attorney and that less than one in five used attorneys to resolve consumer problems.

A number of legal clinics were established to remove some of the mystique from the law and to make legal services more accessible and affordable. However, a 1977 survey found that, of 33 legal clinics throughout the U.S., eleven were insolvent, five relied on subsidies to fund losses, fourteen were solvent, and only three could be described as prospering. Part of the problem was that state bar associations prohibited lawyers from using advertising to solicit professional employment. This barrier was eliminated in mid-1977, when the United States Supreme Court ruled in *Bates* v. *State Bar of Arizona*, 433 U.S.

EXHIBIT 1

Location and Characteristics of Lewin & Associates in Offices in Lakeshore Area, 1983

Location	Neighborhood	Employees		Type of Client	Average Consultations Per Month	Average Monthly Income
Market Street Lakeshore	Business	Atty. Sec.	2 2	Mixed ethnically Status: Professional	145	$19,600
1st Avenue Lakeshore	Business Residential	Atty. Sec.	2 2	Mixed ethnically Status: Middle management	108	$17,800
15th Avenue Lakeshore	Business Residential	Atty. Sec.	1 2	Mixed ethnically Status: Middle management	49	$11,400
Broadmoor	Residential	Atty. Sec.	2 2	Black Status: Blue collar	97	$18,000
Royal Highway	Residential	Atty. Sec.	2 2	White Status: Blue collar	87	$26,000
Town Park	Residential	Atty. Secy.	1 2	White Status: Blue collar	75	$20,900
Logan	Residential	Atty. Secy.	1 2	Mixed ethnically Status: Blue collar	66	$10,500
Green Lake	Residential	Atty. Secy.	1 1	Black/Hispanic Status: Middle management	98	$ 8,400
Black Plains	Residential Business	Atty. Secy.	1 1	Mixed ethnically Status: Professional	112	$10,500
Arlmont*	Residential	Atty. Secy.	1 2	Black Status: Blue collar	35	$ 7,900
Georgeville*	Residential	Atty. Secy.	1 1	Black Status: Blue collar	75	$11,200
Fittburg*	Residential	Atty. Secy.	1 1	White Status: Blue collar	129	$12,400
East Bulbeck*	Residential	Atty. Secy.	1 1	White Status: Middle management	29	$ 7,400
Bulbeck Center*	Residential	Atty. Secy.	1 1	White Status: Blue collar	103	$13,100
Vienna	Residential	Atty. Secy.	1 2	White Status: Blue collar	119	$16,800
Petit Lac*	Residential Business	Atty. Secy.	1 2	White Status: Middle management	71	$ 9,000
Plymouth	Business	Atty. Secy.	1 1	Mixed ethnically Status: Middle management	32	$ 6,000

*Denotes unprofitable or financially marginal office. (*Note:* Vienna and Fittburg were located in Valu-Rite stores.)

350 (1977), that lawyers had a constitutional right to advertise. Associate Justice Blackmun wrote:

> Since the belief that lawyers are somehow above trade has become an anachronism, the historic foundation for advertising restraint has crumbled . . . (I believe that advertising by lawyers would reduce the cost of legal services . . . without encouraging any more shoddy work than now exists.)

Two months later, the four-office legal clinic of Jacoby & Meyers in Los Angeles became the first law firm to advertise on television. Within 18 months, that firm had expanded to a total of 22 offices. An independent study reported that since the firm began its TV campaign, it had attracted approximately 2,500 new clients each month. By 1983, Jacoby & Meyers boasted a total of 63 offices in California and New York. Other multioffice legal clinics expanded rapidly. Hyatt Legal Services, based in Kansas City and affiliated with the H&R Block chain of income tax preparers, operated 114 offices in 14 states and Washington, D.C.

THE LAKESHORE AREA LEGAL MARKET

Although there were no other chains of legal clinics or law offices in the Lakeshore area, Elizabeth Lewin had noted increased television and newspaper advertising by law partnerships and solo practitioners. Most of these solo practitioners specialized in a particular area of law, such as personal injury, immigration, or bankruptcy. A few had formalized referral services from other attorneys on a statewide basis and offered a toll-free number for initial consultation. The *Lakeshore Area Yellow Pages* featured 30 pages of listings under the category of "Lawyers," including separate listings grouped by type of practice and by location of practice. There were a number of eye-catching display advertisements for lawyers in the *Yellow Pages*, including one for Lewin & Associates.

Consumer Use of Legal Services

A telephone survey of randomly selected Lakeshore area residents commissioned by Lewin found that fewer than half of the respondents had previously used legal services. These users were more likely to be middle-aged, male, white, with above-average incomes, and professionals or managers. Half of these individuals had used legal services at least twice before. The most frequent case types were business, real estate, personal injury, and divorces (*Exhibit 2*).

When previous users were asked how they chose their attorney, they listed, with equal frequency: quality, reputation, and fees. Among nonusers, the most cited criterion for future selection was fees. The survey revealed that 65 percent of respondents (mostly previous users) would refuse to consult a lawyer whose office was located in a depart-

EXHIBIT 2
Types of Legal Needs Encountered Among Residents of Greater Lakeshore

Type of Case	Percent of Total Cases Reported
Business	22.9
Real estate	20.0
Wills	15.9
Other	11.3
Personal injuries	8.7
Divorce	6.1
Criminal	3.8
Workers compensation	3.2
Estate	2.6
Motor vehicle	2.0
Landlord/tenant	1.2
Immigration	1.2
Malpractice	0.9
Social Security	0.6
Adoption	0.3
Employment	0.3
Name change	0.3
Guardianship	0
Bankruptcy	0
Unemployment	0

SOURCE: Telephone survey of 402 randomly selected residents of L&A's service area, 1982.

ment store. Eighty-nine percent of respondents said they did not believe that a price-quality tradeoff existed. The survey also asked what sources people would consider most helpful in finding an attorney: 76 percent of respondents cited referral from a friend or relative, 16 percent listed word-of-mouth, and 5 percent mentioned the *Yellow Pages*. However, combined mentions of all other media totaled only 3.5 percent. More than half the respondents said they would not feel comfortable consulting an attorney who advertised on television or in a newspaper. This feeling was unrelated to prior experience with lawyers. Aversion to advertising generally increased with income level and correlated with refusal to consult an attorney whose office was in a department store or shopping mall.

In contrast to the profile of the "typical" Lakeshore legal client, L&A records showed that the firm attracted a larger proportion of clients who had a below average income, were black, or aged between 25 and 35. Each of these groups was more receptive to legal advertising. Although half of the firm's clients had used an attorney before, only 3 percent had consulted L&A previously—a fact that Lewin attributed to the firm's relative youth. Some clients wanted a "second opinion" on a matter about which they had already consulted another attorney. The most frequent type of case brought to L&A was divorce (*Exhibit 3*).

When asked how they chose their attorney, L&A's clients most frequently cited fees (61 percent), personal attention (44 percent), and convenient location (36 percent). Those who listed fees were most likely to be young and white; there was no correlation between fee sensitivity and income level. Almost three quarters of the firm's clients had learned of L&A through TV advertisements, which emphasized fees and personal attention. Only 13 percent heard of the firm from a friend. Another 15 percent learned of L&A through the *Yellow Pages*. About 70 percent of clients came to the firm's offices directly from their homes; more than half of this group of clients lived 2 to 10 miles from the office in question.

EXHIBIT 3
Composition of the Firm's Caseload, Fall 1982

Type of Case	Proportion of Total Cases
Divorce	33.4%
Criminal	10.7
Money claims	7.3
Landlord/tenant	6.9
Wills	6.6
Bankruptcy	5.9
Real estate	5.5
Business	5.4
Personal injuries	3.4
Employment	2.0
Dept. of Motor Vehicles	1.9
Adoption	1.8
Name change	1.6
Immigration	1.2
Social Security	1.0
Workers compensation	0.8
Guardianship	0.7
Other	4.0

SOURCE: Company records.

Competition Among Providers of Legal Services

Providers of legal services in the Lakeshore area ranged from prestigious firms in downtown office towers to neighborhood solo practitioners. Lewin & Associates competed primarily with solo proprietorships, local partnerships, legal clinics, and do-it-yourself legal kits. Within this group it did not provide the lowest-priced services (*Exhibit 4*). Rather, it served those clients who could not or did not want to pay the high-priced prestige firms, yet did not seek out the lowest fees available.

The firm had had some difficulties with the organized bar. One attorney observed:

> We're not well liked by the legal community because we take business away from the little guys. And judges have a bone to pick with Lewin & Associates from time to time. They see our ads on TV and become suspicious that the level of service is not what it should be.

Lewin acknowledged that her firm was encroaching on the turf of solo practitioners, but emphasized that L&A had tried to avoid antagonizing the bar through advertising:

> We try to make our ads as informative as possible. We try to stay within all the guidelines that are required. And if something is potentially controversial, we'll analyze it and decide whether we think we're justified in trying it. There's no reason to make the legal community angry with us. We try to do things professionally.

ORGANIZATION AND MANAGEMENT

Lewin & Associates had developed a two-tiered system of management. Certain administrative functions were handled centrally. Individual offices were headed by a managing attorney who both practiced law and supervised office personnel and financial matters.

The head office employed six administrators. Two of these, Elizabeth Lewin and Gordon Kane, were attorneys. The major functions of the head office were pricing decisions, monitoring of office management, quality control, and attorney hiring, training, and compensation. It collected business statistics from the individual offices, handled client complaints, and coordinated advertising efforts with the firm's advertising agency. Excluding advertising costs, Lewin estimated that head office expenses consumed about 25 percent of the firm's total earnings. Lewin took responsibility for office locations and attorney incentive and compensation plans. She participated with her financial partners in decisions regarding financing and future growth strategies. Kane handled personnel hiring and supervision of individual offices.

Pricing

Each attorney had a fee manual which listed categories of cases, covering nearly every option a client might need, and identified the appropriate fees in each instance. Lewin determined the fee based on the dollar and cents costs of running the business and an evaluation of what the market would bear. The goal was to set a price in advance, rather than to charge on an hourly basis. L&A was not the cheapest legal service in the Lakeshore area. For example, the firm offered to undertake uncontested divorce for $328 plus court costs; individual practitioners charged from $100 to $700 (*Exhibit 4*). Kane trained new attorneys to use the fee manual. He went over fact patterns or situations that might be encountered, and

EXHIBIT 4
Comparative Fees for Different Types of Cases

Type of Case	Lewin & Assoc.	Solo Practitioners	Legal Clinic	D-I-Y Legal Kit
Uncontested divorce	$328	$100–700	$250–350	$99–150
Simple bankruptcy	459	500–750	350–550	N/A
Real estate closing	1% of value*	250 or 1% of value*	250 or 1% of value*	N/A
Legal name change	250	200–250	200–350	N/A
Wills:				
Single	60	0–200†	40–100	N/A
Reciprocal	110	0–300†	80–300	N/A

Note: Fees cited exclude court costs (where applicable).

*That is, 1% of the selling price of the property.

†Some practitioners made no charge for a will in expectation of subsequently handling the estate work.

SOURCE: Company records plus local research in Greater Lakeshore.

demonstrated how that case should be categorized.

On arriving at an L&A office, a new client was requested to complete a brief form and pay a $25 consultation fee. The client then met with an attorney for approximately 30 minutes to discuss the problem. After analyzing the case, the attorney selected the appropriate fee category, gave the client a written estimate, and sent a copy to the main office. Approximately one consultation in three resulted in a client's retaining L&A to handle the case.

For the estimated fee, the client would receive a certain number of the attorney's hours, at a rate averaging more than $100 per hour. If the required time exceeded that included in the fee, the client was charged for the balance at an hourly rate of $85, which approximated the actual cost to L&A of providing legal services. Lewin claimed that her firm's more efficient procedures enabled it to offer clients greater value for their dollar than conventional law firms.

If the nature of the case changed—for example, if an uncontested divorce became contested—the attorney had to file a case-type change form to adjust the fee as appropriate. Certain cases, such as legal name changes, were charged at a flat rate regardless of the amount of time spent. Wills were priced as loss leaders. Although fees on a few cases, such as contested divorces or felony charges, could be as high as $3,000 or more, the average case at L&A yielded fees to the firm of about $350.

There was still some variability in fee quotes. Kane explained that the difference could arise if one attorney was more optimistic about settling the case through negotiation while another foresaw lengthy litigation. In 1981, a disguised visit to two L&A offices by a reporter for the *Lakeshore Tribune* revealed a $600 variance in fee estimates to do a contested divorce. Kane believed that training had narrowed such differences. Fees were usually changed once a year. The situation would be reviewed if attorneys complained that a fee was too high and that they were not retaining clients, or if they claimed that a fee was too low for the time required. Proposed revisions were submitted to attorneys for comment.

Recruitment

Most attorneys at Lewin & Associates came to the firm from their own practice or from a small law firm. L&A's official qualifications were five years of general practice experience for a managing attorney and one to three years for an associate. Each attorney had a personnel handbook which outlined basic firm policies such as working hours and dress codes. Practicing law on the side was strictly forbidden. When Kane interviewed an applicant, he looked for attorneys with a broad base in general practice and experience in dealing with people:

> I look for someone with the ability to elicit facts from clients expeditiously and to tell clients what to expect in terms of representation and fees. I look for someone who is generally well-organized and has the ability to follow up, because what we are looking for is a solo practitioner in a sense.

Applicants who passed Kane's screen were then sent to visit managing attorneys of offices to which they might be assigned. The managing attorney determined whether the applicant would be able to retain clients and do a reasonable share of the work. About 30 percent of the firm's attorneys were women, none were black. There was a scarcity of black attorneys, Lewin explained, and most of them went to work for large firms.

Monitoring Office Management

Each office called the head office daily with figures on the number of appointments kept, the fees collected the previous day, and the number of appointments booked for the present day. Monthly rankings were assigned to each office based on number of clients, rate of retention, and profitability. Kane visited all offices periodically. Those with new attorneys or poor statistics were visited more frequently—for example, once a month—whereas a more established office might not be visited more than twice yearly.

By 1983, each office had enough of a track record to allow Kane to know if it should be doing better. He reviewed files to ensure that cases were being moved along expeditiously. Depending on the office, 50 to 150 files would be open at any one time. A file might remain open for anything from two weeks to as long as two and a half years. The average uncontested divorce case file remained open for 16 weeks.

L&A's policy required offices to call and confirm appointments, but not to call and inquire about an already missed appointment. "People feel that's a little too aggressive and pushy," said Lewin. To minimize the number of missed appointments, L&A policy required that offices schedule appointments at the earliest possible date, preferably the same day that a client called. Lewin commented:

> We have trouble with this. The attorneys in the offices don't really believe it, but the faster you get clients in after they phone, the less likely they are to be no-shows. Offices can be really lax about this sometimes. You can understand the tendency to say, "Oh no, another client—book them tomorrow, book them Wednesday." But that's not good for business.

When Kane had finished reviewing files at an office, he sat down with the managing attorney to discuss his impressions and to make suggestions on how to manage the case load more efficiently. "One of the things I tell the attorney," he said, "is that we're a 'pay-as-you-go' law firm. The faster the work can be accomplished, the sooner the file can be closed and the better off that office is economically."

The firm had an of counsel[1] litigation specialist, whom Lewin urged the attorneys to use since she felt litigation was disruptive to an office. The more experienced attorneys, she said, would handle a case up to trial before turning it over to the specialist.

---

[1]An of counsel attorney is neither a partner nor an employee of the firm. He or she maintains a relationship not unlike that of a consultant, providing assistance to the firm on some matters, but working independently on others.

Both Lewin and Kane described the task of evaluating the quality of service as a matter of judgment. Kane observed that one of the most direct ways of evaluating an attorney's advice was being in the office frequently. "You have to have a feel for what goes on in an office: how does it look, how does the attorney handle his staff, how does he greet the client, how does he behave with the client?" The firm also relied on client complaints to alert it to problems, which Kane then investigated.

Every year, L&A reviewed the performance of each office and each attorney; this review was based on Kane's and Lewin's impression of the office, and the office statistics. The results helped the firm decide on salaries and on whether an attorney should stay with the firm.

Not all attorneys felt that the administrators were able to control quality effectively. Said one: "The administrators say they ensure consistency because of the forms, training, hiring process. But not really. They find out when there's a problem. They have carried some people for a long time when they've known the attorney had problems, when the problems were pretty consistent." Another attorney agreed that the firm's quality control was not that effective but felt, in general, that the attorneys had been good and hard working.

Attorney Compensation

After some experimentation, L&A had adopted a compensation formula whereby each office was assigned a certain gross earnings target per month, such as $12,000 for a one-attorney office. The attorney was paid a salary plus 10 percent of anything the office earned over that gross amount. The annual salary, including bonus, for a managing attorney, ranged from $27,000–$45,000; for an associate, it was between $17,000 and $22,000. The additional cost to L&A of benefits and payroll taxes amounted to about one fifth of the salary totals.

Lewin was still unsure whether the compensation scheme provided enough incentive for the attorneys "to go that extra mile which you really need to make these offices very effective." It appeared that the stronger offices were carrying the weaker, and Lewin felt that many managing attorneys had lost all sensitivity to the cost of their offices. She was not happy with the plan, stating that she wanted to see some change:

> This kind of firm really needs an entrepreneurial type of attorney. It's a retail business. You've got to be out there hustling. You've got to be on top of your office. It's a nickel and dime business in a way, with lots of small cases. So unless attorneys really feel they're going to be getting something out of the office, you're going to have a situation where you're not getting the maximum amount you can from each operation.

Monetary compensation was an especially important incentive, since L&A attorneys could not look forward to rising in the firm's ranks. Lewin had no plans for taking on new partners nor additional executive personnel. One managing attorney described his probable career path as: "Associate, manager, out . . . . I don't see my future with L&A. I can see myself opening a competitor and becoming an entrepreneur. I'm not crazy about the practice of law. I'd rather be the owner." The turnover rate was described variously by attorneys as "extremely high" and "not as high as you'd think."

INDIVIDUAL OFFICES

The typical L&A office was staffed by a managing attorney and a paralegal secretary. Where the volume of cases warranted it, an associate attorney and additional secretarial help were hired. Secretaries were paid, on average, $320 per week. Benefits and payroll taxes added another 21 percent to these wage costs. Most offices were small, ranging in size from 700 to 1000 square feet. Annual rental costs averaged $15 per square foot. Miscellaneous office expenses, such as supplies, copying, electricity, heating or cooling, telephone, etc., amounted to around $280 per week for the average office.

The managing attorney was responsible

for office management and for compliance with firmwide policies with regard to the keeping of statistics, fee quotes, and appointment booking procedures. He or she also had full responsibility for handling the case load and supervising the associate attorney. The firm was considering extending office hours (currently Monday–Friday, 9:00 A.M.–5:30 P.M.) into two evenings each week and opening for a full day every fourth Saturday.

L&A offices were simple and unpretentious. The firm accepted credit cards. Wherever possible, all brochures and written materials, including legal documents, were prepared in straightforward language. Attorneys were encouraged to be direct and matter-of-fact in their dealings with clients.

The Market Street Office in Lakeshore

Four blocks from Union Station, across from a coffee shop and wedged between two banks, was the L&A office managed by Steven Farmann, who worked with an associate. Serving a substantial area of midtown Lakeshore, it had been one of the firm's highest-revenue offices, averaging a gross of about $19,600 per month with a record high month of $26,000 and a record low month of $14,000.

Farmann had held a responsible position in a family sportswear company before graduating from Illiana Law School. After passing the bar, he opened his own practice in a suburban town 20 miles from Lakeshore. For 10 months he worked as an attorney during the day and as a waiter at night for additional income. When he decided to marry, Farmann began applying for jobs in Lakeshore and joined Lewin & Associates.

The work itself could be repetitive, Farmann felt. What made it interesting was the variety of people: "At the bottom end, I see an alcoholic postal worker who wants a divorce. At the top end, I see a psychiatrist at a major hospital. I also see nurses, middle managers—mostly women—people who work for Blue Cross and in health-related fields." They came to Lewin & Associates, he thought, because they didn't know any lawyers, and had seen the firm's advertisements. Due to the nature of the cases—predominantly divorce—there was little repeat business from the same clients.

In summarizing his role, Farmann said:

Once I became managing attorney, it became a challenge to bring the office from an average of $12,000 or $13,000 per month up to $20,000 or $21,000. So that's where I put all my energy. I got a paralegal who was like a diamond in the rough. She got so good at her job that I could give her verbal instructions and half an hour later something would be completed on my desk. This gave me time to sit with clients. L&A can succeed only if an attorney is in the office a maximum number of hours. An attorney can't afford to go to court to answer motions, go to trials, do real estate closures, because time is precious and should be spent in the office.

However, Farmann did not turn down cases involving court time: "I can't turn down clients because I have to make the money. It's all about making the money. I have a second attorney, so if I go to court, there's coverage here." He estimated that he spent only 5 percent of his time in court.

Despite Farmann's efforts, business during the third quarter of 1982 had not been good. The office scheduled as many appointments as possible, but there was an exceptionally high rate of missed appointments. Lewin estimated the firmwide average at 35 percent. Farmann attributed the increase in no-shows to the firm's austerity program under which radio spots replaced TV advertisements when the cost of television spots rose seasonally. He felt that radio advertising attracted a different kind of client, who was surprised, on calling for an appointment, to learn that the firm charged an initial consultation fee and who was less likely to keep an appointment.

Farmann had other concerns about the firm:

The organization is so unusually informal that each office basically is fairly autonomous. The manual with fee schedules dictates the policies of the firm. But, whether we follow it closely varies office by office. There's no strict monitoring like Kentucky Fried. Lots of things go by the board here because we don't have the time.

Beth Lewin feels that if attorneys have direct control over costs, offices will be more profitable. But she needs to put more time into sitting down with the attorneys and figuring out what it is about their offices that isn't profitable in terms of time and consultation management. Most office expenses are fixed. The only thing to maximize is performance of individual attorneys and the head office administrators have us pigeonholed in such a way following their procedures that they lose a lot of people along the way. They've tried to standardize and make the operation so uniform that they don't take attorney preferences to heart. We're not pushing lingerie over the counter. I like to think of myself as a professional, not a retail store operator, and this as a law firm, not Valu-Rite or Sears.

In November 1982, about a month after making these observations, Farmann resigned to go back into private practice. Lewin remarked that she and Kane had not regarded Farmann as a good manager. The new managing attorney appointed to Market Street had taken the initiative in establishing a better work flow, thereby lowering costs, while also moving aggressively to increase revenues. The net result had been a significant improvement in profitability of this office, which had hitherto been operating at close to breakeven.

The Nuffield Street Office in Broadmoor

The Nuffield Street office was located on a side street just off a busy and colorful shopping street in Broadmoor, an old neighborhood just west of central Lakeshore. It was on the top floor of a three-story building populated by small retail businesses and fast-food chains. There was a family dental practice on the second floor. The waiting room had the same utilitarian carpeting found in nearly all L&A offices. Brochures were available on a small table. A receptionist sat behind a glass window. Hanging on the wall was a framed quotation from Abraham Lincoln. It read: "A lawyer's time and advice are his stock in trade."

Martha Ross was managing attorney at this office. She was also the firm's bankruptcy specialist. Ross, a graduate of Ohio State Law School, had worked for legal aid in Cleveland for two years, and then for a two-person firm in Lakeshore before joining Lewin & Associates in 1980. She had left the small firm because she felt she was being exploited, "doing 75 percent of the work for 25 percent of the income," as she put it. Discussing her work at L&A, Ross commented: "I kind of enjoy what I do. It really is my own office. I feel fairly entrepreneurial. I do basically what I want within certain guidelines which are rational, so there's no reason to argue." Six months had gone by since Lewin or Kane had been out to check on her office.

Ross supervised one general practice attorney, two bankruptcy attorneys (located in other offices), and three paralegal secretaries (two of whom worked in other offices). By early 1983, she was spending 75 percent of her own time on general legal work, the balance on bankruptcy work. The typical bankruptcy client had been out of work for six months and had just become employed again. Most had fallen in arrears on their mortgage payments and faced foreclosure, but given time, they would be able to pay off their debts. Chapter 13 of the Bankruptcy Code allowed them three years. Ross preferred to see as many first-time clients as possible, believing that she was best able to evaluate a case, establish a fee and make referrals where necessary. She remarked:

I do virtually no routine work. The secretaries do all the routine work, all the pleadings, papers, simple matrimonials. I quickly skim it before it goes to court. Basically, it's all done by the secretaries. They've done it countless times, they're perfectly competent. When I have a question I ask them.

Three-quarters of the business that came into Ross's office consisted of matrimonial and family court cases. The rest included bankruptcy, real estate, and wills. Criminal cases were referred to the firm's criminal law expert in the First Avenue Office. Ross remarked:

I don't turn anything down. The head office may encourage it indirectly. I think they're concerned about people getting caught in cases that are going to require a lot of time and take them out of the office. I wouldn't like what I'm doing if I was turning down everything that was a little complex and therefore interesting, leaving myself only uncontested divorces.

The area where Ross worked was largely populated by blacks. This was reflected in her client mix. Many clients worked for Lakeshore Transit, Henderson's Department Store, Union Electric, and the Illiana Telephone Company, all of which had offices nearby. Most clients' incomes ranged from $15,000 to $30,000. Many had pensions, some had credit union accounts, fewer than half owned homes.

Ross kept a record of the time she spent on each case on strips of paper attached to the side of her desk. Like the firm's other attorneys, she worked with L&A's standard fee schedule, but noted:

I tend to give higher fee estimates than indicated by the schedule because experience tells me that it's really hard to explain to someone that what you said would be $1,000 will now be $4,000. If there's a real problem paying, I take less money up front. The general policy is to take at least half the fee in advance. I may take a quarter. Still, there are billing collection problems. Five percent, maybe, are bad debts.

COMMUNICATION EFFORTS

L&A's business was heavily dependent on advertising. Lewin estimated that the firm spent 12 percent of every dollar earned to cover advertising expenses. The firm's advertising agency selected advertising media by comparing efficiencies. The goal was to reach the largest number of potential clients for the least cost. Advertising was bought on a quarterly basis, with the same amount of money budgeted for each quarter. During the first and third quarters of the year, television advertising was relatively cheap, and so L&A ran about fourteen 30-second TV spots per week. During the second and fourth quarters, when TV advertising was seasonally more expensive, the firm switched to 60-second radio spots. Several attorneys noted a drop in business during the second and fourth quarters.

Lewin & Associates did not advertise on transit vehicles or on billboards. In 1978, the firm had run some full-page advertisements in the *Lakeshore Examiner*, a large circulation daily newspaper; these showed a man with a mask over his eyes saying, "The way lawyers charge, there ought to be a law." The advertising did not generate many calls to L&A offices. It did, however, offend many members of the legal community. Lewin remarked:

> We have not done print advertisement on a consistent basis. I think there might be some print opportunities we haven't taken advantage of. On the other hand, it's expensive and we face a lot of competition. Every other lawyer who advertises in print quotes specific fees. We don't want to do that. We're usually more expensive.

Community Contacts

Lewin said she would like to see her attorneys taking out local advertisements, joining more local neighborhood activities, and putting up billboards near their offices. However, she wanted to retain control over their efforts. One managing attorney observed that if the office were his own, he'd be out in the field more, making contacts and trying to get referrals. "I want to know why L&A has no community-based contacts and why they rely strictly on advertisements," he said.

Another attorney said he would not invest in local print advertising because it was expensive and not cost effective. He had thought about giving seminars on common legal problems for employees of major businesses in the area, but was not sure how to go about this. It had occurred to him to give discounts to members of large groups; this would re-

quire Lewin's approval and he had never pursued his idea so far as to ask for that.

A third L&A attorney said he had no time to organize meetings with local clubs and churches. "If the firm took one month's worth of advertising money," he remarked, "they could get a PR person for 12 months, but they think each individual attorney has enough time. An organization with these resources should do a lot more local PR."

THE PARTNERS DELIBERATE

After Lewin had summarized the firm's difficult economic situation, she and her financial partners considered possible solutions. One was to reduce the number of offices. However, the tension level among employees was rising as word spread that drastic changes were in the offing. Lewin worried about the impact of office closings on attorney morale. Reducing the number of offices would also increase the burden of advertising expense on the remaining offices.

The partners next considered changing the compensation plan to a 50–50 split of gross income between the managing attorney and the head office, with a guaranteed minimum salary of $2,000 per month. According to this plan, the managing attorney would be required to pay all office expenses out of the 50 percent share, including the salary of the associate attorney, if the office had one, and that of the office secretaries. The managing attorney would then take home whatever was left over as salary. Lewin felt that this arrangement would give the attorneys an incentive to keep office costs down. Any office which was not able to meet its expenses out of its 50 percent would be closed.

But the partners foresaw several problems. New offices would need to be carried until they could establish themselves. Moreover, the gross income of some offices was highly variable from month to month; employment contracts, hitherto unused at L&A, might be necessary to give attorneys the security they required. The location of new offices would become extremely important since these might dilute business at existing offices if established nearby. Further, the fee-sharing arrangements between the general practice attorney and the specialist might have to be changed.

The partners also considered providing additional services to increase volume. Tax service was one possibility. As Lewin perceived it, the problem with this option was that L&A's image would then become blurred, and expensive changes in the advertising would have to be made. In addition, L&A personnel lacked the necessary expertise for complicated, specialized areas of the law, such as tax.

PART III
Designing and Delivering Services

The ABCs of Service System Blueprinting

JANE KINGMAN-BRUNDAGE

Service system blueprints present marketers with a new tool for the strategic management of service details. Blueprinting helps to communicate the details of a service in ways that are useful to managers and employees, often revealing systems that might otherwise remain invisible.

Managing a service system effectively is intricate work. The intangibility surrounding a service complicates the traditional management tasks of planning, organizing, directing and controlling the performances which go into creating a service. If a way can be found to depict the service system concretely, the service management task is not only simplified but important elements of control are gained as well. Service system blueprints are a reliable, practical tool for simplifying the daily management of the most complex service systems (Shostack 1984).

WHAT'S THE PROBLEM?

Consider the difficulty of trying to use narrative text to give instructions to the builder of a house. How would you convey accurately the spatial relationships and connections which form your mental picture of the house? Suppose for the sake of argument that you found a builder willing to construct your house based on your verbal description, and that you were confident in his ability to do so. Suppose that midway through construction you changed your mind about the layout of a room. How would you communicate your change of mind to the builder, and how would the builder communicate the message to his workers and subcontractors? Yet that is precisely the situation facing most managers in service systems. The simple truth is most service systems are not designed: they grow like topsy, or are instituted by management fiat.

Architects have refined graphic techniques for accurately describing the buildings they design. To extend the metaphor, architects prepare several different kinds of drawings for a single project. For the client, the architect prepares drawings designed to convey the architectural idea: Floor plans and various elevations communicate the essential concept, assisting the client to visualize the intended structure, or outcome. For the builder and various subcontractors, the architect prepares working drawings which detail the technical plans and specifications, assisting electrical, plumbing and heating contractors to perform their work accurately. If the drawings are not clear, the likelihood of error increases. Managers in service systems face communications problems similar to those faced by architectural designers.

WHAT IS A SERVICE SYSTEM BLUEPRINT?

In the simplest terms, a service system blueprint is a picture of a service system. A *concept blueprint* is a macro-level blueprint. It conveys the service concept by showing the service at an overview level. A concept blueprint demonstrates how each job or department functions in relationship to the service as a whole. Concept blueprints do not normally stand alone.

A *detailed blueprint* is a micro-level blueprint. It conveys details of the service system identified but not described on the concept blueprint.

WHO USES SERVICE BLUEPRINTS?

Service system blueprints simplify service complexities by displaying the operation of existing systems. When the current operation is explicit, managers are enabled to make rational choices about how they will operate in the future. Service system blueprints are task-oriented; that is, they focus on observable actions or events (tasks). This characteristic makes service system blueprints useful to managers in a wide range of departments and at various levels.

Business unit managers employ concept blueprints to assist in the decision making activities associated with strategy-setting, allocation of resources, integration of service functions and evaluation of performance overall. Marketing managers use concept blueprints in developing advertising and promotion campaigns which are consistent with actual internal operating capability.

Detailed service blueprints are useful to marketing and communications people. Marketing managers can employ them in consumer research, as a guide to the key service elements contributing to consumer satisfaction. Communications managers can use them as the starting point for development of consumer materials geared to convey the "invisible actions" (i.e., those performed backstage or even in support areas) taken on the consumer's behalf to assure service quality. Marketing managers performing an R&D function can use detailed blueprints to communicate operational details when it is time to shift the new service from R&D into routine operations.

Human resource managers can use detailed service blueprints in the preparation of job descriptions, selection criteria, performance standards and appraisal systems, and compensation schemes. Training managers can use the service blueprint as a foundation for setting realistic training objectives and creating task-based training materials. Because a detailed service blueprint is primarily a flowchart, technology managers can adapt detailed service blueprints as the technical basis for evaluating the need for new software, and for ordering or developing it.

Finally, but certainly not least in importance, a detailed service blueprint is, in effect, an expert system, and it can be used as the first step in developing an automated expert system such as the one developed by American Express. Drawing on the technology of artificial intelligence, the expert system at American Express assists customer representatives to make credit decisions. Beginning with a service system blueprint avoids the need for the involvement of expensive knowledge engineers until much of the basic analysis has been completed, and kinks in the manual system are identified and removed.

THE ANATOMY OF A SERVICE BLUEPRINT

Service blueprinting derives its methodology from the systems approach, especially as practiced in data processing, and from industrial engineering. In systems analysis, a flowchart is a picture of the program. Flowcharts map the set of instructions which make up the program: procedures (Do this first, Do that second); and conditional branches (If this condition, Then do that).

Although the flowchart is the methodological foundation of service system blueprinting, there are important differences. Flowchart technique is based on on-off, yes-no rules. Service system blueprints do not always adhere strictly to flowcharting conventions. Service blueprints follow the service path, an operations route which is neither black and white nor entirely consistent in terms of flowchart logic.

Performance is the unit of analysis in a blueprint. For the purposes of this paper, performance is defined as the series of actions, or tasks, undertaken in rendering a service understood to be an instrumental interaction.

A service is *instrumental* because it is a means to a definite end or outcome. Unlike many other social interactions, a service is purposeful: It is goal-directed. This need to achieve specified outcomes sets a service apart from other kinds of interactions. A service is *interactive* because at its core rest a series of reciprocal or mutual actions undertaken respectively by consumer and service contact person. The consumer's potential active involvement in creation of the service characterizes a service and uniquely distinguishes it from a manufactured good.

A service, however, is more than a process. It is also *structure*. It is easier to discuss structure because structural issues are more familiar. Physical setting is the most obvious structure, but there are other equally familiar ones: organizational structure, accounting structure, communications (internal and external) and information system structure, even the motivational structure created by the net result of the service firm's personnel practices.

But structure alone doesn't explain a service either. A restaurant just before opening, an empty airline seat, a physician without patients — we recognize the essential incompleteness of these service structures. Without the customer, service structure is latent possibility, nothing more than a statement of hope.

To see a service as an integrated whole, a technique is needed for plotting *process* against *structure*. As Richard Normann observes, "...the ability to think in terms of *wholes* and [in terms] of the integration of structure and process is indispensable to the creation of effective service systems" (Normann 1984). If the first question is, "What does it mean to 'think in wholes'?", then the second must be, "How are *managers* to 'think in wholes'?"

A service system blueprint depicts process and structure by employing the horizontal and vertical dimensions of a flat surface. (See Figure 1.) Process is depicted from left to right on the horizontal axis as a series of actions (rectangles) plotted chronologically along the horizontal axis of the service system blueprint. A flow line marks the service path by connecting discrete actions chronologically.

FIGURE 1
Service System Management

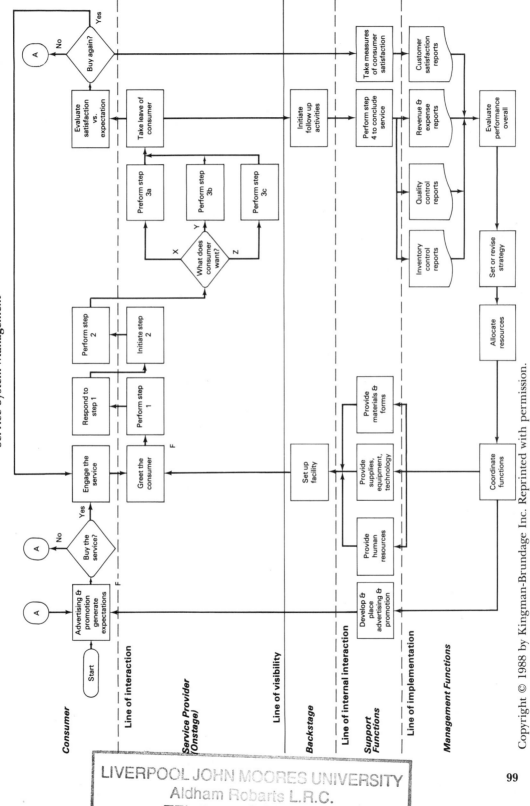

Copyright © 1988 by Kingman-Brundage Inc. Reprinted with permission.

Service structure is depicted on the vertical axis as organizational strata, or structural layers. Three primary structural strata are common to all services: consumer interaction, support functions, and management. Within these three primary strata, finer distinctions can be made. In essence, a service system blueprint turns the traditional organizational chart upside down and adds action to it.

In the consumer stratum, a *line of interaction* demarcates actions performed by the consumer from actions performed by contact personnel. Consumer actions are placed above the line. Actions performed by contact people are located below the line. As noted earlier, these actions are charted on the service path proceeding from left to right.

The actions of contact personnel are further classified by a *line of visibility* which separates *onstage* from *backstage* actions. Onstage actions refer to the public performance of the service, or actions visible to the consumer. Not surprisingly, onstage actions often represent the tip of the service iceberg.

Contact people *set-up* aspects of the service environment prior to the consumer's arrival, and they frequently *follow-up* in order to complete the service following the customer's departure. These *backstage* activities, conducted below the line of visibility, are the behind-the-scenes actions performed by contact people in order to create the service experienced by consumers.

Contact people do not normally work in a vacuum. Other departments contribute services or materials (facilitating goods) used in rendering the service.

Lines of internal interaction separate support functions from the backstage, contact stratum. Lines of internal interaction delineate the service firm's *internal customers,* whether across departmental lines, or from one work station or professional specialty to another within the same department. It is this characteristic which makes the concept blueprint useful as a communications tool for conveying the service "big picture" to all service employees. Such a device builds awareness of how an individual's job contributes to creation of the service overall.

Finally, the concept blueprint demonstrates management's true role in facilitating the operation of the service system. A *line of implementation* separates the planning and organizing functions from "doing" activities. By documenting process and structure, both concept and detailed blueprints support management's task as decision-maker.

Service system blueprints animate service details. They show managers the underlying pattern, that is, connections and relationships among key elements of the service system. When the patterns and connections are explicit, the rational basis for key decisions can be demonstrated objectively.

HOW TO READ A SERVICE SYSTEM BLUEPRINT

Learning to read a service blueprint is similar to learning to read a map. It is necessary to learn the conventions — north is up, south is down. The conventions are few in service blueprinting but it is important to understand them.

A service system blueprint answers this question: Who Does What, To Whom, How Often, Under What Conditions? On a service blueprint, the process symbol (rectangle) describes "Who Does What, to Whom"; the flow of lines denote "How Often"; and the decision symbol (diamond) describes "Under What Conditions."

The basic operations paradigm — Input · Processing · Output — is a second framework for reading service blueprints: *input* refers to the action, event or condition that initiates the services; *processing* refers to changes made to the input during the service process; and *output* refers to the final outcome or result.

A service blueprint scanned with these frameworks in mind conveys to the reader a sense of its basic contours and dynamics. To gain a sense of the basic service path and interaction, scan the blueprint horizontally along the line of visibility. To gain a sense of the backstage and support functions, scan the blueprint vertically.

To read a service blueprint in detail, begin at the line of interaction. Who does what to initiate the service? First, trace the service process by following the service path from the consumer's point of view. Note any branching (IF consumer is or wants X, THEN do X; IF consumer is or wants Y, THEN do Y) in the service path.

From a service design standpoint, existing or potential branching may present an opportunity to distinguish the service competitively. Shostack discusses issues of divergence and complexity as they pertain to service positioning (Shostack 1987). Finally, how/when is service concluded? Is the service discrete (shoeshine), or is the service relatively continuous — as in the case of club members?

Second, trace the contact person's path. Note set-up and follow-up activities in the backstage area.

Third, trace the path of support functions, noting the points of initiation and termination and noting how and when hand-off's occur.

Finally, examine the management stratum, paying special attention to management information reports. What is included? What is left out? What do these reports tell you about management values and priorities?

Reading a service system blueprint from left to right gives a sense of its horizontal integration — the rationality of the service from the consumer's point of view. Reading a service blueprint from top to bottom gives a measure of the vertical integration — the rationality and economy of hand-offs between departments and/or work stations.

The design of a service blueprint should meet two criteria: economy and symmetry. Economy in a service blueprint is achieved when two points are linked by the shortest possible distance, and when the service system blueprint is free of redundancy. Symmetry in a service system blueprint is achieved by iden-

tifying the decisions (branching) or procedural sequences which are of equal weight, and by placing them on the blueprint at the same line or row. The communications power of a service blueprint is enhanced when these criteria are met.

CONCLUSION

The advantages of service system blueprinting lie in the technique's ability to reveal what is currently implicit. Most service systems are complex operations which call upon the collective expertise of individuals scattered in diverse parts of the organization. Finding ways to objectify and integrate this expertise is a first step toward increasing the rationality of key management actions: service system design, marketing, quality control, human resource and technological management.

Ultimately, the real advantage may lie in the ability of service system blueprints to communicate the details of a service in a way that is efficient, intelligible and useful to managers at all levels in service organizations. American managers are currently undergoing considerable criticism over their perceived failure to gain intimate familiarity with the details which are the heart and soul of a business.

In earlier years managers developed this intimate understanding by serving prolonged apprenticeships in various parts of a single business. Times have changed. Today's service organizations need a way to communicate the details of their businesses efficiently and accurately to managers who need to master details of the business *now*. Service system blueprints are a reliable shortcut for acquiring the information their management predecessors gained through experience.

Service system blueprints simplify the complexity associated with a service by systematizing it, or by revealing systems which are otherwise invisible. When a service system is thus revealed in objective and explicit terms, management is in a position to make rational choices about how the process is to be structured to create the services desired by consumers.

REFERENCES

NORMANN, RICHARD (1984), *Service Management,* New York: John Wiley & Sons, 16.

SHOSTACK, G. LYNN (1984), "Designing services that deliver," *Harvard Business Review* (January-February), 133-139.

SHOSTACK, G. LYNN (1987), "Service positioning through structural change," *Journal of Marketing,* 51, 34-43.

Measuring Productivity in Services

CURTIS P. MCLAUGHLIN AND SYDNEY COFFEY

Productivity measures for service industries have not only developed more slowly than for manufacturing, but are often industry specific. A classification scheme is presented to assist in the description and selection of available service productivity measures according to the complexity of inputs and outputs, degree of customization, and level of aggregation — from a single service to an entire industry.

Service managers need service productivity measures. Productivity measures provide bench-marks for evaluating methods and for improving the use of labor, automation and logistics, as well as for developing equitable, motivational employee reward systems. Without them, the competitive improvements available in manufacturing will not be available to services and they will fall prey to substitute goods and competing services[1, 2, 3].

While productivity measures for manufacturing are widely understood and used, productivity measures specific for services have developed more slowly[4]. This slower development of productivity measures for services has been attributed to intangibility[5], labor intensity, perishability and simultaneity[1], complexity, entrepreneurial independence and lack of attention from professional societies[6], smallness of individual firms leading to inability to amortize development costs[7] and complacency[2]. Despite these problems, services managers can and do improve productivity — including managers in the developing world[8]. The effort at productivity measurement has been particularly intensive in the health services industry where the pressures for cost reductions are especially strong[9].

This article will consider these measurement issues in greater detail, provide a review of available productivity measurement methods in terms of their ability to overcome these problems, suggest ways of dealing with them, and highlight issues for further research on productivity measures for services. A classification scheme is presented to assist in the description and selection of available service productivity measures. The classification scheme is based on (1) complexity of inputs and outputs, (2) degree of customization, and (3) level of aggregation. Available measurement approaches for services productivity reviewed are then considered and presented in terms of this classification.

The diversity of the service industries has meant that each field has developed its own productivity measures. Yet these have not been widely disseminated due to the lack of common professional literature. This article, therefore, also serves to bring together a number of these approaches.

MEASUREMENT PROBLEMS

Productivity measures express relationships between the outcomes or outputs of service processes and the resources or inputs required to operate them. Having appropriate definitions of outputs and inputs is critical to meaningful productivity analysis. Without the right specification of inputs and outputs derived from careful process analysis and matched with the right measurement techniques productivity measurement in services cannot succeed. The section which follows deals with (1) the inherent problems of measuring inputs and outputs, (2) tactical problems of process analysis, and (3) the selection of measurement techniques given the other two.

Inherent Problems

The intangibility aspects of services — the fact that the quality of the consumer contact and customization is highly variable and reflects personal values and that most customers must be dealt with in real time — all make the measurement of service productivity and service quality a difficult task[10]. Yet both the input and output indicators for services must be quantifiable if productivity is to be measured.

In consumer services such as fast foods, inputs and outputs are easily defined. Schmenner[6] has referred to these as "service factories." But there are also many services that are "made up chiefly of human relationships consisting of advice, transmission of knowledge, and creative activity where the result does not apply in the main to an objective, unique piece of advice"[10, p.71]. Common to all of these, but more important to professional services, are the inseparability of the server from the service[11], the participation of the client in the process, and the subjective role of the client in evaluation.

While intangibility complicates the process of productivity measurement, managers must do the best they can in spite of it. While intangibles may be an inherent problem, they are not an excuse for avoiding productivity analysis. Drucker[5] suggests using proxies such as the number of people attending church rather than the indeterminate number of souls saved. Gadrey[10] suggests separating immediate outputs from mediate ones, and Flipo[12] recommends separating out controllable and noncontrollable intangibles and attempting to measure those that are controllable and "tangiblising" those that can be. Intangibility makes measurement difficult, but it is seldom a reason to avoid measurement even if proxies must be used.

Quality. Intangibility makes quality harder to measure. Yet service organizations must seek to maximize productivity consistent with the goals of the system[13] which always include quality. This is nothing new. Although many forget to state it, productivity is always measured subject to meeting a specified level of quality. In manufacturing it is easy to measure the tolerances or functionality of the finished product, but in services much of the end-product quality is in the eye of the consumer. Service quality is often defined as the difference between expectation and perceived performance. With this in mind Parasuraman *et al.*[14] have developed a set of measures of perceptions of intangible attributes of services. Haywood-Farmer and Stuart[15] have worked to expand the range of attributes beyond the intangibles associated with service factory firms and into the professions by adding functional attributes of the service, knowledge and information, and customization constructs. To these generic intangibles one must also add specific measures of the performance of a specific service. Since the 1989 San Francisco earthquake US insurers have been showing television advertisements of satisfied customers indicating that they were expecting cold, hard insurance adjusters but received warm, sensitive people. These ads also emphasize the high level of adjuster training and the speed of settlement which is easily measurable.

While data on service quality are difficult to obtain directly and are more variable than data concerning product quality, they can be obtained from the customer, or by someone playing the role of the customer, or by direct observation of the process and/or the results. Research on consumer perceptions of services is enabling us to capture more of quality in an output, ensuring that the attributes being measured are closely linked to customer desires[4]. Moreover, services have many directly observable attributes in terms of waiting time and speed of delivery, physical characteristics (cleanliness, temperature, color), effectiveness, expertise, courtesy, following the script, etc. Each service sector will continue to develop objective measures relevant to its particular business.

The inspection criteria adopted by many franchisers show that a great deal of creativity can and does go into the measurement process, motivated by the necessity of making the corporate strategy work. Many of the criteria used seem to be related to the *precursors* and the *reinforcers* of the less tangible qualities. For example, inspectors of fried chicken restaurants report whether or not the person serving them was courteous. They also report whether or not the training script, a precursor of quality, was followed and whether or not an assistant manager witnessed the transaction, a reinforcer of courtesy. They might taste the chicken, but that can be very subjective and jading, so instead they measure the temperature of the rolls and the chicken and use color comparison charts. Temperature and color are precursors of expected taste and they are also reinforcers of taste with the consumer and with the workers.

In the health field a significant amount of research effort in recent years has gone into the development of measures for case mix, case severity, quality of life and functional status. Without them, the evaluator is left with little but cost and mortality measures. Costs alone can easily be minimized by reducing levels of care. Most major health studies today include some measures of quality of life and of patient functional status on entry, during processing and on exit.

What is important to remember is that productivity measures work effectively in services only if first accompanied by a clear definition of the services strategy and its related performance characteristics[13], and then by an effective parallel system of quality measurement based on those characteristics[16]. Once that quality has been defined, directly or indirectly, productivity measurement can start.

Timing of demand and capacity impacts. In manufacturing the productivity of the firm is related to scheduled production, not necessarily to consumer orders. In services the demand must usually be met at the time that it is generated. In fact, staffing and, therefore, labor productivity are a function of forecast demand rather than actual demand[17], further complicating productivity analysis.

One of the major dilemmas when measuring the productivity of a service unit is knowing whether or not it is at capacity at the time of the measurement. If the organization lacks control over customer arrival rates directly or through an appropriate reservation system, productivity becomes highly variable and, therefore, more difficult to measure[4]. This can be overcome by recording with the output rates whether or not the system was at capacity, which can be determined very quickly by observing whether or not there are significant numbers of people waiting.

Mundel's work[18] raises another form of productivity constraint often found in the public sector — the budget. The budget in the governmental context may constrain the resources used to a maximum as well as a minimum, if "programming" all one's resources is considered a mark of effective management. In that case productivity is merely an accident of the volume of services requested. Productivity analysis is meaningful only when the levels of both inputs and outputs are free to fluctuate in response to managerial decisions.

Process Analysis

The decision maker has to have a clear picture of the process being studied before undertaking the analysis. The right unit of analysis must be selected. Is it to be a firm or a unit (aggregate) or a product or process (disaggregate)? Service operations have their flows and bottlenecks just as factories do, and the study of methods and processes is just as important in services as a step prior to productivity measurement as it is in factories.

If a service involves a multistage process with successive stages — some affected by the same and some by different factors — then an overall analysis of output/input relationships is likely to yield little useful information. Yet analysis of each specific stage for factors affecting quality and productivity might yield very useful relationships. With the disaggregated flows management can specify and then test much less complex theoretical models for the individual stages. For most service businesses there are at least two specific stages — front-office and back-room — and often many more within those two. Complex processes, ones where an overall model often fails to yield significant analytical results, can often be decomposed into a number of stages, each of which can be analysed relatively simply. Harvey[19] has presented a similar argument with respect to the design of social service processes, recommending flowcharting the processes to identify design decisions.

We often see in students a reluctance to do process analyses in services in the same detail that they would normally do in manufacturing settings. It comes through in their analyses of cases[20, 21]. Good process analysis precedes good productivity analysis.

Selecting a Method

One of the first problems of measurement in services is the variety of situations which are to be assessed. To make any meaningful generalizations about which measurement approaches are appropriate for which situation we must next develop a classification scheme to classify situations and provide a basis for comparing them.

CLASSIFICATION

Haywood-Farmer[22] has reviewed the difficulties of classifying services for quality control purposes. He suggests a three-dimensional cube based on (1) labor intensity, (2) degree of contact and interaction with the customer, and (3) degree of customization. He acknowledges that Schmenner[6] linked degree of contact and interaction with customization. Yet labor intensity is not as much of a problem to productivity measurement as it is to service quality measurement. Riddle and Brown[1] dismiss labor intensity as a "myth" for productivity concerns, since firms and countries increasingly have choices among labor-intensive and capital-intensive modes of services production.

We propose instead two other classifications to accompany contact and customization. It is important to know the *complexity* of the service inputs and outputs to be measured. Some techniques measure only simple ratios of one input to one output, while others handle multiple, sometimes joint, outputs resulting from multiple inputs. Furthermore, it is necessary to know whether a study needs to measure productivity of a single service (disaggregate) or the aggregate productivity of a unit, firm or industry.

Figure 1 shows these three dimensions and also suggests the positioning of a number of the productivity measures commonly used in manufacturing superimposed on it. It is a rough classification of these methods along the three dimensions of complexity, degree of aggregation and customization. We urge discretion in its use. It is based only on observed tendencies. Undoubtedly some creative investigator somewhere has adapted each of these techniques to some specific application that could be classified outside the regions illustrated. Our main objective is to illustrate the utility of these dimensions for conceptualising the classification problem and to stimulate discussion and further research in this field.

Consumer Involvement and Customization

Consumer involvement and customization have often been cited as key characteristics

FIGURE 1
Traditional Manufacturing Productivity Measures

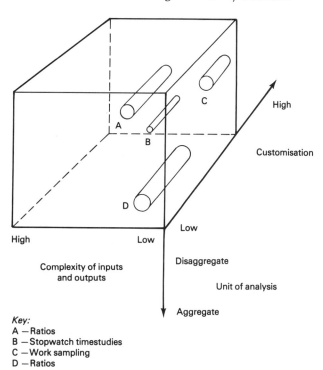

Key:
A — Ratios
B — Stopwatch timestudies
C — Work sampling
D — Ratios

of services. A number of authors have suggested them as *the* classification variables for services[6, 23, 24]. Each adds variability to the services whose productivity is being studied.

Customization affects the definition of the product and introduces a great deal of variability in outputs. Custom outputs are hard to group discretely for analysis. This variety of outputs which may be difficult to define can have significant impact on the choice of a means of productivity measurement and can often force the analysis to a higher level of aggregation.

Consumer involvement introduces variability. It alone does not affect the product as much as the customization which often accompanies it. Consumer involvement, however, does affect the design of a productivity measurement program by requiring larger samples or longer time-frames for measurement to cope with the process variability.

Complexity of Inputs and Outputs

Service process may have one, several or many input factors and one, several or many outputs. Service mix refers to the number and type of services offered and is analogous to product mix in manufacturing. In the latter case, product mix creates few problems for disaggregate productivity measurement, but can complicate aggregate measures considerably. This is also true of services. For example, "if one hospital provides patient care at $300 per day and another provides patient care at $350 per day, can a manager draw any conclusions about their relative productivity without also considering the mix and nature of product care provided? Measuring the productivity of these and other service business requires techniques that are more sensitive than accounting and ratio measures and that can explicity consider the mix of service outputs produced"[25, p. 11]. Gadrey notes that volume of transactions cannot be used effectively as a measure of outputs where service mix is variable[10].

Where service mix is a problem, there are two strategies. The first is to focus the productivity measurement effort on the disaggregated components of the mix. Inputs and outputs for each component are measured separately and compared separately. The second approach is to use a model which deals with multiple inputs and multiple outputs simultaneously. Although sometimes controversial, such a model is available in data envelopment analysis[25, 26].

Such a model is especially useful if some of the outputs are joint products of a single process. This is often the case in the professional services fields. Travel agents provide information, dispense advice and issue tickets[24]. Academic departments provide graduate teaching and research by a process which defies separate time allocations[26].

Aggregation and Disaggregation

Inputs and outputs can be measured on an aggregate (e.g. firm or unit) or a disaggregate (e.g. product or process) basis. Some aggregate comparative measures require a substantial number of similar units to compare and analyze. Measurement of performance of any activity requires careful specification of the appropriate unit of analysis[28], the choice of which depends on end use of the productivity measure. Aggregate measures are best for: (1) evaluating overall economic policy, (2) making decisions about what products or services to produce, including analysis of comparative advantage, (3) deciding on relative inputs of labor and capital, and (4) determining pricing strategies and policies. Aggregate information, however, does not help identify specific sources of inefficiency and cannot help much with improving firm efficiency and effectiveness. For example, "a bank branch may have high profitability based on revenues earned on funds less costs of funds less operating expenses. This aggregate measure, however, tells the manager little about whether or not the branch is us-

ing its resources efficiently or whether it could reduce its operating costs and increase profits further"[25].

Since the main objective of productivity measurement for the operations manager is productivity improvement, disaggregate measures are of special interest. They are useful when (1) making operational decisions such as the choice of work methods, and (2) developing reward systems for workers. Disaggregate measures, however, are generally difficult to develop for complex services[29]. Therefore, much of the emphasis on services productivity research needs to focus on disaggregate measures.

A SERVICES ADVANTAGE

The literature has emphasized the disadvantages of productivity measurement in services. Therefore, it has often overlooked the major advantage for productivity measurement that services have over manufacturing — larger numbers of similar delivery units. The typical manufacturing firm has a few plants which serve large geographic areas. Services have to be delivered where the consumers are, often to hundreds of communities. The greater the consumer interaction involved, the greater the number of service units required to cover an area. The need for consistency in the service package and its delivery leads to a drive towards consistency among units. With comparable units it is practical to study productivity in comparative terms. Many of the newer productivity measurement approaches are comparative and derive from specific studies of services systems. The notion of comparative productivity is more relevant for services and, therefore, will continue to be of greater interest to service operations managers and scholars.

AVAILABLE SERVICE PRODUCTIVITY MEASURES

A variety of productivity measures are available for services. The strengths and weaknesses of each are discussed below. We have suggested a three-dimensional clas-

FIGURE 2
Available Service Productivity Approaches

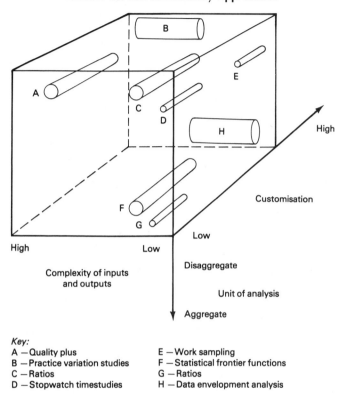

Key:
A — Quality plus
B — Practice variation studies
C — Ratios
D — Stopwatch timestudies
E — Work sampling
F — Statistical frontier functions
G — Ratios
H — Data envelopment analysis

sification scheme for services productivity measurement — customization, complexity, and degree of aggregation, so that we can see where existing measurement techniques work best and where more development is needed. Figure 1 illustrates these dimensions and the positioning of widely known manufacturing productivity measuring techniques. In Figure 2 we have a larger array of techniques available for measuring services productivity, all of which are discussed below. It should be apparent to the reader that there are still large domains of this cube for which appropriate methods do not exist.

Do not ignore manufacturing measures. All of the methods used for measuring productivity in the factory — input/output ratios, time study and other time standards methods, especially work sampling — have been used effectively by service organizations. Airlines normally use synthetic time standards to improve the productivity of cabin crews. Household Finance[30] reported how a work sampling study of its branches showed that only 20 per cent of its personnel time was spent on front-office work and 80 per cent was backroom. Centralization, automation and teleprocessing have enabled the company to improve its productivity in consumer loan processing by 36 per cent in three years. Do not ignore traditional industrial engineering approaches to the delivery of services.

Output/Input Ratios

Output/input ratios are frequently used in both manufacturing and services. They are often referred to under the rubric of "factor productivity". The first tendency in services is to look at labor productivity as a single ratio, assuming that services are mostly labor intensive. Yet that is becoming a less and less safe assumption[1].

Output/input ratios can be used at both the aggregate and disaggregate levels. They are used at the aggregate level to evaluate economic policy (e.g. deregulation) and are compiled regularly by government agencies such as the Bureau of Labor Statistics[31]. They are frequently used at the firm-wide level. For example, the capital recovery department of Ameritech Services studied whether or not telephone company decisions benefited customers. Using ratios such as employees/10,000 telephones, they were able to identify significant long-term productivity improvements due to the substitution of capital for labor[32]. Here the aggregate ratio proved useful as a measure of the effect of past policy decisions, but it cannot help much in identifying which new incremental (disaggregate) substitutions of capital for labor are preferable in the future. One problem with productivity ratios is that they tend to consider only one input and one output at a time.

Output/input ratios are often followed at the disaggregate level, especially staffing ratios. They are frequently criticized for their narrowness, however. For example, the ratio of home health visits per home health aide as a standard, can be questioned as having (1) the potential to compromise quality standards, and (2) a negative effect on morale by focusing too much attention on the raw numbers[33]. Sometimes ratios are built into the control system. One retail clothing chain uses considerable part-time labor and budgets the hours allocated for these workers as proportional to the store's previous week's sales. This guarantees a constant labor to sales ratio over time. Similarly, commissions are frequently used in service organizations, stabilizing the labor to sales ratio and motivating employee effort in the customer contact process.

One can also question the appropriateness of comparing disaggregate ratios in the face of joint production and of variability in service mix, capacity constraints, consumer interaction, problems in quality measurement and customization. Therefore, such ratios seem to work best at the disaggregate level with the simplest of services, the service factories.

Work Measurement Methods

Manufacturing plants have long relied on measurement techniques such as stopwatch timing, predetermined time standards, historical standards and time reporting. All of these have been and are used in the service sector. Predetermined time standards have been used to plan the work of personnel in hospital laboratories. Stop watches have been used in many service factories[34]. Work sampling can be used for jobs that are more varied[35] and can incorporate the variability inherent in consumer interaction. Work sampling with worker review has been used to try to make the resulting productivity measures acceptable to nurses[36]. Historical standards, expert estimates, and time reporting as well as time study, output/input ratios, standard data and predetermined time systems are reported for a wide variety of professional situations by Mundel[18].

Most work measurement methods based on time reporting are highly disaggregate ratio methods. They require that the work be identified, recorded and standardized before any significant measurement takes place. Therefore, they seem to be most appropriate to services where the outputs and inputs are simplest and most easily measured.

OTHER APPROACHES TO PRODUCTIVITY MEASUREMENT

A number of other methods have been used for services productivity analysis, especially in the health field where federal and state governments are the primary payers and have been willing to invest substantially in process and productivity analysis.

These other techniques can be further divided into two categories: (1) those that deal with a single firm as the unit of analysis, and (2) the approaches which compare a large number of provider units with each other for diagnostic purposes. Most of the newer methods of analysis are comparative methods based on comparing a number of similar service delivery units. The approach that is suitable for the individual delivery unit we have dubbed "quality plus".

Quality Plus Techniques

The above cited techniques all face the final response, "But what about quality?" Attempts are now being made to develop productivity measures that deal more adequately with service quality. These we call quality plus systems because they attempt to make quality a measured output of the service.

In the health field where the government and large corporations are major payers, there are many attempts to integrate aspects of quality and outcome into productivity measures. Thompson[37] reports on the use of a 300-question patient questionnaire related to aspects of care. In addition to problems with the length of the questionnaire, this approach assumes that the patient is a good judge of quality and outcomes, which may be questionable. Other attempts have been made to incorporate information about aggregate characteristics of health care provided into the productivity measures (e.g. severity of patient condition being treated)[38, 39] and consumer utilities[40].

The Service Assessment Matrix (SAM) is one interesting approach developed to incorporate aspects of quality into service product measurement. In this approach individual clients specify a potential set of service performance and quality criteria which are then assembled into a matrix to guide the development of standards. The SAM approach has been used in an engineering department of a manufacturing firm and to evaluate the document control department of an electronics firm[41].

A more generic quality plus approach is being used by an insurance company to measure performance over time by programmers. By identifying inputs such as group time need, number of edits, data manipulation and outputs such as program complexity, the firm has developed a process of output/input weightings based on peer review to evaluate programmer productivity. This approach seems to take into account the difficulties of gaining acceptance by those being evaluated[42].

Those quality plus techniques which include some type of peer quality assessment provide face validity for those using the measures and probably represent the future for disaggregated productivity assessment for complex services. Clearly, however, this is an area where much research remains to be done.

Practice Variation Studies

In the health field there are also disaggregate comparative attempts to measure productivity which parallel the quality plus techniques. Here teams of health experts use the considerable statistical variability apparent in hospital discharge and insurance records to identify variations in cost and outcomes of the practice of medicine within small local areas and then analyze the local case records for differences in technological approach. These studies are attempting to include patients' utilities for outcomes in the analysis[40, 43]. Wennberg's outcome study of prostate surgery is just the first of many planned by the US government which use naturally occurring variations in physician practice patterns to identify and evaluate alternative means, costs and outcomes of delivering specific types of care. Presumably, these analyses of natural experiments will lead to improvements in productivity in health care as well as enhance consumer satisfaction. It is not difficult to envision such an approach applied to other areas of complex professional services where methods have never been standardized, such as eduction, management consulting and brokerage analysis. Such studies would come under intense scrutiny by professional and technical experts and, therefore, should impact on the behavior of service deliverers.

AGGREGATE COMPARATIVE METHODS

There are a number of promising analytical methods for the comparison of aggregate service unit productivities. They are both deterministic and statistical. The statistical methods include studies of central tendencies of cost and frontier cost functions. The deterministic methods often involve mathematical programming models, including Data Envelopment Analysis (DEA).

Statistical Comparisons

Studies of central tendencies of cost and output do not identify the most productive units directly, but it is sometimes useful to develop a cost or output relationship through regression analysis, using those data to forecast the output of each unit, and then identifying and studying the higher- and lower-than-expected performers for the specific correlates of productivity[44]. Lewin and Minton's criticism of least squares methods[45] is correct in that they do not identify and analyze the most efficient organizations directly.

Statistical frontier production functions, however, seek to find the maximum output for a given set of inputs.

> A standard definition of a production function is that it is a function giving the maximum possible quantity of some output given quantities of a set of inputs...to answer certain economic questions, notably the measurement of the level of efficiency of a firm or plant, the maximum possible output is relevant, and a literature has developed which attempts to estimate it as a function of input quantities. Such a function is often called a *frontier* production function, with the word "frontier" emphasizing the idea of maximality of which it embodies[46, pp. 289-90].

They usually deal with single outputs, although Schmidt argues that multiple outputs should not be a major problem. They are based on maximum likelihood estimation or corrected ordinary least squares. The difference between an observed productivity and the estimated upper bound relationship is assumed to be a mixture of statistical noise and inefficiency[46]. Several functional forms of the frontier estimation are often specified including the Cobb-Douglas and translog. Unfortunately, rather large numbers of units are required for statistical significance and different parameterizations of the frontier function yield quite different results. An advantage of these stochastic models is that they do deal with random error as well as technical inefficiency. For a stochastic frontier production function a one-side error distribution is assumed, usually half-normal but occasionally exponential.

Technical inefficiency is the amount of improvement that is feasible without changing the input ratios. Also of importance, but harder to measure, is *allocative inefficiency,* the improvement that can be achieved by changing factor input combinations.

Deterministic Models

If an analyst assumes that the differences between the less productive and the most productive organizations are due to technical efficiency, then mathematical programming techniques can be used to fit a frontier function that minimizes the sum of the errors or the sum of the squared errors. In this case the parameters are specified. A recent article on handicapping 5K runners by Camm and Grogan[47] illustrates this approach.

Data Envelopment Analysis (DEA)

There is considerable current interest in the multiple output deterministic frontier analysis technique called Data Envelopment Analysis (DEA). There is an ongoing debate comparing the utility and accuracy of deterministic and stochastic frontier estimation models and strong partisans of each. Banker *et al.*[48] provide one example. A similar debate between economists and operations researchers occurred between Charnes *et al.* and Evans and Heckman[49, 50].

DEA is a mathematical programming technique for evaluating productivity which allows for multiple outputs and multiple inputs simultaneously[51]. It has been found to be a valuable tool for a variety of service operations[25]. DEA is most valuable in complex situations where there are multiple outputs and inputs which cannot be readily analyzed with other techniques such as ratios and where a number of similar service units are being evaluated. It is an aggregate productivity measure method which uses the branch or unit as its unit of analysis. It does not actually specify the steps needed for improvement, but identifies the areas of concern. Epstein and Henderson suggest that DEA is currently better suited to diagnosis than to control, but suggest some research avenues to strengthen its use for control purposes[52]. It requires many very similar units for comparison, so it is adapted to a wide range of process complexity with multiple inputs and outputs, but is limited to a narrow range of product composition (customization) within a given application.

DEA is similar to other frontier analysis methods in that different parameters and different functional forms offer different re-sults[53]. There is also the sometimes disturbing characteristic that there can be a considerable proportion of technically efficient decision-making units (DMUs) with their number increasing with model dimensionality and with the heterogeneity of the DMUs.

ATTACKING A SERVICE PRODUCTIVITY PROBLEM

With a classification scheme and knowledge of available measurement techniques in hand we can now consider how the services manager can go about tackling a productivity issue in services. We suggest the following:

1. First the services manager should specify the reason for investigating productivity. This will force a review of the strategic issues behind the analysis and help focus it on analyzing the level of aggregation important to the desired solution. This effort should involve a multifunctional team that looks at the system as a whole.

2. Then analyze the service delivery system in place (or planned) and decompose it into its process stages and key decision areas. This process analysis will focus attention on key, specific operational areas for productivity measurement.

3. Next specify the service characteristics that are of strategic importance at each service process stage and key decision area. This means that the management team must be absolutely clear about what service package it desires to deliver. From this derives (a) specifications for service outputs, (b) definitions of alternative inputs required, (c) service quality standards that must be met before productivity becomes an issue, and (d) the dimensions and limits of trade-offs allowable between process characteristics and output characteristics. Where intangibles cannot be measured directly, measure their proxies and measure their precursors and reinforcers.

4. Select and investigate the methods of productivity measurement which seem most appropriate to the team's analytical objectives. If there are a large number of service units, consider the newer comparative techniques carefully. The selection criteria should include concern for complexity, customization and degree of aggregation.

5. Be prepared for all kinds of objections about "quality". One of our health service research col-

leagues often argues that when professionals object to productivity measures on the basis of quality, just substitute the word "money" and it will all become clear. There is no substitute for measurement and review. As Stankard puts it "Don't expect what you don't inspect"[54, p. 72].

6. Involve the implementers all along the way. Staff acceptance of any proposed productivity measures is critical to their ability to enhance productivity. Because productivity systems affect the effort expended and rewards offered, they are a critical part of the psychological contract that controls service worker behaviors[55, 56]. How those standards are imposed are as important as what they are. Stankard argues that an effective productivity effort will need:

(1) ideas about *what* changes or opportunities will benefit your business, (2) sponsorship from someone with enough authority to put money or people's time into working on the idea, (3) specialized technical or analytical thinking about the best way to make the idea work, and (4) the energy and commitment of all who have to do anything to implement the idea to make it successful[54, p. 298].

He emphasizes an organizational development approach to productivity in services, increasing employee participation so that the productivity measures developed can be perceived as equitable by most of the people being measured. Given the subjective nature of service attributes, employee participation consensus is also a way to utilize the knowledge and creativity of the service deliverers, especially since their day-to-day interaction with customers makes them expert judges of what customers consider efficient, quality services[16, 25, 36].

CONCLUSIONS

It is appropriate to emphasize the lack of productivity measures for services. Major advances are being made. The managers of services have an increasing number of tools available and should be willing to use them. While some attributes of services make productivity measurement difficult, this article suggests that it is not as problematic as some would think and that a number of approaches are available, especially if the analyst takes advantage of the fact that service units tend to be far more numerous and homogeneous than factories.

As Figure 2 indicates, the greatest gaps in the ability to measure service productivity come in the areas of disaggregate, customized services. Aggregate approaches are not as sensitive to detailed issues of quality measurement, joint outputs, and cost allocation. Because of problems with these issues, it is also harder to provide managerially useful insights at the disaggregate level.

Managers should be trained to utilize the available productivity measures in services. A wide variety is available and services with their larger number of dispersed delivery units are especially suited for using comparative pro-

ductivity methods of productivity analysis that are not often used in manufacturing productivity analyses. These include practice variation studies, statistical frontier production analyses, and data envelopment analysis. This article also suggests steps that management should follow in developing a productivity analysis in a service organization. This is summarized in Figure 3.

While many new ideas in the areas of quality measurement and productivity measurement are emerging in specific service industries, it is clear that there are still many opportunities for expanding this field. The

FIGURE 3
Procedure for Service Productivity Analysis

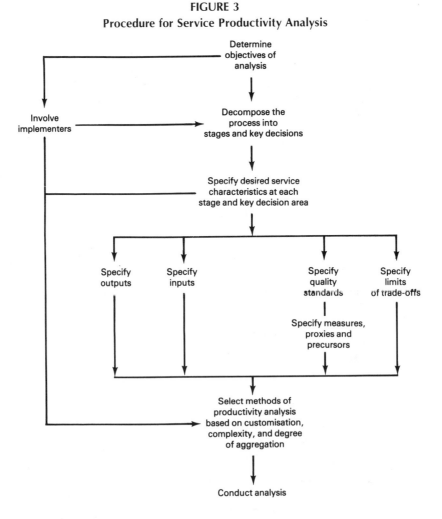

activities of operations scholars today need to focus on encouraging further utilization of these techniques by:

1. developing quality measures to incorporate into disaggregate analysis in specific industries;
2. developing procedures for the use of these techniques in a wider variety of settings, building on the principles outlined above;
3. publicizing the availability and applicability of productivity measurement techniques for services and looking out for some new ones as they arise in the various specialized service sectors;
4. participating in the further development of these techniques to ensure greater flexibility and utility in their use in the field.

REFERENCES

[1] RIDDLE, D. I. and BROWN, K. J., "From Complacency to Strategy: Retaining World Class Competitiveness in Services", in Starr, M. K. (Ed.), *Global Competitiveness: Getting the US Back on Track*, W.W. Norton/The American Assembly, New York, 1988, pp. 239-70.

[2] JOHNSTON, R., "Service Industries — Improving Competitive Performance", *The Service Industries Journal*, Vol. 8 No. 2, 1988, pp. 202-11.

[3] QUINN, J. B. and GAGNON, C. E., "Will Services Follow Manufacturing into Decline?, *Harvard Business Review*, Vol. 64 No. 6, November- December, 1986, pp. 95-103.

[4] MILLS, P., CHASE, R. B. and MARGULIES, N., "Motivating the Client/Employee System as a Service Production Strategy", *Academy of Management Review*, Vol. 8 No. 2, 1983, pp. 301-10.

[5] DRUCKER, P., *Management: Tasks, Responsibilities, Practices*, Harper & Row, New York, 1974.

[6] SCHMENNER, R.W., "How Can Service Businesses Survive and Prosper?", *Sloan Management Review*, Vol. 27 No. 3, Spring 1986, pp. 21-32.

[7] BERG, S.V., "Determinants of Technological Change in the Service Industries", *Technological Forecasting and Social Change*, Vol. 5, 1973, pp. 407-26.

[8] KORETZ, G., "Economic Trends: Productivity in Services is Not a Problem Abroad", *Business Week*, 22 May, 1989, p. 28.

[9] BOLSTER, C.J. and BINION, R., "Linkages between Cost Management and Productivity", *Topics in Health Care Financing*, Vol. 13 No. 4, Summer 1987, pp. 67-75.

[10] GADREY, J., "Rethinking Output in Services", *The Service Industries Journal*, Vol. 8 No. 1, 1988, pp. 67-76.

[11] KOTLER, P. and BLOOM, P. N., *Marketing Professional Services*, Prentice-Hall, Englewood Cliffs, NJ, 1984.

[12] FLIPO, J-P., "On the Intangibility of Services", *The Service Industries Journal*, Vol. 8 No. 3, 1988, pp. 286-98.

[13] DEANE, L. M., "Hospital Productivity Measurement in a Changing Environment", *Hospital Material Management Quarterly*, Vol. 8 No.3, February 1987, pp. 59-65.

[14] PARASURAMAN, A., ZEITHAML, V. and BERRY, L. L., *SERVQUAL: A Multiple-item Scale for Measuring Customer Perceptions of Service Quality*, Report 86-108, Marketing Science Institute, Cambridge, MA, August 1986.

[15] HAYWOOD-FARMER, J. and STUART, F. I., "Measuring the Quality of Professional Services", *The Management of Service Operations: Proceedings of the UK Operations Management Association Annual International Conference*, Coventry, 1988.

[16] HELMER, T. and SUVER, J.D., "Pictures of Performance: The Key to Improved Nursing Productivity", *Health Care Management Review*, Vol. 13 No. 4, Fall 1988, pp. 65-70.

[17] GARDNER, E.S. JR. and MCLAUGHLIN, C.P., "Forecasting — A Cost Control Tool for Health Care Managers", *Health Care Management Review*, Vol. 5 No. 3, Summer 1980, pp. 31-8.

[18] MUNDEL, M.E., *Measuring and Enhancing the Productivity of Service and Government Organizations*, Asian Productivity Organisation, Tokyo, 1975.

[19] HARVEY, J., "Designing Efficient and Manageable Public Professional Service Processes", *International Journal of Operations & Production Management*, Vol. 9 No. 1, 1989, pp. 35-44.

[20] AXELROD, D. and WALLACE, W. A., "Licensing Day Care Facilities", in Collier, D. A. (Ed.), *Service Management: Operating Decisions*, Prentice-Hall, Englewood Cliffs, NJ, 1987, pp. 250-73.

[21] DOYLE, S., PIGNERI, R. and MAISTER, D.H., "University Health Service: Walk-in Clinic", in Lovelock, C. H. (Ed.) *Managing Services: Marketing, Operations and Human Resources*, Prentice-Hall, Englewood Cliffs, NJ, 1988, pp. 198-207.

[22] HAYWOOD-FARMER, J., "A Conceptual Model of Service Quality", *International Journal of Operations & Production Management*, Vol. 8 No. 6, 1988, pp. 19-29.

[23] CHASE, R. B., "The Customer Contact Approach to Services: Theoretical Bases and Practical

Extensions", *Operations Research*, Vol. 29, 1981, pp. 698-706.

[24]MAISTER, D. H. and LOVELOCK, C. H., "Managing Facilitator Services", *Sloan Management Review*, Vol. 23 No. 4, Summer 1982, pp. 19-31.

[25]SHERMAN, D. H., "Improving the Productivity of Service Businesses", *Sloan Management Review*, Vol. 25 No. 3, Spring 1984, pp. 11-23.

[26]HUANG, L. G.-Y., and MCLAUGHLIN, C. P., "Relative Efficiency in Rural Primary Care: An Application of Data Envelopment Analysis", *Health Services Research*, Vol. 24 No. 2, June 1989, pp. 143-58.

[27]HARRISON, M. E. JR. "Measuring the Technical Efficiency of Universities", unpublished PhD, dissertation, Graduate School of Business Administration, University of North Carolina at Chapel Hill, 1988.

[28]UTTERBACK, J., "Innovation and Industrial Evolution in Manufacturing Industries", in Guile, B. R. and Brooks, H. (Eds.), *Technology and Global Industry*, National Academy Press, Washington, DC, 1987, pp. 16-48.

[29]SHIFFLER, R. E. and COYE, R. W., "Monitoring Employee Performance in Service Operations", *International Journal of Operations & Production Management*, Vol. 8 No. 2, 1988, pp. 5-13.

[30]Household Finance Corporation, *1988 Annual Report*, 1989.

[31]MARK, J. A., "Measuring Productivity in Service Industries", *Monthly Labor Review*, Vol. 105 No. 6, June 1982, pp. 3-8; expanded in Guile, B. R. and Quinn, J. B. (Eds.), *Technology in Services: Policies for Growth, Trade and Employment*, National Academy Press, Washington, DC, 1988, pp. 139-59. See also Kendrick, J.W., "Productivity in Services", pp. 99-117 in the same volume.

[32]NOUSAINE, T. and BRANT, S., "A Case for Capital Investment", *Telephony*, Vol. 212 No. 5, February 1987, pp. 58, 60.

[33]MATTERN, K. M., "Public Health Nursing and Productivity Measurements: Are Home Visit Numbers the Right Focus?", *Nursing Management*, Vol. 19 No. 3, March 1988, pp. 99-104.

[34]KISRO, F. and LEYVA, S., "Developing Productivity Standards for Performance in the Central Processing Department", *Hospital Material Management Quarterly*, Vol. 9 No. 4, May 1988, pp. 70-76.

[35]DENTON, D. K., "Work Sampling: Increasing Service and White Collar Productivity", *Management Solutions*, March, 1987, pp. 37-41.

[36]VENTRONE, J., ZANOTTI, M. and HEIDTMAN, M., "Dressing for Success: Measuring Productivity Can Ensure Continuing Success", *Healthcare Financial Management*, Vol. 42 No. 8, April 1988, pp. 30-40.

[37]THOMPSON, A. G. H., "The Soft Approach to Quality of Health Care", *International Journal of Quality & Reliability Management*, Vol. 3 No. 3, 1986, pp. 59-67.

[38]EASTBAUGH, S. R., "Hospital Quality Scorecards, Patient Severity, and the Emerging Value Shopper", *Hospital and Health Services Administration*, Vol. 31 No. 6, November-December 1986, pp. 85-102.

[39]SMITH, G. R., "Using a State-of-the-art Approach", *Business and Health*, Vol. 5 No. 11, September 1988, pp. 20-3.

[40]WENNBERG, J. E., MULLEY, A. G., HANLEY, D., TIMOTHY, R. P., FOWLER, F. J., ROOS, N. P., BARRY, M. J., MCPHERSON, K., GREENBERG, E. R., SOULE, D., BUBOLZ, J., FISCHER, E. and MALENKA, D., "An Assessment of Prostatectomy for Benign Urinary Tract Obstruction: Geographic Variations and the Evaluation of Medical Care Outcomes", *Journal of American Medical Association*, Vol. 257 No. 7, 20 February, 1987, pp. 933-6.

[41]LONG-BECKE, L. and LANDAUER, E., "Service Assessment Matrix: A Measurement Technique for Service Group Evaluation", *Industrial Management*, Vol. 29 No. 5, September/October 1987, pp. 10-16.

[42]SCHULTZ, W. T., "Systems Programmer Productivity", *Information Management*, Vol. 7 No. 1, Winter 1986, pp. 25-9.

[43]WENNBERG, J. E., ROOS, N., SOLA, L., SCHONI, A. and JAFFE, R., "Use of Claims Data Systems to Evaluate Health Care Outcomes", *Journal of the American Medical Association*, Vol. 257 No. 7, 20 February, 1987, pp. 933-6.

[44]TALUKDAR, R. and MCLAUGHLIN, C. P., "Monitoring and Improving the Productivity of Semiautonomous Human Service Units", *Journal of Operations Management*, Vol. 5 No. 4, August 1985, pp. 375-93.

[45]LEWIN, A. Y. and MINTON, J. W., "Determining Organizational Effectiveness: Another Look, and an Agenda for Research", *Management Science*, Vol. 32 No. 5, May 1986, pp. 514-38.

[46]SCHMIDT, P., "Frontier Production Functions", *Econometric Reviews*, Vol. 4 No. 2, 1985-6, pp. 289-328.

[47]CAMM, J. D. and GROGAN, T. J., "An Application of Frontier Analysis: Handicapping Running Races", *Interfaces*, Vol. 18 No. 6, November-December 1988, pp. 52-60.

[48]BANKER, R. D., CONRAD, R. F. and STRAUSS, R. P., "A Comparative Application of Data Envelopment Analysis and Translog Methods: An Illustrative Study of Hospital Production", *Management Science,* Vol. 32 No. 1, January 1986, pp. 30-44.

[49]CHARNES, A., COOPER, W.W. and SUEYOSHI, T., "A Goal Programming/Constrained Regression Review of The Bell System Breakup", *Management Science,* Vol. 34 No. 1, January 1988, pp. 1-26.

[50]EVANS, D. S. and HECKMAN, J. J., "REJOINDER: Natural Monopoly and the Bell System: Respose to Charnes, Cooper and Sueyoshi", *Management Science,* January 1988, pp. 27-38.

[51]CHARNES, A., COOPER, W.W. and RHODES, E., "Evaluating Program and Managerial Efficiency: An Application of Data Envelopment Analysis to Program Followthrough", *Management Science,* Vol. 27 No. 6, June 1981, pp. 668–97.

[52]EPSTEIN, M. K. and HENDERSON, J. C., "Data Envelopment Analysis for Managerial Control and Diagnosis", *Decision Sciences,* Vol. 20 No. 1, Winter 1989, pp. 90-119.

[53]AHN, T., CHARNES, A. and COOPER, W.W., "Efficiency Characterization in Different DEA Models", *Socio-Economic Planning Sciences,* Vol. 22 No. 6, 1988, pp. 263-7.

[54]STANKARD, M. F., *Productivity by Choice: The 20-to-1 Principle,* Wiley-Interscience, New York, 1986.

[55]ANANIA, L., "Services: Low Productivity/High Cost", *Review of Business,* Vol. 9 No. 1, Summer 1987, pp. 21-3.

[56]WILSON, M. P. and McLAUGHLIN, C. P., *Leadership and Management in Academic Medicine,* Jossey-Bass, San Francisco, 1984.

Courtyard by Marriott: Designing a Hotel Facility with Consumer-Based Marketing Models

JERRY WIND   PAUL E. GREEN
DOUGLAS SHIFFLET   MARSHA SCARBROUGH

Marriott used conjoint analysis to design a new hotel chain. The study provided specific guidelines for selecting target market segments, positioning services, and designing an improved facility in terms of physical layout and services. The effectiveness of the study and associated processes also changed Marriott's approach to new product development.

Innovative new products and services have traditionally been created by the designers, architects, R&D engineers, or artists. Can marketing science be of help in this process? Marriott used conjoint analysis to design the new hotel chain, *Courtyard by Marriott,* illustrating the power and value of marketing science in designing such complex services as hotels.

Marriott hired outside consultants (the academic authors of this paper) to conduct a large-scale consumer study among business and nonbusiness travelers, aimed at establishing an "optimal" hotel design. The hotel features included seven sets (called "facets") of attributes (Table 1).

1. External factors — building shape, landscape design, pool type and location, hotel size;
2. Rooms — room size and decor, type of heating and cooling, location and type of bathroom, amenities;
3. Food-related services — type and location of restaurant, room service, vending services and stores, in-room kitchen facilities;
4. Lounge facilities — location, atmosphere and type of people (clientele);
5. Services — including reservations, registration and check-out, limo to airport, bellman, message center, secretarial services, car rental and maintenance;
6. Facilities for leisure-time activities — sauna, exercise room, racquetball courts, tennis courts, game room, children's playroom and yard; and

7. Security factors — security guards, smoke detectors, 24-hour video camera, and so forth.

Overall, the study considered 50 attributes, each ranging from two to eight levels. (Indeed, to our knowledge, this is the most complex trade-off study ever conducted.)

We designed the study as a hybrid conjoint analysis task [Green 1984] and also included a price elasticity task using the ELASTICON model [Mahajan, Green, and Goldberg 1982] and a variety of other analyses (for example, multidimensional scaling and cluster analysis) related to consumers' demographic and psychological characteristics, attitudes, and usage of hotels.

The results of the study provided specific guidelines for selecting target market segments, positioning the hotel within the market, and designing an improved facility in terms of physical layout and services. Using these strategy and design recommendations, Marriott developed the *Courtyard by Marriott* concept, test marketed it successfully, and subsequently introduced it nationally.

This application clearly demonstrates the value of consumer-based information to the design of products and services, even those as complex as a hotel chain aimed at specific target segments.

THE PROBLEM

In the early '80s, the Marriott Corporation was concerned that it was running out of good sites to place typical-design Marriott Hotels at a high enough rate to assure the firm's continued high rate of growth. It made a preliminary (and tentative) decision to develop a new hotel chain for the segment of travelers who were not satisfied with current hotel offerings. Two a priori segments were identified: business travelers (who travel at least six times a year and stay in mid-level hotels or motels) and pleasure travelers (who travel at least twice a year and stay in hotels or motels). Management faced a critical question: what type of hotel facilities and services should Marriott design and offer to attract these travelers away from the competitive facilities they were currently using.

To position and design a hotel that would meet management's profit and growth objectives, it was essential to (1) assure that the new hotel offered consumers good value for their money; (2) minimize cannibalization of Marriott's other hotel offerings; and (3) establish a market positioning that offered management a substantial competitive advantage.

We designed and implemented a large-scale consumer study to provide explicit answers to the following interrelated questions:

- Does sufficient demand exist for a new hotel concept aimed at the low business and pleasure segment to meet growth and financial return objectives?
- What is the best competitive positioning for the new hotels?
- Of the various hotel features and services listed in Table 1, which combination should be offered?
- What should be the pricing strategy for rooms in the new hotels?
- What should be the location strategy for the new hotels?

The Approach

We conducted a consumer study for Marriott management in the first quarter of 1982 (Figure 1). The study surveyed 263 midlevel business travelers, 83 high-end business travelers, and 255 nonbusiness travelers.

The concept-testing methodology we developed to help answer management's first three questions centered on a hybrid categorical conjoint analysis augmented by computer simulations and a number of related analyses.

Hybrid conjoint models [Green, Goldberg, and Montemayor 1981; Green, Goldberg, and Wiley 1982] adapt an old idea — self-explicated utility assessment [Wilkie and Pessemier 1973] — to conjoint analysis [Green and Rao 1971; Green and Wind 1973; Johnson 1974]. While a number of hybrid models have been proposed, each procedure entails the prior consideration of some type of self-explicated utility task where respondents evaluate the levels of each attribute (one attribute at a time) on some type of desirability scale. This is followed by an evaluation of the attributes themselves on an importance scale and the collection of data on each respondent's evalu-

TABLE 1
Hotel Features and Services*

1. **EXTERNAL FACTORS**
   Building Shape
   L-shaped w/landscape
   Outdoor courtyard
   Landscaping
   Minimal
   Moderate
   Elaborate
   Pool type
   No pool
   Rectangular shape
   Free form shape
   Indoor/outdoor
   Pool location
   In courtyard
   Not in courtyard
   Corridor/View
   Outside access/
   restricted view
   *Enclosed access/
   unrestricted view/
   balcony or window*
   Hotel size
   *Small (125 rooms,
   2 stories)*
   Large (600 rooms,
   12 stories)

2. **ROOMS**
   Entertainment
   Color TV
   Color TV w/movies
   at $5
   Color TV w/
   30 channel cable
   *Color TV w/HBO,
   movies, etc.*
   Color TV w/free
   movies
   Entertainment/Rental
   None
   Rental Cassettes/
   in-room Atari
   Rental Cassettes/
   stereo cassette
   playing in room
   Rental Movies/
   in-room BetaMax
   Size
   Small (standard)
   *Slightly larger
   (1 foot)*
   Much larger
   (2 ½ feet)
   Small suite
   (2 rooms)
   Large suite
   (2 rooms)
   Quality of Decor (in
   standard room)
   Budget motel decor
   Old Holiday Inn
   decor
   New Holiday Inn
   decor
   New Hilton decor

   New Hyatt decor
   Heating and Cooling
   Wall unit/full control
   *Wall unit/soundproof/
   full control*
   Central H or C
   (seasonal)
   Central H or C/
   full control
   Size of Bath
   Standard bath
   *Slightly larger/sink
   separate*
   Much larger bath
   w/larger tub
   Very large/tub for 2
   Sink location
   In bath only
   In separate area
   In bath and separate
   Bathroom Features
   None
   Shower Massage
   Whirlpool (Jacuzzi)
   Steam bath
   Amenities
   Small bar soap
   *Large soap/shampoo/
   shoeshine*
   Large soap/bath
   gel/shower cap/
   sewing kit
   Above items +
   toothpaste,
   deodorant,
   mouthwash

3. **FOOD**
   Restaurant in hotel
   None (coffee shop
   next door)
   *Restaurant/lounge
   combo, limited
   menu*
   Coffee shop, full
   menu
   Full-service
   restaurant, full
   menu
   Coffee shop/full
   menu and good
   restaurant
   Restaurant nearby
   None
   Coffee shop
   Fast food
   Fast food or coffee
   shop and moderate
   restaurant
   *Fast food or coffee
   shop and good
   restaurant*
   Free continental
   None
   Continental included
   in room rate

   Room service
   None
   Phone-in order/guest
   to pick up
   Room service,
   limited menu
   Room service, full
   menu
   Store
   No food in store
   Snack items
   Snacks, refrigerated
   items, wine, beer,
   liquor
   Above items and
   gourmet food
   items
   Vending service
   None
   Soft drink machine
   only
   Soft drink and
   snack machines
   *Soft drink, snack, and
   sandwich machines*
   Above and microwave
   available
   In-room kitchen
   facilities
   None
   Coffee maker only
   Coffee maker and
   refrigerator
   Cooking facilities in
   room

4. **LOUNGE**
   Atmosphere
   Quiet bar/lounge
   Lively, popular bar/
   lounge
   Type of people
   Hotel guests and
   friends only
   *Open to public —
   general appeal*
   Open to public —
   many singles
   Lounge nearby
   None
   Lounge/bar nearby
   Lounge/bar w/
   entertainment
   nearby

5. **SERVICES**
   Reservations
   Call hotel directly
   800 reservation
   number
   Check-in
   Standard
   Pre-credit
   clearance
   Machine in lobby
   Check-out
   At front desk

   *Bill under door/
   leave key*
   Key to front desk/
   bill by mail
   Machine in lobby
   Limo to airport
   None
   Yes
   Bellman
   None
   Yes
   Message service
   Note at front desk
   Light on phone
   Light on phone
   and message
   under door
   Recorded message
   Cleanliness/upkeep/
   management skill
   Budget motor level
   Holiday Inn level
   *Nonconvention
   Hyatt level*
   Convention Hyatt
   level
   Fine hotel level
   Laundry/Valet
   None
   *Client drop off and
   pick up*
   Self-service
   Valet pick up and
   drop off
   Special Services
   (concierge)
   None
   Information on
   restaurants,
   theaters, etc.
   Arrangements and
   reservations
   Travel problem
   resolution
   Secretarial services
   None
   Xerox machine
   Xerox machine and
   typist
   Car maintenance
   None
   Take car to service
   Gas on premises/bill
   to room
   Car rental/Airline
   reservations
   None
   Care rental facility
   Airline reservations
   Car rental and
   airline reservations

6. **LEISURE**
   Sauna
   None
   Yes

TABLE 1 (continued)
Hotel Features and Services*

Whirlpool/jacuzzi	Game room/	Pool extras	Sprinkler system
None	Entertainment	None	None
Outdoor	*None*	Pool w/slides	Lobby and hallways only
Indoor	Electric games/pinball	Pool w/slides and	*Lobby/hallways/rooms*
Exercise room	Electric games/pinball/	equipment	24-hour video camera
None	ping pong	7. SECURITY	None
Basic facility	Above + movie	Security guard	Parking/hallway/public
w/weights	theater, bowling	None	areas
Facility w/Nautilus	Children's playroom/	11 a.m. to 7 p.m.	Alarm button
equipment	playground	*7 p.m. to 7 a.m.*	None
Racquet ball courts	*None*	24 hours	Button in room, rings
None	Playground only	Smoke detector	desk
Yes	Playroom only	None	
Tennis courts	Playground and ployroom	*In rooms and throughout*	
None		*hotel*	
Yes			

*The 50 factors that describe hotel features and services and the associated (167) levels are categorized under seven facets. The italicized items were included in the final design of the hotel.

FIGURE 1
Overall study design, research analysis, and output.

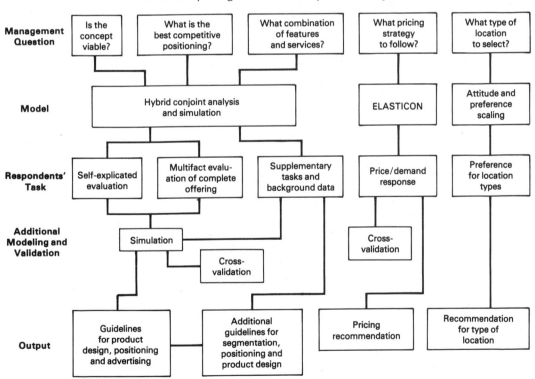

ation of a limited set (usually eight or nine) of complete (all-attribute) stimulus profiles. These stimulus profiles are, in turn, drawn from a much larger master design (usually ranging between 64 and 256 profiles) that permits statistical estimation of all main effects and selected two-way interactions. Moreover, profiles are "balanced" (to prevent bias) within respondent by means of various blocking designs. The respondent evaluates each complete stimulus profile on some type of likelihood-of-purchase or intentions-to-buy scale. (We discuss the hybrid conjoint model briefly in Appendix 1.)

We analyzed the hybrid conjoint analysis data to produce individual utility functions. We input these, in turn, into a computer simulation that allowed management to assess any desired new concept formulation (for example, a specific combination of any of the attributes listed in Table 1) for the potential share of nights as well as the source of those nights (for example, the switching pattern from the other hotels). In addition, the simulation allowed management to identify the characteristics of each subsegment — those who switched to the new concept and those who did not.

To answer the pricing question, the study also focused on establishing the respondent's price elasticity among various new hotel concepts and established hotels. We used the ELASTICON model and algorithm [Mahajan, Green, and Goldberg 1982] discussed in Appendix 1 to determine elasticity.

To provide input to the location decision, we scaled each respondent's preferences for various locations. In addition, we used a number of other analytical approaches including the following:

- To establish and rank order the various segments' perception and preference for various hotel features and services, we employed multidimensional scaling (MDS) algorithms.
- To identify the key discriminating characteristics of the various segments (low-business vs. high-business vs. pleasure), we used multiple discriminant analysis (MDA).

THE EMPIRICAL STUDY

We conducted the study among 601 consumers, selecting four metropolitan areas — Atlanta, Dallas, San Francisco, and Chicago — on the basis of the results of an earlier psychological segmentation study. Within each market, we selected suburban areas and nearby small towns randomly. Within each subarea, we screened respon-

dents (who were also selected randomly) by telephone to learn the number and type of trips they took, their incomes, and the type of accommodations they usually chose.

Data Collection

We conducted a pretest prior to conducting our final survey. Both the pretest and the main interviews were administered in a central location setting, with supervisors available to explain any task a respondent did not immediately understand. We designed both the pretest and the main surveys to maintain high respondent involvement in the various ranking and rating tasks. In addition, we paid the respondents a monetary incentive that varied by city and averaged $35 per respondent. The respondents did not find the tasks too long or complex. Only three respondents refused to complete the tasks. Clear discrimination in the responses of all subjects was evident, indicating both understanding and lack of respondent burnout.

Overall, post-interview debriefing indicated high levels of interest in and completion of the tasks. We will discuss the various respondents' tasks in relation to the models and analytical methods employed.

Task 1a.

For the categorical conjoint analysis we first administered a questionnaire designed to question respondents on characteristics they prefer in hotels. This questionnaire is termed a "univariate self-explicated evaluation" because the respondent determines his or her preference for various hotel features and services based on a single rather than multiple comparison.

After explaining the task and the focus on the respondent's preferences for hotel amenities related to business trips (or nonbusiness trips), we gave each respondent seven cards, one at a time. Each card dealt with one of the seven facets (sets of attributes) of hotel facilities, including external factors and physical layout, and six other factors (the room itself, services, and so forth, see Table 1).

Figure 2 shows a card describing the "Rooms" facet. This set of features ("factors") includes nine attributes; for each factor three

FIGURE 2
Example of stimulus cards for room features*

Most Frequently Used Hotel Chain
_____

ROOMS

"X" the TRIANGLE (△) in the block that comes closest to describing your current hotel (ONLY "X" ONE)
"X" the CIRCLE (○) in the block(s) that you find to be completely unacceptable
    (YOU MAY "X" NONE, ONE, OR MORE THAN ONE)
"X" the SQUARE (□) in the block that represents what you want and are willing to pay for (ONLY "X" ONE)

Features	Alternative Descriptions					Enter Price of Wanted Block
Entertainment	Color TV	Color TV with movies which are 9 months ahead of HBO, $5 each	Color TV with 30 channel cable	Color TV with HBO movie channel, sports news channel	Color TV with free in-room movies (choice of 3)	
	(.00) △○□	(.00) △○□	(.25) △○□	(.40) △○□	(2.50) △○□	
Entertainment/ Rental	None	Rental cassettes available for use with in-room Atari or Intellivision	Rental cassettes available. In-room stereo cassette player	Rental movies, in-room video cassette player (BetaMax)		
	(.00) △○□	(.40) + △○□	(1.35) + △○□	(1.35) + △○□		
Size & Furniture	Small— typical size motel/hotel room	Somewhat larger— 1 foot longer	Much larger— 2 1/2 feet longer	Small suite— 2 rooms	Large suite— 2 rooms	
	△○□	△○□	△○□	△○□	△○□	
Quality of Decor (in standard room)	Similar to Days Inn and other budget motels	Similar to older Holiday Inn, Ramada, Rodeway	Similar to newer and better Holiday Inns	Similar to newer and better Hilton and Marriott	Similar to Hyatt Regency and Westin "Plaza" hotels	
	△○□	△○□	△○□	△○□	△○□	
Heat/Cooling	Through-wall unit. Full control of heating & cooling year round	Through-wall unit (soundproofed). Full control of heating & cooling year round	Either central heating or cooling (not both), depending on season	Full control of central heating & cooling year round		
	△○□	△○□	△○□	△○□		
Bath size	Standard bathroom and tub/shower as in most hotels. Sink in bath only.	Somewhat larger bath and standard tub/shower. Sink in separate area outside bathroom	Much larger bathroom with large tub/shower	Large bathroom with sunken tub for 2		
	△○□	△○□	△○□	△○□		
Sink location	Sink in bath only	Sink in separate area outside bathroom	Sink in bathroom and a sink outside bathroom			
	△○□	△○□	△○□			
Bathroom features	None	Shower massage	Whirlpool (Jacuzzi)	Steam bath		
	△○□	△○□	△○□	△○□		
Amenities	Small bar of soap	Large soap, shampoo packet, shoe shine mitt	Large soap, bath gel, shower cap, sewing kit, shampoo, special soap	Large soap, bath gel, shower cap, sewing kit, special soap, toothpaste, etc.		
	△○□	△○□	△○□	△○□		

↑
Importance Ranking

TOTAL _____

*This is the stimulus for the second facet. Each respondent received cards corresponding to all seven facets for the self-explicated conjoint analysis task.

(Transfer Total Cost to Worksheet)

to five attributes are described, with the associated price included for each profile. For example, in the case of entertainment, the five levels range from color TV at no extra cost to color TV with a choice of three in-room movies for $2.50. Marriott's cost-accounting department developed the specific price levels used.

The respondents were asked to think about their usual hotel stay (for business purposes or pleasure) and to check the triangle in each row that best described the hotel they currently used. Next, the respondents supplied one of three possible responses to each amenity-price combination:

- The combination is completely unacceptable;
- The combination is most preferred; and
- The combination is acceptable (by implication, that is, if they expressed a preference for each of the amenities or prices individually, we could infer their implied acceptance of the combination).

In addition, the respondent was also asked to rank the various factors within the facet on their relative importance. Similar cards were used for the remaining six facets. A total of 50 attributes, across the seven facets, were included. The total number of attribute levels exceeded 160; pictures were used, where appropriate, to describe the various attribute levels (for example, a hotel pool).

When the respondents had evaluated all seven facets, they were asked to add the total incremental costs of the features and services they selected. If the total of the charges plus the base room price were higher than they were willing to pay on a regular business (or pleasure) trip, they were asked to go back and select the enhancements they were willing to forego in order to arrive at an acceptable total room price.

Task 1b.

In the second phase of the categorical conjoint analysis we obtained a multifaceted evaluation of "complete" hotel offerings. In this phase, each respondent was shown, one at a time, five cards, each containing a full-profile description of a "complete" hotel offering (Figure 3). Each set of five cards was drawn from a possible 50 cards and was balanced within subject. Using factorial design (aided by computer analysis), we arranged for respondents to receive various combinations of the 50 profiles. This approach provided the respondents with choices that made sense to

them, provided the researchers with sufficient information to be statistically significant and unbiased, and provided Marriott with the practical knowledge necessary to design a new hotel.

In this case we treated each of the seven facets as an experimental factor with five levels each. Thus, we obtained a large range of combinations: five to the seventh power (five levels, seven facets). What this means is that we used statistical computing and a complex experimental design (the 5^7 full-factorial design) called a fractional orthogonal main effects plan. This experimental design, although complicated to explain, can help management determine what qualities the respondents preferred in a hotel, given the trade-offs they have to make for comfort versus price.

Within each facet, Marriott personnel constructed the five levels so as to "cover" the range of interest. As might be expected, attribute levels tended to be correlated within each facet so that premium priced amenities often clustered together. Despite these clusters of answers at the attribute level, which might bias a study, the orthogonality of the master design across facets was respected. For each of the five hotel descriptions that each respondent received, he or she was asked to indicate the likelihood of staying there.

Task 2. The ELASTICON Model

We evaluated each of the hotels likely to compete with the new hotel (for example, LaQuinta, Marriott, newer and older Holiday Inns) and the tested hotel concepts under various prices. We first described the hotel concepts in terms of price, external factors, rooms, food and beverage services, entertainment, recreation and other services and security. Each respondent received five cards. Each card listed four existing hotels and two new hotel concepts, each at a specific price. We based the specific prices on an experimental design involving 32 combinations. The respondents were asked to allocate 100 points among the hotel-price combination based on how likely they would be to stay at each hotel at the given price.

FIGURE 3
Sample hotel offering*

ROOM PRICE PER NIGHT IS $44.85

BUILDING SIZE, BAR/LOUNGE
    Large (600 rooms) 12-story hotel with:
      •Quiet bar/lounge
      •Enclosed central corridors and elevators
      •All rooms have very large windows

LANDSCAPING/COURT
    Building forms a spacious outdoor courtyard
      •View from rooms of moderately landscaped courtyard with:
      —many trees and shrubs
      —the swimming pool plus a fountain
      —terraced areas for sunning, sitting, eating

FOOD
    Small moderately priced lounge and restaurant for hotel guests/friends
      •Limited breakfast with juices, fruit, Danish, cereal, bacon and eggs
      •Lunch—soup and sandwiches only
      •Evening meal—salad, soup, sandwiches, six hot entrees including steak

HOTEL/MOTEL ROOM QUALITY
    Quality of room furnishings, carpet, etc. is similar to:
      •Hyatt Regencies
      •Westin "Plaza" Hotels

ROOM SIZE & FUNCTION
    Room 1 foot longer than typical hotel/motel room
      •Space for comfortable sofa-bed and 2 chairs
      •Large desk
      •Coffee table
      •Coffee maker and small refrigerator

SERVICE STANDARDS
    Full service including:
      •Rapid check in/check out systems
      •Reliable message service
      •Valet (laundry pick up/deliver)
      •Bellman
      •Someone (concierge) arranges reservations, tickets, and
       generally at no cost
      •Cleanliness, upkeep, management similar to:
      —Hyatts
      —Marriotts

LEISURE
      •Combination indoor-outdoor pool
      •Enclosed whirlpool (Jacuzzi)
      •Well-equipped playroom/playground for kids

SECURITY
      •Night guard on duty 7 p.m. to 7 a.m.
      •Fire/water sprinklers throughout hotel

"X" the ONE box below which best describes how likely you are to stay in this hotel/motel at this price:

Would stay there almost all the time	Would stay there on a regular basis	Would stay there now and then	Would rarely stay there	Would not stay there
☐	☐	☐	☐	☐

*This full profile description of a hotel offering is one of the 50 cards developed by a fractional factorial design of the seven facets each at the five levels (developed by the Marriott's development team). Each respondent received five cards following a blocking design.

Task 3. Location Analysis

To provide guidance in positioning the hotel location competitively, we asked respondents to allocate 100 points among a set of locations based on their importance in selecting a hotel. We defined the locations in terms of closeness to business, shopping, sightseeing, night life, theaters, airport, major highways, and so forth.

Task 4.

In addition to these major tasks, we asked the respondents for demographic information and for information on the type of overnight hotel accommodations used for business and nonbusiness stays, the frequency and length of stay, the price usually paid, and so forth.

To provide further guidelines for the room design, we conducted a secondary conjoint analysis on seven additional design factors, including room size, quality of decor, type of heating and cooling unit, bath size, bathroom features, and the amenities and type of entertainment available in the room. As in the preceding full-profile task, we gave each respondent only a small number of cards — four in this case — for evaluation.

To provide additional information for the design of the hotel, we asked the respondents to rank the importance of several features, including an alarm clock, carpeted bathroom, baby-sitting service, hot tub, king-sized bed, plants in the room, remote TV controls, windows that open, X-rated movies, and AM/FM radio.

To help Marriott management select the hotel name, we asked respondents to indicate how much they liked each of 11 names, and following this to rank the names that best fit the hotel concept. *Courtyard by Marriott* was one of the 11 names.

To help position the hotel's image, we gave the respondents a number of supplementary tasks. We asked them to evaluate hypothetical hotels on the degree to which they had each of several desired characteristics and the degree to which they would compare favorably or unfavorably on these attributes to a Holiday Inn. The stimulus set included such characteristics as "a place kids really like," "gives

a complete break from usual routine," "gives safe and secure feeling," "has stimulating/exciting atmosphere," "is good for people who do not want to be hassled," "is a good place for people on a budget," "provides a comfortable room for when you are alone," and "has charm, warmth" and so forth.

In addition, we gave respondents a number of descriptions of different types of hotels derived from the segmentation study. These descriptions included such positionings as "a busy, efficient, modern hotel," "a good, no-frills, basic hotel," "an informal, quiet, relaxing hotel with charm and personality," "a casual feeling in a hotel with understated elegance," "and an exciting, action-oriented hotel with spectacular, modern architecture."

THE ANALYSIS

The core of our analysis centered on computing consumer utility functions for the hotel amenity-price evaluation. Using data collected in the two phases described for the categorical conjoint analysis, we performed the following steps:

- For each of the seven facets, we employed a categorical conjoint analysis for the facet's response data.
- We computed each respondent's self-explicated utility (with individualized importance weights) to obtain a set of predictor variables.
- We then computed parameters of the hybrid conjoint model for each cluster of respondents.
- We found the residuals from this step and regressed them on the total room price (the five cards shown to the respondent in Task 1b). We then determined if including this variable accounted for significant variance in the residuals.

These steps constituted the main thrust of the analysis and generated the data used in the computer choice simulation described in the appendix. The simulation was designed to evaluate the market attractiveness of various bundles of features and services. It allowed the design team to specify alternative design concepts and to obtain, for each specific bundle of services, the estimated share of choice for that "concept," vis-a-vis its intended competitors.

We augmented these various analyses to consider such methodological questions as: How accurate are the results at the individual level? How sensitive are the predictions to changes in facet importance weights? What is the effect of the blocking variable (that is, the particular five profiles out of 50 evaluated by the respondent in the first place)?

We conducted other analyses to answer management's questions:

- to provide further guidance in selecting hotel features, we ran a conjoint analysis on the additional room features evaluated in Task 4 and ran an MDS on the 16 secondary features examined in Task 4;

- to establish price elasticity, in addition to performing conjoint analysis on Tasks 1a and b, we analyzed the data from Task 2 using the ELASTICON model and methodology;

- to determine the profile of the segments, we conducted a series of multiple discriminant analyses; and

- to help name, position and locate the hotel, we conducted cross-tabulations and preference mapping for the data from the relevant tasks.

RESULTS

The study clearly suggested that some business and pleasure travelers were dissatisfied with current hotel offerings. Some hotels cost too much and offer features not valued by the traveler while others that cost less offer too few of the desirable features. Both types of hotels also tend to lack the personalization of features that travelers seek. Thus, a new hotel concept tuned to travelers' needs at an acceptable price seemed to be the most viable product for Marriott to consider.

The respondents' dissatisfaction with hotels that cost too much for the value given and with others that offer too little, combined with the set of hotel amenities they selected as most desirable and the level of price sensitivity, all suggested the chosen positioning of "a special little hotel at a very comfortable price." This market positioning was further reinforced by the pleasure and nonbusiness travelers' selection of the following description as the most preferred hotel — "an informal, quiet, relaxing hotel or motel with charm and personal-

ity." The respondents' clear specification of desired product attributes and price defined the competitive positioning of *Courtyard by Marriott* vis-a-vis other Marriott hotels (providing important guidelines to a product line strategy) and vis-a-vis the industry's other hotels aiming at the same target segment. This selected positioning was found to be superior to the original positioning management considered, namely, that of a small Marriott hotel.

The study provided extremely detailed guidelines for the selection of close to 200 features and services. Table 2 is an example of the output for various external features or facilities. It suggests how powerful the study was in directing the design of the hotel. The attributes selected for the hotel are those that are numbered in bold type — the ones with the highest utility for the target segments. In Table 1, the underlined items are the levels of the various factors selected for the hotel. Some of the specific attributes Marriott selected for inclusion were amenities such as shampoo and medium soap; in-room kitchen facilities (for regular rooms — either coffee makers or coffee makers and refrigerators); and "limo" to airport (a van at airport location). For the most part, indoor whirlpools or jacuzzis were installed except in Arizona and California, where some outdoor ones were installed. Marriott postponed installation of complete exercise rooms based on their management expertise (weight rooms were included).

Similar output and patterns of implementation were found for the other six sets of attributes. We presented the results to management in cross-tabulation form for each of the 50 features. The computer simulation provided additional and most significant insight into the value of various features and services. The simulation output offered the design team and management a clear idea of

1. The likely share (of nights) any hotel concept (presented as a specific combination of features and services from those listed in Table 1) would get by any target segment(s).

2. The source of business — the hotels from which the new hotel is most likely to draw business,

TABLE 2
Sample Output for External Features and Facilities*

Attribute	Levels	Description	Part Worths
Hotel Size	1	Small (125 rooms) 2-story hotel (.00)**	1.06
	2	12-story (600 rooms) with large lobby, meeting rooms, etc. (7.15)	0.00
Corridor/View	1	Outside stairs and walkways to all rooms. Restricted view. People walking outside window. (.00)	0.00
	2	Enclosed central corridors and stairs. Unrestricted view. Rooms have balcony or large windows. (.65)	1.85
Pool Location	1	Not in courtyard (.00)	0.00
	2	In courtyard (.00)	1.37
Pool type	1	No pool (.00)	0.61
	2	Rectangular pool (.45)	1.25
	3	Freeform pool (.50)	0.29
	4	Indoor/outdoor pool (.85)	0.00
Landscaping	1	Minimal landscaping (.00)	0.81
	2	Moderate landscaping (.10)	0.97
	3	Elaborate landscaping (.50)	0.00
Building Shape	1	"L" shape building with modest landscaping (.00)	0.00
	2	Building forms an outdoor landscaped courtyard for sitting, eating, sunning, etc. (.45)	0.37

* Part worths are shown for attribute levels within the external factors/facilities facet. Similar output was developed for the other facets for each target segment (for example, low-end business travelers) and the total market.

**Figure in parentheses after each description = price premium.

including the likelihood of cannibalization of the Marriott.

3. The characteristics of the specific segment attracted to the specific configuration of attributes and services.

The final design — the italicized items in Table 1 — was quite different from the original design idea of a small Marriott, but it reflected the highest expected share from the target business and pleasure segments.

The results of the ELASTICON tasks and analysis included

1. the expected share for each of the concepts tested by each price versus their current competition,

2. the likely source of business for the concept, and

3. the self-elasticity and cross-elasticity of demand for the concept. We presented this most critical information for each segment in a table similar

to Table 3. In addition, the price/demand relationship for each segment was also presented graphically.

The analysis of the respondents' answers to questions concerning the desired location of the hotel in terms of its proximity to business, shopping, theaters, airports, and so forth, greatly aided management in deciding on location. In addition, because target segments had a utility for a restaurant, one criterion for a site became the availability of a nearby restaurant.

IMPLEMENTATION

Development team members from several corporate departments were involved in the design of the study and provided expertise in the direct translation of the research results into final product design. The resulting hotel follows almost to the letter the recommenda-

TABLE 3

Hampton Elasticon Results for Low-End Business Segment

Reference Conditions:	
La Quinta at $30/night	
Older Holiday at $35/night	Share of Nights
Newer Holiday at $48/night	18.0%
Newer Marriott at $66/night	
Hampton at $42/night	
Alternative Price Conditions:	
La Quinta at $26/night	
Older Holiday at $31/night	
New Holiday at $42/night	
Newer Marriott at $60/night	
Hampton at $38/$46/$50/night	

Self-Price/Demand Relationships
If Hampton is priced at $38, add 7.8 points to Hampton's share.
If Hampton is priced at $46, subtract 5.1 points from Hampton's share.
If Hampton is priced at $50, subtract 12.3 points from Hampton's share.

Other Price/Demand Relationships
If newer Holiday is priced at $42, subtract 2.6 points from Hampton's share.
If older Holiday is priced at $31, subtract 1.3 points from Hampton's share.

tions of the study. Every one of the features and services offered were among the highest valued by the consumer.

Validation

We implemented internal cross-validation of the conjoint analysis by using a leave-one-out procedure. We predicted each individual's actual first choice (among the five full profiles evaluated) from model parameters computed across the rest of the sample. Each person's data were held out and predicted, one respondent at a time. Predictions covered not only first choice but the ranking of each respondent's five profiles.

The leave-one-out procedure indicated that approximately 40 percent of first choices were predicted (versus 20 percent by chance). Given the complexity of the profiles (and respondent heterogeneity), this performance, while not outstanding, was statistically significant. (Predictions of the market share level were much higher: mean absolute deviations of four to five share points were obtained from a bootstrap resampling procedure.)

We also used a leave-one-out procedure for the ELASTICON model with even better results. In this case we predicted market share by using the model demand from the remaining conditions; the mean absolute difference in share of market was quite small (0.031).

The most effective validation of the study results is the success of the *Courtyard by Marriott*. Currently, *Courtyard by Marriott* has 175 hotels either open, under construction, or under contract; 111 were opened by the end of 1988. Marriott committed over $450 million a year to national expansion. Figure 4 shows the expansion pattern of the new chain, which is the fastest growing, moderately priced hotel chain in the country. The actual market share of *Courtyard by Marriott* was within four percentage points of the share predicted by the conjoint simulation.

The validity of the study's conclusions was also evident when we analyzed the results of the guest-tracking studies. These studies revealed that the features and services offered are very important to the consumer and are perceived as better at *Courtyard by Marriott* than at its competition.

IMPACT

The study has had a major impact on the profitability and growth of Marriott Corporation. The *Courtyard by Marriott* chain is a success. The in-depth hotel experience of Marriott executives led them to expect that a smaller version of a typical Marriott hotel was needed. Surprisingly, the study resulted in a new product that was markedly different from the normal Marriott with a clear appeal to a distinct target market segment. In fact, the important differences identified for the *Courtyard by Marriott* product led Marriott to create an operating division separate from Marriott hotels.

Direct Benefits

The study gave Marriott executives the confidence to expend the large amount of personnel time and funds necessary to develop this new product from the ground up. The close tie between the study results and the exe-

FIGURE 4
Growth of Courtyard chain

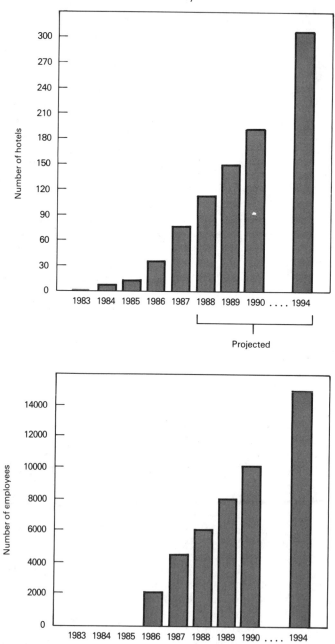

cuted product demonstrates the importance of the study in guiding development.

Since the results focused not only on what the travelers wanted, but also identified what they did not want to pay for, the design team was able to meet the specified price while retaining the features most desired by the target market. Features often provided based on traditional hotel management beliefs were not retained, for example, an "action" lounge, a more upscale restaurant and room service, and more meeting space. This focus on guest needs allowed more funds to be spent on better executions of highly desired guest features. The resulting design filled a gap in the market with a product that represented the best balance between price and desired product and service features.

The addition of *Courtyard by Marriott* to the Marriott hotel product line allowed the Marriott Corporation to continue rapid hotel expansion and profitability by placing hotels in locations where a typical Marriott hotel could not be profitably justified: (1) in lower demand areas and smaller sites in major markets; and (2) in smaller markets.

One important additional benefit is the positive psychological impact the study had on Marriott's personnel, who know that the hotel is based on consumer perceptions and preferences and is therefore designed to serve consumers better and offer them the best value.

An important by-product of the study was the effective incorporation of the study's results in Marriott's advertising and promotion programs.

Indirect Benefits

The project fostered an orientation of employee attitudes toward the identification and satisfaction of customer preferences. This impact ranged all the way from entry level training programs to top management.

The success of the *Courtyard by Marriott* study led to the development of additional customer-driven products (Fairfield Inn and Marriott Suites), all using the methodology and models similar to those employed in the original study.

The occupancy rate of the chain is higher than the industry average, and the consumer satisfaction with the hotel and its services is very high.

Financial Impact

The *Courtyard by Marriott* chain has been a success, growing from three test hotels in 1983 to 90 hotels in 1987 (with sales exceeding $200 million). The chain is expected to grow to 300 hotels by 1994 (with sales exceeding $1 billion). *Courtyard by Marriott* thus contributes significantly to Marriott's overall growth goals and related stock values. It has already created 3,000 new jobs. By 1994, that figure is expected to reach 14,000.

The impact of *Courtyard by Marriott* on the hotel industry has also been substantial. The targeted design and positioning of *Courtyard by Marriott* has filled an identified gap or niche in the market. The success of this effort has caused a restructuring of the midprice level of the lodging industry.

1. Older hotels in the *Courtyard by Marriott* price range found themselves losing market share. They generally decided to upgrade their properties, to reduce prices in order to compete, or to sell out.

2. Relatively new and often more upscale hotels located near *Courtyard by Marriott* hotels found themselves losing market share and decided to refurbish their hotels ahead of schedule, to reduce rates on competitive business (weekday transient guests and weekends), or to add popular features available at *Courtyard by Marriott*.

3. At least five new *Courtyard by Marriott* clone chains have been initiated by other hotel groups. They all offer a high-end hotel room at a midlevel price. In some cases, they add a feature for differentiation, but the basic consumer appeal is the same.

In addition to the industry impact and specific benefits to Marriott, the approach demonstrates to marketing management and the marketing science community that

• Products and services can, and should, be developed using targeted consumer perception, preference, and attitudinal inputs;

- Complex and large products, such as hotels (with close to 200 attribute levels), can be studied effectively using creative conjoint analysis designs; and
- Categorical hybrid conjoint analysis models can be used in commercial applications.

Many products and services — cars, boats, electrical appliances, single homes, condominiums, stereo and video equipment, computer terminals, copy machines, word processors, financial services — are often sold as basic units with various add-ons that are optional at extra cost. The methods described here (or some variation of them) can be applicable to this wide class of problems.

APPENDIX 1

Technical Background

While a variety of marketing research tools were employed in the *Courtyard by Marriott* study, the primary set of techniques was drawn from conjoint analysis. Conjoint analysis was introduced to marketing research in the early 1970s [Green and Rao 1971]. Since that time, applications to industry and government problems, both in the US and abroad, have been extensive and varied.

Conjoint analysis is a survey-based technique for measuring consumers' trade-offs among product and service attributes [Green and Wind 1973]. In traditional conjoint analysis, respondents are shown profiles of product or service offerings. Each profile (see Figure 3) is made up of a set of attribute levels. The specific combination of attribute levels is drawn from a balanced experimental design, often referred to as an orthogonal array. Table 1 shows the extensive set of factors and levels used in the *Courtyard by Marriott* study.

Each respondent receives a set of profiles and evaluates each profile's "worth" to him or her on some type of preference or likelihood-of-purchase scale. In our study, we were concerned with the likelihood that a respondent would stay at a specified hotel or motel (see Figure 3). In traditional conjoint studies involving seven or fewer product/service attributes, conventional dummy variable re-

gression (or perhaps isotonic regression in which the response variable, likelihood of staying, is expressed only on an ordinal scale) is used to find parameter values. These parameter values are called part worths; one such part worth is obtained for each attribute level, for each respondent.

The set of part worths derived for a particular respondent represents the building blocks for predicting how the respondent would value some *new* combination of attribute levels. The part worths may be simple (so-called main effects) parameters, or they may include various sets of interactions. Often the researcher employs small holdout samples to determine the accuracy of the predictions. (However, in larger-scale studies, the logical number of combinations and predictions may be enormous, amounting to hundreds of thousands or possibly millions of possible products or services.)

In virtually all conjoint studies, a computer choice simulator is employed to forecast shares of choice as new product/service profiles are introduced to the market. The part worths are used in various ways to estimate shares of choice for competing market offerings. Recently, choice simulators have been augmented by the development of optimal product and product-line design models that systematically explore the product or service "space" to find attribute combinations that maximize share or profits, conditional on the characteristics of competitive offerings. Another recent development is the appearance of commercial software packages that include modules for preparing experimental designs, product profile presentation by computer, part worth estimation, and choice simulators, all integrated for personal computer implementation.

In the *Courtyard by Marriott* study, we employed two fairly recent innovations in conjoint analysis — hybrid models for data collection, for use when the number of product or service attributes is extensive, and ELASTICON, a version of conjoint analysis that is particularly well suited for measuring price/demand relationships. These developments (and a short description of how choice simulators were used in our study) follow. (Material for the technical appendix is drawn from

Goldberg, Green, and Wind [1984] and Mahajan, Green, and Goldberg [1982].)

Hybrid Conjoint Models

Hybrid conjoint models have been developed recently to cope with a practical problem in applied conjoint analysis, namely, the need to streamline the data collection task while still preserving individual differences in utility functions [Green, Goldberg, and Montemayor 1981]. The name *hybrid* is used to denote the fact that the technique incorporates both compositional and decompositional procedures to obtain utility functions. While a number of hybrid models have been proposed, each procedure entails the consideration of some type of self-explicated utility where respondents evaluate the levels of each attribute (one attribute at a time) on some type of desirability scale (phase 1); this is followed by an evaluation of the attributes themselves on an importance scale (phase 2). These two phases together represent the compositional part of the model.

For the *Courtyard by Marriott* study, Figure 2 shows an illustration of the self-explicated section. Each attribute (for example, entertainment) and its levels are evaluated, one at a time, in terms of their acceptability. In addition, each attribute (that is, feature) is evaluated with respect to its importance in the facet.

A respondent's self-explicated utility for the hth stimulus profile is usually assumed to be given by a simple additive model,

$$U^h = \sum_{j=1}^{J} w_j u_{i_j}^h \qquad (1)$$

where
U^h = the respondent's total utility for alternative h,
w_j = the respondent's self-explicated importance weight of attribute j, and
$u_{i_j}^h$ denotes the fact that alternative h has a desirability score of u on level i_j of attribute j, and J is the number of attributes. (For ease of presentation the respondent index is suppressed.)

The next phase of data collection (the decompositional part) involves presenting each respondent with a limited set (usually eight

or nine) of complete (all-attribute) stimulus profiles (phase 3). These stimulus profiles, in turn, are drawn from a much larger master design (usually ranging between 64 and 256 profiles) that permits orthogonal estimation of all main effects and selected two-way interactions. Moreover, profiles can be "balanced" within respondent by means of various blocking designs. The respondent then evaluates each complete stimulus profile on some type of likelihood-of-purchase or intentions-to-buy scale. Call each of these responses Y^h for the stimulus profile h.

Figure 3 shows a sample stimulus profile drawn from the *Courtyard by Marriott* study in which the attribute descriptions are composed from the basic attribute level design of Table 1. The respondent is asked for an overall response: to rate the profile in terms of his or her likelihood of staying there. From the self-explicated part of the hybrid model, the researcher already has parameter estimates of the attribute levels' part worths when attributes are considered one at a time. The next step is to integrate the full profile responses with the self-explicative estimates.

The self-explicated task of phase 1 provides a matrix of utility functions, of order N by ΣI_j for the N respondents, where I_j is the number of levels for attribute j. This matrix is row centered or standardized to zero mean and unit standard deviation or both. That is, each respondent's specific set of $w_j u_{i_j}$'s in equation (1) — there are ΣI_j of these for each respondent — are often expressed as deviations from his or her mean. Respondents are then clustered on the basis of similarities in their self-explicated utility functions. Assume that K clusters are found.

The hybrid model's parameters are then separately estimated for each cluster by means of OLS (ordinary least squares) regression. The full hybrid model is defined as follows:

$$Y^h \cong a + b\,U^h + \sum_{j=1}^{J} v_{i_j} + \sum_{j<j'} t_{i_j i_{j'}}, \qquad (2)$$

where stimulus profile h has level i_j for attribute j. U is separately computed for each respondent and each profile via equation (1): a is an intercept term, b is a regression slope parameter representing the contribution of the self-explicated utility to Y, and the v's and t's are also regression parameters, estimated at the cluster level. The v's denote main effects while the t's denote selected two-way interactions, where the arguments are attribute-level descriptions. Hence, each respondent's utility function consists of two sets of parameters — one set measured at the individual level and one set measured at the subgroup (or cluster) level.

The last step, then, is to integrate the various sets of parameter values into a vector of part worths (including interactions, if necessary), one vector for each respondent. Thus, in terms of Table 1, we obtain an individual part worth for each respondent for each attribute level shown in that table. To illustrate, Table 2 shows a set of averaged part worths for only one facet of the design: external factors.

Categorical Hybrid Conjoint Analysis

In the *Courtyard by Marriott* study, we employed a form of conjoint analysis called categorical conjoint analysis for estimating the part worths of the individual attribute acceptabilities, prior to applying equations (1) and (2). Full details of the method are available in Goldberg, Green, and Wind [1984] and Green and Goldberg [1981].

The ELASTICON Model

An important case of conjoint modeling entails the trade-off of price versus nonprice attributes in a competitive context. The ELASTICON model is a type of conjoint analysis approach in which the respondent sees not one supplier's profile of attribute levels but a composite profile that explicitly shows each competitive offering and its associated price. For example, in the *Courtyard by Marriott* study, the profile may consist of five alternative motels or hotels: La Quinta, older Holiday Inns, newer Holiday Inns, and Hampton Inns, each shown at different prices. The respondent's task is to indicate, under the stated price conditions, what share of his or her choices would go to each alternative.

This type of design and subject's response is quite different from the usual presentation in which the respondent sees alternative profiles of only a single supplier or product offering. It is also different in that the conjoint part worths now include, as arguments, prices of competitors as well as one's own price levels. First we will describe how price has been conventionally dealt with in conjoint studies. We will then present this alternative formulation and analysis (referred to as the ELASTICON model).

In most applications of conjoint analysis, price is almost always included as an additional attribute in describing brand or supplier profiles. In the simplest case in which only two attributes vary (for example, brand name and price), the respondent may be given all combinations of each brand crossed with each price level and asked to rank or rate the combinations according to preference. These data are then analyzed [Green and Srinivasan 1978] to yield a set of part worths for brand and a set for price.

In the case of three or more attributes (two of which are brand and price), the procedure is similar except that fractional factorial designs are usually employed. In either case, it is often assumed that each price can appear with each brand name (or any other attribute combination) and that all brands are subject to identical variation in permissible price levels. Moreover, it is usually assumed that the derived part worths for the price attribute are independent of the specific brand with which any price level is associated.

An Alternative Formulation

As an alternative formulation of the conjoint analysis problem, consider an experimental design in which each price level is affixed to a specific brand and the respondent sees all brands, appropriately priced, simultaneously (see Mahajan, Green, and Goldberg [1982]). In this case, the respondent is asked to allocate 100 points across the various alternatives so as to reflect the likelihood of choosing each brand-price combination. In this procedure, if there are I_j price levels for the jth brand ($j = 1, 2, \ldots, J$), the full factorial design consists of $I_1 \times I_2 \times \ldots \times I_J$ combinations. Hence, if there are four brands each appearing at five price levels, the full factorial consists of $5^4 = 625$ combinations, not $5 \times 4 = 20$ combinations, as assumed in the conventional trade-off model.

Fractional factorials can also be used in the alternative formulation; each set of permissible price levels can be idiosyncratic to each brand and the number of price levels can vary brand by brand. Futhermore, other attribute levels that are idiosyncratic to each brand (for example, miles per gallon, length of service warranty) also can be added to the profiles.

In the conjoint model formulation, we can fit separate functions for estimating the probability of choosing brand j from the set of J brands as long as two restrictions, inherent in the respondent task, are observed:

1. Each estimated probability for choosing some j^{th} brand should range from zero to one.
2. The sume of the choice probabilities across all J brands (including some other-brand category, if desired) should equal unity.

Satisfaction of the first restriction can be accomplished by use of a logit transformation. To illustrate, consider $P_{j=1|i_1 i_2 \ldots i_J}$, the probability of choosing brand 1, given the specific price levels $i_1 i_2 \ldots i_J$ of all J brands. The logit function [Berkson 1969] is defined as the natural logarithm of the odds favoring the choice of brand 1 to its nonchoice:

$$L_{j=1|i_1 i_2 \ldots i_J} = ln\left[\frac{P_{j=1|i_1 i_2 \ldots i_J}}{1 - P_{j=1|i_1 i_2 \ldots i_J}}\right]. \quad (3)$$

Note that the logit $L_{j=1|i_1 i_2 \ldots i_J}$ increases from $-\infty$ to ∞ as $P_{j=1|i_1 i_2 \ldots i_J}$ increases from zero to one.

The second restriction (and also the first) can be met by defining a *conditional logit* [Thiel 1969]. For example, assume that we examine pairs of responses involving brands j and k $(j \neq k)$; more specifically, let us consider each pair as entailing brand 1 and brand $k = 2, 3, \ldots, J$. If so, we can define the conditional logit for $k \neq 1$ as the natural logarithm of the odds in favor of choosing brand k over brand 1:

$$L_{k(1)|i_1 i_2 \ldots i_J} = ln\left[\frac{P_{k|i_1 i_2 \ldots i_J}}{P_{j=1|i_1 i_2 \ldots i_J}}\right]. \quad (4)$$

Note that each of the equations (for $k = 2, 3, \ldots, J$) is based only on the ratios of the probabilities; absolute values of the probabilities will be determined by the condition that the sum over $j = 1, 2, \ldots, J$ equals unity.

To illustrate, if $k = 2$, the probability of choosing brand 2 is 0.45 and the probability of choosing brand 1 is 0.1, the conditional logit for brand 2 with respect to brand 1 as the reference brand is

$$L_{2(1)|i_1 i_2 \ldots i_J} = ln\left[\frac{0.45}{0.1}\right] = 1.5041. \quad (5)$$

As Theil [1969] shows, by using this type of formulation, we satisfy both of the restrictions listed above.

Parameterizing the ELASTICON Model

In the ELASTICON model, we parameterize the conditional logit transformation by assuming a type of analysis-of-variance (ANOVA) model (with interaction terms if desired) that relates the conditional logit for $k = 2, 3, \ldots, J$ relative to the reference brand, to the appropriate price levels of each set of profiles. That is, we assume a multivariate response: $P_1, P_2, \ldots, P_J$ in which the P_j denotes the amount of probability points assigned to brand j and where each respondent allocates 100 probability points (later converted to decimal fractions) over the set of brands in response to their specified prices.

The ANOVA-type model can be illustrated for $k = 2$ (that is, brand 2, relative to the reference brand 1) as:

$$L_{2(1)|i_1 i_2 \ldots i_J} \approx v_0 + v_{i_1} + v_{i_2} + \ldots + v_{i_j} \quad (5)$$

where $L_{2(1)|i_1 i_2 \ldots i_J}$ as in equation 4, v_0 denotes the case in which all prices are at reference levels (coded zero in dummy-variable form), the v_{i_j}'s denote the incremental (decremental) contribution of some nonreference price level i of the jth brand, and $\approx$ denotes approximation by least squares, dummy-variable regression. However, in this case *generalized* least squares regression is entailed, because the original responses $(P_1, P_2, \ldots, P_J)$ on which the conditional logit is based are not independent (namely, their sum equals 100).

In the *Courtyard by Marriott* study, we used the ELASTICON model to estimate self and cross demand/price relationships if the *Courtyard* concept (or another concept, such as Hampton) was implemented and priced at different levels vis-a-vis its competitors. Table 3 shows how share of nights for a new hotel concept (for example, in this case, Hampton) might change from its base level of 18.0 percent to some other share level, as a function of its price vis-a-vis competitors' prices. Changes in its share are shown as a function of its prices and also as a function of new Holiday and older Holiday prices. (Other effects were not statistically significant.)

Computer Choice Simulation

The input to the computer choice simulation included for each respondent a vector of part worths for all the attributes included in the study and a corresponding vector of perceptions of each of a number of competing hotels. At the core of the simulation is a consumer choice rule [for example, first choice (select the hotel with the highest utility) or probability of choice (assign each hotel a probability of choice corresponding to the ratio of its utility to the total utility of all the hotels in the relevant competitive set)]. In our application the unit of measurement was the share of nights, calculated as the share of trips times the number of trips, times the average number of nights per trip.

The simulation was developed to allow management to find the desired configuration of hotel attributes and services which, in turn, was guided by the results of the hybrid conjoint analysis for each target segment. Once the concept profile was input, the simulator calculated total utility for the given concept versus the relevant set of competing hotels. Management could specify whether they wanted to use a first-choice rule or a probability-of-choice rule.

The control case (the share of choices received by Marriott without the new concept) provided another way to validate the results by comparing the share of choices generated by the simulator with the actual market shares of the various hotels. The particular simulator

used in this study also contains a built-in re-sampling procedure (based on the bootstrap method of cross validation) that permits the researcher to obtain empirically based standard errors share of choices through repeated sampling of respondents' part worth and perceptions data.

APPENDIX 2

Comments by Marriott's Senior Management

A. B. Bryan, Jr., Executive Vice-President and General Manager of *Courtyard by Marriott* writes: "In designing the actual product, the research allowed management to focus on the items customers wanted, and we avoided focusing on things important to management, but not important to the consumer. In the design stage, the focus was on creating a small hotel, with a great room, and excellent security, while being a home away from home.

Courtyard success led the way for the development of other customer-driven products, such as the acquisition of Residence Inn, the development of Fairfield Inn (economy segment) and Marriott Suites. These new products have markedly contributed to the growth of Marriott Corporation.

With a good base on consumer research and the success we have had, it has been relatively easy to "sell" research in the division and to provide information for consumer-based decision making by management....

In order to deliver the *Courtyard* product the consumers wanted and at the price they wanted, we had to dramatically change the operating systems and organization structure standard to Marriott hotels....

The organizational structure surrounding *Courtyard* was designed to maximize customer and employee contact and to allow these people who are on the property to worry about one thing — taking care of the guest. All the support functions such as marketing, reservations, food and beverage, and accounting were centralized in a regional office. (We have four regions with each region ultimately running 50-100 *Courtyard* hotels)...

I am convinced that we would not have had such a great product without the help of the study (Of course, I'm biased.)

REFERENCES

BERKSON, JOSEPH 1968, "Application of minimum logit χ^2 estimate to a problem of grizzle with a notation on the problem of 'no interaction'," *Biometrics*, Vol. 24, No. 1 (March), pp. 75-95.

CAROLL, J. DOUGLAS 1969, "Categorical conjoint measurement," paper presented at the Annual Meeting of Mathematical Psychology, University of Michigan (August).

CATTIN, PHILIPPE and WITTINK, DICK R. 1982, "Commercial use of conjoint analysis: A survey," *Journal of Marketing*, Vol. 46, No. 3 (Summer), pp. 44-53.

GOLDBERG, STEPHEN M.; GREEN, PAUL E.; and WIND, YORAM 1984, "Conjoint analysis of price premiums for hotel amenities, *Journal of Business*, Vol. 57, No. 1, Part 2 (January), pp. S111-S132.

GREEN, PAUL E. 1984, "Hybrid conjoint analysis: An expository review," *Journal of Marketing Research*, Vol. 21, No. 2 (May), pp. 155-159.

GREEN, PAUL E. and GOLDBERG, STEPHEN M. 1981, "A Nonmetric version of the hybrid conjoint analysis model," paper presented at the third ORSA/TIMS Market Measurement Conference, New York University (March).

GREEN, PAUL E.; GOLDBERG, STEPHEN M.; and MONTEMAYOR, MILA 1981, "A hybrid utility estimation model for conjoint analysis," *Journal of Marketing*, Vol. 45, No. 1 (Winter), pp. 33-41.

GREEN, PAUL E.; GOLDBERG, STEPHEN M.; and WILEY, JAMES B. 1982, "A cross-validation test of hybrid conjoint models," Proceedings of the 1982 Annual Meeting of the Association for Consumer Research, San Francisco (October).

GREEN, PAUL E. and RAO, VITHALA R. 1971, "Conjoint measurement for quantifying judgmental data," *Journal of Marketing Research*, Vol. 8, No. 3, pp. 355-363.

GREEN, PAUL E. and SRINIVASAN, V. 1978, "Conjoint analysis in consumer research: Issues and outlook," *Journal of Consumer Research*, Vol. 5, No. 2 (September), pp. 101-123.

GREEN, PAUL E. and WIND, JERRY 1973, *Multi-Attribute Decisions in Marketing: A Measurement Approach*, The Dryden Press, Hinsdale, Illinois.

JOHNSON, RICHARD M. 1974, "Trade-off analysis of consumer values," *Journal of Marketing Research*, Vol. 11, No. 2, pp. 121-127.

KRUSKAL, JOSEPH B. 1965, "Analysis of factorial experiments by estimating monotone transformations of the data," *Journal of the Royal Statistical Society*, Series B, Vol. 27, No. 2, pp. 251-263.

MAHAJAN, V.; GREEN, PAUL E.; and GOLDBERG, STEPHEN M. 1982, "A conjoint analysis model for measuring self and cross-price/demand relationships," *Journal of Marketing Research*, Vol. 19, No. 3 (August), pp. 334-342.

SHOCKER, ALLAN D. and SRINIVASAN, V. 1977, "LINMAP (Version II): A FORTRAN IV computer program for analyzing ordinal preference (dominance) judgments via linear programming techniques and for conjoint measurement," *Journal of Marketing Research*, Vol. 14, No. 1, pp. 101-103.

THEIL, HENRI 1969, "A multinomial extension of the linear logit model.," *International Economics Review*, Vol. 10, No. 3 (October), pp. 251-259.

WILKIE, WILLIAM and PESSEMIER, EDGAR A. 1973, "Issues in marketing's use of multiattribute attitude models," *Journal of Marketing Research*, Vol. 10, No. 4 (November), pp. 428-441.

Domino's Pizza:
A Deadly Delivery Problem

MICHAEL KELLY

Fast home delivery has always been a major service plus for Domino's Pizza. But an increasing number of the firm's delivery personnel — many of them young people — are being involved in traffic accidents, some of them fatal. Critics claim that the firm's pioneering pledge, to deliver each pizza within 30 minutes or knock $3 off the price, is driving many to risk their lives.

Speed has always been of the essence for Domino's Pizza. The Michigan company's pioneering promise to home deliver a pizza within 30 minutes of a phone order boosted it from a single pizzeria in 1960 to the second-largest pizza operation in the world, with 5,000 outlets and $2.3 billion in sales last year. But now a growing number of critics are saying that, in Domino's case at least, speed kills.

Last year, according to the company's own records, accidents involving Domino's drivers cost 20 lives, 18 of them during pizza runs. The company would not say how many of the victims were Domino's drivers. Company spokesman Ron Hingst, while hastening to say that "even one death is too many," said that with 230 million pizzas delivered last year, this works out to only about one death per 11.5 million pies. "We're not minimizing the deaths by any means," Hingst said. "But that is what the mathematics come out to."

Domino's critic Joseph A. Kinney finds little comfort in Hingst's statistic. "Great," he said. "Now we know the value of the life of a 17-year-old: 11.5 million pizzas."

Kinney, the director of the Chicago-based National Safe Workplace Institute, an independent research and advocacy group, has come up with his own statistic.

Domino's employs between 70,000 and 80,000 part-time drivers. Assuming that this amounts to the equivalent of 20,000 full-time drivers — four for each of the 5,000 Domino's outlets — Kinney claims that 20 deaths in

Reprinted from *The Boston Globe,* July 19, 1989, pp. 1, 6.

1988 means that Domino's drivers face a death rate between three and six times higher than that in the construction industry and twice as high as that of miners.

"The point is this," Kinney said. "Would parents let their kids drive for Domino's if they knew they were three times more likely to die doing that than they would be working construction?"

Suzanne Boutros can answer that one. Her 17-year-old son was the latest Domino's driver to die, the only one so far this year. Hustling to deliver pizzas in the semirural area west of Indianapolis, Jesse Colson often covered 100 miles a night. His mother and others who knew him say he was proud that he almost always made the delivery within the 30-minute limit and was determined never to get the "King of the Lates" badge allegedly given every week by his franchise to the driver most often late on deliveries.

Colson died on June 3 when the company-owned Toyota pickup he was driving in a delivery run swerved off a wet road and struck a utility pole. Domino's has offered the family about $4,000 in worker's compensation to cover funeral costs, Boutros said. Kinney estimates that the 20 deaths in 1988 cost Domino's about $70,000 in death benefits, and he and other critics argue that Domino's is unconcerned because the cost is so low.

Kinney has written to Thomas Monaghan, founder and 97 percent owner of the company, asking that Domino's pay $500,000 to each accident victim, abandon the 30-minute rule, and hire only drivers 18 or older.

Colson's mother calls Domino's guarantee to deliver each pizza within 30 minutes or knock $3 off the price "a license to speed," and she and family friends blame it in large part for Colson's death. They have started a petition drive asking for federal restrictions on the policy: the petitioners have delivered their first batch of more than 1,200 signatures to the Indianapolis offices of Republican Sen. Richard Lugar.

"They have made me angry and now I'm fighting," Boutros said, "There's nothing they can do to bring my son back and that hurts — there are days I can hardly stand it — but I feel I am doing this for my son. I know I can't

help him, but I figure maybe the reason he died is so someone would stand up to Domino's on this."

Domino's faces criticism and legal action on other fronts as well:

- In Salem, Mass., Charles Dunbar, a 22-year-old motorcycle driver allegedly struck by a Domino's driver in Lynn last July, has sued the company for damages. Dunbar's attorney, Daniel Crane, says his client suffered a compound fracture of the left femur and was unable to work for a year.

- In Indiana, the state Department of Labor is looking into the Colson case to determine whether Domino's policy constitutes a violation of the 1970 Occupational Safety and Health Act under the agency's jurisdiction, said spokesman David Bear.

- In Pittsburgh, attorney Kenneth R. Behrend has filed suit on behalf of Franklin and Mary J. Kranack, who he says suffered neck, back, and arm injuries when their car was broadsided by a driver leaving a Domino's store in July 1985. Kranack alleges that the store manager rushed to the scene of the wreck and yelled, "Let's get this pizza on the road!"

- In addition to unspecified monetary damages, Behrend is seeking to force Domino's to abandon the 30-minute rule, which he calls "a grossly negligent corporate policy." Behrend is also helping other lawyers around the country press cases against the company and is attempting to organize an information network to coordinate the filing of cases in different jurisdictions.

The unusually widespread attacks have Domino's officials somewhat worried. "We recognize that we have a perception problem," said Hingst. "We are taking a lot of heat now."

But the company has not responded to either the Indianapolis petitioners or to Kinney. And it is not considering dropping or revising its delivery policy, said Hingst. "The 30-minute guarantee is very, very important to our customers," he said.

Hingst said the company has always encouraged drivers to take care, has never penalized late drivers and will now place even greater emphasis on safe driving.

On June 21, after Jesse Colson's death, the company sent a letter to its corporate-owned stores and its franchises stating that it is company policy to hire drivers 18 or older. The directive, however, is not binding on the franchisees, and they constitute two-thirds of the Domino's outlets. Kinney charges that "the vast majority" of Domino's drivers are under 18.

Hingst said the company is also urging franchise owners and store managers to promote safe driving and will soon put into effect a new safety course for its drivers.

Domino's executives say the system does not promote fast or reckless driving. They say the speed takes place in the store — not on the road. "We can custom-make a pizza within 10 to 12 minutes," said Hingst. "And our average delivery area is only 1 to 2 miles, so there is enough time to deliver."

Christopher Rogers, who owns Massachusetts Domino's stores in Medford, Arlington, Somerville, and Winchester, said: "We never ask a driver to break the speed limit. We never want them to do anything to make haste on the road."

However, interviews with current and former Domino's employees suggest the company's critics may be right. While Domino's franchisees, managers and executives do not actively encourage reckless driving, the 30-minute rule acts as an inherent encouragement, putting great pressure on the drivers, they said.

Vivek Handi Parde, a 21-year-old University of Virginia student who has worked at Baltimore-area Domino's outlets off and on for three years, said the company's self-vaunted quality of "hustle" is "just a euphemism for doing everything fast, and that includes driving."

Parde, who says he quit two weeks ago in anger over Domino's policies, said he and other drivers "speeded all the time. I would speed at least 80 percent of the time, run stop signs, anything to make those deliveries."

Paul, a 19-year-old driver in Chicago who asked that his last name not be used, said many managers "get uptight when pizzas are running late and start yelling at everyone to hurry up, hurry up."

Lane Tarleton, a franchise consultant for six months of 1987 in Domino's southern regional headquarters, said: "There's a lot of pressure to speed. It's not written, but it's there. A driver goes out with three or four deliveries, and he ends up with a minute to get to the last one and he's two minutes away, he's going to speed, he's going to cut corners."

Parde would like to see the 30-minute rule abolished. "There's no reason 20 people a year should get killed over pizza," he said. "Period."

BayBank Systems, Inc.

CHRISTOPHER H. LOVELOCK

An innovative bank has built is retail strategy around an intensive electronic distribution network. Now its competitors are catching up and management seeks to maintain the advantage. The bank's systems subsidiary is examining the pros and cons of introducing debit cards using several alternative technologies.

"WELCOME TO X-PRESS 24," read the screen. "WE ARE PLEASED TO SERVE YOU 24 HOURS A DAY, 7 DAYS A WEEK." It was a Friday afternoon in February 1990. All over Massachusetts, people were lining up at automated teller machines (ATMs) to make banking transactions. More than half were using one of the ubiquitous green and blue machines of the BayBank X-Press 24 network. At this busiest time of the week, over 900 X-Press 24 transactions were being made very minute.

"PLEASE INSERT YOUR CARD." Robert P. Shay put his BayBank card into the machine on the third floor of the BayBank Systems office building. "WELCOME. PLEASE ENTER YOUR PASSWORD." He punched in four digits and then touched the keys for Fast-cash and Custom Cash in succession. Within seconds, Shay was collecting his usual customized withdrawal of $80. "PLEASE TAKE YOUR CARD AND RECEIPT. THANK YOU. PLEASE USE OUR BAYBANK X-PRESS 24 AGAIN SOON." "That's one thing you can be sure of," he muttered to the machine. "But my real interest right now is finding other things for people to do with this card."

Shay walked back upstairs and strode into the conference room. The group of young men and women who had been working with him on the POS task force looked up expectantly. Shay, Vice President for Research and Development at BayBank Systems, Inc. (BBSI), had formed the task force to explore the possibility of using BayBank ATM cards to make debit purchases at point-of-sale (POS) in retail outlets. "Well folks," he said cheerfully, "It's decision time! Lindsey Lawrence (BBSI's president) told me this morning that she and Don Isaacs (the chairman) want a recommendation by next Thursday on whether or not to proceed with debit POS and, if so, which approach to adopt."

BANKING IN MASSACHUSETTS

Retail banking in Massachusetts was very competitive, especially in Greater Boston, which accounted for two-thirds of the state's 5.8 million population. As the commercial and financial center of New England, Boston had a large concentration of major financial institutions. Bank of Boston, Bank of New England, BayBank, and Shawmut Bank dominated retail banking in Massachusetts. These four, plus Fleet/Norstar (headquartered in Rhode Island), were also the five largest banks in the six-state New England region (comprising Connecticut, Maine, Massachusetts, New Hampshire, Rhode Island, and Vermont) where interstate banking was already permitted. Observers predicted that national interstate banking would be permitted by 1993.

Two large, regional ATM systems served New England. X-Press 24, owned by BayBanks, Inc., had 1,250 machines at 1,000 locations in Massachusetts and a few in Connecticut; Yankee 24, owned by a consortium that included Bank of Boston, Bank of New England, and Shawmut, had 3,700 machines in every New England state but New Hampshire. In Massachusetts, 50% of all checking account holders had ATM cards. But for BayBank customers the figure was a remarkable 96%. Some banks were also members of national and super-regional networks, such as Cirrus (30,000 ATMs in the US, Canada, and two other countries), NYCE (7200 ATMs), and Plus (31,000 ATMs). MAC, a Philadelphia-based super-regional was trying to expand into Massachusetts from New Hampshire.

After enjoying rapid growth during the 1980s, New England banks were entering the '90s with some trepidation. Economic activity had turned down significantly, due to slowdowns in high tech and real estate in particular. But wages remained high, and it was still difficult for banks to hire and retain people with the skills needed for front-line positions in their urban branches.

Banks which had been aggressive lenders on real estate projects now found they had many non-performing loans. Most seriously affected was the Bank of New England (BNE). In January 1990, BNE stunned financial markets with the news that it had incurred an annual loss of $1.11 billion — one of the greatest losses ever recorded in American banking history. Each of the other large banks had sharply increased its loan loss provisions; Bank of Boston had also been forced to take write-downs on third-world debt. However, Fleet/Norstar was in strong financial shape and appeared eager to penetrate the Massachusetts retail market.

BayBanks, Inc.

BayBank Systems was a wholly-owned subsidiary of BayBanks, Inc. ("BayBank"), a bank holding company. BayBank was the parent company of nine banks with a total of 217 branches in Massachusetts and seven in Connecticut. With total assets of some $10 billion, it ranked about 60th in size among all US banks. Within Massachusetts, BayBank's strong retail focus gave it a 30% market share of all retail accounts in the state.

Several of BayBanks' subsidiaries traced their roots back to the mid-19th century. In 1974, when William M. Crozier, Jr. was named chief executive officer, few customers were aware of the linkages between each subsidiary bank. Crozier pushed hard to create an overall unity and identity, adding the word "BayBank" to each subsidiary's name. Thus the Harvard Trust Company became BayBank Harvard Trust. A new logo and the distinctive green and blue color scheme adopted for all BayBank signage created the impression of a large bank operating across much of the state.

BayBank then moved to standardize the services offered so that they could be promoted by a common advertising campaign.

The first step was a new single-statement banking product named "Something Better." Never before had a Massachusetts bank used television to promote a retail banking service. Customers using the product also received a "Something Better" cash card, allowing them to cash personal checks up to $100 a day at any BayBank office in eastern Massachusetts. This card, printed in green and blue on durable cardboard, was the same size as a credit card. Baybank's officers soon realized that "the more you can make your card do, and make the customer believe it does, the more essential you will be to the customer."

Electronic Banking at BayBank

The next task for the "Something Better" card — now made of plastic and bearing a magnetic stripe — came in 1977, when BayBank introduced its first ATMs. Customers could use these machines to make deposits, withdrawals and transfers between accounts, as well as to obtain account balances. To operate an ATM, customers inserted their bank card into the machine and typed in their Personal Identification Number (PIN), a confidential password.

BayBank expanded its ATM network rapidly. In many parts of the US, people resisted using ATMs. BayBank, however, through advertising and employee support, did everything possible to make its customers comfortable with the machines. By 1979, the company was investing heavily in ATMs at a time when no competitors were doing so. In fact, the only other American bank making a major commitment to ATMs was Citibank in New York. Looking back, a BayBank officer observed:

> ATMs were originally seen as a way of reducing costs by getting machines to replace human tellers. But we noticed that customers responded to the convenience of an easy-to-use, all-hours delivery system, and we saw ATMs as a way to differentiate BayBank from its competitors on a marketing basis. We also found that the people who started opening accounts with us were just the type of customers that banks like to get — they were younger, better educated, and had significant future earning potential.

To ensure reliability and reduce the risk of failure, Bay Bank invested millions of dollars in redundant systems. Hot-line phones were located at each ATM site, so that customers could always call a BayBank employee if they were having problems. One of the bywords at the bank was "There's nothing less convenient than a convenience that doesn't work."

The first ATMs were installed "through the wall" in bank branches, so that they could be used by customers outside on the street. Later, ATMs were installed inside the branches, in an area that could be sealed off from the main bank lobby after hours but was accessible from the street through a card-controlled door. BayBank then sought other locations for what it had named its X-Press 24 network, gaining exclusive rights to install its ATMs in terminals at Boston's Logan Airport. By 1981 BayBank had started placing ATMs in freestanding kiosks or in small storefronts, often far removed from the nearest branch. Bob Shay described the rationale:

> The conventional wisdom is that remote ATMs are too expensive to justify. We view it differently. We have put ATMs in locations where a branch might not be justified but where people still want the convenience. "Why not bring cash to the people?" we asked. We felt it would enhance customer convenience, of course, but with strong signage it also had another impact — the impression that BayBanks was everywhere, because the signage was there on the kiosks. It was like having your own billboards in places where no billboards would ever be allowed and has greatly strengthened our regional image.

In 1984, BayBank teamed up with Bank of Bostom to develop an in-store network of cash dispensing machines called Money Supply, which were located in rented space at supermarkets and other retail stores. Unlike X-Press 24, which was restricted to BayBank customers, use of Money Supply machines was open to other banks. The services offered by these machines were limited to cash withdrawals and information on balances. No deposits could be made. Previously, BayBank had begun franchising its X-Press 24 network to several small banks in Massachusetts and New Hampshire which paid a fee for the service.

Earlier, BayBank had joined with nine other banks across the US to found Cirrus, a national ATM network. Each bank enjoyed territorial exclusivity, so that access to Cirrus was denied to BayBank's competitors. Customers could use their bank cards to withdraw funds from any ATM in the network. In 1986, Cirrus was sold to MasterCard International, parent of the MasterCard credit card. The sale agreement allowed the new owner to open membership in Cirrus to all comers.

In late 1986, BayBank joined a second ATM network, the super-regional New York Cash Exchange (NYCE). This move gave its cardholders, who often traveled to New York for business or pleasure, better access to New York area financial institutions than Cirrus alone could do. Later, BayBank became an equity owner of NYCE. Meanwhile, its major competitors had joined together to create their own local ATM network, Yankee 24. Some of them also joined Cirrus or NYCE, thus enabling their customers to use X-Press 24 machines for cash withdrawals, balance information, and transfer of funds between accounts. Cirrus charged the account holder's bank a fee of $0.60 for each transaction, of which $0.50 went to the owner of the ATM terminal, while NYCE charged the account holder's bank $0.54, of which $0.38 went to the ATM owner.

Around this time, management decided that the focal point of BayBank's advertising and positioning efforts should be the card itself, rather than the network. Research showed that people did not identify with the machines as such, but rather with the personalized card that enabled them to use the ATMs. However, "BayBank machine" seemed to have become a generic term to describe any ATM terminal in Massachusetts — much like "Xerox" for photocopy, "Scotch" for adhesive tape, or "Kleenex" for paper tissues. The brand name on the green and blue card was changed from X-Press 24 to BayBank, and the BayBank name was given prominence over the X-Press 24 logo on all ATMs and kiosks.

By 1990, BayBank had a total of 760 ATMs in operation at 530 locations; 380 ATMs were in branches, and 380 in remote locations. The main branch of BayBank Harvard Trust — across the street from Harvard University — boasted 10 ATMs, each of which often recorded more than 25,000 transactions a month, making them among the busiest ATMs in the world.

BayBank now operated one of the country's largest regional ATM networks; it had also pre-empted most of the best sites in Massachusetts. In addition, the bank had 200 in-store machines, primarily in supermarkets. It had bought out Bank of Boston's share in Money Supply and renamed it BayBank X-Press 24 CASH. This system was open to participants in X-Press 24, Yankee 24, Cirrus, and NYCE. BayBank customers paid a $0.50 fee to use X-Press 24 CASH, but no charges were imposed for using the regular X-Press 24 machines unless a customer's average monthly balance fell below a specified amount.

BAYBANK SYSTEMS, INC. (BBSI)

BayBank had originally established BBSI to manage data processing operations. As the ATM network expanded, BayBank's chairman, Mr. Crozier, charged the subsidiary with maintaining and marketing that network. BBSI was also responsible for exploring other ways in which BayBank could use electronic technology to enhance its productivity and add value to its services.

Few BBSI managers had followed a traditional banking career. Its chairman and CEO, Donald L. Isaacs (who was also executive vice president of the holding company), had joined BayBank in 1974 with an MS from the Sloan School of Management at MIT. His early career was spent as a staff assistant to Crozier, working on development of electronic funds transfer systems. He was named president of BBSI in 1981 and CEO three years later. Isaacs described BBSI as being at the "epicenter of the ATM world." More than ten million transactions a month were routed through BBSI's two separate computer centers, making it one of the largest ATM transaction processors in the United States.

BBSI's president, Lindsey C. Lawrence, a mathematician by training, had worked in both marketing and data processing. She had been the architect of the new branch automation system, and was now involved in systems technology and R&D. In her role as chief op-

EXHIBIT 1
BayBank ATM Terminals and Transactions*

YEAR	TOTAL ATMS IN SERVICE (YEAR-END)	AVERAGE MONTHLY TRANSACTIONS (000s)	
		X-Press 24	X-Press 24 CASH**
1978	39	239	—
1979	78	524	—
1980	136	910	—
1981	235	1,490	—
1982	379	2,780	—
1983	490	3,990	—
1984	703	5,200	36
1985	843	5,830	213
1986	891	6,780	345
1987	977	8,010	329
1988	1,143	9,170	635
1989	1,249	9,000	720

*Totals include X-Press 24 ATMs operated under franchise agreements.
**Originally known as Money Supply.

SOURCE: Company records

erating officer, she oversaw all BBSI operations. As BayBank's explosive growth in ATM installations and transactions began to slow from what Lawrence described as "100 miles per hour down to 55"— BBSI intensified its efforts to extend use of the bank's technological resources (*Exhibit 1*). Although management was monitoring Citibank's use of new touchscreen ATMs, which that bank had custom-designed, BayBank had no immediate plans to develop its own proprietary machines. Instead, it used Diebold ATMs, manufactured in Ohio.

Excluding land costs, a freestanding, two-unit kiosk cost about $35,000; buying and installing two full-service ATMs would add another $65,000. Annual operating and servicing costs for such a kiosk were around $30,000. Although 60% of the sites were equipped with just one machine, most kiosks or storefronts were designed so that a second machine could be added when monthly volume exceeded 17,000 transactions. Customers often made several transactions at an ATM; for instance, a deposit, a request for account balances, and a transfer of funds represented three transactions.

Lawrence and Isaacs were particulary interested in developing informational or transactional products for which a fee could be charged. In 1988, BayBank introduced Account Update at its ATMs. This service offered a "mini-statement," printing out the numbers, dates and amounts of the last five checks received for payment, plus the three most recent card transactions and the latest deposit. This service, which cost $0.50, was debited automatically to the customer's checking account. Check Update, introduced in 1989, cost $0.15. Customers keyed in the number of a specific check to determine whether or not it had been received for payment. *Exhibit 2* compares the services available to BayBank customers with those offered by banks participating in the Yankee 24 network.

The two new products also became available by telephone in August 1989 through the bank's new Telephone Banking service. Customers with a touch-tone telephone could call a local phone number and follow computerized voice instructions to press specific keys, including their account number and password (PIN). Telephone banking offered several free services — account balances, fund transfers, and information on BayBank products and interest rates, as well as the fee-for-service Check Update and Account Update.

EXHIBIT 2

Types of Transactions Available to Cardholder at BayBank X-Press 24 and Yankee 24 ATMs

Transactions	BayBank Cardholder at BayBank ATM	NYCE Cardholder at BayBank ATM	Cirrus Cardholder at BayBank ATM	Yankee 24 Cardholder at Yankee 24 ATM*
Cash Withdrawals	X	X	X	X
Fast Cash Withdrawals**	X			
Custom Cash Withdrawals**	X			
Deposits	X			
Deposits with Cash Back	X			
Account Balances	X	X	X	X
Account Transfers	X	X		X
Check Update	X			
Credit Line Cash Advances	X			
Payments	X			

*at ATMs in Massachusetts

**"Fast Cash" speeded the withdrawal process by saving the customer from having to enter the amount of the withdrawal. Instead four options were presented: $20, $50, and $100, and "Custom Cash" (a personalized amount pre-set by the customer and recorded in the X-Press 24 computer).

SOURCE: Company records

By early 1990, the system was handling 150,000 calls a month.

ATMs in other parts of the country sometimes dispensed more than monty. A bank in Portland, Oregon, used its machines to issue monthly bus and rail passes, printed on ATM receipt paper. Other uses for ATMs included selling discount movie tickets, postage stamps, retail gift certificates and grocery coupons. But Shay was concerned that adding such offerings, or even new banking services, might lead to unacceptable levels of queuing at ATMs. Further possibilities included greater use of telephone-based technology for enhanced transactions. With improvements in microchips and liquid crystal displays, BBSI expected that both desk and public telephones would soon be able to display information on small screens. Another direction lay in extending use of the BayBank card.

THE SEARCH FOR NEW SERVICES

Responsibility for examining new applications for BayBank cards fell to Bob Shay in his role of vice president for research and development. Shay was another of BBSI's "nonbankers." He held a PhD in British History from Columbia University and had briefly pursued an academic career. Seeing options in college teaching as limited, he had gone on to take an MBA at the Columbia Business School. After graduation, he joined a consulting firm where one of his assignments involved working on AT&T's early pilots of videotex technology. (Videotex allowed visual display of information transmitted over telephone lines or other communications media.) In 1982, BBSI hired Shay to head a task force to examine videotex possibilities, particularly ones related to home banking.

Home Banking

Home banking involved the delivery of banking services to consumers at the time and place of their choice, using personal computers linked to telephones. It offered such services as bill paying, account information, account transfers, budgeting and record keeping. Potential applications included stock quotes, brokerage, and financial planning. A full service videotex offering also provided services ranging from news and weather to sports and travel information, plus electronic mail, purchase of travel and entertainment tickets, and shopping.

Shay's task force evaluated several joint venture and franchising opportunities, as well as studying proprietary systems developed by Citibank and Chase Manhattan. At one point, BayBank unsuccessfully sought a pilot contract for Chemical Bank's "Pronto" home banking system. But after monitoring market acceptance of home banking and videotex offerings, including Shawmut Bank's poorly received "Arrive" service, the task force concluded that the technology would not win widespread retail acceptance until the mid-1990s.

Card Technology and Applications

Consumers' wallets were filled with a wide variety of cards. Some, such as driver's licenses and student IDs, simply offered visual proof of identification. Increasingly, though, cards were encoded with machine-readable information.

Some encoded cards were like pass keys, offering admission to restricted parking lots or other secured locations. Others served as financial tools. Prepayment cards, for instance, contained a magnetically stored cash value, which decreased each time the card was used to access a service. In Europe and Japan, such cards could be purchased in many locations, with values typically equivalent to $10 or $20. Used for a variety of purposes, they were a popular alternative to cash in public telephones. In the US, use of prepayment cards was limited mostly to rapid transit systems and photocopy machines.

The most common group of cards were credit, charge, and debit cards. Credit cards — such as Visa, MasterCard, Optima, Discover, and Eurocard — allowed the customer an extended time period to pay off the outstanding balance, but a substantial finance charge was levied on this balance after the monthly settlement date. By contrast, the charge cards issued by retailers, oil companies and American Express typically did not always extend credit beyond the due date.

Debit cards provided no credit at all. Each transaction was deducted directly from the customer's account — just as a check would be — leading some people to describe debit cards as "plastic checks". Some users saw them as an alternative to carrying a checkbook or cash. Others, who worried about getting into debt, saw tham as a way to pay by card without facing large, end-of-the-month bills. All ATM cards were debit cards, too, but confined to accessing ATM machines. Now the issue was how to extend their use to other types of transactions.

Credit, charge and debit cards had to be protected against fraudulent use. Security for bank cards involved use of a PIN (or password) chosen by the customer and revealed only to the bank's computer. Customers had to enter their PINs to access their accounts. Security for other cards was provided by checking a master file to ensure that the card was not stolen and that the account was good for the amount charged; vendors also compared the customer's signature on the sales slip with the one on the back of the card. Visa and MasterCard came in both credit and debit forms, and were issued through retail banks. BayBank offered Visa and MasterCard credit cards; they could also be used in ATMs to obtain cash advances, which were charged as a loan against the monthly credit card account.

In the US, all financial cards used a magnetic stripe to record and store information, but there was growing interest in "smart cards," which used microchip technology. These cards, the same size and shape as a traditional credit card, varied in sophistication. *Memory only* smart cards were passive and could store 1–2 kilobytes (KB) of information. More advanced cards offered *memory plus intelligence* and could do limited processing. The imbedded chip contained 2–16KB of EE-prom (electrically erasable-programmable read only memory) and an 8- or 16-bit processor. So-called *SuperSmart cards* added a two-line liquid crystal display (LCD) and a flat keypad. A smart card cost from $4 to $15, as compared with $0.15 or less for a traditional credit card. To handle smart cards, merchants would need to install new POS equipment. Card readers capable of handling both magnetic stripe and smart cards cost at least $800 each.

The French were the earliest to embrace smart card technology and had conducted over 300 test programs for a wide range of applications — including banking and an electronic yellow pages. These services involved as many as two million customers of the publicly owned telephone and postal authority, and were offered free of charge. The Japanese were also testing smart cards. In Canada, smart cards were being used by corporate customers of the Royal Bank of Canada to control access to cash management software at their own sites. In the US, however, there still were no commercial banking tests underway in the marketplace.

Visa planned to issue a SuperSmart card to its Platinum customers in 1993. Features might include a built-in calculator, world time clock, medical data, personal preferences in travel and accommodations, a transaction journal, and manually entered records and memos. In addition to using the card for credit purchases, the user might also be able to employ it for reserving airline seats, trading shares, checking personal bank records, and transferring funds.

The Toshiba-made Visa card could be used off-line to conduct and authorize transactions; it stored a pre-programmed credit limit that was reduced by the appropriate amount each time a purchase was made. The user had to enter a PIN on the card's keypad (which would be internally validated), followed by the purchase amount. The card would then verify that the user was within the credit limit and display an approval code for the purchase amount, which the clerk would enter on a paper credit card slip in traditional fashion. If the purchase were for an amount greater than the existing balance, the card would display "OVER LIMIT." The user could check the card's credit limit and expiration date at any time. The balance could be updated by entering an amount, an expiration date, and a cryptographic code. If several attempts were made to enter an incorrect PIN or code, the card would "lock up" and only the issuer would be able to unlock it.

Lindsey Lawrence was enthusiastic about the potential of SuperSmart cards. She liked them from a systems standpoint because transactions could be approved and processed off line. Since they generated fewer demands on telecommunication links and central host computers, costs could be reduced.

POINT-OF-SALE DEBIT TRANSACTIONS

As Shay and his colleagues reviewed possible applications of the BayBank card, they looked at payment transactions at the retail point of sale (POS). What was the potential for transforming the card into a broad-based debit card? There were an estimated 258 million transactions a month in Massachusetts (*Exhibit 3*); the payment method varied with transaction size (*Exhibit 4*).

Cash was almost universally accepted, and was handled quickly and easily by both customers and cashiers. Disadvantages included risks of error and employee pilferage, plus the costs involved in obtaining, depositing and storing it.

EXHIBIT 3
Point of Sale Payments in Massachusetts, by Medium

Payment Medium	Cash	Check	Credit Card	Other	TOTAL
POS Transactions/ Month (mn)	226	18	12	2	258
Transactions/Month per Adult (units)	56.4	4.6	3.0	0.5	64.5
Average Transaction Value	$8.90	$72.68	$71.77	$20.00	$16.45
Median Transaction Value	$1.90	$28.00	$30.00	—	$2.40
POS Spending/Month per Adult	$502	$331	$218	$10	$1,061

SOURCE: Company records

EXHIBIT 4
Estimated Distribution of POS Transactions in Massachusetts

	DOLLARS SPENT PER MONTH (MN)				TRANSACTIONS PER MONTH (MN)			
Value Range	Cash	Checks	Credit Cards	TOTAL	Cash	Checks	Credit Cards	TOTAL
<$2	$109	$1	$0	$110	117.32	1.19	0.24	118.75
$2-4	$114	$3	$2	$119	38.36	1.00	0.67	40.03
$4-10	$187	$15	$10	$212	29.33	2.18	1.52	33.03
$10-20	$289	$50	$35	$374	20.31	3.37	2.43	26.11
$20-40	$327	$109	$73	$509	11.28	3.65	2.43	17.36
$40-60	$350	$215	$158	$723	5.64	3.37	2.43	11.44
$100-200	$356	$307	$215	$878	2.59	2.18	1.52	6.29
$200-400	$180	$264	$191	$635	0.64	0.91	0.67	2.22
>$400	$95	$361	$186	$642	0.14	0.38	0.24	0.76
TOTAL	$2,007	$1,325	$870	$4,202	225.61	18.24	12.14	255.99

SOURCE: Company records

Checks had several shortcomings as a retail payment method, including slow handling by both customers and cashiers, as well as substantial risk of fraud. When a check "bounced" because of insufficient funds in the account, it was the merchant's problem, not the bank's. The costs to merchants for processing checks were modest, but the costs incurred for verification or file maintenance were often significant. Only about 20% of all checks were written at POS — most of these at supermarkets. The cost to a bank of processing a check averaged about $0.02.

Credit cards were accepted at many locations, although food stores or small merchants were often unwilling or reluctant to take them; some stores required a $10-15 minimum purchase. Paying by credit card could be a slow and cumbersome process. The sales clerk or cashier had to phone for authorization, imprint the paper charge slip with details from the customer's card, write up purchase details, and have the customer sign. One copy of the slip was given to the customer, a second kept for the store, and a third sent to the bank for collection. New card-reading devices that were linked to telephone lines simplified the process, as the cashier simply had to pass the card through the reader and type in the purchase amount. The machine automatically called for authorization and, if approved, promptly printed out a receipt for the customer to sign. As long as transactions were authorized, there was little risk of fraud for the merchant, since the issuing bank was held responsible for extending credit (even on a stolen card). Merchants paid a fee expressed as a discount from the sales price of any transaction. This "merchant's discount" ranged from 1.2% for a large national retailer to as much as 5% for a boutique; the average was about 2.5%.

The Marketplace for Debit POS Transactions

Some observers felt that transactions under $10 were poor candidates for either credit or debit card use. Merchants discouraged card use for small sums because of processing costs and the transaction time involved. Customers showed little interest in using their debit cards for small purchases, except for gasoline, where they and the retailers were both accustomed to card use. Shay believed that the potential for debit card use was limited above $100, on the grounds that purchasers would either need credit or prefer to gain the four to seven weeks' float available from using a credit card with a monthly billing cycle.

For the purpose of examining POS payments, Shay and his associates had divided merchants into three categories: high volume, high value added, and other. High volume merchants included supermarkets, convenience stores, fast food restaurants, and gas stations. They accounted for half of all transactions, but only 35% of dollars, spent at POS. The average transaction was $11.50 and margins were low. Both customers and stores sought to minimize transaction times. Except for gas stations, many high volume merchants preferred to avoid credit cards and, except for supermarkets, most avoided checks as well.

High value added merchants included department stores, specialty retailers, full-service restaurants, travel services, and personal service providers (such as hair salons). With an average sale of $30, they accounted for 55% of the money spent at point of sale and for 30% of transactions. Customer satisfaction and the opportunity to sell additional goods and services during a visit were important for success, since merchants enjoyed sizeable markups on most sales. Most accepted checks and credit cards; many offered their own charge card services, too.

Typical of the third category of merchants were the classic Mom and Pop stores and newsstands. They accounted for an estimated 20% of transactions but only 10% of POS dollars. The average transaction was about $8. Such merchants were usually reluctant to accept checks, and the few that offered sales on credit were likely to use non-credit card arrangements.

Alternative Method of Implementing Debit POS

Direct debit at the point of sale ("Debit POS") allowed customers to use debit cards for their purchases, with real-time authorization of the amount. Payment was automatically debited from the customer's bank account and credited to the merchant's account. All transactions had to be routed through a computer switch, typically operated by an intermediary organization, which went back and forth twice between the two banks to obtain authorization and then arrange settlement. There were three principal mechanisms for settling payments.

On-line Debit POS worked through an ATM network — either a super-regional network like NYCE or, potentially, a regional network such as X-Press 24 or Yankee 24. Customers could use their ATM cards to make purchases. To prevent fraud, customers were asked to enter their PINs on a keypad at the register before payment could be authorized. This online approach enabled transactions to be settled rapidly, with credits and debits being posted overnight to the relevant accounts. To offer this payment mechanism, merchants had to install terminals, purchasing them at $800 each or leasing them for $50 per month, including servicing. Each POS terminal had to be located beside a register. NYCE currently had only one chain of supermarkets participating in debit POS, located in upstate New York. So BayBank would have to lead the way in persuading New England merchants to accept NYCE or X-Press 24 POS debit.

Each debit card transaction involved two banks (the merchant's and the cardholder's), a switching organization, and a third-party processor. Sometimes, of course, both merchant and customer used the same bank. Merchants paid their own bank an average of $0.20 per transaction. In turn, that bank had to pay $0.04 to the switch and $0.12 to a third-party processor. The cardholder's bank received no revenue unless it imposed a "hard charge" for each customer transaction. (Although some bank charges were waived when a customer's average balance exceeded a certain level, hard charges were imposed regardless of balance levels.) The customer's bank also had to pay $0.04 to the switch. In addition, there was an internal processing cost of $0.05 when a transaction was debited against a customer's account.

MasterDebit and Visa Debit used the switches of these two credit card networks. Debit cards were issued by the banks, which could expand the use of their customers' ATM cards by adding the relevant hologram, printed service mark, and a new numbering configuration. Customers had to be prequalified for a line of overdraft protection, known at BayBank as "reserve credit." Purchase authorization took place in real time, using the same procedures as for credit cards, including signature verification (no PINs were involved). But settlement and posting might take one to ten days to complete, depending in part on whether purchases were recorded electronically or on paper drafts. If the merchant already accepted credit cards, no new equipment was needed. The transaction cost ("discount") to merchants was similar to credit cards — averaging around 2% of sales price — but Shay thought that merchants might insist on a lower discount for debit cards if customers started using them widely instead of cash or checks. The discount was collected by the merchant's bank and shared with the bank issuing the card. The latter received an interchange fee averaging 1.3% of the transaction value, but incurred processing and settlement costs totalling about $0.15.

Proprietary Debit POS used cards issued by the merchant. The task force saw little potential for BayBank in this approach. Customers needed a separate card for each merchant, as with department charge cards or supermarket check-cashing cards. Capital costs for the merchant were $125 or more per terminal. The cost per transaction for the merchant was about $0.25. One advantage of this system for merchants was that they could develop profiles of individual cardholders' buying habits and use them for research and marketing purposes. Shaw's, a local supermarket chain, was exploring proprietary debit cards.

Current Status of Debit POS

A number of on-line debit POS pilots and rollouts were already underway in North America, Europe and Australia. The heaviest activity in the United States was in California (which accounted for 62% of all debit POS transactions in the country), as well as in Arizona and Texas. Interlink was one of the most active networks, providing switching for transactions based on ATM cards in Arizona, California, and Nevada. Some ten million customers — representing about 30% of the population of these three states — were eligible to use the service. Interlink boasted 12,500 terminals in 3,000 stores, including grocery stores, gas stations, convenience stores, and fast food restaurants. About five million

transactions were recorded each month by 32 financial institutions. Two major banks reported that 19% of their cardholders had made debit POS transactions.

Lucky Stores, a California-based supermarket chain, was the largest merchant offering on-line debit POS. Lucky had installed a total of 3,000 terminals in 350 stores, advertised the service heavily and promoted it at the checkout counters. It was recording two million debit POS transactions per month. To discourage banks from charging cardholders for such transactions, Lucky posted a list of banks which did and did not impose such charges.

In New England, on-line debit POS activity was limited. Any merchant accepting MasterCard or Visa would, of course, accept the debit versions of these cards. The only bank in the region offering MasterDebit was Fleet/Norstar. Mobil Oil was the only large merchant promoting use of debit POS. It had invested in a nationwide on-line system with terminals in all stations so as to get float faster on its own charge cards. Users of debit cards issued by other institutions would be able to buy gas (petrol) at the cash discount rate, saving four cents per gallon (about one cent per liter) over the rate for credit card purchases. Many banks declined Mobil's invitation to participate, since the firm offered them no fee for processing transactions. Others found that building the necessary interface was too difficult. All systems, right back to the customer's statements, had to be changed. In Massachusetts, only BayBank was willing to build a link to the Mobil data center and create the software interface needed to allow its customers to use their ATM cards as debit cards at Mobil stations.

BayBank went on line with Mobil in May 1987 and promoted the service actively through statement inserts, dollar-off coupons, and posters at Mobil stations. The $65,000 cost was shared with Mobil. Monthly transactions rose steadily to 61,911 in June 1988. (*Exhibit 5*.) In July, BayBank imposed a hard charge of $0.15 charge per transaction. Transactions then fell sharply, stabilizing at around just under 40,000 a month by a total of 15,000 BayBank ATM cardholders.

EXHIBIT 5
BayBank POS Transactions through Mobil Oil Co., 1987-89

	MONTHLY TRANSACTIONS		
Month	*1987*	*1988*	*1989*
January	—	40,521	37,451
February	—	38,604	35,696
March	—	41,285	39,068
April	—	42,062	38,301
May	8,924	46,997	41,439
June	18,645	61,911	40,595
July	30,250	*55,388	38,721
August	40,874	52,244	38,036
September	57,783	41,774	36,756
October	52,764	41,748	38,975
November	41,259	38,949	36,888
December	41,138	39,575	38,367

A charge of $0.15 per transaction was imposed in mid-July 1988 (debited directly from the customer's account).

SOURCE: Company records

DEVELOPING A DEBIT POS PLAN FOR BAYBANK

As Shay reviewed the information that the task force had collected on debit POS, it was clear to him that BayBank faced a wide array of options. The ideal scenario would be one that allowed BayBank to develop a distinctive advantage for its cardholders that was not available to customers of other banks.

An on-line debit POS system switched through X-Press 24 would achieve that purpose, whereas one switched through NYCE would open participation to many of Bay-Bank's competitors. An important issue, regardless of who performed the switching, was to market the concept of on-line debit POS to merchants, so they would be willing to make needed investments in terminals and staff training. It was not clear who would take responsibility for the necessary marketing effort, which could cost $750,000 or more in Massachusetts alone. Systems development costs for BayBank were estimated at $800,000 for the X-Press 24 option and at $600,000 for the Cirrus or NYCE option. Start-up time would be 8-12 months.

With the MasterDebit/Visa Debit option, it would not be necessary for merchants who already accepted MasterCard and Visa credit-cards to make any upfront investment. If Bay-Bank decided to opt for this alternative, Shay favored MasterDebit. It would be relatively simple to add a hologram to the front of the BayBank ATM card. Upfront development costs for this option would be $500,000.

The task force members debated what proportion of ATM cardholders in Massachusetts might use their cards to make debit POS purchases. They also wondered what percentage of present cash, check, and credit card transactions could be converted to debit card purchases. One important determinant would doubless be the pricing policy that BayBank adopted.

BayBank already had one of the most aggressive fee structures for electronic funds transfers (EFT) in New England. It could employ the same approach for POS debits as for checks and ATM transactions. Customers whose average monthly balance fell below a predefined minimum (typically $1,500) paid 35 cents for each check or ATM withdrawal. Historically, about one-seventh of all transactions incurred such a charge. As with Mobil debit purchases, however, a supplementary hard charge could be imposed on each POS debit transaction by any BayBank customer.

Whichever approach was selected, significant planning and expense was involved when debit card capability was added to ATM cards.

If the bank selected the on-line debit POS route, all 750,000 BayBank ATM cardholders would be eligible to use this service. But a vigorous promotional effort, costing an estimated $250,000, would be needed to encourage BayBank customers to make debit card purchases on a regular basis. Since any competing bank could join NYCE, choosing that option would be unlikely to attract new customers to BayBank; indeed Shay believed that BayBank customers would probably account for only half of all debit POS transactions if NYCE were the switch. If X-Press 24 were used as the switch, the outcome might be very different.

If the MasterDebit option were selected, about 50% of BayBank ATM cardholders could be prequalified because of existing credit relationships with the bank. These customers could be targeted by direct mail at a cost of $0.75 each. Many other BayBank account holders could be qualified on application. One opportunity to reach them would be when ATM cards were reissued every two years. The debit card option could also be promoted to noncustomers as one more reason to open an account with BayBank.

Shay estimated the cost of credit screening at $250,000 and account opening at $50,000 during the first two years. A large-scale promotional campaign, using television and newspapers to attract new customers to a BayBank debit card, would cost an estimated $1,975,000 over two years.

AT THE TASK FORCE MEETING

Bob Shay looked around at his team and declared:

Our task this afternoon is to review the numbers that John and Terry have prepared for us on the proportion of all unit and dollar transactions at POS that debit cards might be expected to capture in Massachusetts for the on-line and MasterDebit options. On Tuesday morning, we'll meet again to finalize our recommendations. Don Isaacs and Lindsey Lawrence have scheduled a meeting with Bill Crozier a week from today, and that's when the final decision will be made.

A key issue is whether this is the right time to act, with the New England economy in a downturn and our profits squeezed. If we recommend a "go" decision on one of these options, will that constrain future directions that BayBank might take as a result of new technological developments, the advent of national interstate banking, evolving trends in retailing, or changes in customer needs and preferences? And what opportunities might we miss if we don't act now?

So there's lots to think about. Right now, Terry and John, let's hear your opinions on POS debit's prospects for penetrating the retail transactions market.

ENDNOTE

[1] One byte (B) of information — equivalent to 8 bits — is the amount of memory required to store one printed keyboard character. A magnetic stripe card in 1990 could store 200 B, equivalent to roughly three lines of typewritten text. A 16 KB smart card could store about five pages of single-spaced typescript. Another, laser-based technology, the optical memory cards, could store as much as 2.8 megabytes (MB); but data, once written, could not be erased and the writer/reader terminals need for these cards cost up to $4,000 each.

PART IV
Managing Capacity and Managing Demand

Strategies for Managing Capacity-Constrained Services

CHRISTOPHER H. LOVELOCK

A major problem facing managers of capacity-constrained service organizations is how to balance demand against available capacity. Unlike manufacturing firms, service businesses cannot rely on inventories of finished products to act as a buffer between a constrained level of supply and a fluctuating level of demand. Opportunities may exist to manage both capacity and demand.

Abraham Lincoln, when practising law, once remarked that "A lawyer's time and expertise are his stock in trade." His comment captured the timebound nature of services. Unlike manufacturers, service firms cannot inventory their "stock" for sale at a later date. This characteristic is not an issue when demand levels are relatively stable and predictable. However, it does raise difficulties for managers of capacity-constrained service organizations that face wide swings in demand. The problem is most commonly found among services involving tangible actions to either customers or their physical possessions — such as transportation, lodging, food service, repair and maintenance, entertainment, and health care. But it also affects professional services, especially accounting, that face cyclical shifts in demand, reflecting factors such as tax-year deadlines.

Financial success in all these services is, in large measure, a function of management's ability to use productive capacity — staff, labor, equipment, and facilities — as efficiently and as profitably as possible.

From Excess Demand to Excess Capacity

At any given time, a fixed-capacity service organization may be faced with one of four conditions (see Figure 1):

- There is *excess demand* — the level of demand exceeds maximum available capacity with the result that some customers are denied service and business is lost.
- Demand exceeds the optimum capacity level — no one is turned away, but all customers are

FIGURE 1
Implications of Cyclical Variations in Demand Relative to Capacity

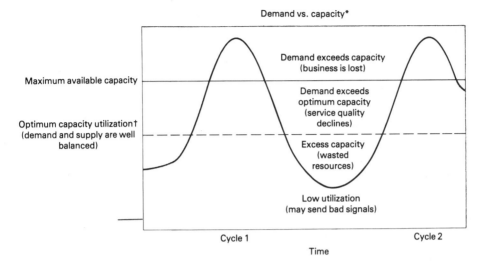

*For simplicity, this diagram assumes no variations over time in the amount of capacity available. In practice, however, some service organizations do seek to manage the level of capacity over the duration of the product-demand cycle. Sometimes, employee illness, labor shortages, and damaged facilites or equipment lead to unplanned reductions in capacity.

†The optimum capacity is that level of utilization above which the perceived quality of service begins to deteriorate due to crowding. In some services, such as theaters and sports arenas, optimum and maximum capacity may be one and the same.

likely to perceive a deterioration in the quality of service delivered.

- Demand and supply are well balanced at the level of optimum capacity.
- There is *excess capacity* — demand is below optimum capacity and productive resources are underutilized; this poses the risk (in some instances) that customers may find the experience disappointing or have doubts about the viability of the service.

Note the distinction between *maximum available* capacity and *optimum* capacity. When demand exceeds maximum capacity, some potential customers may be disappointed because they are turned away — and their business may be lost forever. But when demand is operating between optimum and maximum capacity, there is a risk that all customers being served at that time may receive inferior service and thus become dissatisfied.

Sometimes optimum and maximum capacities are the same. At a live performance in a theater or sports arena, a full house is grand, since it stimulates the players and creates a sense of excitement and audience participation, thereby enhancing the service experience. With other services, customers may feel that they get better service if the facility is not operating at full capacity. The quality of restaurant service, for instance, often deteriorates when every table is occupied, because the staff is rushed and there is a greater likelihood of errors or delays. Passengers traveling alone in aircraft with high density seating usually feel more comfortable if the seat adjacent to them is empty. When repair and maintenance shops are fully scheduled, delays may result if there is no slack in the system to allow for coping with unexpected difficulties in completing particular jobs. Hence, smoothing demand to the optimal level may be a desirable goal even for service organizations that rarely encounter demand in excess of maximum available capacity.

There are two basic solutions to the problem of fluctuating demand. One is to tailor *capacity* to meet variations in demand. This approach, which falls within the province of operations and human resource management, requires an understanding of what constitutes productive capacity and how it is constrained. The second is to manage the level of *demand,* using marketing strategies to smooth out the peaks and fill in the valleys to generate a more consistent flow of requests for service.

MANAGING CAPACITY

The productive capacity of a service organization takes several forms. One concerns *physical facilities* that hold people or things — hotels, medical clinics, supermarket shelves, or railroad freight wagons. A second form of productive capacity concerns *equipment* — such as telephones, hair dryers, machine tools, airport metal detectors, ovens, and cash registers. *Labor* is the third type of productive capacity and the output of service workers may be physical or mental in nature (or both).

Many services, such as health care or repair and maintenance, consist of multiple actions delivered sequentially. Flowcharting is an excellent tool for clarifying the elements in this sequence and for identifying points at which capacity bottlenecks may occur. A single piece of equipment with limited capacity or a workstation staffed by too few employees may represent a bottleneck in the process, backing up the flow and setting an upper limit to the volume and quality of service that can be delivered in a given time by an entire service operation.

Measures of capacity utilization include: the number of hours (or percentage of total time) that facilities, labor and equipment are productively employed in revenue operation, and the percentage of the physical space (for example, seats or cubic freight capacity) actually utilized in revenue operations. Labor is typically more variable than physical elements in its ability to sustain certain levels of output over time. A tired or poorly trained employee staffing one station in an assembly-line service operation such as a cafeteria restaurant can slow the entire service to a crawl.

In a well-designed, well-managed service operation, the capacity of the facility, supporting equipment, and service personnel will be in balance. Similarly, sequential operations will be designed to minimize the risk of bottlenecks at any point in the process. However, this ideal may prove difficult to achieve. Not only does the level of demand vary over time, often randomly, but the time and effort required to process each person or thing may vary widely at any point in the process.

The time required to process customers is more variable than for processing physical objects, reflecting lack of preparedness ("I've lost my credit card"), argumentative versus cooperative personalities ("If you won't give me a table with a view, I'll have to ask for your supervisor"), and so forth. But service tasks are not necessarily homogeneous. In both professional services and repair jobs, diagnosis and treatment times vary according to the nature of the problems presented by customers.

Tailoring the Level of Capacity

Some capacity is *elastic* in its ability to absorb extra demand. A subway car, for instance, may offer 40 seats and allow standing room for another 60 passengers with adequate handrail and floor space for all. Yet at rush hours, when there have been delays on the line, perhaps 200 standees can be accommodated under sardinelike conditions. In certain instances, service personnel may be able to work at higher levels of efficiency for short periods of time, although they would quickly tire and begin providing inferior service if they had to work fast all day long. Where capacity appears fixed, such as being related to seating, there may still be the option of adding extra seats at busy times. Some airlines, for instance, increase the capacity of their aircraft by slightly reducing legroom throughout the cabin and cramming in another couple of rows. Similarly a restaurant may add extra tables and chairs. Upper limits to such practices are often set by safety standards and the capacity of supporting services (such as the kitchen).

Another strategy for stretching capacity within a given time frame is to utilize the facilities for longer periods — for instance, flying aircraft 15 hours a day instead of 12. Alternatively, the average amount of time that customers (or their possessions) spend in process may be reduced. Sometimes this is achieved by minimizing slack time, as when the check is presented promptly to a group of diners relaxing at the table after a meal. In other instances, it may be achieved by cutting back the level of service — say, offering a simpler menu at busy times of day.

Beyond these "elastic" strategies there is the option of tailoring the overall level of capacity to match variations in demand; a strategy known as "chase demand." For example, during peak periods management can add part-time staff and rent extra facilities. During periods of low demand, capacity can be reduced by laying off staff and scheduling employee vacations, renting out surplus equipment and facilities, or taking these elements out of service for maintenance and renovation.

In short, there are several actions that managers can take to adjust capacity to match fluctuating levels of demand:[1]

1. *Schedule downtime during periods of low demand.* To ensure that 100 percent of capacity is available during peak periods, preventive repair and maintenance activities should be conducted when demand is expected to be low. Employee vacations and training programs should also be arranged during such periods.

2. *Using part-time employees.* Many service businesses hire extra workers during their busiest periods. Examples include postal workers and store clerks at Christmastime, extra lifeguards during summer weekends, and additional hotel employees during vacation periods.

3. *Renting or sharing extra facilities and equipment.* To avoid overinvestment in fixed assets, a service organization may be able to rent extra space or machines at peak times. Sometimes service firms with complementary demand patterns enter into formal sharing agreements.

4. *Cross-training of employees.* Even when the service delivery system appears to be operating at full capacity, certain elements — and their attendant employees — may be underutilized. If employees can be cross-trained to perform a variety of tasks, they can be shifted to bottleneck points as needed, thereby increasing total system capacity. In supermarkets, for instance, the manager may call upon stockers to operate cash registers when checkout lines start to get too long. Likewise, during slow periods, the cashiers may be asked to help stock shelves. An effective service manager keeps a watchful eye on the service flow and should be prepared to reassign workers or even lend a hand personally if bottlenecks occur.

Whether a service organization pursues a strategy of level capacity or elects to chase demand, its managers need to understand and forecast the forces determining demand. They should also seek to identify opportunities for smoothing the peaks and valleys through active management of demand.

UNDERSTANDING THE PATTERNS AND DETERMINANTS OF DEMAND

The search for demand management strategies starts with an understanding of what factors govern demand for a specific service at a given point in time. Managers should address the following questions:

1. Does the level of demand for the service follow a regular and *predictable* cycle? If so, is the duration of that cycle
   - One day (varies by hour)
   - One week (varies by day)
   - One month (varies by day or by week)
   - One year (varies by month or by season; or reflects annually occurring public holidays)
   - Some other period

2. What are the underlying causes of these cyclical demand variations?
   - Employment schedules
   - Billing and tax payment/refund cycles
   - Wage and salary payment dates
   - School hours and vacations
   - Seasonal changes in climate
   - Occurrence of public or religious holidays
   - Natural cycles, such as coastal tides

3. If changes in the level of demand are largely random in nature, and not easily predicted, what are the underlying causes?
   - Day-to-day changes in the weather affecting relative use of indoor and outdoor recreational or entertainment services.
   - Health events whose occurrence cannot be pin-pointed exactly (for example, heart at-

---

[1]Based on material in James A. Fitzsimmons and Robert S. Sullivan, *Service Operations Management* (New York: McGraw-HIll, 1982) and in W. Earl Sasser, Jr., "Match Supply and Demand in Service Industries," *Harvard Business Review* (November–December 1976).

tacks and births affecting the demand for hospital services).

- Calls for assistance resulting from accidents, acts of God, and certain criminal activities requiring fast response by emergency services.

4. Can demand for a particular service over time be disaggregated by market segment to reflect such components as

   - Use patterns by a particular type of customer or for a particular purpose?
   - Variations in the net profitability of each completed transaction?

Most periodic cycles influencing demand for a particular service vary in length from one day to 12 months. In many instances, multiple cycles may operate simultaneously. For example, demand levels for public transport may vary by time of day, day of week, and season of year. The demand for service during the peak period on a Monday in summer may be different from the level during the peak period on a Saturday in winter, reflecting day-of-week and seasonal variations jointly.

Disaggregating Demand by Market Segment

Can marketing efforts smooth out *random* fluctuations in demand? The answer is generally no, since these fluctuations are usually caused by factors beyond the service organization's control. But detailed market analysis may sometimes reveal that a predictable demand cycle for one segment is concealed within a broader, seemingly random pattern. For instance, a repair and maintenance shop may know that a certain proportion of its work consists of regularly scheduled contractual business, representing preventive maintenance. The balance may come from "walk-in" business and emergency repairs, and it may be hard to predict or control the timing and volume of such work.

The ease with which total demand can be disaggregated depends on the nature of the records kept by the service organization. If each customer transaction is recorded separately, and backed up by detailed notes (as in a hospital visit or accountant's audit) then the task of understanding demand is greatly simplified. In subscription services, where each

customer's identity is known and itemized monthly bills are sent, managers can gain some immediate insights into usage patterns. Some services — such as telephone — even have the ability to track subscriber consumption patterns by time of day. Although these data may not always yield specific information on the purpose for which the service is being used, it is often possible to make informed judgments about the volume of sales generated by different user groups.

Analysis may also show that part of the demand for a particular service is undesirable — for instance, calls to emergency services to rescue cats from trees. Discouraging undesirable demand through marketing campaigns or screening procedures will not, of course, eliminate random fluctuations in the remaining demand. But it may bring the peaks of that demand within the service capacity of the organization.

No strategy for smoothing demand is likely to succeed unless it is based on an understanding of *why* customers from a specific market segment choose to use the service when they do. For example, most hotels find it difficult to convince business travelers to remain on Saturday nights since few executives do business over the weekend. Instead, hotel managers should consider promoting use of their facilities for other purposes at weekends, such as conferences or pleasure travel. Similarly, attempts to get commuters on public transport to shift their travel to off-peak periods will probably fail, since the timing of most commute travel is determined by people's employment hours. Instead, marketing efforts should be directed at employers to persuade them to adopt flextime or staggered working hours.

STRATEGIES FOR MANAGING DEMAND

Optimizing the use of capacity requires looking at the *mix* of business obtained as well as at the total volume. Some market segments may be more desirable than others because the customers fit particularly well with the organization's mission, reinforce the ambience that the service organization is trying to create, have needs that match the professional skills and interests of staff members, or pay higher rates and are more profitable. Marketing managers should examine the components of overall demand and seek to stimulate or discourage demand from particular segments on a selective basis.

Five common approaches to managing demand exist. The first involves taking no action and *leaving demand to find its own levels.* This approach has the virtue of simplicity: eventually customers may learn from experience or word of mouth when they can expect to stand in line to use the service and when it will be available without delay. The second and third strategies involve *shaping demand:* taking active steps to reduce demand in peak periods and to increase it when demand is low, respectively. The fourth and fifth approaches involve *inventorying demand.* This objective can be accomplished either by introducing a reservations system or by adopting a formalized queuing system (or by a combination of the two).

Table 1 links these five approaches to three alternative demand/capacity situations and offers a strategic commentary on each of the 15 resulting cells. To achieve the best results over the duration of the demand cycle, service organizations should consider using a combination of two or more of the options described.

All the elements of the marketing mix have a role to play in stimulating demand during periods of excess capacity and in decreasing it (demarketing) during periods of insufficient capacity. Price is often the first variable to be proposed for bringing demand and supply into balance, but product changes in distribution strategy, and communication efforts can also play an important role. Although each element is discussed separately below, effective demand management efforts often require changes in two or more elements jointly.

Product Variations

Offering a different type of service is sometimes the only way to attract customers to a service facility when demand for the original service is seasonally based. A rather obvious example is provided by the respective problems of a ski manufacturer and a ski slope operator during the summer. The former can either produce for inventory or try to sell skis in the summer at a discount. If the skis are sufficiently discounted, some customers will buy before the ski season in order to save money. However, no skiers would buy ski lift tickets for use on a midsummer day at *any* price. To encourage summer use of the lifts, the operator has to change the product by installing an alpine slide or by promoting the view at the summit. Solutions of a similar nature have been adopted by tax preparation firms that now offer bookkeeping and consulting services to small businesses in slack months, and by landscaping firms in many parts of the United States and Canada that seek snow removal contracts in the winter. These firms recognize that no amount of price discounting is likely to develop business out of season.

Many service offerings remain unchanged throughout the year, but others undergo significant modifications according to the season. Hospitals, for example, tend to offer the same array of services throughout the year. By contrast, resort hotels sharply alter the mix and focus of their peripheral services such as dining, entertainment, and sports to reflect customer preferences in different seasons.

There can be variations in the product offering even during the course of a 24-hour period. Restaurants provide a good example, marking the passage of the hours with changing menus and levels of service, variations in lighting, changes of decor and even employee uniforms, opening and closing of the bar, and the presence or absence of entertainment. The goal is to appeal to different needs within the same group of customers, to reach out to different customer segments, or to do both, according to the time of day.

Modifying the Timing and Location of Delivery

Rather than seeking to modify demand for a service that continues to be offered at the same time in the same place, some firms respond to market needs by modifying the time and place of delivery.

TABLE 1
Alternative Demand Management Strategies for Different Capacity Situations

APPROACH USED TO MANAGE DEMAND	CAPACITY SITUATION RELATIVE TO DEMAND		
	Insufficient Capacity (Excess Demand)	*Sufficient Capacity** (Satisfactory Demand)	*Excess Capacity* (Insufficient Demand)
Take no action	Unorganized queuing results. (May irritate customers and discourage future use.)	Capacity is fully utilized (But is this the most profitable mix of business?)	Capacity is wasted. (Customers may have a disappointing experience for services like theater.)
Reduce demand	Pricing higher will increase profits. Communication can be employed to encourage usage in other time slots. (Can this effort be focused on less profitable/desirable segments?)	Take no action (but see above).	Take no action (but see above).
Increase demand	Take no action, unless opportunities exist to stimulate (and give priority to) more profitable segments.	Take no action, unless opportunities exist to stimulate (and give priority to) more profitable segments.	Price lower selectively (try to avoid cannibalizing existing business; ensure all relevant costs are covered). Use communications and variation in products/distribution (but recognize extra costs, if any, and make sure appropriate trade-offs are made between profitability and usage levels).
Inventory demand by reservation system	Consider priority system for most desirable segments. Make other customers shift (a) to outside peak period or (b) to future peak.	Try to ensure most profitable mix of business.	Clarify that space is available and that no reservations are needed.
Inventory demand by formalized queuing.	Consider override for most desirable segments. Seek to keep waiting customers occupied and comfortable. Try to predict wait period accurately.	Try to avoid bottleneck delays.	Not applicable.

*"Sufficient capacity" may be defined as *maximum available capacity* or *optimum capacity,* depending on the situation.

Three basic options are available. The first represents a strategy of no change: regardless of the level of demand, the service continues to be offered in the same location at the same times. By contrast, a second strategy involves varying the times when the service is available to reflect changes in customer preference by day of week, by season, and so forth. Theaters often offer matinees at weekends when people have leisure time throughout the day; during the summer in hot climates, banks may close for two hours at midday while people take a siesta, but remain open later in the evening when other commercial establishments are still active.

A third strategy involves offering the service to customers at a new location. One approach is to operate mobile units that take the service to customers, rather than requiring them to visit fixed-site service locations. Traveling libraries and vans equipped with primary care medical facilities are two examples that might be copied by other service businesses. A cleaning and repair firm that wishes to generate business during low demand periods might offer free pickup and delivery of portable items that need servicing.

Alternatively, service firms whose productive assets are mobile may choose to follow the market when that, too, is mobile. For instance, some car rental firms establish seasonal branch offices in resort communities. In these new locations, they often change the schedule of service hours (as well as certain product features) to conform with local needs and preferences.

Pricing Strategies

For price to be effective as a demand management tool, the marketing manager must have some sense of the shape and slope of a product's demand curve (that is, how the quantity of service demanded responds to increases or decreases in the price per unit) *at any one particular time*. It's important to determine whether the aggregate demand curve for a specific service varies sharply from one time period to another. If so, significantly different pricing schemes may be needed to fill capacity in each time period. To complicate matters further, there may be separate demand curves for different segments *within* each time period, reflecting variations between segments in the need for the service or ability to pay.

One of the most difficult tasks is to determine the nature of all these different demand curves. Research, trial and error, and analysis of parallel situations in other locations or in comparable services are all ways of obtaining an understanding of the situation.

Many service businesses explicitly recognize the existence of different demand curves for different segments during the same time period by establishing distinct classes of service, each priced at levels appropriate to the demand curve of a particular segment. In essence, each segment receives a variation of the basic product, with value being added to the core service in order to appeal to the higher paying segments. For instance, top-of-the-line service in airlines offers travelers larger seats, more personalized service from flight attendants, free drinks, and better food; in computer service bureaus, product enhancement takes the form of faster turn-around and more specialized analytical procedures and reports.

In each case, the objective is to maximize the revenues received from each segment. However, when capacity is constrained, the goal in a profit-seeking business should be to ensure that as much capacity as possible is utilized by the most profitable segments. For this reason, various usage conditions may have to be set to discourage customers willing to pay top-of-the-line prices from trading down to less expensive versions of the product. Airlines, for instance, may insist that excursion tickets be purchased 21 days in advance and that ticket holders remain at their destinations for at least one week before returning — conditions that are too constraining for most business travelers. We will return to pricing issues in a later segment on yield management.

Communication Efforts

Even if the other variables of the marketing mix remain unchanged, communication efforts alone may be able to help smooth demand. Signing, advertising, and sales messages can remind prospective customers of the peak periods and encourage them to travel at uncrowded, off-peak times when service is, perhaps, faster or more comfortable. Examples include postal service requests to "Mail Early for Christmas," public transport messages urging noncommuters — such as shoppers or tourists — to avoid the crush conditions of the commute hours, and communications from sales reps for industrial maintenance firms advising customers of periods when preventive work can be done quickly. In addition, management can ask service personnel (or intermediaries such as travel agents) to encourage customers with discretionary schedules to favor off-peak periods.

Changes in pricing, product characteristics, and distribution must be communicated clearly. If the firm wants to obtain a specific response to variations in marketing mix elements it must, of course, inform customers fully about their options.

Short-term promotions, combining both pricing and communication elements as well as other incentives, may provide customers with attractive incentives to shift the timing of service usage.[2]

INVENTORYING DEMAND THROUGH QUEUING AND RESERVATIONS

What is a manager to do when the possibilities for shaping demand have been exhausted and yet supply and demand are still out of balance? Taking no action at all and leaving customers to sort things out for themselves is no recipe for service quality and customer satisfaction. Instead, the search must turn to strategies for ensuring order, predictability, and fairness in place of a random free-for-all. Although service businesses can rarely inventory supply, they can often inventory demand.[3] This task can be achieved in one of two ways: by asking customers to wait in line (queuing), or by offering them the opportunity of reserving space in advance.

Queuing

In fast-moving modern societies, customers increasingly demand fast service — and are unhappy when they don't get it.[4] Unfortunately, waiting in line is sometimes inevitable. But careful design and management of queuing systems has important implications for the

perceived quality of the service experience and the speed of service delivery.[5] Operational approaches to queue management often focus purely on logistical issues without taking human ones into account. When queuing involves people rather than inanimate objects waiting to be serviced, then a marketing approach to queuing is needed. What is the maximum amount of time that customers will wait for service? How can we find ways to make this time pass quickly and pleasantly?

Strategies for accomplishing this latter goal include providing agreeable surroundings (for example, a comfortable temperature, a seat, and restful music), taking preliminary information from customers while they are waiting for service (rather than making them wait in a separate line to give this information before moving on to another line), offering advance information on service features, promoting other products offered by the organization, or delivering supplementary services (for instance, entertainment, reading materials, or food and drink).[6]

Not all queuing systems work on a first-come, first-served basis. Market segmentation is sometimes used to design queuing strategies that set different priorities for different types of customers. A higher priority or allocation to a separate queuing area may be based on the importance of the customer (or urgency of the job — as in medical care), how long it will take to provide service (with "express lanes" for shorter jobs), or faster service in return for a premium price (separate check-ins for first class and economy-class passengers).

Reservations

Ask someone what services come to mind when you talk about reservations and most likely they will cite airlines, hotels, restaurants and car rentals. Suggest a synonym like

---

[2]See Christopher H. Lovelock and John A. Quelch, "Consumer Promotions in Services Marketing," *Business Horizons*, May–June 1983. Also, Christopher H. Lovelock, *Services Marketing*, 2nd edition (Englewood Cliffs, NJ: Prentice Hall, 1991), Chapter 9, 247–59.

[3]Inventorying the supply of a service is usually only possible for repair and maintenance services directed at homogeneous, interchangeable goods. For instance, an industrial service shop may handle large numbers of identical electrical motors. Regular customers who bring in such a motor for repair can be given a substitute motor, already serviced and sitting on the shelf, then billed subsequently for the work on their own motor, which will be offered later to another customer bringing in a similar piece of equipment at some future time.

[4]Leonard L. Berry and Linda R. Cooper, "Competing with Time-Saving Service" (page 169 in this book).

[5]See David H. Maister, "The Psychology of Waiting Lines," in J. A. Czepiel, M. R. Solomon, and C. F. Surprenant, eds., *The Service Encounter* (Lexington, MA: Lexington Books — D. C. Heath, 1985).

[6]For further ideas, see K. L. Katz, B. M. Larson, and Richard C. Larson, "Prescription for the Waiting in Line Blues: Entertain, Enlighten, and Engage." *Sloan Management Review* (page 176 in this book).

"bookings" and they may add theaters, sports events, haircuts, and doctors' appointments. In each case, a reservation is supposed to guarantee that the service will be available when the customer wants it. Reservation systems may vary from a simple appointment book for a doctor's office, using handwritten entries, to a central, computerized data bank for an airline's worldwide operations.

When goods require servicing, their owners may not wish to be parted from them for long. Households with only one car, for example, or factories with a vital piece of equipment, often cannot afford to be without such items for more than a day or two. So a reservations system may be necessary for service businesses in fields such as repair and maintenance. By requiring reservations for routine maintenance, management can keep time free for handling emergency jobs at premium prices which yield a much higher contribution margin.

Taking reservations serves to presell the service. In theory, it benefits customers by avoiding the need for queuing and guaranteeing service availability at a specific time, thus helping the service firm balance capacity. Demand can be deflected from a first-choice time to earlier or later times, and even from first-choice locations to alternative locations. However, problems arise when customers fail to show or when service firms overbook. Marketing strategies for dealing with these operational problems include: requiring an advance fee for all reservations (not always feasible); canceling nonpaid reservations after a certain time; and providing compensation to victims of overbooking.

YIELD MANAGEMENT

When demand is low relative to capacity, then any business might seem welcome, but when demand exceeds capacity, then some business will have to be turned away or put on a waiting list. In the latter instance, a key question for service managers is to decide which business to accept and which to defer (or even reject).

Most capacity-constrained organizations have a high fixed-to-variable-cost ratio, re-

flecting the presence of expensive physical facilities and equipment plus a pool of full-time personnel. In effect customers "rent" the use of service facilities and personnel. Assuming for the moment that the costs associated with serving different segments remain constant, then the higher the price and the greater the volume of usage, the greater the profits. However, different customer segments vary in their ability and willingness to pay for use of these services and also in their potential to use the full breadth of services offered on a single occasion. To complicate matters further, the volume of demand from a specific segment and even the price sensitivity of that segment may vary sharply over time.

Many service organizations use percentage of capacity sold as a measure of operational efficiency. For instance, transport services talk of the "load factor" achieved, hotels of their "occupancy rate," and hospitals of their "census." Similarly, professional firms can calculate what proportion of a partner's or an employee's time is classified as billable hours, and repair shops can look at utilization of both equipment and labor. By themselves, however, these percentage figures tell us little of the relative profitability of the business attracted, since high utilization rates may be obtained at the expense of heavy discounting — or even outright giveaways.

More and more, service firms are looking at the *yield* per unit of capacity — that is, the average revenue received. The goal is to maximize this yield in order to improve profitability. Strategies designed to achieve this goal are collectively known as yield management and are widely used in such industries as passenger airlines, hotels, and car rentals.[7] One limitation of the concept of yield management is that it focuses on revenues and often assumes that costs are fixed; a second weakness is that the yield measure is a relative one — unlike capacity utilization, which provides a more absolute target to shoot for.

---

[7]For a detailed description, see Sheryl E. Kimes, "Yield Management: A Tool for Capacity-Constrained Service Firms," *Journal of Operations Management* 8, (October 1989), 348–63. (Page 188 in this book.)

Asset Revenue Generating Efficiency

What is needed is a measure of the extent to which the organization's assets are achieving their full revenue-generating potential. This must take into account the relationship between the average price actually obtained per unit of service and the maximum price that might potentially have been charged for that same service unit — what we'll call the yield percentage. By multiplying the capacity utilization rate by the yield percentage, we can derive an index of *asset revenue-generating efficiency* (ARGE). Consider, for example, a 400-room hotel where all rooms carry a maximum posted price of $100. If only 60 percent of rooms is occupied one night, with 120 rooms being sold at $100 and another 120 at the discounted price of $60, then the yield percentage is 80 percent and the ARGE is (0.6 × 0.8) = 48 percent. Another way to arrive at the ARGE is to divide total revenues received ($19,200) by the theoretical maximum revenues that could have been obtained by selling all rooms at the highest unit price ($40,000).

Improving Advance Sales Decisions

The value of the ARGE approach to performance measurement is that it forces explicit recognition of the opportunity cost of accepting business from one segment when another might subsequently yield a higher rate. Consider the following problems facing sales managers for different types of capacity-constrained service organizations:

- Should a hotel accept an advance booking from a tour group of 200 room nights at $80 each when these same room nights might possibly be sold later at short notice to business travelers at the full rack rate of $140?

- Should a railroad with 30 empty freight cars at its disposal accept an immediate request for a shipment worth $300 per car or hold the cars idle for a few more days in the hope of getting a priority shipment that would be twice as valuable?

- How many seats on a particular flight should an airline sell in advance to tour groups and passengers traveling at special excursion rates?

- Should an industrial repair and maintenance shop reserve a certain proportion of productive capacity each day for emergency repair jobs that

offer a high contribution margin and the potential to build long-term customer loyalty, or should it simply follow a strategy of making sure that there are sufficient jobs, mostly involving routine maintenance, to keep its employees fully occupied?

- Should a computer service bureau process all jobs on a first-come, first-served basis, with a guaranteed delivery time for each job, or should it charge a premium rate for "rush" work, and tell customers with "standard" jobs to expect some variability in completion dates? Good market information supported by good marketing sense is the key to making appropriate decisions in such instances. The decision to accept or reject business should represent a realistic estimate of the probabilities of obtaining higher rated business, together with a recognition of any damage to customer relations that might result from rejecting low-rated business.

Based upon past experience and an understanding of current market conditions, prices can be set that reflect the demand curves of different market segments. At the same time, "selective sell" targets can be assigned to advertising and sales personnel, reflecting how management expects to allocate available capacity among different market segments at a *specific time.* (See Figure 2 for an example from a hotel that sets different sales targets by both day of the week and by season.) These allocation decisions by segment also constitute vital information for reservations personnel, indicating when to stop accepting reservations from certain segments. To simplify the task, customers from different segments can be assigned different phone numbers or mailing addresses for making reservations.

Service organizations often offer different *classes* of a particular service, with the premium version containing added value elements such as more comfort, more speed, and extra amenities. Sometimes it's possible to change the mix of capacity assigned to different classes of service. In effect the product mix is changed over time in order to better meet the needs of a changing customer mix. Marketers of multiclass services need to develop a framework for establishing pricing policy and capacity allocation decisions by both service class and time period.

FIGURE 2
Setting Capacity Allocation Sales Targets over Time

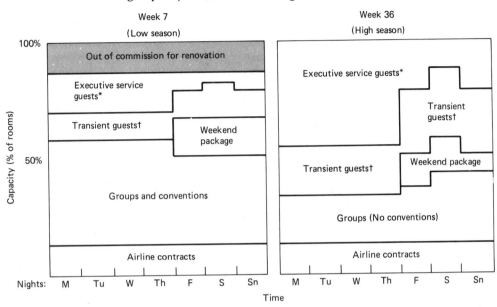

*Employees of corporations called upon by sales force (pay full price and book rooms through special reservations line

†Individual customers paying full price but reserving rooms via publicized telephone number or by just "walking in

Figure 3 shows an example in which 3 service classes — top-of-the-line, standard, and budget — have been combined with 4 time periods to form a matrix of 12 cells, each of which may require a distinctive marketing approach. The size of each cell reflects the percentage of total capacity allocated to it. Clearly, accurate demand forecasting and understanding of customer behavior are important to this assignment process. Fine tuning can be achieved by monitoring results and changing capacity allocations, prices, and other marketing actions for future demand cycles.

Cost Analysis

Managers attempting to maximize the contribution to profits generated by each asset unit cannot assume that the associated costs will remain unchanged. In practice, these costs often vary. Average costs per seat mile for an airline, for instance, vary with distance; such costs tend to decline with longer-stage flights where aircraft can cruise economically

for many hours at high altitudes without incurring the expenses associated with frequent take-offs, landings, and terminal handling fees.

Meeting profitability goals requires identification of the variable cost per sales unit, such as a seat, a room, or a specific repair task. This cost is likely to vary by service class when extra value is added by providing extra service — such as more floor space, more personal attention, or use of superior equipment. In some instances, however, as in theaters with identical seat sizes, the extra value to customers is created by better locations, and no extra costs are incurred by the marketer unless additional benefits are offered involving further expenses for the theater.

A decision must then be made on how to allocate fixed costs among the different cells (as exemplified in Figure 3). When the marketer would like to price close to variable cost in order to stimulate off-peak demand for budget-class service, it may be appropriate to allocate no fixed costs to that cell at all. (How-

FIGURE 3

Developing a Pricing Matrix: Allocating Capacity over Time by Service Class

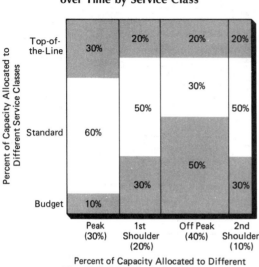

Percent of Capacity Allocated to Different Time Periods Within the Product Demand Cycle

Transportation operations pose a particular problem in that their productive assets are mobile. Airlines, for instance, dispatch aircraft of different seating capacity on a wide variety of routes both domestically and internationally. The task of yield management involves not only thinking of the number and price sensitivity of passenger segments wishing to travel on a given schedule on a particular route, but also comparing alternative allocations of aircraft between routes. Assigning a jumbo jet such as a Boeing 747 or an Airbus A-310 to one route may mean that a smaller aircraft will have to be flown on another route at that time.

Hence the relevant unit of analysis is the number of seats, vehicles, or cubic feet of carrying space available at a particular location on a given day. A decision by an airline, trucking firm, railroad, or shipping company to accept a one-way load of freight for a non-scheduled service must be evaluated not only on the basis of the relative attractiveness of that load, but also with reference to the opportunities for obtaining a profitable backhaul; the effect of taking that return load on the firm's ability to attract and hold particular classes of customers should also be evaluated.

Some of these tasks may sould like the responsibility of operations, and traditionally they have been, often with limited regard for the relative profitability of accepting different mixes of business. Hence the need for injecting a strong marketing orientation and for developing a balance between operational and marketing considerations.

ever, all fixed costs must be allocated and recovered *somewhere* within the matrix!) The final issue is to recognize that 100 percent utilization of the assigned capacity within each cell may not be achieved. Hence, cost allocations per sales unit must reflect the anticipated utilization rate in each cell. Again, this places a premium on accurate forecasting.

Capacity allocation charts similar to those presented in Figures 2 and 3 could be developed for most other capacity-constrained businesses. In some instances, capacity is measured in terms of seats or rooms; in others it may be in terms of machine time, labor time, vehicle units, or cubic capacity—whichever is the scarce resource. Unless there is the option for easy diversion of business from one facility to a similar alternative, allocation planning decisions have to be made at the level of geographic operating units. Thus, each hotel, repair and maintenance center, or computer service bureau may need its own plan. For service operations where speed of turnaround or ability to respond to emergencies are important, a good understanding of the time value of the service to customers is a necessary ingredient to development of profitable pricing strategies.

The Role of Marketing in Yield Management

Marketing's task in yield management is sixfold. It involves the following procedures:

1. Identifying the principal market segments that might be attracted to the service facility and that are consistent with its capabilities and mission.

2. Forecasting the volumes of business that might be obtained from each segment at specific price levels (through supply-and-demand analysis).

3. Recommending the "ideal business mix" at each specific time in terms of maximizing net

revenues, which may not, in fact, be the same as maximizing capacity utilization.

4. Providing the sales force with specific sales targets on specific dates for each segment. This information may also be useful for planning advertising and related communication efforts.

5. Providing guidelines for the prices to charge each segment at specific points in time. For some segments, these guidelines should be adhered to rigorously; in other instances, they may simply provide targets for negotiation.

6. Monitoring performance over time, evaluating the reasons for achieving a higher or lower than predicted yield or performance on the ARGE index, and modifying future strategy accordingly.

A consistently high ARGE index may indicate the need for a price increase, while a below-target ARGE may reflect failure to achieve the business mix anticipated, due to poor forecasting or unanticipated changes in the environment. In this case, changes will have to be made in the ideal business mix at specific points in time. Alternatively, a poor ARGE performance could be due to sales or reservation personnel overriding the business mix targets or charging lower prices than recommended in the plan.

Clearly, the adoption of customer mix sales targets that may vary from day to day—or even from hour to hour — puts a premium on accurate market analysis and forecasting. But the economic and strategic benefits are likely to outweigh greatly the planning and research costs involved. Setting specific sales targets by segments, with recommended prices for each segment, reduces the risk that business will be booked in advance at a discount when there is a high probability of later obtaining business for the date in question from a higher-paying segment.

Sales targets also reduce the risk that potential business from lower-rated segments will be turned away in the hope of obtaining a higer priced sale when the chances of obtaining the latter are actually very small. Similarly, operations personnel will be better able to plan service levels, staffing, and availability of special features if they have a good idea of the business mix that is likely to be obtained on specific dates.

Constraints

One possible constraint on management's desire to maximize yield in the short term is the need to maintain good customer relations, especially with customers that provide extensive repeat business or use substantial capacity during periods of low demand. In the former instance, perceived price gouging during peak periods may alienate customers and result in bad word-of-mouth publicity. In the second instance, it may sometimes be necessary to take low-rated business in the peak period in order to ensure continued patronage by that organization during off-peak periods. Each case should be taken on its own merits, with careful assessment being made of who needs whom the most — the buyer or the seller.

The pricing strategy outlined earlier presumes that the organization is in a position to charge different customer segments different prices at the same point in time. This, in turn, presumes no legal restraints against such a strategy and general acceptance of such practices as discounts for bulk purchases or premiums for providing emergency service at short notice. If different segments are being charged different prices for similar service under more or less identical conditions and the higher-paying segment learns of this price differential, then ill will may result. Such a strategy may only be feasible, therefore, when the different segments are unlikely to share information with each other.

In many instances prices have to be advertised up front and equal treatment provided to all parties (or certainly to all individual purchasers). This does not alter the need to adjust price to reflect variations in demand over time. Nor does it mean that the customer mix may not vary significantly over the time cycle. Hence, it may still be appropriate for the marketer to identify the most likely sources of business at a specific point in time and to direct sales and advertising efforts accordingly.

INFORMATION NEEDS

Service managers require substantial information to help them develop effective strategies for planning capacity allocation and managing demand. Information needs include

- Historical data on capacity utilization, financial yield per unit of capacity, and ARGE per unit.
- Historical data on the level and composition of demand over time, including responses to changes in price or other marketing variables.
- Forecasts of the level of demand for each major segment under specified conditions.
- Segment-by-segment data to help management evaluate the impact of periodic cycles periodic cycles and random demand fluctuations.
- Availability of incremental capacity (both labor and facilities) in specific locations.
- Good cost data to enable the organization to distinguish between fixed and variable costs of capacity, as well as to determine the relative profitability of incremental unit sales to different segments at different prices.
- Customer attitudes toward queuing under varying conditions.
- Customer opinions on whether the quality of service delivered varies with different levels of capacity utilization.

Where might all this information come from? Although some new studies may be required, much of the needed data are probably already being collected within the organization — although not necessarily by marketers. A stream of information comes into most service organizations, especially from reservations and other records detailing the multitude of individual transactions of the business. Sales receipts and tickets often contain vast detail.

Almost all service businesses collect information for operational and accounting purposes. Although some do not record details of individual transactions (examples include urban public transportation, cinemas, and sports arenas), a majority have the potential to associate specific customers with specific transactions. Information technology offers the potential to make this data easy to store and easy to retrieve, if the right hardware and software are used. Unfortunately, the marketing value of these data is sometimes overlooked and the information is not always formatted and stored in ways that permit easy retrieval and analysis for marketing purposes.

CONCLUSION

Since many capacity-constrained service organizations have heavy fixed investments and incur substantial fixed labor costs, even modest improvements in capacity utilization can have a significant effect on the bottom line. Similarly, changes in the mix of business to emphasize the most profitable segments during periods of excess demand can also have an important impact on profits. Service organizations that combine a strong marketing management orientation with the management information systems needed to develop effective demand management strategies will be well placed to achieve — or improve upon — success. An important by-product of such actions is likely to be better quality service which, of course, is what keeps customers coming back.

Competing With Time-Saving Service

LEONARD L. BERRY
AND LINDA R. COOPER

While managers may be attentive to locational and time-of-day convenience, many ignore process convenience — that is, providing goods and services quickly at the service site. By identifying the bottlenecks and other conditions leading to service delays, a large bank was able to reduce waiting times.

Today's consumers perceive they have a "poverty of time"; that is, they have insufficient time to do all they *have* to do and all they *want* to do.

Several studies document the extent to which Americans perceive time is in short supply. In a 1987 Newspaper Advertising Bureau study, 76% of working women, and 58% of all Americans, felt pressured for time, and in a 1987 *USA Today* poll, 70% of two-income couples claimed they did not have enough time.

In 1965, 1975, and 1985-87 studies, national samples of adult Americans were asked whether they "always," "sometimes," or "almost never" felt rushed to do the things they have to do. In the most recent study, 32% of the sample reported that they "always" feel rushed, up from 28% in 1975 and 25% in 1965.

Working mothers with young children and educated, affluent individuals aged 35 to 54 with long workweeks are most likely to always feel rushed.[1]

Time has, in fact, become a precious resource. Consequently, enterprises that steal their customers' time — that sell inconvenience instead of convenience — will surely have fewer customers in the future.

To make our case, we first explore the concept of convenience and show how consumers' sense of what is convenient is shifting. We then present a case study of how one company, The First National Bank of Chicago (First Chicago), launched an all-out effort to improve its convenience. We conclude with a discussion of what the case study teaches us about the "how" and "why" of time-efficient operations.

A CLOSER LOOK AT CONVENIENCE

Convenience is a dynamic concept. What was convenient yesterday may not be convenient today. Indeed, the synergy of technology, innovative distribution systems, and perceived time scarcity are significantly altering consumers' concepts of convenience. In just a few years, for example, consumers' expectations for photo-processing service have shifted from one week to one night to one hour. A similar compression of acceptable "delivery" time has occurred for services ranging from lens grinding for eye glasses to mail delivery. The current soaring sales of facsimile machines indicates our shifting concepts of time and convenience.

Just as consumers are responding to time-compressed services, so are they responding to location-compressed services. Advertising executive John Considine concludes that consumer time consciousness is the main reason for the resurgence of strip shopping centers in America, from 22,000 centers in 1980 to 41,000 in 1990. Considine believes the malls are too far away, too big, and too congested for many busy consumers to patronize for routine shopping.[2]

Moreover, a growing number of consumers are doing considerable shopping without even venturing from their homes, as demonstrated by the dramatic increase in consumer mail-order sales from $29 billion in 1980 to $70 billion in 1989.[3] Another instructive trend is the stepped-up pace of home-ordered, home-delivered local goods and services. Boosted by the success of Domino's Pizza, this mode of marketing is spreading to wallpaper, video-tapes, and automobile care, among other categories.

Convenience is multifaceted as well as dynamic. Executives interested in making their companies more time-efficient for consumers need to consider three primary types of convenience:

- *Locational convenience* — offering goods and services at the right place.
- *Time-of-day convenience* — offering goods and services at the right time.

- *Process convenience* — offering goods and services quickly at the service site.

We believe many managers pay too little attention to process convenience, even when they are quite attentive to locational and time-of-day convenience. Most retailers, for example, place a high premium on making their stores easy to get to, yet from the consumers' standpoint, one can waste time just as easily when standing in a check-out line as when driving to the store. Precious time is being diverted from other activities in either case.

A recent study of over 2,000 Texas supermarket shoppers illustrates the importance of process convenience. The purpose of the research was to measure shopper perceptions of the time-saving value of various supermarket operating practices. The questionnaire included 18 existing or potential practices that could conceivably save customers time in food shopping. The respondents were asked to rate each of these practices on a scale of 1 ("would definitely *not* save me time") to 7 "would definitely save me time"). The three top-rated practices and their mean scores on the 7-point scale were as follows:

- A supermarket that would open up more check-out lanes whenever lines were too long. (6.71)
- A supermarket with signs at the end of each aisle to let you know where products are located (6.40)
- A supermarket that puts frozen foods on one side of the store so that you can pick them up last, before checking out (5.91)[4]

Analyzing these and other data from the study confirms that operating a time efficient supermarket involves far more than location and store hours. Indeed, the data over-all suggest that given the opportunity, food shoppers would design and run food stores *differently* than do food store operators!

Further evidence of the importance of process convenience comes from a 1989 *Wall Street Journal* survey in which a national sample of consumers was asked to select from a list of 19 situations the 2 or 3 that most annoy them. The most frequently selected item — chosen by 36% of the sample — was waiting in lines for service while other windows or cash registers are closed. As one consumer stated in the survey: "The bank tellers are going to lunch while everybody else is trying to get their business done before their lunch hour ends."[5]

IMPROVING PROCESS CONVENIENCE AT FIRST CHICAGO

Process convenience is important to time-impoverished consumers, and managers can improve it for their customers with some ingenuity, commitment, and resources. In this section we describe how First Chicago, the nation's eleventh largest bank and Chicago's dominant retail bank, reduced significantly the amount of time its customers wait in line for teller service. First Chicago's approach and success is instructive for managers of any enterprise that has customer queues, from discount stores to theme parks to government offices. The setting for this case study is banking; the principles apply to many different types of organizations.

First Chicago faced a daunting challenge in the mid-1980s in reducing teller line delays. Part of the problem was the sheer size and complexity of its operation, with a main office lobby almost the size of a football field and with an average of 17,000 transactions daily. Also problematic was the attitude of managers and staff. Prior to banking deregulation, customer convenience was not a principal concern of management, and it was not uncommon on a busy day for customers to stand in the teller line for 45 minutes or more. In fact, movies were sometimes shown to waiting customers during busy periods; the bank chose to entertain its customers rather than fix the problem.

Deregulation, however, meant that financial service customers no longer had to patronize a bank to open a checking account and First Chicago and other area banks no longer had a "captive" market for these services. For First Chicago, the loss of customers to savings and loan associations, credit unions, and securities brokerage houses jolted management to attention and became the impetus for change.

Of particular concern was Citicorp's 1984 move into the Chicago retail financial services

market through acquisition of a failing savings and loan association with 44 branches. Virtually overnight, one of America's most aggressive and deep-pocketed financial service competitors had taken over a thrift institution having a large network of branch offices and gone into competition with banks that were restricted from opening new branches by Illinois banking law. In the aftermath of deregulation in general, and with Citicorp's arrival in particular, the idea of quick, competent service started to gain support at First Chicago.

The Role of Leadership: Deregulation created a climate for change, but someone still had to assume the mantle of leadership and take positive action. In this case, First Chicago's Community Banking Group, responsible for retail banking, was catalyzed by a new group head who decreed: "No more lines. I don't care what it takes."

A second catalyst was the newly created Consumer Affairs Department, which was given the task of helping to improve service quality in the Community Banking Group. Staff from the Consumer Affairs Department and line managers from the retail bank planned and implemented the changes.

In effect, the group head provided the mandate, and an empowered group of middle managers provided the strategies to meet it. The group head was the champion; the middle managers, the architects and implementors. It is unlikely that material change would have occurred absent either level of leadership.

Mechanisms for Change: First Chicago tackled the teller-line problem on multiple levels. It invested in technology that assisted or eliminated labor-based functions, took steps to improve the caliber and motivation of the people performing the service, and provided customers with more service delivery alternatives.

First Chicago's actions to improve teller process convenience can be grouped into three broad categories: *service system*, *service provider*, and *customer options*. These actions, by category, include those that follow:

For the Service System —

- A computer-based, customer information system that consolidated a household's account information. For the first time, the bank's contact personnel could answer customer account inquiries completely and quickly from one central system. A new IBM teller terminal system was integrated into the customer information system, improving productivity further. For example, through the IBM system, tellers could check customers' identification (including signatures) without leaving their stations.

- An electronic queuing system called Camtron. This system measures the length of time a customer waits in line through an infrared sensor and displays it for both customers and employees to see. It automatically routes customers to the next available teller via a flashing light, and provides supervisors with a wealth of on-line information, for example, number of customers in line, number of teller windows open, and the average time customers wait. The system also projects staffing requirements.

- Cash dispatch machines that eliminate the need for tellers to select bills and count them twice. The cash needed for a customer is keyed into the machine, which produces that specific amount. These machines save about 30 seconds per transaction.

- A revised job description for teller managers, making them responsible for the front side of the teller counter (managing the lines and ensuring quick transactions) in addition to their traditional responsibilities for the back side of the counter, such as, balancing. Broadening the scope of the teller managers' role to include customer flow has resulted in these managers floorwalking and "working the lines" on busy days to expedite transactions.

- An officer-of-the-day program in which a designated bank officer, equipped with a beeper, is quickly available to tellers for approvals on exceptions and assistance with complicated transactions.

For the Service Provider —

- A "peak-time" teller program in which individuals are hired at premium wages (up to $12 an hour at this writing) to work during the noon rush, before holidays, and during other high-volume periods. Peak-time hours (15-18 hours a week) are particularly attractive to homemakers and students, who tend to be more educated than the teller group as a whole.

- Improved pay and recognition for full-time tellers, including a new teller-of-the-month recognition program to reward productivity, accu-

racy, and service. Special cash incentives are offered for improved productivity on high-volume days, such as the Friday before the July 4th weekend.

- A new approach to teller lunch breaks, including half-hour lunch periods and catered lunches on busy days. The bank cafeteria now opens at 10:30 a.m. to serve lunch to peak-time tellers.

For the Customer —

- "Quick Drop" desks set up in teller lines on busy days to accept deposits, provide routine information, and handle simple service requests such as address changes.

- Express teller stations for customers who need only to make deposits or cash checks.

- Expanded lobby hours, from 38 hours a week in 1988 to 56 hours, including Sunday, at the end of 1989. Opening earlier and closing later has deflected some of the "noon rush" to before-work and after-work periods.

- A customer brochure entitled "How to Lose Wait" that alerts customers to when the bank is likely to be busiest, and offers suggestions on how to avoid delays.

Improved Performance: First Chicago has been successful in improving teller process convenience for its customers. Collectively, the bank's actions have increased teller productivity, expanded capacity, and spread out demand. These outcomes have helped the bank to better synchronize service availability with demand patterns, resulting in reduced teller line delays for customers and improved service quality.

Exhibits 1 and 2 document the bank's progress. Exhibit 1 shows the percentage of customers who waited less than five minutes for teller service during 1988 and 1989. Although the installation of the Camtron system in January 1988 resulted in quick improvement, performance worsened during the summer of 1988 due to an unexpectedly slow internal controller mechanism in the new IBM teller system, and to the assimilation of 100,000 new retail customer accounts purchased from Continental Illinois National Bank. By September, with upgraded circuit boards benefiting the IBM system and with the teller managers regularly working the

EXHIBIT 1
Customer Queuing — Percent Served under Five Minutes by Tellers

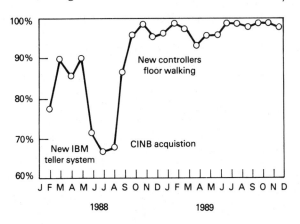

1988   1989

lines, the bank was achieving much better results. By October, the bank was achieving its best results ever.

Exhibit 2 shows that First Chicago has been able to improve teller process convenience even as its total customer count has increased. In the latter half of 1989 the bank served more than 95% of its nearly 200,000 monthly customers in under five minutes. In the first half of 1988, it was serving between 80% and 90% of 100,000 to 125,000 monthly customers in under five minutes.

First Chicago's customers are noticing the improvement. Every quarter the bank tabulates customer responses to an ongoing study of its service quality. Customers check off one of three categories for different aspects of service: "You are the best:" "OK, but no better than the competition:" "Need a lot of improvement." In October 1988, 29% rated First Chicago as "the best" for teller line waits. In March 1989, the figure was 41%, in August 1989 it was 58%, and in December 1989 it was 66%.

EXHIBIT 2
Customer Queuing Compared to Total Customers Served

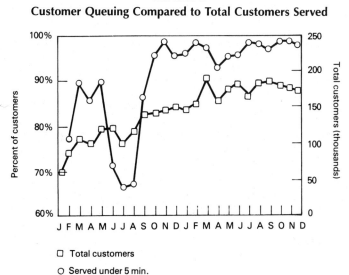
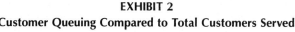

☐ Total customers

◯ Served under 5 min.

Implications of Time Scarcity: Managers who approach the 1990s believing their customers have time to waste, and are willing to waste it, are inviting failure. The implications of consumers' perceived time scarcity extend to many types of enterprises. Institutions that steal consumers' precious resource time — whether they be banks, supermarkets, department stores, restaurants, or even the post office — are committing competitive suicide.

As we have shown in this article, convenience involves more than location and hours; it also involves serving customers efficiently at the service site. To position their enterprises as time-efficient, managers must concern themselves with improving process convenience, in addition to locational and time-of-day convenience.

It is tempting to view long queues at airline counters, hotel front desks, or big banks and assume that it is impossible to do anything about them. This assumption is easy — and incorrect.

No American company has a tougher queue-management challenge than Disney World which serves as many as 150,000 "guests" on a busy day. Just recently, to reduce delays, Disney World replaced four-seat cars with six-seat cars on its popular Space Mountain ride. Marriott's development of its "Express Checkout" service is another example of a customer-minded company marrying technology and creativity to address the seemingly intractable problem of many guests needing to check out of the hotel at the same time.

For years First Chicago provided little process convenience to its customers. The problem was just as bad at the other banks and management had other concerns. However, when customers and competitors started to change, First Chicago's management discovered that it had to forge in new directions in order to be competitive. The change model at First Chicago is a common model. Since internal change typically involves uncertainty and risk, conventional practice wins out over innovation without the countervailing influence of leadership — which is often prompted by adverse external conditions. And since improved performance is unlikely without innovation, change mechanisms are a must.

First Chicago's progress in reducing teller-line delays teaches several key lessons. One lesson is the value of multirole, multilevel leadership in inducing change. The combination of the group head's transformational leadership, the middle managers' strategic leadership, and the teller supervisors' tactical leadership proved to be powerful. The boss made the problem a priority and told staff and line managers to fix it. The middle managers in turn figured out the strategies that were needed, including making the teller supervisors responsible for day-to-day results.

A second lesson derives from breaking down a "big problem" into a series of smaller, more manageable problems. By identifying the various bottlenecks and conditions that contributed to teller-line delays, First Chicago's strategists were able to focus on solutions to each of them. Some solutions centered on the service system, some on the service provider, some on the customer. Some, like Camtron, were high tech, some were high touch, like the teller-of-the-month program, and some were both high tech *and* high touch, like the beeper-equipped officers-of-the-day. The strategists looked for multiple causes to a complex problem, and then for solutions to each of the causes.

Managers can make headway against difficult problems if they make the problems priorities and apply ingenuity, muscle, and money to solving them. Improving process convenience may not be the most glamorous of problems, but it is important to time-impoverished customers, and does influence their perceptions of service quality. One study of customer dissatisfaction with waiting time in bank branches found that the shorter the length of time customers spent in line, the greater their satisfaction with waiting time, and the greater their overall satisfaction with the bank's service quality.[6]

First Chicago used to steal considerable time from its teller service customers. Now the bank steals less time from its customers. The problem is not completely solved, and never will be. Improving process convenience, like the larger issue of improving service quality, is an ongoing journey, not a destination.[7]

REFERENCES

[1]JOHN P. ROBINSON, "The Time Squeeze," *American Demographics* (February 1990): 30-33.

[2]Presentation at Texas A&M University Center for Retailing Studies Symposium, 12 October 1988, Houston, Texas.

[3]Mail-order data supplied by Maxwell Sroge Publishing, Inc.

[4]LEONARD L. BERRY and VALARIE A. ZEITHAML, "Time is Money," Progressive Grocer Executive Report (January 1988): 36-38, 45.

[5]DAVID WESSEL, "Sure Ways to Annoy Consumers," *Wall Street Journal*, 6 November 1989, Section B.

[6]ELIZABETH CLEMMER and BENJAMIN SCHNEIDER, "Toward Understanding and Controlling Customer Dissatisfaction with Waiting," *Marketing Science Institute Research Program Working Paper* (September 1989): 9 and 18.

[7]The first to use the now popular phrase "quality is a journey, not a destination" were MARY RUDIE and J. BRANT WANSLEY, in "The Merrill Lynch Quality Program," *Services Marketing in a Changing Environment,* proceedings of American Marketing Association Services Marketing Conference, 1985: 9.

Prescription for the Waiting-in-Line Blues: Entertain, Enlighten, and Engage

KAREN L. KATZ
BLAIRE M. LARSON
RICHARD C. LARSON

As consumers experience a greater squeeze on their time, even short waits seem longer than ever before. If firms can improve customers' perceptions of the time they spend waiting to be served, then customers will experience less frustration and may feel more satisfied with the service encounter. This paper examines customer perceptions of waiting in line and investigates methods for making waiting more tolerable.

Historically, service businesses interested in customer satisfaction have focused on hiring and training knowledgeable, pleasant servers. Today this approach is insufficient. Consumers not only demand quality, they also demand speed. They do not tolerate waiting in line for long periods of time. Firms must respond to this change if they wish to remain competitive. In this paper, we argue that improving customers' *perceptions* of the waiting experience can be as effective as reducing the actual length of the wait, and we focus on methods for managing perceptions.

WHY IS SPEED IMPORTANT TO CONSUMERS?

Americans today work longer, more varied hours than they have since World War II. The past decade has seen stagnating wages and drastic unemployment shifts. Consequently, many Americans have been forced to work overtime or hold second jobs in order to maintain middle-class lifestyles. The average work week has risen from 40.6 hours in 1973 to 47 hours a week in 1988.[1] During the same period, U.S. leisure time has declined from 26.2 hours to 16.6 hours a week.[2] Furthermore, as the service sector expands, the structure of the traditional forty-hour work week erodes. Today, weekends are workdays for many people, and twenty-four-hour service operations are common-place. These changes have shifted consumer values. Since workers have fewer nonworking hours, they place a greater value on their free time — witness the increase in time-buying and time-saving services,[3] and the concept of "quality time."

As consumers experience a greater squeeze on their time, short waits seem longer and more wasteful to them than ever before. The lesson for managers, then, is that transactions should seem brief. There are two ways to approach that goal: through operations management and through perceptions management.

The logic behind perceptions management — the focus of this research — is that when it comes to customer satisfaction perception is reality. If customers think that they are satisfied, then they are satisfied. Similarly, if customers think that their wait was short enough, then it was short enough, regardless of how long it actually was. A major benefit of perceptions management is that it is often very inexpensive to implement.

PREVIOUS WORK
IN QUEUE PSYCHOLOGY

Empirical research into the psychology of waiting dates back to at least 1955, when I. J. Hirsch et al. studied the effects of auditory and visual backgrounds on perceptions of duration. They asked subjects to replicate a tone heard in either a quiet or a noisy environment. Short durations tended to be overestimated, while long durations tended to be underestimated. In addition, subjects thought they heard the tone for a longer time in a quiet environment than in a noisy environment.[4]

A more recent study focused on the perceptions of commuters waiting for and traveling on a train in the Boston subway system. Arnold Barnett and Anthony Saponaro found that, while recent construction had not disturbed the trains' operations, it had disturbed perceptions. The authors concluded that riders experienced an asymmetry in perceptions: although they were quick to sense a decline in service quality, they were far slower to recognize when the problem had been corrected.[5]

David Maister has developed a theory of queue psychology that focuses on a combination of perceptions and expectations management.[6] In particular, he has defined a concept he calls the "First Law of Service":

Satisfaction = Perception − Expectation

According to Maister,

> If you expect a certain level of service, and perceive the service received to be higher, you will be a satisfied customer.... There are two main directions in which customer satisfaction with waits (and all other aspects of service) can be influenced: by working on what the customer expects and what the customer perceives.

Maister proposes eight principles that organizations can use to influence customers' satisfaction with waiting times:

- Unoccupied time feels longer than occupied time.
- Preprocess waits feel longer than in-process waits.
- Anxiety makes waits seem longer.
- Uncertain waits are longer than known, finite waits.
- Unexplained waits are longer than explained waits.
- Unfair waits are longer than equitable waits.
- The more valuable the service, the longer people will wait.
- Solo waiting feels longer than group waiting.

Richard Larson has observed that a key determinant in waiting satisfaction is the degree of "social justice." Even when waiting times are very short, customers may become infuriated if the system violates the first in, first out principle.[7] Larson's research has also uncovered instances where perceptions of queuing have influenced satisfaction. For example, for fast food customers, satisfaction in a single-queue system (such as Wendy's) may be higher than in a multi-queue chain (such as McDonald's) — even though customers wait longer in a single-queue system.[8]

Two of the world's foremost test sites for queuing psychology experiments are Disneyland and Disney World. Disney management realizes that "there's a real art to line management," and does its utmost to make the waiting experience less psychologically wearing.[9] Lines at Disney theme parks are always kept moving, even if only to dump customers into one of a series of preride waiting areas. A *Newsweek* reporter observed that, to influence customer expectations,

> the waiting times posted by each attraction are generously overestimated, so that one comes away

mysteriously *grateful* for having hung around 20 minutes for a 58-second twirl in the Alice in Wonderland teacups.

Their effort appears to have paid off: even though Disney's theme park lines get longer each year, customer satisfaction, as measured by exit polls, continues to rise.

THE STUDY

In November 1988, the Bank of Boston was contemplating installing two different technologies intended to influence customers' waiting line experiences. The first, by a firm called SilentRadio, is an electronic newsboard. One of these had been installed at an off-premise ATM site, and managers considered it a great success. They were interested in determining if customers waiting for human tellers would respond well to a similar installation. The second, by Camtron Corporation, utilizes "electric eyes" at the entrance and exit of the queue channel to estimate line waits and provide statistics for improving staffing and service levels.

The bank's managers had many questions they wished to answer before investing further. They wondered if the equipment worked accurately, how employees would adapt to the equipment, and, most important, how customers would perceive the improvements. Our own interests focused primarily on the psychology of queuing. We believed that if we could improve customer satisfaction by managing perceptions in a real-world setting, then altering perceived waiting times would be further legitimized as a management tool.

The purpose of the study was to measure customer perceptions of waiting under different conditions. We tested the following hypotheses:

- As the perception of waiting time increases, customer satisfaction decreases.
- Increased distractions reduce the perception of waiting time, increase customer interest level, and may improve customer satisfaction.
- A wait where the length is known in advance is less stressful than an open-ended wait; such knowledge may improve customer satisfacton.

In addition, we explored differences between customers' perceptions of waiting and their actual waiting times, as well as what customers considered a "reasonable" waiting time.

Methodology

Our study site was the Bank of Boston's 60 State Street branch in downtown Boston. We gathered data on Wednesdays, Thursdays, and Fridays, when the branch had the heaviest traffic. In two of the three phases, our data-gathering days included the first or the fifteenth of the month, which are the most common paydays.

Two video cameras filmed customers as they entered the queue and as they left the queue to see a teller; the cameras recorded the time as they filmed. We and our research assistants then interviewed approximately one-third of the customers after they finished their transactions, and asked them about perceived waiting times. Later, when we identified each interviewed customer on the videotape, we were able to compare individual customers' perceptions with how long they actually waited. (To our knowledge, no earlier studies have matched individual perceptions to reality in this way. Most compare individuals' perceptions with *average* waiting periods.)

We also asked customers to rate their wait on three attributes: duration, boredom, and stress level. We asked an open-ended question of what a "reasonable" wait would be. We measured general satisfaction by asking customers to rate the branch's service overall, and on that day in particular.

The study took place in three phases. The first phase served as a control. In the second and third phases, we introduced variables that we hypothesized would alter the perceived waiting times and customer satisfaction levels. The second-phase variable was Silent-Radio — implemented as a large, black electronic board that displayed two lines of bright red print in "Times Square" fashion. Everyone waiting in line could see the board, which transmitted fifteen minutes of up-to-date news and information, interspersed with Bank of Boston ads. During phase three, we removed SilentRadio and introduced Camtron's digital clock feature. The clock, positioned at the entrance to the line, gave an estimate of how long the customer's wait would be.

During the newsboard and clock phases, we asked customers whether they had noticed the new installations and, if so, whether they had read them.

Altogether we conducted 324 personal interviews, which were distributed fairly evenly over the three phases. In analyzing them, we omitted responses from 14 newsboard-phase respondents who had not noticed the installation and from 33 electronic-clock phase respondents who had not noticed the time indicated.

RESULTS

Table 1 provides summary statistics for the 277 questionnaires included in our analysis.

Actual Waiting Times

We determined actual waiting times by analyzing videotapes of customers entering and leaving the teller line. Figure 1 shows the distribution of actual waiting times for the 277 customers we interviewed. Nearly 60 percent of the customers we interviewed waited less than four minutes to be served, and only 3 percent waited over twelve minutes. On average, survey respondents waited in line 4.2 minutes before seeing a teller. Actual average waiting time for all customers was somewhat shorter because we did not interview customers who did not have to wait before being served.

Perceived Waiting Times

We asked subjects, "How long do you think you waited in line today (in minutes)?" Figure 2 shows the distribution of perceived waiting times for the 277 customers we inter-

TABLE 1
Summary Statistics for All Respondents

	Phase I (Control)	Phase II* (Board)	Phase III** (Clock)	Total
# Responses	116	89	72	277
Actual Wait				
0-4 minutes	75%	40%	56%	59%
4-12 minutes	19%	60%	44%	38%
> 12 minutes	6%	0%	0%	3%
Average actual wait (In minutes)	3.6	4.8	4.3	4.2
Perceived Wait				
Average perceived wait (In minutes)	4.7	6.0	4.6	5.1
Average overestimate (In minutes)	1.1	1.2	0.2	0.9
Average % overestimate	78%	43%	22%	52%
Reasonable Wait				
Average reasonable wait (In minutes)	5.8	5.9	6.1	5.9
Description of Time in Line (Averages on 1 to 10 scales):				
Short/long	2.9	3.4	3.3	3.2
Boring/interesting	3.9	5.4	3.8	4.3
Stressful/relaxing	6.9	6.6	6.8	6.7
Overall Satisfaction (Averages on 1 to 10 scales):				
Today	9.1	9.2	9.0	9.1
Usually	8.1	8.1	8.0	8.1

*Respondents who noticed the newsboard.
**Respondents who noticed the time on the clock.

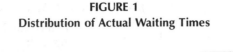

FIGURE 1
Distribution of Actual Waiting Times

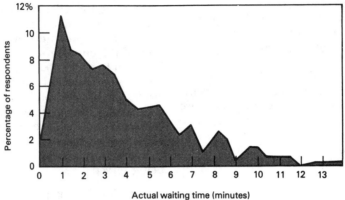

Actual waiting time (minutes)

FIGURE 2
Distribution of Perceived Waiting Times

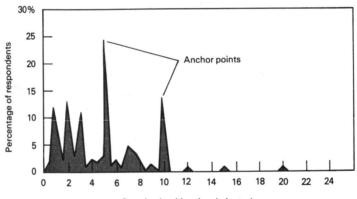

Perceived waiting time (minutes)

viewed. On average, respondents thought they waited 5.1 minutes to see a teller. Twenty-five percent of respondents believed they had waited five minutes. In general, we observed perceptual "anchor points" at five-minute intervals.

As we had expected, people tended to overestimate the amount of time they spent waiting in line. Figure 3 shows the distribution of differences between perceived and actual waiting times. Differences between perceived and actual waiting times were approximately normally distributed, with a mean overestimation of just under one minute and a standard deviation of 2.5 minutes. Waits of less than one

minute typically were not perceived to be waits at all.

Reasonable Waiting Times

Customers had very different notions of how long a reasonable wait is. Many said that their concept of "reasonable" varied based on when they came into the bank; for example, they were willing to wait longest during lunchtime or on payday. Figure 4 shows the distribution of responses to the question about reasonable waiting times. On average, customers thought that 5.9 minutes was a reasonable amount of time to wait. However, as with

FIGURE 3
Perceived vs. Actual Waits

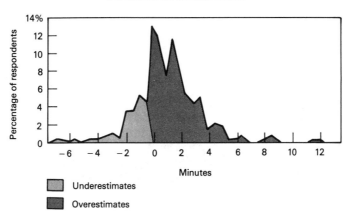

Underestimates

Overestimates

FIGURE 4
Distribution of Reasonable Waiting Times

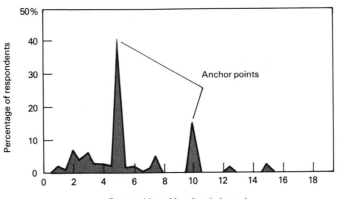

perceived waiting time responses, descriptions of what constitutes a reasonable waiting time tended to anchor around five-minute intervals. More than 40 percent of respondents specified exactly five minutes.

Descriptions of Time Spent in Line

Subjects tended to fall into one of three groups, which we called "watchers," "impatients," and "neutrals." "Watchers" enjoyed observing people and events at the bank. "Impatients," on the other hand, could think of nothing more boring than waiting in line. "Neutrals," as their name indicates, fell somewhere in the middle.

Interest Level. When customers were asked to describe how interesting their wait was, on a 10-point scale, with 1 being the least interesting, the three most frequent responses were 1 (26%), 5 (22%), and 10 (11%). Figure 5 provides the distribution of responses to this question.

Length of Time in Line. When asked to describe the length of the wait on a 10-point scale (1 = short, 10 = long), most respondents described their waits as relatively short. On average, customers rated the length of their wait as a 3.2 out of 10. Eighty-five percent rated the wait as 5 or lower.

FIGURE 5
Overall Customer Interest Level

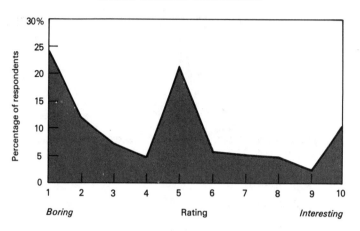

Anxiety Level. We asked customers to describe the waiting experience on a 10-point scale (1 = stressful, 10 = relaxing). The majority of respondents did not find waiting in line stressful. The average response to this question was 6.7, and 83 percent of subjects responded with a 5 or greater.

Overall Customer Satisfaction

In general, we found that customers were very satisfied with the bank. Overall satisfaction "today" received a rating of 9.1, with 64 percent of respondents indicating their satisfaction was at 10. Overall satisfaction with the bank's usual service received a rating of 8.1, with 41 percent rating it at 10. As a result, it became difficult to detect effects of the installation of the electronic newsboard and clock on customer satisfaction; there simply was not much room for improvement.

Correlations

Correlations between the variables were as expected. Changes in actual waiting time tended to influence customer perceptions: as actual waiting times increased, overall customer satisfaction tended to decrease and stress levels tended to increase. In addition, as actual waiting times increased, both perceived waiting times and "reasonable" waiting times increased. Thus, customers recognized that they were waiting longer, but also indicated that they were *willing* to wait longer. This cor-

relation suggests that customers' definitions of a reasonable wait may be based on the length of the current service encounter.

Similarly, increases in perceived waiting times were associated with decreases in satisfaction and with increases in stress levels and definitions of a reasonable wait.

Overall satisfaction with the service received on the day of the survey was correlated with descriptions of what constitutes a reasonable wait and with usual satisfaction. Customers who had a longer definition of a reasonable wait tended to be more satisfied than customers with a shorter definition. In addition, customers who were usually satisfied were more likely to be satisfied with the service on the survey date. Customers may have used their survey date satisfaction as a reference point for rating their usual satisfaction.

High interest levels and low stress levels were associated with high levels of customer satisfaction, both in general and on the survey date.

Customer satisfaction appeared to depend on how closely reality matched expectations. During the study, several customers commented that the teller lines were much shorter than usual, and thus that they were very satisfied.

Comparisons between the Three Phases

In order for us to make comparisons between the survey phases, actual waiting times needed to be equivalent across the three phases. We controlled for this by looking at two subgroups with comparable mean waiting times: those who waited less than four minutes, and those who waited between four and twelve minutes.

This division may have some operational significance. Since customers typically said they were willing to wait around five minutes, but tended to overestimate their waits by around one minute, they may actually be willing to wait only four minutes before the wait becomes "unreasonable."

Impact of the Electronic Newsboard. Newsboard installation did not significantly affect perceived waiting times nor the amount by which respondents overestimated their waits. Nor did it affect how customers rated the length of the wait on a 10-point scale.

However, the newsboard did make the time spent in line more palatable. Interest level, measured on a 10-point scale, increased from 3.9 to 5.0 for customers who waited less than four minutes, and from 3.8 to 5.6 for customers who waited four to twelve minutes. Figure 6 shows the effects of the electronic newsboard on customer interest levels.

When asked to describe the wait in line on the boring-to-interesting scale, many respondents said that the line was usually very boring, but having the newsboard to watch made it much more interesting. After the newsboard had been removed, many customers noticed it was gone and said they wished the bank would reinstall it. Respondents who spent a greater percentage of their time in line watching the newsboard were more interested and relaxed than other customers and tended to overestimate the length of the wait by a smaller amount.

In addition, overall satisfaction with the service received from the bank on the survey date increased from 9.3 to 9.5 for customers who waited less than four minutes and from 8.5 to 9.0 for customers who waited from four to twelve minutes when the newsboard was present. While the increase was not statistically significant, the trend was clearly in the hypothesized direction.

The newsboard had a noticeable physical effect on the line, as well. Normally, customers face the back of the person in front of them. This formation can have the symbolic effect of crowding, which is often linked to stress.[10] In order to view the electronic newsboard, customers had to either twist their heads or turn their bodies so they stood shoulder to shoulder. In so doing, customers may have subconsciously felt less crowded.

FIGURE 6
Effect of Newsboard on Customer Interest

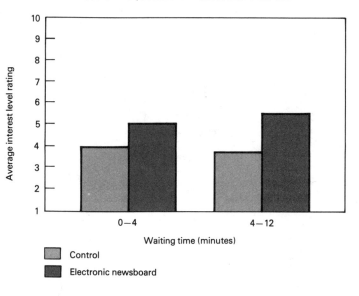

In addition, customers tended to stand completely still with their arms at their sides while watching the newsboard. During other phases of the study, subjects were extremely fidgety; they constantly moved around and touched their faces and hair. We believe that a relaxed customer will have a more positive experience than a tense one.

Impact of the Electronic Clock. Installation of the electronic clock appeared to influence perceived waiting times and overestimation of waiting times. Specifically, perceived waiting times were lower for clock-phase respondents than for control-phase respondents. Clock-phase respondents also tended to overestimate their wait by less than control-phase respondents. While these differences are on the borderline in terms of statistical significance, they are clearly in the hypothesized direction (see Figure 7).

There are two reasons why the clock may have improved the accuracy of perceived waiting times. Customers may have believed what the clock told them about their waiting time and thus adjusted their perceptions. Alternatively, the clock may have made customers more aware of time, and thus more aware

than usual of exactly how much time they spent in line.

We had hypothesized that a wait where the length is known in advance would be less stressful than an open-ended wait, so we hoped to find that the clock reduced stress levels. However, control-phase and clock-phase respondents did not rate their stress levels differently.

Nor did the clock improve customers' overall satisfaction with the service they received. This may be because the clock made respondents more aware of the time wasted standing in line.

We observed that customers like to play "beat the clock" and felt as if they were "winning" if they spent less time than the clock had indicated that they would. Since the clock tended to overestimate waiting times by about one minute, most respondents did beat the clock; however, some customers became annoyed when their wait turned out to be longer than estimated. In addition, the balking rate appeared to increase during the electronic-clock phase: more people looked into the bank, saw the clock, and left (presumably because the wait was too long) than did so when the clock was not there.

FIGURE 7
Effect of Clock on Time Perception

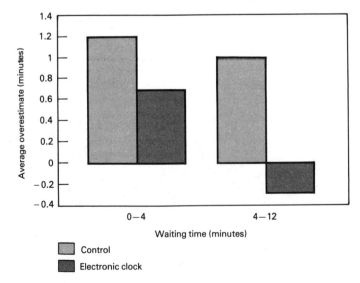

Waiting time (minutes)

Further Observations

Throughout the electronic newsboard and clock phases, customers commented that service had improved dramatically over the last few weeks and that lines were much shorter than they had been in the past. Some even commented that they thought the improvements were due to the addition of new staff members (even though there were no additional staff at the time they made the comments!). These observations may have surfaced because the installation of the Camtron system affected teller productivity or because February was a slow month at the bank. Or these perceptions may have occurred simply because customers were being entertained and interviewed, and they felt that the bank cared about their concerns.

SUMMARY OF FINDINGS

In general, our findings supported our preliminary hypotheses. However, there were a couple of surprises. The major findings were as follows:

- In this setting, the average overestimate is about one minute, and waits of five minutes or less are considered reasonable.
- As perceptions of waiting time increase, customer satisfaction tends to decrease.
- Increased distractions make the waiting experience more interesting and tend to increase customer satisfaction.
- However, information on expected time in queue tends to improve the accuracy of customer perceptions of waiting but does not influence customer satisfaction.

Management Implications

Every line is different. Therefore, when attempting to manage customer perceptions of waiting, managers should consider the experience from the customer's point of view. Important issues include the following:

- Fairness. Can newcomers cut in front of customers who arrived before them, or is the line first come, first served?
- Interest Level. Are interesting things happening that the customer can watch?

- Customer Attitudes. What time pressures do customers face?
- Environment. Is waiting comfortable? Does the customer have to freeze in the cold or bake in the sun?
- Value of Service. How important is the result of the transaction to the customer? Could it easily be obtained elsewhere? Can the customer come back another time, or is the transaction urgent?

Suggestions

We have formulated ten suggestions for managers. Some are direct applications of our research results, while others are based on qualitative observations and previous work in the field of queue psychology.

1. Do not overlook the effects of perceptions management: consumer concern about waiting is growing. There is no limit to the frustration that waiting can cause. Cities are becoming more crowded, the work week is expanding, the economy is worsening, and people need more free time to deal with their frustrations. Now, more then ever, excellent service is the key to success. Using perceptions management to improve customer satisfaction is only a tool, but it's a good tool.

2. Determine the acceptable waiting time for your customers. One minute of waiting in a bank will probably go unnoticed, whereas a minute on hold on the telephone can be infuriating. Determining an acceptable waiting period will help managers set operational objectives and, if those are met, will improve customer satisfaction.

3. Install distractions that entertain and physically involve the customer. Keep the content lighthearted. Piped-in music or live piano players may create a more pleasant atmosphere, but they do not effectively rope the customer into the activity. If the content of the distraction is light, fresh, and engaging, customers remain interested and entertained for many visits. Customers at the bank preferred horoscopes and tabloid headlines to more informative headline news.

   The SilentRadio used in our study managed perceptions effectively. It was inexpensive, easy to operate, and did not disrupt normal operations. In addition, since most customers had to stand still to read the screen, they became physically involved with the distraction and did not mind waiting as much. Screen placement forced customers to turn slightly in order to read it; thus they stood shoulder to shoulder rather than front to back.

4. **Get customers out of line.** Whenever customers can be served without having to stand in line, both company and customer can benefit. For example, queues can be avoided by advance reservations, by mail or telephone service, or by better automation.

   In banking, there are many ways to conduct transactions without using a teller — for example, direct deposit, ATMs, automatic loan payments, and check-cashing machines. The challenge is to increase customer awareness and use of these tools.

5. **Only make people conscious of time if they grossly overestimate waiting times.** There is a tradeoff between the accuracy of waiting time perceptions and the awareness of time. In the bank, perceptions were fairly close to reality, perhaps because customers had previous experience with the branch, or because the lines were short. For whatever reason, informing customers of their expected waiting time backfired. The clock made people more aware of the waiting time. It also appeared to increase balking rates.

   However, there may be numerous instances in which information on expected waiting times is helpful. Airline passengers, for example, have no way of knowing when a plane sitting on the runway will take off unless they're told. In such cases, Maister's principle that an informed wait is better than an uninformed wait may still hold.

6. **Modify customer arrival behavior.** Customers are often aware of peak times before they arrive at a service location, but they show up then anyway. If some customers could be convinced to arrive at other times, everyone would be better off. To achieve this, signs that list off-peak hours could be posted in stores and banks. Servers could also mention off-peak hours to customers who have waited an inordinate amount of time. In addition, incentives could be used to encourage off-peak arrivals.

7. Keep resources not serving customers out of sight. Several customers commented that they do not mind waiting so long as the tellers seem to be working as hard as they can. Customers tend to become annoyed if they see several unstaffed teller windows or if tellers are present but not serving customers. To address this perception, managers can adopt several policies:

- Keep idle employees out of view.
- Conduct activities that do not involve customer interactions out of the customer's sight.
- Staff stations closest to the exit point of the queue first. The practice creates a better first impression for the customer.
- Keep unused physical capacity out of view (e.g., portable cash registers for the Christmas season).

8. **Segment customers by personality types.** The three types of customers we observed — watchers, impatients, and neutrals — want different types of service from the bank. Watchers find the bustle of the bank entertaining and prefer a friendly teller with a smile to a shorter line. The impatient group is more apt to emphasize the length of the queue in their definition of overall satisfaction.

   The needs of the "impatients" can be met through innovative products, services, and educational programs that either avoid or reduce the waiting experience. The airline and hotel industries, for example, have developed club memberships that provide express check-in and check-out policies. Some retailers satisfy convenience-seeking consumers by creating express check-out cashier lines. The emergence of convenience-oriented businesses proves that people are willing to pay more for services that save them time.[11]

9. **Adopt a long-term perspective.** In our research, respondents rated their overall satisfaction significantly lower on a historical basis than on the survey date itself. And, although daily satisfaction improved as the study progressed, historical satisfaction did not. It evidently takes a tremendous number of "good days" before customers' historical opinions change. Managers must take a long-term approach when attempting to improve perceptions.

10. **Never underestimate the power of a friendly server.** Although waiting is an issue worth addressing, managers should not lose perspective. Servers should continually be trained and rewarded for good service, since their efforts can overcome many negative effects of waiting.

REFERENCES

This work was supported in part by the National Science Foundation, Grant No. SES 8709811.

[1]"More Time Spent Winning Bread, Less Enjoying It," *Boston Globe*, 16 January 1989, p. 1.

[2]J. RICHARD, "Out of Time," *New York Times,* 28 November 1988, Sec. L, p. A25.

[3]C. L. ANDERSON, "Selling Time: Emerging Trends in the Consumer Service Industries" (Cambridge, Massachusetts: MIT Sloan School of Management, Master's Thesis, May 1988).

[4]I. J. HIRSCH et al., "The Effects of Auditory and Visual Background on Apparent Duration," *American Journal of Psychology* 69 (December 1956): 561–574.

[5]A. BARNETT and A. SAPONARO, "The Parable of the Red Line," *Interfaces* 15 (March-April 1985): 33–39.

[6]D. H. MAISTER, "The Psychology of Waiting in Lines" (Boston: Harvard Business School Note 9-684-064, Rev. May 1984), pp. 2–3.

[7]R. C. LARSON, "Perspectives on Queues: Social Justice and the Psychology of Queuing," *Operations Research* 35 (November-December 1987): 895-905.

[8]Several studies have examined the concept of the "time budget": How do consumers choose among numerous activities, given the constraint of limited available time? An excellent review of this literature is provided by M. VENKATESAN and B. B. ANDERSON, "Time Budgets and Consumer Services in *Service Marketing in a Changing Environment,* ed. T. M. Block et al. (Chicago: Proceedings Series, 1985), pp. 52–55.

[9]C. LEERHSEN, "How Disney Does It," *Newsweek,* 3 April 1989, p. 52.

[10]B. SCHWARTZ, *Queuing and Waiting* (Chicago, Illinois: University of Chicago Press, 1975), pp. 177–178.

[11]ANDERSON (May 1988).

Yield Management: A Tool for Capacity-Constrained Service Firms

SHERYL E. KIMES

The objective of yield management is to maximize the revenue or yield of the firm. A good yield management system will help the firm decide how much of each type of inventory (whether it be seats on an airplane, rooms in a hotel, or cars in a rental car fleet) to allocate to different types of demand. This article attempts to structure the concept of yield management by reviewing current literature, classifying types of solution approaches, discussing the managerial implications of yield management and presenting a future research agenda.

INTRODUCTION

Yield management, a method for managing capacity profitably, has recently gained widespread acceptance in the airline and hotel industries. Yield management is a method which can help a firm sell the right inventory unit to the right type of customer, at the right time, and for the right price. Yield management guides the decision of how to allocate undifferentiated units of capacity to available demand in such a way as to maximize profit or revenue. The problem then becomes one of determining how much to sell at what price and to which market segment.

The concepts behind yield management can easily be seen in the airline industry. Yield refers to either yield per available seat mile or yield per revenue passenger mile. Airlines typically offer several classes of service such as full-fare, maxi-savers, and super-savers. The airlines would prefer filling their planes with full-fare customers, but since this rarely occurs, they try filling the plane by offering reduced fare incentives. A tradeoff develops between the desire for high capacity utilization (or load factor) and the desire for selling seats at the maximum price. Due to the perishable nature of an airline's inventory, an empty seat represents an opportunity cost. The airlines must decide how many discount fares to sell while at the same time making sure they have enough seats left to sell to later-booking full-fare passengers.

Reprinted with permission from the *Journal of Operations Management*, Vol. 8, No. 4 (October 1989), pp. 348–63. Copyright © 1989, American Production and Inventory Control Society.

Many airlines have solved this problem with yield management and use a combination of seat inventory management and pricing tools to achieve their goal of maximum revenue. Since more revenue can be obtained from a relatively fixed capacity, yield management becomes a very attractive option. The airline industry was the first to systematically address the capacity allocation problem with yield management and has achieved a great deal of success (Lloyd's (1985), Cross (1986), Belobaba (1987)). Many airlines report increases in revenue of 5 percent or more after starting a yield management program (Lloyd's (1985), Belobaba (1987)).

Other firms, most notably in service industries such as lodging, car rental and freight transport, have noticed the success of yield management in the airline industry and have tried adapting yield management concepts to their particular industries. Extending the airline definition of yield to other industries would result in yield per available inventory unit. For example, yield for a hotel would be measured as revenue per available room. While these other industries are certainly not identical, they do share one characteristic: fixed capacity. In addition, all have easily segmented markets and stochastic demand for each type of service.

When service firms are constrained by capacity (i.e., transportation, lodging, health care, entertainment, and food service), financial success is often a function of management's ability to use capacity efficiently. Yield management in capital-intensive service industries such as airlines is often equated with revenue (or yield) maximization because of the high fixed-cost nature of the industry. The marginal costs of selling another seat and transporting the passenger in it are so small compared to the marginal revenue as to render the marginal costs inconsequential.

Lovelock (1984) proposed a concept similar to yield management, by advocating capacity allocation to different market segments over time. He believed that, rather than measuring capacity utilization (whether load factor, occupancy, or another parameter), service firms should measure the Asset-Revenue Generating Efficiency (ARGE) of the firm. The ARGE, the product of capacity utilization and the unit price efficiency rate, provides a measure of both productive efficiency and pricing efficiency. This concept is very similar to yield management since both combine capacity utilization and pricing efficiency.

In this paper, I will address the characteristics of the yield management, identify basic solution techniques and associated problems, describe possible implementation concerns, and discuss possible directions for future research.

APPROPRIATE SITUATIONS FOR EFFECTIVE YIELD MANAGEMENT APPLICATION

Yield management techniques are appropriate (1) when a firm is operating with a relatively fixed capacity, (2) when demand can be segmented into clearly-identified partitions, (3) when inventory is perishable, (4) when the product is sold well in advance, (5) when demand fluctuates substantially, and (6) when marginal sales costs and production costs are low, but capacity change costs are high. Although these traits are characteristic of the firms in which yield management is used, they are also characteristic of firms which have a problem of allocating fixed capacity efficiently. These characteristics are necessary conditions for the proper adoption of yield management. Each characteristic will be further discussed below.

1. *Relatively fixed capacity.* Since the focus of yield management is efficient allocation of shared fixed capacity, it is only appropriate for firms which cannot quickly adapt available capacity to available demand. For example, if all rooms in a hotel are occupied, another room cannot easily be added, although the customer may be accommodated in a sister hotel in a different part of the city. For airlines, if all seats on a flight are occupied, the plane cannot be enlarged, but it may be possible to put the passenger on a later flight. Essentially, capacity is fixed, although there may be some limited flexibility.

2. *Ability to segment markets.* In order for a yield management program to be effective,

the firm must segment its market into different types of customers. For example, the airline industry distinguishes between time-sensitive and price-sensitive customers by requiring a Saturday night stay for most discounted fares. Basically, the business must know which customers are most likely to use variously-priced classes of service, and must develop different marketing strategies for each market segment.

3. *Perishable inventory.* One of the key factors distinguishing service firms from manufacturing firms is that the inventory is perishable. In the case of capacity-constrained service firms, the problem is even more severe in that additional capacity cannot be obtained. Seats unsold on an airplane, rooms unsold in a hotel, or cars unrented at a rental car agency all represent spoiled or wasted inventory. If a firm can minimize its inventory spoilage, it will operate much more efficiently.

4. *Product sold in advance.* One of the capacity management tools that service businesses use is a reservation system in which units of inventory are sold in advance of actual use. Reservations systems provide the firm with some measure of security, in that they know that their capacity will be used in the future, but when the product is sold in advance, the manager is also faced with uncertainty. The manager must decide whether to accept an early reservation of a customer who wants low price, or wait and see if higher paying customers will appear. With a good yield management system, this type of situation can be addressed.

5. *Fluctuating demand.* Many service firms face highly erratic demand patterns, and managers must devise some method of dealing with this uncertainty. Yield management can be used to help temper some of the demand fluctuations by increasing utilization during slow demand times (by decreasing price), and by increasing revenue during times of high demand (by increasing price). If a manager knows when demand peaks and valleys will occur, he/she will be better able to plan for them.

6. *Low marginal sales costs/high marginal capacity change costs.* For a yield management system to be effective, marginal sales costs, the cost of selling an additional unit of inventory, must be low, but marginal capacity change costs should be high. For capacity-constrained firms, providing additional capacity is a very expensive proposition, but selling another unit of available capacity is relatively inexpensive.

COMPONENTS OF THE PROBLEM

Yield management must address a myriad of problems including:

1. demand patterns for various rates/fares,
2. overbooking policy,
3. demand elasticities,
4. information system.

Of these problem components, the existence of an accurate information system is most critical, because without it, none of the other information will be available for use.

1. *Demand patterns.* Information on historical demand patterns for various rate classes must be available. Most yield management systems in commercial use are based strictly on historical demand patterns. Generally, in the airline industry, demand is assumed to follow a normal distribution (Belobaba (1987)). The probability distribution of demand in other industries has not yet been rigorously studied. In addition, information on the booking pattern for each rate class must be obtained in order to better understand the behavior of the different customers. Generally, bookings have been assumed to follow a random Poisson probability distribution (Beckman (1958), Thompson (1961), Taylor (1962)). Finally, the demands for different rate classes must be studied to determine the possibility of correlation among rate classes. By knowing the interaction between rate classes, a firm can better understand how many inventory units which could have been sold at a high price may be cannibalized by selling too many inventory units at a lower price.

Several other assumptions often made include the forgetfulness property which states that the probability of cancellation is not dependent upon when the reservation was made, and that customers will freely upgrade or downgrade their class of service (Thompson (1961)). The latter hypothesis may be based on unrealistic price elasticity assumptions which will lead to inaccurate model results.

2. *Overbooking policies.* Overbooking policies must also be assessed and include information on historical no-show rates and current policies on overbooking. The overbooking problem has been studied rather extensively (Rothstein (1971), Rothstein (1974), Schlifer and Vardi (1975), Ladany (1976), Ladany (1977), Hersh and Ladany (1978), Rothstein (1985), Alstrup et al. (1986)). Generally, cancellations are assumed to follow a binomial distribution, although this assumption has not been rigorously tested in all industries. The overbooking policy must be integrated with the yield management program or sales will be limited to an arbitrarily low level.

3. *Demand elasticities.* The effect of price changes on demand must also be assessed. As mentioned above, yield management consists of both pricing and inventory management components. Although pricing has a direct impact on revenues, most firms cannot change price without taking the reactions of competitors into account. To fully use the potential of a yield management system, management must know the elasticity of demand for various rate classes and be able to make corresponding changes.

4. *Information system.* The biggest problems facing a firm contemplating adoption of a yield management program are data availability and accuracy. A completely computerized management information system is not required; what matters is the type and accuracy of data collected. Without a good information system, the yield management system will be doomed to failure. For example, an airline which does not keep track of the number of discount seats sold for a particular flight can encounter a severe problem when all of the potential passengers arrive at the gate only to find an extremely-overbooked plane.

SOLUTION TECHNIQUES

Yield management solution techniques vary in sophistication, but generally fall into four different categories: (1) mathematical programming, (2) economics-based, (3) threshold curve, and (4) expert systems. One of the key characteristics of the yield management problem is that it must be solved repeatedly. Because of this, any solution method must be fast, fairly accurate and not too expensive. Optimality is desirable, but may not be as important as solving the problem quickly with a fair degree of accuracy. Due to computer limitations, marginal revenue models and threshold curve approaches seem to be the most popular methods. Mathematical programming and expert systems approaches may produce better results than the popular models currently in use, but the time and computer resources necessary to solve the problem on a frequent basis have reduced their attractiveness to decision-makers. Still, if the computational problems can be overcome, these approaches offer viable alternatives.

Belobaba (1987) gives a comprehensive review of yield management research in the airline industry. His description and approach to the problem provide an excellent framework from which to address the issue of yield management. Most published research on yield management has occurred in the airline industry, and this will be the focus of the discussion on methodology. Although the research was developed for the airline industry, it is certainly applicable to yield management problems in other industries. Before describing each of the methods, terminology associated with yield management will first be defined, and the framework developed by Belobaba will be discussed.

Terminology

Buckets of Inventory, Booking Limits and Booking Curves. Different types of inventory (be they seats, rooms, or cars) are commonly referred to as *buckets* of inventory. Frequently, an inventory bucket will have a *booking limit,* which refers to the maximum number of inventory units of that bucket which can be sold. The *booking curve* refers to the way in which reservations for an inventory bucket are made over time.

Types of Rate Classes. Rate classes within the shared fixed capacity can be considered to be either *distinct* or *nested* (Belobaba (1987)). Shared fixed capacity might refer to the coach cabin of a plane (Belobaba (1989)), or all similar rooms within a hotel. Distinct rate classes provide separate inventories of capacity (or buckets) for each rate class. For example, an airline might decide to sell 20 full-fare coach seats, 20 super-saver seats, and 20 max-saver seats. The concept of distinct rate classes is related to the classic aircraft design problem of where to locate the partition between classes, although in the case of yield management, all capacity is shared. The booking limits for each capacity bucket must sum to the shared capacity, but if overbooking is allowed, should sum to the maximum number of reservations allowed for the shared capacity (Belobaba (1989)). This type of system sets aside a fixed amount of inventory for each rate class and does not allow for allocating unsold lower-price inventory to higher-paying customers.

With nested systems, a high-rate request will not be refused if inventory is available at lower rates. Booking limits are binding for lower rate classes, but do not exist (other than for service capacity) for the highest rate class. For example, consider the hypothetical case of a 100 room hotel with four rate classes (ranked from highest rate to lowest rate): tran-

sient, corporate, government and group (Figure 1). The maximum number of rooms which could ever be sold to the highest rate class (transient) is 100. This is referred to as the *booking limit*. After looking at relative price and demand, management might decide to protect at least 20 rooms for this class of service. This is referred to as the *nested protection level*. Next, if managment wanted to determine the booking limit for the corporate guests, the nested protection level of the transient guests would be subtracted from the booking limit for that class (100-20) and 80 rooms would be the maximum number of rooms which should ever be booked for the corporate class. This logic continues for all other rates of service.

Static Versus Dynamic Problems. When static solution approaches are used, the problem is solved once and is not updated when additional information becomes available. Dynamic approaches allow booking limits to be revised as actual bookings are accepted. In reality, many dynamic approaches simply involve resolving the static problem when additional information becomes avaiable. When addressing the dynamic problem, the value of accepting a current reservation relative to the decrease in expected total revenue from re-

FIGURE 1
Nested Reservation System

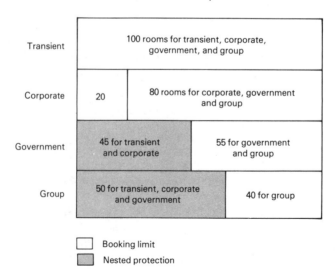

☐	Booking limit
▨	Nested protection

moving one item from the available inventory of the service can be assessed.

Demand is assumed to be either deterministic or probabilistic. Deterministic demand is easier to model, but probabilistic demand is more realistic. Research in airline seat allocation among distinct fare classes generally assumes that demand for each fare class is separate and noncorrelated, that cancellations and no-shows do not exist, and that rejected revenues represent a loss of revenue (Belobaba (1987)).

Early research in the airline industry tended to overlook the relationship between overbooking and seat inventory control and made some assumptions which were not necessarily true. For example, refused requests do not necessarily represent lost revenue, since passengers may upgrade or switch to another flight on the same airline. In addition, the possibility of correlation of demand among fare classes exists, but this problem has not been systematically addressed.

The ideal method should be efficient, adaptable and match the solution with the practical constraints of the problem which mostly stem from data availability and computer capability. The method should also incorporate realistic demand assumptions and should use nested fare classes.

Mathematical Programming Approaches

A widely-used approach for solving the static problem is mathematical programming (Rothstein (1971), Hersh and Ladany (1978), Alstrup et al. (1986)). Mathematical programming works well with distinct rate classes, but will not necessarily give the true revenue-maximizing allotments for a nested reservations system. Mathematical programming and network approaches (Glover et al. (1982)) with multiple rate classes, flight legs and customer itineraries have been developed but suffer from problems in dealing with nested rate classes, using deterministic demand, and computational power required.

Linear Programming. The linear programming formulation of the yield management problem is fairly simple, with an objective of maximizing revenue subject to constraints on

(1) the sum of the number of units of inventory allocated to each inventory bucket must be less than the capacity of the service, and (2) the number of units of inventory allocated to an inventory bucket must be less than the expected demand for that inventory bucket.

$$\text{MAX} \sum_{i=1}^{n} r_i x_i$$

subject to:

$$\sum_{i=1}^{n} x_i \leq C$$

$$x_i \leq d_i \text{ for all } i$$

$$x_i, d_i \geq 0$$

i = Rate class.

x_i = Number of items sold in rate class i.

d_i = Demand for rate class i.

r_i = Revenue from selling items at rate i.

C = Capacity of service.

Although the linear programming solution can be found, the assumption of deterministic demand makes the solution to the problem unrealistic. In addition, most basic linear programming formulations of the problem assume distinct, rather than nested rate classes.

Probabilistic Linear Programming. An optimal solution can be found using probabilistic linear programming, but unfortunately, the computational intensity of such an approach may render it an impractical solution method. The basic linear programming formulation is modified to include the demand constraints in the objective function (although in a probabilistic form) with the objective of maximizing expected revenue. Capacity constraints and binary integer restrictions on all decision variables are the only constraints on the objective function.

$$\text{MAX} \sum_{j=1}^{m} \sum_{i=1}^{n} p_{ij} r_{ij} x_{ij}$$

Subject to:

$$\sum_{j=1}^{m} \sum_{i=1}^{n} x_{ij} \leq \sum_{j=1}^{m} C_j$$

i = Rate class.

j = Inventory item.

x_{ij} = 0 if item j not sold at rate i,

   = 1 if item j sold at rate i.

p_{ij} = Probability of selling item j at rate i.

r_{ij} = Revenue from selling item j at rate i.

C_j = Capacity of service.

Solution of this problem is very computationally intense, and solution of even a simple problem can lead to an enormous and unworkable number of decision variables (Williamson (1988)). The number of decision variables is equal to the number of inventory items multiplied by the number of rate classes. For example, a 100-seat plane with five rate classes would have 500 binary decision variables. Although the solution to the problem is optimal, it is not at present a practical technique for repetitive solution of the yield problem. As with simple linear programming, most probabilistic linear programming approaches are based on distinct rate classes.

Dynamic Programming Approaches. Because of the repetitive, sequential, and probabilistic nature of the yield management problem, many researchers have attempted to model the problem using stochastic dynamic programming (Rothstein (1971), Hersh and Ladany (1978), Alstrup et al. (1986)). Most early research applied this approach to the overbooking problem, although it could easily be extended to the yield management problem. Generally, the objective is to maximize expected revenue subject to operating constraints with states defined as the demand (or reservations) recorded at any given time prior to the service delivery. Stages are defined as time prior to service delivery. Transition probabilities are based on the probability distributions of demand for reservations, cancellations, and no-shows. The computational intensity of this approach leads to solution difficulties given current computing capabilities.

Network Approaches. Glover et al. (1982) modeled passenger itineraries for Frontier Airlines as a network flow problem. Given a daily forecast of the demand for passenger itineraries at the various fare classes, they sought to find the passenger itinerary and associated fare-class mix on each segment of each flight that would maximize revenue for that day.

The problem was modeled as a minimum cost (maximize profit) network flow diagram with side constraints. The forward arcs designated flight legs, and represented the number of passengers on a flight segment. The upper bound for each forward arc was limited by aircraft capacity. The backward arcs represented the passenger itineraries by fare class and were defined as the number of passengers on each passenger itinerary at each fare class. The flow on the backward arcs were limited by the demand for the passenger itinerary and fare class. Generally, the network formulation was found to be too loose, and the authors found that additional constraints were needed.

The model was tested for Frontier Airlines for 600 flights with 30,000 passenger itineraries. An additional 1800-2400 side constraints were also imposed. Computer solution was fast and was conducive to frequent, interactive runs. The linear programming formulation of the same problem would have required 200,000 variables with 3,000 constraints, and solution would be much too time-consuming for any practical implementation.

Wollmer (1989) extended the network approach of Glover et al. (1982) by including probabilistic demand and multiple flight legs. Wollmer (1989) first formulated a probabilistic linear programming model similar to the one given above, reformulated it to a network flow approach, and finally solved the problem as an acyclic network.

The beginnings and ends of flight legs were represented as nodes. Arcs corresponded to a seat k being sold at fare j. Maximum flow on an arc was set at 1, while minimum flow was 0. Arc lengths were equal to the expected marginal revenue from selling seat k at fare j. Any probability distribution could be used with the model.

Wollmer (1989) showed that the expected revenue for an aircraft could be represented as a function of the number of empty seats on each leg. The acyclic network possessed a large number of arcs (number of seats times the number of fares), but only a few needed to be present during solution. The problem became one of solving a series of longest path problems in a relatively small network.

Economics Approaches

Marginal Revenue Models. Early research in the airline industry (Littlewood (1972)) showed that at any point in time, an airline should protect a certain number of seats for potential high fare demand, to the point at which the expected revenue from an additional protected high fare seat was equal to the actual fare level of the lower fare class. This indifference point determined the optimal number of seats to allocate. The optimal seat allocation occurs when the marginal revenue for the last seat sold in one fare class is the same as for another fare class. This point, lambda, is the Lagrange multiplier and represents the marginal revenue for the last seat allocated to each fare class (Belobaba (1987)).

Belobaba developed the expected marginal seat revenue (EMSR) model to address both the static and dynamic nested seat allocation problem. The objective of the model was to incorporate probabilistic demand into a seat inventory control method that could be applied to multiple fare classes on a single flight leg in a nested reservation system. He assumed normally distributed demand, that demand densities for different fare classes were not significantly correlated and that the number of requests received for various fare classes during different periods were not correlated.

With the nested problem the seat inventory problem is "to determine how many seats *not to sell* in the lowest fare classes and to retain for *possible* sales in higher fare classes closer to departure day" (Belobaba (1987), 120). The model is directed at finding protection levels for higher fare classes which can then be converted into booking limits for lower fare classes. The protection limits are the maximum number of seats that should be retained for a particular fare class (and available to all higher fare classes). Booking limits are the maximum number of seats that may be sold to a fare class, including all lower fare classes with smaller booking limits. The booking limits for the highest fare is equal to the capacity of the cabin. The protection level for a

higher fare is the difference between its booking limit and that of the next lower class. In the initial stages of this model, he assumed no vertical or horizontal choice shifts, and no cancellations or no-shows. Since he assumed a normal probability distribution, the probabilities are found by determining the z-score and the value corresponding to it. Obviously, any probability distribution could be used with this model.

In general, solution models that treat classes as distinct inventories (as in mathematical programming) can produce less than optimal results when applied to a nested fare structure. The logic of accepting all lower fare requests as long as the lower fare exceeds the expected marginal revenue of the higher marginal revenue fare class being displaced suggests that the EMSR will generate at least as much in total expected revenue as the stand-alone solution applied to nested fare classes for a range of demand and booking assumptions.

The static EMSR approach can be applied to the dynamic problem by updating information over time. Additional information on requests at a given time are required, and basically the static model is applied repetitively over time with the revised input data. Both the static and dynamic approaches can be modified to include cancellations, no-shows, overbooking and passenger choice shifts.

Another possible extension is to the virtual nesting problem. Most airlines operate on a hub and spoke system and are more concerned with origin-destination itineraries than with individual flight legs. These airlines maintain a primary inventory of 5-8 fare classes while establishing a relationship between a fare class and the itinerary combination and one of a much larger number of hidden inventory classes. The classes are internal to the reservation system. The objective is to maximize expected revenue over an airline's complete network of routes and flights and to give the airline greater control over seats made available to passengers that generate different revenue levels for the airline. Virtual inventory classes (VIC) are associated with each specific flight leg and itinerary. The EMSR can be applied to the VIC concept, by nesting the VICs hierarchically for each flight so that the top inventory class can not be shut down without closing down all lower-ranked classes. EMSR can be used as long as the demand density for each inventory class can be determined. EMSR can then be used to determine the optimal protection levels and booking limits for each VIC and flight leg. Adding in over-booking and upgrades causes this to become a heuristic rather than optimizing approach.

Belobaba applied the EMSR to Western Airlines reservation data for 210 high-demand flights in 1987. When compared with the Western Airlines method of seat allocation, the EMSR increased revenue by 6.2 percent. The EMSR consistently allocated more seats to lower-fare classes than did the seat inventory analysts for the airlines. In some cases this proved to be highly advantageous, but in others it proved to be detrimental to overall revenue. Several problems were noticed, including that the fare differentials of Western were fairly low and that only the most basic formulation of the EMSR model was used. In addition, since only flights with high demand were used, a comparison of the methods for a variety of demand scenarios was not performed.

Combining Mathematical Programming and Economics Approaches. Curry (1988) developed equations which allow mathematical programming to handle nested problems. Since EMSR is good with nested problems, but can handle only legs, and mathematical programming can handle multiple origin-destinations and side constraints, but can not include nesting, a combination of the two approaches seems ideal. By proving that the expected revenue function for nested fare classes was convex, he was able to show that a piecewise linear approximation of the expected revenue function could be developed and that mathematical programming approaches can adequately handle nested problems.

The objective of his problem is to maximize revenue over the entire origin-destination network, subject to capacity constraints. The optimal solution gives booking limits for a given nest allocation which ensures maximum revenue whatever the allocation for the nest. Assumptions made by Curry do not vary much

from those of Belobaba and include: 1) fare classes within a nest are ordered by value, 2) the lower value fares book first, 3) no cancellations occur in closed fare classes, 4) independent demand of fare classes, 5) a demand request denied represents lost revenue, and 6) no upgrades are allowed.

Comparison of Methods. Williamson (1988) tested six yield management methods: (1) leg-based EMSR, (2) prorated EMSR, (3) virtual nesting EMSR, (4) deterministic linear programming, (5) probabilistic linear programming, and (6) deterministic linear programming nested on shadow prices. The test problem, which consisted of flying from Atlanta to four cities, with the fare, and mean and standard deviation of three different levels of demand given, was evaluated for each of the methods.

The EMSR models were based on the work of Belobaba (1987). The leg-based EMSR was Belobaba's basic model, the prorated EMSR tried to allocate revenue over the appropriate flight leg, and the virtual nesting EMSR was an attempt by Belobaba to model the role of the network of flight legs. Deterministic linear programming was limited by the restriction of nonprobabilistic demand forecasts and the use of distinct instead of nested inventories. The probabilistic linear programming was solved with a binary integer program in which the decision variables represented every possible seat. The objective was to maximize expected marginal revenue. Williamson then used the standard linear programming approach, but ordered the shadow prices in such a way as to give priority to those seats with the highest shadow price.

At low demand levels, deterministic linear programming gave the worst result, while probabilistic linear programming had the best performance. At medium and high levels of demand, the virtual nesting EMSR had the worst performance and probabilistic linear programming had the best performance. Unfortunately, the size of the probabilistic linear programming formulation was much too large, and would probably not be a practical approach for a firm which must dynamically allocate seats. The EMSR and prorated EMSR displayed similar results. Although they did not account for the network of flights, they proved easy to use and understand. The shadow price method worked well, but suffered from the limitation of deterministic, rather than probabilistic, demand.

Threshold Curve Method

Another method frequently used with yield management systems is the threshold curve (Cross (1986), Relihan (1989)). Much of the research on threshold curve methodology is proprietary, but it appears to be a popular yield management method used by many hotels and airlines. Essentially, data on past booking behavior over time (usually 60 to 90 days) are collected, curves based on historical aggregate demand patterns are constructed, and actual booking patterns are plotted against the forecast (Cross (1986)). Generally, different threshold curves are built for different days of the week and seasons of the year for particular blocks of inventory (individual hotels or flights). Given that some fluctuations in demand are likely to occur, an acceptable range of variation is calculated using standard deviations of demand (see Figure 2). If demand is higher than expected, one or more rate classes may be closed, while if demand is lower than expected, one or more rate classes may be opened. A simple threshold curve can be built using historical mean and standard deviations of demand, although many of the commercial applications of this methodology are fitted using cubic spline methodology. In Figure 2, the heavy line represents the average demand, while the other lines represent between ±.25 through ±2 standard deviations of demand. The function of the cubic spline methodology is to smooth out the threshold curves.

Belobaba (1986) views this approach as a statistical data management program which is not designed to find optimal booking limits.

FIGURE 2
Threshold Curve

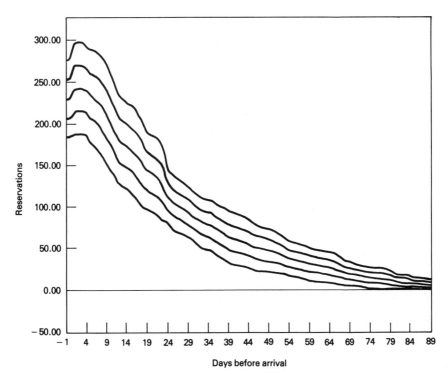

Days before arrival

Despite this limitation, the threshold curve methodology is fairly simple to use and appears to give good results. In addition, aggregate demand, rather than demand for different rate classes, is used to develop the threshold curve. As with other methods, the most critical problem is obtaining timely and accurate information.

Expert Systems Approaches

Several systems purporting to be expert system or neural network approaches have been developed, but too little information is available to assess their validity. Certainly, such an approach would be extremely useful to managers of capacity-constrained service organizations, but before adopting such a sophisticated method, managers must first be aware of the fundamentals of the problem with which they are faced.

SPECIFIC PROBLEMS WITH YIELD MANAGEMENT TECHNIQUES

Yield management techniques developed in one industry are not always immediately applicable to other industries. Yield management systems need to address the problems of multiple-phase services, such as legs of a flight, or multiple-night stays in a hotel. The multiplier effect of the inventory items (seats, rooms, cars) on other business functions must also be assessed.

MULTI-PHASE SERVICES.. Many services consist of more than one phase. For example, most airlines operate hub-and-spoke systems in which passengers purchase different flight legs, hotel guests may stay for more than one night, and car rental customers may rent the car for more than one day. Developing an optimal solution for the single phase of the service may not prove useful when considering the entire service network. Some commercial yield management systems have considered this problem on an ad hoc basis, but no published research systematically addresses this issue.

MULTIPLIER EFFECT. One of the underlying assumptions of yield management is that the inventory item being allocated is independent of other portions of the service business. For example, sales of airline seats do not affect other portions of the airline business. This assumption may be violated in some industries, such as the hotel industry, because customers purchase more than just rooms, and allocating reservations on only the basis of room rate may lead to less than optimal solutions when considering the overall revenue of the hotel.

MANAGERIAL IMPLICATIONS OF YIELD MANAGEMENT SYSTEMS

Very little has been written on the managerial implications associated with yield management. Yield management may give a firm a competitive edge, but it could also result in (1) a loss of competitive focus, (2) customer alienation, (3) severe employee morale problems, (4) a change in reward systems, and (5) a need for intensive employee training. As with any new approach to business, (6) proper organization and (7) a firm commitment from top management are essential.

1.   *Loss of competitive focus.* Since most yield management systems focus on maximizing revenue or yield, companies using such a system may develop an undue focus on short-term profits and ignore long-term profits which could result from managerial attention to producing and delivering good service. As Hayes and Abernathy (1980) point out, although financial success is imperative to any firm, an over-emphasis on short-term financial gains may lead to disastrous results. Many service organizations are successful because they offer very high quality services which are in high demand. The focus on efficient resource use that yield management implies may take managerial attention away from customer service, and fundamentally change the service concept. The net result may well be a loss of customers at considerable financial cost.

2.   *Customer alienation.* Consumers seem to be resigned to the fact that airlines charge different prices depending on how far ahead a ticket was bought, and on what restrictions were met, but will customers of other types of services do the same? In industries with only

a few major competitors (such as the airline or rental car industries) this may work, but in industries with a large number of competitors (such as the hotel industry), a customer who does not like paying different prices for the same room may decide to patronize the competition. Likewise, customers may find it unfair to be paying a higher price for a service than someone who reserved it a few weeks earlier. Firms adopting yield management programs may face a consumer education problem.

3. *Employee morale problems.* Yield management systems take much of the guess work out of how many items of inventory to sell at what price, but they also take some of the judgment out of the jobs of reservationists. Unless properly structured to allow for some judgment, yield management systems could be met with resentment from people having to use them.

4. *Incentive and reward systems.* Yield management systems could also cause a problem for group sales departments. Typically, salespeople in such departments are rewarded by the amount of sales they make. With a yield management system, it might not be beneficial for the business to accept a group sale at a low rate when that block of inventory could be sold at a higher rate. Unless incentive systems are changed, group sales workers might find that yield management works against them.

In a similar vein, managers are often rewarded on the basis of capacity utilization or average rate. With a yield management system, the manager needs to be concerned with both of these factors. Unless the incentive system is changed to reflect this, managers may resent using yield management.

5. *Employee training.* As with any new system, a yield management system will require extensive training of all employees. The employees must clearly understand the purpose of yield management, essentially how it works, and how it affects their jobs. Top management cannot assume that yield management will just happen: it requires careful planning and training.

6. *Organization of yield management function.* One of the major problems confronting most firms adopting yield management systems is degree of centralization of reservations systems. Airlines have traditionally had highly centralized reservations systems, but other industries, such as the hotel, rental car, and freight shipment industries tend to have more decentralized reservations systems. This problem can be overcome by developing a strong information system which integrates both central and branch reservations systems.

In terms of what department within the business should be responsible for the yield management system, arguments for several departments (sales, operations, reservations, MIS) could be made. Ideally, all areas of the firm will be involved with the yield management program. Only when this occurs will the program be truly successful.

7. *Top management commitment.* Without a commitment from top management, yield management systems may be doomed to failure. Unless all employees know that the yield management system is considered essential to the success of the company, they may be inclined to treat it less seriously than top management may prefer.

DIRECTIONS FOR FUTURE RESEARCH

Research in yield managment should address the following concerns.

1. *Integrate multiple-phase services into the solution technique.* Solution methods which include provisions for multiple flight legs, multiple night stays, multiple services, and multiple rental days must be developed if yield management systems are to be truly useful.

2. *Develop a method for solving problems with nested rate structures.* Nested rate structures seem to provide a more reasonable reservation model. Currently, only the EMSR (Belobaba (1987)) uses a nested rate structure. Mathematical programming methods which can use such a structure should be developed.

3. *Further develop solution techniques for quick and easy application.* One of the major problems confronting firms considering yield management is the frequency with which the problem must be resolved. Optimal methods are of little value when they take a long time to solve. Solution techniques which lend themselves to quick and

repetitive solutions will prove invaluable to firms using yield management.

4. *Analyze demand distributions and correlations.* Demand distributions and correlations have been studied thoroughly in the airline industry, but no published research has addressed this issue in other capacity-constrained industries. Without knowing the probability distribution of demand, cancellations and overbooking, improper assumptions may be made, and the results from the yield management program may be highly inaccurate.

5. *Analyze model sensitivity to data.* Models are often best designed for the data on which they were built (Mosteller and Tukey (1977)). Very little work on analyzing the performance of different methods on different types of data sets has been performed. This research would lend itself nicely to a simulation approach and would help determine which methods are better in which situations.

6. *Analyze booking rates over time.* One of the most difficult factors that firms practicing yield management must face is collecting the information necessary for implementation. A thorough study of how reservations are made for various classes of service must be made and integrated into the yield management system.

7. *Incorporate pricing decisions into solution methods.* Most current yield management approaches assume price is a given (Belobaba (1989)). Since yield management consists of both inventory management and pricing, techniques which can better integrate pricing into the yield management decisions would be extremely desirable.

8. *Develop centralized reservations and information systems.* Since information availability is often a problem, developing a centralized information system is of utmost importance. If the firm cannot access its demand history easily, the yield management system will become unworkable.

CONCLUSION

Yield management presents a tremendous opportunity for profitably managing capacity in capacity-constrained service firms. Research on solution techniques is fairly advanced in the airline industry, but much is left to be done in other industries. Emphasis should be placed on developing quick and easy-to-use methods which can immediately begin producing results. Operations management researchers

can provide an invaluable service to capacity-constrained firms by helping them manage their capacity more efficiently.

REFERENCES

[1]ALSTRUP, JENS, SOREN BOAS, OLI MADSEN, and RENE VIDAL. "Booking Policy for Flights with Two Types of Passengers." *European Journal of Operations Research*, vol. 27, 1986, 274–288.

[2]BECKMAN, M.J. "Decision and Team Problems in Airline Reservations." *Econometrica*, vol. 26, 1958, 134–145.

[3]BELOBABA, PETER PAUL. *Air Travel Demand and Airline Seat Inventory Management.* Unpublished doctoral dissertation, Massachusetts Institute of Technology, 1987.

[4]BELOBABA, PETER PAUL. "Application of a Probabilistic Decision Model to Airline Seat Inventory Control." *Operations Research*, vol. 37, no. 2, 1989, 183–197.

[5]CROSS, ROBERT G. "Strategic Selling: Yield Management Techniques to Enhance Revenue." Presented to Shearson-Lehman Brothers 1986 Airline Industry Seminar. Key Largo, Florida, February 1986.

[6]CURRY, RENWICK E. "Optimum Airline Seat Allocation with Fare Classes Nested by Origins and Destinations." Unpublished paper, Aeronomics, Inc., 1988.

[7]DEETMAN, C. "Booking Levels." *AGIFORS Proceedings*, vol. 4, 1964, 210–235.

[8]GLOVER, FRED, RANDY GLOVER, JOE LORENZO, and CLAUDE MCMILLAN. "The Passenger-Mix Problem in the Scheduled Airlines." *Interfaces*, vol. 12, no. 3, 1982, 73–79.

[9]HAYES, ROBERT H., and WILLIAM J. ABERNATHY. (1980). "Managing Our Way to Economic Decline." *Harvard Business Review*, vol. 58, no. 4, 1980, 67–77.

[10]HERSH, MARVIN, and SHAUL P. LADANY. "Optimal Seat Allocation for Flights with One Intermediate Stop." *Computers and Operations Research*, vol. 5, 1978, 31–37.

[11]LADANY, SHAUL P. "Dynamic Operating Rules for Motel Reservations." *Decision Sciences*, vol. 7, no. 4, 1976, 829–840.

[12]LADANY, SHAUL P. "Bayesian Dynamic Operating Rules for Optimal Hotel Reservation." *Z. Operations Research*, vol. 21, 1977, B165–176.

[13]LIEBERMAN, V., and U. YECHIALLI. "On the Hotel Overbooking Problem: An Inventory Problem

with Stochastic Cancellations." *Management Science*, vol. 24, 1978, 1117–1126.

[14]LITTLEWOOD, KENNETH. "Forecasting and Control of Passenger Bookings." *AGIFORS Proceedings*, vol. 12, 1972, 95–117.

[15]*Lloyd's Aviation Economist*. "Yield Managers Now Control Tactical Marketing." May 1985, 12–13.

[16]LOVELOCK, CHRISTOPHER. "Strategies for Managing Capacity-Constrained Service Organizations." *Service Industries Journal*, November 1984.

[17]MARTINEZ, R., and SANCHEZ, M. "Automated Booking Level Control." *AGIFORS Proceedings*, 1970.

[18]MOSTELLER, FREDERICK, and JOHN W. TUKEY. *Data Analysis and Regression*. Reading, MA: Addison-Wesley, 1977.

[19]ORKIN, ERIC B. "Boosting Your Bottom Line with Yield Management." *Cornell Hotel and Restaurant Administration Quarterly*, February 1988, 52–56.

[20]RELIHAN, WALTER J. "Yield Management Approach to Hotel-Room Pricing." *Cornell Hotel and Restaurant Administration Quarterly*, May 1989, 40–45.

[21]ROTHSTEIN, MARVIN. "An Airline Overbooking Model." *Transportation Science*, vol. 5, 1971, 180–192.

[22]ROTHSTEIN, MARVIN. "Hotel Overbooking as a Markovian Sequential Decision Process." *Decision Sciences*, vol. 5, 1974, 389–394.

[23]ROTHSTEIN, MARVIN. "Operations Research and the Airline Overbooking Problem." *Operations Research*, vol. 33, no. 2, 1985, 237–248.

[24]ROTHSTEIN, MARVIN, and A. W. STONE. "Passenger Booking Levels." *AGIFORS Proceedings*, vol. 7, 1967.

[25]SCHLIFER, E., and Y. VARDI. "An Airline Overbooking Policy." *Transportation Sciences*, vol. 9, 1975, 101–114.

[26]TAYLOR, C. J. "The Determination of Passenger Booking Levels." *AGIFORS Proceedings*, vol. 2, 1962, 93–116.

[27]THOMPSON, H. R. "Statistical Problems in Airline Reservation Control." *Operational Research Quarterly*, 12, 1961, 167–185.

[28]TOH, REX. "Airline Revenue Yield Protection: Joint Reservation Control Over Full and Discount Fare Sales." *Transportation Journal*, Winter 1979, 74–80.

[29]TOH, REX. "An Inventory Depletion Overbooking Model for the Hotel Industry." *Journal of Travel Research*, Spring 1985, 24–30.

[30]WILLIAMS, FRED E. "Decision Theory and the Innkeeper: An Approach for Setting Hotel Reservation Policy." *Interfaces*, vol. 7, no. 4, 1977, 18–30.

[31]WILLIAMSON, ELIZABETH L. *Comparison of Optimization Techniques for Origin-Destination Seat Inventory Control*. Unpublished MS thesis, Massachusetts Institute of Technology, 1988.

[32]WOLLMER, RICHARD D. "An Airline Reservation Model for Opening and Closing Fare Classes." Unpublished Douglas Aircraft report, 1989.

The Parker House:
Sales and Reservations Planning

PENNY PITTMAN MERLISS
CHRISTOPHER H. LOVELOCK

The management of a successful hotel finds itself on the horns of a dilemma. A large tour group seeks to make a major booking, with the possibility of additional bookings at two other hotels in the same chain. Yet management is reluctant to allocate too much of the hotel's capacity to this type of client, preferring to attract business travelers who pay top rates and are more consistent with the image desired for the Parker House.

"Could I speak to you for a minute, Mac?"

Robert McIntosh, general manager of the Parker House, Boston's oldest hotel, looked up from his desk. William Murphy, the hotel's director of sales, was standing in the doorway. McIntosh smiled. "Any time, Bill," he replied, hoping no more surprises had surfaced since last week, when a group of athletes sponsored by one of the hotel's leading corporate clients had smoked enough marijuana to render their rooms uninhabitable for 24 hours. Or perhaps another VIP was complaining about the need to book early at the Parker House; the hotel was often filled to capacity during the fall season, and this October was proving to be no exception.

"We've got a problem on our hands with TransAm Tours," Murphy began. "My sales force has been doing its best to cut down on tour groups, especially since the hotel's done such a good job of attracting clients who will pay the full rate. Some of our other properties—I am thinking of the Berkshire Place in Manhattan—can't afford to turn down a lot of tour business."

McIntosh nodded. He was well aware of the Parker House's 85 percent occupancy rate, significantly above the national average and the second highest in the Dunfey Hotels system.

"Well, I just got a call from Harvey Kimball" [Dunfey's national tour sales director], Murphy continued. "He's worked out a

---

This case was prepared as the basis for class discussion. Copyright © 1980 by the President and Fellows of Harvard College, Harvard Business School case 9-580-152.

deal with TransAm Tours for next summer and fall. They've agreed to block out approximately 2,000 guest nights at the Berkshire Place, weekends as well as midweek, from June through October of next year. The problem is that TransAm is trying to leverage the Berkshire deal into roughly 4,000 guest nights with us during the same period. Now, not only are we trying to avoid tour groups — we're also trying to maximize our room revenues. On the other hand, Mac, the Berkshire is a Dunfey hotel, and it needs our help. What do you think we should do?"

DUNFEY CLASSIC HOTELS

The Parker House was the most profitable of the company's 23 hotels. Generally considered to be the flagship of the corporation, it was the premier member of Dunfey's Classic Hotels division, directed by Yervant Chekijian. Management felt that the Classic hotels — each of which was a unique unit — offered discriminating travelers a welcome opportunity to escape the monotony of the chains. The Classics also provided a retreat from the noise and crowds of conventions. As Chekijian explained:

> A Dunfey Classic is not a convention hotel. While we will accommodate small executive and professional groups, our marketing approach is not to pack the house with large groups. We are seeking a quiet, peaceful atmosphere.... Our feeling is that corporate travelers who are regular customers of the hotel will appreciate knowing that they can get rooms with us even if the rest of the town is sold out to a convention.

Each Classic hotel was a formerly elegant property located in the city center which had fallen into decay prior to Dunfey's purchase. The renovation process involved more than refurbishment of facilities. In the words of William Dunfey:

> A Dunfey Classic hotel is not just an old hotel that we've slapped a new coat of paint onto. Even though some of the properties may have been neglected or run down when we took over, they all had a tradition of excellence and quality. Turning them into Classic hotels involves restor-

ing that level of service as well as restoring the physical plant.

In keeping with Dunfey management's belief in the individuality of the Classic hotels, each had a very different decorating scheme. The Berkshire Place, in Manhattan, where major renovations had recently been completed at a cost of over $9 million, had a contemporary tone, with large green plants, hand-woven Oriental rugs, and imported Italian marble columns and floors in the lobby. the Ambassador East, in Chicago, restored a year earlier for over $7 million, was decorated in a mixture of eighteenth-century English antiques and Oriental and contemporary accessories.

Renovations at the Parker House had been designed to establish the air of understated luxury considered most congenial to cultivated New England tastes. Old oak paneling and rich Oriental carpets decorated the lobby; burnished, ornately patterned brass doors glowed on the elevators; a two-tiered brass chandelier was suspended from the elaborately carved central wooden ceiling. Encouraged by the success of the first round of room renovations, the Dunfey management had begun even more luxurious redecorating. The cuisine served in Parker's Restaurant had become widely recognized for its excellence among Boston diners; according to *Boston* magazine, Parker's was one of the ten best restaurants in the city and offered the best Sunday brunch in town.

Situated on the Freedom Trail, a self-guided walking tour through the heart of historic Boston, the Parker House was closer to Boston's financial, governmental, and trade centers than any other major hotel in the city. Much of the waterfront area, once decayed, now contained new apartments, offices, shopping areas, and parks; the recently restored Faneuil Hall-Quincy Market retail and restaurant complex, which had become enormously popular, was less than a ten-minute walk from the hotel. However, over the next three years, three new luxury hotels were scheduled to open in the same area as the Parker House. Offering a combined total of over 1,200 rooms, these new hotels would be operated by Inter-Continental, Meridien, and Marriott Hotels, respectively.

The Parker House was the oldest continuously operating hotel in the United States. The original building, constructed in 1855, quickly attracted a large and cosmopolitan clientele. The hotel had been almost totally rebuilt in 1927, but during the fifties and sixties it fell into decline. By 1969, occupancy at the Parker House was down to 35 percent, and the hotel that had hosted presidents was forced to declare bankruptcy.

Subsequently, the Parker House was rescued by Dunfey Hotels, a privately owned chain. The Dunfey family hired the former head of Sheraton's international marketing, Jon Canas, as vice president of sales and marketing.

Well aware of the heavy fixed costs of operating a hotel, Canas and his team knew that their major source of profits lay in room sales rather than food and beverage revenue. Accordingly, they went after all the business they could find: tour groups, conventions, training sessions, anything to "keep the lights on." As occupancy rose, they began to upgrade the appearance of the Parker House, renovating, restoring, and finally repositioning rooms, restaurants, and public areas. Room prices rose accordingly, and many of the customers who had initially enabled the hotel to survive were replaced by less price-sensitive corporate clients. Successful renovation of the Parker House, combined with Canas's marketing efforts and the improving national economy, led the Dunfey hotels' revenues to double.

MARKETING STRATEGY

The key to successful marketing, in the opinion of Dunfey management, was segmentation. Ron Gustafson, Dunfey's manager of sales administration, stated:

> What we want to say is, "We are this type of a hotel: now what do we need to do to reach these segments?" First we canvass an area door to door. We talk to customers and find out their needs. Then we bring them down and show them the hotel. When business begins to pick up, we try

to monitor whether we're taking share from the correct hotels. We want to build our business with the correct market segments — not just fill rooms — because we're building for the future and the profile of customers we take in has a tremendous impact on creating a position for the hotel in the minds of the customers. For example, if our hotel is in the luxury class appealing to the upscale business executive and professional traveler, we don't want the badge-and-bottle conventioneers running around the lobby because, frankly, it destroys the atmosphere.

Extensive segmentation was very unusual in the hotel business. Most hotels segmented their guests into tourists, corporate travelers, and groups. However, the Parker House segmented its clients as follows:

1. *Pure Transient* — the customer, either tourist or corporate traveler, who simply picked up the phone and made a reservation at the rack rate,[1] attracted through general advertising or word of mouth. No direct sales effort reached this person.

2. *Outside Reservation* — the customer whose room (also at rack rate) was arranged through Dunfey's toll-free reservations number, often used by travel agents. This number, operated for Dunfey by an independent reservation service, cost the Parker House $100 per month, plus $5.43 for each individual reservation made. Management was interested to see how well this service performed.

3. *Executive Service Plan (ESP)* — executives traveling singly or in groups smaller than ten who reserved their rooms through an unlisted number and paid rack rate. Because this group was, to a large extent, drawn to the Parker House as a result of personal sales calls by ESP representatives, it was important to measure the success of the sales effort.

4. *Special Transient* — a limited category composed of friends of management, favored travel agents, etc. This segment was traced so that the lower rates charged to it would not skew other rate data. the hotel tried to limit these bookings to slow periods, such as weekends or the first quarter of the year.

---

[1]The published rate charge for each accomodation, as established by hotel management.

5. *Patriot* — the government segment. The Parker House had 36 extremely small rooms, each containing a single bed, which were offered to government employees for a price considerably below the rack rate. Annually, 7,000 room nights in this category were billed.

6. *Mini-Vacation* — a standard weekend package comprising two nights (Friday-Saturday or Saturday-Sunday) and two breakfasts. It cost $88.

7. *Classic Package* — the luxury weekend package, including a wine and cheese platter in the room, Godiva chocolates in the evening, sheets turned down before bedtime, dinner at Parker's Restaurant. It cost $186.

8. *Corporate Groups* — corporate clients reserving rooms at the same time in blocks of ten or more. It was very unusual for the Parker House to book sleeping space for groups of over 150 people, though meetings of up to 500 were accepted.

9. *Associations* — professional associations reserving rooms in blocks of ten or more. Their rates varied, depending on the time of the year and the desirability of the groups. Medical associations, for example, were highly prized, because they spent heavily on food and beverage and often planned their meetings during the weekends.

10. *Bus Tours* — the hotel attempted to limit these groups to weekends and the months of July and August, traditionally slower periods. The Parker House also tried to upgrade its bus tours from American groups to European, Japanese, and other foreign tourists, who were willing to pay higher rates.

11. *Airline* — 117 small rooms, overlooking airshafts, were secured through annual contracts with airlines using Boston's Logan International Airport and were occupied seven nights a week. European and other foreign airlines were courted because they were willing to pay more than American carriers.

The other categories were: *permanent residents* (at present, the Parker House had none); *complimentary rooms,* provided free of charge, sometimes to compensate for a previous error made by the hotel; and *house use rooms,* given to employees who were forced to stay overnight or who wished to appraise the hotel's service.

A quarterly breakdown of room revenue by segment is presented in *Exhibit 1.*

In some cases the market was segmented further by seasons of use, geography, and industry. When all rooms were full, or when a guest was turned away because of overbooking, management made sure that well-heeled transients and top-rated corporate clients were referred to Boston's best hotels, such as the Ritz, the Copley Plaza, and the Hyatt Regency. More price-sensitive guests were directed to middle-rank hotels or motor lodges.

Pricing varied for each segment and depended on competition. Boston hotel rates were much lower than rates at similar hotels in New York City. Competitive information was gathered at regular intervals. Projected rack rates at the Parker House for the coming year are reproduced in *Exhibit 2.*

One important benefit of the detailed segmentation employed by the Parker House was the guidance it offered to the sales division. Jon Canas commented:

> With the rooms merchandising plan you know what to ask sales and reservation people to do. In general, in the industry, salespeople do not know who to see, they do not know how many rooms are available, and they definitely do not know what rate to charge. At Dunfey we provide these guidelines as closely as possible to maximize our profitability and productivity.

The Sales Division

The Parker House sales division was led by Bill Murphy, who had previously directed sales at the Ambassador East in Chicago. He directed a group of five salespeople and eight inhouse telephone and clerical staff. Direct sales efforts were targeted toward the most desirable market segments, according to the hotel's mission statement. The sales manager handled professional associations; the corporate sales executive covered corporate groups; and the two ESP account executives, Lyssa O'Neill and Pamela Roberge, were responsible for sales to individual business travelers. Since most ESP reservations were made by secretaries or corporate travel managers, O'Neill

EXHIBIT 1
The Parker House Room Revenue by Segment, (quarterly)

Segment	(1) Jan.–Mar.	(2) April–June	(3) July–Sept.	(4) Oct.–Dec.	Annual Total
1. Pure transient	$ 448,087	$ 335,103	$ 387,227	$ 338,141	$1,508,558
2. ESP	382,287	605,889	594,414	594,224	2,176,814
3. Weekend packages	45,894	48,855	40,098	67,388	202,235
4. Patriot and airline	243,438	247,121	251,300	252,002	993,861
5. Associations and corporate groups	156,500	314,541	208,669	276,268	955,978
6. Bus tours	12,819	64,914	172,910	83,388	334,031
7. Other*	38,095	21,353	23,276	32,555	115,279
Total	$1,327,120	$1,637,776	$1,677,894	$1,643,966	$6,286,756

*Includes Special Transients and Outside Reservation System guests.

EXHIBIT 2
Projected Parker House Room Rates, Next Year

Room Category	Number	RATE Single	RATE Double	Furnishings
1. Standard	130	$ 70	$ 80	Double bed, clock radio, color TV, Drexel furniture, Thermopane windows, individually controlled heat and air conditioning. The least expensive room available to ESP clients.
2. Deluxe	181	80	90	Similar to standard; larger room.
3. Top of the line	20	90	100	King-size beds; other furnishings similar to standard; larger room.
4. Mini-suite	48	105	115	Very large room (often constructed from two smaller rooms, with a wall removed) with walk-in closets and dividers between living and sleeping areas.
5. Parlor suite	16	$125		Living room, bedroom (1 or more), and some kitchen facilities such as a sink or wet bar.
6. Deluxe suite	2	250		Larger rooms, complete kitchen facilities, luxurious furnishings.

and Roberge directed the majority of their calls to people in these positions. Banquets were handled by another representative who also reported to Murphy.

One of the hotel's goals was to shift its market base toward customer segments more likely to pay full rates. Very seldom were all 546 rooms in the Parker House sold at the rack rate; most often about 30 percent were discounted. To raise room sales efficiency[2]

and reduce discounting, management had decided to aim for a lower occupancy rate — 83.5 percent — in the hope of bringing in more guests at rack rate and raising revenues and profits. The latest renovations and rate increases were an essential part of this strategy. As Yervant Chekijian put it: "We are going to have no compromises on our product offering, and at the same time, we are not going to apologize for our rates."

Executive Service Plan

Rates for tours, groups, and associations were often discounted, but ESP clients were

---

[2]Defined as the ratio of total room sales revenue over a period divided by the potential revenues that might be obtained if all available rooms were sold at full rates during the same period.

always charged the rack rate. The ESP plan was considered the key to the hotel's new room sales efficiency target. Designed to make it convenient for individual corporate travelers to use the hotel, the plan included a direct unlisted telephone number reserved for ESP clients (out-of-town customers could call collect); "preferred" (i.e., larger) rooms; preregistration to ensure easy check-in; an express check-out service; bill-back privileges; a welcome packet, including a complimentary newspaper each morning; and a special ESP privilege on Friday and Saturday nights entitling the spouse of an ESP guest to stay at the hotel free of charge.

Direct sales calls were an essential element of ESP marketing strategy. The Parker House sales division kept files on 710 ESP companies, categorized as red, blue, green, or yellow depending on how frequently their employees used the hotel. Red clients, who booked over 150 room nights annually, were called on monthly; blue clients (75-150 rooms annually), every two months; green clients (25-75 rooms annually), every three months; and yellow clients (less than 25 rooms annually), once or twice a year. In order to cover these accounts, ESP reps Roberge and O'Neill made approximately 40 calls (including 16 key accounts) weekly.

The ESP job was the hotel's entry-level sales position. Selling to groups and associations, according to Dunfey management, required dealing with experienced travel and convention planners and was handled by more senior members of the sales staff. In fact, since many of the ESP accounts were steady clients of the Parker House, and the demand for hotel space in Boston was high for a large part of the year, the ESP reps tended to view their job as customer service or client education rather than sales. "As salespeople we're not strictly solicitors at all," said O'Neill. "We're more personal contact. We are the company's liaison to the hotel, and they can call us if they have a problem. They know our faces, our names."

Neither ESP representative considered it very difficult to distinguish the hotel's most valuable clients. Commented O'Neill:

The least desirable people are those who are very price-sensitive and concerned about the rates. For instance, one guy who ran a shoe outlet wanted to have a function here and bring his own liquor and his own dry snacks. People like that — or people who have reservations made on short notice in spring and fall only — I really want to discourage because the hotel is full during that time and their volume is nothing we can put our finger on. I'll bring up rates during the call, which is something a salesperson usually doesn't do. Alternatively, I would encourage such a client to go through the front desk or the 800 number, which offers the smaller, less expensive rooms that we don't sell to ESP guests.

The sales staff saw one of its major challenges as determining how many rooms should be set aside for clients desiring long lead time, how many rooms should go to shorter lead-time groups, and how much capacity should be saved for walk-in business. Faced with average occupancy rates ranging from 90–97 percent, Monday–Thursday, during many periods, many clients tried to book well in advance. (Occupancy rates Friday–Sunday during the same periods averaged 80–83 percent.) The Parker House, however, refused to quote rates more than six months in advance and had set a 45-day maximum on advance banquet bookings at lunch; such banquets could potentially interfere with the needs of groups booking rooms as well as meal service. Jon Canas summed up the situation:

Consider New England during the middle of October. For us success at this time is to have 100 percent walk-in transient business at the rack rate — and to have raised the rate the day before! It wouldn't be to our best interest to have booked a group at a very low rate way in advance when we know we're going to get this excellent, high-rated transient business at this time of year. On the other hand, there are cases which crop up when it's necessary to give people a discount in the middle of October — when you could have had the highest rate — in order to get that business back on January 2 when you will otherwise have nothing. So, it's a constant game of balancing.

Roberge and O'Neill made a point of reminding their accounts about the hotel shortage in Boston. There were a total of 6,925 rooms in the city; all major hotels were fully booked for close to 90 days of the year. The sales division published a special quarterly newsletter for ESP clients which publicized problem dates, and also kept a waiting list, for ESP accounts, after space closed.

The hotel continued to solicit some new business, primarily in New York City, where Roberge and O'Neill had recently traveled on a sales trip. It was hoped that the highly desirable, less price-sensitive accounts solicited there would crowd out smaller, rate-conscious clients and increase the number of ESP guests.

Managers believed that no other hotel in Boston offered significant competition to the Parker House's ESP account coverage program. The Sonesta sent representatives out to corporate accounts about once every two months; other hotels invited clients to occasional public relations functions.

Tour Groups

Although Harvey Kimball, Dunfey's director of tour sales, maintained his office at the Parker House, the greater part of his marketing efforts were directed toward other Dunfey hotels which considered tours an important part of their business mix. His task was to uncover leads; it was the responsibility of the individual hotel's Executive Operating Committee (EOC), aided by the regional director of sales, to decide whether the business was good for the hotel. Kimball received a yearly salary, plus a bonus based on the number of room nights he brought in.

Janet Morin, the Parker House tour coordinator, was a secretary in the general manager's office who received no incentive and made no direct sales calls of any kind. "It really isn't necessary," she stated. "The tour wholesalers call us — in fact, I usually get about 18 calls a day and end up referring most of them to the Park Plaza,[3] which is more eager to get tours than we are." Rates for groups of 15 or more

---

[3]A large hotel, not part of the Dunfey organization, located on the fringe of the downtown area.

varied according to the time of year, ranging from $44 to $58 (single), with a $10 additional charge per person for double, triple, and quadruple occupancy. The hotel did not encourage tours during the middle of the week, because ESP and transient guests brought in much more revenue. During the weekend, however, ESP guests almost vanished, and as Morin noted, "We need anything we can get." Tour rooms as a percentage of total rooms sold monthly ranged from 0.3 percent to 11 percent; tour room revenues as a percentage of total monthly revenues ranged from 0.3 percent to 8 percent.

Tours usually reached the hotel in groups of 46, a standard bus load. Most tour group guests were older people who preferred not to drive themselves, and they spent relatively little money in the hotel. "Our restaurants are in the moderate to expensive range," Morin explained, "and tour operators want the least expensive rate they can get on everything. They'll put inexpensive restaurants on the itinerary and herd the group in and out." The one meal which tour groups usually ate in the hotel was breakfast, and this had caused problems in the past, according to Morin:

> The breakfast scene is at its worst in the fall. We may have several tours in the hotel and they'll all come down for breakfast at 8:15 or 8:30, because their buses leave at 9. You have hundreds of people waiting to eat breakfast, lines in the lobby, buses leaving at 9, people getting edgy, and then if they have to miss breakfast to catch the bus they all want vouchers for another meal. It gets very confusing.

Tour wholesalers also tended to submit their passenger lists to the hotel at the last minute, a habit which both the sales division and the front desk found intensely annoying. "We like to get a rooming list three weeks beforehand for forecasting," Morin explained, "but tour groups will sell space in a tour till the day they leave. They'll send us a list with four names on it to meet the deadline, and then they'll give us any excuse to keep putting more names on. That's okay on weekends, but terrible on weeknights." Tours also often failed to meet their pre-established check-in times of 1 p.m. Groups coming in late were asked to wait in their buses until the lobby was clear of other tours, "but they always get out anyway and end up crowding around the desk."

Despite these frustrations, Morin felt that tour wholesalers offered one advantage to the hotel in addition to raising weekend occupancy: they did occasionally bring in corporate bonus trips. Fifty top sales representatives from a large corporation, for example, might be rewarded with a weekend in Boston and brought to the hotel in a group. Since corporations were less price-sensitive than tourists, the hotel could charge rack rate for each room.

TransAm Tours [disguised name] operated out of the West Coast and put together packaged tours for travel agents and individuals. This firm was considered a relatively "exclusive" tour wholesaler by the Parker House. "They're price-sensitive," Morin commented, "but their customers aren't." TransAm tourists were flown to Boston and then put aboard a bus which would transport them through New England. A typical group would come in late Thursday night, spend Friday exploring Boston and return after dinner, spend Saturday in New Hampshire, return to the hotel Saturday night, and leave early Sunday for Vermont. "They don't spend any money in the hotel, outside breakfast," Morin noted, "because they're never here."

Advertising, Promotion, and Customer Relations

The Parker House advertising strategy, as devised by Bill Murphy and Dunfey's senior marketing executives, was twofold. The hotel was promoted locally, as an individual property, and nationally, as a Dunfey Classic hotel. Although the need for strong promotion had been questioned, Paul Sacco, Dunfey's corporate director of sales, felt the Parker House's high average occupancy rate was very deceptive:

The hotel is favored with a very heavy demand on Monday, Tuesday, and Wednesday nights. But we fight like hell to get people to stay on Sunday night, and we beg them to stay over Thursday and check out Friday — maybe stay for the weekend, bring their spouse. When we have an occupancy in the high 90s Sunday through Saturday, we will be satisfied. That's not presently the case.

Bill Murphy added:

It's important not to look at it as though we do not need to sell any more. Actually, we have to work even harder — it's easier to get soft at the top. Our sales reps don't have a quota of 25 new accounts per week any more, but they do have a firm quota of 40 calls. That's necessary just to keep up with movement within firms and within the city.

Classic hotel advertising, budgeted at close to $800,000 per year, promoted the Parker House, the Berkshire Place, and the Ambassador East as a group, and was supervised by Dunfey's director of advertising and public relations.

The Classic hotels advertisement was designed to upgrade and promote the Dunfey corporate image while it simultaneously linked the three hotels as a group. A four-color, one-page ad, it first appeared in the Boston, New York, Chicago, and Los Angeles editions of leading national news and business magazines. Local promotion of the Parker House as a Classic hotel was particularly important, according to Dunfey's advertising director:

The Boston market is a very important source of guests for New York and Chicago. The Dunfey corporate image still needs to be supported. And also, though from a rooms point of view and an occupancy point of view they may not seem to need it, the combination of the Parker House with the Ambassador and the Berkshire is helping to further position the Parker House, further upgrade its image ... as well as positioning Dunfey.

Local promotion for the Parker House was supervised by Bill Murphy, whose combined advertising and sales budget totalled approximately $260,000. Except during December, January, and February, when occupancy averaged 75 percent, promotions (such as parties for clients or inexpensive desk items for travel agents) were not a major concern at the hotel.

Management placed a good deal of emphasis on customer reaction to the hotel. Questionnaires were distributed to clients after banquets; they were also placed prominently in every room. The cards were signed by Roy Dunfey, vice president of employee and guest relations, and designed to be mailed directly to him. Although comments were not tabulated by segment, it was McIntosh's opinion that bus tours complained the most. As he put it: "They are on limited budgets, they have high expectations because their vacation is a big thing for them, they have time on their hands for complaining, and they give lots of reinforcement to each other's objections."

THE CONTINUED DEBATE

The Parker House's dislike for tour groups was not totally shared in Dunfey headquarters, and by mid-October, as the deadline for responding to TransAm's offer for the following year approached, discussions grew increasingly heated. From the beginning, there had been no doubt that the Berkshire Place business would be accepted. TransAm had originally offered to pay a flat $25 (double), mid-week and weekend, for 2,000 Berkshire guest nights. After bargaining the rate up to $55, Dunfey sales executives felt that the revised contract was almost indispensable, considering the Berkshire's recent occupancy rate: 60 percent in July, 70 percent in August (breakeven was 62 percent). Then came a strong intimation from TransAm that the Berkshire business next year might ultimately depend on a guarantee of all 4,000 guest-nights requested at the Parker House.

Terry Flahive, Dunfey's regional director of sales for New England, told Paul Sacco, the corporate director of sales:

> We're desperate for business in New York. From a corporate point of view, we want those room nights to make the Berkshire Place successful. I think we're going to have to bite the bullet at the

Parker House, even though it might be bad rooms merchandising.

Sacco tended to agree. As he pointed out to Bill Murphy:

> It isn't a big bite, because we definitely want the business at the Berkshire Place, and at the Parker House we want the weekends. What we're arguing about is weeknights, mid-week, and the question is whether we should cut some of that revenue to capture the rest.

Murphy, on the other hand, was strongly opposed:

> We're already booked very heavily to other tour brokers, and if we accept TransAm for evey date they've requested, we're going to be rolling the dice a little bit, hoping we get some cancellations. What is even more important, in my opinion, is that if we add another tour group of this volume, we're going against the entire mission of the hotel.

TransAm's Parker House room requests are reproduced in *Exhibit 3.* Approximately half of these requests were accepted immediately, at a rate of $32/39, single/double (weekend) and $53/61 (weekday). TransAm then requested that the hotel accept the remaining tour bookings at a rate of $32/39 (weekend) and $63/73 (weekday); it was implied that all TransAm business for the following year would hinge on the hotel's acceptance of this latest offer.

Murphy and Flahive immediately began an intensive review of the specifics of the TransAm proposals, attempting to calculate exactly how much tour space was available and how much revenue the tours might generate, compared with expected transient and corporate business. The key to establishing room availability was the Group Rooms Control Log (GRC), which listed "selective sell targets" for groups broken down by room night. By starting with the total number of rooms in the hotel (546) and subtracting projected transient, ESP, "patriot," and airline business, the sales department could apportion a certain number of rooms each night to be sold to groups of all kinds, including corporate groups, associa-

EXHIBIT 3
Transam's Requested Future Bookings at the Parker House, June–October

	S	M	T	W	T	F	S
June					[26]a	[27]a	
July			1	2	3	4	5
	6	7	8	9	(10)a	(11)a	12
	13	14	15	16	17	18	19
	20	21	22	23	[24]a	[25]a	26
	27	28	29	30	(31)a		
August						(1)a	2
	3	4	5	6	(7)a	(8)a	9
	10	11	12	13	14	15	16
	17	18	19	20	[21]b	[22]b	23
	24	25	26	27	28	29	30
	31						
September		1	2	3	[4]a	[5]a	6
	7	8	9	10	[11]a	[12]a	13
	14	15	16	(17)*	△18 b	◇19 d	△20 a
	(21)a	22	(23)*	[24]*	△25 *	◇26 c	[27]a
	(28)*	(29)*	(30)*				
October				[1]*	△2 *	◇3 *	[4]*
	(5)*	(6)*	(7)*	△8 *	△9 *	◇10 b	[11]b
	(12)*	(13)*	(14)*	[15]*	△16 b	◇17 d	[18]a

Bookings Requested by TransAm Tours for Specific Dates:

○ One group (2 singles, 20 doubles, 1 complimentary for tour escort).

□ Two groups (4 singles, 40 doubles, 2 complimentary).

△ Three groups (6 singles, 60 doubles, 3 complimentary).

◇ Four groups (8 singles, 80 doubles, 4 complimentary).

Parker House's Initial Response to TransAm Requests:

a All reservations requested for that date were immediately accepted by the hotel.

b Only one group of requested bookings was accepted.

c Only two groups of requested bookings were accepted.

d Only three groups of requested bookings were accepted.

* None of requested bookings were accepted.

SOURCE: Company records.

EXHIBIT 4
Extract from Group Rooms Control Log

Type of Group	Number of rooms requested* Gross	Net	Day	S	M	T	W	T	F	S	Rates
			Aug.	17	18	19	20	21	22	23	
			SST†	193	135	135	135	140	253	258	
Assoc./Corp.‡											
Definite	800	500		125	125	125	125				53/61
Tentative	600	600		100	100	100	100	100	100		NRQ#
Tours											
Definite	52	40					40				28/31/36
Tentative	169	164						47	72	45	NRQ

Type of Group	Number of rooms requested Gross	Net	Day	S	M	T	W	T	F	S	Rates
			Aug.	24	25	26	27	28	29	30	
			SST†	103	110	75	75	90	233	258	
Assoc./Corp.‡											
Definite	200	160		40	40	40	40				NRQ
Tentative	0	0									
Tours											
Definite	25	20					20				28/31/36
Tentative	632	593		25				67	238	263	28/43

Type of Group	Number of rooms requested Gross	Net	Day	S	M	T	W	T	F	S	Rates
			Sep.	21	22	23	24	25	26	27	
			SST	128	100	75	75	90	233	258	
Assoc./Corp.‡											
Definite	267	220					70	70	70	10	58/68
Tentative	100	80				80					NRQ
Tours											
Definite	50	40					20			20	28/31/36
Tentative	827	769		114				35	311	309	28/43

Type of Group	Number of rooms requested Gross	Net	Day	S	M	T	W	T	F	S	Rates
			Sep.	28	29	30	Oct. 1	2	3	4	
			SST†	138	90	75	75	75	218	238	
Assoc./Corp.											
Definite	298	293		50	60	50	61	61	11		NRQ
Tentative	0	0									
Tours											
Definite	225	198						20	45	133	NRQ
Tentative	576	500			85	20			185	210	30/43

Type of Group	Number of rooms requested Gross	Net	Day	S	M	T	W	T	F	S	Rates
			Oct.	5	6	7	8	9	10	11	
			SST	108	75	75	75	75	218	238	
Assoc./Corp.											
Definite	69	54						18	18	18	50/58
Tentative	0	0									
Tours											
Definite	200	170		40				20	45	65	28/43
Tentative	689	650			90	40		25	220	275	28/43

Type of Group	Number of rooms requested		Day Oct.	S 12	M 13	T 14	W 15	T 16	F 17	S 18	Rates
	Gross	Net	SST	148	50	50	60	60	208	188	
Assoc./Corp.											
Definite	120	90							45	45	NRQ
Tentative	0	0									
Tours											
Definite	75	70		20					25	25	28/49
Tentative	717	659		162	20			22	226	229	33/46

*Gross = the number of rooms reserved by a group; net = salesperson's estimate of the number of rooms a group would actually occupy.

†SST = "selective sell target," the optimum number of rooms to be sold to associations, corporate groups, and tours.

‡Assoc./Corp. = professional or special-interest associations and corporate groups.

#NRQ = no rate quoted.

SOURCE: Company records.

tions, and tours. GRCs for the remaining dates requested by TransAm are reproduced in *Exhibit 4*.

Potential TransAm revenues were then compared to the revenues to be derived from the sale of comparable rooms at the following year's projected summer and fall rack rates (*Exhibit 2*). Since it was not possible to know how guests would make their choices between room categories (e.g., standard vs. deluxe vs. top of the line), an average of standard and deluxe rates was used for calculations.

Murphy felt he was faced with three questions. Did the Parker House have space for TransAm on the data not yet accepted (*Exhibit 3*)? Would the TransAm business be as profitable as reservations which might be booked simultaneously by other segments? And how many tours could the Parker House accept without altering the desired positioning of the hotel?

As he wrestled with these issues, the phone rang. Harvey Kimball was on the line. "Bill, I just talked to TransAm Tours," he announced. "They told me they're putting things together for Chicago — and under certain circumstances, might consider booking at the Ambassador East. Can we give them the go-ahead for the Parker House?"

University Health Service:
Walk-In Clinic

SHAUNA DOYLE
ROCCO PIGNERI
DAVID H. MAISTER

The administrator of a walk-in health clinic is evaluating the performance of a triage system designed to reduce delays experienced by patients seeking different types of treatment. She wonders whether further changes are needed.

Kathryn Angell stared out her office picture window, oblivious to the bustle on Mount Auburn Street. Shortly after receiving her Master's degree in Health Policy and Management from the Harvard School of Public Health, Angell was hired into a new University Health Service position as Assistant Director for Ambulatory Care. A major objective of the new position was the reorganization of the Walk-In Clinic — the exact topic of Angell's thesis.

As the chief administrator of the clinic, responsible for its daily functioning, the organization of medical and support services and its overall planning, the emphasis of Angell's position was clearly placed on the improvement of the delivery of medical care through better services coordination and the implementation of new programs. Soon after assuming her duties in July, Angell implemented a triage system in the Walk-In Clinic, whereby arriving patients were screened by a triage coordinator to determine whether they should be treated by a nurse practitioner or a physician. After almost a year's operation under the new system, Angell's concern shifted from implementation to evaluation of the clinic's performance.

THE UNIVERSITY HEALTH SERVICE

The University Health Service offered medical care to Harvard University students, staff, faculty and their dependents who elected certain health care plans in which the services of UHS were included. Since the system was prepaid for over 90 percent of the potential users, UHS operated primarily as a health maintenance organization.

The medical services provided to patients by UHS included surgical and 24-hour emergency facilities, an inpatient infirmary, four outpatient clinics (including the Walk-In and three primary care clinics associated with specific Harvard professional schools), mental health services, laboratory and x-ray facilities, and a variety of other specialized services. Patients were free to choose a personal physician, who could be seen by appointment and who would, if necessary, refer the patient to an appropriate specialist. Ailments of an acute or emergency nature were treated by the outpatient clinics.

For the 1979–1980 fiscal year, UHS was budgeted approximately $10 million to meet its total health care expenses (*Exhibit 1*). Of

the $10 million, the Walk-In Clinic, including its emergency facilities, expended approximately 20 percent, including salaries to its medical professionals and clerical staff as well as its portion of overhead and supplies.

Physicians worked 46 forty-hour weeks in the year. Of the 40 hours, approximately 12 were spent in the Walk-In Clinic, 16 hours in meeting patients by appointment in the physician's office, 5 hours on duty at the UHS infirmary, and 7 hours on administrative and other matters. Included in the time for appointments (which were normally scheduled by the physician's secretary in half-hour intervals) were two half-hour periods per week known as "reserve time." These were periods when the doctor might ask patients to come to see her or him in the office, perhaps to check on the progress of treatment. Reserve time differed from regular appointments in that patients could not, by themselves, book appointments at these times: only the physician could schedule them. The physician could sometimes see up to 4 patients in one half-hour of reserve time. By well-established precedent, all UHS doctors were required to undertake duty in the Walk-

EXHIBIT 1
Income and Expense Statistics

INCOME	1979–80	%1978–79	%1979–80
Student health fee	$3,390,023	38.2	34.4
Student insurance	1,636,925	17.3	16.6
Harvard University			
Group Health Program	900,212	7.0	9.1
Payroll assessment	1,589,497	16.9	16.1
Care for Medicare	252,074	1.6	2.5
Radiation protection	435,603	3.8	4.4
Other services	1,628,448	15.2	16.9
Total	$9,832,782	100.0%	100.0%
EXPENSE			
Salaries, wages & benefits	$5,223,685	53.5	53.7
Student insurance	1,636,925	17.2	16.8
Building operations & maintenance	388,870	4.3	4.0
Medical/dental supplies	278,987	2.3	2.8
Outside laboratories	176,309	2.2	1.8
Malpractice insurance	49,048	1.1	.5
All other	1,967,436	19.4	20.4
Total	$9,721,260	100.0%	100.0%

In Clinic. Doctors who were associated with UHS on a part-time basis were normally allocated a proportionate share of their time in the clinic. While exceptions existed, most doctors preferred seeing patients in their office to Walk-In Clinic duty—partly because of the hectic pace of the Walk-In Clinic, but also because in their appointments they could deal with patients they knew and with whose medical records they were familiar. Salaries for physicians ranged from $35,000 to $55,000 for primary care physicians. Nurses were paid a range of $16,000 to $26,000, depending upon their level of practical experience. For both physicians and nurses, UHS incurred additional costs of 18.5 percent of salary in the form of benefits.

THE WALK-IN CLINIC

The Walk-In Clinic at the Holyoke Center provided the most comprehensive ambulatory care of the four walk-in clinics by offering the patient a portion of the total available UHS services. Patients with acute medical and surgical problems, who had not chosen a UHS personal physician, or who were unable to wait for appointments with their personal physicians, were served on a first-come, first-served basis Monday through Friday, 8 A.M. to 5:30 P.M. The clinic was also open on Saturday mornings, 8 A.M. to 12:45 P.M. Emergencies, of which there were relatively few, were of course treated immediately.

In 1979, over 37,400 patients visited the Walk-In Clinic for treatment of problems ranging from common ailments such as colds, nausea, and respiratory illnesses to those with more serious problems such as acute appendicitis and chest pains. Of the patients who visited the clinic, 67 percent were students, 23 percent staff, and 10 percent dependents and Medex and Medicare subscribers. One UHS study, conducted in 1980 over a three-week period, demonstrated that an average of 143 patients were seen per day (*Exhibits 2 and 3*).

Staffing levels for the Walk-In Clinic were scheduled on the basis of past experience

EXHIBIT 2
Daily Average of Patient Visits by Day of the Week

Monday	163
Tuesday	151
Wednesday	136
Thursday	137
Friday	128
Average	143

Average Number of Patient Arrivals per Hour

8–9 A.M.	18.2
9–10 A.M.	17.6
10–11 A.M.	16.8
11–12 noon	15.2
12–1 P.M.	11.8
1–2 P.M.	16.9
2–3 P.M.	16.2
3–4 P.M.	15.9
4–5 P.M.	11.6
5–6 P.M.	2.8

EXHIBIT 3
Patient Distribution by Reason for Visit*

Reason	Percent of Total
Emergency	1.4
Medical: initial visit**	41.3
Medical: return visit	11.3
Medical: specific provider	24.0
Surgical: initial visit**	0.1
Surgical: return visit	0.8
Lab result	2.0
Premarital test	0.4
Blood pressure	2.2
Prescription: confirmed diagnosis	0.8
Prescription refill	2.0
Administrative	1.0
Other	1.7
Unspecified (missing)	11.0
	100%

*As indicated by the patient.

**Initial visit for the specific complaint: this is not to be interpreted as the patient's first visit *ever* to the Walk-In Clinic.

EXHIBIT 4
University Health Service—Walk-In Clinic:
Medical Professional Scheduling 1979 Walk-In Clinic

	Monday		Tuesday		Wednesday		Thursday		Friday	
	# MDs	# NPs	# MDs	# NPs	# MDs	# NPs	# MDs	# NPs	# MDs	# NPs
8–9 A.M.	2	2	2	2	2	2	2	2	2	2
9–10 A.M.	2.5	4	3	4	2.5	4	2	4	2.5	4
10–11 A.M.	5	4	4	4	5	4	5	4	5	4
11–12 noon	3	4	3	4	3	4	3	4	4	4
12–1 P.M.	3	2.5	2	2.5	2.5	2.5	3	2.5	2.5	2.5
1–2 P.M.	3	2.5	3	2.5	3	2.5	2	2.5	3	2.5
2–3 P.M.	3	4	4	4	3	4	3	4	4	4
3–4 P.M.	4	4	4	4	4	4	4	4	4	4
4–5 P.M.	3	2.5	2	2.5	2	2.5	3.5	2.5	3	2.5
5–6* P.M.	1	2	1	2	1	2	1	2	1	2

MD = Medical Doctor.
NP = Nurse Practitioner.
*The clinic admitted its last patient at 5:30 P.M. Staff were required to stay until 6 P.M.

with peak periods of patient visits, which typically occurred between 10 A.M. and 4 P.M., according to the generally accepted impression of the UHS staff (*Exhibit 4*). No set criteria existed for establishing staffing levels; only minor adjustments were made year-to-year, at times that were felt to be too busy. Twenty-two physicians treated all patients in the clinic as part of their overall UHS responsibilities, and were scheduled by Ms. Angell for specific hours throughout the week, usually in blocks of 3 to 4 hours at a time. The Walk-In Clinic was also staffed by two registered nurses and eleven nurse practitioners, the latter being registered nurses with additional medical training capable of treating minor ailments without direct consultation with a physician. In a small number of cases, nurse practitioners also treated patients by appointment. Nurses and nurse practitioners worked 8-hour shifts, including one hour for lunch.

Nurse practitioners staffed the UHS emergency room at nights and weekends, and performed a variety of semiadministrative duties, such as receiving test results over the phone. Approximately 45 percent of nurse practitioner hours were available to treat patients in the Walk-In Clinic.

The Walk-In Clinic had 12 rooms available for seeing patients, 4 for nurses and 8 for doctors. However, 3 of the doctors' rooms were permanently assigned to individuals as their UHS offices, and were only available for Walk-In Clinic use at the times when those three individual physicians were scheduled for Walk-In Clinic duty.

PRE-TRIAGE ORGANIZATION

Before the triage system was instituted, a typical patient's visit to the Walk-In Clinic proceeded in the following way. On arrival, the patient signed in at the front desk, by providing basic identification information on a small, sequentially numbered sheet, and was then asked by a receptionist to take a seat in the waiting area. The receptionist next requested the patient's record from the Medical Records Department, who retrieved and sent down the record to the Walk-In Clinic in approximately 8–9 minutes. The receptionist then brought the record to the "medical desk" where a clerk checked to ensure that the patient's address and phone number were current and that all recent lab reports were present. When checking was completed, which took approximately 5 minutes, the clerk placed the record and the numbered sheet in a pile ordered according to the arrival of patients. Each patient was subsequently seen by the first available nurse when his or her medical record reached the top of the pile. If the problem was minor (such as a cold), the nurse would treat the patient definitively. However, if, after the nurse had done all she or he could, it was still necessary for the patient to see a physician, the patient would return to the waiting area and the nurse would put the record in a pile for the physicians, again according to the order of initial arrival. The patient would be seen, in turn, by the first available physician.

Widespread dissatisfaction had developed concerning the Walk-In Clinic. Waiting time between sign-in and treatment constituted the major complaint, specifically the waiting time to the first contact with a professional staff member capable of assessing the patient's problem. This time period averaged 23 minutes; however, as many as 22 percent of all patients who saw a nurse had to wait over 35 minutes for this first contact. A study of the Walk-In Clinic done in November 1978 found that patients who requested specific nurses or physicians at sign-in waited an average of 40 minutes before seeing the desired staff member; this group comprised approximately 19 percent of the total patient load. If a nurse had to refer a patient on to a doctor, an average of 10 minutes elapsed between the end of the nurse visit and the meeting with the doctor. Some patients complained that the length of their wait often had no relation to the nature of the visit such as a 55-minute wait for a prescription renewal. Other patients reportedly decided to avoid potential visits to the Walk-In Clinic because of the anticipated wait. Consequently, patients viewed the Walk-In Clinic as cold, inefficient, and impersonal since there was such a time gap between sign-in and treatment.

Members of the UHS administrative and medical staff also expressed feelings that the Walk-In Clinic could function better than it had. Sholem Postel, M.D., the Deputy Di-

rector and Chief of Professional Services (physicians and nurses) at UHS, and the person to whom Angell reported with respect to the Walk-In Clinic, commented on the pre-triage system's problems:

> All the nurses were involved in seeing all the patients initially. This created a bottleneck as each nurse independently decided the extent of care for a patient and then provided as much of that care as possible before, if necessary, having the patient wait to be seen by a physician for the rest of the care. This led to inconsistency and too much variation in treatment, given the different skills and experience levels of individual nurses. Furthermore, though nurses saw 100 percent of the patients, they treated only 40 percent definitively. The result: duplicated efforts (time, questions and examinations) for 60 percent of our patients.

THE TRIAGE SYSTEM

To overcome these problems, a "triage system" was introduced in September 1979 by the UHS administration. The system was defined as "the preliminary evaluation and referral of patients to the necessary health resource, based on decisions about the nature of the patients' problems and knowledge of the priorities and capabilities of the available health care resources."

Under the triage system, the patient upon arrival filled out an Ambulatory Visit Form (AVF) which requested the patient's reason for visit as well as identification information (*Exhibit 5*). If the patient checked off "emergency care," the front desk personnel immediately notified a physician, nurse practitioner or triage coordinator who then more thoroughly assessed the patient's condition. In most cases, however, the front desk simply reviewed the AVF for completeness and requested the patient's record from Medical Records. Upon arrival of the record in 8–9 minutes, the appropriate clerical personnel matched the record with the AVF, ensured that all personal information and prior tests were properly filed and updated in the record, and then placed them chronologically in a "triage pile."

In turn, one of two "triage coordinators" called for the patient and provided the initial contact. The two triage coordinators were both highly experienced registered nurses. It was felt that experience was necessary so that they could make accurate assessments and preliminary diagnoses. The triage coordinator visited with the patient in a private room and, on the basis of the immediately available information and a brief discussion with the patient, summarized the nature of the patient's problem. If the triage nurse, in determining the severity of the patient's problem, decided the ailment warranted more immediate care, she would then put the patient ahead of others waiting to see a physician.

As one triage coordinator explained:

My duties are to determine the chief complaint of the patient and to triage him or her to an MD or nurse practitioner. I'll spend 3–4 minutes per patient in an average encounter and I rarely have to deviate from this—only when people are unable to clearly describe their symptoms or when they overestimate the severity of their illness. However, there is no time constraint in determining the status of a patient.

The triage coordinator did not treat the patient but determined, according to guidelines and her discretion, whether the patient needed to see a nurse practitioner or a physician in the Walk-In Clinic and whether the problem could be better handled by an appointment or referral to another service within UHS. Patients were triaged to a nurse practitioner if their ailments fell under one of thirteen categories (*Exhibit 6*). All other ailments outside the guidelines required the attention of a physician, unless the triage nurse, by using her discretion, felt a nurse practitioner could treat the problem. If, however, the nurse practitioner attended a problem which was not included under the thirteen categories, a physician was required to countersign the treatment. This required the nurse to find a doctor who would sign the medical record, thereby authorizing the treatment recommended by the nurse. In some cases, the doctor might choose to meet with or examine the patient before signing. Other doctors would sign without examining further. Expansion of the guidelines beyond the thirteen specific ailments would, by state law, require the drafting of detailed treatment guides so that a nurse practitioner could be allowed to treat the patient without consulting a physician. The UHS planned on such expansion in the near future. However, it was not known how many patients this might affect.

After the visit with the triage coordinator, the patient returned to the waiting area while his/her record was placed by the triage nurse chronologically in either the nurse practitioner or the physician "pile," unless more immediate care was deemed necessary by the triage coordinator. As physicians and nurse practitioners then finished with their previous patient, they summoned the next patient in their respective piles for treatment. Although significant variation existed, MDs saw an average of 3.10 patients per hour while approximately 1.83 patients per hour were seen by nurse practitioners.

When the triage system was instituted, it was expected that the waiting time to see a triage coordinator would be about 15 minutes, and waiting time to be seen by a nurse practitioner or a physician would be less than 10 minutes. A 1980 UHS study reported, however, that patients waited a mean length of 19.7 minutes to the point of being triaged and a mean time of 18.6 minutes from the start of the patient's visit with the triage coordinator to the point of being seen by either a nurse practitioner or a physician. The average total waiting time was 37.5 minutes, including the actual time to be triaged (*Exhibit 7*). Approximately 67 percent of the patients were triaged to a physician whereas 33 percent were triaged to a nurse practitioner. Ms. Angell commented,

When we introduced the triage system, we thought the nurse practitioners would accept more of the patient load and leave the physicians more time on a per patient basis. Unfortunately, it has not worked out that way. Among the reasons for this might be the fact that, as we discovered, the triage coordinators

EXHIBIT 5

Ambulatory Visit Form

Nº 82336

UNIVERSITY HEALTH SERVICES : WALK–IN CLINIC

AMBULATORY VISIT FORM

FOR PATIENT USE: PLEASE FILL OUT THIS SECTION COMPLETELY

TIME & DATE

UHS/
HARVARD
I.D. NO.

NAME:
PLEASE
PRINT

First   Middle   Last

BIRTHDATE   Mo.   Day   Yr.   MALE ☐
                                  FEMALE ☐

LOCAL ADDRESS

PHONE DURING THE DAY

LOCATION OF VISIT:
☐ Holyoke Center ☐ Law School
☐ Business School ☐ Medical Area

IS THIS YOUR FIRST VISIT TO
A UHS FACILITY? YES ☐

IF YOUR MEDICAL RECORD IS KEPT AT A UHS FACILITY OTHER THAN
HOLYOKE CENTER, PLEASE CHECK HERE: BUSINESS ☐ LAW ☐ MEDICAL AREA ☐

STATUS

☐ H/R UNDERGRAD, CLASS _____
☐ GRAD, SCHOOL (Name) _____
☐ LESLEY COLLEGE
☐ EPISCOPAL DIVINITY SCHOOL
☐ STAFF WITH HARVARD BC/BS
☐ STAFF WITH HARVARD UNIVERSITY
    GROUP HEALTH PROGRAM (HUGHP)
☐ STAFF WITH NO HARVARD INSURANCE
☐ HARVARD MEDEX
☐ MEDICARE (ONLY)

☐ STUDENT DEPENDENT WITH UHS COVERAGE
☐ STUDENT DEPENDENT WITH UHS COVERAGE
    – UNDER 14 YEARS OLD
☐ HUGHP DEPENDENT
☐ HUGHP DEPENDENT—UNDER 14 YEARS OLD
☐ MEDEX DEPENDENT
☐ SUMMER SCHOOL: STUDENT _____
    FACULTY _____ FAC. DEPENDENT _____
☐ NON-MEMBER OF HARVARD UNIVERSITY _____
☐ OTHER _____

FOR WALK-IN PATIENTS ONLY

The following information is designed to help us treat you promptly and efficiently.
All information will be kept confidential. If you do not wish to complete the rest of
the form, please check "personal" and you will be seen in turn.

WHAT IS THE REASON FOR YOUR VISIT?   PLEASE CHECK:

☐ I NEED **EMERGENCY CARE.**   ☐ BLOOD PRESSURE CHECK ONLY

GENERAL MEDICAL PROBLEM
☐ FIRST VISIT FOR THIS PROBLEM
☐ RETURN (REPEAT) VISIT FOR THIS
    PROBLEM
☐ TOLD TO SEE:

    NURSE OR DOCTOR

PRESCRIPTION(S) **ONLY**
☐ DIAGNOSIS CONFIRMED; INSTRUCTED
    TO OBTAIN PRESCRIPTION
☐ PRESCRIPTION REFILL:
    UHS _____ OTHER _____

ADMINISTRATIVE PROBLEM
☐ SPORTS CLEARANCE
☐ MEDICAL EXCUSE FOR EXAM
☐ MEDICAL FORMS TO BE COMPLETED

GENERAL SURGICAL PROBLEM
☐ FIRST VISIT FOR THIS PROBLEM
☐ RETURN (REPEAT) VISIT FOR THIS
    PROBLEM
☐ TOLD TO SEE:

    NURSE OR DOCTOR

LABORATORY PROCEDURES ONLY
☐ LAB RESULTS DESIRED
☐ PREMARITAL TESTS DESIRED
☐ PREGNANCY TEST REQUISITION

☐ PERSONAL

☐ OTHER _____

FOR UHS USE ONLY

TRIAGE TIME   TIME PT. SEEN

PROVIDER 1 NUMBER _____

NAME _____

PROVIDER 2 NUMBER _____

NAME _____

SERVICE

☐ MEDICAL
☐ SURGICAL
☐ EMERGENCY
☐ ALLERGY
☐ DENTAL
☐ DERMATOLOGY
☐ EAR, NOSE, & THROAT
☐ EYE
☐ GASTROENTEROLOGY
☐ GYNECOLOGY

☐ IMMUNIZATION
☐ MENTAL HEALTH
☐ NEUROLOGY
☐ NUTRITION
☐ OBSTETRICS
☐ ORTHOPEDICS
☐ PEDIATRICS
☐ PHYSICAL THERAPY
☐ UROLOGY
☐ OTHER _____

☐ INITIAL VISIT FOR THIS PROBLEM

☐ RETURN VISIT

TYPE OF CONTACT
☐ WALK-IN
☐ APPOINTMENT
☐ BROKEN APPOINTMENT
☐ CANCELLED BY UHS
☐ CANCELLED BY PATIENT
☐ LEFT BEFORE BEING SEEN
☐ RESERVE
☐ OTHER

HEMATOLOGY
PROVIDER NO.:
1 2
☐ ☐ COULTER CBC
☐ ☐ DIFFERENTIAL
☐ ☐ OCCULT BLOOD (GUAIAC)
☐ ☐ PLATELET COUNT
☐ ☐ PROTHROMBIN TIME
☐ ☐ RETICULOCYTE COUNT
☐ ☐ SEDIMENTATION RATE
☐ ☐ OTHER _____

Please circle as many lab test boxes as apply.

CHEMISTRY
PROVIDER NO.:
1 2
☐ ☐ BILIRUBIN
☐ ☐ BLOOD GLUCOSE
☐ ☐ BLOOD UREA NITROGEN (BUN)
☐ ☐ CHOLESTEROL
☐ ☐ CREATININE
☐ ☐ ELECTROLYTES
☐ ☐ SGOT
☐ ☐ SMA 12/60
☐ ☐ T3 UPTAKE
☐ ☐ T4
☐ ☐ TRIGLYCERIDES
☐ ☐ URIC ACID
☐ ☐ OTHER:

SEROLOGY
PROVIDER NO.:
1 2
☐ ☐ HETEROPHILE
☐ ☐ RPR
☐ ☐ RUBELLA
☐ ☐ OTHER:

BACTERIOLOGY
PROVIDER NO.:
1 2
☐ ☐ CERVICAL/URETHRAL CULTURE
        & GRAM STAIN
☐ ☐ STOOL FOR CULTURE
☐ ☐ STOOL FOR OVA & PARASITES
☐ ☐ THROAT CULTURE
☐ ☐ URINE CULTURE
☐ ☐ OTHER:

MISCELLANEOUS
PROVIDER NO.:
1 2
☐ ☐ BLOOD TYPE & RH
☐ ☐ ELECTROCARDIOGRAM
☐ ☐ MONILIA
☐ ☐ PAP SMEAR
☐ ☐ PATHOLOGY
☐ ☐ PREGNANCY TEST
☐ ☐ PULMONARY FUNCTION
☐ ☐ TRICHOMONAS (WET PREP)
☐ ☐ URINALYSIS
☐ ☐ OTHER:

are sometimes classifying patients as "MD/NP" (physician/nurse practitioner) to maintain the flow when they feel the practitioners are backed up. The MD's share of patients thus gets increased in overload situations. We did not want to have "MD/NP" as a classification, and have asked the triage coordinators to stop using it. When in doubt, they are to triage the patient to a nurse practitioner.

Among the patients who were initially seen by a nurse practitioner, about 5 percent were then referred to a second provider, usually a physician. Either the patient would remain in the NP's room while the NP fetched an MD, or, if longer MD treatment time was anticipated, the patient would join the MD waiting line, their file being placed in the MID pile according to the AVF number. Thus, if any other patient still in the MD queue had arrived before the referred patient, that other patient would be seen first. Though the mean times to be triaged to an MD or NP were relatively equal (approximately 19 minutes), as would be expected, the mean waiting time to see a physician was much longer (25.2 minutes) than the mean waiting time to see a nurse practitioner (6.7 minutes).

It was suspected that one of the factors creating differences in the waiting time to be seen by a physician versus a nurse practitioner was the percentage of patients who asked to see a specific provider of medical care. This percentage increased, for physicians in particular, after the institution of the triage system to a total of 24 percent of all patients. These patients still had first to see a triage nurse, who might attempt to dissuade them from waiting for a specific provider. If, however, the patient chose to wait, he or she did not obtain any priority over patients who were ahead in the system. For almost one-third of the physicians, more than 40 percent of the patients they saw in the Walk-In Clinic specifically asked for them (*Exhibit 8*).

Though the waiting time for triage was the same for the patients who asked for a specific physician or nurse practitioner and for patients who did not, the waiting time to be seen by the specific provider requested was 8.6 minutes longer on average for the

EXHIBIT 6
Categories Treatable Under Guidelines by Nurse Practitioners

1. Acute viral respiratory illness (primarily colds)
2. Amenorrhea (missed menstruation)
3. Cerumen (wax in ears)
4. Enterobiasis (pinworms)
5. Lower urinary tract infection (females)
6. Mononucleosis
7. Nausea, vomiting, diarrhea
8. Pediculosis capitus (lice)
9. Pediculosis pubis (lice)
10. Pharyngitis (sore throat)
11. Rubella (German measles)
12. Seasonal rhinitis (hayfever)
13. Vaginitis (vaginal infection)

EXHIBIT 7
Percentage of Patients Waiting, by Time Waited

Interval (minutes)	Waiting Time to be triaged	Waiting Time to be seen (after triage)	Total Waiting Time
0–4	1%	24%	0%
5–9	8	14	3
10–14	24	12	7
15–19	25	11	10
20–24	19	9	10
25–29	11	8	14
30–34	6	8	11
35–39	2	5	10
40–44	1	4	8
45–49	1	3	6
50–54	1	2	7
55+	1	0	14
	100%	100%	100%
Average	19.7	18.6	37.5

patients who asked. But as Mary Dineen, Supervisor of Outpatient Nursing, commented:

It seems doctors are allowed "walk-in appointments" with their own regular patients. Patients whose doctors have heavily booked appointment schedules become aware of the doctor's walk-in schedule and come into the

EXHIBIT 8
Summary of Patients Seen and Waiting Time to First Available Appointment, by Physician

Physician*	Total No. of Patients Seen	No. of Patients Who Asked to See Specific MD (%)	Total No. of Hours	No. of Patients Seen per Hour	Calendar Days to First Available Appointment
Zuromskis	113	33 (29.2)	36	3.14	9
Bogota	50	23 (46.0)	17	2.94	24
Wellington	89	— —	18	4.94	5
Byrd	76	26 (34.2)	33	2.30	15
Recife	78	48 (61.5)	24	3.25	25
Brunei	113	45 (39.8)	36	3.14	17
Lobito	28	10 (35.7)	6	4.67	21
Santiago	91	43 (47.3)	29	3.14	3
Hobart	59	27 (45.8)	24	2.46	28
Seoul	90	34 (37.8)	28	3.21	5
Kingston	113	26 (23.0)	25	4.52	7
Java	78	16 (20.5)	27	2.89	13
Rome	74	32 (43.2)	19	3.89	7
Ottawa	82	31 (37.8)	26	3.15	5
Caracus	53	17 (32.1)	18	2.94	7
Manila	25	18 (72.0)	9	2.78	23
Durban	48	41 (85.4)	18	2.67	29
Luanda	61	5 (8.2)	21	2.90	8
Papua	34	— —	9	3.78	—
Glasgow	35	2 —	9	3.89	12
Cristobal	33	3 (9.1)	19.5	1.69	2
Aukland	16	1 (6.3)	12.5	1.28	—
	1439	481 (33.4)	464	3.11	17

*Some names in this exhibit have been changed.

Walk-In Clinic at prearranged times to meet. This may be a necessary evil to some degree, but today, for example, two of the five doctors on duty are 100 percent occupied with "walk-in appointments." This decreases our available MD resources by 40 percent for true walk-in patients today and fills up our waiting room.

Peter Zuromskis, M.D., a physician in the Walk-In Clinic, also suggested reasons for the misuse of the walk-in operation:

My evaluation of the dissatisfaction our patients have sometimes expressed with this system is that it represents an approach to acute ambulatory care which is quite different from that which they have previously experienced. Patients understandably find appealing the nostalgic image of the general practitioner who knows his patients well and is able to provide advice and treatment of minor illnesses in his office with an apparent minimum of clerical encumbrances. This is clearly impossible in a clinic which provides the volume and variety of medical care services that UHS offers to a large and heterogeneous population with a wide variety of diseases, from relatively minor complaints to major medical emergencies. Our aim is not and should not be to provide an atmosphere reminiscent of the country doctor's office, but rather to provide the best possible care to all our patients, particularly to those whose medical needs are most urgent.

Although people, for the first time ever, had been giving unsolicited praise to the new system, Angell knew that it still had problems and didn't always work as it had been designed. Some patient complaints still noted "excessive" waiting times and misunderstanding of the triage systems illustrated by the following specific, though not average, opinion submitted to the UHS Patient Advocate:

> In order to see a doctor about a very simple problem (a mild sore throat), I have seen a "triage nurse" (who stamped my form and passed me on) and a "nurse practitioner" (who looked, felt, and probed, but dared not offer an opinion). I am now 30 minutes into my visit, much handled, but not within sight of a doctor.

The medical, clerical, and administrative staff within the Walk-In Clinic, however, felt that although the efficiency of the clinic was still at less than a desirable level, the triage system was an improvement. As Warren Wacker, M.D., the Director of UHS, commented:

> Right now, I'm satisfied with the results of the triage system and I expect the system to be operating very well in another year. Of course, we'll have to resolve some sticky issues in the meantime. For instance, we need to expand the 13 nurse practitioner guidelines and further define the roles of nurse practitioner and physician within the Walk-In Clinic. Another item is how do we educate students in the Walk-In Clinic concept? Expectations of traditional medicine don't fit with the walk-in concept.

ANGELL'S DILEMMA

Angell now had the difficulty of sorting through a year's performance data, the concerns raised by several distinct groups associated with the clinic, and her own subjective observations. What changes needed to be made, if any? Were waiting times now acceptable? What was, after all, acceptable? Ms. Angell knew that work was in progress to expand the 13 nurse practitioner guidelines, but would this be enough to solve any remaining problems?

Among her biggest concerns was the issue of "walk-in appointments." She commented:

> We have tried in the past to ask the doctors to refrain from encouraging their patients to meet them in the Walk-In Clinic. However, we have not had very much success, since the practice continues. Some of the doctors feel that they want *their* patients to see only them. Part of this is for medical reasons (the doctors wish to check on their patient's progress) and part of it is a general philosophy that medical care involves more than just treatment, and that personal relationships add to both the quality of health care and the patient's perception of good service. Many patients, perhaps appropriately, have the attitude of wanting to see "*my*" doctor." Apart from the fact that you can never dictate to doctors, the UHS has always had a philosophy of not trying to tell physicians how to practice medicine.

> Part of the problem is the general availability of appointment time. All our patients have the freedom to select their own "personal physician" from among any of our doctors. However, this often means that some are overloaded. Our overall staffing level at UHS is set approximately to provide one physician per 2,000 people covered by our various health plans. At the moment, the only way we try to limit the number of patients "assigned" to any given doctor, is by pointing out to the potential patient the difficulty of getting an appointment with an overloaded physician, and this is generally only done if the patient asks about it. We do not know how many patients each doctor is seeing as the patient's "personal physician," since this is an arrangement made by the doctor and the patient and not a formal "assignment."

> There are a number of potential alternatives for dealing with this problem. We could try to educate our patient public on the separate purposes and missions of doctor appointments and the Walk-In Clinic—try to get them to use each appropriately. We could ask the triage coordinators to be a little more aggressive in asking patients who request a specific physician whether they really need to see that person and suggest alternatives. Ultimately, we could establish a firm policy of not accepting specific physician requests in the Walk-In Clinic.

Angell had these questions and more to consider over the next two weeks. At that time, she would share her findings and proposals with Ms. Dineen and Dr. Postel, since they would all have to agree on necessary changes and be involved in their implementation, if any changes were to succeed.

Five Imperatives for Improving Service Quality

LEONARD L. BERRY
VALARIE A. ZEITHAML
A. PARASURAMAN

It is time for companies to raise their service aspirations signifi-cantly and for executives to declare war on mediocre service and set their sights on consistently excellent service, say the authors. This goal is within reach if managers will provide the necessary leadership, remember that the sole judge of service quality is the customer, and implement what the authors call the "five service imperatives."

The downtown Chicago Marriott hotel had been open for fifteen years before its management determined that two-thirds of all guest calls to housekeeping were to request ironing boards. This discovery prompted the idea of simply placing irons and ironing boards in all of the hotel's guest rooms, an idea that would cost $20,000. The hotel manager reviewed the capital budget and saw that $22,000 was earmarked to replace black-and-white television sets in the bathrooms of concierge-level guest rooms with color sets. The manager then inquired how many VIP guests had requested color television sets for their bathrooms and learned that no guest had ever made such a request. So the manager eliminated the color television sets and added the irons and iron-ing boards with no net addition to the capital budget, a big productivity boost for housekeeping, and a new, important guest room feature.

We begin with this story to make two critical points. The first is that customers are the sole judge of service quality. Customers assess service by comparing the service they receive (perceptions) with the service they desire (expectations). A company can achieve a strong reputation for quality service only when it consistently meets customer service expectations.

The second point is how easy it is for managers to forget the first point. Managers nod their heads in agreement when convention speakers stress the importance of customer focus and then go back to work and buy the equivalent of color TVs for the bathroom instead of ironing boards. We know it because we have spent most of the 1980s studying service quality in the United States. We have done extensive research with customers, front-line service providers, and managers in our studies of six service sectors: appliance repair, credit cards, insurance, long-distance telephone, retail banking, and securities brokerage. We describe our research program in more detail in the Appendix.

Through our studies, we have been able to identify the principal dimensions customers use to judge a company's service:

- Tangibles. The appearance of physical facilities, equipment, personnel, and communication materials.
- Reliability. The ability to perform the promised service dependably and accurately.
- Responsiveness. The willingness to help customers and to provide prompt service.
- Assurance. The knowledge and courtesy of employees and their ability to convey trust and confidence.
- Empathy. The provision of caring, individualized attention to customers.

Knowing what customers expect is, of course, only part of the challenge. Another part — a big part — is actually meeting these expectations. In this article we attempt to answer a fundamental question: What must every company interested in improving service do to actually improve it? We answer in terms of five service imperatives: define the service role, compete for talent (and use it), emphasize service teams, go for reliability, and be great at problem resolution.

DEFINE THE SERVICE ROLE

There are no standards for quality. We tell them to provide a high level of service to the customer.
— A bank marketing officer, referring to branch office employees

It's hard to say what our manager expects because he is no longer in our building.
— A customer service representative at one of the branches

In our unit, it's sell, sell, sell. And — oh yeah — give good service, too. But that's an afterthought.
— A lender from one of the branches

The above quotations from our research illustrate a common failing in service organizations: management's failure to properly define and reinforce the service role for employees. The result is *service role ambiguity;* the concept of service is vague and noncredible.

The potential causes of service role ambiguity are many. They include the following:

- No service standards, which drains the credibility from management rhetoric about the importance of service.
- Too many service standards, which diminish employees' awareness of the most urgent service priorities.
- General service standards, which offer employees little direction and provide a limited basis for measuring their performance.
- Poorly communicated service standards, which make the standards a guessing game for employees, or, more likely, a nonentity.
- Service standards unconnected to the performance measurement, appraisal, and reward systems, which render the standards "toothless" while conveying management's low priority for service.

Service standards are customer expectations stated in a way that is meaningul to employees. If well conceived, the standards *guide and energize* employees; they clarify the service task, convey a sense of priority, and provide benchmarks against which employees can judge their own performance and managers can judge the employees' and the organization's performance. Service standards bring a customer focus into the employee's day-to-day reality of service delivery.

A common assumption is that contact personnel understand their customers' service priorities by virtue of regular customer contact. Our research shows otherwise. Our data reveals that managers in five major service companies had a more accurate grasp of customer expectations than did front-line contact employees.

What it boils down to is this: If employees are unsure of how to deliver excellent service, if they think they know how but are wrong, of if they believe management does not really care about service, they are unlikely to deliver excellent service.

Start with Research

Defining the service role effectively starts with formal research to identify customers' principal service expectations. Guessing at what customers value most in service introduces a "Russian roulette" dynamic into the entire chain of service-improving actions, from setting service standards to the staffing, training, measuring, appraising, and rewarding decisions required to support the standards.

Although the five service dimensions presented earlier provide a framework of customer expectations, each company must still do its own research to measure the relative importance of the service dimensions among customers, prospects, and different market segments. The firm must also assess company and competitor performance against customer expectations. Company-specific research lends insight to the process of setting service standards that generic studies cannot provide. For example, a firm will want to set standards for service dimensions that are important to target markets and on which the company's performance is weak compared to competitors.

Research also helps managers make choices among service standards and pare down the list of standards to the pivotal ones that will make a difference for customers. Customers judge a company's service on the basis of a very few important service factors, and managers should establish a limited set of service standards for individual employees that contributes to the limited set of service goals for the organization.

The most successful service companies focus employee attention on the preeminent service factors. At Deluxe Corporation (formerly Deluxe Check Printers), the focus is on error-free printing and next-day order shipment. At Southwest Airlines, it is on fifteen-minute turnaround of an aircraft once it arrives at the gate and on creating a "fun" atmosphere for passengers. At Sewell Village Cadillac in Dallas, Texas, it is on convenient, reliable after-sale service. Indeed, Sewell Village is one of the few automobile dealerships where the service manager's income is as handsome as the sales manager's!

Communicate and Reinforce Service Standards

Still another key to defining the service role is to use every opportunity to communicate and reinforce service standards — in meetings and training sessions; in internal media such as wallet cards, desk signs, and wall posters; and in performance measurement, appraisal, and reward systems. Palais Royal, a successful Houston-based chain of apparel stores, posts service standards on a large sign in the employee area of each store and furnishes employees with personal copies of the standards. The explicit standards (for example, greeting or acknowledging every customer within 30 seconds) form a basis for training, performance measurement, appraisal, and compensation.

Defining employees' service roles clearly, consistently, and credibly is important to any organization's efforts to improve service. The behavior-guiding and motivational benefits of service standards are well worth the investment necessary to develop and reinforce them. Service employees need to know what excellent service means — and why they should care about delivering it.

COMPETE FOR TALENT — AND USE IT

> We should be more aggressive and active in seeking qualified tellers, rather than just waiting for them to walk in off the street.
> — *A bank branch manager*

Nothing has changed about the raw material. It's as bad today as it has always been. We draw from the bottom of the barrel because that's the way we compensate.
> — *Another branch manager*

> We have so many rules and regulations that we can't think anymore. We can't bend the rules. We can't be entrepreneurial. Our customers suffer.
> — *A branch lender*

Defining the service role is an important step, but it won't get a company very far unless the company has personnel with the attitude, ability, and flexibility to fulfill the role. Our studies indicate that two of the principal causes of poor service quality are placing the wrong people in the service role and giving employees too little control over the service. Contact employees who believe their units are *not* meeting service standards *disagree* with the following statements:

- My company hires people who are qualified to do their jobs.
- I have the freedom in my job to truly satisfy my customer's needs.

Services are performances, and most of the time it is people who render these performances. From the customer's perspective, the people performing the service *are* the company. An incompetent insurance agent is an incompetent insurance company, and a rude waiter is a rude restaurant.

So why do managers allow the wrong people to carry the company flag in front of customers? One reason is that most managers do not think like marketers when it comes to human resource issues. They view marketing as something you do to win over customers but not something you do to win over employees.

Read the employment ads in your local newspaper. Is this any way to compete for talent? The same companies that advertise imaginatively to compete for customers advertise with no imagination at all to recruit employees. The employment ads are look-alike ads in fine print selling "jobs" rather than careers.

Moreover, managers often do not have a well-defined profile of people to hire. They do not base hiring standards on service standards, which contributes to a mismatch between the type of people the company actually hires and the type of people the company *needs* to hire to deliver excellent service.

Compounding the mismatch problem is anachronistic thinking about "affordable" wage rates, with the goal of "saving money" dominating the goal of "serving customers." The tendency we observe among service firm managers to spend more liberally on things than people runs counter to our research findings that customers value the human dimensions of service more than the "tangibles" of service. If you believe we are overstating our

case, we invite you to visit your local department stores. Notice the expensive floor space, displays, and inventory, and then try to find salespeople who are knowledgeable about the merchandise and who tune into your needs with commitment and grace.

The Problem is Getting Worse

The problem of hiring the wrong people is getting worse due to labor-force shortfalls. Service sector employment is expanding rapidly, and the skills needed are being elevated just at the time that changing demographics are shrinking the labor pool of young people, who in many instances are not receiving the education they need to be marketable.[1]

The implications for service quality are sobering. Rather than leave positions unfilled or pay what they consider to be exorbitant wages, many managers are hiring people who are woefully ill equipped to deliver excellent service. The pressure to hire "just about anyone" is very real in many industries.

Squelching Talent through Rule Book Management

Service managers frequently add to their problems by not fully using the capabilities of those they do employ. By using thick policy and procedures manuals to control service delivery, managers stifle creativity, diminish the opportunity for employees to grow in their work, and chase the most able employees out the door in search of more interesting work.

Thick rule books serve customers no better than employees. They produce regimented, "by-the-book" service when a flexible, "by-the-customer" one is needed. While managers are demanding that employees be "robot servers," customers are demanding that they be "thinking servers."

One reason rule book management is so prevalent is that many managers believe it is essential to standardize service among different employees and service units. To some degree they are probably right. However, another factor is that many managers simply do not trust employee's judgment and make rules to replace it with their own. "Thinking" employees also threaten the control and power of insecure managers. The labor shortfall issue is also a factor. If you can't get good people, the theory goes, you at least need to make sure you control their work tightly. This theory is nonsense. People who are unqualified for a position should not be in that position. People who are qualified will perform better and stay with the company longer if given room to maneuver, achieve, and grow.

The Search for Fresh Ideas

Excellent service is too integral to a firm's future to accept yesterday's ideas about whom to hire, how to hire them, and what to do with them once hired. Managers need to compete as hard and creatively for *talent* market share as they compete for *sales* market share.

Here is what we recommend: Market careers rather than jobs, market them in multiple ways, link hiring standards to service standards, and leverage the freedom factor. Companies that do these things will do just fine in the talent market.

The idea of "career" may seem at odds with the demographically fragmented labor pool available and the high cost of employee benefit programs (which make part-time workers desirable), but in fact it is smart to look for the countertrend when prevailing routines are not working. Selling "just a job" does not typically inspire commitment and loyalty from employees or a willingness to invest in employee development from companies.

This is why Nordstrom and Wal-Mart Stores, two of America's most successful retail chains, take a different tack. Unlike most department store companies, Nordstrom resists the lure of part-time salespeople, preferring to staff the store with full-time personnel. Earning wages plus commissions, Nordstrom salespeople earn well above retailing standards. Indeed, the most successful Nordstrom salespeople earn more than some of the managers of competing stores in the same malls.

Wal-Mart provides scholarship assistance to employees so that they can attend college while continuing to work part-time. Once these employees graduate from college, they are promoted into management. Approximately 40 percent of Wal-Mart's managers started as hourly trainees.

Using good old-fashioned marketing fundamentals also makes sense. McDonald's "McMaster" program to attract older workers, Century 21's "Career Opportunity Week" advertised in national media, and Disney World's training of existing employees to recruit new employees illustrate the use of such familiar marketing concepts as market segmentation, market development, and personal selling.

It is also important to use service standards as a basis for hiring decisions. This requires having written service standards for the various positions, written "ideal candidate" profiles that reflect the service standards, and extensive line involvement in actual hiring decisions. Getting good people requires tenacity. There are no shortcuts. Jim Daniel, president of the high-performing Friendly Bank in Oklahoma City, makes the point well:[2]

> A continual challenge is finding people...who have the qualities necessary to provide the top-notch customer service that we require. Creative interviewing techniques must be utilized to obtain a clear picture of how the applicant truly feels about the public. Most applicants have had some degree of customer contact in previous employment. However, very few really *thrive* on customer contact. We look until we find *that* person.

Of course, it does little good to recruit capable, service-minded people only to frustrate them into leaving. Competing for talent means having good careers to market, not just marketing them well. And having good careers to market is a principal reason why service freedom is so important. Human beings were not meant to be robots.

To leverage the freedom factor, managers have to select their people well, provide them with a strong foundational culture in which to work, offer them strategic direction, and give them the company-specific training and education they need to perform their roles. And then managers need to get out of their way!

We agree with Robert Waterman, who writes in *The Renewal Factor:* "When managers guide instead of control, the sky's the limit on what people can accomplish."[3] We do recognize that some policies are necessary in most companies. What we are arguing for is *thinning the rule book down to the bare essentials.* Most companies would benefit from task forces that systematically review existing policies and procedures expressly to revise or eliminate those that unnecessarily restrict service freedom. Companies should also tackle head-on the issue of empowerment in the education and training of managers. Managers must learn the dangers of overmanagement; they must learn to widen the solution boundaries for their people.

EMPHASIZE SERVICE TEAMS

> We're not working as a family and as a group. We may all come together again but it hasn't happened yet.
>
> *—A bank branch customer service representative*

> Our cashier sits there and smokes cigarettes and drinks coffee. She doesn't help with any of our work. She says it isn't in her job description.
>
> *— A customer service representative*

> Our customers are used to walking in, talking to us, and getting the money tomorrow. Now that doesn't happen. Your priority becomes someone else's C drawer.
>
> *— A lending officer*

Service work is frequently frustrating and demoralizing. Customers can be rude and insensitive. The sheer number of customers to be served can be psychologically and physically overwhelming. Control over service can be dispersed among multiple organizational units that function without cohesion or a unified spirit, limiting contact employees' ability to come through for their customers.

It is very common for service workers to get "beat up" by the service role and become less effective even as they gain technical experience that should theoretically produce the opposite result. In numerous cases, however, what customers perceive as inhospitable behavior is actually the "coping" behavior of weary servers who have taken too many punches. Many service workers, of course, do not succumb to the stresses of the service role. They may be indomitable personalities, have an unusually strong work ethic, or work for support-

ive managers who help them get through difficult periods. Any number of factors can account for the fact that service work pummels and changes some employees more than others.

One dynamic that is particularly important in kindling and sustaining service-mindedness is the presence of service "teammates." An interactive community of coworkers who collaborate, overcome, and achieve together is a powerful antidote to service burnout. Membership on a team can be rejuvenating and inspirational. It can also raise the ante for individual performance. To let down the boss is bad, but to let down the team is often worse. Team participation can unleash one of the most potent of motivators — the respect of peers.

Service teamwork is also important because people in service organizations typically depend on one another. The end service the customer receives is commonly the result of many behind-the-scenes, internal services.

Our research shows convincingly that teamwork is a principal factor in delivering excellent service. Employees who indicate that their organizational units are *not* meeting service standards *disagree* with the following statements:

- I feel that I am part of a team in my unit.
- Everyone in my unit contributes to a team effort in serving customers.
- I feel a sense of responsibility to help my fellow employees do their jobs well.
- My fellow employees and I cooperate more than we compete.
- I feel that I am an important member of this company.

Organizational teamwork is clearly not a new idea, but it is an idea whose time has come. Robert Reich views "collective entrepreneurship" within organizations as the primary route to a better economic future for the United States.[4] Marketing researcher Mimi Lieber admonishes top managers to "reward cooperative farming rather than the number of pelts."[5] Retail executive Allen Questrom states that the biggest challenge in U.S. industry is to develop "team energy."[6]

Working at Teamwork

Service team building cannot be left to chance. Some degree of structuring, assigning, and facilitating is needed to overcome organizational inertia. Managers should strive to nurture teamwork within organizational units (intraunit teams) and between organizational units (interunit teams).

Some firms have already formed teams to accomplish specific tasks or solve problems. But we believe managers must go beyond this focus to fully reap the benefits of service teamwork. Creating the richest form of service teamwork requires long-lasting team membership; frequent team contact and communication; team leadership, direction, and goals; and team measurements and rewards (in addition to individual employee measurements and rewards).

In the 1990s a growing number of service firms will boldly pursue the full benefits of service teamwork by replacing functional organizational structures with market-focused team structures. PHH FleetAmerica, the nation's largest automobile fleet management company, is experimenting with this approach by assigning teams to serve the range of needs of selected large clients. This is in contrast to the firm's predominantly functional structure, in which various departments specialize in specific tasks (such as automobile procurement, titles, and disposal) and clients deal with different units for different needs.

Aid Association for Lutherans (AAL) totally reorganized its $50 billion insurance business from a functional structure to a market-team structure in 1987. Before reorganizing, AAL field agents contacted multiple internal departments for support services, which was a cumbersome and impersonal process. Now, field agents contact an assigned home office team to receive whatever internal service they require. These all-purpose teams perform more than 150 functions previously spread throughout the organization. Management gives the restructuring credit for reducing case-processing time by as much as 75 percent.[7]

In effect, FleetAmerica and AAL are moving from interunit to intraunit service delivery with their new structures. Management is placing people with different specialties together in the same unit and saying, "Work together as a team, take ownership of the customer, and improve the way we do things." This approach is promising because it combines into one package close-to-the-customer decision making, unified control over the service, and — most of all — the team energy about which Mr. Questrom speaks.

GO FOR RELIABILITY

> I was told I would be the first call tomorrow. At 12:30 the next afternoon I called to ask them when their day started.
> *—An appliance repair customer*

> I don't trust their computers or statements. I don't want to be at the mercy of their mismanagement.
> *—A securities brokerage customer*

> If I'm going to charge something, I don't want any problems.
> *—A credit card customer*

Breaking the service promise is the single most important way service companies fail their customers. When a firm is careless in performing the service, when it makes mistakes, when it doesn't do what it said it would do, customers lose confidence in the firm's reliability; they lose confidence in the firm's wherewithal to do what it promises to do dependably and accurately.

We have learned in our research that service reliability is the service "core" to most customers. Little else matters to customers when a company is not dependable. We have now measured the relative importance of the five service dimensions in nine independent customer samples covering a variety of services. In all nine samples, respondents rate reliability as the single most important feature in judging service quality. Unfortunately, the evidence that U.S. companies are delivering service reliability is not reassuring. Our data shows our sample companies, large, well-known U.S. firms, are more deficient on the reliability dimension than on any other.

We sometimes hear executives say that 98 percent reliability is acceptable and that it is cost-prohibitive to do better. We disagree. The flip side of 98 percent reliability is 2 percent unreliability, and more than likely, the actual "cost" of 2 percent unreliability is higher than the cost of improving 98 percent reliability.

If executives were to calculate the true costs of service unreliability — lost customers, unfavorable word-of-mouth, and redoing services not done properly the first time — they would realize just how much sloppiness steals from the bottom line and that a "zero defects" attitude is as important in services as in manufacturing.

And if more executives were to investigate the primary causes of service unreliability in their companies, they would find most of them rooted in poor service design, inattention to service details, and basic carelessness — problems that cannot be solved by throwing money at them.

Reliability is the heart of excellent service. No one reading this article wants to travel on an airline whose pilots are usually dependable, to be operated on by a surgeon who usually remembers where on the body the surgery is to be done, or to bank with a financial institution that usually keeps its records straight. When we have our consumer hats on, "usually" isn't good enough. And it is not just the "high-stake" services involving our health or financial security for which we demand reliability. The dry cleaner that loses our shirts, the automobile repair firm that says a car is fixed when it isn't, the taxi service that forgets to pick us up to go to the airport — these folks also lose our confidence. And our business. Robert Ferchat, president of Northern Telecom Canada Ltd., captures the spirit of a zero-defects approach to service:[8]

> Think for a moment about what it would mean in our daily lives if people got things right only 99 percent of the time: at least 200,000 wrong prescriptions would be processed every year; there would be nine misspelled words on every page of a magazine; we'd have unsafe drinking water four times each year; there would be no telephone service for fifteen minutes every day.

Building a "Do-It-Right-First" Attitude

Managers shoud use every opportunity to build a "do-it-right-first" attitude. This means specifically addressing the reliability issue in company communications, including mission statements; setting reliability standards; teaching the why and how of reliability in training programs; appointing reliability teams to study specific services and recommend ways to improve reliability; measuring error rates; and rewarding error-free service.

Service reliability is so important that we suggest companies ask each employee to make a formal commitment to it. Maryland's Preston Trucking Company, selected in 1987 as one of the ten best U.S. companies to work for, has made service reliability the centerpiece of its Commitment to Excellence statement that each employee signs. The statement, posted in each Preston facility, reads in part:

> ... Once I make a commitment to a customer or another associate, I promise to fulfill it on time. I will do what I say when I say I will do it.... I understand that one claim or one mistake is one error too many. I promise to do my job right the first time and to continually seek performance improvement.

Books and Co., a Dayton, Ohio, bookstore whose sales have grown 30 percent a year since 1984, insists each new employee sign a performance contract that spells out the employee's service responsibilities. Several of the clauses pertain directly to service reliability.

One of the most important opportunities for improving reliability involves analyzing services for "fail points" — the service processes most vulnerable to mishap. Firms can identify fail points by monitoring service delivery through "mystery shoppers" and periodic surveys; by soliciting the input of employees actually performing the service; by studying and categorizing customer service complaints; and by mapping the architecture of the service process — generally referred to as "blueprinting."

Identifying fail points focuses attention on the need for special training, additional inspection, building in corrective subprocesses, or even redesigning the original process. Consider the case of Florida Power & Light and its quest to reduce the duration and frequency of service interruptions, a major cause of customer complaints. Serving a part of the country that averages 80 days a year of thunderstorms and lightning, the company has developed a sophisticated, computer-based lightning tracking system to anticipate where weather-related problems might occur and to strategically position crews to quicken recovery response time. This and other initiatives have enabled the utility to reduce service unavailability (customer minutes interrupted divided by customers served) from 70 minutes at the end of 1987 to 48.37 minutes at the end of 1988. The company's target for 1991 is 36.41 minutes.

Outstanding service reliability is the foundation on which to build a reputation for outstanding service quality. Companies that consider the service promise inviolate are most likely to earn the confidence of their customers. And the confidence of customers is the greatest asset a company can have.

BE GREAT AT PROBLEM RESOLUTION

> If you have a problem, they treat you like you have a disease.
> —*A banking customer*

> You can't get in touch with these people.
> —*A credit card customer*

> When you call in irate, who do you talk to? The office clerk who can't do anything.
> —*An appliance repair customer*

When a customer experiences a problem with a service — when something goes awry — the customer's confidence is jarred but probably not destroyed, unless the problem reflects a pattern of negative experience with the company. Thus, what happens *after* the service problem occurs — the firm's response — becomes crucial. The firm can make things better with the customer — at least to some extent — or much, much worse.

All too often, service companies make things worse. They do not encourage their customers to resolve their problems and set up roadblocks for those who try to do so. They do not put sufficiently trained personnel, or enough of them, in problem-resolution positions. They do not give employees the authority to solve most problems immediately. And they do not invest in the communication and information systems that would support the problem-resolution service.

Three possibilities arise when a customer experiences a service problem:

- The customer complains and is satisfied with the company's response.
- The customer complains and is *not* satisfied with the company's response.
- The customer does *not* complain to the company and remains dissatisfied.

Of these possible outcomes, the first one is good and the last two are very bad. Our sample companies received the most favorable service quality scores from customers who had experienced no recent service problems with them, the next most favorable scores from customers whose problems were resolved satisfactorily, and the worst scores (by far) from customers whose problems were not resolved satisfactorily. Table 1 presents these numbers.

In effect, companies that do not respond effectively to customer complaints *compound* the failure; they fail to come through for the customer *again*. At this point, the customer's shaky confidence in the firm probably collapses.

Many dissatisfied customers do not complain, often making unflattering comments about the firm and taking their business elsewhere instead. The studies of Technical Assistance Research Programs, Inc. (TARP), a Washington, D.C., organization noted for its research on customer complaining behavior, document that large numbers of customers do not complain because they fear a hassle, perceive no easy or efficient way to air their grievances, or believe complaining will not do them any good.[9]

Managers need to come to grips with the seriousness of the lost business and negative word-of-mouth that occurs when customers cannot resolve problems with the firm, or do not even try. How a company handles service problems tells customers (and employees) a great deal about the firm's service values and priorities.

TABLE 1
Service Quality Scores for Different Sample Groups

No Service Problem	Service Problem	Service Problem Resolved Satisfactorily	Service Problem NOT Resolved Satisfactorily
−0.49	−1.50	−1.03	−2.10

Note: We determine a company's service quality by measuring customer expectations for the service and customer percep-tions of the company against these expectations. If perceptions fall short of expectations, the company receives a minus score. The bigger the minus score, the worse the company's service quality.

Three Prescriptions

Being excellent in recovery is easier said than done. We offer these specific prescrip-tions.

- Encourage customers to complain and make it easy for them to do so. Managers who want to im-prove problem-resolution service must overcome the common customer perception that compa-nies don't really care when things go wrong. The solution calls for some creative marketing of the customer feedback idea. Comment cards avail-able in service delivery facilities and toll-free telephone numbers merely scratch the surface of what is possible. British Airways' Video Point booths, in which disembarking passengers can videotape their concerns, make an unusually strong statement that the company want to know when its customers are unhappy.

- Make timely, personal communications with cus-tomers a key part of the strategy. Companies fre-quently make two fatal mistakes in problem resolution: They take too long to respond to cus-tomers, and they respond impersonally. Timely, personal communication with unhappy custom-ers offers a firm the best chance to regain the customer's favor. By responding quickly, a firm conveys a sense of urgency. By responding per-sonally, with a telephone call or a visit, it creates an opportunity for dialogue with customers — an opportunity to listen, ask questions, explain, apologize, achieve closure.

North Carolina's Wachovia Bank & Trust has a "sundown rule" — employees must establish con-tact with a complaining customer before sunset on the day a complaint is received. When Min-neapolis's First Bank System messed up a direct payroll deposit for a client company in 1988, it immediately sent every employee of that com-pany a $15 check and an apology. In addition, the employees were given the name and tele-phone number of a person at the bank who could

answer questions and resolve problems. Silence is not golden when a problem exists and the cus-tomer is waiting to hear.

- Encourage employees to respond effectively to customer problems and give them the means to do so. Companies must market the idea of prob-lem resolution to employees, not just to custom-ers. This involves many of the ideas we have already covered in the article, for example, set-ting and reinforcing problem-resolution stan-dards, and giving employees the freedom to truly solve customer problems. It is no fun trying to solve customer problems if doing so produces a small mountain of red tape or a sneer from a supervisor.

Service employees need specific training about how to deal with angry customers and how to help customers solve service problems. In some cases, they need access to information systems that will tell them more about the cus-tomer, the situation causing the problem, and possible solutions.

When American Express card holders tele-phone the 800 number on their monthly state-ment, they talk to a highly trained customer service representative with the authority to solve *on the spot* 85 percent of the problems that prompt telephone calls. The representatives key billing or other changes directly into an on-line data system, and these adjustments are reflected in the card holder's next statement. Over the years, American Express has made a huge investment in problem-resolution staff-ing, training, and technology, and as a re-sult few, if any, U.S. companies have a stronger reputation for fast, reliable problem-resolution service. Given the strong pricing competition American Express faces from bank credit cards, this is not a bad reputation to have.

Specifics aside, problem-resolution excellence requires that managers view services marketing as a way of cementing customer loyalty through service and trust, rather than only as a way to acquire new customers. Effective services marketing — and its cornerstone, service quality — require that managers take the long view.

AGENDA FOR THE 1990s

Excellent service is within reach if managers are willing to stretch for it. In every single industry in the United States, there are examples of companies delivering superb service and profiting from it. But these are the exceptional stories; in most companies, quality service is still a soft idea, an elusive goal, or a low priority.

Our objective in this article has been to frame an agenda for improving service that will strip away softness and elusiveness, and help galvanize management commitment. The five service-improvement imperatives described here apply whether a company is small or large, new or old, a pure service organization or a manufacturer that supplies product-support service. It is time for U.S. companies to raise their service aspirations significantly. It is time for U.S. executives to declare war on mediocre service and set their signts on excellent service, every day, every week, every month. At stake is market leadership — within industries and among countries. It is hard to imagine any service company faring well in the ultracompetitive decade ahead if its service is suspect. And it is hard to imagine U.S. service industries holding their own against foreign competition if their service isn't strong.

But more is at stake than economics and competitiveness. The service issue is inextricably linked to the issues of craftsmanship, integrity, generosity, and civility in our culture. What many U.S. consumers are *really* anguishing about when they complain of poor service is their perception of a declining culture.

We have an agenda for improving service quality in the United States. We have a new decade ahead of us. What we need now is the will to set our sights higher, provide genuine leadership, and do what it takes to transform potential into achievement.

APPENDIX
RESEARCH PROGRAM

Our service quality research program, initiated in 1983 under the auspices of the Marketing Science Institute, is still underway. We have completed three major phases of our research, the findings of which form the basis for this article.

Phase I was an extensive qualitative study of service customers and executives in four service sectors: appliance repair, credit cards, retail banking, and securities brokerage. In each sector, we conducted customer focus-group interviews and in-depth executive interviews on issues pertaining to service quality. Phase I resulted in our developing a conceptual model that defines service quality from the customer's standpoint, identifies the criteria customers use to judge quality, and outlines potential organizational shortfalls that can cause poor service.

Phase II involved an empirical study that focused on the "customer side" of our service quality model. In this phase, we surveyed nearly one thousand customers in the credit card, long-distance telephone, product repair, and retail banking sectors. On the basis of these empirical findings, we consolidated the criteria customers use to evaluate service quality into five dimensions: tangibles, reliability, responsiveness, assurance, and empathy. We also developed and refined SERVQUAL, a methodology for measuring customers' perceptions of service quality. Phase II included a comprehensive case study of one of the largest U.S. banks. We selected three of the bank's regions (each of which had at least twelve branches) and interviewed managers and employees from these regions individually and in focus groups. We also did a survey of bank customers.

In Phase III, we focused on the "service provider" half of our model, building on what we learned about internal shortfalls from Phase I and the case study from Phase II. In

Phase III, we conducted a large-scale study to verify our hypotheses about potential causes of service quality problems. This study involved mail surveys of customers, contact personnel, and managers in eighty-nine separate field offices of five national service companies — two banks, two insurance firms, and a telephone company. In all, 1,936 customers, 728 contact personnel, and 231 managers responded to our Phase III questionnaires.

REFERENCES

The authors wish to express their gratitude to the Marketing Science Institute.

[1] "Where the Jobs Are Is Where the Skills Aren't," *Business Week*, 19 September 1988, pp. 104–108.

[2] L. L. BERRY, D. L. BENNETT, and C. W. BROWN, *Service Quality — A Profit Strategy for Financial Institutions* (Homewood, Illinois: Dow Jones-Irwin, 1989), p. 51.

[3] R. H. WATERMAN, JR., *The Renewal Factor* (New York: Bantam Books, 1987), p. 73.

[4] R. B. REICH, "Entrepreneurship Reconsidered: The Team as Hero," *Harvard Business Review*, May–June 1987, pp. 77–83.

[5] M. LIEBER, "Managing for Service Excellence in a Turbulent Environment," (Boston: Speech at an American Marketing Association conference, 25 February 1987).

[6] A. QUESTROM (College Station, Texas: Presentation at Texas A&M University, 20 April 1989).

[7] "Work Teams Can Rev Up Paper-Pushers, Too," *Business Week*, 28 November 1988, pp. 64–72.

[8] As quoted in "The Quest for Quality," *The Royal Bank Letter*, November–December 1988.

[9] J. A. GOODMAN, T. MARRA, and L. BRIGHAM, "Customer Service: Costly Nuisance or Low-cost Profit Strategy?" *Journal of Retail Banking*, Fall 1986, pp. 7–16.

New Tools for Achieving Service Quality

D. DARYL WYCKOFF

Service operations can be managed for both quality and cost control without treating staff members like "cogs." Implementing some new quality-management techniques can turn service staff into thinking workers who find ways to exceed the quality standards set for them, while they delight customers with attentive service—as occurred at Rusty Pelican Restaurants and Midway Airlines.

Where manufacturing techniques have been applied to the service industries for improved consistency and productivity, services have too often become standardized, and personal interaction lost.[1] Particularly in the hospitality industry, some managers and customers feel that the loss of the personal touch is too severe a penalty to pay for productivity gains through "production-line" approaches. In the effort to improve some aspects of service, other important service qualities were sacrificed. Customers now ask where the *service* has gone from the service industries.[2] As Stanley Marcus remarked about the large hotel and fast-food chains: "They have perfected training methods to provide the guest with adequate but imper-

---

[1]Theodore Levitt, "Production-Line Approach to Service," *Harvard Business Review*, September–October 1982, pp. 41–52.

[2]See: Barbara Tuchman, "The Decline of Quality," *New York Times Sunday Magazine*, November 2, 1980, p. 38; Jeremy Main, "Toward Service without a Snarl," *Fortune*, March 23, 1981, p. 58; and Frank S. Leonard and W. Earl Sasser, "The Incline of Quality," *Harvard Business Review*, September–October 1982, pp. 163–177.

---

sonalized attention and unvarying hamburgers."[3]

The distortion of services to allow the application of production methods is only one problem attendant on the use of manufacturing concepts. Another problem is that the types of production concepts applied have often been steeped in "Taylorism," an attitude that workers are unintelligent and unthinking cogs who must be told what to do to make the machine run.[4]

Fortunately, more recent manufacturing techniques stress the thinking, quality-oriented worker. These new methods give caring workers the tools for self-improvement in delivering service quality—and substantially reduce the need to denigrate service quality by sacrificing customization, choice, flexibility, and personalized services.

This article discusses these new techniques, using the experience of two firms, Rusty Pelican Restaurants and Midway Airlines, as examples of how service firms can apply these concepts.

IMPROVING ON EXCELLENCE

Rusty Pelican is a group of full-service restaurants that serve well-prepared, fresh seafoods in a setting of "sophisticated casualness." Originated in California, the company was one of the first to sense consumers' demand for lighter, more healthful foods, and their turning away from the limited menus of theme restaurants and from heavy meals of red meat. A typical Rusty Pelican restaurant might serve as many as 25 different varieties of fresh fish, which can be prepared in any of several ways, accompanied by fresh vegetables. The restaurants are pleasing to the eye and are often located in unusual and striking settings, such as on a waterfront.

A major component of Rusty Pelican's service strategy is hiring knowledgeable servers to provide attentive and personal-

ized cocktail and food service. Maintaining the firm's service standards is a significant challenge, because of the wide variety of seafood offered (and the fact that the availability and prices of seafood items change daily), because of the alternatives in preparation, and because the service style of sophisticated casualness requires a delicate balance to provide the appropriate pacing.

By most measures, Rusty Pelican was a success. The company was doing well financially, it received positive customer comments, and the number of repeat customers was large. Management recognized, however, that the service was too inconsistent in some of the restaurants and seemed too mechanical in others. The company was providing coaching and training, of course, but many of the employees were not really convinced that one way of providing the service was necessarily better than another. Performance, while generally good, was more a matter of the enthusiasm of a given staff or particular individuals than the result of design.

Management was concerned about how to recruit and train enough capable servers, especially since it didn't seem appropriate in this market segment to resort to a paramilitary-style application of detailed handbooks and industrial engineering, as has happened in many restaurant chains. The company also realized that increasing server productivity would reduce the number of servers needed and increase the individual servers' earnings through tips. Management set a goal of increasing productivity by ten to 20 percent. It chose a self-improvement strategy to achieve this goal.

Skills. Rusty Pelican hired a consultant to meet with small groups of employees and discuss how they believed they could increase productivity without reducing service quality. At this stage, most of the attention was devoted to how servers could improve their selling and merchandising skills to increase sales per employee hour. The groups decided to pay particular attention to their communication skills.

The results of this effort were measured

---

[3]Stanley Marcus, *Quest for the Best* (New York: Viking Press, 1979), p. 42.

[4]Also called scientific management, this approach breaks every job into small elements.

by the employees against the targets they had set for themselves. Productivity improvements were seen almost at once, partly because the employees wanted to see how much improvement they could bring about. Management's original targets for productivity improvements were easily met and sustained. In informal interviews, customers also rated the service quality as being higher.

Rusty Pelican then anonymously conducted a customer-satisfaction study, and found that the firm's service was rated significantly higher than that of competing restaurants. The company could easily have been satisfied with this result, but there was better news. Research had shown that customers were willing to pay considerably more for innovative service.

With the servers' assistance, the company began to examine every step in its service process to find opportunities for improvement and to pinpoint instances of failures. The servers identified several bottlenecks that were causing service problems. More space was needed in the kitchen to assemble orders, for example, and rearrangement of the bar and service bars would allow the cocktail servers to achieve their goals for prompt service.

Employees began to coach each other, and the experiences of team problem-solving promoted greater teamwork on the job. As the servers became more productive and quality-minded, they began to find that they could deal with more detail. Rather than simply going through the motions of service, they were *thinking* about service as they delivered it.

FROM WHOLESALE SKIES TO EXECUTIVE SKIES

Midway Airlines began life as a no-frills airline spawned by deregulation. Midway had dubbed its service the "wholesale skies"—a play on the "friendly skies" slogan used by United Airlines. Midway provided a simple service at cut-rate fares, a strategy that succeeded only as long as the major air carriers ignored Midway (i.e., while their own ca-

pacity was heavily utilized). At that point, Midway was easy to ignore, for it was small in comparison with the large trunk carriers that were focusing on long-haul competition.

The "wholesale passengers" were mostly price-sensitive, of course, and demonstrated little loyalty when another airline brought prices down to meet or beat Midway's fares. During periods of heavy traffic, therefore, Midway picked up the low-fare traffic that spilled over from regular-fare carriers. When traffic fell and other airlines offered low fares, Midway's traffic would disappear. The company was in what is known as a "stalled-market" position.[5] If Midway continued to hold this position, the best the company could hope for was meager earnings (with good luck) or great losses (with bad luck).

Breakout. To get *un*stalled, management initiated a "breakout strategy" by repositioning its service to attract the frequent traveler. Research had shown that this market was so badly served by most carriers that many travelers' feelings toward the airlines had gone beyond frustration to outright hostility.

In addition to examining its own customer feedback, Midway undertook formal market research. One step was to run full-page ads (without company identification) in *The Wall Street Journal* and the business sections of other newspapers, inviting experienced travelers to help design an airline that could deliver quality service.

The response was conclusive. Frequent travelers did not want lavish foods or liquor, but they *did* want reliability, timeliness, and comfort. Two-abreast seating was important to the respondents, for example, because they were crowded when they sat in rows of three and couldn't get any work done. Sufficient facilities for carry-on baggage were important, but so was reliable and fast baggage service. Simple, well-prepared food was preferred to more elaborate, reheated "mystery meals." Reliable, on-time departures and ar-

---

[5]This position is also called "stuck in the middle." Michael E. Porter, *Competitive Strategy* (New York: Free Press, 1980), pp. 41–44.

rivals were deemed vital, and knowledgeable and efficient cabin crews and ground staff were considered important to assure smooth services and to help when problems arose.

Businesslike. As a result of these findings, Midway removed some seats and added substantial carry-on luggage facilities. Aircraft interiors and exteriors and crew uniforms were redesigned to convey a new businesslike image. The gate areas were redesigned to provide work stations for passengers. Simple, excellent food offerings of salads, cold meats, and homemade-style breads were substituted for reheated meals, thereby avoiding the systematic destruction of food texture, flavor, and color that is inevitable with rewarming. The meals were presented in specially designed plastic boxes that resembled the sophisticated Japanese *bento* lunchboxes. Since there was no heating and the packaging was done in advance, the cabin crews could serve an entire meal in minutes.

These quality improvements (mostly in product design) answered only part of the challenge of repositioning. Midway felt these steps would help, but the most difficult part of the breakout strategy would be to change the company's culture from that of the "wholesale skies" to one of "executive skies." The mechanical product redesign provided some signals of change to the staff, but the real alterations in service had to come from the employees themselves.

The employees had been involved in the process right from the beginning, working through councils and committees on the redesign of the facilities, aircraft, and uniforms. They had struggled over the marketing research and had worked with designers who translated customer requirements into designs.

Next they turned to service delivery, by establishing priorities for action. It would be wishful thinking to expect to bring everything up to a high quality standard at once, but the most important service-quality issue identified in the marketing research was timely departure. This issue was to receive primary attention.

The first step toward achieving high levels of on-time service was to examine all the causes of late flights. Analyzing different aspects of the operation through flow charts revealed that there were about 30 causes of late departures. The employees identified failure patterns and suggested and implemented corrective actions. Soon the employees felt that their original performance targets for departures had been too modest. They questioned the traditional airline practice of considering any flight operating within 15 minutes of schedule as on time, and changed that standard to five minutes for Midway.

Baggage handling, announcements, onboard services, and the like soon received treatment similar to that of scheduling. A new sense of pride became the company's hallmark, and new quality measures were rapidly added by the employees, who suggested that the performance standards could be tightened further.

There were some interesting side effects of the quality program. Employees' absentee rates dropped by nearly half. Turnover of flight attendants and agents was reduced by 25 percent. Midway was experiencing a phenomenon that has been witnessed in other companies: quality-improvement programs frequently produce positive side effects.

TOOLS FOR QUALITY SERVICE

In both of the cases described here, customers recognized that there had been substantial improvements in service quality. In both cases, customers were willing to pay a premium, because the quality change enhanced their perception of the value of the service. This concept, service quality, may be defined as follows:

> Quality is the degree of excellence intended, and the control of variability in achieving that excellence, in meeting the customer's requirements.

This definition of quality is useful, because it incorporates the following three components: *design quality,* or the intended degree of excellence; *conformance quality,* or the minimizing of variance from the intended design; and *fitness of design,* or the extent to which the product meets the customer's needs.

In fact, it is important to focus first on the last point—namely, on the customer's needs, which usually take two forms. The first are the basic *substantive* needs. To satisfy substantive needs, for instance, hotels provide shelter, restaurants provide food, and airlines provide transportation. In most cases, customers can readily determine through simple observation whether they have received a substantive service.

The second category, *peripheral* needs, goes beyond the needs met at the substantive level. The service attributes that meet these needs surround and complete the substantive service. These needs must not be ignored.[6] Peripheral service attributes (e.g., security, promptness, interpersonal relations) fulfill such needs as the need for a sense of control, for a feeling of trust and confidence, or for a sense of belonging, self-fulfillment, and self-esteem.[7]

STANDARD AND CUSTOM

Two distinctions in services have important implications for service-quality management. The first is whether a particular service is standard (routine) or custom (nonroutine), and the second is the degree

to which the "back-room" parts of the service can be isolated from the customer, so that front-room operations can be minimized and controlled.[8]

Production approaches are often more easily applied to standard or routine services. Indeed, some service companies have *made* their services standard just so production methods could be applied. McDonald's did this with food service, Midas with automobile repair, and H&R Block with accounting services. The problem with these firms' rigid approach is apparent: gone is the chance for custom or nonroutine service. But service variety and service quality need no longer be mutually exclusive; using some new techniques of quality management, one can now deliver variety in service at a given quality standard.

The new methods used in manufacturing easily improve the production-oriented standardized services, but the Rusty Pelican example shows that the thinking employee can also manage a greater range of nonroutine services when given the opportunity.

Front and Back. Whereas past efforts at service management rested on the conceptual division of service into back-room and front-room operations and an emphasis on the back of the house (which was presumed easier to manage with standard production methods, being out of the customer's sight), the new quality-management techniques often stress front-room operations—helping employees manage and improve human-interaction processes.

NEW APPROACHES TO QUALITY MANAGEMENT

Managers have learned a great deal in the past two decades about quality management in manufacturing. In some cases, old truths have been rediscovered or restated in ways that make more sense in modern settings; in other cases, old beliefs have been turned up-

[6]For a more detailed discussion of this view of service, see: W. Earl Sasser, R. Paul Olsen, and D. Daryl Wyckoff, *Management of Service Operations* (Boston: Allyn and Bacon, 1978), pp. 177–179. For other views of the concept of a constellation of attributes for each quality, see: Corwin D. Edwards, "The Meaning of Quality," *Quality Progress,* October 1968, pp. 36–39.

[7]For a complete discussion of the needs fulfilled by peripheral services, see: Robert C. Lewis, "The Positioning Statement for Hotels," *The Cornell Hotel and Restaurant Administration Quarterly,* 22, No. 1 (May 1981), pp. 51–61; Leo M. Renaghan, "A New Marketing Mix for the Hospitality Industry," *The Cornell Hotel and Restaurant Administration Quarterly,* 22, No. 2 (August 1981), pp. 30–35; and Theodore Levitt, "Marketing Intangible Products and Product Intangibles," *Harvard Business Review,* May–June 1981.

[8]Christopher H. Lovelock, *Services Marketing* (Englewood Cliffs, NJ: Prentice-Hall, 1984), p. 5.

side down. The following statements summarize current thinking on the topic of quality management.

- *Quality exists only to the extent that a product or service meets the customer's requirements.* Therefore, design quality must begin with a thorough understanding of those requirements.
- *A product or service of high quality is the result of a total system of quality throughout every aspect of the firm.* A quality orientation and commitment in every part of the firm—by every employee and every supplier—is central to delivering a quality product or service.
- *The costs of poor-quality products and services outweigh the costs of good-quality products.* Doing things right the first time yields substantial reductions in total costs by cutting the costs of inspection, internal failure, and external failure.
- *Management must go beyond thinking of inspection merely as sorting out the good products and services from the bad or as preventing bad products from reaching customers.* Management must instead view inspection primarily as a tool to measure whether the production process is able to deliver the intended products or services—if the process is not capable of producing the desired quality consistently, why not?—and whether the process is under control. Examination of product problems has been simplified by improved means of process analysis and statistical process-control methods.

The following is a closer look at each of these four propositions.

SQUARE ONE

It is a marketing fundamental that one must start with customer requirements. There have been many departures from this principle in the service industries, however, partly because customers' requirements for services may be difficult to identify and articulate, and also because customers' wants are complex and multidimensional.[9] Perhaps for these reasons, service firms have often been dominated by creative individuals who have an

intuitive concept of the services desired by customers. We remember those whose intuition was right—James Nassikas of the Stanford Court, Fred Smith of Federal Express—and we forget (or never know) the multitude who guessed wrong.

Even when intuitive concepts work, their creators may not know why. A mysticism often develops around details that are actually of little consequence to the customer. Because the interior of his first successful pizza store was decorated in a shade of green paint purchased from an Army surplus store, for example, "Shakey" Johnson insisted that the same color paint be used for all subsequent Shakey's Pizza Parlors.

It takes courage to reexamine the offerings and make changes, particularly when a firm has been successful. United Parcel Service, a company founded to deliver packages under contract from downtown department stores to uptown customers, made this reexamination when it observed the movement of retailers to the suburbs after World War II, and accordingly modified its entire service strategy to provide common-carrier service for all types of shippers to all destinations.

Unstated Needs. One must be imaginative in how one goes about learning of customers' requirements, because customers do not always *know* what they need or want. For example, the introduction of the "800" telephone number was important to Holiday Inns' ability to satisfy the customer's need for a familiar service in an unfamiliar location. Yet in consumer research of the time, customers did not explicitly ask for this innovation that proved so vital. Likewise, years ago, few customers even conceived of a reliable, nationwide, overnight parcel-delivery service. But they did have requirements for communication and document delivery that Federal Express was imaginative enough to detect.

In other cases, consumers *do* know what they want and articulate it—but are still left dissatisfied. As an example, such professionals as architects and doctors are now sometimes the targets of lawsuits by unhappy clients and patients. The professionals' fre-

---

[9]This concept is known as a "bundle of desires." Lawrence Abbott, *Quality and Competition* (New York: Columbia University Press, 1955), pp. 30–31.

quent reaction has been to have their clients sign releases rather than to find ways to win loyalty and confidence (i.e., to start with customer requirements).

Many recent management texts have stated that, in "excellent" firms, the customer is prominent in the minds of everybody at all levels. Despite the occasional difficulties, reviewed here, of emphasizing customer needs, service industries can also benefit from this attitude.

TQC

Many Japanese firms have enthusiastically embraced the concept of *total quality control* (TQC).[10] TQC rests on the belief that quality-control techniques or methodology must be used to raise the level of quality for every corporate activity, with a result of better yields, greater efficiency, higher productivity, and lower costs. TQC broadens the definition of quality management to cover all aspects of corporate existence, and quality control becomes the responsibility of everyone in the firm—not just an isolated step in the production line. For the company that practices TQC, accuracy in typing letters, politeness in answering the phone, and fussiness in cleaning the offices are just as important as meeting design and conformance quality standards in its products and services. Each activity represents a commitment to quality. Professional telephone manners do not substitute for poor product or service quality, of course, but care in all operations communicates a message of quality to employees and customers.

Because TQC emphasizes the exchange of information through the entire firm from the bottom up as well as from the top down, it depends heavily on informed, thinking, and involved workers. This does not mean that TQC leads to undisciplined operations—in fact, it promotes strict adherence to standards—but it encourages

continual reexamination of processes and standards and embodies a formal method for changing operations as needed to improve quality and productivity. TQC rejects the notion of doing just enough to get by.

The Japanese "quality circle" builds broad participation in quality thinking. The quality circle is based on a long Japanese tradition of looking down into an organization to find answers to problems, and the quality circle stimulates the initiative for improvement at every level of the company. Although it reflects unique aspects of Japanese culture that are not readily exported, the quality-circle concept may be adapted to any setting, as long as "one respects the brain power of human beings."[11] Regardless of what it is called, the success of this structure stems from employee involvement on a regular and ongoing basis, and simply giving trendy new names to tired old organizational structures will not guarantee quality.[12] As seen in the Rusty Pelican and Midway cases, employees participated in a quality-circle process without ever using that term.

COST OF QUALITY

The concept of the *total cost of quality* provides a framework for analyzing the expenses associated with providing a product or service that meets given standards. The total cost of quality is made up of four components. *Assurance costs* are those expenses associated with inspection, testing, and collecting and processing quality control data. *Prevention costs* are the expenses incurred in avoiding poor quality (e.g., the cost of training programs, quality-improvement pro-

---

[11]Kaorn Ishikowa, quoted in: Sud Ingle and Nima Ingle, *Quality Circles in Service Industries* (Englewood Cliffs, NJ: Prentice-Hall, 1983), p. 8.

[12]For example, see: Elizabeth Faulkner, "Will Quality Circles Work in American Food-Service Operations?," *Restaurants & Institutions*, September 15, 1983, p. 149; Keniche Ohmoe, "Why Quality-Control Circles Succeed," *Asian Wall Street Weekly*, April 5, 1982, p. 12; and Wayne S. Rieker, "QC Circles and Company-Wide Quality Control," *Quality Progress*, October 1983, pp. 14–17.

---

[10]This is sometimes called company-wide quality control.

TABLE 1

Hypothetical Comparison of Two Cost-Control Strategies

The following calculations of the total cost of quality show that the low-price strategy described in the accompanying text is actually more costly than a policy of purchasing a more expensive product and investing in preventive measures.

"LOW-COST" STRATEGY

Lettuce purchased for salad:	$30,000/year (a savings of $9,000 over premium grade produce)
Salads made:	120,000/year
Yield of usable lettuce:	75%
Cost of salad:	$0.25
Salads rejected by food servers:	6,000/year
Salads rejected by customers:	3,000/year
Average cost of placating customers:	$.75/upset customer

COST ANALYSIS (ANNUAL FIGURES)

Cost Category	Item	"Low-Cost" Strategy	Alternative Strategy
Prevention costs:	Lettuce price premium	$ 0	$ 9,000
	Purveyor meetings	0	100
	Employee training	0	100
Assurance costs:	Receiving inspection	0	100
	Chef's inspection	1,800	900
Internal-failure costs:	Lost lettuce	7,500	500
	Server rejections	1,500	100
External-failure costs:	Customer rejections	750	100
	Placating customer	2,250	100
Total cost of quality		$13,800	$11,000

grams, process modifications, and vendor-qualification programs). *Internal-failure costs* arise from scrapping or reworking faulty products that are intercepted before they reach the consumer. *External-failure costs* stem from defective products that reach the consumer.

Management's objective is to minimize the sum of these costs. The simple example in Table 1 shows how this concept is applied. Imagine that a restaurant buys standard-grade lettuce to avoid the 30-percent premium for perfect lettuce. The company also reduces training costs by not telling kitchen helpers how to inspect the lettuce when it is

received. (As standard grade, it can hardly be rejected anyway.) Predictably, some heads regularly fail to meet the freshness-quality requirements for salads, and although the chef spends some time inspecting the produce, he is so rushed that some salads are invariably made with wilted lettuce. Needless to say, either servers or customers reject these salads.

The alternative scheme illustrated in Table 1—spending *more* on the product and on assuring its quality—shows substantially reduced *total* costs. In this case, as is so often true, doing it right the first time saves money by obviating the need for greater spending in other quality-cost categories.[13] Reworking products, recalling defective materials, and placating unhappy customers are expensive. Perhaps the highest cost of all occurs when an unhappy guest never returns but takes every chance to tell friends about a terrible hotel or restaurant.

STATISTICAL PROCESS CONTROL

Among the most important advances in quality management has been the adoption of concepts of *statistical process control*. Statistical process control has changed the role of inspection from one of sorting out good and bad products to that of managing the production process by assessing whether the process is under control and by determining the process's capability when under control. This change in inspection's role has great significance for the service manager. Instead of depending on final inspection, often believed to be impractical in service delivery, operators can manage the service-delivery process, whether custom or standard in nature.

The first step in statistical process control is to chart the process in the form of a table or flow chart. A flow chart helps depict the complete process that must be managed. Rusty Pelican started with the flow chart shown in Figure 1, and expanded it to several pages of detailed design-quality specifications and standards.[14]

The initial standards the Rusty Pelican servers established are listed in Table 2. The next step—applying these standards—was critical to Rusty Pelican's success. Restaurant employees were shown how to measure themselves, rather than being evaluated by

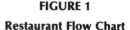

FIGURE 1
Restaurant Flow Chart

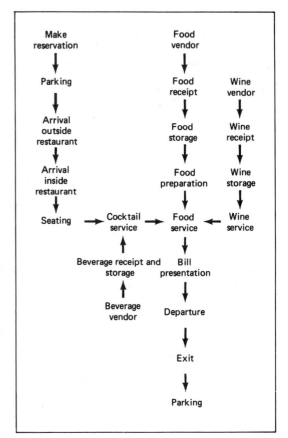

an inspector. In some cases, a control chart (a simple record of activity) is useful for monitoring performance.[15] The key to successful use of control charts is that they are based on data collected and recorded by involved employees who view the results as an opportunity for learning and self-improvement rather than reprimand. Again, such self-inspection reduces the need for inspec-

---

[13]See: Jack Campanella and Frank J. Corcoran, "Principles of Quality Costs," *Quality Progress*, April 1983, pp. 16–22; and Charles A. Aubrey II and Debra Zimbler, "The Banking Industry: Quality Costs and Improvement," *Quality Progress*, December 1983, pp. 16–20.

[14]See: G. Lynn Shostack, "Designing Services That Deliver," *Harvard Business Review*, January–February 1984, pp. 133–139.

---

[15]For additional background on the use of control charts, see: Armand V. Feigenbaum, *Total Quality Control* (New York: McGraw-Hill, 1983), pp. 345–369. For a detailed discussion of quality measurement in the service industries, see: Everett E..Adam, Jr., James C. Hershauer, and William A. Ruch, *Productivity and Quality: Measurement as the Basis for Improvement* (Englewood Cliffs, NJ: Prentice-Hall, 1981).

TABLE 2

Rusty Pelican Service Standards

FOOD-SERVICE STANDARDS

1. **First contact**—cocktail server speaks to customer within two minutes of customer seating.
2. **Cocktails delivered**—beverage service at table within four minutes of order. If no beverage order, request for food order within four minutes of first greeting.
3. **Request for order**—within four minutes after beverage service, customer should be asked whether he or she cares to order.
4. **Appetizers delivered**—salad, chowder, or wine delivered within five minutes.
5. **Entree delivered**—entree served within 16 minutes of order.
6. **Dessert delivered**—dessert and coffee or after-dinner drinks served within five minutes after plates are cleared.
7. **Check delivered**—check presented within four minutes after dessert course or after plates are cleared if no dessert.
8. **Money picked up**—cash or credit cards picked up within two minutes of being placed by customer on table.

COCKTAIL-SERVICE STANDARDS

1. **First contact**—greeting given and cocktail order taken; seafood bar, happy-hour specials, and wine-by-glass menus presented within two minutes.
2. **Cocktails delivered**—cocktails delivered within five minutes after first contact.
3. **Seafood bar delivered**—seafood bar and happy-hour specials delivered within seven minutes of first contact; ten minutes for cooked items.
4. **Next contact**—check for reorder of cocktail, seafood bar, customer satisfaction, and table maintenance within five minutes from delivery of first cocktail.

---

tors (or spies in the skies, as airline staffers call them).

Figure 2 shows the type of control chart used by Midway's employees to monitor their scheduling performance. The chart tells an interesting story, because simply measuring and tracking this critical feature of service quality caused some improvement. An enthusiastic management team was able to gain considerable additional improvement with "locker-room pep talks." Even with this enthusiasm, however, it was difficult to maintain consistent performance. More study was needed to reveal the causes of service failures.

Fishbones. Midway applied another tool of statistical process control, cause-and-effect analysis (also called "fishbone analy-

sis").[16] This technique may appear at first glance to be mechanistic, but its results are usually worthwhile, for the analysis stimulates creative responses from employees and managers.

The initial fishbone analysis of Midway's delayed flights is shown in Figure 3. The cause-effect diagram starts with the effect—namely, delayed flight departures. Then major categories of causes are listed on the "spine." To get the analysis started, it is often useful to start with the five broad causal categories illustrated in Figure 3: material, personnel, procedure, equipment, and "other."

---

[16]First developed by Kaorn Ishikowa of Tokyo University, fishbone analysis was first applied at Fulsai Ironworks in 1953.

FIGURE 2

Control Chart of Midway Airlines Departure Delays

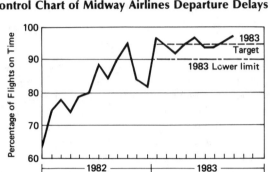

FIGURE 3

Portion of Midway Airlines Fishbone Analysis—Causes of Flight Departure Delays

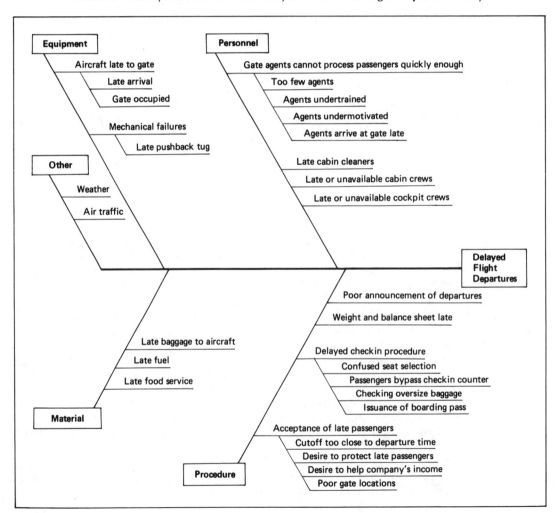

TABLE 3
Pareto Analysis of Flight Departure Delays

ALL STATIONS, EXCEPT HUB	Percentage of Incidences	Cumulative Percentage	NEWARK	Percentage of Incidences	Cumulative Percentage	WASHINGTON (NATIONAL)	Percentage of Incidences	Cumulative Percentage
Late passengers	53.3	53.3	Late passengers	23.1	23.1	Late passengers	33.3	33.3
Waiting for pushback	15.0	68.3	Waiting for fueling	23.1	46.2	Waiting for pushback	33.3	66.6
Waiting for fueling	11.3	79.6	Waiting for pushback	23.1	69.3	Late weight and balance sheet	19.0	85.6
Late weight and balance sheet	8.7	88.3	Cabin cleaning and supplies	15.4	84.7	Waiting for fueling	9.5	95.1

There may be several factors contributing to each cause.

Because of their personal experience, Midway's employees had little difficulty suggesting the causes of late departures. One problem, late arrival of passengers, quickly received considerable attention when it was discovered the company's policy on how to handle late passengers was vague. It was essential to determine how significant late arrivals were as a cause of late flights. To answer this, Midway applied "Pareto analysis," a technique that arranges data so that problems are ranged in order of importance.[17]

Discipline. The Pareto analysis revealed that nearly *90 percent* of the departure delays for all airports other than the hub were accounted for by only *four* of the many causes listed in Figure 3. The actual causes of late departures for one month of operation are listed in Table 3 in order of their frequency. Obviously, accommodating late passengers *was* a major cause of flight delays. These were not passengers who were late from connecting flights; they were simply passengers who were casual about getting to the airport. Individual gate agents had been making their own decisions about what was best for Midway in these circumstances. Most agents were anxious that Midway not lose the fares of the latecomers, and most agents were also sympathetic to the late passenger (although they forgot the inconvenience to the many passengers who had made the effort to arrive on time). Midway established a policy that it would operate on time and give top service to passengers who were ready to fly on schedule. This discipline was appreciated by the passengers, and the number of late passengers soon declined.

The delays in "pushback" (moving the aircraft away from the gate with motorized tugs) were reduced by better scheduling of tugs in some locations and by working more closely with subcontractors in other locations. Similar programs were initiated with cabin-cleaning contractors and fuel suppliers, and the Midway staff placed greater priority on promptly supplying the plane's weight and balance calculations to the pilot.

More specific information was generated by "stratification," dividing the data into useful subcategories or segments. Different patterns showed up in the Pareto analysis when the data were separated into different services, times, or locations. In Table 3, for instance, note the difference in problems of Newark departures and Washington depar-

---

[17]Named for Vilfredo Pareto, the 19th-century economist and social scientist. The Pareto rule, also referred to as the "80-20 rule," assumes that in a normal population roughly 80 percent of sales come from 20 percent of customers, or in this case, that 80 percent of the failures come from 20 percent of the causes.

tures. These differences could not have been discerned in the "total station" data.[18]

In January 1983, once the flight-departure process was under control, the company set control limits. At first, the *minimum* performance standard was set arbitrarily at 90-percent on-time flights, as shown in Table 4. Soon there were data showing that this lower limit was too generous (but it was probably a good place to start). The company shortly decided that any month that the on-time record was more than three standard errors from the *target* of 95 percent, the process was out of control.

UNCONTROLLED AND UNSTRUCTURED

Measuring the service customer's satisfaction levels is still one of the most subjective and difficult parts of quality management in services. Some service organizations mistakenly rely on unsolicited comments. This is unfortunate, because such a sample is uncontrolled and unstructured.[19] Comments are most likely to come from customers who are writing about exceedingly bad or exceedingly good experiences. Sometimes the comments come from crank letter writers. Worse, many customers who have bad experiences never tell the management; they just complain to their friends and switch their patronage.

---

[18]The other tool frequently used to capture variations that may be lost in averages is the "histogram" or scatter diagram. The histogram shows variability in conformance quality by plotting information on a graph. The time it takes to deliver baggage after landing, for example, could be plotted for every flight. The result should be a mass of dots near the time established in the performance standard. If the diagram shows many dots falling below the standard—a trend that might be obscured in averages if many dots also fell *above* it—management would be alerted and could take corrective action.

[19]For a specific discussion of this problem, see "Improving Guest Surveys" in the *Notes* section of the November 1984 issue of the *Cornell Hotel and Restaurant Administration Quarterly*.

The only satisfactory alternative to unreliable surveys is a controlled sample that is carefully examined for bias. Studies like this are usually tedious and expensive, and often the testing itself can damage the quality of the service experience. But these studies may be an important "reality check" of whether the service is satisfying customers' needs.

Rusty Pelican decided a short in-house restaurant survey was important. While management acknowledged the risk of disrupting a diner's experience, the need for reliable customer feedback was critical. Likewise, Midway found that passengers are quite willing to complete in-flight surveys, partly as a distraction during the flight, and the response rates have been high.

Incomplete. There were two shortcomings with the in-house surveys administered by Midway and Rusty Pelican. First, the companies did not get information about the perceptions of nonusers. Second, the surveys did not capture customers' reactions to the whole service experience, since the questionnaires were given out during the meal or flight (not afterward). Both Midway and Rusty Pelican gained additional information from focus-group research (i.e., interviews with groups of customers).

Although critical, measuring only one's own service quality is not sufficient. Some rude surprises can come to light in surveys of competitors' service offerings. Singapore Airlines, for example, thought it saw steady improvement on every measure of its in-flight services. Several competing airlines, however, were rapidly closing the lead Singapore had established, and it appeared that Singapore might shortly lose its competitive advantage in cabin services. Fortunately for Singapore Airlines, it observed this developing pattern and moved into a quality-improvement program at once.

One final observation: In those companies where the top officers personally made the investment to learn and understand the application of process control to quality management, process control has nearly always been successful. Whether the officers' personal understanding was the critical factor or was just interpreted by employees as a sign of the company's commitment to quality management, the effort paid off.

BEYOND TAYLORISM

When the service businesses have adopted a production-line approach in recent years, the result has frequently been standardized services and diminished personal interaction. The new lessons for quality management learned in manufacturing industries have changed this mechanistic approach to one of cultivating thinking employees, backed up with management methods that enable them to understand, control, and improve the service-management process.

These techniques are not constrained or dictated by the size of the firm. While many of the quality-management methods described in this article may seem to be statistical tools oriented toward industrial engineering, their real strength lies in their ability to augment the human role in the service-delivery system. These tools can give small firms the same efficiency advantages enjoyed by large companies, while large firms can regain some of the flexibility and service quality seen in small firms.[20]

Designing quality around customers' requirements may seem axiomatic, but it has been forgotten or ignored by too many managers and servers; quality is more than slogans and press releases. It requires a company-wide investment in defining and articulating what quality service means, and providing the resources to produce that quality. All parts of the enterprise must be committed to *measuring* quality, because improvement is possible only when quality is measured.

Improving the quality of service is often a slow process. Some of the *fastest* process-control implementations have taken over two years; many will take longer. And recognition by *customers* of an improvement in quality takes still longer. The market is often slow to acknowledge quality changes. As a result, management may think it has gotten away with reduced quality if there is no short-term evidence of a loss in market share. Unfortunately, when the market is lost it may not be regained for years after the quality is restored.

---

[20]G. Michael Hostage, "Quality Control in a Service Business," *Harvard Business Review*, July–August 1975, pp. 98–106.

Zero Defections:
Quality Comes to Services

FREDERICK F. REICHHELD
W. EARL SASSER, JR.

Service businesses must think in terms of relationships, not transactions. The longer a customer relationship lasts, the greater its value to the firm. Tracking defecting customers can help direct management attention to the problems that cause customers to switch to competitors and identify strategies for retaining customers and increasing profits.

The *real* quality revolution is just now coming to services. In recent years, despite their good intentions, few service company executives have been able to follow through on their commitment to satisfy customers. But service companies are beginning to understand what their manufacturing counterparts learned in the 1980s — that quality doesn't improve unless you measure it. When manufacturers began to unravel the costs and implications of scrap heaps, rework, and jammed machinery, they realized that "quality" was not just an invigorating slogan but the most profitable way to run a business. They made "zero defects" their guiding light, and the quality movement took off.

Service companies have their own kind of scrap heap: customers who will not come back. That scrap heap too has a cost. As service businesses start to measure it, they will see the urgent need to reduce it. They will strive for "zero defections"— keeping every customer the company can profitably serve — and they will mobilize the organization to achieve it.

Customer defections have a surprisingly powerful impact on the bottom line. They can have more to do with a service company's profits than scale, market share, unit costs, and many other factors usually associated with competitive advantage. As a customer's relationship with the company lengthens, profits rise. And not just a little. Companies can boost profits by almost 100% by retaining just 5% more of their customers.

While defection rates are an accurate leading indicator of profit swings, they do more than passively indicate where profits are headed. They also direct managers' attention to the specific things that are causing customers to leave. Since companies do not hold customers captive, the only way they can prevent defections is to outperform the competition continually. By soliciting feedback from defecting customers, companies can ferret out the weaknesses that really matter and strengthen them before profits start to dwindle. Defection analysis is therefore a guide that helps companies manage continuous improvement.

Charles Cawley, president of MBNA America, a Delaware-based credit card company, knows well how customer defections can focus a company's attention on exactly the things customers value. One morning in 1982, frustrated by letters from unhappy customers, he assembled all 300 MBNA employees and announced his determination that the company satisfy and keep each and every customer. The company started gathering feedback from defecting customers. And it acted on the information, adjusting products and processes regularly.

As quality improved, fewer customers had reason to leave. Eight years later, MBNA's defection rate is one of the lowest in its industry. Some 5% of its customers leave each year — half the average rate for the rest of the industry. That may seem like a small difference, but it translates into huge earnings. Without making any acquisitions, MBNA's industry ranking went from 38 to 4, and profits have increased sixteenfold.

THE COST OF LOSING A CUSTOMER

If companies knew how much it really costs to lose a customer, they would be able to make accurate evaluations of investments designed to retain customers. Unfortunately, today's accounting systems do not capture the value of a loyal customer. Most systems focus on current period costs and revenues and ignore expected cash flows over a customer's lifetime.

Served correctly, customers generate increasingly more profits each year they stay with a company. Across a wide range of businesses, the pattern is the same: the longer a company keeps a customer, the more money it stands to make. (See the bar charts depicting "How Much Profit a Customer Generates over Time.") For one auto-service company, the expected profit from a fourth-year customer is more than triple the profit that same customer generates in the first year. When customers defect, they take all that profit-making potential with them.

It may be obvious that acquiring a new customer entails certain one-time costs for advertising, promotions, and the like. In credit cards, for example, companies spend an average of $51 to recruit a customer and set up the new account. But there are many more pieces to the profitability puzzle.

To continue with the credit card example, the newly acquired customers use the card slowly at first and generate a base profit. But if the customers stay a second year, the economics greatly improve. As they become accustomed to using the credit card and are satisfied with the service it provides, customers use it more and balances grow. In the second year — and the years thereafter — they purchase even more, which turns profits up sharply. We found this trend in each of the more than 100 companies in two dozen industries we have analyzed. For one industrial distributor, net sales per account continue to rise into the nineteenth year of the relationship.

As purchases rise, operating costs decline. Checking customers' credit histories and adding them to the corporate database is expensive, but those things need be done only once. Also, as the company gains experience with its customers, it can serve them more efficiently. One small financial consulting business that depends on personal relationships with clients has found that costs drop by two-thirds from the first year to the second because customers know what to expect from the consultant and have fewer questions or problems. In addition, the consultants are more efficient because they are familiar with the customer's financial situation and investment preferences.

How Much Profit a Customer Generates Over Time

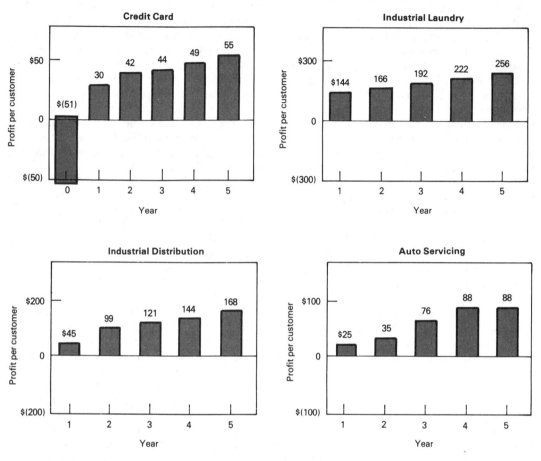

Also, companies with long-time customers can often charge more for their products or services. Many people will pay more to stay in a hotel they know or to go to a doctor they trust than to take a chance on a less expensive competitor. The company that has developed such a loyal following can charge a premium for the customer's confidence in the business.

Yet another economic boon from long-time customers is the free advertising they provide. Loyal customers do a lot of talking over the years and drum up a lot of business. One of the leading home builders in the United States, for example, has found that more than 60% of its sales are the result of referrals.

These cost savings and additional revenues combine to produce a steadily increasing stream of profits over the course of the customer's relationship with the company. (See the chart "Why Customers Are More Profitable over Time.") While the relative importance of these effects varies from industry to industry, the end result is that longer term customers generate increasing profits.

To calculate a customer's real worth, a company must take all of these projected profit streams into account. If, for instance, the credit card customer leaves after the first year, the company takes a $21 loss. If the company can keep the customer for four more years, his or her value to the company rises sharply. It is equal to the net present value of the profit streams in the first five years, or about $100.

Why Customers Are More Profitable Over Time

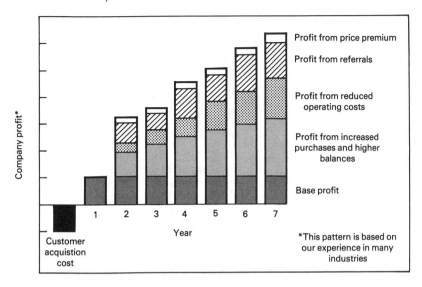

A Credit Card Company's Defection Curve

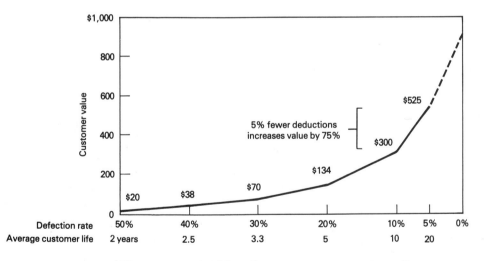

* The net present value of the profit streams a customer generates over the average customer life. At a 10% detection rate, for example, the average customer life is ten years (1 divided by the defection rate); the customer value is the net present value of the profit streams for ten years.

When a company lowers its defection rate, the average customer relationship lasts longer and profits climb steeply. One way to appreciate just how responsive profits are to changes in defection rates is to draw a defection curve. (See the graph, "A Credit Card Company's De-fection Curve.") This shows clearly how small movements in a company's defection rate can produce very large swings in profits.

The curve shows, for example, that as the credit card company cuts its defection rate from 20% to 10%, the average life span of its relationship with a customer doubles from five years to ten and the value of that customer more than doubles — jumping from $134 to $300. As the defection rate drops another 5%, the average life span of a customer relationship doubles again and profits rise 75% — from $300 to $525.

The credit card business is not unique. Although the shape of defection curves vary across industries, in general, profits rise as defection rates fall. Reducing defections by just 5% generated 85% more profits in one bank's branch system, 50% more in an insurance brokerage, and 30% more in an auto-service chain. (See the chart "Reducing Defections 5% Boosts Profits 25% to 85%.") MBNA America has found that a 5% improvement in defection rates increases its average customer value by more than 125%.

Understanding the economics of defections is useful to managers in several ways. For one thing, it shows that continuous improvement in service quality is not a cost but an investment in a customer who generates more profit than the margin on a one-time sale. Executives can therefore justify giving priority to investments in service quality versus things like cost reduction, for which the objectives have been more tangible.

Knowing that defections are closely linked to profits also helps explain why some companies that have relatively high unit costs can still be quite profitable. Companies with loyal, long-time customers can financially outperform competitors with lower unit costs and high market share but high customer churn. For instance, in the credit card business, a 10% reduction in unit costs is financially equivalent to a 2% decrease in defection rate. Low-defection strategies can overwhelm low-cost strategies.

And understanding the link between defections and profits provides a guide to lucrative growth. It is common for a business to lose 15% to 20% of its customers each year. Simply cutting defections in half will more than double the average company's growth rate. Companies with high retention rates that want to expand through acquisition can create value by acquiring low retention competitors and reducing their defections.

DEFECTIONS MANAGEMENT

Although service companies probably can't — and shouldn't try to — eliminate all defections, they can and must reduce them. But even to approach zero defections, companies must pursue that goal in a coordinated way. The organization should be prepared to spot customers who leave and then to analyze and act on the information they provide.

Watch the door. Managing for zero defections requires mechanisms to find customers who have ended their relationship with the company — or are about to end it. While compiling this kind of customer data almost always involves the use of information technology of some kind, major investments in new systems are unnecessary.

The more critical issue is whether the business regularly gathers information about customers. Some companies already do. Credit card companies, magazine publishers, direct mailers, life insurers, cellular phone companies, and banks, for example, all collect reams of data as a matter of course. They have at their disposal the names and addresses, purchasing histories, and telephone numbers of all their customers. For these businesses, exposing defections is relatively easy. It's just a matter of organizing the data.

Sometimes, defining a "defection" takes some work. In the railroad business, for instance, few customers stop using your service completely, but a customer that shifts 80% of its shipments to trucks should not be considered "retained." The key is to identify the customer behaviors that both drive your economics and gauge customer loyalty.

For some businesses, the task of spotting defectors is challenging even if they are well defined, because customers tend to be faceless and nameless to management. Businesses like retailing will have to find creative ways to "know" their customers. Consider the example of Staples, the Boston-based office products discounter. It has done a superb job of gathering information usually lost at the cashier or sales clerk. From its opening, it had a database to store and analyze customer information. Whenever a customer goes through the checkout line, the cashier offers him or her a

Reducing Defections 5% Boosts Profits 25% to 85%

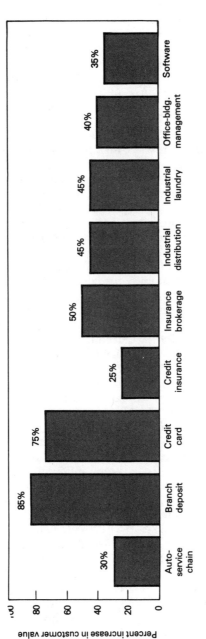

Percent increase in customer value

	Auto-service chain	Branch deposit	Credit card	Credit insurance	Insurance brokerage	Industrial distribution	Industrial laundry	Office-bldg. management	Software
	30%	85%	75%	25%	50%	45%	45%	40%	35%

*Calculated by comparing the net present values of the profit streams for the average customer life at current defection rates with the net present values of the profit streams for the average customer life at 5% lower defection rates.

membership card. the card entitles the holder to special promotions and certain discounts. The only requirement for the card is that the person fill out an application form, which asks for things like name, job ittle, and address. All subsequent purchases are automatically logged against the card number. This way, Staples can accumulate detailed information about buying habits, frequency of visits, average dollar value spent, and particular items purchased.

Even restaurants can collect data. A crab house in Maryland, for instance, started entering into its PC information from the reservation list. Managers can now find out how often particular customers return and can contact those who seem to be losing interest in the restaurant.

What are defectors telling you? One reason to find customers who are leaving is to try to win them back. MBNA America has a customer-defection "swat" team staffed by some of the company's best telemarketers. When customers cancel their credit cards, the swat team tries to convince them to stay. It is successful half of the time.

But the more important motive for finding defectors is for the insight they provide. Customers who leave can provide a view of the business that is unavailable to those on the inside. And whatever caused one individual to defect may cause many others to follow. The idea is to use defections as an early warning signal — to learn from defectors why they left the company and to use that information to improve the business.

Unlike conventional market research, feedback from defecting customers tends to be concrete and specific. It doesn't attempt to measure things like attitudes or satisfaction, which are changeable and subjective, and it doesn't raise hypothetical questions, which may be irrelevant to the respondents. Defections analysis involves specific, relevant questions about why a customer has defected. Customers are usually able to articulate their reasons, and some skillful probing can get at the root cause.

This information is useful in a variety of ways, as the Staples example shows. Staples constantly tracks defections, so when cus-

tomers stop doing business there or don't buy certain products, the store notices it immediately and calls to get feedback. It may be a clue that the competition is underpricing Staples on certain goods — a competitive factor management can explore further. If it finds sufficient evidence, Staples may cut prices on those items. This information is highly valued because it pinpoints the uncompetitive products and saves the chain from launching expensive broad-brush promotions pitching everything to everybody.

Staples's telemarketers try to discern which merchandise its customers want and don't want and why. The company uses that information to change its buying stock and to target its catalogs and coupons more precisely. Instead of running coupons in the newspaper, for instance, it can insert them in the catalogs it sends to particular customers or industries that have proved responsive to coupons.

Defections analysis can also help companies decide which service-quality investments will be profitable. Should you invest in computerized cash registers or a new phone system? Which of the two will address the most frequent causes of defection? One bank made a large investment to improve the accuracy of monthly account statements. But when the bank began to study defectors, it learned that less than 1% of its customers were leaving because of inaccurate statements.

A company that is losing customers because of long lines can estimate what percentage of defectors it would save by buying new cash registers, and it can use its defection curve to find the dollar value of saving them. Then, using standard investment-analysis techniques, it can compare the cost of the new equipment with the benefit of keeping customers.

Achieving service quality doesn't mean slavishly keeping all customers at any cost. There are some customers the company should not try to serve. If particular types of customers don't stay and become profitable, companies should not invest in attracting them. When a health insurance company realized that certain companies purchase only on the basis of price and switch health insurers every year, for example, it decided not to waste its efforts seeking their business. It told its brokers not to write policies for companies that have switched carriers more than twice in the past five years.

Conversely, much of the information used to find defectors can point to common traits among customers who stay longer. The company can use defection rates to clarify the characteristics of the market it wants to pursue and target its advertising and promotions accordingly.

THE ZERO DEFECTIONS CULTURE

Many business leaders have been frustrated by their inability to follow through on their public commitment to service quality. Since defection rates are measurable, they are manageable. Managers can establish meaningful targets and monitor progress. But like any important change, managing for zero defections must have supporters at all organizational levels. Management must develop that support by training the work force and using defections as a primary performance measure.

Everyone in the organization must understand that zero defections is the goal. Mastercare, the autoservice subsidiary of Bridgestone/Firestone, emphasizes the importance of keeping customers by stating it clearly in its mission statement. The statement says, in part, that the company's goal is "to provide the service-buying public with a superior buying experience that will encourage them to return willingly and to share their experience with others." MBNA America sends its paychecks in envelopes labeled "Brought to you by the customer." It also has a customer advocate who sits in on all major decision-making sessions to make sure customers' interests are represented.

It is important to make all employees understand the lifetime value of a customer. Phil Bressler, the co-owner of five Domino's Pizza stores in Montgomery County, Maryland, calculated that regular customers were worth more than $5,000 over the life of a ten-year franchise contract. He made sure that every order taker, delivery person, and store manager knew that number. For him, telling workers that customers were valuable was not nearly as potent as stating the dollar amount: "It's

so much more than they think that it really hits home."

Mastercare has redesigned its employee training to emphasize the importance of keeping customers. For example, many customers who stopped doing business with Mastercare mentioned that they didn't like being pressured into repairs they had not planned on. So Mastercare now trains store managers to identify and solve the customer's problem rather than to maximize sales. Videos and role-playing dramatize these different definitions of good service.

Mastercare's message to employees includes a candid admission that previous, well-intentioned incentives had inadvertently caused employees to run the business the wrong way; now it is asking them to change. And it builds credibility among employees by sharing its strategic goals and customer outreach plans. In the two target markets where this approach has been used, results are good. Employees have responded enthusiastically, and 25% more customers say they intend to return.

Senior executives at MBNA America learn from defecting customers. Each one spends four hours a month in a special "listening room" monitoring routine customer service calls as well as calls from customers who are canceling their credit cards.

Beyond conveying a sense of urgency, training should teach employees the specifics of defections analysis, like how to gather the information, whom to pass it on to, and what actions to take in response. In one company's branch banking system, retention data is sent monthly to the regional vice presidents and branch managers for review. It allows the regional vice presidents to identify and focus on branches that most need to improve service quality, and it gives branch managers quick feedback on performance.

Employees will be more motivated if incentives are tied to defection rates. MBNA, for example, has determined for each department the one or two things that have the biggest impact on keeping customers. Each department is measured daily on how well performance targets are met. Every morning, the previous day's performance is posted in several places throughout the building. Each day that the company hits 95% of these performance targets, MBNA contributes money to a bonus pool. Managers use the pool to pay yearly bonuses of up to 20% of a person's salary. The president visits departments that fall short of their targets to find out where the problem lies.

Great-West Life Assurance Company of Englewood, Colorado also uses incentives effectively. It pays a 50% premium to group-health-insurance brokers that hit customer-retention targets. This system gives brokers the incentive to look for customers who will stay with the company for a long time.

Having everyone in the company work toward keeping customers and basing rewards on how well they do creates a positive company atmosphere. Encouraging employees to solve customer problems and eliminate the source of complaints allows them to be "nice," and customers treat them better in return. The overall exchange is more rewarding, and people enjoy their work more. Not just customers but also employees will want to continue their relationship with the business. MBNA is besieged by applicants for job openings, while a competitor a few miles away is moving some of its operations out of the state because it can't find enough employees.

The success of MBNA shows that it is possible to achieve big improvements in both service quality and profits in a reasonably short time. But it also shows that focusing on keeping customers instead of simply having lots of them takes effort. A company can leverage business performance and profits through customer defections only when the notion permeates corporate life and when all organizational levels understand the concept of zero defections and know how to act on it.

Trying to retain all of your profitable customers is elementary. Managing toward zero defections is revolutionary. It requires careful definition of defection, information systems that can measure results over time in comparison with competitors, and a clear understanding of the microeconomics of defection.

Ultimately, defections should be a key performance measure for senior management and a fundamental component of incentive systems. Managers should know the company's defection rate, what happens to profits when the rate moves up or down, and why defections occur. They should make sure the entire organization understands the importance of keeping customers and encourage employees to pursue zero defections by tying incentives, planning, and budgeting to defection targets. Most important, managers should use defections as a vehicle for continuously improving the quality and value of the services they provide to customers.

Just as the quality revolution in manufacturing had a profound impact on the competitiveness of companies, the quality revolution in services will create a new set of winners and losers. The winners will be those who lead the way in managing toward zero defections.

Centel of Virginia

JAMES R. FREELAND
GEORGE B. BEAM

The management of a telephone company is studying the possibility of introducing quality circles in an effort to increase productivity and improve worker participation and morale.

Dan Martin sat in his office considering the alternatives before him. He had just made a presentation to the division vice-president and his department heads of the Central Telephone Company of Virginia on quality circles, a form of participative problem solving being used by an increasing number of American companies. In his presentation Dan had also recommended the specific implementation plan Centel should use. Daryl Ferguson, the Division Vice-President, and Don Roberton, the Customer Services Manager, believed Centel would make better use of quality circles by changing the concept to fit the structure and work flow at Centel. They were basing their beliefs primarily on the Fall Rush Program at the University of Virginia. Dan Martin had studied the concept of quality circles and was not sure how successful the program would be if changed. Mr. Ferguson asked him to reanalyze the situation taking into account the differences in a service company like Centel and a manufacturing company (where quality circles first originated). Dan knew he had to either come up with a new plan or better defend his old plan and soon. Mr. Ferguson wanted his new recommendations within one week.

Case prepared by George B. Beam under the supervision of Professor James R. Freeland, The Colgate Darden Graduate School of Business Administration, University of Virginia. Copyright 1980 by the Colgate Darden Graduate Business School Sponsors, Charlottesville, Virginia. Reproduced by permission.

COMPANY BACKGROUND

The Central Telephone Company of Virginia was one of seventeen divisions of the Central Telephone & Utilities Corporation (Centel). With corporate headquarters in Chicago, Centel had eleven divisions offering phone service throughout the country. Together, these divisions constituted the fifth largest telephone system in the U.S. Centel also owned and operated electric utilities in Colorado and Kansas. Through its subsidiary Centel Communications Company, the company was involved in other communications-related businesses including cable television, the sale of business communication systems, and the design and marketing of acoustic enclosures for public telephones. Telephone revenues comprised over 70 percent of total sales for the corporation.

Centel of Virginia was the third largest subsidiary of the Central Telephone & Utilities Corporation. Covering a service area of 6,070 square miles, Centel served 142,600 customers in 29 counties throughout the State. For organizational purposes the service areas were broken down into geographic territories. Charlottesville was the location of the division offices and the customer services offices for the surrounding area. Other customer services offices served the Martinsville/Lexington area and the remaining Centel service area in Virginia. Centel employed 1,460 employees in Virginia of which 77 percent were hourly. Most of the hourly workers were represented by the International Brotherhood of Electrical Workers (IBEW). In 1980 Centel's management had a good working relationship with the Union. Centel had rarely had to lay off workers in the past, except for the '73–'74 recession, but with the rapid gains in tele-

EXHIBIT 1
Division Organization Chart

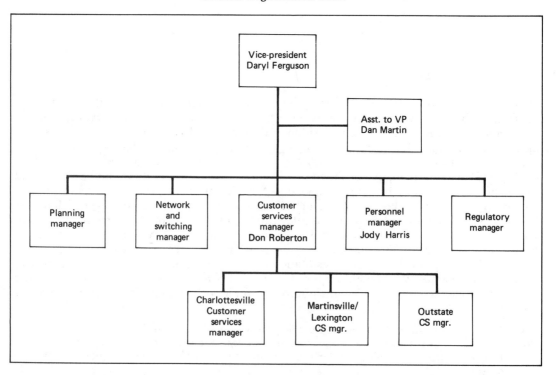

communications technology over the past few years, the practice could change. Turnover was very low and the average worker had been with Centel approximately seven years.

An organization chart of the division management is shown in *Exhibit 1*. Mr. Ferguson had been the head of the Virginia division for almost two years. Mr. Ferguson brought a number of new managers when he came to Virginia. In particular the department heads of Customer Services and Network & Switching who between them had 96 percent of the hourly workforce were replaced by Mr. Ferguson.

The Virginia division had experienced problems in the past which had affected service to customers and management-employee relations. The division management had changed a number of times over the past 10 years. It seemed that as soon as the employees had become accustomed to one management, they were replaced by another team. Service suffered and the gap between management and workers had widened.

Mr. Ferguson and his new managers had made progress in improving the relationship between management and workers. In the winter of 1979, Mr. Ferguson and other managers started meeting with first line supervisors and hourly workers. These meetings became known as Skip Level Meetings and they had a positive effect on the workers. The workers aired their gripe or question, and the attending managers tried to give them an answer. The new attitude of the workers was that "this management cares but let's wait awhile longer before we trust them completely." Because of the success of the program, Mr. Ferguson decided to continue Skip Level Meetings provided they would only be held when scheduling of the managers and workers permitted.

Though progress had been made, there still remained some areas where improvements could be made. One particular area was in the communications and coordination at the lower levels between different groups. The Fall Rush Program demonstrated there were problems in this area that could be corrected.

FALL RUSH PROGRAM

In September of 1979 Mr. Ferguson received a phone call from a professor in the Sociology Department at the University of Virginia. He was calling to complain about Centel's service. Centel's work load typically increased 50 percent during the period August through September when students at the University of Virginia returned to school, so these types of complaints were not uncommon. It was during this conversation that the professor suggested a way that might help Centel improve service in the future to its customers in the Charlottesville area during the Fall Rush. He suggested to Mr. Ferguson that Centel organize two groups of employees from all areas of the company to meet during the spring of 1980 to discuss how Centel could better prepare for the Fall Rush. The groups would be composed of hourly workers and managers chosen by upper management. The professor would provide two sociology graduate students who would serve as facilitators for the two groups. Mr. Ferguson was impressed with the approach and gave the go-ahead for the program.

From January to March the two seven-member teams met weekly to review the results of the 1979 Fall Rush and analyze specific problem areas identified by division management. The first couple of meetings were unproductive as the team members argued over which group in the company was responsible for a particular problem. A number of times the facilitator in each group had to interject to get his team back on the right track.

After the first couple of meetings, the group began to be more productive. In March each group made a presentation of their analysis and recommendations to Mr. Ferguson and Mr. Roberton. The recommendations of both teams were well received. The two teams were then combined into one team that was to come up with a detailed plan for improving service during the Fall Rush. Work continued for another month at the end of which another presentation was made. A number of the recommendations

EXHIBIT 2

Centel's New Fall Rush Procedure for Incoming Students

August 1, 1980

Dear Student:

Welcome back to Charlottesville. Centel looks forward to serving your telephone needs, and to help start the semester out right, we've made some changes this year to make applying for service easier and faster.

Centel's temporary business office will be in a new location this year. We have leased space in the former Sears building (1105 West Main Street) and we'll be open at this site from August 11 through September 15, just to handle student applications. Our hours are 8:30 a.m. to 5 p.m., Monday through Friday. There is plenty of free parking at our new location, which is also on the University bus route.

There are several reasons why we need more space this year. We're taking a larger staff consisting of experienced service representatives, clerks, and storeroom personnel. They will be able to process your orders more quickly, give you a telephone, and in most cases, provide service at your residence in one to three days.

Our temporary office is air conditioned and more spacious than our permanent business office on Arlington Blvd., so you'll be served in comfort.

In order to accomplish our goal of providing you quicker and better service, we'll need your help. First of all, we expect all students to make applications for service at the temporary business office (TBO) location. (Only permanent-resident customers will be served at our Arlington Blvd. location.) Beginning August 11, phone or in-person applicants will be asked to go to the TBO. Secondly, while you're waiting (hopefully the wait will be short) we will ask you to complete your own Service Application Card which will save time when you get to the Service Representative.

There are some additional facts we'd like you to know about our operations this year. In approximately 2500 addresses where students are normally housed, we have left the number and equipment in place. This means that if you move into one of these locations, you will have the telephone number of the student who lived there previously. The advantage of this is that we'll have a good chance of providing same-day service. At locations not "dedicated," we still hope to be able to provide three-day service.

Also, our lease instruments are now limited to standard desk and wall models in black or white (rotary or Touch Call). We will, however, offer phones in a variety of colors for sale to students at a reduced rate. These phones will be refurbished (cleaned and repaired lease instruments that have been returned to the telephone company), but will carry a full one-year guarantee. You can save on your monthly bill by owning your own telephone.

Enclosed is a handbook that Centel has produced especially for students in our serving areas. We hope you'll take the time to read it—it will provide the answer to a lot of your questions. If you need additional information or have questions, please call the business office.

We hope to see you at our temporary business office.

Sincerely,

Larry L. Gorby

Larry L. Gorby
Customer Services Manager

were accepted and implemented in the summer of 1980. One of these was a letter (shown in *Exhibit 2*) sent to every returning U.Va. student detailing Centel's new Fall Rush operations.

At the conclusion of the fall rush, the Fall Rush Program was declared a tremendous success. The program saved Centel an estimated $88,000, but more importantly, Centel's image was greatly enhanced by the better coordination and service offered students. The members of the Fall Rush Program groups were also enthusiastic. One member commented that it was the first time division management had listened to the supervisors' and workers' suggestions.

QUALITY CIRCLES

The Fall Rush Program convinced Mr. Ferguson that an ongoing group participation program could definitely benefit Centel. He had heard about a program used by the Japanese called "quality circles" but was not sure if that was a program Centel could use. He asked his assistant, Dan Martin, a new MBA out of the Darden School at the University of Virginia, to research major elements of the Japanese productivity system including quality circles and study some companies in the U.S. that had implemented a quality circle program. Finally, he wanted Dan to develop an implementation plan that could be initiated within the next six months if Centel chose to use quality circles.

Dan began his research by finding as many articles as he could on quality circles. As it turned out there were many due to the success of the Japanese and the new emphasis on productivity in American industry. After learning as much as he could from the articles, Dan called the American Productivity Center in Houston. From them he learned about three consulting firms on the West Coast which specialized in coming into companies and implementing quality circles. All three firms were established by the original Lockheed team that went to Japan to learn about quality circles and then returned to

Lockheed and started their own program. Dan also contacted two companies on the East Coast which had implemented a QC Program. After visiting these companies he felt he understood what made quality circles work. He now needed to determine if circles would work at Centel.

Dan felt the best way to find out if circles would work at Centel was to talk to the managers and hourly people at all levels in Centel. He specifically concentrated only on the Charlottesville area because he felt it would be the best place to start a program with the division offices there and the success of the Fall Rush Program. If it turned out the program was successful in Charlottesville, it then could be expanded to other areas. Dan also talked to the IBEW Union manager. All the managers and the union manager were receptive to such a program. Dan was really surprised the union manager was for it because his research indicated that most unions take a negative approach to such a program.

The two hourly workers Dan talked to had mixed feelings about quality circles. One felt such a program was needed because there were a number of times he had made suggestions to his supervisor and no one took any action. The other worker felt quality circles would just be another management program that would fail like all the others. Because the circles would be strictly voluntary, Dan was not worried by the last worker's comments. He knew only workers who wanted to participate would.

Dan Martin was convinced quality circles would benefit Centel, but what bothered him was the differences in a manufacturing environment where circles were being used exclusively, compared to a service environment like Centel. Dan knew quality circles should be made up of people with common work-related problems. This was so everyone in the group would be able to contribute in analyzing the problem. In a manufacturing company quality circles were formed from one supervisor's work group because most of the group's problems were within their common work area. This could be an assembly line, a machine, or a procedure. In a service company like Centel this was not the case. *Exhibit 3* shows the work flow in Centel's customer services department for getting one phone hooked up. For the phone to be installed properly, it was important that each of the four groups coordinate their work with the other groups and communicate any problems. If one group had a problem then all the groups had a problem. Thus, in Centel the majority of work-related problems that had the greatest effect on service were *intergroup* rather than *intragroup* problems as in a manufacturing company.

MEETING

Dan knew Centel would eventually have quality circles made up of workers from different groups, but he was hesitant to recommend that approach at the outset. From his research he had determined that two of the most important characteristics of quality circles were that the groups chose their own problems to analyze and that all problems analyzed would be common to the group. With intergroup circles Dan was worried members might choose problems that were not common to all members. He knew this problem could be alleviated by allowing management to choose the problems to be analyzed, but that would undermine the whole concept of quality circles being the workers' program rather than a management-imposed program. One indication of this was that one worker who participated in the Fall Rush Program said he resented management telling him what problems to analyze. Dan felt once some workers had gotten experience in a quality circle made up of members from the same work group,

EXHIBIT 3
Service Order Flow

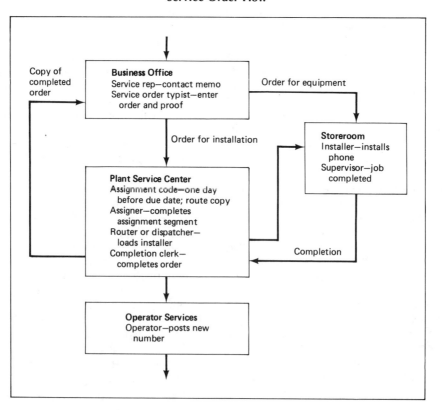

they would better understand how to function in an intergroup circle. He knew from talking with a number of supervisors there were a number of problems that could be work-group analyzed.

Dan prepared the implementation plan (see Appendix) and sent it to Mr. Ferguson and his department heads. Mr. Ferguson called for a meeting with his department heads and Dan to go over the implementation plan. Mr. Ferguson and Mr. Roberton said they felt Centel should go right to intergroup circles. They felt the greatest problems to be addressed were in this area and that the Fall Rush Program had shown such a concept could work at Centel. They both felt they did not have the six months Dan had recommended before going to intergroup circles.

Dan and Jody Harris, the Personnel Manager who would be responsible for the program, did not agree. They felt Centel should get some experience with the QC program as used by other companies before making any changes. Dan tried to point out the differences between the Fall Rush Program and quality circles and explain why he did not recommend intergroup circles to begin with. Mr. Ferguson, still unconvinced, asked Dan to reanalyze the situation and, if necessary, come up with a new plan.

DECISION

Dan returned to his office and thought over what had transpired. He knew why Mr. Ferguson and Mr. Roberton wanted to use intergroup circles, but it bothered him that they did not have six months before forming such circles. Dan wondered if increasing productivity was their only reason for wanting to implement a quality circle program? Dan felt a circle program should be started to increase worker participation and morale. Productivity increases were a benefit of the program and were a primary reason for management implementing such a program. If increasing productivity was the *only* reason Centel wanted to implement circles, Dan was worried what would happen if the program did not generate the magnitude of cost savings ideas the Fall Rush Program had. Whatever their reasons, Dan knew he would have to come up with a new plan or be better prepared to defend his old plan to Mr. Ferguson next week.

APPENDIX
Quality Circle Implementation Plan

September 30, 1980

TO: Daryl Ferguson
FROM: Dan Martin
SUBJECT: QC Implementation at Centel

I recommend that Centel implement a pilot Quality Circle program in the Charlottesville offices of Customer Services and Network & Switching. I first would like to list my reasons for making such a recommendation, followed by some of the problems identified to me by some Centel managers. Finally, I will list the implementation program I recommend Centel use if they choose to have a Quality Circle program.

During the past month, I spent time talking to a number of Centel managers and the IBEW Union Manager in the Charlottesville area. In our meetings, I presented the QC concept and got their reactions to such a program. Also, I talked to these managers about their work environment and how compatible it was to a QC program. A number of strengths and weaknesses of the program as it pertains to Centel were identified.

APPENDIX (continued)

I believe Centel should implement a pilot QC program in the Charlottesville area because:

1. Every manager and supervisor I talked to was favorable toward such a program. There were some problems identified, but all managers and supervisors said they would be willing to support such a program in their area under the right conditions. Also, the managers I talked to felt there were definitely a number of areas where employees could identify problems and make recommendations that would benefit Centel.

2. The IBEW Business Manager is in favor of the program and would like to see it implemented. Even though it is strictly voluntary, he was not sure if the hourly people would accept it, but he said the Union would take no action against the program.

3. The Fall Rush Program has made a favorable impression on the people involved in the program and on a number of employees who did not get to participate in the program now that management has used some of the recommendations of this program. According to first line supervisors, a number of employees feel the current management team will listen to employees' suggestions. Also, I believe the Fall Rush Program has established the idea of participative problem solving at Centel.

4. The Charlottesville area has closer contact with the division offices than any other Centel service area. The QC program will require a number of management meetings in the pre-implementation phase. These meetings will require less management time if the program is implemented in the Charlottesville area due to less traveling.

5. The skip level meetings have given employees a medium for airing grievances. Skip level meetings should be continued. This will help prevent Quality Circles being used by employees as a gripe session.

Some of the problems that will have to be addressed before Centel implements a Quality Circle program are:

1. What would be Centel's policy toward a Circle recommendation that eliminated someone's job?

2. What will Centel's policy be toward scheduling QC meetings? Will they be held during normal working hours or overtime? All the managers believed the program would benefit their area, but they could not see how they could schedule 8-10 people from one work group to meet for one hour each week and still meet their workload.

3. Since the normal workload goes up 25-50 percent during August and September, what would be Centel's policy toward circles meeting during the Fall Rush?

These were the problems identified by the managers I talked to. After the Steering Committee is formed, these should be the first issues they should consider after choosing a facilitator.

QC IMPLEMENTATION PLAN

Below are the steps I recommend to implement a pilot Quality Circle Program at Centel. See the estimated timetable in Table 1 and the estimated costs in Table 2.

1. Hire a consulting firm to make an in-house presentation on Quality Circles to all managers in Customer Services and Network & Switching in the Charlottesville area. If scheduling is a problem the seminar can be presented at night or twice during the work day. I recommend the consulting firm Quality Circle Institute of Red Bluff, California, as a first choice and J. F. Beardsley and Associates of San Jose, California, as a second choice. They both have good programs, but the former is much cheaper.

2. Hire same firm to implement Quality Circles in Charlottesville offices of Customer Services and Network & Switching. The consulting firm will send preliminary information concerning the formation of the Steering Committee, criteria for selecting a facilitator, and information on the formation and training of Quality Circles.

3. Form the Steering Committee, composed of the department heads of Customer Service, Net-

APPENDIX (continued)

work & Switching, and Personnel, the Charlottesville Customer Services Manager, Union Representative, Facilitator (after he is chosen), and the Division Vice-President.

4. Have the Steering Committee select one full-time facilitator and either a second full-time or part-time facilitator. The second facilitator can be used as a substitute at the beginning and then as a full-time facilitator when the program grows.

5. Facilitators begin training with consultant. The Union representative can be included in the training, but he indicated to me at our meeting he was not interested in participating. The Steering Committee begins to meet regularly to prepare guidelines and objectives of Centel program. Consultant will help Steering Committee identify areas to consider.

6. Steering Committee, Facilitator, and Consultant Design Implementation Program for Centel. The program should identify departments that will have pilot circles, schedule for circle meetings, and schedule for group leader training.

   Based on my study of the Charlottesville area, I recommend that a pilot program of six circles be initiated. I would put two circles in both the Charlottesville Customer Services Business Office and Plant Service Center. Because Centel desires to have them in Network & Switching also, I would organize two circles in Northern and Southern.

7. The facilitator should collect some pre-implementation data so as to later demonstrate a before and after comparison. I could not identify any data that Centel presently has to do this. Thus, I would recommend the Personnel Department administer a simple questionnaire to determine employees' attitudes in the Business Office, Plant Service Center, and Network & Switching.

8. The facilitator will next distribute Quality Circle literature to managers of the Business Office, Plant Service Center, and Network & Switching. Though I have already talked to most of these managers, it gives them an opportunity to review materials on circles and ask questions. It will then be up to the managers to select the pilot program circle leaders from the interested supervisory volunteers.

9. The Steering Committee will meet with the pilot program managers and circle leaders to discuss the program and answer any questions. This meeting is necessary to show middle managers and group leaders that the program has top management support.

10. The facilitator and consultant begin Circle Leader training. The Steering Committee and consultant make final review of circle policy, guidelines, and implementation plan.

11. Second level managers of pilot program departments conduct Quality Circle familiarization meetings with employees. The facilitator and possibly a representative of the Steering Committee should be there. Workers should be allowed to openly discuss the program and ask questions.

12. Circle leaders talk to each employee individually in their work groups to find out if employee is interested in voluntarily participating in the group.

13. The facilitator and circle leaders begin group training with training materials supplied by the consulting firm.

This concludes the pilot circle implementation plan. Circles will continue training for one hour each week during the first two months of the program. After two months, the circles will begin to identify problems in their work area and choose the ones they want to work on. The facilitator should schedule circle presentations to management on either recommendations or status once every three months. Members of the Steering Committee or pilot group managers should try and attend all or part of a circle's meeting at least once in the first three months of the program.

After the pilot program gets started, the Steering Committee needs to address the issue of circle expansion. How fast will circles be allowed to grow and in what areas are two primary considerations. Expansion should not be allowed until after approximately three months to give Centel management and employees a chance to experience the program.

The facilitator will meet with all the pilot circles during the first months to help the circle

APPENDIX (continued)

leader. After approximately three months, the facilitator should prepare a report for the Steering Committee on circle activities and any cost savings realized to date. Any problems in implementing the pilot circles should be identified in this report so the Steering Committee can make modifications to the program before future circles are added. Also, after three months of circle activities, the Steering Committee should meet with the managers and leaders of the pilot circles to discuss the attitudes of circle members, non-circle members, and middle management.

During the first six months, the facilitator will be able to contact the consulting group about any implementation problems and, if needed, have them send someone to Charlottesville. At the end of six months, the consultant will return to Centel to make an evaluation of the program and, along with the facilitator, establish goals for the program for the next year.

Once Centel has experienced some success with the pilot program, I would recommend the Steering Committee form two or three interdepartment groups between the Business Office, Plant Service Center, Storeroom, and possibly Operator Services. A number of people who took part in the Fall Rush Program said there are communication problems between groups that would be alleviated by intergroup interaction on problem solving. I do not recommend interdepartment groups initially because I feel the program must be accepted in its original form before making variations to it. Once employees become experienced in identifying and solving problems in their work groups, I feel they will be ready to tackle the more difficult task of interdepartmental problems.

I have tried to make my implementation steps as specific as possible. Once a consulting firm is retained and a facilitator hired more detail can be incorporated into the plan as Centel begins to get into the preliminary implementation phase. It will be up to the Steering Committee to add more detail and make modifications to the program as information becomes available.

TABLE 1
Implementation Timetable Guideline

Action	By Whom	Approximate Working Days
Decision to start.	Division Vice-President	0
Contact consultant to arrange for in-house seminar and implementation. Hopefully, seminar can be scheduled within next 20 days.	Assigned Individual	1
Receive and review preliminary information from consultant concerning organization of steering committee and choosing facilitator.	Assigned Individual	5
Form steering committee and initiate first meeting.	Assigned Individual	8
Steering committee selects facilitator and works on circle objectives and guidelines.	Steering Committee	18
Facilitator begins training with the instructor/consultant. Also, the two work on setting up implementation program to be presented to steering committee.	Facilitator	18
Facilitator collects preimplementation data for before and after comparison.	Facilitator	23
Distribute Quality Circle literature to pilot group managers.	Facilitator	28
Pilot group managers and supervisors meet with steering committee to discuss program and answer any questions.	Steering Committee and Pilot Group Managers	30
Select pilot program circle leaders from interested supervisory volunteers. Begin leader training.	Pilot Group Managers Facilitator	31
Managers conduct Quality Circle familiarization meetings with employees. Facilitator, Circle leaders, and a member of the steering committee participate as speakers.	Managers Facilitator	35

APPENDIX (continued)

Leader contacts each employee to determine circle membership.	Leader	37
Leader and facilitator begin weekly Circle meetings and initiate member training.	Facilitator, Leader	38
Circles learn problem solving techniques from training sessions.	Facilitator, Leader Group Members	78
Facilitator makes progress report to steering committee and arranges Circle presentation.	Facilitator	100
Steering committee decides on program expansion and makes revisions to policy/procedures.	Steering Committee	3 Months

TABLE 2
Cost Analysis—Quality Circles

A. One time costs:

Consultant seminar presentation	$ 500
Consultant implementation cost	3,950
Consultant expenses (estimate only)	4,000
	$8,450

B. On-going costs:
Full-time facilitator
Loss of production due to Circle meetings
Management expenses for participation on steering committee

Federal Express
Quality Improvement Program

CHRISTOPHER H. LOVELOCK

The leading U.S. company in express shipments faces a very competitive marketplace. To maintain its lead, Federal Express has developed an intensive quality improvement program, involving active participation of employees. But this is expensive to implement and, with profits declining, a senior vice president wonders how to maintain future investment in the program.

"The first year of our quality improvement program was really a great success. But the last six months have been tough," said Thomas R. Oliver, shaking his head ruefully. Oliver, senior vice president sales and customer service, was talking about some of the challenges facing Federal Express as it sought to maintain momentum on quality improvement efforts in early 1990.

Last August, we merged with Flying Tigers, which has proved to be more difficult than anyone anticipated in terms of impacting service. In September, Hurricane Hugo, perhaps the most powerful storm of the century, disrupted our operations in the southeastern United States. Then there was the San Francisco earthquake

in October. In December, the Mount Redoubt volcano in Alaska began erupting a huge ash cloud, which totally dislocated our international flights through Anchorage. That volcano's still erupting on and off. The Friday before Christmas, the coldest weather seen in Memphis in the past 50 years caused burst water pipes and a computer foul-up that shut down our Superhub sorting operation. And now we're facing a profit crunch. Our revenues are way up, but we've incurred very heavy costs from the Tiger purchase and the continued expansion of our international operations.

Oliver pushed the company newspaper *Update* across the table. "Earnings drop; costs to be controlled," read the headline. He explained that Federal's third quarter profits for fiscal year (FY) 1990 were down by 79% to $5.2 million on revenues of $1.7 billion (up 35% over last year). Then he added:

> A going concern that is doing reasonably well but not making the desired level of profit can experience a big courage gap on the quality issue. People know what it costs to train management, to train employees, to continuously train new hires, to give people 'time around the clock' to work quality issues, and to organize the implementation of the various ideas that emerge. Yet, they aren't clear about the benefits. I want to ensure that last year's interest in quality doesn't get preempted by this year's interest in cutting costs.

THE EVOLUTION OF A LEGEND

Few companies had achieved legendary status as quickly as Federal Express. People loved to tell stories about the firm, incorporated in 1971 by Frederick W. Smith, Jr., then aged 27. The earliest story told how Smith had sketched out the concept of a national hub-and-spoke airfreight network in a paper written while an undergraduate at Yale. The professor told Smith that his concept was interesting but infeasible because of competition and regulation, and gave the young man a "C" grade. But after service in Vietnam, Smith went on to turn his dream into reality, basing the hub in his home town of Memphis, Tennessee.

The concept was simple. Federal Express couriers, based in cities around the country, would pick up packages and take them to a local station, from where they would be flown by air to a central hub. Memphis was selected since it was centrally located in the US and airport operations were rarely disrupted by bad weather. At the hub, packages would be unloaded, sorted, reloaded, and flown to their destinations, where they would be delivered by couriers driving Federal Express vans. Because of federal regulations, the new airline had to be chartered as an air taxi operator and was restricted to aircraft with a carrying capacity of 7,200 pounds (3.3 tonnes). Initially, Federal flew Dassault Falcons, French-built executive jets converted into minifreighters.

On an April night in 1973, 14 Falcons took off from cities around the US and flew to Memphis. In total, they carried 186 packages. Not surprisingly, the company lost money heavily in its early years. But aided by aggressive sales and clever advertising, package volume built steadily and by 1976 the firm was profitable. Thereafter, growth in revenues, profits and package volume was rapid.

With the 1978 deregulation of the airfreight industry (for which Smith had lobbied heavily), Federal went public and bought larger aircraft. Having redefined service as "all actions and reactions that customers perceive they have purchased," management began a major investment in information technology, creating an online order-entry system known as COSMOS. This was designed to provide superior customer service in the face of increasing competition from UPS, Emery, the US Postal Service, and other express delivery firms.

Federal's early advertising slogan "When it absolutely, positively has to be there overnight" became almost a national byword. By FY 1985, Federal's sales exceeded $2 billion and its advertising jabbed fun at the competition, asking provocatively, "Why fool around with anybody else?" Later, to emphasize its role as a tool for JIT (just-in-time) inventory man-

Fiscal year ending May 31

	1976	1981	1986	1988	1989[1]	1990[2]
Annual revenues ($mn)	75	589	2,573	3,883	5,167	7,000
Annual net income ($mn)	4	58	132	188	185	110
Av. daily express packages ('000)	15	87	550	878	1,059	1,250
Av. daily heavyweight vol. ('000 lbs)[3]	—	—	—	—	4,019	3,300

[1]Includes Tiger International operations for the last four months.

[2]Projections

[3]1,000 lbs = 0.455 metric tonnes

agement procedures, the company began using the slogan, "It's not just a package, it's your business."

Following the purchase of Flying Tigers in August 1989, analysts forecast that Federal's total revenues for FY 1990 could exceed $7 billion. By now the company was an American institution. Its vans with their distinctive purple, orange, and white colors were everywhere; its aircraft could be seen at most airports; and the verb "to Fedex" (meaning to ship a package overnight) had become as much a generic expression for office workers as the term "to Xerox."

For 19 years, Federal Express had had a single leader, its chairman, Fred Smith, who was still only 46 years old. Outside management experts noted that it was unusual for an entrepreneur whose company had grown so large, so fast, to continue to lead the firm. Smith appeared to have a remarkable ability to supply vision, inspire loyalty, and create a climate in which innovation and risk taking were encouraged and rewarded. Although the Federal Express Manager's Guide ran to 186 pages, Smith's core philosophy for the corporation was simple:

> Federal Express, from its inception, has put its people first, both because it is right to do so and because it is good business as well. Our corporate philosophy is succinctly stated: People — Service — Profits (P-S-P).

Line Haul Operations

Federal's operating concept of a hub in Memphis, served by aircraft flying spoke-like routes from cities all around the US, had been only slightly modified over the years. But the technology and scale of the operation had changed dramatically. The sorting facility at Memphis International Airport had been enormously expanded. The Superhub, as it was known, now covered some 23 acres (100,000 m³), consisting of a matrix of 83 conveyor belts moving at right angles to one another. Aircraft arrived at Memphis almost continuously between 11:00 pm and 1:15 am. Using specially designed equipment, a crew of 14 workers could unload 44,000 pounds (20 tonnes) of freight from a Boeing 727 in 12 minutes.

The freight began its journey through the Superhub on a wide belt, known as the Primary Matrix, moving at 10 mph (16 km/h). Watching the packages rush by on this belt and then be diverted by guide arms into specific sort areas reminded one visitor of seeing a mountain torrent in full flood. Although the sort was assisted by computers, much of the process was labor intensive and expected to remain so. Once reloaded, the aircraft left Memphis between 2:15 and 3:45 am.

Regional domestic sorting facilities had been established; packages traveling between two East Coast cities were sorted in Newark, New Jersey, rather than being sent to Memphis; while packages traveling between West Coast destinations were sorted in Oakland, California. A second national hub had been opened in Indianapolis, southeast of Chicago. These facilities were served by large trucks as well as by aircraft; packages traveling shorter distances were frequently transported entirely by truck.

Since 1979, Federal had offered service to and within Canada. In 1985, the company inaugurated international service and began to build up a network of routes around the world. A European hub was established in Brussels, the capital of Belgium (and administrative center of the 12-nation European Community). Federal planned to build up significant intra-European business as well as transatlantic volume. Overseas expansion was aided by the purchase of existing courier firms in each national market (nine were purchased in FY 1989).

In December 1988, Smith announced what the press described as "an ambitious and highly risky plan" to pay $895 million for Tiger International, Inc., the world's largest heavy cargo airline, best known for its Flying Tiger airfreight service. Although Tiger had some domestic business, most of its revenues came from international services. The merger was a key step towards realizing Smith's goal of making Federal "the world's premier priority logistics company." Six "Freight Movement Centers"— located in Anchorage, Memphis, Chicago, New York, Brussels and Tokyo — now coordinated Federal's international traffic, which was expected to generate 30% of the firm's revenues in FY 1990.

A major benefit was Tiger's overseas operating rights, including landing rights in Japan. The merger allowed Federal to operate its own aircraft on routes where transportation had formerly been contracted out to other carriers. It also catapulted Federal into the heavy cargo business; previously, the firm had limited most packages to 150 pounds (68 kg) maximum weight, as well as imposing length and girth restrictions. Another important asset was Tiger's fleet of aircraft, including 21 Boeing 747s. However, these benefits came at the cost of taking on significant debt at a time when margins were being squeezed by price competition and heavy upfront costs were being incurred due to overseas expansion. There was also the challenge of merging two sharply different corporate cultures.

The Scope of the Operation in 1990

By 1990, Federal Express was one of the world's largest airlines, with a fleet of some 350 aircraft. This fleet comprised 170 trunk line aircraft (21 Boeing 747s, 25 McDonnell-Douglas DC-10s, 118 Boeing 727s, and 6 DC-8s) and another 180 feeder aircraft used for shorter-distance operations. The firm served 119 countries and had 1,530 staffed facilities worldwide. Some four-fifths of its 86,000 employees were based in the United States, including 17,300 employees in Memphis. Federal operated over 20,000 vans and almost 2,000 large trucks in the US, plus another 6,300 vehicles in international locations.

A visitor to Memphis might be surprised to see a large fleet of snowplows and other snow-removal vehicles sporting Federal Express colors. The company had purchased this equipment in 1988 after a heavy snowstorm — unusual for Memphis which had almost no snow removal equipment — had badly disrupted operations one night. "We only need this equipment about one night every two years," explained a company official. "But when we need it, we really need it!"

The average daily volume for express packages (up to 150 pounds in the US) was around 1.25 million. Federal's average package weighed 5.4 pounds (2.5 kg) and yielded a revenue of over $16; a significant price increase would take effect on April 1, 1990.

Document shipments weighing just a few ounces (100–200g) had a declining share of package volume; the Fedex Overnight Letter represented 37% of all express packages in FY1989, down from 40% two years earlier. The company offered three levels of delivery speed in the United States: Priority Overnight (next business morning by 10:30 am in most locations); Standard Overnight (next business day for shipments of five pounds or less, with delivery before 3:00 pm in most locations); and Standard Air (second business day). Federal's rates tended to be more expensive than most of its US competitors.

For heavyweight shipments, the average daily volume was around 5,000 units. These shipments weighed an average of almost 800 pounds (360 kg) each — some were so large that they required an entire aircraft — so they were handled separately from the normal hub sorting operations. The revenue for each shipment ranged widely but the average was around $850.

The express package industry was consolidating and the company's chief operating officer, James L. Barksdale, described the challenge facing its 1,300 sales professionals: "We're in a tough business. Our competitors are tough, mean, go-getting folks. They are not a bunch of idiots. I wish they were." Within the US, the key players were Federal Express (with about 45–50% of the market), UPS (15%), Airborne (10–15%), Emery/Purolator (5%), US Postal Service (10%), and others (5%). Federal had purchased Purolator's Indianapolis hub. Overseas, Federal faced UPS, Emery, DHL, and Australian-owned TNT, plus the express divisions of national postal services and airline freight and package services.

INFORMATION TECHNOLOGY

For Federal Express, information about each package was seen as just as important as the package itself. Information also played a key role in achieving the most effective utilization of the entire physical operation. Dr. Ron J. Ponder, senior vice president for information and telecommunications, described the line-haul operations (package sorting and transportation) as one of several parallel fibers running through the entire business. The others included a series of major information networks. "We run three data processing houses at Federal," explained Ponder, a former business school professor. "There are the traditional, commercial revenue systems that every company has; a line-haul flight operations system that is unique to airlines; and COSMOS, our customer service house."

> To me, quality is everything we do. Our goal for availability — communication and systems — is 99.8%. We've cranked that up during the last ten years from about 88%. Each year, we keep raising the bar. We're running some of the highest systems availability numbers in North America. Most companies are happy at 95% or 96%.
>
> Our computer center is now one of the largest in the world under one roof, and we have the highest transaction rates of any shop in North America on a daily basis. Last month, we had 320 million transactions from all over the world go through our computer systems. We measure each one of them. Less than 86,000 exceeded our standard internal compute time of one second, which you have to have to run these massive parallel systems. Each morning at 8:30, we have a conference call in this division with perhaps 50 people in on it. We start off with any problems we've had in the last 24 hours.
>
> In addition to overseeing the systems, I do the strategic architectural planning that lets this company use technology to the greatest possible advantage for customer satisfaction and competitive superiority, and for reducing operational costs to improve productivity.

Ponder believed that Federal Express had a sharply different view of technology from most companies.

> Technology transfer — or being able to absorb new technology — is a cultural thing that we've built in here. One of the keys to our success is that we constantly embrace new technology. For most companies, that's very painful and they don't like it. It's painful to leave what works and is cheap for new, expensive, unknown approaches. So they don't do it. At Federal, we would rather get an innovation a year earlier and develop back-up systems to counter a relatively high failure rate than to wait until the failure rate — and the price — have been reduced to more "acceptable" levels. Most folks prefer to wait until a technology matures.

> You can view technology as a wave in the ocean, washing in debris. Most people concentrate on the debris that floats in. 'Oh, isn't this neat!' they'll say of some device. 'Where can I use it?' And that's where I think they mess up. I view technology as the wave itself, not the individual things that are brought to shore. We knew what we wanted to do ten years ago, but the technology wasn't there. So we were waiting for the wave and constantly prodding manufacturers to create what we needed as that wave rolled in.

Asked what new waves Federal Express was watching, Ponder listed battery technology, continued miniaturization, the maturing of relational databases (essential to maintaining detailed customer files) and, most importantly, a new generation of computer hardware and software using RISC (Reduced Instruction Set Computing) architecture. The net effect would be more computing power and faster access to information for less money.

COSMOS AND DADS

Federal prided itself on having one of the most sophisticated customer service systems in the world. COSMOS (Customer, Operations, Service, Master On-line System) was first installed in 1979 and had been constantly upgraded to cope with the more than 260,000 calls now received, on average, each working day. COSMOS had evolved into a worldwide electronic network that transmitted critical package information to Memphis. Its major components were an order-entry system for customers to request package pickups, a continuously updated record of each package's progress through the Fedex system that could be used to trace a missing package, financial records for billing purposes, and a huge relational database the could also be used for marketing analysis and planning.

The system worked in much the same way around the world. In the US, customers had a choice between requesting a pickup or, for a reduced fee, of dropping off a package at a drop-box or at one of Federal's business service centers. To request a pickup, customers telephoned a toll-free number that connected to a customer service agent (CSA) at one of 17 call centers around the nation. Calls could

EXHIBIT 1
Contents of Federal Express Dispatch Request Screen*

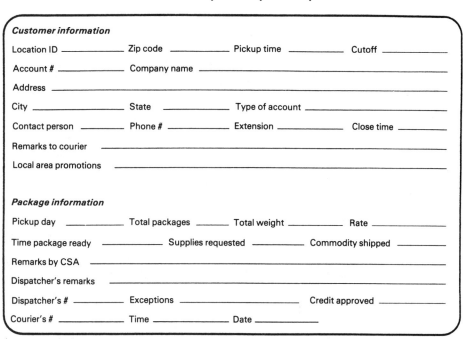

Customer information

Location ID _____ Zip code _____ Pickup time _____ Cutoff _____

Account # _____ Company name _____

Address _____

City _____ State _____ Type of account _____

Contact person _____ Phone # _____ Extension _____ Close time _____

Remarks to courier _____

Local area promotions _____

Package information

Pickup day _____ Total packages _____ Total weight _____ Rate _____

Time package ready _____ Supplies requested _____ Commodity shipped _____

Remarks by CSA _____

Dispatcher's remarks _____

Dispatcher's # _____ Exceptions _____ Credit approved _____

Courier's # _____ Time _____ Date _____

Note: The screen display has been clarified and simplified for purposes of case presentation, with abbreviations written out in full.

be diverted from one center to another to maintain the company's response-time standards. Since most calls were received in the mid to late afternoon, peak volumes could be shifted to centers in other time zones. The CSA requested the shipper's account number which was entered on an electronic order blank on the video screen. (*Exhibit 1.*) Armed with this information, the system automatically provided the CSA with the account name, address, phone number, pickup location, contact name, and other relevant data.

An alternative method was to call a special Automatic Pickup number. In response to the promptings of a recorded voice, callers used the buttons on their touch-tone telephones to enter their account numbers and then, as a cross-check, their postal zip code, followed by the number of packages being shipped. The voice would then provide a confirmation number and latest pick up time. These service requests were transmitted automatically to the nearest origin station.

Federal was also testing a custom-designed desktop unit, smaller than a telephone, called "Hello Federal." This device had a full alphanumeric keypad, an adjustable LCD screen, and buttons to press for pickup, package tracing information, and requests for airbills and packaging. The requested information was displayed on the screen; no voice communication was needed. Since each unit was programmed with the shipper's account number, it was not necessary to provide account identification when calling. If the tests proved successful, the company planned to offer a "Hello Federal" unit free to any customer shipping a predefined volume of packages three or more days per week.

Once a pickup request was received, the CSA entered shipping information through COSMOS to alert the dispatch center nearest to the pickup location. The message was received by the dispatch center's DADS (Digitally Assisted Dispatch System) computer which, in turn, sent the information to a courier. The request was displayed on a small DADS video screen in the courier's van or on a portable unit the size of a slim briefcase used by walking couriers.

One customer, a management consultant working out of a home office, testified to the efficiency of the system:

> It was only the second time that I had used the Automatic Pickup service and I still didn't have 100% confidence in it, but I knew that it was a little faster than talking to a CSA in a call center and I was in a hurry. I had just finished a report for one client and was about to leave for the airport on a visit to another client. So I sealed up the report, phoned for a cab, and then called the Automatic Pickup number to place my order. The taxi arrived in five minutes, which was pretty good. As I was getting into the cab, what should roll up but the Federal Express van to pick up my package. I was so astonished that I got out of the cab and asked the courier how he had arrived so quickly. "I was driving on the next street," he said, "when your request came up on my screen."

When a customer called Federal Express, the customer service agent first asked the caller for a Federal Express account number. When this was typed in, most other customer information (other than details of the caller's request, e.g. pickup) was automatically retrieved from the computer's memory and displayed on the screen, from where it could then be verified with the caller.

Tracking the Package Through the Federal Express System

Each airbill contained a unique 10-digit bar code label which was scanned by an infrared light pen every time the package changed hands. The first scan, known as PUPS (Pick Up Package Scan), took place at the pickup location. Using a handheld terminal called a COSMOS IIB SuperTracker (a little bigger than the remote control for a TV set), the courier scanned the bar code and then entered on a key pad the type of service, handling code, and destination zip code. The SuperTracker recorded this information, added the time of pickup, and responded on its LCD display with a routing and sorting code which the courier then handwrote on the package. Dr. Ponder

noted, "Miniaturization has enabled us to stretch the communications system right to the customer's doorstep."

On returning to the van, the courier plugged the SuperTracker into a shoe within the dispatch computer, which transmitted its information to COSMOS. In many overseas countries, this data transfer took place when the van returned to its station. Once unloaded, each package received a Station Outbound Package Scan (SOPS) before being reloaded into a container for transport to a sorting hub. Any exceptions, such as packages that were damaged or missed the aircraft, received a P.M. eXception (PMX) scan. These data were then transmitted to COSMOS. Similar scans were made at several other points. (*Exhibit 2.*)

Finally, at the delivery point, the package received a Proof of Delivery Scan (PODS). The courier entered the recipient's first initial and last name, as well as a code for delivery location, and the SuperTracker automatically recorded the time. If the package were delivered to an alternative location (for instance, a neighboring building) or no one was available to accept delivery, it received instead a Delivery EXception (DEX) scan and full details were entered.

The records provided by these scans enabled Federal to offer full custodial care of all packages. A trace of a missing package would reveal in seconds the time and location of the latest scan. No competitor could match this level of tracing capability. Said Ponder, "The notion of picking up and delivering a package without being able to offer the customer total information on it is totally unacceptable to us."

Automated Systems for High Volume Customers

Federal had formed a team called Customer Automation to assist customers in managing their shipments more effectively. The result was a family of automated shipping and invoicing systems designed to reduce paperwork and tie the company more closely to its large volume customers.

Tape Invoice offered customers a weekly invoice on magnetic tape, instead of paper. By running the invoice tape on the computer, cus-

EXHIBIT 2
Physical Flows and Information Flows for Federal Express Packages

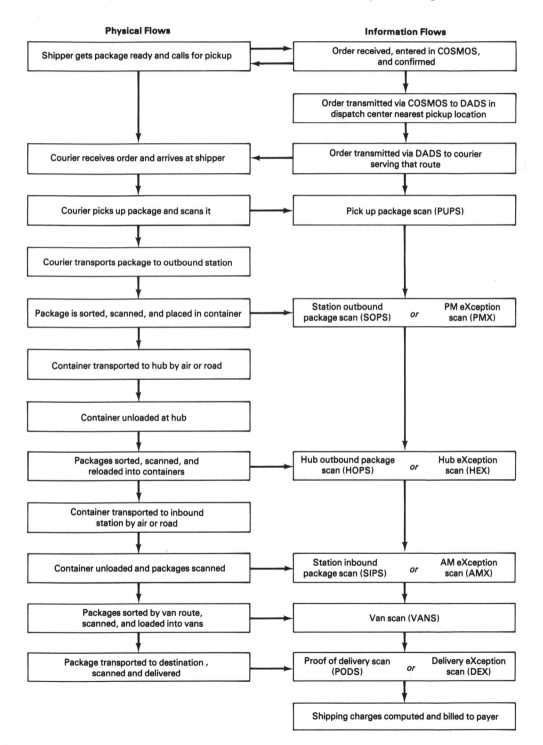

278 The Search for Service Quality

tomers could analyze Federal Express shipping information any way they wished. Such data could be fed directly into the firm's accounting system.

Powership 2 was a shipment management system that streamlined package preparation and billing. Federal provided customers with an electronic weighing scale, microcomputer terminal, bar code scanner, and printer at no charge; all the customer paid was telephone charges. The system eliminated the need for airbills and express manifests, and could be programmed to store up to 32,000 recipient names and addresses. The printer could generate barcoded address labels. Powership 2 rated packages with the right charges, automatically combining package weights by destination to provide volume discounts. Daily invoices could be prepared automatically, as could customized management reports. Customers could trace their own packages through COSMOS.

Powership Plus allowed customers to link their computers with Federal Express's tracking and invoicing systems. If the package weight were known (which was true for many mail order items) users could quote shipping rates, delivery schedules, and tracking numbers to their own customers at the very time they entered the purchase order. Next, they transmitted information directly to the warehouse, where the barcoded address label could be printed and applied. When each night's shipping was complete, users would transmit their shipping data to Federal. At the end of the week, they would send Federal Express a computer tape containing the week's shipping data, plus a check for the total shipping charges.

NEW QUALITY INITIATIVES

Quality had been implicit in Federal's efforts from the beginning. In 1975, its advertising claimed "Federal Express. Twice as Good as the Best in the Business" (a slogan comparing Federal's performance against its then leading competitor, Emery Air Freight). The firm's emphasis on reliability was captured in its classic slogan, "Absolutely, Positively Over-

night." Management had long recognized the connection between doing things right the first time and improving productivity: "$Q = P$" (quality equals productivity) was the internal rallying cry.

Employee Orientation

As chairman, Fred Smith constantly set goals of improving reliability, productivity, and financial performance to promote the corporate imperative of People — Service — Profits. Particular attention was paid to leading and motivating employees. Regular communication with employees had always been a corporate priority. As the company grew in numbers and geographic scope, increasing reliance came to be placed on the use of videotaped messages for both communication and training. In 1987, Federal launched FXTV, a real-time business television network broadcasting daily by satellite to over 700 locations in the US and Canada from studios in Memphis. Satellite hook-ups with overseas locations were arranged for special occasions. Each month, FXTV produced about 20 hours of broadcast TV, plus 10–15 hours of videotape.

Since 1985, a confidential employee survey had been conducted annually called Survey Feedback Action (SFA). It consisted of 26 statements with which the employee was asked to agree or disagree on a five-point scale ranging from "strongly agree" to "strongly disagree." Scores were reported for employee work groups not for individuals. The first ten questions (*Exhibit 3*) related to employees' views of their managers. The percentage of favorable responses on these items constituted what was known as the SFA Leadership Index.

The full SFA Index represented the percentage of positive responses on all 26 items, including questions on pay, working conditions, views on senior management and feelings about the company. Other companies administered the same survey, so scores could be compared with those from employees in other firms. Federal had consistently obtained above average ratings.

In 1983, Smith initiated "Bravo Zulu" awards (from the US Navy signal flags for, BZ, meaning "Well done!"), which allowed

EXHIBIT 3
Survey Feedback Action Program: Components of Leadership Index

1. I can tell my manager what I think.
2. My manager tells what is expected.
3. Favoritism is not a problem in my work group.
4. My manager helps us to do our job better.
5. My manager listens to concerns.
6. My manager asks for my ideas about work.
7. My manager tells me when I do a good job.
8. My manager treats me with respect.
9. My manager keeps me informed.
10. My manager does not interfere.

Note: The above sentences paraphrase the actual wording used in compiling the Leadership Index. Employees were asked to review each statement carefully and then to express their agreement or disagreement with that statement on a 5-point scale.

managers to provide instant recognition to employees for excellent service within the company. Stickers bearing the signal flags could be placed on paperwork or a memo; managers also had authority to issue a Bravo Zulu voucher worth up to $100.

Outstanding examples of customer service were celebrated with Golden Falcon awards, consisting of a gold pin and ten shares of Federal Express stock (worth about $500 in early 1990). About 20 such awards were made each year. Nominees were often identified by customer calls or letters; a typical example might concern extraordinary effort in tracking down and delivering a missing package. Golden Falcon and Bravo Zulu awards, and the stories behind them, were publicized to motivate employees and create corporate legends.

An Unsuccessful First Look at Quality Training

It was not until 1985, when Smith and senior officers became concerned about a possible slowdown in the business and decline in profitability, that the company first addressed quality improvement techniques at the corporate level. Smith hired a consultant to conduct an off-site meeting with top management, but it was not a success. As Tom Oliver recalled, "Everyone walked away with a calculator and a statistics book, but our interest had not been captured." Some improvements were made, but the idea lost momentum. Smith was soon preoccupied with the problems of ZapMail, the company's same-day facsimile service, which was discontinued in 1986 with a write-off of some $360 million — the company's first major setback since its start-up days.

Two and a half years passed, during which the feared slowdown was replaced by a period of explosive growth. By mid-1987, the sales and customer service division was struggling with service problems that were becoming increasingly serious as the company continued to expand. As senior vice president of the division, Oliver decided it was high time to re-explore the quality issue.

Working with ODI

Disappointed with the previous statistically-based approach to quality improvement, Oliver selected Organizational Dynamics, Inc. (ODI), an international consulting firm headquartered in Burlington, Massachusetts. ODI's great advantage, from Oliver's perspective, was that it paid little attention to statistical techniques but a lot more to the thought processes and involvement of people within the company in developing quality programs.

ODI began by designing and leading quality planning workshops for senior executives from all divisions. The product of each workshop was a series of action plans, setting priorities for problems needing resolution. Next, ODI focused on the sales and customer service division. Under the leadership of ODI vice president Rob Evans, the consultants trained all managers in the division to understand the quality process, then began training employees and creating quality action teams. ODI also trained facilitators from other divisions, including ground operations. A key goal was to get people to analyze what were often complex problems, rather than shooting from the hip with instant solutions. Different versions of the programs were developed for managers and employees.

The Quality Advantage Program began with a module on "The Meaning of Quality," introducing five pillars on which a quality organization must be built:

- Customer Focus — a commitment to meeting customer needs;
- Total involvement — "improving quality is everyone's job";
- Measurement — where and when to take action; documenting progress;
- Systematic support — applying strategic planning, budgeting, and performance management to quality improvement efforts;
- Continous improvement — always reaching for new and better ways to perform one's job.

"The Cost of Quality" module identified the costs of not doing quality work — rework, waste, unnecessary overtime, and job dissatisfaction. The goal was to help participants estimate their own cost of quality, break this down into avoidable and necessary costs, and then plan ways to reduce avoidable costs. The third module, "You and Your Customer," described the customer-supplier chain and helped participants to see that everyone in Federal Express was both a customer and a supplier. Participants learned to identify their own key customers and suppliers within the company, as well as how they were linked, and then to align customer needs and supplier capabilities in order to meet agreed requirements.

The "Continuous Improvement" module emphasized that it was everyone's responsibility to fix and prevent problems, showed how to identify early warning signals, and required that everyone strive to meet customer needs in innovative ways. The fifth module, "Making Quality Happen," was directed at managers, supervisors and professionals; it described how to take a leadership role to implement quality programs.

A separate program, Quality Action Teams (QATs), focused on how to implement quality improvement. ODI taught a problem-solving process consisting of four phases: focusing on a particular problem or opportunity, analyzing data, developing solutions and action plans, and executing plans for implementing solutions. To help the QATs perform each of these tasks, ODI taught participants how to apply 20 problem-solving tools, including fish-bone analysis, flowcharting, and cost-benefit analysis.

Setting Goals for People — Service — Profits

By June 1988 (the beginning of fiscal year 1989), Oliver had concluded that to make quality improvement work for customer service, it was critical to involve domestic ground operations. Most problems at Federal were cross-divisional in nature, in the sense that one division created a certain output and passed it on to the next one. That next division's problems were often directly related to what had happended earlier up the line. Commenting on this, Oliver noted:

> We were able to put across the idea that one of the big difficulties in getting cross-divisional cooperation was the multiplicity of different goals. These goals might individually maximize the performance of each division, but collectively resulted in a deterioration of performance for the system. We realized that the more each unit tried to maximize its own performance, the more it tended to send difficult problems downstream. So we concluded that what we needed for Federal Express were three very simple goals.

> First, we took the existing SFA Leadership Index. The leadership a manager provides has a tremendous impact on the positive attitudes of the employees. We determined to use this index as the single goal in our people management process and established a goal of 72 for FY 1989, up from 71 the previous year.

> People — Service — Profits implied a profit goal, so we set a goal of a 10% operating margin on the domestic business. That goal was irrespective of individual department performance. Service had historically been defined in terms of couriers' on-time delivery efforts, what percentage of packages were delivered by 10:30 am. There were a lot of problems with that service level measure: specifically, we could get that package delivered by 10:30 am on the wrong date! It was also a limited measure, suggesting that Federal could be successful simply by delivering packages on time. That was no longer true!

> We found that the information associated with packages had as much to do with customer satisfaction as did delivery. For instance, "don't know" answers to questions upset customers. As we reviewed customer correspondence, we found that

the angriest of all the letters we got were those where our information processes failed us as opposed to those where we didn't deliver on time. What was needed was a broader measure that also addressed other shortcomings that upset customers, such as failure to answer the phone quickly, damaged packages, etc.

ODI stressed the danger of using percentages as targets. In an organization as large as Federal Express, delivering 99% of packages on time or having 99.9% of all flights land safely would still lead to horrendous problems. Instead, they approached quality from the standpoint of zero failures. Oliver emphasized:

> It's only when you examine the types of failures, the number that occur of each type, and the reasons why, that you begin to improve the quality of your service. For us, the trick was to express quality failures in absolute numbers. That led us to develop the Service Quality Index or SQI, which takes each of 12 different events that oc-

cur every day, takes the numbers of those events and multiplies them by a weight from one to ten points, based on the amount of aggravation caused to customers — as evidenced by their tendency to write to Federal Express and complain about them. Fred Smith calls it our "hierarchy of horrors."

The SQI, pronounced "sky," was computed as a daily average. *Exhibit 4* shows its 12 components. Like a golf score, the lower the index, the better the performance. Based on internal records, it was calculated that the average score during FY 1988 (which ended on May 31, 1988) would have been 152,000 points per day — out of a potential maximum of 40 million per day if everything possible had gone wrong. The goal set for FY 1989 was the same — 152,000 points — but since package volumes were expected to rise by 20%, this goal actually represented a 20% improvement. Employees were urged to "Reach for the SQI!"

EXHIBIT 4
Service Quality Index ("SQI") FY 1990 Goals vs. Actual for First Nine Months

Beginning in FY 1989, the overall quality of service was measured by the Service Quality Index (SQI). This index, which was based on the findings of extensive customer research, weighted service failures from the customers' perspective, and comprised the twelve components shown below.

Failure Type	Weighting Factor	FY 1990 GOALS (JUNE '89–MAY '90) Goal for Average Daily Occurrences	FY 1990 GOALS (JUNE '89–MAY '90) Weighted Daily Failure Points	JUNE 1989 FEBRUARY '90 Actual Average Daily Failure Points
Right Day Late Service Failures	1	22,000	22,000	33,561*
Wrong Day Late Service Failures	5	11,522	57,606	74,674*
Traces (not answered by COSMOS)	1	4,170	4,170	5,165
Complaints Reopened by Customers	5	851	4,255	2,330
Missing Proofs of Delivery (PODs)	1	4,959	4,959	6,260
Invoice Adjustments Requested	1	12,852	12,852	11,921
Missed Pick Ups	10	152	1,526	1,548
Lost Packages	10	72	725	1,102
Damaged Packages	10	181	1,815	2,868
Delay Minutes/Aircraft ("0" based)	5	1,735	8,675	16,821
Overgoods	5	327	1,635	1,788
Abandoned Calls	1	4,782	4,782	8,073
TOTAL AVERAGE DAILY FAILURE POINTS (SQI)			125,000	166,111

*Estimated

Note: SQI points were reported on a daily basis, as well as on a weekly, monthly, or year-to-date daily average.

To reinforce the significance of these three corporate-wide goals, senior management tied the entire management bonus process to achievement of the three goals. Simply put, there would be no bonus for any manager at the end of FY 1989 unless the company achieved all three goals. "Needless to say, that caught everyone's imagination." Oliver smiled wryly and continued:

> It was very different from our previous approach of having managers' bonuses based on their ability to meet individual management-by-objective goals without regard to whether that did or didn't help the corporate process. In the actual unfolding, Fiscal year 1989 turned out to be the best year we had had in a long, long time. We achieved the profit goal despite some difficult circumstances, and the SQI came in at 133,000 points. The Leadership Index reached 76. It was the largest single jump in the history of the SFA process, in terms of managers' relationships with employees.

ODI's Evans believed that one reason for the SQI successes was that Federal had set up 12 QATs, each of which focused on a specific SQI category. As CEO, Fred Smith provided active support and encouragement. Most teams were headed by a vice president. Results were posted weekly, and every three months each QAT reported out to Smith, Barksdale, and other senior executives. Quarterly awards were given in four categories: (1) greatest impact on SQI results; (2) best use of the quality process (using tools that had been taught); (3) best understanding of root causes (identifying and working on underlying problems rather than superficial effects); and (4) best use of line employees (gathering information from the people closest to the process who knew it best).

Activities during FY 1990

While training continued efforts were made to facilitate a bottom-up movement in quality improvement. John West, manager of quality improvement, saw his job as a catalyst to bring about shared approaches to problem solving. West coordinated training efforts with ODI and had established a network of quality professionals in each of Federal's ten divisions. These people formed a quality ad-

visory board which met biweekly to discuss failures and successes.

One of these professionals was Linda Griffin, senior quality administrator for domestic ground operations, which had 40,000 employees working out of 600 stations. Griffin felt that while the quality program had enjoyed many "surface" successes, the challenge was to coordinate the replication of these successes by getting people to describe what they had actually done and how they did it, as opposed to simply talking about the results. Forms and electronic mail systems had been created to make it easy to record this information, while a reward system encouraged people to turn in details of their successes. Said Griffin:

> Recognition programs have a mutual benefit. They motivate and reward employees and create some peer pressure. At the same time, management gets to see the value of the training programs, which reinforces the belief that training is the right thing to do.

One replicated success concerned a sorting table designed by employees in the Phoenix station to prevent missorts caused by envelopes sliding into the wrong destination pile. They sent a videotape of the table design to the company's industrial engineers, who developed several versions of the sort table for different-sized stations. Couriers in a QAT at another station were frustrated with the problems (such as missed pickups) caused when the regular courier on a route had to be replaced by a substitute unfamiliar with obscure addresses, building entrances, location of freight elevators, and pick-up or delivery locations on different floors, etc. So they designed an informational booklet describing each route. The result was a sharp increase in on-time delivery and productivity. This idea had now been incorporated in the "Policy and Procedures" manual for all stations.

Sharing success stories was seen as a way to get more people involved in QATs and to improve working relations within the company through customer-supplier alignments. West commented:

> People tend to gravitate toward QATs, which are more fun. We really have to push the notion of customer-supplier alignment. People and de-

partments don't always work well together. W. Edwards Deming, the American quality pioneer, claims that about 95% of quality problems are management problems, because of the way the system was designed.

Federal's satellite broadcast network, FXTV was employed in both a sharing and training role. Rob Evans participated in a program entitled "Customer/Supplier Alignment: The First Step in Quality," designed to reinforce earlier quality training. Evans began his segment of the live broadcast by reminding viewers of the "Right Things Right" grid, a simple four cell matrix developed by ODI.

That grid is a simple way to look at the work we do from two different angles. The first angle is *how* we do the work we do. We either do things wrong or we do things right. The second angle has to do with *what* work we actually do, doing the right things or the wrong things. When we put these two together, we have four possibilities. We could be doing the right things wrong; that's the old way of looking at quality problems and, of course, that happens. We could be doing the wrong things wrong, really wasting our time. Or we could be doing the wrong things right, things that don't matter to our customers, internal or external, but doing a very good job of them. The fourth possibility is doing right things right. This is the only one that adds value to our customers and our company.

In a quality organization, people spend the great majority of their time doing the right things right. What we've found at ODI is that most managers spend 45–60% of their time doing the right things right, but the rest is wasted — time, effort, money. Of that wasted time, about half seems to fall into the wrong things right category.

Pressures and Distractions

Top management was delighted by improvements in SQI and other measures during FY 1989, but then the picture changed dramatically. The average daily SQI goal of 125,000 points for FY 1990 (on a higher package volume) was ravaged by the dislocations of the Tiger merger and a series of natural disasters during the fall and winter. Mount Redoubt's volcanic ash cloud grounded five of Federal's 747s at the Anchorage hub in Alaska for two days and forced subsequent Far East flights to operate through Seattle, using more fuel and carrying less freight. The computer shutdown at the Memphis Superhub on December 22 resulted in manual sorting, delayed deliveries, and an average daily SQI for that week of 613,842. At the end of February, the year-to-date daily average stood at 166,111.

Meantime, a sharp earnings decline had led to company-wide cost reduction efforts, including some impacting quality facilitation. Some outside financial analysts had suggested that the company's financial situation made it vulnerable to a takeover. Tom Oliver was very concerned that the momentum of the quality improvement efforts not be lost.

Most companies need four to five years of continuous effort before employees and managers alike really understand that this is *the* way to approach problems. The fact that we had some initial successes was certainly positive, but by no means have we gotten it to the point where if you scratch an employee, you're going to get a quality-related response. And that's especially true of first-level managemenet who feel tremendous pressure to achieve budget-related financial results.

We've found that the SQI process works really well for the corporation as a whole, but Federal Express doesn't have the ability to develop a precise tracking of these events down to individual locations, so our station-level goals tend to stay related to the service level measurement (on-time deliveries) instead of the broader SQI perspective. We're trying to work aggressively on measurement systems so that Federal can use that information more precisely in measuring and managing the performance of first line managers. Feedback is critical in any quality process.

Much remains to be done. But it always comes back to these questions: Is it financially feasible to spend the dollars and take the time to train the people? Will we spend the time and money to let them work the issues after they are trained? Are investments in quality high enough in the corporation's competing priorities? In the sales and customer service division's case, feedback systems require substantial investments in data systems resources. We want to make them, but we're always fighting the allocation process.

Right now, everyone is trying to minimize their own costs and efficiency; in the process, they're sending enormous costs downstream. The tendency in corporate management is to seek good budgets and financial controls for every individual unit in your operation. A well-managed corporation has a very strong financial system — but a strong, department-oriented financial system is precisely what you're trying to get around when you're attempting to approach things from a systematic quality and cost viewpoint. You must expend money at the source of the problem to eliminate the waste expenses later in the process. But people won't do it, because they don't get the benefits; some other department and the customers do.

Almost every change we've made in Federal's services has no measurable ROI (return on investment). You cannot, in effect, prove the reductions in cost because they're systemic reductions, as opposed to individual area reductions. In any case, changes in the quality of service impact customer revenues as much or more than they impact costs. In the final event, one needs to make these decisions based on the impact on customers and on the system, as opposed to precisely measured return-on-investment calculations.

Oliver glanced at the clock. It was almost time for another senior executive meeting on cutting costs. ODI had submitted a proposal for the next phase of the quality training program, and there were numerous internal projects as well. His best estimate was that future training and other key quality initiatives would, if properly funded, cost as much as $200 per employee in the first year and half of that in subsequent years. "It all comes down to that courage gap," he said to himself as he gathered up his papers and strode out of the office.

PART VI
Adding Value Through Customer Service

Designing and Managing the Customer-Service Function

CHRISTOPHER H. LOVELOCK

Customer perceptions of value and quality are often strongly influenced by the customer service accompanying the core product. Creating an effective customer-service function that will enhance the firm's competitive posture requires a good understanding of the tasks to be performed, a clear definition of employee responsibilities, and attention to detail.

Service must change in response not only to continuing technological advances but also to more demanding customers, who seek better information, faster service, and a variety of enhancements of the core product. How is the customer service function evolving in response to these needs as they occur in both manufacturing and service businesses? What sorts of people and systems are needed to deliver good customer service? And what is entailed in designing this function and managing it effectively?

Parts of this chapter have been adapted from Chapter 10, "Developing and Managing the Customer Service Function," in my book *Services Marketing, 2nd edition* (Englewood Cliffs, NJ: Prentice Hall, 1991).

DEFINING CUSTOMER SERVICE

One of the most fundamental concepts in analyzing service operations, as emphasized earlier in this book, is the distinction between the "front stage" (or "front office") and the "backstage" (or "back office").[1] Front stage procedures are those experienced by the consumer. In some instances, they represent a very small proportion of the service firm's total activities. For instance, the extent of per-

---

[1] See, for example, Christopher H. Lovelock, "A Basic Toolkit for Service Managers," (pp 17–30), and Richard B. Chase, "The Customer Contact Approach to Services: Theoretical Bases and Practical Extensions (pp 37–49).

---

sonal contact between customers and their credit card companies is limited to receiving and paying a monthly statement, and perhaps an occasional letter or telephone call when problems arise. All other activities, such as the review of credit card applications, credit checks, and processing of credit card slips, take place behind the scenes. In a hotel, by contrast, the customer is exposed to a variety of physical facilities and to numerous hotel personnel, ranging from telephone reservation agent to front desk, from bellhop to room service, and from waitress to concierge.

The quality of customer service plays an increasingly important role in overall evaluations of service quality. Designing and managing front stage interactions should be approached strategically, taking a "big picture" view of how customers experience the total service experience — as opposed to considering each procedure separately.

Recognizing how important front stage interactions are for customer satisfaction, let's define customer service as follows:

> Customer service is a task, other than proactive selling, that involves interactions with customers in person, or by telecommunications, mail, or automated processes. It is designed, performed, and communicated with two goals in mind: operational productivity and customer satisfaction.

This definition is much broader than the traditional view of customer service as a strictly reactive function that simply responds, on an exception basis, to customer problems or complaints. Essentially, it embraces all personnel whose jobs bring them into contact with customers on a routine as well as an exception basis. Such personnel become part of the overall service product, even though their jobs may have been defined in strictly operational terms. Note that the definition extends beyond human resource management to embrace automated processes where self-service machines and information technology supplement — or replace — service personnel.

Looking at customer service in this way requires close collaboration between marketing, operations, and human resource managers. Operational productivity must be balanced against customer satisfaction, and both goals must be pursued without confusing or alienating customer service personnel, who may otherwise feel caught in the middle between conflicting demands. When the customer service function is well designed, it may be possible to obtain simultaneous improvements in service quality (as perceived by customers), productivity, and employee satisfaction.

As firms grow larger and extend their operations across regions, countries, and continents, corporate managers often find themselves far removed from the day-to-day operations of the business—and thus from their customers. This development requires new efforts to achieve product consistency across time and geography.

Service firms with multisite operations are trying to develop programs for building closer ties with customers by centralizing certain functions that don't require face-to-face contact. Computer technology and telecommunications make it possible to provide national (or even global) on-line service out of a central location to serve customers requiring information, wishing to place orders, or needing to resolve problems.

Customer Service in the Manufacturing Sector

Customer service facilitates enhancement of the manufactured core product by adding one or more service components. As the quality of the core product improves, and as new technological advances are cloned by competitors, the competitive battleground in manufacturing starts to shift from physical product features to service features.[2]

The original use of the term "customer service" in manufacturing firms was relatively narrow, being applied to physical distribution services, usually in companies that supplied their products to industrial buyers or to wholesale and retail intermediaries. Typically, customer service concerns emphasized such issues as inventory reliability, order accuracy, and order cycle times. Only lip ser-

---

[2]William H. Davidow and Bro Uttal, *Total Customer Service: The Ultimate Weapon* (New York: Harper & Row, 1989).

vice was paid to the need for a corporatewide policy on customer service.

The first attempt to explore customer service in a broader context was by LaLonde and Zinszer, who expanded the concept beyond the strictly order-cycle-related components. They defined customer service as "Those activities that occur at the interface between the customer and the corporation which enhance or facilitate the sale and use of the corporation's products or services."[3] Their major contribution was to divide customer service into the following temporal sequence:

1. *Pretransaction* Written statements concerning distribution and warranty policies, and information on system flexibility.
2. *Transaction* Order placement, document processing, inventory policies, order assembly, and transportation of the shipment.
3. *Posttransaction* Delivery of the shipment and installation of the product.

Rakowski took this model and broadened it further by subdividing customer-service activities into five phases: precontact, personal contact, predelivery, delivery, and postdelivery. He argued that "Customer service activities are necessary before an order is ever placed and must continue long after the product is delivered. The generally accepted view of customer service which focuses on order cycle-related activities is far too limited in scope."[4]

Customer service embraces different activities within the various departments of a manufacturing firm. It could involve such tasks as:

- Providing information and technical advice to customers.
- Taking orders over the phone and passing these to the department responsible for order fulfillment.
- Communicating with customers following receipt of orders and providing information on availability and shipping dates.

[3]Bernard J. LaLonde and Paul H. Zinszer, *Customer Service: Meaning and Measurement* (Chicago: National Council of Physical Distribution Management, 1976).

[4]James P. Rakowski, "The Customer Service Concept," *Review of Business and Economic Research* (Winter, 1982), pp. 55–66.

- Maintaining conta[...] pervising assembly an[...] customized orders.
- Scheduling transportation[...] deliveries.
- Handling installation at the cust[...] physical equipment, components, or[...]
- Diagnosing problems and undertaking[...] tive actions, including repairs, maintenanc[...] replacements.
- Investigating and resolving complaints and giving refunds.
- Documenting work performed, arranging credit, sending out invoices, accepting payment, and maintaining accurate account records.

Customer Service in Service Industries

The key distinctions between the service and manufacturing organizations center on differences between the core products. But many customer service tasks are remarkably similar in both sectors. In service businesses, as in manufacturing firms, service personnel may be called on to provide information and advice, take and confirm orders (reservations), work with customers on creating and delivering custom-designed services, diagnose and solve problems (including repair of physical equipment used to deliver the core service), document work performed, arrange credit, and maintain billing and payment systems.

To an increasing extent, many of these tasks are being redefined in both sectors by new technologies. Information technology (IT), for example, speeds order entry, allowing it to be processed automatically through computers linked by telecommunications to distant terminals. Customers need no longer speak with service personnel to place routine orders, since they can do so on a remote terminal, in response to the promptings of a computer-generated voice or on-screen displays. Similarly, information on the status of orders or accounts can be obtained by accessing data banks directly.

When customers are themselves part of the service process — as in services such as airlines, restaurants, and hotels — then a variety of other customer service features may have to be added, reflecting the need to be hospi-

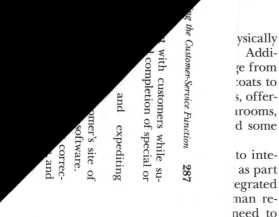

ysically
Addi-
ge from
coats to
s, offer-
rooms,
d some

to inte-
as part
egrated
man re-
need to
iount.

with customers while su-
completion of special or
and expediting
omer's site of
software.
correc-
and

BETTER CUSTOMER SERVICE AS A RESPONSE TO COMPETITIVE PRESSURES

As competition intensifies in the service sector, the need for meaningful competitive differentiation is sharpened. To an increasing degree, this differentiation includes a search for superior performance on supplementary product elements, especially those included under the expanded definition of customer service provided earlier in this reading.

The managerial process necessary for creating competitively superior customer service consists of six key tasks. Each task may have to be approached on a segment by segment basis in situations where customer service features are tailored to the needs of different market segments. For instance, first class airline passengers expect a higher level of customer service than those in economy class, and additional features should be designed into the overall product to match their expectations.

The six tasks in customer service design are as follows:

1. Conducting research to determine and monitor customer needs, wants, and satisfaction levels as they relate to customer contact with service personnel and automated systems.

2. Identifying the key sources of customer satisfaction (or dissatisfaction) with current customer service elements, for both the firm's services and those of leading competitors.

3. Adding or deleting service elements to the overall service concept so that the resulting "package" meets or exceeds customers' requirements within the price range that they are prepared to pay, while still enabling the firm to make a profit.

4. Setting service-level standards that will match or exceed customer expectations for each element. These standards may include speed of response, extent of choice available, degree of personalization, and so forth.

5. Designing technology, staffing requirements, job specifications, and systems so that the delivered service will meet the standards.

6. Recruiting personnel who have the right personality for the job and possess (or can be trained to have) the desired skills and attitudes.

Historically, many service organizations were operations driven rather than marketing driven. And many lacked a clear understanding of the role of human resource management in delivering high quality service. As a result, only limited efforts were made to measure customer satisfaction through formal research or to seek feedback from employees (especially those who had direct contact with customers). A growing number of service firms have begun to reexamine their operations with a view to making them more responsive to customers on both the core product and supplementary service elements.

An Example from American Express

At the credit card division of American Express (AmEx) customer service used to be measured by the number and content of customer complaints through letters and telephone calls.[5] AmEx made what was, for its time, the radical departure of recognizing that the customer-service department was only the "catcher's mitt" for problems that arose in other departments such as data processing, mail room, new accounts, and accounts receivable.

New programs were then put into place to set standards, improve work procedures,

[5]"How American Express Measures Quality of Its Customer Service," *AMA Forum* 71, March 1982, pp. 29–31.

foster teamwork between departments, and monitor performance. Back office output was categorized into "service elements," such as processing applications, issuing new cards, responding to billing inquiries, authorizing charges on accounts, and issuing replacement cards. More than 180 measures were developed to track the level of each service element against previously established quality assurance standards.

The company claims that substantially improved efficiency, productivity, and service levels have resulted from its quality assurance program. Interestingly, the refocusing of company attention on customer needs has also improved employee morale in both the front and back offices.

High Contact, Low Contact, and the Customer Experience

Like the credit card division of American Express, many other service firms have a large back office and a small front office. In these low-contact organizations, customer service is most appropriately viewed as the output of the operations department, and is usually channeled through a limited number of employees. In high-contact organizations that serve customers in person — rather than dealing with them at arms' length — the front office is relatively much larger. Customers come into contact with more employees, whose services may be delivered sequentially and independently of each other. Earlier in the book, we showed how sequential delivery of services could be flowcharted to display the customer's experience with different service elements.[6]

Airline service provides a good example, with customers first making inquiries and reservations, then checking their baggage, getting seat assignments, being checked at the gate, receiving on-board service in flight, and retrieving their baggage at the destination airport (a task that may or may not en-

tail further contact with service personnel). Each of these activities is an operations task, generally employing human resources. Although these tasks are secondary to the core product of physically transporting passengers between two airports, they have great potential to generate customer dissatisfaction if performed poorly.

Poor performance may include bad manners as well as incompetence. In such a situation, the responsibility of an expanded customer-service function might be to develop a stronger customer perspective on the part of all these service personnel, including such activities as developing recruitment guidelines, employee training, performance monitoring, obtaining customer feedback, and then redefining tasks and retraining personnel as appropriate.

DESIGNING AN EFFECTIVE CUSTOMER SERVICE ORGANIZATION

Each business has some distinctive characteristics that should be recognized in designing its customer service activities. Managers must understand the factors shaping the way in which customer service can best be delivered and they must clarify the nature of the tasks to be assigned to the customer service function. Determining where the organization stands at present can be accomplished by conducting a customer service audit.

Factors Shaping the Customer Service Function

The nature of the customer-contact function inevitably varies by industry and by type of organization. Table 1 lists some of the key factors that serve to shape the tasks performed and the place of customer service within the organization. Each of these factors is discussed briefly below.

Presence or absence of intermediaries. Some customer-contact tasks may be more efficiently performed by intermediaries. Often these relate to contacts with customers prior to delivery of the core service. Examples include travel agents and theater ticket agen-

---

[6]See, for example, Christopher H. Lovelock, "A Basic Toolkit for Service Managers," (pp 17–30) and Jane Kingman-Brundage, "The ABCs of Service System Blueprinting" (pp 96–102).

TABLE 1
Factors Shaping the Customer Service Function

- Presence or absence of intermediaries in the delivery system for different service elements
- Extent to which contacts with customers are high contact versus low contact in nature
- Access to, and acceptance of, technologically based communication and delivery systems
- Whether purchases are made by institutional buyers, members of the general public, or both
- How long the service delivery process lasts
- Whether or not the service is capacity constrained
- How frequently customers use the service and repurchase it
- How complex the service is to deliver and use
- How much risk is involved for customers in consuming the service and what the consequences of service failure are for them

cies that provide information and advice, make reservations, and collect payment. Some smaller hotel chains offer a toll-free telephone reservations service but contract out this task to a specialist firm. Although this strategy weakens the control of the firm over performance of key customer-contact tasks, it may result in better service at a lower cost.

High contact versus low contact. The more involvement the customer has with the service firm, the greater the number of customer-contact points and the more likely these are to take place in locations that are geographically far removed from the head office. This situation offers more opportunities for mistakes or poor service to occur and is thus more complex to manage. By contrast, low-contact services entail few interactions with customers, with contacts often being limited to mail and telephone interactions with personnel located in a central office, where management controls can be much tighter.

Access to, and acceptance of, technology. Information-based customer service activities such as reservations, confirmations, simple consultation, updates, billing and payment lend themselves to use of information technology. And certain simple transactions such as purchasing tickets may be made through automated dispensing machines. Whether such approaches can be used, however, de-

pends on the availability of terminals and modern telecommuncation links, as well as customer acceptance of such technology.

Institutional versus individual purchases. Greater variability may be introduced into customer-service activities when serving the general public (who are often infrequent users of a particular service) versus working with institutional customers. The latter tend to purchase in greater volume and with greater frequency, but there may be multiple contact persons within the client organization. This requires good record keeping on the part of the service deliverer.

Duration of service delivery process. The longer it takes for service delivery to be completed, the more likely it is that customers will require information on work in progress — such as estimated completion dates, projected costs, and so forth. Good internal monitoring systems are required to generate and communicate the needed information.

Capacity-constrained services. In most instances, this group of services will need to offer either a reservation system or a queuing-control mechanism. The former requires on-line access to a reservations data base, and is usually handled by telecommunications; the latter requires friendly but firm interactions with customers standing in line and realistic projections of the estimated wait for service.

Frequency of use and repurchase. When the bulk of consumption is accounted for by repeat use, it is important to separate proactive selling (which is expensive and requires more training) from simple order taking. A computerized data base should allow authorized personnel immediate access to customer records. To stimulate repurchase, some service businesses encourage their customer-contact personnel to remember regular customers and to offer them special recognition and favors. A good information system, which identifies repeat users, can be employed to brief staff members who might not otherwise be aware that a specific customer merited special treatment.

Level of complexity. Some services are simple for customers to use and easy for the operations department to deliver. Other services are more complex — sometimes because they offer more choice and more features.[7] As a result, inexperienced users often require assistance. A related problem in complex services is that there are more things that can go wrong. So these services require customer-contact personnel who can provide information and help to educate the customer. They also require contingency plans for problem resolution, necessitating careful training of personnel on what actions to take when a particular problem arises. Superior performance by service personnel in restoring operations (or providing an acceptable alternative) can create a very favorable impression in customers' minds, distinguishing the excellent organization from the mediocre ones.

Degree of risk. Service managers must understand the consequences for customers of a service failure. Safety precautions and contingency planning may be required by government regulations where personal safety is a factor. Other consequences involving risks for customers can range from personal inconvenience to monetary loss. The higher the probability of a service failure and the more serious the consequences, the more important it is to employ mature, well-trained contact personnel who not only behave calmly and tactfully when faced by upset customers, but also work to resolve the problem as quickly as possible.

Assignment of Tasks to Customer Service

The array of tasks that may fall under the rubric of customer service is quite broad. An important question for any service organization that is developing or expanding its customer-service function is which specific tasks should be assigned to the customer service function and which should be the responsibility of other groups or departments.

Potential tasks can be divided into selling-related and nonselling activities, and also into customer-initiated and firm-initiated interactions (Figure 1). Although customer-service personnel can become involved in selling-related activities, this should normally be seen as an adjunct to their work, not its principal focus. For instance, an employee might mention the availability of new products in the course of delivering service to customers, or information on new service features might be included with an invoice or statement of account activity.

As the number of retail-banking products expands, tellers are being encouraged (or required) to inform customers of these new services. Similarly, airline and hotel reservations personnel may encourage callers to make additional purchases. But there's a risk of annoying customers by making continual sales pushes.

Note that service delivery may be initiated by either the provider or the customer. An example of the former is the serving of airline meals; in economy class, the cabin crew select the time at which meals will be given to passengers. However, restaurant patrons normally take the initiative in choosing where, when, and what to eat. Some airlines are now experimenting with a new approach in which first class passengers select the time that they would like to eat and are also given more choice over the type of meal.

Customer service has historically focused on reactive problem solving and responding to complaints. Effective complaint handling and problem solving remain key tasks. Every effort should be made to surface problems by making it easy for customers to complain, and then to solve these problems promptly. But progressive service firms also try to identify potential problems before they occur. For instance, if a service garage determines that repair work on a car cannot be completed by the promised time, it should notify the car owner so that he or she can make alternative plans.

Rather than waiting for complaints, a proactive firm will regularly telephone or write to all recent customers (or a sample of them) to determine if they are satisfied. This is, of course, a form of market research which may serve to uncover simmering problems before

---

[7]For a good discussion of complexity in the service process, see G. Lynn Shostack, "Service Positioning Through Structural Change," *Journal of Marketing,* 51 (January 1987), 34–43.

FIGURE 1
The Customer Contact Matrix

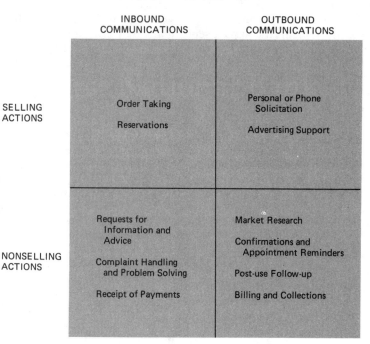

they reach the boil, as well as identifying service features that customers appreciate.

Ultimately, a service firm may wish to involve customer service in all four cells of the customer-contact matrix. But developing an incremental strategy that expands the scope and professionalism of the customer-service function on a step-by-step basis may be wiser than attempting all tasks immediately.

Conducting a Customer-Service Audit

To determine the current nature and scope of its customer-service function, each service organization should conduct a customer-service audit. Table 2 outlines a basic format for such an audit, although greater detail will be required to cover the situation in any specific organization.

The audit begins by identifying all customer-contact tasks and the standard procedures prescribed for each. It then considers performance goals for each task and current measures of performance. Next comes a detailed review and evaluation of all per-

sonnel elements, and finally identification and evaluation of support systems available to customer-contact personnel. To determine the current utilization of customer-service personnel, it is useful to maintain a log of all calls to customer service (in person, by telephone, or by mail). The format for a simple customer-service log should include space for information on the date and time of the call, information on the caller, the reason for the call, and the disposition of that call.

The findings of the audit will establish the current situation and provide a basis for planning the future scope and quality of the customer-service function. Since customer service is potentially an important tool in competitive differentiation, an appraisal should also be made of competitors' customer-service efforts.

Organizing the Customer Service Function

What should a fully fledged customer service department look like? And to whom

TABLE 2
Outline Format for a Customer Service Audit

1. *Identify customer-contact tasks* (other than sales), for example:
   - Information, reservations
   - Service delivery tasks
   - Billing and customer-record transmittal
   - Problem solving, complaint handling
2. *Review standard procedures* for each task
   - Written standards (procedures manual) for each task
   - Oral/written instructions (ad hoc)
   - Availability (hours/days, locations)
   - Interactions with other personnel
3. *Identify performance goals by task*
   - Specific quantitative goals
   - Qualitative goals
   - Contribution to related activities
   - Contribution to long-term success of system
4. *Specify measures of performance by task*
   - Money based
   - Time based
   - Management/supervisor evaluations
   - Customer evaluations
5. *Review and evaluate personnel elements*
   - Recruiting/selection criteria and practices
   - Nature, content of training
   - Job definition, career path (if any)
   - Interactions with other employees
   - Nature of supervision, quality control
   - Evaluation procedures
   - Corrective actions available
   - Employee attitudes, motivation
   - Hours, extent of paid/unpaid overtime
6. *Identify and evaluate support systems*
   - Instruction manuals, brochures, form letters
   - Office facilities, furnishings, layout
   - Office equipment (phones, fax machines, answering machines, computers, word processors),
   - Vehicles and equipment for repair/maintenance
   - Radio or cellular telephone communications
   - Record-keeping devices (e.g., log books, portable computers, bar code scanners)

should it report? Specific answers to these questions will vary according to the nature of the service and the firm's own characteristics, as determined through auditing and analysis.

In service businesses with a high level of customer contact, we may be seeing the beginning of a trend to place all front-stage service operations under the control of marketing, essentially splitting the front stage and back-stage operations functions. American Airlines and British Airways are examples of service firms where the drive for customer satisfac-tion has led to new reporting relationships, with all customer service activities under a senior manager who has responsibilities for both marketing and operations. However, there still remains an active need for coop-eration between the front and back halves of the operation, since the former cannot func-tion without the support of the latter.

Increased use of information technology (IT) often leads to creation of central data bases serving either centralized or distributed reservations and customer accounting sys-tems. Examples are found in many types of industries, including transportation, finan-cial services, and lodging. IT has radically changed both the power and the responsibili-ties of the customer service function.

A good example is provided by the COS-MOS system at Federal Express, where a world-wide reservations, package tracking, and accounting system is linked to a central com-puter in Memphis, Tennessee.[8] In Federal's case, the customer service department re-ports to a senior vice president — sales and customer service. Other senior executives are responsible separately for such areas as flight operations, station operations, marketing planning, and communications activities. However, the customer service function works in close cooperation with both field sales and ground operations (couriers, local sta-tions, and sorting hubs).

The evolution of an IT-based customer ser-vice function is not without impact for sales and operations personnel. As diagrammed in Figure 2, the customer service function can take over certain routine tasks and simple problem-solving activities from sales and op-erations, leaving these other two functions to focus on the tasks that they are uniquely qualified to perform. Making the change is expensive and sometimes painful, but the long-term benefits in terms of both produc-tivity and service quality can be enormous. At the same time, the customer service func-tion's data base can become a vital input to other management groups such as human re-sources, accounting, and strategic planning.

---

[8]See "Federal Express: Quality Improvement Pro-gram" reproduced on pages 270–84 of this book.

FIGURE 2
Role of the Customer Service Function

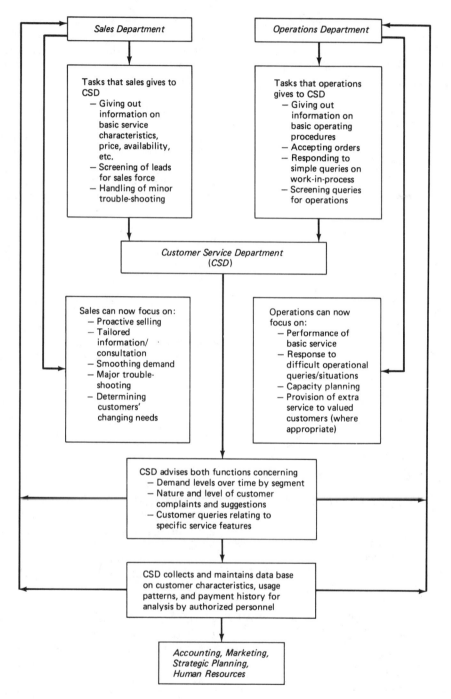

GUIDELINES FOR EFFECTIVE PROGRAM IMPLEMENTATION

Once the customer-service program has been designed, it must be implemented effectively, giving careful consideration to each of the following tasks.[9]

1. *Recruit the right employees.* Individuals whose jobs require them to interact with customers must possess the right technical skills as well as the appropriate personal characteristics. Depending on the job, the latter may include appearance, mannerisms, voice, personality, and so forth.

2. *Train employees properly.* First, develop the necessary level of technical proficiency to perform specific tasks properly. Second, instruct employees in personal appearance and/or telephone manner, behavior toward customers, and use of correct language. Third, develop skills in handling anticipated situations, particularly as these relate to personal interactions under difficult or stressful situations. The use of role-playing exercises is often very helpful in this regard. Finally, educate all employees to see problems as a source of useful information for the firm rather than as a source of annoyance.

3. *Create a user-friendly environment.* This objective applies to both customers and staff. Facilities should be easy to find and pleasant to visit (or work in). All equipment — mechanical or electronic — should be in good working order and designed for fast, foolproof operation (especially if customers need to use it for self-service). Managers should periodically check that telecommunications systems have sufficient capacity to avoid unnecessary queuing and that recorded messages or instructions are both clear and polite.

4. *Educate the customers.* They should know both how to use and how *not* to use the service. It's helpful to offer customers information in printed form; good signing is very important at service delivery sites and on self-

service equipment. At large service facilities, customer-service desks or courtesy telephones should be available to help customers with queries or problems. When customers and the service organization transact remotely, consideration should be given to installing toll-free telephone numbers for customers to call if they need assistance. In any location where customers are likely to come from several different language populations, consideration should be given to providing multilingual instructions and access to multilingual staff.

5. *Be efficient first, nice second.* A customer-service program should aim to resolve problems, not provide cheerful sympathy. While basic courtesy is important to convey a caring attitude and to mitigate consumer confusion or anger, too much friendliness can be inefficient. At busy times, especially when other clients may be waiting, the primary responsibility of a customer-service agent (CSA) is to resolve the problem quickly.

6. *Standardize response systems.* Using standard forms for handling inquiries and complaints provides a checklist for each CSA and simplifies data entry into an information system. This not only speeds follow-through, but also facilitates monitoring of changes in the mix and level of customer-initiated contacts. Effective response also requires rapid forwarding to specialist personnel of difficult problems that the agent cannot handle.

7. *Develop a pricing policy.* High quality customer service does not necessarily mean free service; consideration should be given to charging for certain categories of service that have traditionally been offered free of charge. This is especially necessary if delivering the service in question costs the company money or if customers abuse the service relationship (for example, calls to directory assistance for telephone numbers that are already in the phone book, frequent requests for copies of mislaid bank statements, deinstallation of cable television connections for the summer followed by reinstallation in the fall).

8. *Consider using subcontractors.* Fast, good quality response is sometimes more easily and cheaply obtained by subcontracting cer-

---

[9]Several of these guidelines have been adapted from Hirotake Takeuchi and John A. Quelch, "Quality Is More than Making a Good Product," *Harvard Business Review* (July–August 1983), pp. 139–145.

tain customer-service functions to outside firms. Examples include use of travel agents for airline information and reservations, and use of an independent reservations service for toll-free hotel telephone reservations. The negative side of such an approach is that the primary service supplier loses control over the quality of customer service, may fail to capture the valuable marketing information inherent in customer-service calls, and may even find the subcontractor actively promoting the competition.

9. *Be proactive.* Look for opportunities to do more for customers. This may consist of letting specific customers know about new products that are likely to interest them (as some retailers do), reminding patients that it's time for a new health or dental checkup, or checking back with customers who have had a problem to see if all is now well.

10. *Evaluate performance regularly.* Quantitative performance standards must be set for each element of the customer-service package. Actual performance should be measured against these standards and reasons for any variances determined. In addition, efforts should be made to solicit customers' opinions on customer-service elements at regular intervals. This may be done by distributing comment forms to all customers and relying on those who experience above-average or below-average service to respond with compliments or complaints; this is the strategy adopted by most hotels, which leave guest comment cards in each room. It can also be used quite inexpensively by firms that have an ongoing relationship with their customers and send out monthly statements; a short survey could be enclosed, say, once a year. Alternatively, a service firm may choose periodically to survey a representative cross section of customers to solicit their appraisals and suggestions.

11. *Acknowledge and affirm good work.* Superior performance by customer-contact employees should be recognized. Initiative should be rewarded. Employee feedback and suggestions should be encouraged. Many service managers are quite removed from their customers and fail to recognize the insights that employees may develop from their day-today contact with customers.

12. *Take corrective actions on defective work.* Such actions may include retraining employees, reassigning employees who are unsuited to perform customer-contact tasks but are otherwise motivated and proficient, and terminating incorrigibles. It may also be necessary to revamp support systems, restructure the work environment, and reassign responsibilities within the customer-service group to improve efficiency. Finally, in order to catch problems before they become too serious, it may help to develop improved performance monitors.

Effective Implementation

Implementation involves transforming written plans and verbal guidelines into specific actions. Unlike some marketing activities, which may perhaps be executed only once (or just a few times) a year, many customer service tasks may be performed dozens of times a day by each employee. Getting an effective customer service program in place is only half the battle. The continuing challenge is to ensure that good service (as defined by the customers) is being delivered on an ongoing basis. All members of the management team, as well as both front-office and back-office personnel, have a role to play in meeting this challenge.[10]

CONCLUSION

The customer-service function is changing dramatically in many service businesses. It's evolving from a purely reactive function, often grudgingly performed, to a responsive and even proactive function designed to enhance the firm's competitive posture. Previously haphazard procedures are being standardized and professionalized. Modern computer technology is an important factor in improving the efficiency and effectiveness of customer-service activities.

---

[10]See Linda M. Lash, *The Complete Guide to Customer Service* (New York: John Wiley, 1989). Most chapters in this book conclude with guidelines for chief executives, middle management, and for front- and back-office personnel.

As service firms grow larger and as the number of each firm's service delivery sites increases, the customer-service function is becoming an important element in knitting the service organization together. It also helps to ensure that operations managers recognize the need to strive for both customer satisfaction and operational efficiency.

The more customers are exposed to high-quality execution of customer-service tasks, the more they will come to expect it of all service suppliers. Many service firms survived in the past with inadequate or mediocre performance of customer-service activities. However, they are liable to find themselves severely disadvantaged in the future unless they take steps to develop and implement an improved customer-service function.

The Market Power Is in the Services: Because the Value Is in the Results

SANDRA VANDERMERWE

Customers want results. The power to deliver results lies in value added services that are responsive to customers' needs and expectations at each stage in the cycle of service delivery. Customers of both manufacturing and service firms increasingly look for solution systems, consisting of product-service components that are directed at achieving the desired results.

Why would Volvo, one of the world's largest truck manufacturers, decide to enter the mobile information system business? Discovering that the average capacity utilization of a truck company in Sweden is only 40%, they took the initiative and developed a way to cut down on empty mileage time, i.e. when the vehicle is not fully loaded, by providing truck buyers with electronic links to in-house information and logistic networks and various real-time traffic and transportation services. By increasing the owner's usage of the vehicle by as little as 1%, tens of million of Kroner have been added to their bottom line.

Volvo is no different from many companies who now recognize that their basic offer-ing has become no more than a commodity. They also acknowledge that customers take a lot more for granted. New world values and patterns are challenging these corporations to discard their long-held beliefs and ways of doing business and find more appropriate models to satisfy customers.

When corporations do not confront the issues, they lose out. France's superfast, 290 kilometer-an-hour Train à Grande Vitesse (TGV), for example, recently lost an opportunity to enter the huge, 50 billion dollar US market because the French proposal required a 25% government subsidy up-front. A US railroad executive explained that the French company had missed the point: there

Reprinted by kind permission of the *European Management Journal*, Vol. 8, No. 4, December 1990.

was more to the deal than a high speed train. The customer needed a firm able to assume a developer's role, offering and integrating the whole package from financing and real estate through to construction. In short, the customer needed a total solution system. (*International Herald Tribune*, June 18, 1990.)

The message in these examples and in this article is a simple one. First, the power to create and hold customers today rests largely on the ability to deliver solution systems. And, second, services comprise an ever more significant portion of these customer systems.

In this article the notion of solution systems will be explored in an end market context. Simply put, from toothpaste to aerospace new consumer drivers are transforming the way managers do business, both in a direct and derived sense. The discussion centers on these issues: what motivates this trend? What are some of the critical success factors gleaned from current examples? What is the impact on marketing formats and on the overall organization? A diagnostic tool is then suggested to assist corporations assess their current situation and future needs in order to align their corporations to current market requirements.

Based on a literature review and a survey of recent and on-going manufacturing and service corporation tendencies, four premises have been formulated, listed below.

1. Unlike the industrial period, when value was associated with the tangible, today larger groups of customers value results more than the actual products or services.

2. Forward-thinking firms are responding by offering solution systems consisting of product-service components throughout the customer's activity cycle; these increasingly contain more and more services.

3. Successful corporations embracing the results-driven solution system philosophy display common principles and themes in their thinking and strategies.

4. Their approach is a more appropriate framework for dealing with today's consumer issues than that encompassed in traditional industrial models.

YESTERDAY...

In past decades industrial corporate effort was geared at producing better, faster and cheaper products for defined target segments. Services tended to be a remedial, low key activity. The business landscape has changed. Now it is crowded with fierce global competitors in both price and non-price driven categories, within and cross-industry, who can (and do) clone and deliver similar products in record time.

The underlying premise in the industrial era was that physical products satisfied the desired customer needs, both explicit and implicit. People bought hope not cosmetics, holes not drills, status not cars, transport not trains, all common refrains and all true.

What's changed?

In the 60s and 70s traditional manufacturers, computer companies to take only one example, built market share on two main strategies — one, maximizing the tangible quality attributes of the product to raise perceived value in the eyes of the buyer, and two, increasing productivity and perfecting standardization techniques to keep price down.

At the beginning of the 80s, however, it became obvious that services were an integral part of the marketing "package." Computers weren't as easy to use as some of the advertising suggested. Customers wanted effective training, software that was useful, manuals they could understand and, above all, someone there when things went wrong. Thus the "soft" aspects of product offerings and organizations took on a higher order meaning.

At the same time such traditional service operations as financial institutions (with some exceptions), had once relied exclusively on intangible and highly customized offerings and relationships with customers. Technology and products were to improve internal efficiencies and pull costs down. By the 80s advances in technology, especially electronic delivery channels, made products, including their design, manufacture and delivery, fundamental to the service corporations' ability to compete.

TODAY AND TOMORROW...

The 90s will be the decade of the solution system, in which customer relationships will be strengthened by value added services accompanying products. This fact has already been established by many industries and academics (Vandermerwe and Rada, "Servitization..." 1988; Canton, 1988; Davis, 1987).

Figure 1 shows the evolution of *standardized* goods producers and *customized* service producers to full solution system operators. In the 60s and 70s, there was a distinct dichotomy. Advances in technology and push from consumers led firms to augment offerings which in turn led to the "mass customized systems" of the 90s. Such systems enable the seller to build economies of scale while at the same time giving single buyers or market groups variety and flexibility.

The convergence of traditional manufacturing and service organizations today makes rigid distinctions erroneous when discussing strategies. Whether they began as essentially or exclusively goods or service producers, greater numbers of market leaders now offer product-service combinations (Vandermerwe and Rada, "Servitization...", 1988; Chase and Garvin, 1989).

AN ATTEMPT TO DEFINE WHAT CUSTOMERS VALUE

In order to understand the drive towards solution systems, and thus the main elements of customer satisfaction, it is essential to know what customers value now and will value in the future. In preceding decades this task was easier: the classic economic definition of value prevailed—value was something tangible and hence exchangeable. Since services shared in neither characteristic, little definable economic value could be assigned to them (Giarini and Stahel, 1989).

For the marketer, however, life was more complicated. Marketing people instinctively knew that value embraced materialistic, emotive and functional product attributes. The customers' perception of value was in fact a complex accumulation of all the bits and pieces of the marketing mix, including the firm's or brand's image, the corporation's reputation, and the relationship of buyers and sellers.

The point is that historically value was related to the *means* to some desired end which customers were expected to accomplish. Today value is more closely associated with *the overall performance of the whole system,* i.e. it is

FIGURE 1
Convergence of Goods and Services

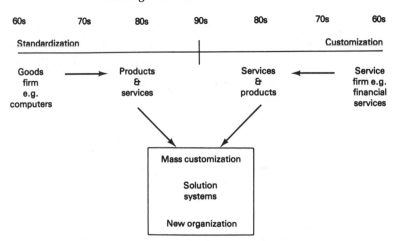

the *end* in itself, and firms are part of that process.

The difference is not simply semantic. It represents a fundamental change in values and hence managerial logic. The materialistic (what is it?), emotive (how does it make me feel?), and functional (how does it work?) buying motives variables still operate but there are additional issues. Rather than simply asking "what does it do?", customers now want to know "what can it potentially do?" What counts is not just "is it guaranteed?" or "can I get it repaired?", but "how can it optimize my performance/enjoyment/wellbeing/productivity/profitability?"

In short, customers don't want goods or services: to varying degrees they want *results*. Results, as Drucker points out in his latest book, are only valid in terms of customers (Drucker, 1989). So far firms have been better at producing results for themselves than for customers, for whom they have been good at producing goods or services.

NEW ORDER WINNING CRITERIA

These new and significant customer demands have led a noticeable shift in emphasis to service-loaded market strategies. Without attempting to generalize, given the differences from product to product and from market to market, certain service-loaded tendencies, if not trends, are discernible. These are summarized below:

From Conformance to Performance. In former years the acid test for industrial markets was whether a product conformed to quality specifications. Sellers called on buyers who bought according to preset strict standards on ingredients, features and benefits that were tangible, measurable and predictable. This is still important, but not enough.

What really matters today is applied performance or, put differently, a functioning system. For an international specialty water-treatment chemical company this meant moving from the traditional product/price mindset to the development of systems enabling users to simply switch on a tap to get the right amount of water at the appropriate temperature.

Digital Equipment Corporation (DEC) followed the same principle. Rather than simply relying on its reputation as a provider of state-of-the-art computers and after sale installation and repair services, DEC now concentrates on networking total systems to facilitate people and information linkups across functions, divisions, companies and even continents.

From Repair to Prevention. Prevention is a hot theme today with the pressure for "green" products and processes coming from legislators as well as from consumers (Vandermerwe and Oliff, 1990; Business International, *Managing the Environment...*, 1990; Economist Intelligence Unit, *Generating Profit from Waste...*, 1989). This aside, prevention, as opposed to simple repair, has become a pervasive concept in many industries, obliging firms to shift their focus to the service aspects even if it means de-emphasizing their basic product lines. The pharmaceutical industry is a case in point, where the market leaders will be those firms promoting health and disease prevention (service logic) rather than simply making and selling more pills (industrial logic). Also in pursuit of a "vision"—to give customers "trouble free operations"—SKF, the huge worldwide bearing corporation, went from a traditional industrial product to a service-focused organization.

From Responsive to Speed, Presence and Joint Development. Being responsive to needs is not good enough anymore. Customers demand instant attention and the dedicated presence of their suppliers. They want suppliers in their space, i.e. in their value creating process. An example is the ICI/Du Pont joint venture paint company, where teams are permanently allocated to automobile customers to deliver application paint services and fix whatever goes wrong on the spot.

DEC also dedicates staff to its customers, but as more than just a handholding exercise. Account executives form part of the clients' strategic teams and assist in the overall ongoing development of the firm. Teams "live in" as an integral part of managing the delivery process, so being able to monitor and update the bits of the system on an ongoing basis. DEC even involves clients in such new developments as software applications, once considered a "secret" activity.

As a general rule, industrial customers are pushing suppliers for more technology and know-how transfer, and co-developments are becoming the norm in many industries. Although this certainly cements partnerships and relationships, certain complications are inherent as well. For instance, who maintains ownership and control?

From Quality and Cost-of-Product to Quality and Cost-of-Use. Customers are assessing value in terms of quality-in-use over the entire period of their investment. Corporations must thus attempt to understand and quantify this shift. A division of Du Pont Europe, for instance, found that more R&D investment in high quality carpet fiber was getting them nowhere. Research revealed that what home-owners were actually after was better stain resistance and easier after-care.

Since consumers are buying a functioning system, they are interested in the cost-of-usage over time as opposed to the cost-of-product at a moment in time. Partek, a Finnish sealant and lubricant manufacturer, found that by looking at the total lifetime costs of customer projects, rather than at the price of sealants and lubricants, the scope of the market changed. Forty percent of total costs were due to decisions taken during the feasibility and specification phase of a project, 20% due to purchase and installation, and the remaining 40% due to decisions taken once the system was up and running (including the cost of sealants and lubricants). Partek now sells a solution system to customers covering all the activities mentioned, thus minimizing their overall cost of use and maximizing productivity.

COMMON PRINCIPLES IN SOLUTION SYSTEM STRATEGIES

To get the flavor of successful solution systems in action four current examples have been chosen from industry: Scandinavian Airline Systems (SAS) (services); SKF (industrial); Du Pont (consumer); and DEC (business-to-business). They have been deliberately selected to give readers as wide a perspective as possible. Although the circumstances and details are different, common principles and themes can be detected and are discussed below.

Principle 1

The company has a profound understanding of who the end users are, their usage behavior and their objectives.

Most of the energy in the past was directed at professional buyers. The buyer cannot, of course, be underestimated or bypassed. However, in the process the user was often missed (ignored?). Solution systems by definition solve problems for users, either in a direct or derived sense.

Digging deeper into why the carpet fiber sales were deteriorating despite a strong market share, Du Pont went directly to the homeowners. What did they find? Unlike PCs, holidays, videos, electrical appliances and curtains, end users simply don't like buying carpets and actually delay their purchase for as long as possible. They regard buying a carpet as a depressing experience which starts before they go shopping because they don't know what to buy and continues in retail stores, where they become confused by poor display information and service. The ordeal does not end there. Once they make a carpet purchase, delivery is invariably late, fitting bad and after-care services non-existent. Du Pont has responded by offering carpet mills, retailers and final customers a full array of information, fashion and after-care services including a 24-hour telephone hotline.

Similarly SKF, which traditionally regarded the distributor as the customer, found through research that their two end user markets, the automotive and factory after market and the Original Equipment Market (OEM) have very different needs. Speed is critical for the after market, where how quickly the bearing could be replaced, so minimizing downtime, and how it could be placed and monitored, to decrease breakdown risk, are fundamental. The OEM machine builder, on the other hand, wants to maximize productivity and thus requires advice on what bearing to put in, and how to configurate it.

Principle 2

The company understands the customer's activity cycle as a process over time.

Classic marketing literature (Kotler, 1988) acknowledges that customers go through a buying process in reaching a decision: from awareness of the need through searching for alternatives, making the decision and, finally, enduring what is known as post-purchase dissonance (after-buying trauma). This process, however, centers around the buying sequence of the product or service rather than the holistic experience over time.

After-sales service is a well-established concept, and Levitt dealt with the issue in his work on relationship management (Levitt, 1983). However, rather than examining the relative attributes of the customer's whole activity cycle, Levitt concentrated on analyzing the sales dynamics between the customer and the seller, and what the latter must do in order to be assured of the customer's return and loyalty.

Corporations which excel at marketing value over time have a keen sense of the *process* and they understand their customer's activity cycle in a holistic way. Although SKF is dealing with two distinct markets, their consumers have one thing in common: they don't want to buy bearings. They want to maximize productivity of their machines over the whole investment.

Successful firms map each of the critical points over this activity cycle. The SAS example in Figure 2 is a simplified illustration of mapping the critical activities customers have to undergo when taking a journey.

Once management has mapped these points, two goals need to be focused on: the design of the product-service components, and the delivery of the system.

Principle 3

The company designs a system consisting of product-service components aimed at maximizing performance over the customer's activity cycle.

When SAS targeted the business market they adopted a new total travel package. Having found punctuality and comfort to be critical, an "unbroken chain" of product-services was designed, as shown in Figure 3 over the entire customer's activity cycle. The objective? To minimize time and maximize the experience. The various customer activities were catered to by obtaining information about flights, the trip to and from airports, the facilities at the airport, services while waiting for a flight, services at the hotel, e.g. boarding pass at breakfast and baggage delivery, and so on.

For SKF, Du Pont, DEC or anyone else for that matter, the principle can be applied in the same way. Map the customer's activity. Then design an integrated product-service system which offers ongoing performance throughout the process.

Du Pont did this for homeowners and now offers services to facilitate the smooth buying and utilization of carpets. DEC similarly offers, in addition to their products, a huge port-

FIGURE 2
Mapping the Customers' Activity Cycle

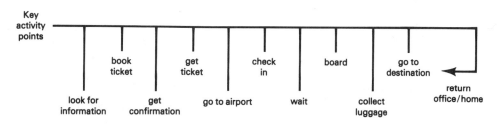

FIGURE 3
Designing the Solution System Over the Customer's Activity Cycle

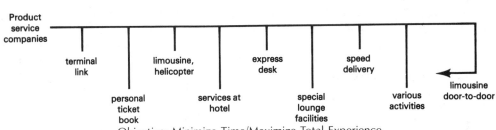

Objective: Minimize Time/Maximize Total Experience

folio of integrated services including strategic consulting, knowledge transfer, problem identification and systems design, services management, e.g. project and facilities management, and service delivery, e.g. logistics support and maintenance.

SKF's portfolio includes a battery of services designed to provide "trouble-free operations," including factory and machine design, temperature control and monitoring, inventory management, replacement and repair, fitting and so on. These are all in addition to actually making and supplying the bearing products and new products such as temperature monitoring equipment.

Principle 4

The company delivers the solution system throughout the activity cycle either on their own or in collaboration with suppliers or other corporations.

The next stage is to deliver the solution system. To match the offering to the customer's cycle, product-service activity components may be conveniently categorized into the Pre-Purchase, Purchase or Post-Purchase activities described below. In Figure 4 this is illustrated for DEC. However, the concept has proven to be a useful working model and can be applied, to a greater or lesser extent, to most product/market situations:

Pre-Purchase Activities before the sale or exchange, to provide information or expert advice on problem identification and solution, availability or needs;

Purchase Such project management activities during the exchange as sourcing, buying, logistics, installation and set-up;

Post-Purchase Systems management activities after delivery takes place, to ensure ongoing optimum functioning and productive

FIGURE 4
A Working Model for Product-Service Delivery Over the Customer's Activity Cycle

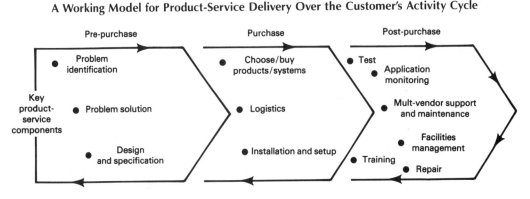

use, including training, support, maintenance and facilities management.

Consequent to these new consumer demands, companies report that the Pre- and particularly the Post-Purchase activities have become more important to both customer relationships and revenues. Purchase activities, more price sensitive, are less significant in the overall scheme of things.

"Who does what?" is the real issue in delivery today.

Looking again at the Pre-Purchase, Purchase and Post-Purchase model, Figure 5 indicates that corporations can no longer stick to an industrial functional mode. The delivery function is an ongoing and interdisciplinary process. In working closely with customers, firms increasingly rely upon cross-functional teams coming from R&D, manufacturing, application engineering, sales and technical service. At each point in the activity cycle these areas of expertise will of course take on differing roles and amounts of responsibility. However, the idea is that they work as a dedicated, cohesive and integrated whole. Special experts or support teams are called in when needed.

It follows then that customer relationship management cannot be left solely to marketing. Other functions are taking initiative in this activity. DEC, for instance, has five customer "reference sites" in Europe. These are located in their plants, where over 500 "manufacturing" personnel do nothing but talk to customers, who come year round to see such application systems as Just-in-Time (JIT) live and in action.

Solution systems invariably require new skills which the company may or may not have. Some corporations are investing in acquiring these core skills or repackaging and refining what is already in-house (Vandermerwe, Rada and Matthews, 1989). Others who feel that someone else can deliver cheaper or better are speedily forming collaborative alliances with suppliers and other corporations, or subcontracting out. In many cases a real competitive edge is gained thanks to a carefully thought out partnership plan. The train deal referred to earlier, which the TGV had lost, is close to being finalized with ABB and Bechtel not because they propose the fastest trains — the TGV is faster — but because they have come up with the right consortium and partnership packages, including finance companies and real estate developers (*International Herald Tribune,* June 18, 1990).

Some corporations are establishing collaborative alliances in order to expand globally. The SAS strategy for the 90s is to create a co-

FIGURE 5

Interdisciplinary Delivery of Product-service Components Over the Customer's Activity Cycle

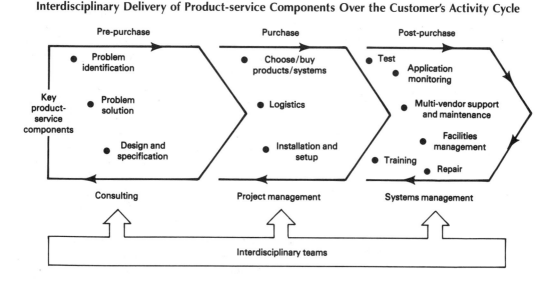

herent travel system by knitting together a group of airlines, hotels and various other types of companies around the world that fit the concept. The object of the giant groupings is to cover the global traveller's total activity cycle and facilitate this flow without interruption.

IMPACTS ON THE MARKETING FUNCTION

The customer activity solution approach goes beyond conventional marketing. Figure 6 summarizes the old and new approach.

From Per-Product/Segment Strategy to Per-Customer Strategy. Where previously industrial or business-to-business marketing strategies were handled on a product or consumer group basis, now it is more focused on individual customers who have specific needs and objectives to fulfil in both the short and long term.

From Market Shares to Share of Market Activity. Market share goals tend to chase volumes and therefore often lead to price cutting (Quinn, Doorley and Paquette, 1990). The solution approach concentrates on "bundles" of "mass customized" product-service components which cut across traditional definitions and boundaries, and lead to the most effective market offering or activity.

From Buyer/Seller to Strategic Relationships. Instead of the buyer/seller interface which dominated the firm's connection to its

customer, relationships are now conducted at many levels, strategically on a global or regional basis and operationally on a local basis. The important thing is that no one relationship can do the full job. Paradoxically, customers want to "see one face" and therefore coordination is vital. "Account management," a concept borrowed from the service world, is now popular among manufacturers, some of whom term it "strategic partnering" and see it as a way to get both the involvement and ongoing connection to customers (Shapiro, 1987). These account executives work at a high level in unison with customers and typically know as much (if not more) about their client's business than about their own.

From Product to Service-Loaded Concepts. The so-called intangibles delivered either electronically or by people are the glue that binds the solution concept together. These range from traditional support services to self-service and remote services information and high value added knowhow.

From Product to Knowhow-Based Pricing. As new concepts rely increasingly on information and knowhow, which to a large extent is the "thoughtware" (Edvinsson, in Bressand, 1989) and expertise in the heads of personnel within the network, the whole area of pricing has to be revised. Do corporations know what their knowhow is worth? Research done so far indicates a resounding "no." Until companies find a way to quantify and cost knowhow they will not be able to realistically price their offerings and so make the investments which lead to a competitive edge.

From On-Time/JIT to Anytime/All-the-Time. With relationships and involvement ongoing, a firm's logistics function will be more intertwined with that of its customers. Some goods may still be on an on-time/JIT basis, particularly those that are routine. Logistics, however, will become a product-service function with a more fluid and ongoing stream delivered anytime and all-the-time, with flexibility becoming the key feature.

From Sales to Project/Interdisciplinary Team Management. Rather than sales management, entire projects will have to be man-

FIGURE 6
A Customer Activity Service Approach to Marketing

60s, 70s and 80s	90s and beyond
Per Product/Segment Strategy	Per Customer/Strategy
Market Share	Share of Market Activity
Buyer/Seller Relationship	Strategic Relationships
Product-Loaded Concepts	Service-Loaded Concepts
Product-Based Pricing	Knowhow-Based Pricing
On-Time, JIT	Anytime, All the Time
Sales Management	Interdisciplinary Projects
Output Based Rewards	Outcome Based Rewards

aged and led. This is complex since participants in customer projects are likely to include cross-functional teams coming from within and without the firm, and including the customers themselves. Coordination is the key, with "coaches" rather than "bosses" facilitating rather than controlling. In an endeavour to capture the synergies from the specialized skills within their corporations and free individuals from red tape, more corporations are using the concept of "self organization," wherein people come together when and where needed around some core customer focus, project or activity. The actual sales role in this setting is more of a consultative than a vending task.

From Output to Outcome-Based Rewards. It is clear then that historic performance criteria and time frames must change. Previously the object was to get as many units sold as quickly as possible. This led to an "output" production and sales mentality and short term tactics often at the expense of long term relationships. Today the reverse is true. "Outcome" for customers is what matters. Firms are switching to rewards over longer periods awarded to teams based on various relationship criteria and not solely on units sold.

FRAMING THE CORPORATE CHALLENGE

If, as this article suggests, the power to deliver results lies in the value added services, then corporations must face two important challenges: how to capture and harness the necessary service skills, and how to organize the firm to handle the complexities of the convergences and networks both within and among functions and companies.

How to Capture and Harness the Needed Skills. This boils down to having the right people, no easy task given changing demographic tendencies. In a nutshell, companies need people who know the customer's business. Computer companies are employing automobile executives as account managers, while banks are seeking genetic engineering graduates to handle this growing investment area. In some instances customers participate

in choosing the individuals with whom they will be closely working.

Companies also need people, both within the firm and on the front line, with a service mentality. This is a cultural issue and requires recreating role models and heroes to transform behavior patterns. Training programs must also change. Firms such as DEC are looking at interfunctional training rather than the more traditional, sales management type program. SKF, whose program for decades emphasized mechanical and technical training in bearings, now obliges their engineers to follow rigorous courses in their customers' businesses, e.g. steel, paper or texiles.

Another subtle but ever more important challenge is to find and package the knowhow within corporations. Increasingly, individuals will need to transfer knowhow in a way which gives the corporation a differentiated and profitable edge. Resources will have to be redirected into such services as R&D, for example.

How to Organize and Handle the Complexities of the Convergences Both Within and Between Functions. Contrary to the erstwhile industrial models, partnering means convergences not separations, sharing not secrets. Having to cooperate and compete, sometimes simultaneously, with partners in order to serve customers over their full experience investment cycle can of course make life complicated! How, then, to create a common vision, culture and, on a more mundane note, common performance standards? And how to do this on a global scale?

Much attention is being directed at reshaping the corporation, which in essence means creating information networks so as to demolish old barriers and build bridges and interdependence among organizations, functions and individuals, both inter- and intracompany. Some executives call this the "boundaryless" organization. To achieve the required linkage and joint working spirit, firms are flattening their organization and adopting more egalitarian ideals which call for consensus, common goals and what one executive referred to as "win-win scenarios."

Where to physically locate is another current issue. Firms are making huge investments

FIGURE 7
Customer Activity-based Diagnostic Tool

Question 1
Do we know what customers and end users (our customers and our customers' customers) value?
If "yes": Proceed
If "no": Do focus group research with suppliers, customers and end-users

Question 2
Can we map our customers' activity cycle over time? (Pre, Purchase, Post)
If "yes": Proceed
If "no": Do focus group research with suppliers, customers and end-users

Question 3
Are relevant product-service components offered at each key point in the cycle?
If "yes": Proceed
If "no": Do focus group research with suppliers, customers and end-users

Question 4
Are there any potential gaps which interrupt the activity flow or lead to vacuums?
If "yes": Fill with product-service components
If "no": Proceed

Question 5
Do we have the core competence skills to deliver these product-service components at the correct quality level?
If "yes": Proceed
If "no": Develop, buy-in, or find partners

Question 6
Do we have the organization form to facilitate/drive customer activity-based behavior?
If "yes": Proceed
If "no": Restructure

Question 7
Do we have the information system to facilitate/link the flow of people, information and knowhow?
If "yes": Proceed
If "no": Develop, buy, set-up, integrate

in service and support centers in central positions and local locations to handle both face-to-face and remote service activities for customers. Individuals form part of this centralized and decentralized network in a kind of "floating matrix" arrangement.

A CUSTOMER ACTIVITY-BASED COMPANY DIAGNOSTIC TOOL

The underlying principles discussed in this article have been converted into a customer activity-based diagnostic tool to give managers the opportunity to ask the right questions and set themselves specific goals for their customer strategy in the years ahead. This is shown in Figure 7. The tool, of course, is a general one and should be approached as such: no one pat formula can be offered which will apply to the full spectrum of intermediary and end-users in the market. At the end of the exercise some may conclude that their firm needs a marginal shift in existing operations. For others a more radical change will be needed. Either way managers will find that marketing is still about satisfying customers. And as the customers change, so too must the marketer, and the organization.

BIBLIOGRAPHY

Business International. *Managing the Environment: The Greening of European Business,* London, 1990

CANTON, IRVING D. "How Manufacturers Can Move Into the Service Business," *The Journal of Business Strategy,* July/August 1988

CHASE, R. B. and GARVIN, D. "The Service Factory," *Harvard Business Review,* July/August 1989

DAVIS, STANLEY. *Future Perfect,* Reading, MA: Addison-Wesley, 1987

DRUCKER, PETER. *The New Realities,* New York: Harper & Row, 1989

Economist Intelligence Unit. *Generating Profit from Waste: Economic Incentives for Waste Management,* London: Economist Publications, 1989

EDVINSSON, LEIF and RICHARDSON, JOHN. "Services in Thoughtware: New Dimensions in Service Business Development" in *Strategic Trends in Services,* edited by Bressand, Albert and Nicolaidis, Kalypso. New York: Ballinger Publishing, division of Harper & Row, 1989

GIARINI, ORIO and STAHEL, WALTER. *The Limits to Certainty: Facing Risks in the New Service Economy,* Dordrecht: Kluwer Academic Publishers, 1989

International Herald Tribune. *US Rail Race Not to the Swift,* June 18, 1990

KOTLER, PHILIP. *Marketing Management,* 6th edition, Englewood Cliffs, NJ: Prentice Hall, 1988 (for example)

LEVITT, THEODORE. "After the Sale is Over...," *Harvard Business Review,* September/October 1983

QUINN, J. B., DOORLEY, T. L. and PAQUETTE, P. C. "Beyond Products: Services-Based Strategy", *Harvard Business Review,* March/April 1990

SHAPIRO, BENSON. "Close Encounters of the Fourth Kind," *Harvard Business School Working Paper,* 1987

VANDERMERWE, SANDRA and OLIFF, MICHAEL. "Customers Drive Corporations Green," IMD Working Paper, to be published in *Long Range Planning,* December 1990

VANDERMERWE, SANDRA, RADA, JUAN and MATTHEWS, WILLIAM. "European Manufacturers Shape Up for Services," *The Journal of Business Strategy,* November/December 1989

VANDERMERWE, SANDRA and RADA, JUAN. "Servitization of Business: Adding Value by Adding Service," *European Management Journal,* vol. 6, no. 4, 1988

Breaking the Cycle of Failure in Services

LEONARD A. SCHLESINGER
JAMES L. HESKETT

Most managers recognize that good service is a direct result of having effective, productive people in customer contact positions. You need winners at the front lines, not just warm bodies. Most service companies perpetuate a cycle of failure by tolerating high turnover and expecting employee dissatisfaction. But others are developing winning customer service teams. Instead of submitting to the cycle of failure, managers should take advantage of ways to break it, and get their organizations onto the cycle of success.

Does this sound familiar? A large retail company (or bank or fast food chain) designs its customer contact positions to be filled by people who are willing, at least temporarily, to work for wages marginally above statutory minimums. It simplifies the jobs, reducing them to a series of repetitive, boring tasks that require minimal training. It makes little effort to develop either dedication to the work or loyalty to the company. The results of this strategy are quite predictable: inordinately high employee turnover and increasing customer dissatisfaction.[1]

Unfortunately, traditional management responses to this scenario only exacerbate the problem. High turnover reinforces the wisdom of decisions to minimize efforts in selection, training, and commitment-building activities. "After all," most managers say, "why invest in people who aren't going to stay with you? There are plenty of bodies available to fill these jobs."

This cycle produces indifferent attitudes toward customers and poor service, which translate into poor perceptions of service by the customer and lower sales. Customer dissatisfaction fuels further decreases in employee satisfaction, thus encouraging turnover. High turnover further deteriorates service, particularly where the continuity of the customer-servicer relationship is important. With the departure of each frontline employee comes

Reprinted from "Breaking the Cycle of Failure in Services" by Leonard A. Schlesinger and James L. Heskett, *Sloan Management Review*, Spring 1991, pp. 17–28, by permission of the publisher. Copyright © 1991 by the Sloan Management Review Association. All rights reserved.

the arrival of another who, at best, is just as inept. Or in tight labor markets, the customer is often greeted by a help wanted sign and an empty server position.

This self-perpetuating "cycle of failure" seems to ensure continuing deterioration of service quality, managerial headaches, and long-term decreases in sales and profits (see Figure 1). When there is an abundance of "cheap" labor, such a cycle may seem acceptable. But as we enter an era of slowed labor market growth, dramatic increases in the de-

mand for service workers, tightened immigration policies, and increasing consumer demands for improved service, the business consequences of the cycle are increasingly untenable.

The cycle of failure also has significant individual and societal implications. According to the Department of Labor, as of 1986 there was a pool of 16 million nomadic service employees roaming from one low-paying employer to the next, experiencing a stream of personal failures with employers unwilling

FIGURE 1
The Cycle of Failure

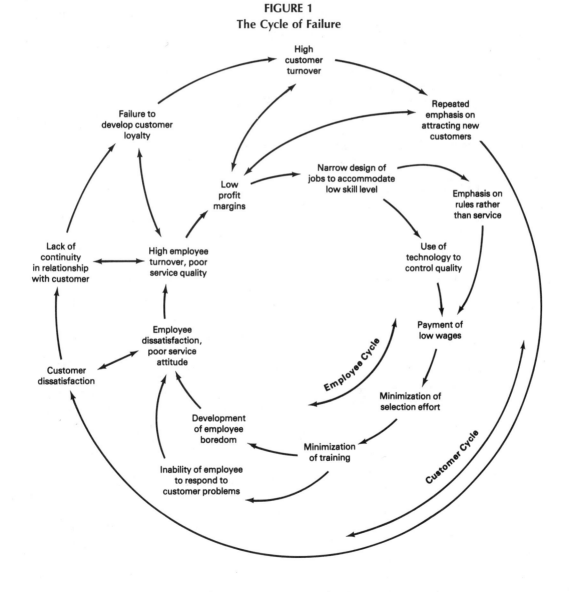

to invest in efforts to break the cycle.[2] This group of low-tenure employees who move to new jobs with decreasing confidence and self-respect is expanding at the same time that labor markets are getting increasingly tight.[3]

The limited number of academic studies to date support the relationships shown in Figure 1. For example, Schneider and Bowen found a direct relationship between well-designed service encounters that enhanced bank customer satisfaction and the satisfaction levels of tellers.[4] Another study suggested a direct relationship between customer satisfaction and employee motivation.[5] Others have related employee satisfaction to management's emphasis on serving customers as opposed to adhering to rules and procedures.[6] Perhaps most important of all, from a business standpoint, are studies that have linked satisfied customers directly to increased sales volumes.[7] We have thus far collected more than two dozen sets of data from service firms and consulting organizations that confirm one or more of the relationships shown in Figure 1.

In spite of this evidence, many service organizations that are generally considered well managed continue to perpetuate the cycle. Some even build it into their strategic plans. Why do managers bring this problem on themselves?

Managers we talk with are often resigned to the possibility that the cycle of failure is inevitable and well beyond their control. They present a litany of excuses:

- You can't find good [or any] people today.

- People just don't want to work today.

- To get good people would cost too much and you can't pass on these cost increases to customers.

- It's not worth training our frontline people when they leave you so quickly.

- High turnover is simply an inevitable part of our business. You've got to learn to live with it.

At the same time, the number of low-paid, unskilled positions is growing in many retail and consumer service companies. Half of all retail jobs pay less than $13,000 per year and a third of all health care jobs pay less than $250 per week. And most growing areas of the service sector rely disproportionately on part-time workers.[8]

Most troubling is that many managers acknowledge the cycle of failure but continue to take actions that perpetuate it. Fortunately, there are alternative ways of viewing and addressing the problem.

Some service firms employing large numbers of people in daily customer contact have taken steps to break the cycle of failure and create an alternative "cycle of success" as shown in Figure 2. Consider the following examples.

Wells Fargo and Company pays its people, from tellers on up, significantly more than competitor banks while maintaining the lowest operating expenses as a proportion of taxable revenue. It currently has over forty-five distinct pay-for-performance plans. Chairperson Carl Reichardt says, "You can see that our people are being rewarded because they're productive. And that to me is the right way to go."

ServiceMaster is a labor market intermediary that directly supervises maintenance, janitorial, and food service personnel in health care and educational institutions. Its management invests extraordinary amounts of time and energy designing jobs and defining tasks, along with creating personal development and training activities for the workforce. Its goal is to recruit 20 percent of its managers from its frontline workers. The results are reduced turnover, increased productivity, and customer cost reductions ranging from 10 percent to 15 percent.

An important element in the economic and service improvements at Dayton's department store, a division of Dayton Hudson, is the "Performance Plus" program, which involves extensive training, job redesign, and supervisory role modeling activities. In a number of test stores the program has dramatically increased the wages of frontline salespeople by 100 percent to 200 percent, while increasing sales and profits and improving the quality of customers' shopping experiences.

FIGURE 2
The Cycle of Success

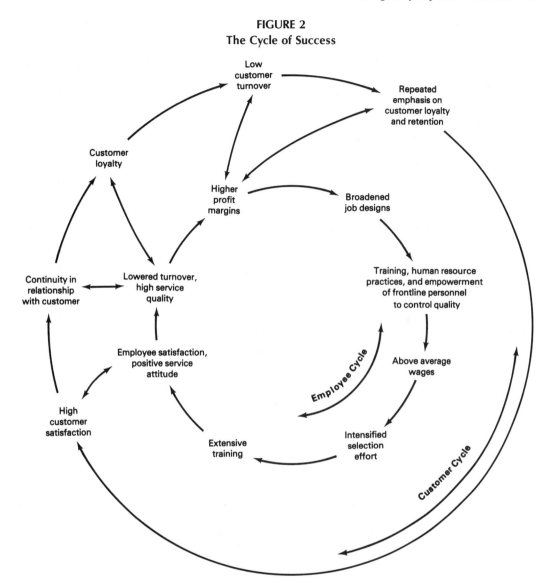

Au Bon Pain, an operator of quick-service French bakery cafés, has introduced a Partner-Manager program under which restaurant managers have earned twice the industry average and as much as $160,000 per year, five times more than managers at competing restaurants. The program has resulted in double digit sales and profit increases for individual units, significant reductions in employee turnover, and service quality improvements.

Fidelity Bank of Philadelphia has increased customer service representatives' wages by 58 percent over a two-year period and authorized the representatives to resolve all customer problems involving less than $1,000. Customer satisfaction, as measured by customers' willingness to recommend the bank to a friend, has jumped from 65 percent to 90 percent! This level of loyalty translates directly into increased profits. At the same time, the total cost of resolving small-scale customer problems has actually declined owing to the elimination of bureaucratic and time-consuming steps.

What differentiates these five firms from many of their competitors? They are hiring from the same population, but they believe that to develop and sustain a position as a preferred service provider they must simultaneously become a preferred employer. These firms have all achieved high levels of service quality and productivity. It is important that we understand why organizations tend to perpetuate the cycle of failure, and how companies are differentiating their service by effectively managing entry level personnel.

PERPETUATING THE CYCLE

Managers by and large are not irrational. How then have so many fallen into the cycle of failure trap? At least five factors provide partial explanations: (1) their assumptions about the labor pool, (2) their attitudes and biases about technology, (3) the availability of excuses for company inaction, (4) pressures for short-term performance, and, most important, (5) the lack of relevant information about the cost of perpetuating the cycle of failure.

Assumptions about the Labor Pool

The United States has been blessed with a huge influx of people into the labor pool in the past two decades. Many of these people, particularly those reentering the pool for a second career, have had strong educational backgrounds. They have been easy to train and have accepted responsibility relatively soon after hiring.

As a result, many organizations have wasted this plentiful resource. But the character of the labor pool is changing rapidly, as suggested by Table 1. New entrants to the pool will increasingly come from minority backgrounds. Cultural and language differences will require that training, jobs, and assignments be redesigned to tap into these new entrants' potential.

Of equal concern, however, should be the increasingly scarce supply of labor for service industries. Projections assume a steadily lower rate of unemployment. Even the potential for fewer jobs in the U.S. armed forces does not significantly alter the trend toward a labor shortage. This suggests the increasing importance of both designing less people-intensive services and becoming the employer of choice in targeted labor markets.

Yet another issue will be attracting qualified entry level workers. Table 2 gives labor force supply projections by race and current education statistics. If the disparity in education levels between whites and minorities continues, by the year 2000 a higher percent of the U.S. workforce will have attained only a high school degree or less. In addition, the value of a high school diploma seems to be deteriorating; with an increasing degree of illiteracy among those students who do graduate, the outlook for job application qualifications is grim.

Of course, managers are aware of these numbers today. But confronted with the day-to-day demands of recruiting, development, and compensation, few service company executives have had time to contemplate long-term trends. And in all fairness, regional short-term swings in labor availability have obscured general trends and distracted managers from long-term issues.

Technology as Savior

Managers in all sectors of the economy have placed tremendous faith in the ability of technological development to solve a wide variety of problems. Time and again that faith has been justified. So there is no reason to believe that technology would be any less useful in services than in manufacturing, particularly those services that are information intensive.

However, for several reasons technology will not significantly alter the service employment demand and supply pattern. First, much of the service sector is already as technology intensive as the manufacturing sector. Investment per worker is higher in information-intensive services than in manufacturing in the United States today.[9]

Second, despite the practical mandate to reduce people intensity in many services, some services require a core element of personal

TABLE 1
Projected Labor Force Demand and Supply, 1986–2000

| | LABOR FORCE DEMAND | | |
	1986 (000s)	2000* (000s)	Percentage Change
Goods producing			
Mining	783	724	−7.5%
Construction	4,904	5,794	+18.1
Manufacturing	18,994	18,160	−4.4
Total, goods producing	24,681	24,678	0.0%
Service producing			
Transportation and public utilities	5,244	5,719	+9.1
Wholesale trade	5,735	7,266	+26.7
Retail trade	17,845	22,702	+27.2
Finance, insurance, and real estate	6,297	7,917	+25.7
Services (medical, educational, and other professional)	22,531	32,545	+44.4
Government	16,711	18,329	+9.7
Total, service producing	74,363	94,478	+27.0%
Agriculture	3,252	2,917	−10.3
Private households	1,241	1,215	−.2
Nonfarm self-employed and unpaid family workers	8,086	9,742	+20.5
Total, all industries	111,623	133,030	+19.2%

| | LABOR FORCE SUPPLY | | |
	1986 (000s)	2000 (000s)	Percentage Change
Men			
16 to 24	12,251	11,506	−6.1%
25 to 54	44,406	53,024	+19.4
55 and older	8,766	8,606	−1.8
Total, men	65,423	73,136	+11.8%
Women			
16 to 24	11,117	11,125	+.1
25 to 54	35,159	47,756	+24.5
55 and older	6,138	6,758	+10.1
Total, women	52,414	65,639	+25.2%
Total, men and women	117,837	138,775	+17.8%

SOURCE: R. E. Kutscher, "Overview and Implications of the Projections to 2000," *Monthly Labor Review,* September 1987, pp. 3–9.

*Projections for labor demand in the year 2000 are "moderate" (mid-range) estimates.

contact that will be very difficult, if not impossible, to reduce through technology. For example, while the use of automated teller machines will continue to increase, customers will still demand to interact with tellers for certain transactions. In fact, as service technology increases, it does not take tremendous foresight to predict a backlash in favor of certain personal services and the use of personal interaction as a means of differentiating one's

TABLE 2
Detail of Labor Force Supply

LABOR FORCE SUPPLY BY RACE*

	1986 (000s)	2000 (000s)	Percentage Change
White, 16 and older	101,801	116,701	+14.6
Black, 16 and older	12,684	16,334	+28.8
Hispanic origin, 16 and older	8,076	14,086	+74.4
Other, 16 and older	3,352	5,740	+71.2

SOURCE: R. E. Kutscher, "Overview and Implications of the Projections to 2000," *Monthly Labor Review,* September 1987, pp. 3–9.

*Total does not equal the "total for men and women" in Table 1 because Hispanics may be included in either the white or African American population groups.

YEARS OF SCHOOL COMPLETED BY EMPLOYED PERSONS, MARCH 1988**

Years of School	Total	Whites	Blacks	Hispanics
Less than high school	16.4	15.8	22.7	39.0
High school	39.7	39.8	42.4	33.5
1 to 3 years of college	20.5	20.5	20.5	15.9
4 years of college or more	23.4	23.9	14.3	11.5

**SOURCE: G. Silvestri and J. Lukasiewicz, "Projections of Occupational Employment, 1988–2000," *Monthly Labor Review,* November 1989, p. 63.

service. Clearly, becoming the employer of choice is much less risky and allows for more organizational flexibility.

The Availability of Excuses

How often have we heard lately about the inadequate and declining level of talent in the labor pool, the failure of the education system to adapt to changing social needs, the continuation of government programs that replace the desire to work, and even the declining importance of values that made this country great? Often the people who most frequently voice these laments are moved least to respond. They act as if the problem is so great as to defy solution, particularly at the level of the individual business organization. This leads managers to design jobs and assignments that assume the worst in people.

The private sector cannot take responsibility for changing the basic labor pool, educating the population, or teaching the values that made the country great, whatever they are. But we have noticed that in companies that have broken the cycle of failure and moved toward the cycle of success, managers continue to have faith that many people want to do good work. These managers design strategies that find and retain such people before their competitors do.

Pressures for Short-Term Performance

While many managers know that improving personnel recruitment, selection, training and development, and rewards and recognition is important, they acknowledge that improvement efforts simply take a back seat to budgets, operating plans, and profit and loss statements.

A 1989 Forum Corporation survey of 611 Fortune 500 executives makes the point.[10] When interviewed, 92 percent of CEOs, 87 percent of COOs, and 83 percent of division VPs said service quality in their business was extremely important. This is a difference of 9 percentage points between the CEO and the VP.

At the same time, 51 percent of CEOs, 69 percent of COOs, and 70 percent of VPs said immediate financial results were extremely important. This difference of 19 percentage points between division VPs and CEOs suggests that top management believes and says one thing and signals another to middle management.

Because long-term trends occur more slowly and less dramatically than other business events, managers tend to push them down the agenda. As a senior human resource executive in one of the United States' largest service employers said to us recently, "It's like the attitudes of San Francisco residents toward earthquakes. They know they're important, but will they happen tomorrow?" It's hard to quantify the negative impact of long-term events on intermediate-term earnings. This explains why so few companies can break the cycle even after they recognize that it exists.

In addition, one cannot underestimate the short-term pressures inflicted by the wave of financial restructurings affecting a number of large service firms. Obsessive focus on short-term cash generation has exacerbated the cycle of failure in some firms to the point that they are likely never to recover.

The Lack of Relevant Information

It is a well-known management axiom that what gets measured gets managed. Wages and training costs are measurable. But the most important costs of all, those deriving from poor service, rarely get measured. We have reviewed the measurement systems of twenty large service employers to discern their capabilities for tracking the total economic toll taken by the cycle of failure. Our dismal assessment is outlined in Table 3.

Measurement lays the foundation for a number of activities, such as engineering and development. Measuring wages and other operating costs allows us to redesign jobs to be performed at a lower cost. It allows managers, other than those directly involved in opera-

TABLE 3
How Well Cycle of Failure Costs Are Measured

Category of Cost	Quality of Measurement 1 (poor)–5 (outstanding)
Aggregate employee turnover	4
Effects on service quality	2
Direct recruiting and hiring costs associated with turnover	4
Quality of new employee replacements	2
Ability to maintain internal wage levels as turnover increases	1
Productivity loss with new employees	3
Impact of turnover on customer retention	1
Customer acquisition vs. customer retention costs and their relationship to employee contact	1
Ongoing vs. entry level training costs	3

These rough estimates of measurement quality are based on examination of the reporting systems of twenty large service employers.

tions, to decide whether wages paid for a certain job are too high or too low.

Measurement also helps us make cost-cutting decisions with certainty in bad times. If we know what we are spending for training and development, we know what we can "save" if necessary. Without this knowledge, human resource development tends to be on-again, off-again, unlike steady machine maintenance, which is conducted with a full understanding of its costs.

But cost measurement is not enough. We must also try to measure the value to customers of our expenditures. If you emphasize costs over customer value you will lose customers. Unfortunately, customer value is hard to measure. Studies that measure the cost of turnover must do more than estimate what it will take to recruit and train new hires. They must also place a value on the reduced productivity that will affect customers for a period of time after a position is refilled.

Our research did begin to uncover some comprehensive approaches to measuring the impact of turnover on customers. Two divisions of Marriott Corporation recently carried out a study that included as an assumption, based on management estimates, that a 10 percent reduction in the industry's historically high turnover rate would reduce "customer nonrepeats" by 1 percent to 3 percent, providing revenue increases of $50 million to $150 million. The study concluded that even at the upper range of estimates for recruiting, training, and lost customer costs, an overall reduction of 10 percent in labor turnover would yield savings significantly greater than the total current profits of the two divisions.

Impact on Strategic Options

The cycle of failure has a subtle but devastating impact on strategic options. Good ideas for new services are aborted early because "the operating organization is not able to deliver that." Unfortunately, this assumption is often based on reasonably good historical information, such as the failure to deliver new services in the past. The result? Failure to capitalize on competitive opportunity.

What is being done about all of this?

STRATEGIES FOR BREAKING THE CYCLE OF FAILURE

No one strategy will lead to a cycle of success. Countless factors influence the policies for managing relationships among managers, frontline service personnel, and customers. However, in our examples of leading service firms patterns have emerged. They include both the underlying assumptions that managers bring to the task and the way that they go about setting in motion the cycle of success.

Winning Assumptions

Many managers who have broken the cycle of failure begin by assuming that there is a limited pool from which to draw entry level service providers, especially those that fit particular strategies. This does not mean that these firms look only for individuals with ready-made talent and attitudes. But it does mean they take extra care to select and develop people to ensure that the pool is not depleted. They attach unusual significance to new hires and departures.

These organizations carefully assess the traits they need in entry level people and determine which can be imparted through training and which cannot. They select people based on those traits that must be hired rather than trained into the organization.

These traits largely have to do with attitudes and personalities — psychographic characteristics, which vary from firm to firm. The emphasis is on how people think, not who they are. As a result, the growing demographic heterogeneity of the labor pool is largely irrelevant. Firms select a workforce from a heterogeneous population that is homogeneous on psychographic dimensions.

These organizations consider technology an essential supporting resource for face-to-face service delivery. For some transactions, technology may play a primary role, as in the use of automatic teller machines. But for the overall service, it is just one element in a package.

Further, these organizations often believe that technology provides limited competitive advantage because it is usually available to all competitors that can afford it. Positive,

customer-oriented attitudes, however, are considered much more difficult to introduce than new technologies and thus provide competitive advantage.

Managers in the firms we observed make no excuses for the turnover rates among their entry level employees or the quality of service they deliver. While they realize that they cannot solve society's ills, they simply refuse to accept that these problems must disable them. They recognize that real competitive advantage comes to those who confront such issues successfully.

Pressures for short-term performance are every bit as great among these managers as others, and are often self-imposed. But these managers assume that appropriate responses are to hire or train "winners," individuals whose own standards are at least as high as the organization's. This requires a one-time major investment to raise the organization's standards, communicate new expectations, and implement new ways to achieve expectations. Once hired and trained, winners attract winners. The organization will not tolerate others. And winning performances provide the resources for hiring and developing people that will contribute to winning performances.

Finally, managers in many of these firms religiously measure the costs associated with the employee and customer life cycles. They know that new customers are more costly and less profitable to serve than existing ones. They know what it costs to hire, develop, and replace preferred employees. They know what it costs to lose customers and key employees. And they have a pretty good idea of the relationship between customer and employee loss. They know these things not only because they have taken the time to measure them, but because they track them continuously.

These assumptions lead to distinctly different strategies and programs for dealing with the cycle of failure.

Winning Programs

One thing that differentiates our employers of choice is that each of them has made a conscious and exhaustive effort to link their human resource, service, and business strategies. Consider the following three examples.

Fairfield Inn. This chain of economy inns operated by the Marriott Corporation was designed to break the cycle of failure before its first room was rented. Fairfield offers its customers, what management terms "road warriors," just two things: the cleanest rooms and the friendliest staff available, at a budget price (often less than $40 per night). Given the simplicity of the service package, the inns are staffed with only two categories of frontline employees — front desk and housekeeping personnel.

Management decided which qualities it would seek in employees, commissioned a questionnaire and interview intended to identify those qualities, and then selected people carefully. It was looking not only for dependable people with good work habits, but also for people to whom a pay-for-performance evaluation system, called Scorecard, would appeal.

With Scorecard, guests answer four questions on a computer-administered touch screen at check out. By correlating their reactions to questions such as "How would you evaluate the cleanliness of your room?" and "How personable was the hotel inn personnel at the time of check in?" with data indicating which employees were responsible for a particular guest, management can keep a running tab on individual performance. The questionnaire process is easy enough to bring in a 50 percent response rate, which provides the necessary volume of observations.

In addition to providing base pay comparable to local wages, Fairfield awards monthly bonuses of up to 10 percent of base pay to service employees, depending on their individual and unit Scorecard results. Performance results are posted on a regular basis for the unit, the region, and the chain.

To combat one of the most difficult problems in the lodging industry, absenteeism, Fairfield replaces all but one week of vacation with "earned leave," days off with pay that are earned with perfect attendance for one- and three-month periods. Dependable attendance makes work schedules more predictable for everyone and helps build a winning team attitude.

Feedback from customers and employees has been overwhelmingly positive, and the chain has staked out a successful position in an incredibly crowded market segment, although some employees have discovered that the Scorecard system is not for them and have left quickly. Others have been encouraged to leave by their peers, who were being penalized by poor unit performance.

Few organizations have the opportunity to avoid the cycle of failure from the first day of operation. Like Dayton's of Dayton Hudson and Au Bon Pain, most organizations have to take actions to reverse the turn of the wheel.

Dayton's. This full-line department store chain has concluded that restoring the high service levels that were prominent among major retailers in their early days is absolutely critical to retaining their current customers and regaining those customers who left for the more personalized treatment available in specialty shops. Three major assumptions drive Dayton's "Performance Plus" strategy:

- Job candidates who historically move toward white collar jobs in large organizations must see retailing as an attractive option.
- Pay for performance must be a central part of any differentiation strategy.
- Supervision must return to the selling floor and provide a role model for selling associates.

The program focuses on selection, training, and incentives all aimed at providing superior customer service performed by sales "consultants" who "go the extra mile" for the customer. On the sales floor, consultants are encouraged to take customers into different departments when needed and to develop a repeat clientele by sending thank you notes and informing customers of sales on new merchandise. Sales consultants are rewarded on a commission basis.

The company believes that selection plays an important role in the system. Interviewers look for candidates hoping to make retail sales a career. Because the compensation is, on average, 20 percent higher than at prior wage levels, the company can attract college graduates and others who would normally apply for jobs in sales and manufacturing companies. After hiring, new employees go through a two-day "celebration training" in which the underlying theme is "It's my company."

The "Performance Plus" program has expanded to eleven stores in the thirty-four unit chain over the past three years. Sales have improved dramatically (as much as 25 percent in individual sales per hour), wages have escalated to the extent that increasingly capable salespeople can be recruited, and total operating costs have shifted but remained stable. At the same time, customer response to the changes, as measured by the chain's service quality survey, has been dramatic.

The program has not yet stemmed turnover; in fact, frontline turnover has increased as an outgrowth of the transition process to the new style of salesperson. And the program has not been without its negative consequences. A successful union organizing drive among long-term employees in Detroit was traced to job insecurities and fears of performance pressures. However, management believes the program will eventually address these problems appropriately.

The chain continues to fine-tune the program as it adds three to four stores to the program each year. Many issues remain, but management believes that results to date absolutely justify the investment.

Breaking the cycle of failure for entry level jobs often means breaking it as well for the supervisors. That's what happened at Au Bon Pain.

Au Bon Pain. Au Bon Pain, a chain of French bakery cafés concentrated between Washington, D.C., and Boston, was a sitting duck for the cycle of failure. (In fact, one of us helped coin the term while serving as a senior executive in the company.) Store managers were paid salaries comparable to or marginally above those at local fast food restaurants and given very little latitude. Results were predictable: the usual "revolving door" of store managers and employees in a business that thrives on relationships built with frequent customers who have acquired the Au Bon Pain "habit."

To reverse the cycle, management negotiated "contracts" with willing store managers that established targets for each store. Company and store management would split equally profits over and above targets. At the same time, managers were given great latitude to change procedures, staffing policies, and even store layout, provided they met certain standards for store decor, core service, and food and service quality. These standards are evaluated frequently by mystery shoppers hired by the company.

Instead of acting as supervisors or controllers, corporate managers shifted their roles to become coaches, consultants, cheerleaders, and increasingly enthusiastic observers as store volumes under the program quickly doubled in a number of cases. In an effort to boost his performance beyond even this mark, one store manager decided to initiate his own program. Gary Aronson, the manager of The Au Bon Pain at Boston's Prudential Center, is now in the midst of his fourth year under the Partner-Manager Program. He has, over this period, earned as much as $160,000 a year, while paying his frontline employees, some of them in their first jobs, up to $23,000 a year when the industry norm is $10,000 to $12,000. How can Aronson afford to do this? He only hires people willing to work fifty to sixty hours per week, with overtime pay over forty hours. He has cut his head count by nearly 70 percent as a result of the longer hours and higher productivity. Employee absenteeism is nearly unheard of; a missed day means lost overtime pay. And Aronson has cut turnover to roughly 10 percent per year in entry level jobs, in which 200 percent is quite normal. Better yet, sales have soared as customers patronize the people they see every day behind the counters.

In short, Aronson has built a "lean, mean team" composed of entry level people who think and act like winners. And like most such teams, they deliver quality as well as quantity. Au Bon Pain's mystery shoppers regularly report perfect scores under the Partner-Manager Program. Celebrations for such occasions are becoming commonplace. And Au Bon Pain spends very little to attract new employees. By word-of-mouth, it can choose from the best talent not only for management but for entry level jobs in most of its markets. Corporate management has been freed to plot strategies for growth and profitability.

Common Elements of Strategy

Increasingly, we can begin to identify common elements in these programs (see Table 4). We discuss them below.

Careful Selection. Service organizations that have broken the cycle of failure have the luxury of being selective in hiring. Fairfield Inn, for example, often considers as many as twenty-five candidates for each housekeeping or front desk position. As discussed earlier, it searches for individuals whose basic values appear congruent with the organization's service ethic. Its managers and others have expressed great confidence in validated employment interviews designed to address issues of fit. In a labor market in which employers often convey the impression of searching for warm bodies rather than valued employees, employees who successfully complete a rigorous screening process can be quite committed to their work.

Realistic Previews of the Job and Organization. A tried and true axiom of service management is "start as you intend to continue." Many of our example organizations increase the likelihood of long-term success by providing prospective job candidates with accurate information about the job. Such information helps new employees become more strongly linked to the job and the organization. An in-

TABLE 4
Strategies for Breaking the Cycle of Failure

- Careful selection
- Realistic previews of the job and organization
- A focus on the nature and quality of early job experiences
- Employee empowerment and latitude
- Employees' awareness of their roles in customer satisfaction and economic success
- Scorekeeping and feedback
- Integration of employees into a winning team
- A focus on aggregate labor cost instead of individual wage levels
- Concentration on quality at the service core

tegral part of the Au Bon Pain selection process is a paid two-day work experience in the stores prior to final selection interviews. This experience weeds out applicants both through self-selection and through management observation of behavior.

Focus on Early Job Experiences. The turnover data for large service employers provides ample evidence that employees' attitudes are shaped in their earliest jobs. This is true across almost all demographic and job categories and is especially relevant given the broad diversity of entry level service jobs and employees. Early employee feelings of disaffection are likely to affect their own behavior profoundly, especially in relationship to customers. The Disney organization is legendary in its attention to up-front acculturation and training for initial job assignments.

Employee Empowerment and Latitude. Several organizations have empowered frontline employees, especially those who take care of customers, to go beyond the routine in performing their jobs. Research clearly demonstrates the role of enhanced authority and supervisory latitude in increasing both overall job satisfaction and customer satisfaction.[11]

In turn, such acts beyond basic service are recognized and applauded by management whenever brought to their attention. Wells Fargo even instituted a peer recognition program to applaud the often unrecognized acts that make for an outstanding coworker.

Employees' Awareness of Their Role in Customer Satisfaction and Economic Success. These companies continuously provide information and rewards to show employees how they affect the whole firm. A broad range of tactics beyond compensation can be helpful in this regard. Service-Master, for example, has invested considerable energy in developing an appreciation among its hospital housekeeping employees of their link to overall patient care. It regularly schedules meetings, on company time, at which medical professionals speak to entry level employees on critical issues such as AIDS in the workplace and the transmission of germs and viruses in hospitals.

Scorekeeping and Feedback. In high-performance service organizations, employees as well as managers like to see the performance "score," whether it is tied directly to compensation or not. It is no surprise, then, that results, whether obtained from customer "votes" at Fairfield Inn, from mystery shopping at Au Bon Pain, or from peer recognition at Wells Fargo, are important. Communicating the results provides management with a number of opportunities to express its enthusiasm for general performance or individual deeds. Recognition, regardless of the accompanying rewards, is at the heart of these programs.

Integration of Employees into a Winning Team. "Winners want to be with winners" is an old management maxim. Through job design and rewards, many organizations have successfully built winning teams. Fairfield Inn combines extensive team-building activities with incentives that foster group effort. For example, at the hotel pre-opening workshop, management and hourly employees have a roundtable discussion of mutual expectations. The session begins with employees and management identifying what they would want if they were a guest at the hotel. They then go on to examine their expectations for each other, employee to management, and employee to employee. All of the data generated is prominently displayed in the employee breakroom as a reminder of commitments made.

At a basic level, organizations need to recognize that employees often feel disaffected when poor performers are carried on the payroll. Recent national surveys of employees indicate that as many as 75 percent of those surveyed believe that management carries "dead wood" employees for too long.[12] The "warm bodies" approach that drives many service employers promotes not only bad service but deteriorating attitudes among solid performers.

Focus on Aggregate Labor Cost Instead of Individual Wage Levels. Each of the firms we have discussed has successfully escalated employee wages, often dramatically, without lowering economic performance. How have they accomplished this seemingly impossible feat?

Simply stated, they have aggressively focused on the total cost of doing business, including the aggregate wage bill and individual productivity levels, without taking their eye off customer service levels. Each of these high-paying firms has successfully demonstrated the potential for individuals to achieve peak performance when expectations and rewards are high.

Pay for performance is an integral element of some, but not all, of these programs. Those that employ it take care to base it on measures of both the quantity and quality of results. This requires a conscious effort to measure, communicate, and reward results associated with quality.

Concentration on Quality at the Service Core. Au Bon Pain's store managers have a great deal of latitude in how they run their businesses. But their employment contracts can be terminated if the quality of their offerings falls below minimum standards in areas such as speed of service, availability of product, and cleanliness.

Similarly, at Dayton's each salesperson must maintain minimum service quality levels to qualify for productivity incentives. This is particularly critical in services in which quality could be neglected in pursuit of sales volume or other forms of productivity.

WHICH WAY FOR THE CYCLE?

The realities of the labor market over the next decade are clear. More people with less relevant job preparation will earn higher wages as frontline service providers. Service levels and economic performance will deteriorate in firms that fail to engage in a fundamental rethinking of the employee-organization-customer relationship.

What are the consequences of a widespread effort to break the cycle of failure? Will it produce a "skimming" of the most able from the labor pool with a growing competition for a small subgroup of people? Managers ask us these questions frequently. They assume that all organizations will be selecting for the same sets of traits, a phenomenon that we have not yet observed in our examination of corporate human resource strategies. Nevertheless, this possibility suggests there might be a modest "early mover" advantage for firms in certain industries or geographic areas who recruit and retain employees fitting their service strategies particularly well.

In nearly every service industry and labor market with which we are familiar, at least one organization has broken the cycle of failure. Its managers have made the commitment and the up-front expenditure of money and effort to achieve a vital but largely invisible competitive advantage. The real value of these efforts will become more visible in the restricted labor market that all service firms will face in the coming decade. Day after day, these firms will spend less than their competitors for recruiting and training. They will attract the most performance-minded managers and frontline personnel, people whose personal philosophies toward work fit those of their employers. They will provide a more satisfying work environment for effective performers. But most critically, they will retain those people who provide the most satisfactory continuing relationships with valued customers.

The next decade will belong to those firms that break the cycle of failure. Even more important, it will belong to their customers and employees.

REFERENCES

[1] Entry level service jobs often have annual turnover rates of 100 percent to 300 percent. See: R. H. Woods and J. F. Macaulay, "Rx for Turnover: Retention Programs that Work," *Cornell HRA Quarterly*, May 1989, pp. 78–90.

[2] *Current Population Survey* (Washington, D.C.: U.S. Government Bureau of Labor Statistics, 1986).

[3] L. C. THUROW, *Toward a High-Wage, High-Productivity Service Sector* (Washington, D.C.: Economic Policy Institute, 1990).

[4] B. SCHNEIDER and D. E. BOWEN, "New Services Design, Development, and Implementation and the Employee," in *New Services*, eds. W. R. George and C. Marshall (Chicago: American Marketing Association, 1985), pp. 82–101.

[5] E. E. LAWLER III, *Motivation in Work Organizations* (Monterey, California: Brooks/Cole, 1973), pp. 153–165.

[6] J. J. PARKINGTON and B. SCHNEIDER, "Some Correlates of Experienced Job Stress: A Boundary Role Study," *Academy of Management Journal* 22 (1979): 270–281; W. G. Bennis, "Beyond Bureaucracy," in *American Bureaucracy*, ed. W. G. Bennis (Chicago: Aldine, 1970), pp. 3–17; and P. M. Blau, *On the Nature of Organizations* (New York: John Wiley & Sons, 1974), pp. 80–84.

[7] See, for example, E. M. Johnson and D. T. Seymour, "The Impact of Cross Selling on the Service Encounter in Retail Banking," in *The Service Encounter*, eds. J. A. Czepiel et al. (Lexington, Massachusetts: D. C. Heath, 1985), pp. 225–239.

[8] L. WALDSTEIN, *Service Sector Wages, Productivity, and Job Creation in the United States and Other Countries* (Washington, D.C.: Economic Policy Institute, 1989), pp. 24–25.

[9] S. S. ROACH, "America's Technology Dilemma: A Profile of the Information Economy," *Morgan Stanley Special Economic Study,* 22 April 1987.

[10] *Wall Street Journal,* 9 August 1989, p. B1.

[11] L. A. SCHLESINGER and J. ZORNITSKY, "Job Satisfaction, Service Capability, and Customer Satisfaction: An Examination of Their Linkages and Management Implications," *Human Resource Planning,* forthcoming, Spring 1991.

[12] Hay Associates, personal correspondence, 1989.

First National Bank

CHRISTOPHER H. LOVELOCK

Problems arise when a big bank, attempting to develop a stronger customer service orientation, enlarges the tellers' responsibilities to include selling activities.

"I'm concerned about Karen," said Margaret Costanzo to David Reeves. The two bank officers were seated in Costanzo's office at the First National Bank's branch in Federal Square.

Ms. Costanzo was a vice president of the bank and manager of the Federal Square branch, the third largest in First National's 92-branch network. She was having an employee appraisal meeting with Mr. Reeves, customer service director at the branch. Reeves was responsible for the Customer Service Department, which coordinated the activities of the customer service representatives (CSRs, formerly known as tellers) and the customer assistance representatives (CARs, formerly known as new accounts assistants).

Costanzo and Reeves were discussing Karen Mitchell, a 24-year-old customer service rep, who had applied for the soon-to-be vacant position of head CSR. Mitchell had been with the bank since graduating from junior college with an associate in arts degree three and a half years earlier. She had applied for the position of what had then been called head teller a year earlier, but the job had gone to a candidate with more seniority. Now that individual was leaving — his wife had been transferred to a new job in another city — and the position was once again open. Two other candidates had applied for the job.

Both Costanzo and Reeves were agreed that, against all criteria used in the past, Karen Mitchell would have been the obvious choice for head teller. She was both fast and accurate in her work, presented a smart and professional appearance, and was well liked by customers and her fellow CSRs.

However, the nature of the teller's job had been significantly revised nine months earlier to add a stronger marketing component. (*Exhibit 1* shows the previous job description for teller; *Exhibit 2* shows the new job description for customer service representative). CSRs were now expected to offer polite suggestions that customers use automated teller machines for simple transactions. They were also required to stimulate customer interest in the broadening array of financial services offered by the bank. "The problem with Karen," as Reeves put it, "is that she simply refuses to sell."

THE NEW FOCUS ON CUSTOMER SERVICE AT THE FIRST

Although it was the largest bank in the state, the "First" had historically focused on corporate business and its share of the retail consumer banking business had declined in the face of aggressive competition from other financial institutions. Three years earlier, the Board of Directors had appointed a new CEO and given him the mandate of developing a stronger consumer orientation at the retail level. The goal was to seize the initiative in marketing the ever-increasing array of financial services now available to retail customers. The new CEO's strategy, after putting in place a new management team, was to begin by ordering an expansion and speed-up of the First's investment in electronic delivery systems. The bank had tripled the number of automated teller machines in its branches during the past 18 months, and was engaged in an

---

EXHIBIT 1
First National Bank: Position Description for Teller (Effective September 1982)

Function: Provides customer services by receiving, paying out, and keeping accurate records of all monies involved in paying and receiving transactions. Promotes the bank's services.

Responsibilities:

1. Serves customers.
   - Accepts deposits, verifies cash and endorsements, and gives customers their receipts.
   - Cashes checks within the limits assigned or refers customers to supervisor for authorization.
   - Accepts savings deposits and withdrawals, verifies signatures, posts interest, and balances as necessary.
   - Accepts loan, credit card, utility, and other payments.
   - Issues money orders, cashier's checks, traveler's checks, and foreign currency and issues or redeems U.S. savings bonds.
   - Reconciles customer statements and confers with bookkeeping personnel regarding discrepancies in balances or other problems.
   - Issues credit card advances.
2. Prepares individual daily settlement of teller cash and proof transactions.
3. Prepares branch daily journal and general ledger.
4. Promotes the bank's services.
   - Cross-sells other bank services appropriate to customer's needs.
   - Answers inquiries regarding bank matters.
   - Directs customers to other departments for specialized services.
5. Assists with other branch duties.
   - Receives night and mail deposits.
   - Reconciles ATM transactions.
   - Provides safe deposit services.
   - Performs secretarial duties.

EXHIBIT 2

First National Bank: Position Description for Customer Service Representative
(Effective February 1988)

Function: Provides customers with the highest quality services, with special emphasis on recognizing customer needs and cross-selling appropriate bank services. Plays an active role in developing and maintaining good customer relations.

Responsibilities:

1. Presents and communicates the best possible customer service.
   - Greets all customers with a courteous, friendly attitude.
   - Provides fast, accurate, friendly service.
   - Uses customer's name whenever possible.

2. Sells bank services and maintains customer relations.
   - Cross-sells retail services by identifying and referring valid prospects to the customer assistance representative or customer service director. When time permits (no other customers waiting in line), should actively cross-sell retail services.
   - Develops new business by acquainting noncustomers with bank services and existing customers with additional services that they are not currently using.

3. Provides a prompt and efficient operation on a professional level.
   - Receives cash and/or checks for checking accounts, savings accounts, taxes withheld, loan payments, Mastercard/Visa, mortgage payments, Christmas clubs, money orders, traveler's checks, cashier's checks, premium promotions.
   - Verifies amount of cash and/or checks received, being alert for counterfeit or fraudulent items.
   - Accepts deposits and withdrawals, verifying signatures where required by policy.
   - Cashes checks in accordance with bank policy. Identifies payees; verifies signatures; checks dates and endorsements; compares written dollar and figure amounts; ensures that numbers are included on all counter checks, deposit slips and savings withdrawal and deposit slips; watches for stop payments and holds funds per bank policy.
   - Where applicable, pays credit card cash advances and savings withdrawals. Accepts credit merchant deposits. Receives payment for collection items, safe deposit rentals, and other miscellaneous items. Confers with head CSR or customer service director on nonroutine situations.
   - Sells traveler's checks, money orders, and cashier's checks and may redeem coupons and sell or redeem foreign currency.
   - Handles sale and redemption of U.S. savings bonds.
   - Sells monthly transit passes.
   - Ensures timely batching and preparation of work for transmittal to proof department.
   - Prepares coin and currency orders as necessary.
   - Services, maintains, and settles automated teller machines as required.
   - Ensures only minimum cash exposure necessary for efficient operation is kept in cash drawer; removes excess cash immediately to secured location. Ensures maximum control over cash drawers and other valuables on hand throughout daily operation.
   - Prepares accurate and timely daily settlement of work.
   - Performs bookkeeping and operational functions as assigned by customer service director.

active branch renovation program. One year ago, the First had also joined a regional ATM network, which boasted freestanding 24-hour booths at shopping centers, airports, and other high-traffic locations.

These actions seemed to be bearing fruit. In the most recent six months, the First had seen a significant increase in the number of new accounts opened, as compared to the same period of the previous year. And quarterly data released by the Federal Reserve Bank showed that the First was steadily increasing its share of new deposits in the state.

Customer Service Issues

New financial products had been introduced at a rapid rate. But the bank found that existing platform staff—known as new accounts assistants—were ill equipped to sell these services because of lack of product knowledge and inadequate training in selling skills. Recalled Ms. Costanzo,

The problem was that they were so used to waiting for a customer to approach them with a specific request, such as a mortgage or car loan, that it was hard to get them to take a more proactive approach that involved actively probing for customer needs. Their whole job seemed to revolve around filling out forms.

As the automation program proceeded, the mix of activities performed by the tellers started to change. A growing number of customers began to use automated teller machines for cash withdrawals and deposits, as well as for requesting account balances. The ATMs at the Federal Square branch had the highest utilization of any of the First's branches, reflecting the large number of students and young professionals served at the location. Costanzo noted that customers who were older or less well educated seemed to prefer being served by "a real person, rather than a machine."

A year earlier, the head office had selected three branches, including Federal Square, as test sites for a new customer service program. The Federal Square branch was in a busy urban location, about one mile from the central business district and three blocks from the campus of the state university. The branch was surrounded by retail stores and close to commercial and professional offices. The other two branches were among the bank's larger suburban offices and were located in a shopping center and next to a big hospital, respectively. As part of the branch renovation program, each of these three branches had previously been remodeled to include no fewer than four ATMs (Federal Square had five), a customer service desk near the entrance, and two electronic information terminals that customers could activate to obtain information on a variety of bank services. The teller stations were redesigned to provide two levels of service: an express station for simple deposits and for cashing of approved checks, and regular stations for the full array of services provided by the tellers. The number of stations open at a given time was varied to reflect the volume of anticipated business. Finally, the platform area in each branch was reconstructed to create what the architect described as "a friendly, yet professional, appearance."

HUMAN RESOURCES

With the new environment came new training programs for the staff of these three branches and new job descriptions and job titles: customer assistance representatives (for the platform staff), customer service representatives (for the tellers), and customer service director (instead of assistant branch manager). The head teller position was renamed head CSR. Position descriptions for all these jobs are reproduced in *Exhibits 2* through *5*. The training programs for each group included sessions designed to develop improved knowledge of both new and existing retail products. (CARs received more extensive training in this area than did CSRs.) The CARs also attended a 15-hour course, offered in three separate sessions, on basic selling skills. This program covered key steps in the sales process, including building a relationship, exploring customer needs, determining a solution, and overcoming objections. The sales training program for CSRs, by contrast, consisted of just two 2-hour sessions designed to develop skills in recognizing and probing customer needs, presenting product features and benefits, overcoming objections, and referring customers to CARs.

All staff members in customer service positions participated in sessions designed to improve their communication skills and professional image: clothing and personal grooming and interactions with customers were all discussed. Said the trainer, "Remember, people's money is too important to entrust to someone who doesn't look and act the part!" CARs were instructed to rise from their seats and shake hands with customers. Both CARs and CSRs were given exercises designed to improve their listening skills and their powers of observation. All employees working where they could be seen by customers were ordered to refrain from smoking, drinking soda, and chewing gum on the job.

Although First National management anticipated that most of the increased emphasis

EXHIBIT 3
First National Bank: Position Description for Head Customer Service Representative
(Effective February 1988)

Function: Supervises the customer service representatives in the designated branch office, ensuring efficient operations and the highest-quality service to customers. Plays an active role in developing and maintaining good customer relations. Assists other branch personnel on request.

Responsibilities:

1. Supervises the CSRs in the branch.
   - Allocates work, coordinates work flow, reviews and revises work procedures.
   - Ensures teller area is adequately and efficiently staffed with well-trained, qualified personnel.
   - Assists CSRs with more complex transactions.
   - Resolves routine personnel problems, referring more complex situations to the customer service director.
   - Participates in decisions concerning performance appraisal, promotions, wage changes, transfers, and terminations of subordinate CSR staff.
2. Assumes responsibility for CSRs' money.
   - Buys and sells money in the vault, ensuring adequacy of branch currency and coin supply.
   - Ensures that CSRs and cash sheets are in balance.
   - Maintains necessary records, including daily branch journal and general ledger.
3. Accepts deposits and withdrawals by business customers at commercial window.
4. Operates teller window to provide customer services (see Responsibilities for Customer Service Representative).

EXHIBIT 4
First National Bank: Position Description for Customer Assistance Representative
(Effective February 1988)

Function: Provides services and guidance to customers/prospects seeking banking relationships or related information. Promotes and sells needed products and responds to special requests by existing customers.

Responsibilities:

1. Provides prompt, efficient, and friendly service to all customers and prospective customers.
   - Describes and sells bank services to customers/prospects who approach them directly or via referral from customer service reps or other bank personnel.
   - Answers customers' questions regarding bank services, hours, etc.
2. Identifies and responds to customers' needs.
   - Promotes and sells services and identifies any existing cross-sell opportunities.
   - Opens new accounts for individuals, businesses, and private organizations.
   - Prepares temporary checks and deposit slips for new checking/NOW accounts.
   - Sells checks and deposit slips.
   - Interviews and takes applications for and pays out on installment/charge card accounts and other credit-related products.
   - Certifies checks.
   - Handles stop payment requests.
   - Responds to telephone mail inquiries from customers or bank personnel.
   - Receives notification of name or address changes and takes necessary action.
   - Takes action on notification of lost passbooks, credit cards, ATM cards, collateral, and all other lost or stolen valuables.
   - Demonstrates automated teller machines to customers and assists with problems.
   - Coordinates closing of accounts and ascertains reasons.
3. Sells and services all retail products.
   - Advises customers and processes their applications for all products covered in CAR training programs and updates.
   - Initiates referrals to the appropriate department when a trust or corporate business need is identified.

EXHIBIT 5

First National Bank: Position Description for Customer Service Director (Effective February 1988)

Function: Supervises customer service representatives, and other staff as assigned to provide the most effective and profitable retail banking delivery system in the local marketplace. Supervises sales efforts and provides feedback to management concerning response to products and services by current and prospective banking customers. Communicates goals and results to those supervised and ensures operational standards are met in order to achieve outstanding customer service.

Responsibilities:

1. Supervises effective delivery of retail products.
- Selects, trains, and manages the customer service representatives and customer assistance representatives.
- Assigns duties and work schedules.
- Completes performance reviews.

2. Personally, and through those supervised, renders the highest level of professional and efficient customer service available in the local marketplace.
- Provides high level of service while implementing most efficient and customer-sensitive staffing schedules.
- Supervises all on-the-job programs within office.
- Ensures that outstanding customer service standards are achieved.
- Directs remedial programs for CSRs and CARs as necessary.

3. Develops retail sales effectiveness to the degree necessary to achieve market share objectives.
- Ensures that all CSRs and CARs possess comprehensive product knowledge.
- Directs coordinated cross-sell program within office at all times.
- Reports staff training needs to branch manager and/or regional training director.

4. Maintains operational adherence to standards.
- Oversees preparation of daily and monthly operational and sales reports.
- Estimates, approves, and coordinates branch cash needs in advance.
- Oversees ATM processing function.
- Handles or consults with CSRs/CARs on more complex transactions.
- Ensures clean and businesslike appearance of the branch facility.

5. Informs branch manager of customer response to products.
- Reports customer complaints and types of sales resistance encountered.
- Describes and summarizes reasons for account closings.

6. Communicates effectively the goals and results of the bank to those under supervision.
- Reduces office goals into format which translates to goals for each CSR or CAR.
- Reports sales and cross-sell results to all CSRs and CARs.
- Conduct sales- and service-oriented staff meetings with CSRs/CARs on a regular basis.
- Attends all scheduled customer service management meetings organized by regional office.

on selling would fall to the CARs, they also foresaw a limited selling role for the customer service reps, who would be expected to mention various products and facilities offered by the bank as they served customers at the teller window.

For instance, if a customer happened to mention a vacation, the CSR was supposed to mention traveler's checks; if the customer complained about bounced checks, the CSR should suggest speaking to a CAR about opening a personal line of credit that would provide an automatic overdraft protection; or if the customer mentioned investments, the CSR should refer him or her to a CAR who could provide information on money market accounts, certificates of deposit, or the First's discount brokerage service. All CSRs were supplied with their own business cards. When making a referral, they were expected to write the customer's name and the product of interest on the back of a card, give it to the customer, and send that individual to the customer assistance desks.

In an effort to motivate CSRs at the three test branches to sell specific financial products, the bank experimented with various incentive programs. The first involved cash bonuses for referrals to CARs that resulted in sale of specific products. During a one-month period, CSRs were offered a $50 bonus for each referral leading to a customer's opening a personal line of credit account; the CARs received a $20 bonus for each account they opened, regardless of whether or not it came as a referral or simply a walk-in. Eight such bonuses were paid to CSRs at Federal Square, with three each going to just two of the seven full-time CSRs, Jean Warshawski and Bruce Greenfield. Karen Mitchell was not among the recipients. However, this program was not renewed, since it was felt that there were other, more cost-effective means of marketing this product. In addition, Mr. Reeves, the customer service director, had reason to believe that Bruce Greenfield had colluded with one of the CARs, his girlfriend, to claim referrals which he had not, in fact, made. Another test branch reported similar suspicions of two of its CSRs.

A second promotion followed and was based upon allocating credits to the CSRs for successful referrals. The value of the credit varied according to the nature of the product — for instance, a cash machine card was worth 500 credits — and accumulated credits could be exchanged for merchandise gifts. This program was deemed ineffective and discontinued after three months. The basic problem seemed to be that the value of the gifts was too low in relation to the amount of effort required.

Other problems with these promotional schemes included lack of product knowledge on the part of the CSRs and time pressures when many customers were waiting in line to be served.

The bank had next turned to an approach which, in David Reeves' words, "used the stick rather than the carrot." All CSRs had traditionally been evaluated half-yearly on a variety of criteria, including accuracy, speed, quality of interactions with customers, punctuality of arrival for work, job attitudes, cooperation with other employees, and professional image. The evaluation process assigned a number of points to each criterion, with accuracy and speed being the most heavily weighted. In addition to appraisals by the customer service director and the branch manager, with input from the head CSR, the First had recently instituted a program of anonymous visits by what was popularly known as the "mystery client." Each CSR was visited at least once a quarter by a professional evaluator posing as a customer. This individual's appraisal of the CSR's appearance, performance, and attitude was included in the overall evaluation. The number of points scored by each CSR had a direct impact on merit pay raises and on selection for promotion to the head CSR position or to platform jobs.

To encourage improved product knowledge and "consultative selling" by CSRs, the evaluation process was revised to include points assigned for each individual's success in sales referrals. Under the new evaluation scheme, the maximum number of points assignable for effectiveness in making sales — directly or through referrals to CARs — amounted to 30 percent of the potential total score. Although CSR-initiated sales had risen significantly in the most recent half-year, Reeves sensed that morale had dropped among this group, in contrast to the CARs, whose enthusiasm and commitment had risen significantly. He had also noticed an increase in CSR errors. One CSR had quit, complaining about too much pressure.

Karen Mitchell

Under the old scoring system, Karen Mitchell had been the highest-scoring teller/CSR for four consecutive half-years. But after two half-years under the new system, her ranking had dropped to fourth out of the seven full-time tellers. The top-ranking CSR, Mary Bell, had been with the First for 16 years, but had declined repeated invitations to apply for a head teller position, saying that she was happy where she was, earning at the top of the CSR scale, and did not want "the extra worry and responsibility." Mitchell ranked first on all but one of the operationally related criteria (interactions with customers, where she ranked second), but sixth on selling effectiveness (*Exhibit 6*).

EXHIBIT 6
First National Bank: Summary of Performance Evaluation Scores for Customer Service Representative at Federal Square Branch for Two Half-Year Periods

CSR NAME[1]	LENGTH OF FULL-TIME BANK SERVICE	OPERATIONAL CRITERIA[2] (MAX: 70 POINTS)		SELLING EFFECTIVENESS[3] (MAX: 30 POINTS)		TOTAL SCORE	
		1st Half	*2nd Half*	*1st Half*	*2nd Half*	*1st Half*	*2nd Half*
Mary Bell	16 years, 10 months	65	64	16	20	81	84
Richard Dubois	2 years, 3 months	63	61	15	19	78	80
Bruce Greenfield	1 year 0 months	48	42	20	26	68	68
Karen Mitchell	3 years, 7 months	67	67	13	12	80	79
Sharon Ronsky	1 year, 4 months	53	55	8	9	61	64
Naomi Rubin	7 months	—	50	—	22	—	72
Jean Warshawski	2 years, 1 month	57	55	21	28	79	83

[1]Full-time CSRs only (part-time CSRs were evaluated separately).

[2]Totals based on sum of ratings against various criteria, including accuracy, work production, attendance and punctuality, personal appearance, organization of work, initiative, cooperation with others, problem-solving ability, and quality of interaction with customers.

[3]Points awarded for both direct sales by CSR (e.g., traveler's checks) and referral selling by CSR to CAR (e.g., ATM card, certificates of deposit, personal line of credit).

Costanzo and Reeves had spoken to Mitchell about her performance and expressed disappointment. Mitchell had told them, respectfully but firmly, that she saw the most important aspect of her job as giving customers fast, accurate, and courteous service.

I did try this selling thing (she told the two bank officers) but it just seemed to annoy people. Some said they were in a hurry and couldn't talk now, others looked at me as if I were slightly crazy to bring up the subject of a different bank service than the one they were currently transacting. And then, when you got the odd person who seemed interested, you could hear the other customers in the line grumbling about the slow service.

Really, the last straw was when I noticed on the computer that this woman had several thousand in her savings account so I suggested to her, just as the trainer had told us, that she could earn more interest if she opened a money market account. Well, she told me it was none of my business what she did with her money, and stomped off. Don't get me wrong, I love being able to help customers, and if they ask for my advice, I'll gladly tell them about what the bank has to offer.

Selecting a New Head CSR

Two weeks after this meeting, it was announced that the head CSR was leaving. The job entailed some supervision of the other CSRs (including allocation of work assignments and scheduling of part-time CSRs at busy periods or during employee vacations), consultation on — and, where possible, resolution of— any problems occurring at the teller stations, and handling of large cash deposits and withdrawals by local retailers (see position description in *Exhibit 3*). When not engaged on such tasks, the head CSR was expected to operate a regular teller window.

The pay scale for a head CSR ranged from $7.00 to $12.00 per hour, depending on qualifications, seniority, and branch size, as compared to a range of $5.40 to $9.00 per hour for

CSRs. The pay scale for CARs ranged from $6.20 to $10.50. Full-time employees (who were not unionized) worked a 40-hour week, including some evenings until 6:00 P.M. and certain Saturday mornings. Ms. Costanzo indicated that the pay scales were typical for banks in the Midwest, although the average CSR at the First was better qualified than those at smaller banks and therefore higher on the scale. Karen Mitchell was currently earning $7.80 per hour, reflecting her associate's degree, three and a half years' experience, and significant past merit increases. If promoted to head CSR, she would qualify for an initial rate of $9.50 an hour.

When applications for the positions closed, Mitchell was one of three candidates. The other two candidates were Jean Warshawski, 42, another CSR at the Federal Square branch, and Curtis Richter, 24, the head CSR of one of the First National Bank's smaller suburban branches, who was seeking more responsibility.

Warshawski was married with two sons in high school. She had started working as a part-time teller at Federal Square three years previously, switching to full-time work a year later in order, as she said, to put away some money for her boys' college education. Warshawski was a cheerful woman with a jolly laugh. She had a wonderful memory for people's names and Reeves had often seen her greeting customers on the street or in a restaurant during the lunch hour. Reviewing her evaluations over the past three years, Reeves noted that she had initially performed poorly on accuracy and at one point, while still a part-timer, had been put on probation because of frequent inaccuracies in the balance in her cash drawer at the end of the day. Although Reeves considered her much improved on this score, he still saw room for improvement. The customer service director had also had occasion to reprimand her for tardiness during the past year. Warshawski attributed this to health problems with her elder son who, she said, was now responding to treatment.

Both Reeves and Costanzo had observed Warshawski at work and agreed that her interactions with customers were exceptionally good, although she tended to be overly chatty

and was not as fast as Karen Mitchell. She seemed to have a natural ability to size up customers and to decide which ones were good prospects for a quick sales pitch on a specific financial product. Although slightly untidy in her personal appearance, she was very well organized in her work and was quick to help her fellow CSRs, especially new hires. She was currently earning $7.20 per hour as a CSR and would qualify for a rate of $9.10 as head CSR. In the most recent six months, Warshawski had ranked ahead of Mitchell as a result of being very successful in consultative selling (*Exhibit 6*).

Richter, the third candidate, was not working in one of the three test branches, so had not been exposed to the consultative selling program and its corresponding evaluation scheme. However, he had received excellent evaluations for his work in the First's small Longmeadow branch, where he had been employed for three years. A move to Federal Square would increase his earnings from $8.20 to $9.10 per hour. Reeves and Costanzo had interviewed Richter and considered him intelligent and personable. He had joined the bank after dropping out of college midway through his junior year, but had recently started taking evening courses in order to complete his degree. The Longmeadow branch was located in an older part of town, where commercial and retail activity were rather stagnant. The branch had not yet been renovated and had no ATMs, although there was an ATM accessible to First National customers one block away. Richter supervised three CSRs and reported directly to the branch manager, who spoke very highly of him. Since there were no CARs in this branch, Richter and another experienced CSR took turns to handle new accounts and loan or mortgage applications.

Costanzo and Reeves were troubled by the decision that faced them. Prior to the bank's shift in focus, Mitchell would have been the natural choice for the head CSR job which, in turn, could be a stepping stone to further promotions, including customer assistance representative, customer service director, and, eventually, manager of a small branch or a management position in the head office.

Mitchell had told her superiors that she was interested in making a career in banking and that she was eager to take on further responsibilities.

Compounding the problem was the fact that the three branches testing the new customer service program had just completed a full year of the test. Costanzo knew that sales and profits were up significantly at all three branches, relative to the bank's performance as a whole. She anticipated that top management would want to extend the program systemwide after making any modifications that seemed desirable.

Nordstrom Stores

SUSAN C. FALUDI

*A department store chain, famed for its exceptional service to
customers, faces problems when a state agency finds that the
company is violating the law by failing to pay employees for a
variety of service-related duties. Retail sales clerks claim that
they face unreasonable pressure to meet selling quotas and work
overtime without extra pay.*

SEATTLE — Recently, a too-thin woman
walked into employment counselor Alice
Snyder's office here, slumped in a chair and
burst into tears. "I know this is going to sound
strange," Ms. Snyder recalls the woman saying,
"but I'm sure they're going to fire me." Never
mind that she had worked for weeks without
a day off, pulled 15-hour shifts without a break
and stockpiled stacks of service awards and
customer thank-you letters. None of this mat-
tered. She missed her sales quota and now
management was questioning her "commitment" to the company.

She knew her days were numbered.

Ordinarily, Alice Snyder might classify such
thinking as paranoid. But not in this case:
The woman is a salesclerk at Nordstrom.

"You're not alone," Ms. Snyder says she
told the woman. "You're the fourth person
from that store I've seen this week." Nervous
"Nordies," as they call themselves, have limped
through her office so regularly — suffering
from ulcers, colitis, hives and hand tremors —
that Ms. Snyder finally went to speak with
Nordstrom Inc.'s personnel office at the company's headquarters here. She says a manager
insisted the company was one happy "family,"
then briskly showed her the door.

Pressure to Perform

But if this prospering retailer is a family,
then reports from some of the "children" suggest it's a dysfunctional one. The retailer, re-
nowned for pampering its customers, expects

---

its salesclerks to work many hours without pay in an environment of constant pressure and harassment that incites employees to prey on each other, according to nearly 500 complaints filed with the workers' union and interviews with several dozen employees in stores from Seattle to Los Angeles.

Last Thursday, a three-month investigation by the Washington state Department of Labor & Industries reached similar conclusions: The agency found the company systematically violated state law by failing to pay employees for a variety of duties, from delivering merchandise to inventory work, and by short-changing employees on overtime pay. The agency ordered Nordstrom to pay back wages — which the union estimates at $30 million to $40 million — or face possible legal action. (State authorities wouldn't confirm the union's estimate.)

Large Claim

"We're looking at what is likely to be the highest wage claim in the history of the state," says Mark McDermott, the agency's assistant director for employment standards. "These are employment-practice patterns the company engaged in, not isolated incidents."

Nordstrom's working conditions are the flip side of the company's phenomenal success as a retailer. In the past decade, low labor costs and a system that compels employees to compete for their paychecks have generally helped generate big earnings, a soaring stock price and sales per square foot that are the envy of the industry. Though the company says it expects to report a drop in profit for its fiscal year ended Jan. 31, its overall success in recent years has spurred the retailer to undertake a big, national expansion.

Nordstrom's customers have been a major beneficiary of the exceptional service the department store chain demands. And, no doubt, thousands of salespeople have thrived in the Darwinian struggle on the sales floor. Pat McCarthy, a longtime salesman in the flagship store's men's clothing department, is one of them. He's turned two decades of cultivating customers into commissions that yield an $80,000-plus yearly salary. "It's really a people

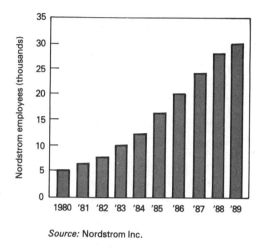

Nordstrom Employees

Source: Nordstrom Inc.

job, which I love," says Mr. McCarthy. "Every year my sales have gotten progressively better."

But for thousands of other Nordstrom employees, the working arrangements aren't so congenial. Just as retail chains of all kinds — from Bloomingdale's to Macy's — are rushing to duplicate the Nordstrom commission system, the stories of unhappiness at the company are spreading.

Salespeople were reluctant to tell their story until recently, when the union representing Nordstrom workers in the Seattle area began looking into complaints that employees are told to punch out on their timeclock before turning to the many "non-sell" duties — such as stock work and deliveries to customers. Otherwise, they were warned, the hours would dilute their critical sales-per-hour performance. A low "SPH" is grounds for dismissal.

The union, the United Food and Commercial Workers, is in the midst of contract negotiations with five Nordstrom stores in the Seattle area and has obviously been scouting for damaging data. Of Nordstrom's 30,000 employees nationwide, only 1,500 are unionized, and the union is eager to win more members and boost its influence. When union leaders began an informal inquiry into working conditions, they say they struck a mother lode of discontent, with possibly big ramifications for Nordstrom. "Unionization of other stores easily could happen as an offshoot of these developments," says Joe Peterson, president of local 1001 of the union.

Within two months, the union had received certified letters from hundreds of Nordstrom employees who have worked, on average, eight to 10 hours a week "off the clock." So many complaints came in, the union set up an 800 hotline to handle them all.

Nordstrom management says it will study the state's report and pay wage claims it considers legitimate. "We haven't seen any complaints" from the union says Jim Nordstrom, co-chairman of the company with his brother John and cousin Bruce. He dismisses the labor board's findings as "simple record-keeping stuff" and the union's stack of claims as "a bargaining ploy." If employees are working without pay, breaks or days off, then it's "isolated" or by "choice," he says.

"A lot of them say, 'I want to work every day.' I have as many people thank us for letting them work all these hours as complain." In fact, Jim Nordstrom suspects employees aren't putting in as much time as they might. "I think people don't put in enough hours during the buy time," he says. "We need to work harder."

Nordstrom's incentives, some employees say, tend to be more stick than carrot. While good customer service is rewarded with cheers at company meetings, occasional $5, $10 and $100 bonuses or "All-Star" honors, a steady flow of threatening management memos seems to be the preferred motivational tool. One Aug. 29, 1989 memo, issued by a Nordstrom cosmetics manager in a California store, is typical. It set a long list of goals for the cosmetics counters and made clear that, "In the next 60 days if any of these areas are not met to our expectations you will be terminated." Another manager's memo reminds employees that it is considered "a lot" to call in sick once every three months and will bring into "question your dedication."

Stoking the Volume

"It reminds me of a cult the way they program you to devote your life to Nordstrom," says Cherie Validi, a salesperson in the women's clothing department who has spent her share of days off making home deliveries and attending Nordstrom's pep rallies, where blond bathing beauties prance on stage, chanting "Vol-ume! Vol-ume!" "Granted, the customer gets treated like a hundred bucks. And Nordstrom gets rich off it. So nobody loses — except the employee," she says.

Ms. Validi, one of the top saleswomen in her department, came out the loser herself recently when she received a $100 paycheck for two weeks of work. Why? The commission on a customer's $6,000 return was deducted from her wages, standard practice at Nordstrom. Ms. Validi complained that the sale wasn't hers, that it took place on a day she didn't work. But the company held firm.

Nordstrom insists the system works. It says that employees get one of the highest base pay rates in the industry — as much as $10 an hour — and especially industrious employees can make as much as $80,000 a year. The company also says it only promotes from within and, under its corporate policy of decentralization, managers have unusual freedom to make decisions. "A lot of what comes out makes it sound like we're slave drivers," says Jim Nordstrom, or "Mr. Jim," as he is called by his employees. "If we were that kind of company, they wouldn't smile, they wouldn't work that hard. Our people smile because they want to."

But employees say Nordstrom's high base pay isn't much comfort. Workers only receive base pay if they don't sell enough to qualify for commission — and if they miss that sales quota several times, they're fired. Moreover, of the 1,500 salespeople in the union, the company lists only seven as having made more than $40,000 last year. (Nordstrom won't reveal the number for its roughly 20,000 non-union salespeople, but says union and non-union employees make an average of $20,000 to $24,000 a year. The national average, for all retail salesclerks, is $12,000 a year.)

Be Happy

Even the smiles aren't necessarily a reliable gauge of employee sentiment. Nordstrom periodically dispatches "Secret Shoppers," people hired to dress up as customers, to check on workers' demeanor. A frown can wind up as a demerit in an employee file. The company also encourages Smile Contests. "They would go around and take pictures of whoever smiled the most" and then hang the photos in the lunchrrom, recalls Andrea Barton, who worked for three years at a Nordstrom cosmetics counter in Seattle; she says she lost 20 pounds in the process. "I'd look at those pictures and go, 'Boy, some day I hope I'm up here.'" She groans. "I mean, the way I got when I was [working] there, it's just sickening."

She is only one of the more than 30 Nordstrom veterans, both current and former employees, who voiced such sentiments in interviews. Here are a few of their stories:

A divorced California homemaker who returned to the job market at 40, Patty Bemis joined Nordstrom in 1981, lured by the promise of a bigger income and the "status" of induction in the Nordie elite. She stayed for eight years.

"They came to me," she recalls of the Nordstrom recruiters. "I was working at The Broadway as Estee Lauder's counter manager and they said they had heard I had wonderful sales figures." Ms. Bemis was thrilled. "We'd all heard Nordstrom was the place to work. They told me how I would double my wages. They painted a great picture and I fell right into it."

She soon found herself working progressively harder — for less money and amid more fear.

"The managers were these little tin gods, always grilling you about your sales," she recalls. "You felt like your job was constantly in jeopardy. They'd write you up for anything, being sick, the way you dressed." Once, she had to get a doctor's note so she wouldn't get in trouble for wearing low-heel shoes to work. Sufficiently cowed, she reported to work even when she had strep throat.

Worn down by the pressure, "the girls around me were dropping like flies," she says. "Everyone was always in tears. You feel like an absolute nothing working for them."

Taking Out the Trash

Ms. Bemis was consistently one of her department's top sellers, but some years she only made $18,000, far below what she had expected she would earn. She won a company-wide sales contest, and received "a pair of PJs," she recalls. "Whoopie-doo!" And she logged many unpaid hours, delivering cosmetics to customers and unpacking hundreds of boxes of makeup. The department rarely had more than one stock person and, in some of the stores, the salesclerks are expected to empty the trash. Jim Nordstrom explains: "Yes, we're always cutting back on stock people." He adds: "It may have happened that some people were asked to pitch in" and carry out the trash. "That would be great if that happened. If people don't want to, then obviously some people don't want to work hard."

Ms. Bemis recalled that "working off the clock was just standard," crucial to elevating sales per hour. "In the end, really serving the customer, being an All-Star, meant nothing; if you had low sales per hour, you were forced out."

During a big Clinique sale, Ms. Bemis says she worked 12 and 15 hour shifts for a number of days without overtime pay or a day off. On the drive home at 10:30 on the tenth night, she passed out at the wheel and slammed into the freeway's center divider, she says. While she was at home recovering from head injuries, she recalls, "The manager kept calling me and saying, 'Patty, we can't hold your job much longer.'" Her doctor told her she should stay out a few more weeks but she didn't dare. "Now, I know I have all these rights. But at the time all I knew was I had to have that job."

She finally left last spring. "I just couldn't take it anymore — the constant demands, the grueling hours. I just said one day, life's too short." She took a sales post at Scandia Down Shops, where she says she makes $400 more a month than at Nordstrom. "And I can sleep at night."

A Broken Clock

The first time Lori Lucas came to one of the many "mandatory" Saturday morning department meetings and saw the sign —"Do Not Punch the Clock"— she assumed the managers were telling the truth when they said the clock was temporarily out of order. But as weeks went by, she discovered the clock was always "broken" or the timecards were just missing.

Finally, she and several other employees just marked the hours down on their timecard manually. She and another employee recall that their manager whited-out the hours and accused the two of not being "team players." The employees took the tampered timecards to the California labor board. In response to the state agency's inquiry, the company reimbursed four employees for the time, according to a notification the company filed with the labor board.

The department meetings "were unbelievable," Ms. Lucas recalls. "There you'd be at seven in the morning and they had all these security guards dressed up like the California Raisins, with plastic garbage bags stuffed with M&Ms around their midriffs. And all you can hear is people chanting, "We're number one!' and 'You want to do it for Nordstrom.' Finally I went up to the store manager and said 'What is this all about?' and she said, 'You are here to learn the Nordstrom Way.'"

The Nordstrom Way involved an endless round of contests ("Who Looks More Nordstrom" was a popular one, intended to encourage employees to shop at the stores) and the daily recital of "affirmations" ("I only sell multiples," was one chanted by salespeople). And the Nordstrom Way, Ms. Lucas discovered, meant working for free. "My manager would say, 'You go clock out and come down and we'll talk.' That was her little trick way of saying there's non-sell work to do." Ms. Lucas's manager declines to comment.

Like most salesclerks at Nordstrom, Ms. Lucas also had daily quotas of thank-you letters to write, and monthly customer-service "books" to generate — photo albums that are supposed to be filled with letters from grateful customers. ("People would get so desperate they would have their friends and relatives write fake letters for them," Petra Rousu, a 10-year salesclerk veteran, recalls.) Such duties, Ms. Lucas says, were supposed to be tackled only after hours. "I'd be up til 3 a.m., doing my letters, and doing my manager's books," she says. "Before you know it, your whole life is

Nordstrom. But you couldn't complain, because then your manager would schedule you for the bad hours, your sales per hour would fall and next thing you know, you're out the door."

The pressure eventually gave Ms. Lucas an ulcer, she says. One day, after working 22 days without a day off, she demanded a lunch break. On her hour off, she applied for and got a new job elsewhere and gave notice as soon as she returned. "I remember thinking, I'm making less than $20,000 a year. Why am I killing myself? Nordstrom was the most unfair place I ever worked."

Staying on Top

Every pay period, the Nordies gather around the bulletin board in the back room to view the chart. It ranks employees by sales per hour, and woe to anyone whose name falls below the red line.

Over the years, the need to stay above the line has inspired an ingenious set of scams and predatory maneuvers on the sales floor, some employees assert. "Sharking," as it's called, is so rampant that at one pep rally, the saleswomen did a skit to the music from "Jaws" and presented a shark mask to an employee they considered particularly conniving.

Some Nordies boost their sales per hour by hogging the register and taking all the "walk-ups," or customers who haven't been helped, workers say. Some have been known to cut a deal with the few non-commission cashiers on the floor, who then ring up sales on the employee's identification number. Others get their rival's number and use it when accepting returns.

When all else fails, there's one way to push your name up the list: Bump off the number-one seller.

For nearly two years, Cindy Nelson had stayed on top of the chart in one of the Bellevue, Wash., stores. She was on her way to making "Pacesetter" again — a prestigious title bestowed upon the employees with the top sales. A clique of salesclerks on the floor — led by numbers two and three on the charts —

held a pow-wow one day, decided that Ms. Nelson must be stealing their sales and vowed to have her "watched," according to court depositions that later became part of a suit filed by Ms. Nelson against Nordstrom in Bellevue, Wash.

On September 29, 1986, Cindy Nelson reported for work and was immediately whisked into the personnel office. The department manager had before her five notes of complaint from the salesclerks, all unsigned, which claimed Ms. Nelson had been stealing sales.

Due Process

Ms. Nelson asked to inspect the sales receipts in question and confront her accusers, but the manager, Rhoda Eakes, refused. "I just didn't feel that it was any of her business," Ms. Eakes explained later in a deposition. Then she told Ms. Nelson that she was fired. (All of the managers and employees involved in Ms. Nelson's firing declined comment, referring queries to Mr. Nordstrom, who said, "That gal wasn't a good employee.")

"I was totally stunned," recalls Ms. Nelson, who had a stack of customer-service citations in her file and had been told she was about to make manager. She was also, up until then, "your 100-percent gung-ho Nordie. This whole time I thought I was going to be this great Nordstrom person and now I was nothing, a nobody. I became an emotional wreck."

She tried applying to other Nordstrom stores but was repeatedly rejected. Finally, she took a job in a small dress shop — and filed suit. Last October, a King County Superior Court jury awarded her $180,000 in damages. The company and Ms. Nelson later settled out of court for an undisclosed sum.

In Ms. Nelson's court case, Nordstom's Achilles heel proved to be its employee handbook, which outlined the terms and procedures for warning and firing employees. The company has subsequently replaced the 20-page rulebook with a one-page sheet, and one rule: "Use your good judgment in all situations," it says.

Jim Nordstrom says management chose to rewrite the manual after receiving a raft of lawsuits from ex-employees. "Our wrongful termination problems have gone way down since we got rid of that darn handbook," he says.

That Special Look

Part of becoming a Nordie, employees say, involves acquiring a certain look. Lupe Sakagawa, a top saleswoman, recalls that on her first day on the job, her manager strong-armed her into buying $1,400 of the "right" clothes — all from the department. But that wasn't enough: The store manager then called her in and told her: "Correct your accent." Ms. Sakagawa is Mexican. "It was very hard for me to prove myself," she says, "because of that image of the Nordstrom Girl — blonde hair, young and cute."

For years, moreover, minority leaders in Seattle have complained of the company's failure to hire and promote blacks. In 1987, after the company was hit with seven discrimination complaints filed with the Equal Employment Opportunity Commission, Nordstrom hired a consulting firm to rebut the charges. But the consultant's confidential report — subsequently leaked — turned out to be a stinging attack on Nordstrom's "band-aid approach" to affirmative action. "The current lack of definitive personnel policies and procedures...perpetuates a system of institutional racism," the report said, "and has had little utility in preventing previous overt racist acts."

Since then, Jim Nordstrom says, the company has hired a black human resources officer and "our minority numbers are outstanding." But he declines to reveal them. Charles Dudley, the human resource officer, won't supply the statistics either: "You'll have to talk to Mr. Jim about that," he says. He did confirm that no company vice presidents are black or Hispanic.

Then there's the case of Sean Mulholland, a salesman who says he paid the price for failing to fit another aspect of the "Nordstrom image." He is gay.

In 1986, Mr. Mulholland started working in the men's clothing department in the Alderwood, Wash., store. He was careful to keep his private life a secret. A Nordie true believer, Mr. Mulholland accumulated a dozen company awards and a sales rating that never fell below No. 3 on the charts, according to records he has saved. "To me, Nordstrom was the Golden Fleece," he says. "I was so proud to work there. I strived to be what they wanted."

Raining Dollars

His faith remained unshaken in spite of some of the company's more bizarre rituals, like the time employees were sent outside for a "surprise." On the roof, a Nordie tossed down $1 bills tied in yellow ribbons. Mr. Mulholland recalls watching, dumbfounded, as fellow clerks scrambled for the cash. "I got this picture in my head: peasants groveling for the loaves of bread from the castle," he says.

But Mr. Mulholland stuck by the company until soon after he discovered he had AIDS. He told no one at the store about his illness. He had heard the jokes around the store about "fag" customers —"don't shake their hands."

When Mr. Mulholland contracted a lung infection, he had to call in sick. His manager phoned him repeatedly at home and demanded an explanation. After four days, Mr. Mulholland reported to work. He was at once summoned to personnel.

"They just dug into me, 'Why were you sick?' 'Where's your doctor's excuse?'" He told them he had an upper respiratory infection, but still they pressed him, he says.

"Finally I broke down crying. As a last resort to save my job, I told them I had AIDS," he says. Honesty backfired. The manager sent him home and told him to stay there. When he tried to return, he says, she told him the company had filled his job and there were no openings.

Nordstrom spokeswoman Kellie Tormey maintains that Mr. Mulholland "asked to leave. It was entirely his choice." Nordstrom made "numerous attempts to find something else for him, but he never once followed up on these opportunities."

But Mr. Mulholland has saved copies of the rejection letters he received from Nordstrom

managers as he attempted, 16 times in the course of the ensuing year and a half, to apply for job postings at four Nordstrom stores in the area. He was always turned away. "Finally I got the picture. They just cut the chain. One day I'm great, the next day I'm garbage."

Valuing Team Spirit

Nordstrom officials brush aside such stories as the gripes of a few bad seeds. "Our people development is probably the most significant advantage our company has," Ms. Tormey says. "If you speak to employees in the stores, you'll see that it's a company that really values the team spirit. But an attempt to walk in the stores and do that is resisted. Ms. Tormey explains: "If you want to interview someone, we need to know ahead of time. That's just one of the things we're sensitive to." Finally, the public relations office picks a slate of employees for interviews. Kathleen Sargent is one of them.

"It's a feeling, it's family," Ms. Sargent says enthusiastically, as she settles into a vinyl chair in the employee cafeteria. A public relations official sits at her side.

"Sure, during the busy seasons, you do work six to seven days a week," Ms. Sargent says. "But being in the store with the Christmas tree here, you create your own memories." Ms. Sargent, who has worked for Nordstrom in Seattle for seven years, says she doesn't mind working for free. "When I go home and do follow-ups or write thank-yous, I think it's inappropriate to be charging the company for that."

It turns out that Ms. Sargent is also the goddaughter of Anne Nordstrom, Bruce Nordstrom's sister. "I don't see what that has to do with anything," Ms. Sargent says, when she is asked about it later. "I'm sure the advertising people didn't even know that when they they picked me to talk to the press."

At the San Francisco store, another set of company-approved employees testify to the company's virtues. "Here at Nordstrom, I feel I can be the best that I can be," says Doris Quiros, a salesperson in the women's sportswear department. While other retailers "give you a big book of rules, when I came here, Nordstrom gave me one with only one rule:

Use your best judgment. That's because they want me to be my own boss."

In the women's shoes department, Tim Snow, a former waiter, says people are impressed now when they learn where he works. "You can be at the grocery store and you show them your ID card they'll start right off on how much they love to shop there."

The reasons people do love to shop at Nordstrom are plainly evident one recent Saturday afternoon in Mr. Snow's department. Sitar and tabla players serenade shoppers with soothing music as salesclerks proffer Nordstrom's much-vaunted service. But the scene isn't nearly so genteel back in the stockroom, where harried employees clang up and down metal stairs, balancing towers of shoeboxes. Lining the walls are the ubiquitous performance charts and sales contests. "Make Your Goal," instructs one sign. "Don't Let Us Down!" says another. "Be a Top Dog Pacesetter! Go for the Golden Milk-bones!!" says a third. One salesclerk stops for a second to eye a visitor taking notes. Finally she asks, only half-joking, "Are you with the Nordstrom Secret Service?"

PART VII
The Human Dimension in Services Management

Development of a Personnel Selection System for Service Jobs

BENJAMIN SCHNEIDER
DANIEL SCHECHTER

A major requirement for quality service delivery is having effective service personnel in place. The chapter proposes a six-step system for selecting employees who possess the right service inclinations and competencies and are likely to remain on the job.

INTRODUCTION

Research and theory about service have focused on services marketing and/or the management of service organizations. The literature has been characterized by the development of models for understanding how services differ from goods and, thus, how service organizations may need to be organized and/or managed differently than goods-producing organizations to achieve effectiveness (Bowen and Schneider 1988; Parasuraman, Zeithaml, and Berry 1985).

Services marketing scholars and practitioners have made some impressive progress in identifying some specific issues consumers consider in the evaluation of service quality (Parasuraman, Zeithaml, and Berry 1986). In contrast, specification of the management and organizational design issues requiring attention to facilitate the delivery of excellent service quality has lagged. Thus, although a number of books exists detailing some broad categories of issues that organizations must attend to in managing the service encounter (Czepiel, Solomon, and Suprenant 1985; Lovelock 1988; Normann 1984), little practical help is provided with respect to the actual steps required to make changes happen.

Obviously, any one of a number of organizational issues might serve as a focus of organizational change. For example, organizations might focus on appraisal and reward systems (Kerr 1988), on training programs (Goldstein 1986), on the creation of climate or culture (Schein 1985; Schneider 1987a), or any of the issues conceptually related to ultimate service effectiveness. One or all of these topics would make for an interesting chapter. This chapter, however, focuses on a topic almost nonexistent in the literature on service and service organizations — personnel selection.

PERSONNEL SELECTION AND SERVICES MARKETING

Much literature on services marketing and the design of service organizations emphasizes the importance of the quality of the people delivering service (e.g., Berry, Parasuraman, and Zeithaml 1988). These literatures include ideas about the basic service inclination of employees and the importance of basic competencies. Service inclinations refer to individuals' interests in doing service-related work; the term *competencies* refers to the various skills and knowledge necessary to be effective in this type of work.

Exactly how or when employees acquire the inclinations and competencies is usually unspecified. Indeed, it is sometimes assumed that all employees have these inclinations (often through self-selection into these jobs) and that it is inhibitive managerial practices that keep employees from providing excellent service (Schneider and Bowen 1985).

While the majority of service organization employees may have this service inclination, some employees clearly have more than others. This has been demonstrated by Hogan, Hogan, and Busch (1984) who showed that service effectiveness is correlated with having service-oriented personality characteristics (e.g., helpfulness, thoughtfulness, etc.). Perhaps most interesting in the Hogan, Hogan, and Busch research was the fact that the people studied were all applicants for a service job at the same organization. It is safe to conclude, then, that not all applicants for a service job are equally inclined toward providing excellent service.

Beyond the issue of inclination to provide service is the question of service competencies. As with service inclinations, it seems clear that people are differentially competent in their ability to deliver, or in their ability to learn to deliver, excellent service. In a typical applicant pool for a service position, one might expect even *more* variability in service-related skills than inclinations or interests in doing service work.

Parasuraman, Zeithaml, and Berry (1986) have clearly shown that service quality is multidimensional in nature; it follows that the delivery of excellent service requires people who are multidimensional in their service inclinations and competencies. Thus, because service quality is perceived by customers along many dimensions (e.g., courtesy, reliability, responsiveness, and so forth), service providers must demonstrate inclinations toward and competencies in these areas to be effective in meeting customer expectations.

The present chapter is about selecting employees who are service oriented both in terms of their inclinations and their competencies. The chapter is based on a number of premises:

1. An organization can be only as effective as the typical people in it; this is especially true in organizations that require interdependent behavior for achieving organizational goals (Bass 1982). This is so because individual excellence cannot compensate for poor performers when it takes a team effort to achieve success. Most service organizations, especially consumer service organizations, require interdependent behavior for effectiveness, as evidenced in Albrecht and Zemke's (1985) service "cycle" diagnostic model. Furthermore, given the highly interactive nature of service "production," often no *opportunity* exists to compensate for poor service.

2. An organization's climate or culture is a function of the kind of people who predominate there (Schneider 1987b). Therefore, it will be difficult to find an organization that is service-oriented if the modal interests of workers are not in service-related work (i.e., the predominant interests are in isolated work or the predominating competencies are

in analytic or mathematical areas). Indeed, service-related inclinations and competencies, like other inclinations and competencies, appear to be relatively stable individual attributes. The dramatic, stable effects of collective employee attributes have some depressing potential consequences for those interested in effecting organizational change. It suggests that some organizations may find it extremely difficult, if not impossible, to create a (service) climate without radically changing the composition of their work force.

3.   The best predictor of future behavior is past behavior — this principle argues for the selection of people based on information about, and optimally observation of, behaviors essential to the provision of quality service.

These are the fundamental premises that have led to emphasis on the role of selection in achieving organizational effectivness (Schneider 1987b; Schnieder and Schmitt 1986). Selection is *not* the only crucial issue for organizational effectiveness. However, when an organization makes initial staffing decisions that yield people with the appropriate competencies and service inclinations, the goal of service excellence will be more easily achieved. People are likely to learn more quickly and effectively, to function more on their own (important in consumer service facilities because of the interactive "real-time" nature of service production and service delivery), to stay longer in the service position, and to contribute to the kind of climate important for service excellence (Schneider and Bowen 1985).

DESIGNING A SERVICE-ORIENTED SELECTION PROCESS

Six steps comprise the design of any selection process:

1.   *Task analysis* — identifying the specific tasks accomplished by job incumbents.

2.   *Personal attributes analysis* — identifying the inclinations and competencies required to do and enjoy the tasks *and* identify which must be present when the person is hired (as compared with those for which people can be trained).

3.   *Selection system design strategy* — selecting existing and/or building new selection procedures to assess the inclinations and competencies required on day one of the new hire's tenure. The eventual procedures are chosen based on their anticipated contribution to the achievement of the selection program's objectives.

Optimally, multiple procedures relevant to each objective are included to increase the reliability of the selection process. Where this is the case, a multiple hurdle approach in which early stages screen out the candidates with the least potential for success is often effective.

Legally and practically, the selection procedures chosen or built must focus heavily on the most important skills and inclinations — the ones shown in the job analysis to be critical for job performance.

4.   *Train people to use the selection processes and pilot them* — this step provides for uniformity in administration of each selection procedure (e.g., interview or job simulation). It also is an opportunity to assess the logistical feasibility of the procedures.

5.   *Assess systems logistics and political feasibility* — this should occur throughout the development of the selection process, for a new selection process is, in fact, a major organizational intervention. This assessment involves the consideration of any practical implementation constraints, including politically sensitive areas that may need high levels of internal support before implementation. Examples might include a legal department's obvious concern over the use of paper and pencil tests, employee fears that job analysis is really designed to eliminate jobs, identification of those who will monitor and manage the selection process, or geographical dispersion of the units for which hiring decisions need to be made.

6.   *Make the system operational and begin tracking results* — this step is called validation and evaluates how well the selection system performs against important criteria of effectiveness. In the present case these criteria include effective job performance and retention on the job for at least one year. The

logic for job performance is straightforward but an explanation of retention as an important issue may be useful.

Research (Schneider and Bowen 1985) suggests that organizations in which employee turnover is low are also organizations in which customers report they receive superior service. In fact, Schneider and Bowen demonstrated that where employee turnover intentions are high, *customer* account retention intentions are low. It is extremely important for service organizations to have relatively low turnover rates, especially when compared to potential competitors.

A brief overview of each of these steps for a telephone sales and service job follows. The job is typically filled by young people or returning homemakers who possess few marketable skills (e.g., computer programming) or knowledge (e.g., legal or accounting knowledge).

TASK ANALYSIS

The following steps isolate task components of jobs:

1. Choose random samples of incumbents in groups of four to six people and hold a meeting to discuss (1) the goals of the job and (2) the tasks that need to be accomplished for the goals to be met. Incumbents are used based on a finding by job analysts that if one wants to know what gets done on a job, the people who do it should be asked. Several first-line supervisory groups are also interviewed to provide a broader view of the important goals and tasks.

2. Observe the work being done to gather any tasks that may have been missed and to gain increased understanding of the job and job context.

3. Prepare a task survey for all incumbents to complete. This will be used to gather quantitative job information; incumbents report on the criticality/importance of each task and the relative amount of time they spend at each task.

Table 1 shows excerpts of some specific tasks included in the survey. The tasks listed in Table 1 were the twenty most critical tasks as rated by job incumbents. Those twenty tasks were statistically analyzed to reveal their underlying dimensions. This statistical procedure, technically called principal components factor analysis, yielded the four factors identified in Table 1.

These factors are called Attention to Detail (Detail), Sensitivity, Informing Customers (Informs), and Courtesy. These same twenty task statements were used in the present study as the basis for the measure of effectiveness. Thus, supervisors were asked, approximately one year after the new employees were hired, to complete the appraisal of how effectively the newcomers were performing these twenty critical tasks. Obviously, the challenge for the selection procedure is to predict these ratings (and retention, as mentioned earlier).

PERSONAL ATTRIBUTES ANALYSIS

The compiled task analysis results are used as input to help discover the kinds of personal attributes the job requires. The following steps are taken to identify these attributes:

1. In group meetings (ranging in size from six to twelve participants), supervisors and managers are asked to review the important job tasks and report the kinds of attributes incumbents must have to do these tasks.

2. An inventory of the attributes emerging from these sessions is created and supervisors make a series of ratings for each. These ratings include:
   - the importance of possessing each attribute for effective job performance
   - the degree to which possession of the competency is required the first day on the job
   - how difficult it is to acquire the competency if it is not present the first day on the job

These ratings, in combination, provide the data required to identify which attributes need to be focused on at selection — versus those more efficiently or effectively gained through training, for example.

Table 2 presents examples of some categories of the important competencies identified as being necessary for effective task performance.

Although only competencies are listed in Table 2, in actuality the measurement of work-related inclinations follows closely from

TABLE 1

Critical Tasks for the Job Identified in the Task Analysis

Task	Factor			
	I	*II*	*III*	*IV*
1. Guides customer through questions.	.39	.36	.58	.33
2. Compiles information to prepare cost quotations.	.66*	.25	.45	.22
3. Determines present situation.	.49	.39	.56	.24
4. Obtains supervisor authorization.	.68	.27	−.06	.44
5. Uses appropriate sources for cost quotes.	.74*	.30	.28	.09
6. Explains contract to applicant.	.30	.48	.60	.29
7. Identifies customers' needs.	.35	.67*	.39	.28
8. Solves service problems.	.38	.77*	.25	.22
9. Calms distressed callers.	.31	.81*	.27	.16
10. Completes documents while on phone.	.71*	.25	.26	.12
11. Adjusts language to customer.	.29	.67*	.30	.35
12. Gives own name and thanks customer.	.18	.30	.23	.82*
13. Uses customers' name.	.10	.23	.36	.80*
14. Gives complete information.	.52	.36	.50	.30
15. Reviews own paperwork.	.69*	.15	.38	.07
16. Explains contract and assists customer.	.32	.29	.72*	.19
17. Informs customers to check and complete application in mail.	.34	.22	.62*	.37
18. Establishes customer rapport.	.24	.61	.42	.41
19. Answers customer questions.	.30	.42	.68*	.22
20. Reviews memos on changes and updates.	.70*	.31	.32	.08

Note: Factor I = Detail; Factor II = Sensitivity; Factor III = Informs; Factor IV = Courtesy. Factor loadings with an asterisk (*) were scored as that factor in later analyses as the performance data. Sample size for this analysis was $N = 531$.

the critical skills identified and used on the job. Thus, in the service selection research, the authors operationally define service inclination as interest in carrying out activities using the skills and abilities required by the tasks of the job. More detail about how these inclinations and competencies are assessed is provided in the next section.

CHOOSING AND DESIGNING PROCEDURES

The choice and design of selection procedures is where the selection researcher really gets to assess his or her skills as a psychologist, playwright, and director! The challenge is to choose and/or create a series of procedures that permit an assessment of the degree to which job candidates possess the attributes required by the job. The procedures must not only assess the attributes identified, but must also be such that some group or groups in the

organization (e.g., supervisors or managers) can be trained to administer the procedures. Also, the total selection process should appear to candidates to be relevant for the job.

Fortunately, all of these considerations are served when selection procedures are chosen that mirror the important characteristics of the job. Thus, interactive selection procedures are most appropriate for positions in which effectiveness is heavily dependent on interaction with others. Aptitude testing is appropriate when the job requires the ability to learn highly technical information and/or procedures related to the aptitude.

Perhaps the most useful way to demonstrate the process is to describe some of the procedures selected and designed for the sales and service job.

Basic Competencies

Basic reading and arithmetic competencies were assessed with two paper and pencil tests

TABLE 2

Examples of Competencies Required for a Sales and Service Job

1. *Persuasion* — Ability to influence the opinions and actions of others through skillful use of information

2. *Comprehension and memory* — Ability to understand the written and spoken language of others; skilled at listening; ability to learn, understand, and remember large amounts of facts, rules and procedures, and codes.

3. *Reasoning* — Ability to apply learned rules and procedures, use judgment, combine pieces of information, and make decisions.

4. *Social sensitivity* — Ability to act enthusiastically in interpersonal situations. Involves skillful adjusting of behavior to fit demands of a call and requires figuring out how others are likely to act or react. Involves the skillful use of control and assertion.

5. *Understandability* — Ability to express oneself through written and/or spoken language so that others will understand.

6. *Clerical speed and accuracy* — Ability to quickly and accurately look up, write down, and/or key in facts, codes, data, numbers, and so forth that are heard, looked up, or already in memory.

7. *Dealing with pressure* — Ability to act and react without losing effectiveness given the very strong requirements on rapid, efficient, and courteous sales and service.

that matched the level of requirements in the job. This match was accomplished by careful review of numerous off-the-shelf tests for a fit to the job. In particular, the arithmetic test was such that applicants had to respond to verbal problems similar to those actually encountered on the job and requiring competency at arriving at solutions (as in Reasoning) and being able to pick up details (as in Clerical Speed and Accuracy).

Choosing tests like these is complicated by the fact that so many are available on the market. The authors required the tests to have demonstrated validity for similar jobs in similar circumstances and to be a significant predictor of performance on the job simulation designed. The latter requirement was established because the paper and pencil tests were to be used as a screening process to get to the more time-consuming interview and job-simulation procedures.

In fact, the two tests eventually chosen were two of five tests actually piloted; the two dropped were discarded based on evidence of

weaker correlations with performance on the job simulation as well as appearing less job relevant for the context. An additional consideration in choosing the tests concerned adverse impact. Thus, the two tests that were dropped revealed more adverse impact against protected minority groups than the tests that were retained.

The Interview

The selection process was designed so that people who qualified on the paper and pencil tests then appeared for an interview. The interview process attempted to measure the level of an applicant's inclinations to do the kind of work offered in the kind of environment in which it exists. Although many companies employ interviews for the assessment of skills, the evidence indicates that skill assessment is problematic in an interview — except for the assessment of verbal skills (Schneider and Schmitt 1986).

This interview process emphasizes assessment of the following issues:

1. To what extent has the applicant worked in or otherwise encountered (through school or hobbies) conditions and job activities similar to those connected with this job? To what extent has she or he enjoyed and/or felt comfortable with these kinds of activities?

   Detailed probing into the applicant's work and educational history, as well as reactions to a realistic description of the current job and work setting, provides much of the evidence needed to assess the applicant's appropriateness for the position.

2. Often applicants for these kinds of service jobs are young and without much prior work history. Where no similar work experiences exist, the interview focuses more on candidate reactions to a realistic job preview (RJP) of the specific job and job environment (Wanous 1980) and to the interest inventory described next.

3. A basis for one part of the interview process is an interest inventory built around the attributes required for the job. This inventory requires applicants to indicate the degree of interest they have in using the kinds of skills required for effective performance of a particular tasks. High and low interest areas identified by the inventory are probed in the

interview. The result of this probing is data on the job-related inclinations of the applicant.[1]

The interview is a structured interview in that interviewers must obtain responses to specific questions even though they may not ask all of the questions. Interviewers take notes during the interview (the format of the interview leaves space for note-taking regarding each question), and then make a series of ratings at the end of the interview that helps them make the final decision on applicants. These rating items are built around the particular skills, tasks, and context issues found to be important for effective job performance.

Interviewers are trained (for two and one-half days) in interviewing skills, most of the time allotted to structured practice opportunities. This practice includes the use of real candidates who may have recently accepted job offers for the job in question. The interview takes approximately eighty minutes to administer (from scoring the interest inventory through making the ratings). The interview yields a rich picture of the applicant's prior work history, likes and dislikes, and inclinations vis à vis the skills and tasks required to do the job.

The Work Simulation

Because this procedure may be the newest to readers of the present chapter, a bit more detail about the process, including a brief history of the use of simulations in selection, is now presented.

The use of simulations for selection is quite old, but they were primarily used for hiring people for relatively simple physical tasks until the mid-1950s. At that time a major breakthrough in selection was demonstrated by psychologists at AT&T (Bray and Grant 1966). These psychologists built on procedures developed by the British and the Germans for selecting spies during World War II and applied them to the selection of managers in the work setting. They showed that performance by applicants for manager jobs on a three-day series of exercises revealed considerable accuracy in predicting their accomplishments (promotion and salary level relative to their peers) up to eight years after hiring.

In the United States in particular, but now throughout the world, the use of what have come to be called assessment centers for the selection of managers has become commonplace. More recently, industrial and organizational psychologists have been using a broader concept of job simulation for hiring workers in positions as diverse as clerical, sales, police, firefighters, high school principals, equipment repair persons, and so on (Schneider and Schmitt 1986).

Simulation means something special. A simulation is a series of exercises that parallel the demands of a job and thus assess the skills and competencies needed to do a job without requiring the candidate to have the knowledge required by the job. The latter point is important because at the time of selection, candidates for many jobs do not have the knowledge required to do them. Simulations must then be designed to capture skills and competencies in the raw. Industrial and organizational pychologists speak of the necessity to capture the psychological fidelity of the job rather than duplicating the job's physical characteristics or capturing its physical fidelity. Essentially, the goal is to create simulated situations that are psychologically close enough to the real job situation to cause the candidate to duplicate the mental processes and behavior she or he would display on the job. Then the effectiveness of those behaviors can be assessed.

Some feel for the simulation may be gained from a brief description of the instructions and exercises built to assess the attributes required for effective job performance. For each exercise, the competencies most tapped by the exercise are highlighted.

Candidates learn what they are supposed to do in different situations by reading and studying an instruction manual describing rules and guidelines for their job. The manual is written in language at the same level of complexity as materials used on the job and in training; time for reading the manual is precisely monitored and controlled by the assessors. Because the job is a telephone sales and service job, the simulation is administered entirely by telephone.

Exercise one for the simulation is a simple sales call in which the candidate must persuade callers to purchase more than they initially ask for (persuasion) and to accurately complete a series of forms summarizing the sale (clerical speed and accuracy).

Exercise two is a person who is unqualified, uncooperative, and eventually abusive calling to make a purchase. This call offers a number of opportunities to assess how sensitive the candidate can be (*social sensitivity*) as well as how he or she can handle interpersonal pressure (*dealing with pressure*). In addition, because paperwork is completed for this call, an additional assessment of *clerical speed and accuracy* is possible.

Exercise three is a service call and requires the candidate to resolve a dispute over a late payment fee. The caller is an established customer who moved and received his or her statement late, eventually causing a bill for a late payment fee. The customer argues it was not his or her fault, and the candidate needs to handle the issue. One part of the exercise requires the candidate to write a memo to his/her supervisor about the incident.

Obviously, this exercise has many components that can be assessed: *understandability* of the memo and the telephone conversation, *comprehension and memory* regarding the candidate's ability to understand the problem and his or her memory for what the manual says about these kinds of problems, *sensitivity* to the caller's problem and ability to reason out a useful solution for both the caller and the company.

Table 3 shows the checklists used by the assessor to identify the effective behaviors of the candidate in response to the problems confronted in exercise three. As shown in Table 3, a paperwork checklist is used to evaluate the memo to the supervisor, and a series of checklist items rates how the call is handled.

Note that the particular competency being assessed is identified next to the item. This is done so that at the end of the exercises a simple sum of the candidate's performance on each dimension can be obtained. These totals are, in turn, compared with the total

TABLE 3
Sample Behavior Checklists — Exercise Three

Paperwork Checklist			Notes
CompMem	(	)	Candidate completes exception form.
Persuas	(	)	Candidate indicates to supervisor that exception should be granted to maintain customer good will.
CompMem	(	)	Memo written by candidate reflects a correct understanding of the customer's particular circumstances.
UnderStand	(	)	Memo written by candidate is understandable and free from distracting grammatical or spelling errors. (Note: Minor errors that don't cloud the meaning are not distracting.)

Telephone Contact Checklist			
SocialSensi	(	)	Candidate answers call politely.
Reason	(	)	Candidate recognizes that this is a billing-related service call and responds appropriately.
UnderStand	(	)	Candidate explains clearly that a late payment penalty is due when the fee is not received (rather than mailed) by the due date.
CompMem	(	)	Candidate correctly indicates the amount of the penalty (i.e., 1/3 of 1% for each day late).
Reason	(	)	Candidate indicates that an exception may be made no later in the call than immediately after the point when the caller indicates that the company does have his or her new address.
Reason	(	)	Regardless of when he or she does so, candidate indicates that an exception to the policy may be called for.
SocialSensi	(	)	Candidate indicates understanding of the caller's situation without criticizing the late payment policy.

possible scores as a basis for judging the candidate's overall level of competence. It should also be noted that space is left for notes next to the checklist item. This allows for raters to note issues not covered by the checklist. The rule here is that no matter how comprehensive the attempt, all issues are never included.

The point of this description is that the assessment of candidates through this simulation procedure is based on the observation of behavior psychologically similar to the competencies required on the actual sales/service job. People are playing out roles like those required by incumbents, and they are confronting situations requiring responses that have psychological fidelity to the job.

Furthermore, candidates are not just casually observed; they are observed for the display of quite specific competencies enumerated in behavior checklists for each exercise. Unlike an interview where only words are available, or paper and pencil tests that only require marking an answer sheet, simulations permit the development of realistic scenarios that require the display of job-relevant competencies. This behavioral orientation reduces the possibility of bias and hunch as a basis for decisions and enhances the probability that decisions will be based on what candidates can actually do (Latham and Wexley 1981).

TRAINING AND PILOTING THE PROCESS

Supervisors and managers of the job in question are trained to conduct the interviews and to administer the simulation. In the latter case, this includes playing the roles required, as well as completing all checklists and arriving at a pass-fail decision.

It was decided that supervisors and managers should play an active role in the selection process based on the idea that full participation in the choice of new employees breeds commitment to ensuring the success of those employees. In many selection situations supervisors are not involved in the selection of their own subordinates, yielding, perhaps, less commitment to the people hired.

The training program lasts four and one-half days and consists of the following steps:

1. An introduction to the task and attribution analysis results combined with the reasons for the particular selection strategy and system design.
2. A walk through the exercises (or interview) and rating systems followed by a series of paper candidates the trainees must rate.
3. Monitored practice with one another.
4. The final and longest stage of training is to work with real candidates.

Steps 2, 3, and 4 are conducted for both the interview and the simulation.

This brief description of the training illustrates that it is extensive, intensive, and focused on both efficiency and accuracy. Interviewers must be able to ask the appropriate questions and follow-up probes in order to gather all the relevant information and learn to use that information to rate the candidates' inclinations to stick with the job. Assessors must be thoroughly familiar with the exercises for them to flow smoothly and for the candidate to have a full chance to demonstrate his or her competencies. They must also become familiar with and proficient at using the checklist rating systems if valid ratings are to be an outcome of the simulation process. At the end of training, two assessors can process one candidate per hour through the entire simulation, including the ratings and a final decision.

LOGISTICAL AND POLITICAL FEASIBILITY

While all the technical issues are moving forward, several political and logistical issues must be monitored and attended to. For example, how well will the personnel department accept the new procedures, who will monitor the actual day-to-day use of the process, who will be trained to use the process, will new staff be required because of the procedures? In addition, considerations (as noted later) of the consequences of a selection procedure need to be identified. For example, in the present project, new training procedures as well as new procedures for training the *supervisors* of the new people were necessary as a result of the implementation of the selection program described.

VALIDATION

Selection researchers are gluttons for punishment; they attempt to evaluate the effectiveness of the procedures they introduce. As noted in the introduction to the chapter, the purpose of the present effort was to facilitate, through employee selection, increased levels of performance and retention. Performance was operationalized by supervisors' ratings of new employees with respect to effectiveness in carrying out the twenty tasks shown in Table 1. As noted earlier, these twenty tasks were rated as the most important tasks in the task analysis inventory.

Retention was operationalized as the requirement to be employed one year after hiring. This period of time was chosen as reasonable by the organization given the level of the job and the investments it made in recruiting, hiring, and training. It is also a fairly typical retention criterion in selection research for a job at this level (Schneider and Schmitt 1986).

A problem in assessing the effectiveness of selection procedures is that the selection procedures themselves are frequently used to make selection decisions, as was true in the present case. This produces what is called the restriction of range problem (Aitken 1934; Alliger and Alexander 1984). Restriction of range is a problem because any correlations calculated between selection data and performance contains only a portion of the information for both the predictors and the criteria; the information missing is the information for the people *not* hired.

Fortunately, some techniques have been developed for correcting for restriction of range. These techniques take into account existing information on the predictors for those (hired versus not hired), the performance of those hired and the observed relationships among the predictors, and job performance to make a statistically educated guess about the relationship without any range restriction. The correction has been shown to be inherently conservative (Linn, Harnisch, and Dunbar 1981), so the results to be presented can be accepted as reliable.

A second issue in conducting selection validation is that the effectiveness of people hired can be measured only within an organizational context that affects the display of individual competencies and inclinations. Thus, actual success in selection is always something less than 100 percent accurate in predicting employee effectiveness or employee retention. In effect, personnel selection provides only the raw material for effectiveness, not the finished product. By analogy, auto manufacturers do not evaluate the utility of their steel acquisition procedures by how well the car that is produced sells or how well it runs; the steel is the raw material but everything else that happens to the steel also determines the eventual product. It is the selection process that should provide the raw human resources who possess the potential to be effective and stay on the job. It is the organizational context that constrains or facilitates the development of this potential.

The multiple correlations, R (corrected for range restriction), of the selection system against the four performance criteria were:

- Detail $R = .07$
- Sensitivity $R = .17$
- Informs $R = .19$
- Courtesy $R = .12$

These relationships are modest and may be interpreted as indicating that, with respect to Informs, for example, the selection system is accounting for 19 percent of what a perfectly valid selection system would accomplish. A perfectly valid selection system here would be one that predicts with 100 percent accuracy each employee's ratings.

In predicting the retention of new hires for a minimum of one year, the selection system was more successful, yielding a multiple correlation, R (corrected for range restriction), of .30.

Internal analyses of the various components of the selection system revealed that the paper and pencil tests contributed more to the prediction of retention than did the job simulation, with the interview contributing an intermediate amount. This may be due to the fact that the paper and pencil tests were selected specifically because they correlated with the simulation, yielding a somewhat duplicate measurement. The interview, however, was not significantly correlated with either the paper and pencil tests or the simulation, permitting it to account for a proportion of variance in retention unaccounted for by the tests or the simulation. For this particular effort, the interview was also the strongest correlate of the various performance criteria. This is an unusual finding in that performance is usually more effectively predicted by competency assessments than by interviews. It may be that for service jobs like the one studied here, so much of the job involves interpersonal issues that interviewers are picking up enough information to make a somewhat accurate prediction. This issue requires attention in subsequent efforts.

It may be informative to note some of the other positive organizational consequences that the implementation of this selection system has triggered (Schneider 1990). First, the trainers of the newly hired employees noted how much quicker the new hires caught on to the training. Subsequently, the training has been redesigned and made more efficient as a result of the improved competencies of the new hires. The task analysis information provided the foundation for the training redesign effort. Second, the service focus of the new employees has highlighted some of the weaknesses of the supervisory staff. This has caused the supervisors of the job in question to undergo training in an attempt to increase their competencies and service focus to keep pace with the competencies and needs of this somewhat different employee.

Finally, to take advantage of the increased competencies and tenure of the new job incumbents, the organization has designed ways for employees to stick with this job without suffering financially. Thus, in the past, the best job incumbents would post out of this job to obtain a raise; now the job has been given additional steps and incentives so that

employee effectiveness can be capitalized on by retaining the best performers. Together, and over time, these systems side effects are profoundly impacting the climate for service of the organization (Schneider 1990).

A result of this stream of changes has been a significant decrease in turnover. So even though the selection system only accounted for a portion of the prediction of turnover, turnover has, in fact, been cut by nearly one-third as the result of the *stream* of efforts instituted. These data support the raw materials metaphor presented earlier and emphasize the fact that personnel selection alone cannot be expected to achieve dramatic results; it often takes a system of organizational efforts to produce the desired performance and retention.

CONCLUSION

This chapter outlines the logic and procedures underlying a system for selecting employees with service inclinations and competencies who will remain on the job. The different phases used to do this have been presented. These have included some examples of how jobs, inclinations, and competencies are described so that procedures can be built that have psychological fidelity to the actual job.

The purpose was to clarify for a services marketing and service management audience some of the conceptual and practical realities of actually doing something about selecting service workers. Prior to concluding this description, however, it is important to comment on the time and money the company invested in the design of the system.

The costs to the company for designing the simulation included:

- hiring a consulting firm to carry out the task and competency analyses and to design the system.
- partial salaries for the three company persons who worked closely with the consulting firm to facilitate access to the various persons required to carry out the different phases.
- expenses involved in traveling around the United States to train supervisors and managers to use the simulation process; salaries and lost productivity for the supervisors and managers while in training.

Why would a company invest so much money in enhancing its selection system? Because organizations can be no more effective than the people in them. In other words, this company made the decision to build its service climate from the ground up based on the hypothesis that the people who interact with the customer are critical for service effectiveness. Of course, excellent evidence in the literature now shows the quite dramatic payoffs companies of all kinds can obtain from investments in selection systems (Hunter and Schmidt 1982).

This particular company had an extremely broad definition of service effectiveness. Its definition was that everything had to be done correctly, that the goal of the company was to make it easy for customers to conduct business, and that it required more than a smile to be effective. The company became convinced that an essentially one-time, up-front, commitment of resources would yield an acceptable return on investment within less than two years and that profits would grow as a function of the improved competencies of the people controlling the service encounter.

One of the critical support features necessary for the success of the intervention described was an organizational focus on longer term gains. The organization knew that changes in an organization through selection is a slow process because new people are added to veterans slowly. Thus, the effectiveness of a selection intervention may be felt only after a significant portion of the incumbents in a job have been hired through that process. Perhaps it is when the newcomers hired through the new process become old-timers that the effects are fully realized.

Indeed, subsequent to the implementation of the service simulation described here, the company has developed four more selection systems for other jobs and designed a simulation to provide data for the promotion of the supervisors of the employees in the sales/service job. This information is presented to show how an organization can promote a service climate through more than words spouting how important service is. This organization is literally putting its money where its mouth is by investing in the people who

are the conveyers of that climate to the customer world.

Two messages channel through. First, delivering excellent service is as difficult as any business task can be because it requires appropriately directed compulsive attention to so many details, and this requires people with appropriate inclinations and competencies. Second, there *is* something companies can do about service excellence besides talk about it but, like service itself, the something that can be done requires compulsive attention to the details — like personnel selection.

NOTES

1. The first version of the interest inventory used in this project actually asked people to report on their skills. However, this version was subsequently changed to interests. We are unable to tease apart the impact of the different forms for the present project but we are working on this for a future effort. Our opinion is that the appropriate issue for the interview is interests (inclinations).

REFERENCES

ALBRECHT, K., and R. ZEMKE. (1985). *Service America: Doing Business in the New Economy.* Homewood, IL: Dow-Jones Irwin.

ALLIGER, G. M. and R. A. ALEXANDER. (1984). "Correcting for Multivariate Range Restriction: Two Computer Programs." *Educational and Psychological Measurement,* Vol. 44, 677–78.

BASS, B. M. (1982). "Individual Capability, Team Performance, and Team Productivity." In M. D. Dunnette and E. A. Fleishman (eds.), *Human Performance and Productivity: Human Capability Assessment.* Hillsdale, NJ: Erlbaum.

BERRY, L. L., A. PARASURAMAN, and V. A. ZEITHAML. (1988). "The Service-Quality Puzzle." *Business Horizons,* Sept–Oct., 35–43.

BRAY, D. W., and D. L. GRANT. (1966). "The Assessment Center in the Measurement of Potential for Business Management." *Psychological Monographs,* 80, Whole No. 625.

BOWEN, D. E., and B. SCHNEIDER. (1988). "Services Marketing and Management: Implications for Organizational Behavior." In B. M. Staw and L. L. Cummings (eds.), *Research in Organizational Behavior* (Vol. 10). Greenwich, CT: JAI Press.

CZEPIEL, J. A., M. R. SOLOMON and C. SUPRENANT. (eds.). (1985). *The Service Encounter.* Lexington, MA: Lexington Books.

GOLDSTEIN, I. L. (1986). *Training in Organizations: Needs Assessment, Development, and Evaluation.* (2nd Ed.) Monterey, CA: Brooks/Cole.

GOLDSTEIN, I. L., and M. J. GESSNER. (1988). "Training and Development in Work Organizations." In C. L. Cooper and I. Robertson (eds.), *International Review of Industrial and Organizational Psychology.* London: Wiley.

HOGAN, J., R. HOGAN, and C. M. BUSCH. (1984). "How to Measure Service Orientation." *Journal of Applied Psychology,* 69, 167–73.

HUNTER, J. E., and F. L. SCHMIDT. (1982). "Fitting People to Jobs: The Impact of Personal Selection on National Productivity." In M. D. Dunnette and E. A. Fleishman (eds.), *Human Performance and Productivity: Human Capability Assessment.* Hillsdale, NJ: Erlbaum.

KERR, S. (1988). "Some Characteristics and Consequences of Organizational Reward." In F. D. Schoorman and B. Schneider (eds.), *Facilitating Work Effectiveness.* Lexington, MA: Lexington Books.

LINN, R. L., D. HARNISCH and S. B. DUNBAR. (1981). "Corrections for Range Restriction: An Empirical Investigation of Conditions Resulting in Conservative Corrections." *Journal of Applied Psychology,* Vol. 66, 655–63.

LOVELOCK, C. H. (ed.). (1988). *Managing Services: Marketing, Operations, and Human Resources.* Englewood Cliffs, NJ: Prentice Hall.

NORMANN, R. (1984). *Service Management: Strategy and Leadership in Service Business.* New York: Wiley.

PARASURAMAN, A., V. A. ZEITHAML, and L. L. BERRY. (1985). "A Conceptual Model of Service Quality and Its Implications for Future Research." *Journal of Marketing,* 49, 41–50.

PARASURAMAN, A., V. A. ZEITHAML, and L. L. BERRY. (1986). *Servqual: A Multiple-Item Scale for Measuring Consumer Perceptions of Service Quality.* Cambridge MA: Marketing Science Institute.

SCHEIN, E. A. (1985). *Organizational Culture and Leadership.* San Francisco: Jossey-Bass.

SCHNEIDER, B. (1986). "Notes on Climate and Culture." In C. Marshall, D. Schmalansee, and V. Venatesan (eds.), *Creativity in Service Marketing.* Chicago: American Marketing Association.

————. (1987a). "Imperatives for the Design of Service Organizations." In C. Suprenant (ed.), *Add Value to Your Service.* Chicago: American Marketing Association.

————. (1987b). "The People Make the Place." *Personnel Psychology,* 40, 437–53.

————. (1990). "Alternative Strategies for Creating Service-Oriented Organizations." In D. Bowen and T. Cummings (eds.), *Service Management Effectiveness.* San Francisco: Jossey-Bass.

SCHNEIDER, B., and D. E. BOWEN. (1985). "Employee and Customer Perceptions of Service in Banks: Replication and Extension." *Journal of Applied Psychology,* 70, 423–33.

SCHNEIDER, B., and N. SCHMITT. (1986). *Staffing Organizations.* 2d ed. Glenview, IL: Scott, Foresman.

WANOUS, J. P. (1980). *Organizational Entry.* Reading, MA: Addison-Wesley.

We appreciate the people in the organization who helped us carry out this project. In addition, we thank Paul Hanges for his assistance in analyzing the data reported here. Finally, we express our appreciation to the Computer Science Center of the University of Maryland, College Park, for supporting the data analyses we did.

The Humanization of Service: Respect at the Moment of Truth

GABRIEL R. BITRAN
JOHANNES HOECH

To a large extent, firms can assure quality in high contact service settings by training and motivating employees to treat customers respectfully. This chapter discusses the issues of communication, control, power, and respect in an integrated way that should help managers design and monitor more effective service encounters. It includes a discussion of how one electronics equipment company redesigned and managed its service encounters.

Many employees who deal with customers do not care about *satisfying* them. At best, they fail to create an impression good enough that customers recommend the firm to others. At worst, they cause customers to take their business elsewhere. In firms that have used sophisticated planning and appropriate automation to fine-tune service design and execution, employee contact skills may be the one factor that separates good service from bad. Contact skills can become a competitive weapon — and customers welcome such competition. In a 1988 Gallup survey, 1,005 consumers were asked what "quality in services" meant to them. The largest group, one-third of all respondents, named employee contact skills such as courtesy, attitude, or helpfulness.[1]

Managers are frequently aware of lapses in front-line service, but lack the procedural tools, the necessary staffing, or worse, the support from their superiors to do much about those lapses. Or their own approach to service quality may be too narrow. They may focus on important issues like transportation logistics, response time, or repair service efficiency, but forget crucial intangibles. Customers *do* want well-designed, cheap, efficiently delivered services, but they also want to be treated respectfully and to know that the service provider cares about their satisfaction.

PROBLEMS WITH CURRENT APPROACHES

All services fall somewhere between the extremes of *high contact* and *low contact* with the customer. Many service products, in fact, have elements of both. Banking, for example, has the low contact back office and the high contact branch operation. Restaurants and hotels have cooks and cleaners behind the scenes, and waiters and receptionists interacting with customers. High and low contact services differ considerably in terms of quality attributes and their implementation. In low contact services, quality essentially means "conformance to specifications." The production of french fries in fast-food outlets, for example, is carefully specified to maintain taste, color, temperature, and appearance.

In high contact services, it is not sufficient to define quality simply as "conformance to specifications," because the human encounter cannot be completely specified. Similarly, more technology does not necessarily increase customer satisfaction. High contact services must satisfy higher order human needs to a much larger extent than low contact services.[2] Thus, to train people to provide high quality in high contact services, it is first necessary to understand the server-customer interaction. We believe that actively understanding and managing the relationship between server and customer can yield higher service revenues through increased repurchase rates.

AN ALTERNATIVE APPROACH

The Service Relationship as a Power Play

The queueing phenomenon is an aspect of service in which "hard" factors (design and execution) and "soft" factors (server-customer interaction) both affect customer satisfaction. Most literature on the subject deals with mathematical modeling of queueing systems. But a few authors have analyzed the interpersonal interaction in service delivery independent of the quality of the underlying core service. Fitzsimmons and Sullivan, for instance, focus on waiting from three interpersonal perspectives: waiting as psychological punishment, as ritual insult, and as opportunity for social interaction. They state:

> Waiting is an anticipatory condition where the consumer's desires can be consummated only upon the initiative of the server. The server, therefore, has power over the consumer, and waiting reinforces the consumer's subordinate status. To be kept waiting is to acknowledge that one's time and social worth are less valuable than those of the person who imposes the wait.[3]

Maister very directly addresses the power relationship involved in wait times. He points out that, "waiting in ignorance creates a feeling of powerlessness, which frequently results in visible irritation and rudeness on the part of customers as they 'harass' serving personnel in an attempt to reclaim their status as paying clients."[4]

Building on these perceptions, we make the following hypothesis — *The way server and customer share benefits and costs in a service relationship depends on:*

- the amount of exercisable power held by each;
- the interest of each party in exercising that power (i.e., assuming control) for their own benefit; or
- the willingness of each party to forgo their power for the benefit of the other party (i.e., show respect for the other party).

Exercisable power can come from three primary sources: the external setting (for example, the business is a monopoly); the phase of the relationship (for example, the customer has already paid without having consumed the service); and the personal presence of the players (for example, the customer is tall and strong). Customers are aware of their status as paying clients and are willing to defend it should they feel challenged. If a business threatens that status, the customer may well initiate a power struggle, the likely outcome of which is a dissatisfied customer unwilling to return. On the other hand, business opportunities arise when a firm demonstrates respect for the customer's status by offering higher quality service without compromising its own need for profits and efficiency. In this context, it will be useful to explore the meaning of respect in services. We will also examine the different types of power to understand when and how to use power to increase customer satisfaction.

Showing Respect

At the onset of a service relationship, the customer is uncertain about how genuine the server's concern for his or her satisfaction is. The server can address that uncertainty and reduce the risk of a power struggle by explicitly showing respect for the customer's well-being.

By respect we do not mean the respect a subordinate shows to a superior, or the respect an art lover shows for a great painting. Instead, we refer to the special consideration that servers pay to the needs and wishes of the customer. The attitudes and behaviors that express respect depend on the socioeconomic and cultural contexts in which a service is delivered, as well as on the type of service. Respect is manifested differently in a sophisticated restaurant, a fast-food outlet, or a bar, for example. What it always includes, though, is a felt and communicated concern for the customer's satisfaction.

Forms of Server and Customer Power

To be able to genuinely and consistently express respect for the customer, one must first understand how power is distributed between frontline employees and customers.

The most obvious form of potential *server* power arises from being in a *unique position to deliver a service* through some form of market dominance. Examples range from outright monopolistic power, as is often attributed to certain governmental services, to oligarchic power, as in the airline industry, to simpler forms of market dominance, like being the only locally available, higher quality service

provider. While such organizations do not *need* to heed calls for higher quality services, being the only game in town can create a complacency that leaves the firm unprepared to survive changing conditions.

Another source of potential server power is *customer quality elasticity*. Comparable to price elasticity, quality elasticity is a measure of how important quality is to the customer's purchase decision. Quality elasticity can be a source of server power *if* the server is capable of providing the level of service that customers demand. *Customer quality inelasticity*, on the other hand, plays into the hands of service providers when inferior services are acceptable because of other factors. Customers waiting patiently in the freezing cold for entrance to popular nightclubs, for example, exhibit service quality inelasticity: the inconvenience does not affect their purchasing decision.

A third source of potential server power develops after the provision of a service has been authorized by the customer, when *he or she has no easy way to back out of the service commitment*. At some point during the service process, the customer normally becomes dependent on the server to satisfy his or her need. The purchase of an airline ticket illustrates this power transfer quite well. Holders of cheaper tickets often cannot change their itinerary after a certain deadline has passed, whereas holders of more expensive tickets can do so up to or even beyond the time of departure. Allowing customers flexible retreat from their commitments is an interesting service strategy that can encourage customers to come back later out of a sense of obligation. In addition, the company develops a reputation for being easy to do business with.

The primary source of potential *customer* power is the *customer's authorization of and payment for a service*. This type of power depends on how directly the customer decision to authorize or pay for a service can be linked to the quality of a service and how well that link can be communicated to the server. In the case of waiters, for example, tipping improves service quality because tips make up a considerable portion of waiters' income. Similarly, employee bonuses or promotions based on customer satisfaction ratings increase the server's incentives to treat customers well.

A closely related type of power is the *ability not to repurchase a service*. A company's loss of market share due to low service quality basically results from the customers' collective choice not to repurchase a service. Unless a single customer is large enough to have an impact, using this form of power effectively depends on how much customers learn from prior experiences and on how well they can act as a collective force. For example, consumer groups and consumer-loyal quality assessment organizations attempt to realize potential consumer power by educating and motivating consumers not to buy low quality products and services. They also spur competitiveness by publishing information about alternative service providers. When possible, companies should clearly communicate their superior quality ratings to consumers.

Another form of customer power is *legal recourse*. Most customers are swayed from its use by the money and effort required, but the old maxim "caveat emptor" (let the buyer beware) is losing meaning as the amount of litigation increases. Malpractice suits are major incentives for physicians to take service quality seriously, for example. However, it is unclear how far the law can protect customers from shoddy treatment if the consequences of bad service are less catastrophic than they are in industries like health care or air transportation.

Moral, psychological, social, or political power is available to *both* consumers and service providers. Companies are aware of the nega-

tive forms these types of power can take — when, for example, customer behavior becomes abusive. The Beacon Hotel Corporation of Boston, Massachusetts, strikes a good balance. It encourages employees to respect customers and give up their own potential power, but it doesn't leave them unprotected. Their customer relations motto is: "The customer is always right until he or she is wrong."[5] In dealing with governmental services, social and political power are often customers' only resources for influencing service quality short of a tax revolt. Differences in social status can become sources of power when the party of apparent higher social standing consciously or unconsciously claims privileged status.

To summarize, we propose viewing the service process as an active relationship between the server and the customer. This perspective augments models that interpret service as a one-way delivery of objective service quality attributes. Viewing service as an *interaction* encourages practitioners to look at things from the consumer's perspective. Table 1 illustrates our server-customer interaction framework. In the next section, we discuss its implementation and describe how a high contact service can be modified to increase customer satisfaction.

IMPLEMENTING HIGH CONTACT SERVICES

We have emphasized the importance of the interaction between servers and customers in

TABLE 1
Server-Customer Interaction Framework

A player	has this type of power	to demand and	give intangibles
Server	• unique ability to deliver a service resulting in market dominance • quality (in)elasticity • customer committed	• reward	• respect
Customer	• authorize and pay service • repurchase refusal • legal recourse	• quality, respect	• thankfulness
Both	• moral, psychological, social, political	not applicable	not applicable

a high contact service setting, and its potential to result in a destructive power struggle. If we can analyze this relationship in sufficient depth and detail, then we should be able to manage the risk of a power struggle and improve customer satisfaction as well. This analysis requires complementing the *degree of customer contact* with the dimensions of *customer communication* and *control*.

Contact, Communication, and Control

Adequate server-customer *communications* is a central ingredient of service quality in high contact services. Hence, a service can be classified by the amount of communication appropriate between provider and consumer. Sometimes a high contact service does not involve much direct communication. In the interaction between a masseur and a customer, for example, the two parties may not speak to each other, yet contact is high. At other times, as in counseling, consulting, or teaching, the way the customer is spoken to is critical. Thus, lumping both services into one category would not do them justice.

Another dimension of service quality is customer *control* over the delivery process. This dimension is of particular importance in some expensive services, and in services requiring customer cooperation. However, giving customers control over the service process has a great destabilizing potential that a service organization must be prepared to deal with. For example, many expensive restaurants strive to give customers control by taking special requests. If employees are not trained to give customers what they want without giving away the store, the likely outcome is flustered service personnel, frustrated customers, and angry owners. Who controls the service delivery process is related to how much power each side holds. While *having control* means being able to choose a course of action, *power* refers to the ability to determine unilaterally who controls all or part of the relationship. Thus power, in this sense, is potential control.

The Electronic Equipment Company Case

An electronic equipment company's customer sales and service organization used our framework to redesign and manage its repair hotline in a four-week trial. (The company's industry has been disguised for proprietary reasons.) To describe this trial, we focus on three principal tasks: service design or redesign, operational performance measurement, and employee feedback methods. These important cornerstones of service delivery are part of the analysis sequence outlined in Figure 1.

Service design or redesign begins with research about how customers perceive the current service offering. This information becomes input for the service design or redesign. The new design includes detailed implementation plans, as well as specifications and control tools to monitor service delivery. Once implemented, the new service is monitored for adherence to the plan, and for whether it can be further improved. Such measurement should focus on actual service performance as well as customer-perceived performance, as we explain below. Finally, in order to make a difference at the frontline, this data is eventually fed back to employees in the form of new procedural guidelines or personal performance feedback.

Monitoring service performance should be done from four viewpoints. One viewpoint rates a service descriptively (i.e., describes the actual condition). In essence, this rating views a service as frontline servers deliver it. Another dimension is a normative rating (i.e., the planned, ideal condition) of a service from management's viewpoint. The third and fourth ratings describe a service as perceived and expected by consumers. Important discrepancies between ratings from the actual, planned, or consumer viewpoints can point to an uneven power distribution between servers and customers, or to a mismatch between interaction intensity requirements and server abilities. Such a comparison led to the redesign analysis presented below.

Service Design or Redesign. The electronic equipment company's sales and service organization analyzed its major service components using the framework shown in Table 2. The components were rated on the basis of their levels of server-customer contact and on how much communication the interaction

FIGURE 1
Service Organization Quality Improvement Cycle

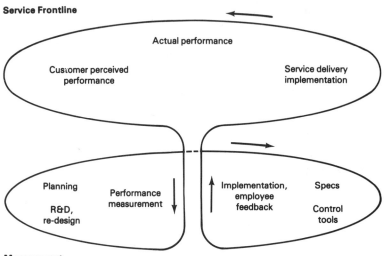

Service Frontline

Actual performance

Customer perceived
performance

Service delivery
implementation

Planning

R&D,
re-design

Performance
measurement

Implementation,
employee
feedback

Specs

Control
tools

Management

TABLE 2
Interaction Dimension-Based Service Rating Example

Service Component	RATING DIMENSIONS*			POWER DISTRIBUTION*		
	Customer Contact	*Communication*	*Customer Control*	*Server Power Due to:*		
				Unique service	*Quality elasticity*	*Committed customer*
Sales	High	High	High	Low	Med	Low
Trouble Hotline	High	High	Low	High	High	High
Repair Service	Med	Med	Low	High	High	High
Shipping	Low	Low	Low	High	Low	High
Financing	Low	Low	Low	Low	Med	Low

*These ratings are specific to the case discussed.

required. That rating was then compared with the amount of power actually held by frontline servers. To look at one example, the analysis uncovered an inappropriate discrepancy between server and customer power on the trouble hotline component. Customers would have liked to exercise some control over when repair technicians showed up, or over the quality of repair work, but employees held so much power that this wasn't possible. Since the repair hotline is a high contact, high communication service, this power imbalance frequently led to emotional exchanges that diminished customer satisfaction.

Management thus concluded that customer satisfaction could be improved if hotline representatives' customer contact skills were enhanced and if customers were given more control over when their problems were fixed. When the trial was initiated, the company redesigned its repair hotline script to give customers more control over technician arrival times. Instead of simply assigning an arrival time, the new approach gave customers the option of requesting faster service — in other words, same day versus next day service.

Employees were also given training in communication skills — specifically, in how they

TABLE 3
Principal Customer Interactions and Associated Process Skills

Principal Tasks	Process Skills
Diagnosing problems	• Active listening • Guiding customer's problem self-diagnosis
Gathering, checking, and disseminating information	• Active listening
Disseminating cost information	• Nonthreatening communication style • Controlling tone of voice
Managing waits	• Generating customer understanding and tolerance for waits
Conflict resolution	• Disengaging emotionally • Active listening • Reflective style • Controlling tone of voice • Nonthreatening communication style

handled four important tasks: diagnosing problems, gathering and disseminating information, managing waiting periods, and resolving conflicts (see Table 3). The skills needed to perform these tasks were further subdivided into detailed subskills. Examples of best and worst practices were used in the training process.

The test's aim was to determine whether improved communication skills and enhanced customer control were equally important. The impact of enhanced customer control was of special concern, since we expected customers to want more "same day" as opposed to "next day" repairs, and thus to demand faster service than the company would ordinarily provide. To allow independent measurement of the two variables, communication and control, four randomly assigned call receipt teams assumed the roles illustrated in Figure 2. All teams had three representatives. Team D was the control group.

Performance Measures. Operational performance measures in high contact services include both external measures relating to customer satisfaction and internal, quantitative measures. These measures should be sampled frequently and regularly. Monthly customer satisfaction data may not be sufficient to match changes in operational performance. If an unusual event occurs during a particular week, for example, its impact on customer satisfaction will be lost in monthly averages, and it cannot be used for training or improvement purposes.

Such data collection should emphasize objectivity and measurability. These are harder to achieve with qualitative than with quantitative measures, obviously. To forestall ambiguities and biases, qualitative data collection should be done using precise rating guidelines. (See Table 4 for the scheme used to collect internal and external qualitative and quanitative data in the electronic equipment company's test.)

We measured customer satisfaction by administering a short customer survey within

FIGURE 2
Trial Team Setup

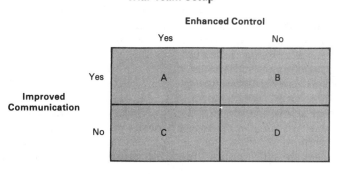

TABLE 4
High Contact Services Performance Measures and Data Sources

PERFORMANCE MEASURES	DATA SOURCES		
	Peer Review	Management Review	Customers
Quantitative	• Not applicable	• Operational data (e.g., productivity, lost customers, re-work, timeliness)	• Customer satisfaction surveys • Market share • Repurchase rates • Complaint frequency
Qualitative	• Demonstrations of good/bad practices	• Evaluation of server skill, effort, and attitude based on: • Mystery shopping • Monitoring • Interviews of customer contact personnel	• Customer comments • Written complaints • Customer interviews

one hour of the customer's initial call. One of the survey's four questions asked customers how satisfied they were with the quoted technician arrival time because, before the test, customers had been most *dis*satisfied with those quoted times. This performance parameter became the focus of improvement efforts. Customers could answer "very satisfied," "satisfied," "neutral," "dissatisfied," or "very dissatisfied." Satisfaction was measured as the percentage of very satisfied and satisfied customers. On the operational side, the performance parameters we tracked were the time per call, the ratio of technician dispatches to incoming telephone calls, and the percentage of dispatches responding to "same day" repair requests.

Fortunately, both improving communication skills and enhancing customer control worked well in the test. While enhancing control improved customer satisfaction with the arrival times more than improving communication skills did, the latter reduced the number of dispatches to "same day" repair requests. This result indicated powerfully that customers, properly influenced, could be satisfied with a course of action cheaper for the company to administer (i.e., they would accept "next day" responses). Figure 3 presents the improvements in customer satisfaction concerning technician arrival times and the changes in the percentage of "same day" dispatches that resulted from each improvement strategy. The absolute values of both variables — 85 to 93 percent, 40 to 45 percent, respectively — have been disguised. However, the individual change coefficients (light shading) and the total impact (dark shading) are the authentic improvements.

We also obtained an interesting result when service throughput — time per call — was compared with customer satisfaction. Our hypothesis was that customers would not be satisfied with a phone call that was either too short (too brief to explain a problem) or too long (too long an interruption of their own work). However, we did not know what the appropriate timeframe would be. Results indicated that the optimal time on the phone was between one and two minutes longer than the operational throughput target. Customer satisfaction with servers who operated within those limits was nine percentage points higher, on average, than with servers who did not.

Employee Feedback Methods. Collecting performance data is not much more than an accounting exercise unless that data is continually fed back to frontline servers and their

FIGURE 3
Improved Communication and Enhanced Control Effects

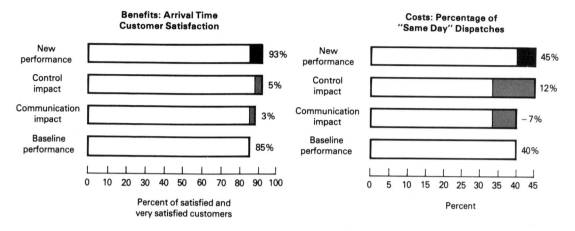

supervisors. This data — like the analogous data in manufacturing — forms the basis for corrective action and improvement through, for example, the well-known "seven tools" of quality analysis (Pareto diagrams, cause-and-effect diagrams, histograms, control charts, scatter diagrams, graphs, and checksheets). However, there are two important differences between performance feedback in a high contact service setting and in a manufacturing setting.

First, in high contact services, frontline servers also receive feedback on how they relate to other people through tone of voice, smiles, friendliness, or empathy. Feedback on such qualities can be very personal and, if not handled correctly, very devastating. Thus, the person administering such feedback should remember three principles: be fact based, be objective, and be friendly. Second, first class customer interaction cannot be demanded; it must be carefully groomed. In high contact services, for customers to be happy, generally employees must be happy. A much greater emphasis must be placed on motivating employees to achieve peak customer contact performance. Doing so is best accomplished by sensitively explaining the reasons for needed changes and by role modeling desired behavior.

During the electronic equipment company's test, employees responded positively to

such feedback. In fact, they enjoyed the opportunity to improve their interpersonal skills. After an initial Hawthorne effect, customer satisfaction improved on average six percentage points over the course of the test. Feedback sessions were instrumental in achieving this improvement. They not only helped servers focus on their weak spots; they also made the work more interesting. Servers developed a stronger sense of being able to control their own performance by seeing the results of their efforts in the next day's survey results.

Once the appropriate performance measurement and feedback techniques were in place, we witnessed the development of a subtle, positive quality and satisfaction feedback loop between frontline servers and customers.[6] A friendly server was more likely to receive friendly customer responses, thereby increasing his or her own motivation to please customers. And a customer who had been treated respectfully seemed more inclined to express his or her satisfaciton.

Thus, a critical objective for a high contact service organization should be the creation of a work environment in which employees are encouraged to give high quality service and in which their job satisfaction is of primary concern to management. Most employees will derive greater satisfaction from their work efforts if they have a feeling that what they do matters and if they are rewarded for it. This dynamic is of central importance to high contact service quality, since job satisfaction translates directly into customer satisfaction.

CONCLUSION

Our discussion of communication, control, power, and respect stresses the close ties between service quality in high contact services and the personal relationship between server and customer. This view prompts the hypothesis that quality assurance in high contact services means focusing to a great extent on frontline employees by training and motivating them to treat customers respectfully. An organization's ability to match its managerial techniques and styles to its service quality mission is therefore crucial to delivering high quality, reliable service. Many leading quality authorities, including Juran and Deming, contend that striving to deliver quality, with all the organizational and managerial implications of that striving, is precisely what keeps a company in top fighting shape.

REFERENCES

1. The Gallup Organization, Inc., "Consumers' Perceptions Concerning the Quality of American Products and Services," survey conducted for the American Society for Quality Control, ASQC Publication No. T711, October 1988.

2. R.B. CHASE and D.A. TANSIK, "The Customer Contact Model for Organization Design," *Management Science* 29 (1983): 1037–50.

3. J.A. FITZSIMMONS and R.S. SULLIVAN, "Service Operations Management," (New York: McGraw-Hill, 1982).

4. D.H. MAISTER, "The Psychology of Waiting Lines," (Boston: Harvard Business School, Note No. 9-684-064, 1984, Revised May 1984); and J.A. Czepiel et al., ed., "The Service Encounter," (Lexington, MA: Lexington Books, 1985).

5. R.M. KELLEHER, president, Beacon Hotel Corporation, personal interview with the authors on 2 February 1988.

6. This was somewhat analogous to the one described by Heskett. See: J.L. Heskett, "Lessons in the Service Sector," *Harvard Business Review,* March–April 1987, p. 118.

This research has been partially supported by a grant from Coopers & Lybrand and by the Leaders for Manufacturing Program.

Many friends and colleagues not only provided valuable comments and examples, but also suggested improvements to the ideas developed in this paper. In particular we would like to thank Professors John Carroll, Charles Fine, Don Kleinmuntz, Peter Senge, and Steve Star of MIT, Thin Yin Leong of MIT, Vincent O'Reilly of Coopers & Lybrand, Cynthia Schuyler of Lotus Development Corporation, and Belden Menkus of McKinsey & Company.

Mrs. Fields' Secret Ingredient

TOM RICHMAN

The real recipe behind the phenomenal growth of Mrs. Fields Cookies cannot be found in the dough. Instead it lies in the information system linking each retail cookie store with the company's headquarters. Information technology provides a way for Debbie Fields to simulate personal contact with hundreds of store managers, supplementing the personal visits she makes. It helps managers with such tasks as hourly sales goals, scheduling crew, interviewing crew applicants, and maintaining equipment.

Part of the late Buckminster Fuller's genius was his capacity to transform a technology from the merely new to the truly useful by creating a new form to take advantege of its characteristics. Fuller's geodesic designs, for instance, endowed plastic with practical value as a building material. His structures, if not always eye-appealing, still achieved elegance — as mathematicians use the word to connote simplicity — of function. Once, reacting to someone's suggestion that a new technology be applied to an old process in a particularly awkward way, Fuller said dismissively, "That would be like putting an outboard motor on a skyscraper."

Introducing microcomputers with spreadsheet and word-processing software to a company originally designed around paper technology amounts to the same thing. If the form of the company doesn't change, the computer, like the outboard, is just a doodad. Faster long division and speedier typing don't move a company into the information age.

But Randy Fields has created something entirely new — *a* shape if not *the* shape, of business organizations to come. It gives top management a dimension of personal control over dispersed operations that small companies otherwise find impossible to achieve. It projects a founder's vision into parts of a company that have long ago outgrown his or her ability to reach in person.

In the structure that Fields is building, computers don't just speed up old administrative management processes. They alter the process. Management, in the Fields organizational paradigm, becomes less administration and more inspiration. The management hierarchy of the company *feels* almost flat.

What's the successful computer-age business going to look like in the not-very-distant future? Something like Randy Fields's concept — which is, in a word, neat.

What makes it neat, right out of the oven, is where he's doing it. Randy Fields, age 40, is married to Debbi Fields, 31, and together they run Mrs. Fields Cookies, of Park City, Utah. They project that by year end, their business will comprise nearly 500 company-owned stores in 37 states selling what Debbi calls a "feel-good feeling." That sounds a little hokey. A lot of her cookie talk does. "Good enough never is," she likes to remind the people around her.

But there's nothing hokey about the 18.5% that Mrs. Fields Inc. earned on cookie sales of $87 million in 1986, up from $72.6 million a year earlier.

Won't the cookie craze pass? people often ask Debbi. "I think that's very doubtful . . . I mean," she says, "if [they are] fresh, warm, and wonderful and make you feel good, are you going to stop buying cookies?"

Maybe not, but the trick for her and her husband is to see that people keep buying them from Mrs. Fields, not David's Cookies, Blue Chip Cookies, The Original Great Chocolate Chip Cookie, or the dozens of regional and local competitors. Keeping the cookies consistently fresh, warm, and wonderful at nearly 500 retail cookie stores spread over the United States and five other countries can't be simple or easy. Worse, keeping smiles on the faces of the nearly 4,500, mostly young, store employees — not to mention keeping them productive and honest — is a bigger chore than most companies would dare to take on alone.

Most don't; they franchise, which is one way to bring responsibility and accountability down to the store level in a far-flung, multi-store organization. For this, the franchisor trades off revenues and profits that would otherwise be his and a large measure of flexibility. Because its terms are defined by contract, the relationship between franchisor and franchisee is more static than dynamic, difficult to alter as the market and the business change.

Mrs. Fields Cookies, despite its size, has not franchised — persuasive evidence in itself that the Fieldses have built something unusual. Randy Fields believes that no other U.S. food retailer with so many outlets has dared to retain this degree of direct, day-to-day control of its stores. And Mrs. Fields cookies does it with a headquarters staff of just 115 people. That's approximately one staffer to every five stores — piddling compared with other companies with far fewer stores to manage. When the company bought La Petite Boulangerie from PepsiCo earlier this year, for instance, the soft-drink giant had 53 headquarters staff people to administer the French bakery/sandwich shop chain's 119 stores. Randy needed just four weeks to cut the number to 3 people.

On paper, Mrs. Fields Cookies *looks* almost conventional. In action, however, because of the way information flows between levels, it *feels* almost flat.

On paper, between Richard Lui running the Pier 39 Mrs. Fields in San Francisco and Debbi herself in Park City, there are several apparently traditional layers of hierarchy: an area sales manager, a district sales manager, a regional director of operations, a vice-president of operations. In practice, though, Debbi is as handy to Lui — and to every other store manager — as the telephone and personal computer in the back room of his store.

On a typical morning at Pier 39, Lui unlocks the store, calls up the Day Planner program on his Tandy computer, plugs in today's sales projection (based on year-earlier sales adjusted for growth), and answers a couple of questions the program puts to him. What day of the week is it? What type of day: normal day, sale day, school day, holiday, other?

Say, for instance, it's Tuesday, a school day. The computer goes back to the Pier 39 store's hour-by-hour, product-by-product performance on the last three school-day Tuesdays. Based on what you did then, the Day Planner tells him, here's what you'll have to do today, hour by hour, product by product, to meet your sales projection. It tells him how many customers he'll need each hour and how much he'll have to sell them. It tells him how many batches of cookie dough he'll have to mix and when to mix them to meet the demand and to minimize leftovers. He could make these estimates himself if he wanted to take the time. The computer makes them for him.

Each hour, as the day progresses, Lui keeps the computer informed of his progress. Currently he enters the numbers manually, but new cash registers that automatically feed hourly data to the computer, eliminating the manual update, are already in some stores. The computer in turn revises the hourly projections and makes suggestions. The customer count is OK, it might observe, but your average check is down. Are your crew members doing enough suggestive selling? If, on the other hand, the computer indicates that the customer count is down, that may suggest the manager will want to do some sampling — chum for customers up and down the pier with a try of free cookie pieces or try something else, whatever he likes, to lure people into the store. Sometimes, if sales are just slightly down, the machine's revised projections will actually exceed the original on the assumption that greater selling effort will more than compensate for the small deficit. On the other hand, the program isn't blind to reality. It recognizes a bad day and diminishes its hourly sales projections and baking estimates accordingly.

Hourly sales goals?

Well, when Debbi was running *her* store, *she* set hourly sales goals. Her managers should, too, she thinks. Rather than enforce the practice through dicta, Randy has embedded the notion in the software that each store manager relies on. Do managers find the machine's suggestions intrusive? Not Lui. "It's a tool for me," he says.

Several times a week, Lui talks with Debbi. Well, he doesn't exactly talk *with* her, but he hears from her. He makes a daily phone call to Park City to check his computerized PhoneMail messages, and as often as not there's something from Mrs. Fields herself. If she's upset about some problem, Lui hears her sounding upset. If it's something she's breathlessly exuberant about, which is more often the case, he gets an earful of that, too. Whether the news is good or bad, how much better to hear it from the boss herself than to get a memo in the mail next week.

By the same token, if Lui has something to say to Debbi, he uses the computer. It's right there, handy. He calls up the FormMail program, types his message, and the next morning it's on Debbi's desk. She promises an answer, from her or her staff, within 48 hours. On the morning I spent with her, among the dozen or so messages she got was one from the crew at a Berkeley, Calif., store making their case for higher wages there and another from the manager of a store in Brookline, Mass., which has been struggling recently. We've finally gotten ourselves squared away, was the gist of the note, so please come visit. (Last year Debbi logged around 350,000 commercial air miles visting stores.)

Here are some other things Lui's computer can do for him.

- Help him schedule crew. He plugs his daily sales projection for two weeks hence into a scheduling program that incorporates as its standards the times Debbi herself takes to perform the mixing, dropping, and baking chores. The program gives him back its best guess of how many people with which skill levels he'll need during which hours. A process that, done manually, consumed almost an hour now takes just a fraction of that time.
- Help him interview crew applicants. He calls up his interview program, seats the applicant at the keyboard, and has him or her answer a series of questions. Based on the answers given by past hirees, the machine suggests to Lui which candidates will succeed or fail. It's still his choice. And any applicant, before a hire, will still get an audition — something to see how he or she performs in public. Maybe Lui will send the hopeful out on a sampling mission.
- Help with personnel administration. Say he hires the applicant. He informs the machine, which generates a personnel folder and a payroll entry in Park City, and a few months later comes back to re-

mind Lui that he hasn't submitted the initial evaluation (also by computer), which is now slightly past due. It administers the written part of the skills test and updates the records with the results. The entire Mrs. Fields personnel manual will soon be on the computer so that 500 store managers won't forget to delete old pages and insert revised ones every time a change is made.

• Help with maintenance. A mixer isn't working, so the manager punches up the repair program on the computer. It asks him some questions, such as: is the plug in the wall? If the questions don't prompt a fix, the computer sends a repair request to Park City telling the staff there which machine is broken, its maintenance history, and which vendor to call. It sends a copy of the work order back to the store. When the work gets done, the store signs off by computer, and the vendor's bill gets paid.

That's a lot of technology applied to something as basic as a cookie store, but Randy had two objectives in mind.

He wanted to keep his wife in frequent, personal, two-way contact with hundreds of managers whose stores she couldn't possibly visit often enough. "The people who work in the stores," says Debbi, "are my customers. Staying in touch with them is the most important thing I can do."

It's no accident, even if Lui isn't consciously aware of why he does what he does, that he runs his store just about the same way that Debbi ran her first one 10 years ago. Even when she isn't there, she's there — in the standards built into his scheduling program, in the hourly goals, in the sampling and suggestive selling, on the phone. The technology has "leveraged," to use Randy's term, Debbi's ability to project her influence into more stores than she could ever reach effectively without it.

Second, Randy wanted to keep store managers managing, not sweating the paperwork. "In retailing," he says, "the goal is to keep people close to people. Whatever gets in the way of that — administration, telephones, ordering, and so on — is the enemy." If an administrative chore can be automated, it should be.

Store managers benefit from a continuing exchange of information. Of course, Park City learns what every store is doing daily — from sales to staffing to training to hires to repairs — and how it uses that information

we'll get to in a minute. From the store managers' perspective, however, the important thing is that the information they provide keeps coming back to them, reorganized to make it useful. The hour-by-hour sales projections and projected customer counts that managers use to pace their days reflect their own experiences. Soon, for instance, the computer will take their weekly inventory reports and sales projections and generate supply orders that managers will only have to confirm or correct — more administrative time saved. With their little computers in the back room, store managers give, but they also receive.

What technology can do for operations it can also do for administration.

"We're all driven by Randy's philosophy that he wants the organization to be as flat as possible," says Paul Quinn, the company's director of management information systems (MIS).

"There are a few things," says controller Lynn Quilter, "that Randy dislikes about growth.... He hates the thought of drowning in people so that he can't walk in and know exactly what each person does.... The second thing that drives him nuts is paper."

"The objective," says Randy, "is to leverage people — to get them to act when we have 1,000 stores the same way they acted when we had 30."

He has this theory that large organizations, organizations with lots of people, are, per se, inferior to small ones. Good people join a growing business because it offers them an opportunity to be creative. As the company grows, these people find they're tied up managing the latest hires. Creativity suffers. Entropy sets in. Randy uses technology to keep entropy at bay.

He began by automating rote clerical chores and by minimizing data-entry effort. Machines can sort and file faster than people, and sorting and filing is deadly dull work, anyway. Lately he's pushed the organization toward automated exception reporting for the same reason. Machines can compare actual results with expected results and flag the anomalies, which are all management really cares about anyway. And within a few years,

Randy expects to go much further in his battle against bureaucracy by developing artificial-intelligence aids to the running of the business.

Understand that it's not equipment advances — state-of-the-art hardware — that's pushing Mrs. Fields Cookies toward management frontiers. The machines the company uses are strictly off the shelf: an IBM minicomputer connected to inexpensive personal computers. It is, instead, Randy's ability to create an elegant, functional software architecture. He has, of course, had an advantage that the leader of an older, more established company would not have. Because Mrs. Fields is still a young enough company, he doesn't have to shape his automated management system to a preexisting structure. Every new idea doesn't confront the opposition of some bureaucratic fiefdom's survival instinct. Rather, the people part and the technology part of the Fields organization are developing simultaneously, each shaped by the same philosophy.

You see this congruence at corporate headquarters and in the company's operational management organization.

Between Debbi as chief executive officer and the individual store managers is what seems on paper to be a conventional reporting structure with several layers of management. But there's an additional box on the organization chart. It's not another management layer. It transcends layers, changing the way information flows between them and even changing the functions of the layers.

The box consists of a group of seven so-called store controllers, working in Park City from the daily store reports and weekly inventory reports. They ride herd on the numbers. If a store's sales are dramatically off, the store controller covering that geographical region will be the first to know it. If there's a discrepancy between the inventory report, the daily report of batches of cookies baked, and the sales report, the controller will be the first to find it. (It is possible for a smart thief to steal judiciously for about a week from a Mrs. Fields store.) "We're a check on operations,'" says store controller Wendy Phelps, but she's far

more than just a check. She's the other half of a manager's head.

Since she's on top of the numbers, the area, district, and regional managers don't have to be — not to the same degree, at any rate. "We want managers to be with people, not with problems," says Debbi. It's hard, Randy says, to find managers who are good with both people and numbers. People people, he thinks, should be in the field, with numbers people backing them up — but not second-guessing them. Here's where the company takes a meaningful twist.

Problems aren't reported up the organization just so solutions can flow back down. Instead, store controllers work at levels as low as they can. They go to the store manager if he's the one to fix a discrepancy, a missing report, for instance. Forget chain of command. "I'm very efficiency minded," says Randy.

So the technology gives the company an almost real-time look at the minutiae of its operations, and the organizational structure — putting function ahead of conventional protocol — keeps it from choking on this abundance of data.

Some managers would have problems with a system that operates without their daily intervention. They wouldn't be comfortable, and they wouldn't stay at Mrs. Fields. Those who do stay can manage people instead of paper.

If administrative bureaucracies can grow out of control, so can technology bureaucracies. A couple of principles, ruthlessly adhered to, keep both simple at Mrs. Fields.

The first is that if a machine can do it, a machine *should* do it. "People," says Randy, "should do only that which people can do. It's demeaning for people to do what machines can do. . . . Can machines manage people? No. Machines have no feelie-touchies, none of that chemistry that flows between two people."

The other rule, the one that keeps the technological monster itself in check, is that the company will have but one data base. Everything — cookie sales, payroll records, suppliers' invoices, inventory reports, utility charges — goes into the same data base. And whatever anybody needs to know has to come out of it.

Don't enforce this rule, and, says Randy, "the next thing you know you have 48 different programs that can't talk to each other." Technology grown rampant.

Having a single data base means, first, that nobody has to waste time filing triplicate forms or answering the same questions twice. "We capture the data just once," says controller Quilter.

Second, it means that the system itself can do most of the rote work that people used to do. Take orders for chocolate, for instance. The computer gets the weekly inventory report. It already knows the sales projection. So let the computer order the chocolate chips. Give the store manager a copy of the order on his screen so he can correct any errors, but why take his time to generate the order when he's got better things to do — like teaching someone to sell. Or, take it further. The machine generates the order. The supplier delivers the chips to the store and bills the corporate office. A clerk in the office now has to compare the order, the invoice, and what the store says it got. Do they all match? Yes. She tells the computer to write a check. The more stores you have, the more clerks it takes. Why not let the computer do the matching? In fact, if everything fits, why get people involved at all? Let people handle the exceptions. Now, the clerk, says MIS director Quinn, instead of a processor becomes a mini-controller, someone who uses his brain.

The ordering process doesn't happen that way yet at Mrs. Fields, although it probably will soon as Randy continues to press for more exception reporting. You can see where he's going with this concept.

"Eventually," he says, "even the anomalies become normal." The exceptions themselves, and a person's response to them, assume a pattern. Why not, says Randy, have the computer watch the person for a while? "Then the machine can say, 'I have found an anomaly. I've been watching you, and I think this is what you would do. Shall I do it for you, yes or no. If yes, I'll do it, follow up, and so on. If no, what do you want me to do?'" It would work for the low-level function — administering accounts payable, for instance. And it would work at higher levels as well. "If," Randy says, "I can ask the computer now where are we making the most money and where are we making the least and then make a decision about where not to build new stores, why shouldn't that sort of thing be an automatic pilot too? 'Based on performance,' it will say, 'we shouldn't be building any more stores in

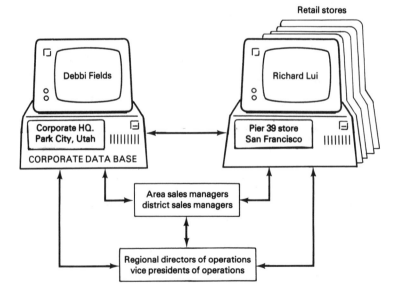

The Information Flow

Installing A System That Works
Keep it simple, and make sure the information flows both ways

No formula exists for applying information technology to a growing company that will assure success. And there are costs of applying technology that are easily overlooked.

Phone Mail, for instance, looked like a great way to battle paper within the Mrs. Fields organization. Debbi Fields wanted to be able to talk to her store managers and wanted them to be able to talk to her without the formality or the delay inherent in paper memos. Voilà, PhoneMail — a computerized system that answers your phone, takes messages, stores them, plays them back, and transfers them to other people. But Debbi soon found herself with scores of messages and no way to classify them by importance and no way to skim quickly through them. Even the computer's memory began to choke on the glut of mail. For routine communications between one person at headquarters and hundreds of store managers in the field, high-tech PhoneMail didn't work.

But FormMail does. Debbi still uses PhoneMail to pass routine messages on to the field. That puts her voice into every store. Managers can still phone her, too. But for routine messages on less than acute issues, Debbi doesn't need to hear their voices. So the managers call up the FormMail program on their personal computers, type in their messages, and the boss can scan through them all quickly the next morning.

Using *appropriate* technology is more important than using technology.

Giving technology to people in doses they can handle is another principle the Fieldses try to practice. "It's not the lack of technology that's slowing us down," says Randy, "but the rate at which people can become comfortable with it."

To increase the rate, they make the technology *look* as simple as possible. The software programs are tutorial and menu driven. If store managers can put a plug into a wall socket, they can operate the PCs that Park City supplies.

But why would store managers want to use one? They wouldn't unless, as at the cookie stores, their efforts are rewarded by feedback that helps them save time and energy. At La Petite Boulangerie (LPB) stores, only recently acquired by Mrs. Fields Inc., the computer isn't yet the manager's friend. LPB store managers have to punch numbers into the machine, but they, unlike the cookie store managers, get nothing in return. There's no data base yet for LPB stores, so the machine, in effect, doesn't know anything useful it can send back. Temporarily, the new computers in LPB stores are a one-way communication channel, just another burden on a busy manager. In many companies, that's all the computer *ever* is. At LPB, at least, there will soon be a concrete payback when managers get interactive software that they can call on for help.

And the cost of installing technology? If a particular technology won't pay back its full cost in two years or less, according to Mrs. Fields's management information systems director Paul Quinn, they don't buy it. They recaptured the cost of the in-store Tandy computers, Quinn says, in well under two years by eliminating touch-tone reporting of daily store operating data and reducing huge telephone toll charges.

East Jibip. Want me to tell [real-estate manager] Mike [Murphy]?' We're six months away from being able to do that."

The ability to look at the company, which is what the data base really is, at a level of abstraction appropriate to the looker, is the third advantage of a single data base — even if it never moves into artificial-intelligence functions. It means that Debbi Fields and Richard Lui are both looking at the same world, but in ways that are meaningful to each of them.

The hurdle to be overcome before you can use technology to its best advantage — and that isn't equivalent to just hanging an outboard motor on a skyscraper, as Buckminster Fuller said — isn't technical in the hardware sense. Randy buys only what he calls plain vanilla hardware. And it isn't financial. For all its relative sophistication in computer systems, Mrs. Fields spends just 0.49% of sales on data processing, much of which is returned in higher productivity.

Much more important, Randy says, is having a consistent vision of what you want to *accomplish* with the technology. Which functions do you want to control? What do you want your organization chart to look like? In what ways do you want to leverage the CEO's vision? "Imagination. We imagine what it is we want," says Randy. "We aren't constrained by the limits of what technology can do. We just say, 'What does your day look like? What would you *like* it to look like?'" He adds, "If you don't have your paradigm in mind, you have no way of knowing whether each little step is taking you closer to or further from your goal."

For instance, he inaugurated the daily store report with the opening of store number two in 1978. The important thing was the creation of the report — which is the fundamental data-gathering activity in the company — not its transmission mode. That can change, and has. First transmission was by Fax, then by telephone touch tone, and only recently by computer modem.

Having a consistent vision means, Randy says, that he could have described as far back as 1978, when he first began to create it, the system that exists today. But he doesn't mean the machines or how they're wired together. "MIS in this company," he says, "has always had to serve two masters. First, control. Rapid growth without control equals disaster. We needed to keep improving control over our stores. And second, information that leads to control also leads to better decison making. To the extent that the information is then provided to the store and field-management level, the decisions that are made there are better, and they are more easily made.

"That has been our consistent vision."

Ten Service Workers
and Their Jobs

CHRISTOPHER H. LOVELOCK ET AL.[1]

*Service workers in a variety of industries talk about their jobs,
their backgrounds, and their interactions with customers, managers, and fellow workers.*

How often do users of a service get a chance
to interact with senior managers? Unless they
are VIPs, the answer is: rarely. Except
in professional service firms, most personal contact takes place with low-level
employees—receptionists, flight attendants,
service engineers, bank tellers, restaurant
servers, letter carriers, bus drivers, customer
service reps, and gas pump attendants. To
succeed in a service business, as one executive wrote, "you have to turn the organization chart upside down."

Since service personnel at the bottom of
the totem pole are often the major points of

contact between customers and the organization, the performance and demeanor of
these individuals can have a powerful effect
on the quality of service delivered.

A few companies require executives from
the head office to spend a certain amount
of time each year in the field, observing—
or even working—in service positions. There's
probably no better way to get a feel for the
nature of the demands placed on employees,
the variety of customer situations encountered, or the problems entailed in trying to
deliver good service.

Managers who are really effective in get-

The ten profiles in this chapter were prepared under the direction of Christopher H. Lovelock by
Elizabeth Gans, Douglas MacKinney, Jane R. Borthwick, Stephen Harper, David Harmuth, Jeffrey Duke,
Merideth Durden Dolan, Lisa H. Rakov, John Fess, and Gordon Wilson.

ting the best possible performance out of their employees take time to understand each individual's personal background, needs, and career aspirations. This chapter provides brief profiles of ten service employees, working in a variety of different customer contact jobs, in an attempt to portray both the people behind the jobs and the environments within which they try to deliver service. The names of the individuals profiled have been changed and, in a few instances, so have the names of the organizations they work for.

SHERRY—RESTAURANT WAITRESS

Sherry, a 22-year-old Ivy League graduate, works as a "waitron" at a new, chic little restaurant while applying to medical school. She prepares the restaurant for opening, greets customers seated at one of her seven tables, offers them beverages and explains specials, memorizes orders, delivers food, watches a customer's progress through drinks/salad in order to time the cook's preparation of the entree, anticipates a customer's need for water refills, etc., checks on the customer two or three times during a meal, delivers the bill without rushing the customer, and collects payment.

As stated in the menu, the restaurant's service concept is to provide "a dining experience prepared with quality ingredients and attention to presentation that comes from truly caring." The basic structure of Sherry's job supports this concept. Sherry's low wage rate ($2.00/hour) induces her to provide good service in order to earn good tips. Also, the job allows her the discretion necessary to personalize service and present an attitude of "caring." For example, she suggests her own unusual drink combinations, such as hot cider and saki. She can request rush or special orders, as long as she stays in the good graces of the cook. Her skill at personalizing service comes from her own intelligence and intuition rather than from training at the restaurant.

Difficulties Sherry has in performing as a caring waitron stem from her interactions with management, not with customers. One problem is the way management has at-

tempted to alter her personal style. A restaurant consultant that the owner-manager brought in to make operations more efficient has instructed her to sound more "professional" (e.g., "Say 'house special soup,' not 'regular soup' "). Interpreting his definition of professional to mean "less friendly," Sherry disagrees with his approach. She also resents his efforts to make her "sell" rather than respond to customers' wishes (she quotes him: "I don't care if she says she's on a diet; tempt her with the dessert tray anyway"). She feels that the manager penalizes her for not "selling" by unfairly assigning her to less lucrative shifts. Because of this, her loyalty has dwindled. Management's failure to communicate new performance standards clearly and in a positive framework, and the resultant perception of unfair treatment, may well contribute to the 100 percent turnover Sherry has observed in the last four months.

Sherry's enthusiasm for performing the job has also declined because the consultant-manager has introduced a less benevolent management style, eliminating many job benefits that were important to Sherry and to maintaining her sense of dignity in a service position. He has cut back on the quality of staff meals, no longer allows staff to take home leftovers, makes waitrons feel that they are being "watched," assigns prep tasks to specific waitrons (which has reduced cooperation and increased blame-shifting among waitrons), and relays customer compliments only in a qualified manner. While he complains about the staff's "negative vibes" driving customers away, he may himself be responsible for creating a colder atmosphere.

JOHN—MAILMAN

John works as a substitute mail carrier at the Arlington, Massachusetts, branch of the United States Postal Service. John began working for the Postal Service nine years ago, shortly after graduation from Kent State University with a B.S. After seven years working as a postal clerk, John applied to become a mail carrier. He had three days of classroom and on the job training and then began work as a substitute carrier two years ago.

The typical mail carrier progression is to start as a substitute carrier, advance to utility carrier, and then to regular carrier. Further career movement depends upon the initiative of the individual to apply for posted opportunities in other areas of the Postal Service. The roles of the substitute, utility, and regular carrier are identical except for route assignment. The regular carrier has his own route and delivers mail on five of the six delivery days each week. The utility carrier delivers mail for regular carriers on their respective days off. The substitute carrier fills in on any route as needed. Despite his substitute status, John usually delivers mail five days a week.

John begins work at 7:00 A.M. For the first two to three hours he sorts the mail for his route, sequencing it by street and house number and putting it in bundles. If the route is a "Park and Loop" route John will load the bundles into a Postal Service Jeep or Pinto and be on his way. On a "Park and Loop" route John parks and delivers the mail by foot, usually doing a loop around the block. On a "Walking" route, the mail bundles are delivered by a parcel truck driver to strategically located transfer boxes (those mailboxes painted olive drab) along the carrier's route. The "Walking" route requires good timing between the carrier and the truck driver so that when a carrier has completed one neighborhood the mail for the next neighborhood will be waiting at the transfer box.

The degree of customer contact on a route varies. With businesses, the mail is often delivered in person. Residential customers sometimes wait for their mail and thus also receive it personally. This is more likely the case for regular carriers who often know most of their customers and deliver the mail at a specified time each day. For "signature" mail (certified, registered, insured, special delivery, and express mail) a signature is required from the customer. A final source for customer contact is complaints, which vary widely but often involve not getting mail.

Safety, security, and customer contact are key operating issues for mail carriers. Dog bites and vehicular safety are the most important safety concerns. Dog spray is issued to mail carriers to protect them from bites, and monitoring and training help promote driving safety. Security procedures include signing out mailbox keys and signature mail each morning. Courtesy and neat public appearance are strongly encouraged and monitored.

John likes his job, primarily for the job security, good fringe benefits, and ease of relocation. John complained, though, that as a substitute carrier he was shoved around a bit and given undesirable routes. He also noted that the relationship between supervisor and employee was often one of unquestioned authority, not unlike the military. He attributed this relationship to the vast number of Vietnam veterans hired and to their highly proceduralized work rules. John also noted that mailmen often took a lot of unwarranted criticism from disgruntled customers. He felt more public image advertising might help.

ANNE—FLIGHT ATTENDANT

"I don't think of myself as a sex symbol or a servant, I am someone who knows how to open the door of a 747 in the dark, upside down, and under 30 feet of water."

Anne has been a Delta flight attendant for five years and is convinced she works for the best airline in the industry.

Training

Initially, FAs are trained for one month in service techniques (serving meals, interacting with passengers) and in first-aid and emergency procedures. They annually attend an FAA-mandated "Jet recurrent" program which focuses on aircraft modifications and updated emergency procedures.

Supervision

An FA's actions are always subject to close scrutiny and evaluation. In fact, only when she/he is out of uniform are her/his actions considered private. Evaluation comes from three sources: Delta, the FAA, and passengers. Flight pursers and supervisors check to ensure that Delta service and safety procedures are met. The FAA monitors safety requirements and issues fines for noncompliance. For example, failure to collect glasses prior to landing results in a $1,000 fine which must be paid by the FA personally. In addition to these formal checks, passengers, who view FAs as The Airline, provide constant evaluation through their letters. For each positive letter, an FA receives a tax-free flight, while six negative letters trigger a review. Anne feels there is every incentive to resolve problems quickly and diplomatically. These evaluations, however, are not reflected in compensation. All FAs receive pay increases based solely on seniority.

Career Development

According to Anne, slower advancement is the biggest problem facing FAs today. With the recent down-turn in the industry, turnover is slower and it is taking everyone much longer to achieve the rewards of seniority. Previously, new recruits spent 1–2 years "on call" before they could bid for a regular schedule. Now they must wait up to six years. Seniority translates into a higher salary and fewer and better working hours. FAs are not typically considered for management positions. Because a career track does not exist, the reward of seniority is the freedom to pursue further education, family, and small independent businesses.

Analysis

While passengers may view an FA as a glamorous waitress, the airline and the FAA insist that safety comes above all else. In fact, much of the friction on-board results from a lack of appreciation of the reasons behind many safety procedures. For example, while passengers may feel instructions to "place luggage firmly under the seat in front of you" are annoying, the possibility of a need to evacuate the aircraft necessitates a clear exit-way.

The public stereotype is partly due to the inherent limits of the job, the essence of which is to follow an established routine. Anne characterizes her job as "mindless." The challenge and opportunity for an FA to "show her/his stuff" is in emergencies which thankfully are infrequent. To more fully utilize FAs' capabilities, Delta has increasingly involved them in other airline activities. For example, Delta encourages FAs to suggest specific design modifications for aircraft which will increase comfort and safety. For example, a Delta FA suggested that Boeing place "L" shaped bars under aisle seats to prevent luggage from sliding into the passageway.

While Anne feels less challenged, she is committed to Delta because of steps the airline has taken to "serve" its employees better. Delta is the only airline that has never laid off an FA. Further, it is the only airline that allows FAs unlimited schedule swapping ability. Management also holds annual meetings to solicit employee suggestions. For Delta this has translated into stronger employee loyalty. For example, Delta FAs are willing to tidy airplanes themselves to ensure rapid turnaround, while other airline FAs would insist on waiting for cleaning crews. At the height of the recent recession, three Delta FAs initiated a movement to purchase a Boeing 767 as an expression of their commitment to the airline.

JANE—HOTEL DESK CLERK

As a front desk clerk during the morning shift (7:00 A.M. to 3:30 P.M.) at a first-class hotel in Washington, D.C., Jane spends about 80 percent of her time "checking out" hotel guests. The checkout procedure requires retrieving the guest's file from the computer, pulling the bill out of a file box and presenting it to the guest for verification, accepting payment, and recording the transaction on the computer file. The remaining 20 percent of Jane's time is spent cashiering (cashing checks or exchanging currency), posting charges (telephone, valet, etc.) to guests' bills, checking in guests, and answering inquiries. These latter tasks, however, do not begin until later in the morning. From 7:00 until 9:30 A.M., the front desk clerks rush to keep up with the deluge of checkouts. As the tempo slows to a leisurely pace, the variety of tasks expands.

Like the other clerks, Jane is young (mid-twenties) and has a high school education. She enjoys her work because she likes the guest contact and the perks, particularly the free meals at work and the free accommodations at affiliated hotels in other cities. Also, the glamor of the hotel business is attractive ("Last week, I checked in Tom Selleck!"). Still, the turnover rate of clerks is high. One source of frustration is the uncertainty of shift schedules. Often, the clerks know only one week in advance which days they must work and which days they have off. Another frustration is that the front desk clerk must deal regularly with complaints or problems—typically five to ten per day. These problems frequently pertain to departments in the hotel with which the clerk is unfamiliar. Nevertheless, the guests expect—and deserve—first-class treatment, so that even a seemingly minor problem must be remedied swiftly to ensure that the guests' expectations are met.

The clerks are trained in front desk operations by their shift supervisor for two weeks before actually going behind the desk. The operating procedures are tightly prescribed and each clerk's work is checked closely. It appears that the operating system is designed to minimize errors by extracting as much discretion as possible from the clerk function. For example, if a guest disputes a charge on a bill or wishes to check out after the specified checkout time, the clerk must obtain the supervisor's approval before entering any change into the computer. Ironically, no supervisor ever refuses such requests because of the risk of offending a guest. Since this approval process consumes "real time" with the guest and unnecessarily amplifies the guest's request, the discretional control is questionable. The apparent consequence is that the clerks depend entirely on supervisors to solve even the most simple problems. In effect, the current operating system

fails to offer the promptness and efficiency that guests demand from the front desk.

BILL—ANSWERPHONE SPECIALIST

Dial 1-800-626-2000 and a voice will answer, "General Electric AnswerCenter. May I help you?" 24 hours a day, seven days a week. The Center is staffed in Louisville, Kentucky, by both technical specialists and trained generalists who can answer questions on virtually all GE consumer products and services. From prepurchase and selection through follow-up service and repairs, the staff is available to describe, explain or make referrals. In addition to reference manuals, specialists use computer terminals to call up full parts listings, operating instructions or listings of service centers.

Bill, a 26-year-old graduate of St. Lawrence University, has been an AnswerCenter specialist for 1½ years. Prior to taking the AnswerCenter position, he had worked at GE's Appliance Park in Customer Service. Because of his prior work experience at GE's Major Appliance Division he felt comfortable about the promotion to the AnswerCenter. Upon joining the AnswerCenter he participated in a training program which provided instruction on GE's consumer products, telephone etiquette, and computer terminal operation. In addition to the initial training they have regular meetings explaining new materials, new products, recalls, and general company information. When asked why he left Major Appliances, Bill stated that the AnswerCenter provided him with much more exposure to the Company's other consumer businesses as well as their respective marketing and sales groups.

In response to my queries about his fellow workers and supervisors, Bill described the environment.

Many people think we are just telephone operators. Contrary to this we have a philosophy that we are a hybrid group. We are a crossbreed of a sales/information counselor and a service advisor. Many of the specialists hold advanced degrees and have had some customer relation experience, such as myself. As a result, the AnswerCenter pays significantly higher salaries than operators receive, to attract and retain qualified people. We receive individual evaluations annually as do other GE personnel. However, we receive immediate feedback from our superiors and consumers, particularly if the lines are busy or consumers are on hold for more than a couple of minutes. Supervisors also receive computerized reports detailing telephone efficiency rates and follow-up calls generated by each specialist. The quality of our telephone conversations is also randomly monitored by our supervisors. All these measurement systems and standard procedures frightened me at first, however there is still lots of room for creativity. Let me explain. I receive hundreds of calls daily, not one of them is the same. I find the creativity in talking with the different consumers. For example, if the computer is slow (particularly during busy periods), I will ask the customer more information about the product or his usage patterns. Sometimes we even engage in a conversation about the weather.

Mondays tend to be the busiest days when we handle upwards of 7,000 calls. We use some regular part-time specialists during these times as well as in the afternoons. There is particular pressure during these periods to answer customer questions more quickly so that the next call may be handled. During these peaks we have had as much as a ten minute wait on our switching system. These busy periods can get quite hectic, particularly if I am unable to locate the correct information or provide an answer. In such cases, I usually seek advice from a specialist next to me or from a supervisor. If it appears that it will take too long or that I am unable to answer the question I advise the caller that I will call him back (at a slower time within 24 hours) or that someone who is better qualified to answer his question will call him back (Division Marketing within 72 hours). I usually prefer to take an extra minute or so to locate the information needed to answer the question while the consumer is on the phone. I often have difficulty getting a hold of the consumer on return calls, thus it takes more time.

CRAIG—REGISTERED NURSE

Craig is a registered nurse. He has worked for eight months as an RN, twelve months as an LPN, and twelve months as an orderly. He currently works forty hours a week during the hospital graveyard shift. Craig is a bright, extremely outgoing, compassionate individual who is dedicated to his work. He loves working with people of all walks of life, and enjoys helping individuals, both healthy and ill, to feel good about themselves and the predicaments in which they find themselves.

There are a number of factors that contribute to a nurse's success, but according to Craig, the most important is comforting the patient. This is manifested in medicating, cleaning, and feeding the patient, examining lab reports, and carrying out the attending physician's demands. As a nurse, Craig is the liaison between the physician and his patient, which necessitates the ability to effectively communicate with the physician, the patient, and other hospital staff. Such communication not only takes the form of orders and words of comfort; the nurse is also expected to not only know how a patient feels but why. Because the physician is rarely attending his patients during the early morning hours, the nurse's ability to diagnose a patient's immediate problems is of critical importance.

Nursing is not unlike other medical disciplines in that it is governed by a myriad of rules, regulations, and operating procedures. A majority of these prescribed procedures are itemized in hospital manuals. One's ability to adhere to these rules and regulations is in large part the basis for a quarterly performance appraisal conducted by Craig's supervisor, the floor nurse, who reports to a floor coordinator, who in turn reports to the Director of Nursing. The successful completion of one's tasks coupled with the requisite experience will enable one to progress through the ranks of nursing. According to Craig, progression to supervisory roles in specialty areas is based primarily on skill, while advancement to the position of floor supervisor is based largely on seniority.

When asked what he enjoys most about being a nurse, Craig expressed the satisfaction he derives from making people feel well. He said he also views nursing as an opportunity to continually develop his knowledge and understanding of the human body, and to figure out what causes his patients to ail. He also said the remuneration is excellent for only two years of schooling, although the disparity between what a nurse and a physician make is often discouraging given the amount of time the nurse spends with the patient. On the other side of the ledger, Craig said that it is tough being in the minority as a male nurse. This means receiving many of the physically demanding jobs, as well as the less desirable jobs related to serving male patients. However, Craig was quick to recognize the preferential treatment he often receives when it comes time for layoffs and advancement. Craig said he also disliked working with physicians in many situations. As a nurse working the graveyard shift, Craig often finds himself in a prisoner's dilemma: if he wakes the physician in response to a patient's request, he usually gets yelled at for not waiting until the morning; if he doesn't serve the patient's needs (which usually requires doctor approval), he stands the risk of getting yelled at. This he finds very frustrating. He also finds the charting of patients and shift work to be generally undesirable, although he recognizes that these are necessary elements of the job.

If he could bring about change, Craig would chart less and give nurses more authority, perhaps in the form of standing orders from the physician. This would allow him to spend more time with the patient, which he sees as his primary responsibility. He said it's frustrating to have to call a physician regarding something as simple as the administration of an aspirin.

SARAH—HOSPITAL TRAYGIRL

"Traygirls" are the lowest status workers on the hospital cafeteria staff. But by talking to any one of the four at Mariemont Hospital, you'd think it was an exclusive club.

"We come in together, we get dressed together, we eat together, and then we work hard together," says Sarah, a two-year veteran. "Oh yeah, we also go to school together." Sarah is part of a strong high school clique that works part time at the hospital

during the school year and full time during the summer. They come in right after school daily and work with the seven other full-time cafeteria workers. They work quickly, noisily, and enthusiastically.

The job requires "setting up" certain types of food on to individual patient trays (e.g. "Mr. Johnson—Room 311—Low Salt"). Traygirls can ask one of the two cooks or three other cafeteria workers about which food type is right for which diet, but most traygirls are experienced and knowledgeable enough to work quickly and correctly. At the end of the line the "boss," the dietician, checks each tray. Then traygirls load the trays onto a huge mobile cart and begin another tray. When the cart is full, a traygirl volunteers to push it around the wards and deliver trays. When the cart is empty, she returns to the cafeteria to fill trays.

The two different tasks a traygirl performs are very different; setting up trays requires speed and accuracy, while delivering trays demands a slower, empathetic style. Yet, no distinction is made of the different skills involved, and the crucial selection about which traygirl delivers the trays is very ad hoc. This is unfortunate; not only are some traygirls clearly more suited to one task or the other, many of them also have *strong*, yet unrecognized, preferences about which job they want. So the hospital could have both higher levels of patient *and* employee satisfaction by recognizing the different jobs and letting traygirls volunteer in advance to push carts.

Another big problem with the traygirl job is that speed and efficiency are encouraged when delivering trays, but that is exactly the *opposite* of what the patients want. Patients' only contact with the cafeteria is the traygirls, and they want lavish service and personal attention—actions that primarily involve the traygirls' *time*. But traygirls are encouraged to rush through tray deliveries so they can get back to where the "real" work is done—inside the cafeteria.

"I'm one of the slowest deliverers," Sarah says. She seems proud. If there is an error or omission on a tray, she tells the patient, "I'll come back with it." Yet it is hard to explain to her friends on the clean-up crew just why, as she returns the empty cart to the room where they are madly cleaning up, she must now take a very few food items and disappear for half an hour.

BONNIE—BANK TELLER

Bonnie has been a teller at Barclay's Bank at the Bronxville branch for five years. While she enjoys her job most days, to her it is still "just a job," and from the end of the lunch crunch onward, she looks forward to "proving out" and going home.

Bonnie's daily routine begins with her arrival at 8 A.M. to the branch. She gets out her money tray and puts her receipts in order. The day begins with a buzz as people stop by to do their banking transactions on their way to work. From about 9:30 to 11:30 is a rather quiet period, and she has specific tasks that she performs, such as counting out the money in the night bags and filing checks. Around 11:30 A.M. peak lunch hour traffic begins. Bonnie is kept constantly busy, and her main objective is to keep the line of customers moving and complete transactions as quickly and accurately as possible. The traffic slows around 1 P.M. and she spends the next few hours handling a slower stream of customers and completing half-started transactions from rush hour. After the window closes, she begins the nightly task of "proving out"—accounting for all her receipts and disbursements for the day. This is the part of the job Bonnie likes least, and she states that it is like a daily performance appraisal on how well she's done for the day. If she doesn't prove out, she can spend hours tracking a mistake. "I feel like there's a lot of pressure from my boss to keep customers happy and not make them wait, but if I don't prove out at night, I regret that I hurried so much."

Critical skills for this position are the ability to count money quickly and accurately, a pleasant customer manner, and working as a team with fellow tellers. Because the peak hours are so hectic, this team cooperation is necessary to keep things flowing smoothly. It is important that they help each other with

handling phone calls, exchanging money or obtaining information quickly.

There seem to be two types of tellers: the "career teller," who may be promoted to head teller but is generally content to stay at the current level, and the "mobility teller," who aspires to move on to a position on "the platform." The platform job has much more status attached to it and has less frenzied customer contact. Bonnie states that there is definitely a "WE/THEY" relationship between the tellers and platform assistants, but that they must learn to work effectively together despite their differences to better serve the bank customers. Bonnie feels that she doesn't have either the training or motivation to become a platform teller.

The job is very structured, and procedures for each transaction are very specific. The hours are regular and Bonnie likes being able to arrive home at 5:45 each night. Her lunch hour is a structured half hour and her daily duties are tightly prescribed. Overall, she feels that she is lucky to have this job because it is a "clean and respectable" workplace and she likes her fellow tellers.

Like McDonald's, this job's biggest problem area is managing the uneven traffic flows during the day. Bonnie's greatest frustration is not having the time to be accurate during peak hours, and being bored during slack hours. Rescheduling the lunch breaks may be one solution, so that all four tellers work during that peak time instead of only three. While this may meet with some initial resistance, it would give the tellers slightly longer lunch hours either later or earlier. Another way to ease the traffic would be to install ATM's to handle the more routine transactions. It would also leave the more challenging transactions to the tellers, and would require managers to hire more qualified entry-level tellers.

Another problem is maintaining a teamwork spirit among the tellers. Bonnie feels that she often competes with her peers to be the quickest or most accurate. A more balanced team of old, new, career, and mobility tellers would keep the group dynamic and ease strict peer competition. Finally, training is currently on-the-job with little formal instruction on use of machines or special transactions. A longer training program would mean slower initial start-up, but would result in fewer mistakes longer term.

BETH—TRAVEL AGENT

Beth is a retail "walk-in" travel agent for Crimson Travel Service. Walk-in customers wait up to 30 minutes (average 15) for a free agent, and require from two to sixty minutes of service. Three-quarters of the walk-in customers require only simple ticketing and reservation services, while the other quarter want more elaborate vacation planning. Anomalous situations, such as irate customers, or those who are demanding a refund, are referred to a supervisor. Crimson receives a fixed percentage commission on ticket sales, thus Crimson's success hinges on volume and efficiency. The travel business is characterized by a huge variety of operational procedures required to make bookings and by a high rate of change in these procedures—between one and two each day.

Beth is in her sixth year at Crimson, making her one of the more senior agents. Her job mirrors the variety of the business: she must master a wide variety of tasks, draw on a wide variety of information resources, and interract with customers who can be in widely varying states of mind. Tasks range from simple ticketing to design and arrangement of around-the-world tours. Information resources include travel guides and brochures as well as an on-line information system. The customer's state of mind can range from a newlywed couple planning a honeymoon, to someone in need of an air reservation to attend a funeral. Beth must know how to handle each of these situations and know what questions to ask to most efficiently handle each particular travel request. Crimson's cost and volume focus leads to some very strict procedural rules, but personally developed style is also important in handling the wide variety of situations. Prior to becoming an agent, Beth received six months of training at night while she worked at Crimson as a receptionist. Periodic ongoing

training covers major procedural changes and new-product offerings.

There are two particularly positive elements of Crimson's setup which deserve comment. The first is the on-line computer system which includes, in addition to airline reservation information, an internal bulletin system called "Star." Star is used to communicate—companywide and on an instantaneous basis—the many procedural changes which occur in the business. The system is also used to leverage the agents' experience, making particular agents' expertise available to all. The second element is the "buddy" system, which pairs agents sitting next to one another, formalizing coverage when one or the other is out. Using this system, agents tend to learn each other's style and particular customer circumstances so that when one agent is out the other doesn't need to start out "cold" with repeat customers. This leverages the style and expertise of the more experienced agents and speeds up the training of new agents.

There are a number of conflicts caused by differences between Crimson's business focus and what Beth finds most rewarding about her job. Beth feels most rewarded by travel opportunities and benefits, positive feedback from satisfied customers, recognition of her value as gained through experience, and being able to operate with minimal supervision. Crimson's low-cost focus tends to value lower-paid (newer) agents higher than the more experienced and expensive agents. This leads to high turnover, reducing the experience base. Turnover increases Beth's seniority, thus reducing the level of supervision, but it also causes her to spend undue time helping out the newer agents. The volume and efficiency focus keeps agents unusually busy, which they resist by slowing down. A focus on strict procedures also makes Crimson tend toward staffing with agents who are "trained by the book" rather than those who have developed their own particular style. Crimson's strong desire for scheduling efficiency sometimes causes agents to lose travel opportunities and free trips. Also, it seems that most feedback the agents receive is negative, including angry customers and supervisors who have detected a ticketing error (via a computerized monitoring and control system). Agents' appraisals define "good" as the lack of "bad" occurrences—an emphasis which stimulates Beth to achieve only minimum standards and no more. Finally, the Office Manager seems to concentrate on taking care of special customers rather than taking care of the employees. According to Beth, this leaves agents feeling quite detached from the company.

RICHARD—ELEMENTARY SCHOOL TEACHER

Spring Hill Day School is located on a wooded hill in a wealthy community west of Boston. It is small, with approximately 160 children spread over eight grades. In admissions policy and educational style, the school emphasizes a supportive atmosphere that is conducive to learning. Its students are intellectually above average but not elite; they are chosen just as much for being socially well-adjusted as for being bright. Spring Hill enjoys a strong reputation: it regularly places its graduates into prestigious preparatory schools, and it has a comfortable admissions waiting list. Similarly, there is a heavy demand for teaching positions at Spring Hill.

Richard will be leaving the school at the end of this school year. He is currently the Science Teacher: he teaches fourth and sixth grade science along with fourth grade reading and sixth grade math. He has his own classroom, which is well stocked with pictures of fish, a diagram of the human anatomy, jars of "mystery powders," windows on two sides, squeaky stools, and the largest rabbit this interviewer had ever seen.

Richard has been at Spring Hill for three years. Until this year, he was the third grade homeroom teacher. Before coming to Spring Hill, he taught third grade for three years at Dillingham, Driggs, and Mickel (DD&M), another local private school. Richard left DD&M because it was an "unfriendly place, very competitive, both the parents and the student body. It's hard to serve people you don't like. . . . I think that at Spring Hill, kids

get trained as better thinkers, because they can develop more confidence. They don't just have stuff thrown at them."

Although Richard enjoys Spring Hill's educational approach, he feels that it is now time to move on. A recent divorce makes his teacher's salary insufficient, and "frankly I'm just burned out." Possibilities for the future include graduate school in educational administration, teaching in England, or law school.

Richard's evaluation of his job has two sides: Spring Hill as a place for teachers, and the teaching profession in general. On the balance, he thinks highly of Spring Hill as a place for teachers. He has flexibility with his curriculum and "a nice bunch of kids." Faculty members have a serious decision-making role in hiring teachers and admitting students. Communication among faculty is reasonably good. He also thinks that the hiring is "cautious—and that's good."

On the other hand, the close parental involvement courted by the school can be a nuisance. For example, every Friday afternoon the entire school puts on a "sharing assembly" for the benefit of the parents—or, in Richard's view, for the "1950's PTA mothers." Beside taking enormous amounts of time away from academic work, these assemblies strike Richard as "cutesy." In a similar vein, the headmaster functions less as an educational leader than as a parent-pleaser. He almost never visits the classroom, and Richard has "no idea how he evaluates us." Spring Hill's low salaries are a drawback. Richard's current salary of $15,000 is only a little more than half what he could make in the Boston Public Schools. Then again, "if I were out for money, I wouldn't be in this business. They couldn't pay me enough to teach in the Boston Public Schools."

The teaching profession in general has some strong advantages. First, "It's a noble job. You feel like you are contributing as much to society as anybody could." At least at first, it is "stimulating to learn how people think." At a school like Spring Hill, "you get to work with good people," and the summer vacation is a real plus.

Why, then, do teachers burn out? A principal reason is the emotional intensity of the job: "If you are doing a good job, you've got to be draining your batteries." Also, "the capable ones resent the lack of professional status. You have to be incredibly dedicated and have a strong independent streak" to ignore the opinions of the rest of the world. Money is not a reason by itself, but it fits in with other reasons, both in signalling a lack of respect and in making teaching practically unaffordable as a career. Richard also men-

tioned the lack of a career track: "The only way to rise in teaching is to rise out of it; to administration, or out of education altogether." More than the lack of externally visible career progress, Richard feels the lack of an internal sense of change and personal learning. "I'm still doing essentially the same job I was doing six years ago. After a while it gets to be so much of a muchness. . . . You are about as good after three years as you'll ever be."

Turbulent Skies for TWA

CHRISTOPHER H. LOVELOCK

Determined to make TWA profitable again, the airline's new management has imposed wage cuts and new work rules on its flight attendants, thus provoking a strike. New attendants are hired to replace the strikers, but on-board service is poor and the union claims that TWA flights are unsafe. New talks are scheduled in an effort to settle the strike.

Carl Icahn, Chairman of Trans World Airlines (TWA), was meeting with senior executives of the airline to decide what posture the airline should take in new talks with striking flight attendants on wages and work rules. The Independent Federation of Flight Attendants (IFFA) had agreed to resume negotiations the following day, March 26, 1986, in New York City.

On March 7, 6,500 IFFA members—a union specific to TWA flight attendants—struck the airline after management had imposed new work rules boosting work by 12 hours a month, reducing wages by 22%, and establishing a two-tier wage scale. Management estimated that these changes would save TWA some $100 million per year. Mr. Icahn, who had taken control of the airline two months earlier, insisted that the proposed changes were essential to return the airline to profitability after an extended period of losses.

Negotiations with the union had broken down on February 5, after management rejected the IFFA's counterproposal of wage and benefit cuts amounting to $30 million a year. Both parties were then released from federal mediation for a 30-day cooling-off period, at the end of which the flight attendants went on strike and the company replaced them with 3,000 newly trained attendants working longer hours at lower

384

wages. Union members picketed the airports and distributed press releases claiming that it was unsafe to fly TWA.

CHANGING PRACTICES AND CHANGING FORTUNES IN THE AIRLINE INDUSTRY

From the end of World War II through the early 1970s, the United States airline industry enjoyed a remarkable era of growth and stability. Industry concentration increased as smaller carriers failed or—more commonly—merged into larger ones.

In addition to safety regulation by the Federal Aviation Administration (FAA), the industry was also regulated by the Civil Aeronautics Board (CAB). The latter agency's policies served to discourage entry of new interstate airlines and made it difficult for existing airlines to reshape their route networks. In addition, permission had to be obtained from the CAB if an airline wished to change its fares.

Transcontinental routes within the USA were dominated by three major carriers in the mid-70s: American Airlines, TWA, and United Air Lines. Other large carriers, such as Delta, Eastern, Western, and Continental, focused on route networks covering perhaps one-third to one-half of the United States. Pan American World Airways served international routes exclusively. Only three carriers had both a significant domestic and international presence. These airlines were Braniff International, which served South America; TWA, which had an extensive transatlantic network; and Northwest Orient, which flew to the Far East.

With the notable exception of Delta employees, most airline personnel were unionized. However, different categories of employee belonged to different unions, and the nature of their jobs created different cultures. Cockpit crews at that time were exclusively male, highly paid, and usually members of the Air Line Pilots Association. The cabin crews, by contrast, were almost exclusively female, with the exception of a few stewards or pursers on international routes. Although unionized, they were significantly less well paid than pilots and engineers on the flight deck.

Ground crews included machinists, who maintained the aircraft and belonged to the powerful International Association of Machinists (IAM), gate and ticket agents, and reservations staff.

Until the advent of equal opportunity legislation, many airlines were very restrictive in their hiring practices. They recruited only young single women, forbade them to marry, and terminated them if they did. Since stewardesses over the age of 35 were strongly encouraged—or even required—to take ground jobs, there was continual turnover of stewardesses and only limited seniority.

New Employment Practices

During the first half of the 1970s, the environment of the airline industry changed dramatically. Operations costs rose sharply, due to rising fuel prices. The industry was buffeted by recession in mid-decade. Airport and aircraft security was tightened sharply in response to domestic and international hijackings and terrorist bombings.

Significant changes also occurred in the area of personnel. Lawsuits brought by stewardesses successfully put a stop to a variety of management practices, including termination on marriage, prohibitions against wearing glasses on the job, forced grounding of women in their thirties, and even prohibitions against allowing stewardesses to continue working in the air while pregnant.

Meantime, equal opportunity legislation required the airlines to open cabin crew positions to qualified males and flight deck positions to qualified females. The terms steward and stewardess were eventually replaced by the new job title of flight attendant.

With growing seniority among their ranks, the various airline unions were able to negotiate increased salary scales and more restrictive work rules for their members. Critics alleged that senior flight crews were being paid more and more for less and less work. But lack of significant price competition in the industry enabled the airlines to pass through increased wage and fuel costs to passengers, in the form of higher ticket prices.

The Impact of Deregulation

With the advent of airline deregulation in 1978, the rules of the competitive game changed dramatically. Barriers to entry fell away, new routes became relatively easily available, and restrictions on pricing policy were eliminated. In the words of one observer, deregulation "turned the skies into an aerial free-for-all."

Fourteen new or intrastate carriers entered the interstate airline market within the following five years, including Air Florida, America West, Midway, People Express, Piedmont, Southwest Airlines, and New York Air. Their labor costs ranged from 19% to 27 percent of total operating costs, reflecting use of newly hired personnel working for lower wages on more flexible schedules than those permitted under many union work rules. At major unionized carriers, by contrast, labor costs ran between 33 percent and 37 percent of total costs.

In addition, several new entrants flew secondhand DC-9s or Boeing 727s and 737s purchased at huge savings; Midway, for instance, paid a total of $9.2 million for three used DC-9s that would have cost $12 million each if purchased new. These lower operating and capital costs enabled the newcomers to offer deeply discounted fares, resulting in a surge of new passengers. Older airlines saw reduced profits or larger deficits as they matched discount fares in an effort to protect their market shares.

Two major innovations sprang from the intensely competitive new environment. One was adoption by most airlines of the hub and spoke system of route structure. The second was frequent flyer programs.

Most airlines selected several airports as hub locations, with routes reaching out like the spokes of a wheel. Hub facilities required a significant capital investment to allow terminals to service more aircraft in a short time period. However, the operational payoff was that hubs enabled airlines to make more efficient use of aircraft and crews. From a competitive standpoint, hubs allowed air-

lines to offer passengers a much wider choice of connecting flights, since nearly all flights into a hub were scheduled to connect with departing flights to other destinations. This system also enabled carriers to retain passengers who might otherwise have used another airline for the continuing leg of the journey.

The first frequent flyer program was devised by American Airlines in May 1981 as a way of building brand loyalty. The airlines wanted to give regular business travelers a reason to fly American without resorting to promotional fares that simply eroded revenues. Other airlines quickly followed suit and within eighteen months, all major carriers and many regionals offered their own frequent flyer programs. Subsequent research showed that these programs had become a significant factor in consumers' airline choice decisions; one study showed that they ranked second only to safety as a criterion.

Several major domestic airlines expanded overseas, feeding their international flights with passengers arriving at their domestic hubs. In turn, Pan Am attempted to build domestic routes feeding its international services to defend itself. But some carriers overexpanded, and found themselves unable to achieve the high load factors required to break even at lower fares.

Braniff International became the first casualty of deregulation, filing for bankruptcy in 1982 after selling its South American routes to Eastern. Braniff was later resurrected as a much smaller discount airline, serving domestic routes only. Air Florida went bankrupt in 1984 and was liquidated.

A different style of bankruptcy took place in September 1983 at Continental Airlines, which had been taken over by Frank Lorenzo's Texas Air Corporation (owner of Texas International and New York Air). Unable to win agreement from its unions for $100 million in cost savings, Continental filed for bankruptcy and Lorenzo shut down the airline. Two days later, Continental resumed operations, flying a truncated schedule at sharply lower fares and employing 35 percent of its former workers at half their previous wages. Despite union resistance and court challenges, Continental survived, gradually rebuilt its schedules as a discount carrier, and absorbed Texas International.

Continental's actions sent shockwaves throughout the industry. Several established airlines, including Pan Am and Republic, had previously obtained temporary wage concessions from employees. But now the talk turned to permanent cost-saving measures, such as reduced wages and benefits and more flexible work-rules.

Many observers cited People Express as the model for a new style of airline operation and management. Headquartered in Newark, NJ, just across the Hudson River from Manhattan, People Express was a no-frills discount carrier which had expanded its operations with extraordinary speed during the 1980s. Almost all employees were known as "managers" and were required to own stock in the carrier. Customer service managers were cross-trained in several different jobs, including flight attendant, gate agent, and counter agent at the departure desk. The idea was to maximize their flexibility and give them exposure to as many areas of the operation as possible.

A notable feature of People Express service was that the ticket price did not include meals, beverages, or checked baggage: these services cost an additional fee, enabling People to keep its fares extremely low. Although immensely successful in its early years, People Express incurred a substantial loss in 1985. Critics claimed that the airline had expanded too fast and lost control of quality—disgruntled passengers called it "People Distress." By early 1986, some industry analysts were expressing concern about the carrier's future financial prospects.

American Airlines' response to low-cost carriers such as People was twofold. First it sought to become a low average cost carrier through an aggressive policy of expansion. This airline had long been rated each year as the business traveler's favorite, reflecting its high quality cabin service and wide choice of convenient schedules. The company expanded its routes and schedules to improve its coverage even further. Wishing to preserve good employee relations, American's management reached agreement with the unions to preserve existing salary structures

but to create a two-tiered structure whereby new hires would be paid on a substantially lower scale.

A second element of American's strategy was a very selective policy of discounting—sufficient to attract passengers who might otherwise fly by a discount carrier but not to erode revenues from business travelers with expense accounts. In this way, American could promote itself as offering full-fare service at bargain prices. The airline saw good quality service as a major point of differentiation in an industry where complaints about poor service were becoming increasingly strident.

THE SITUATION AT TRANS WORLD AIRLINES

TWA's response to deregulation was one of cautious retrenchment on domestic routes. In the early 70s, Trans World had focused on increasing its market share, in order to maintain its Number 3 position among domestic carriers (behind United and American). This approach required maintaining competitive flight schedules, even when they were unprofitable. After a $132 million loss during the recession year of 1975, the airline's president and senior vice president-marketing were let go.

As president, the board appointed C. E. Meyer, previously the airline's vice president-finance. Meyer, an accountant by profession, began by getting rid of inefficient, unprofitable operations and sold off older aircraft (such as Boeing 707s) in TWA's aging fleet. In many instances, two 707 schedules were consolidated into one flight by a Boeing 747 or Lockheed TriStar jumbo jet. The airline also retreated from markets that were too competitive and profit-draining, such as Chicago. Instead it built up operations at its St Louis and New York hubs. More than 3,000 jobs were eliminated.

By 1983, however, TWA was finding itself in increasing difficulties. The previous year, it had lost $31 million on revenues of $3.3 billion. Increasing success overseas—an operating profit of $110 million—contrasted with increasing domestic losses.

TWA's declining domestic traffic led competitors to refer to it as "the incredible shrinking airline." Indeed, Eastern Airlines had displaced TWA as the nation's third largest carrier.

Severe capital constraints made it difficult for TWA to buy the new equipment needed for domestic expansion. Attempts to cut labor costs had met with limited success. In 1982, pilots and noncontract personnel accepted a 17-month pay freeze, but machinists and flight attendants rejected a similar freeze and won new contracts that provided for a 30 percent wage increase over three years with no productivity givebacks (in the form of more flexible work rules).

Part of TWA's problem in labor negotiations was that the airline was a subsidiary of TransWorld Corporation, a large holding company that also owned Hilton International Hotels, a car rental firm, and other subsidiaries. "There's always the perception that the parent will bail out a subsidiary," remarked one observer. This crutch was removed when the parent firm spun off the airline as an independent company in February 1983.

A New Owner

During the next two years, TWA was frequently in the news. In June 1985, TWA Flight 847 was hijacked by Shiite Moslems shortly after takeoff from Athens and forced to fly to several airports in Mediterranean countries during the next few days. One passenger was killed but the others and the crew (who were widely praised for their heroism) were eventually released. That same summer, TWA came close to being purchased by Texas Air Corporation. But the deal fell through and Frank Lorenzo turned his attention elsewhere. In late 1985, Carl Icahn, a so-called corporate raider, made a play for Trans World. After prolonged maneuverings, Icahn won control of the airline with 52 percent of the stock and became chairman on January 3, 1986.

However, Icahn's victory proved to be bittersweet. During the months that he had been pursuing his quarry, TWA's financial position had deteriorated significantly. Although 1985 traffic had increased by 13.3 percent to 32 billion passenger miles and the average load factor stood at 65.2 percent, the airline lost $193 million that year; during the fourth quarter alone, losses totalled $123 million.

Icahn moved quickly to cut costs, dismissing hundreds of office workers, and reaching agreements with pilots and machinists for pay cuts of about 15 percent. He then turned his attention to the flight attendants, whose contract was up for renegotiation.

TWA Flight Attendants

Trans World had some 6,500 flight attendants, who were represented by a union of their own called the Independent Federation of Flight Attendants (IFFA). According to the company, the average TWA flight attendant received wages and benefits worth $44,000 a year—up from $20,000 in 1978. The union noted that this period had included several years of rapid inflation and that since the airline had done little hiring in recent years, it employed a higher proportion of senior flight attendants than its competitors.

The great majority of TWA flight attendants were college educated. Some had been recruited directly from college, others had worked previously as teachers, nurses, social workers, or in office positions. Others had previously worked for the airline in reservations, on ticket counters, or as gate agents and saw a cabin position as a step up in pay and prestige.

Candidates were attracted to the job by the pay and benefits (which increased with seniority), the opportunity to travel, free flights for family members, and a working schedule that was limited to about 14-15 days per month. During their time off, many attendants worked at second jobs—some had small businesses of their own—or pursued their education. However, although salaries and benefits improved with seniority, the opportunities for further career progression were minimal. There were possibilities to work on the ground in supervisory or training positions, but the pay was no higher (and sometimes lower) than the earnings of a senior attendant. Also the hours were longer.

The FAA limited the number of hours that attendants could fly each month as well as setting minimum requirements for days off from flying assignments. The flight attendants' union had negotiated work rules that improved upon FAA requirements, so that a TWA attendant would normally fly about 75 hours a month. However, this excluded time spent waiting at airports and on call, as well as overnight stays in distant cities. On average, an attendant could expect to spend about 250 hours a month away from home.

Junior attendants served in the "Ready Reserves," on call for five hours at a time and ready to arrive at the airport within 50 minutes to fly wherever they were needed. Attendants resented the uncertainty and idle time. However, with seniority came priority in bidding on schedules for the following month.

TWA attendants worked in randomly selected teams of five to seven persons, which were changed monthly. Through this bidding system, attendants could ask to fly on their preferred schedules; because of the priority system, senior attendants had a better chance of avoiding weekend and holiday travel, flying on routes which were perceived as more glamorous, and picking schedules that would avoid the need to stay overnight in distant cities and allow them more time with their families, second jobs, or pursuing additional education.

Recruitment and training of flight attendants was strongly influenced by the requirements of the Federal Aviation Administration (FAA), which continued to regulate airline safety. The TWA training program had historically lasted about five weeks. Most of this period was spent in classroom instruction, with more than half the time being devoted to FAA-prescribed sections on safety procedures and medical first aid, including CPR. The course also covered passenger handling and on-board services, as well as personal grooming and familiarization with the company. There were approximately three dozen written tests.

Education in safety procedures included timed emergency exercises, resembling an obstacle course and designed to simulate real-world disaster situations. Trainees found themselves working in darkness, fire and smoke, and even underwater as they sought to help others and themselves escape from a simulated accident. Between 5 percent and 10 percent of trainees failed to complete the program satisfactorily. Training continued after "graduation," with attendants being required to attend short refresher and update courses in safety each year.

In spite of the emphasis on safety training, an attendant's day-to-day work focused on providing service to the passengers. She or he would greet passengers as they boarded, help them to find seating assignments or stow carry-on baggage, and give special assistance to young children traveling alone or to infirm and disabled passengers. Safety procedures were emphasized before take-off, but once the flight was airborne the focus of the job switched to food and beverage service or "glorified waitressing," as many of them described it.

The nature of the attendant's job was tightly prescribed and included strict dress codes and grooming requirements. Yet a flight attendant's work was not closely monitored in the air. One attendant on each flight was given the coordinating role of "flight service manager," and then assigned each attendant specific duties based upon passenger seating. However, the flight service manager did not evaluate her or his fellow attendants. Written complaints and commendations from crew members and passengers were placed in an attendant's employment file; too many negative complaints about poor service could lead to disciplinary action. Failures to observe safety requirements could be punished by fines or termination.

Many attendants expressed regret that there wasn't more time to give personal attention to passengers, since they recognized that the quality of personal service they provided was a significant factor in passenger satisfaction. Although TWA had a good reputation for service on its international flights, many observers felt that the company's food and cabin service on domestic flights could be improved.

THE STRIKE

Having reached agreement for new contracts with pilots and machinists amounting to a 15 percent cut in pay, Carl Icahn proposed even more significant cuts for TWA's flight attendants. A spokesman for the airline stated:

> We are essentially seeking a 22 percent pay reduction and work rule changes that would amount to being available for duty less than two more hours per week.

The spokesman stated that these cuts would save the airline $100 million annually.

The attendants countered with an offer to reduce wages and benefits by 15 percent, a move that they said would save TWA $30 million a year. They stated that a 22 percent cut, which would save the company some $45 million annually, was excessive, as were the work rule changes, which they claimed would be worth $35 to $65 million.

With neither side able to reach an agreement, the two parties entered a 30-day cooling-off period, which Icahn used to train 1,500 reservation agents and other TWA employees as flight attendants. He also recruited 1,500 new employees for attendants' jobs and began training them, too. However the airline gave no guarantee of permanent employment as flight attendants to any of these individuals. Under the proposed new work rules and assuming a continuation of current schedules, TWA would need only 3,500 attendants at the lowest point of the winter season and 5,000 during the summer "high" season.

On March 3, four days before the union would be free to strike, Icahn claimed that a strike that was successful in shutting down the airline for a considerable period might force him to break up TWA and sell off the pieces.

The day before the strike, the two parties were still talking and still trading charges. The airline claimed that the average flight attendant's pay was $35,000—double the starting price at many airlines. The union said the $35,000 figure was inflated. TWA offered to reduce its pay cut demand to 17 percent but refused to budge on work rule changes. The union rejected the offer. It was reported in the papers that personal antipathy between Carl Icahn and IFFA president Victoria Frankovich had not facilitated negotiations. Frankovich accused Icahn of "negotiating in a sexist fashion."

The Strike Begins

The Independent Federation of Flight Attendants struck TWA at 12:01am EDT on May 7th. The airline's newly hired flight attendants crossed picket lines to the jeers of picketing IFFA members. The pilots crossed the picket lines "regretfully," stating that their contract contained a no-strike agreement. And 85% of the company's machinists crossed picket lines, too. Industry observers were not surprised, pointing out that airline unions rarely displayed solidarity in a labor dispute that affected only one of them.

On the first day of the strike, TWA claimed that it had operated 52 percent of its schedule and said that it planned to restore all flights "within the next several days." Substantial fare cuts were offered through the end of the year to lure passengers. Union representatives disputed TWA schedule claims and stated that the newly hired flight attendants were not properly trained on safety procedures.

Three days into the strike, TWA announced that it was continuing to restore flights and that the figure was now up to 54% of the total flight schedule. That day, the airline took the International Association of Machinists to court to force them to stop honoring flight attendant picket lines.

On March 11, TWA announced that it would meet the union with a federal mediator in Philadelphia the following day. However, these talks broke off after four hours with no new meetings scheduled. That same day, striking machinists obeyed a court order to return to work and the airline announced that 62 percent of its flights were now operating.

The Strike Continues

During the next 12 days, TWA continued to rebuild its schedules and the strike continued to receive broad media coverage. Photos showed sign-carrying picketers shivering outside terminals at northern airports. Strikers spoke of their commitment to TWA and claimed that Icahn was just a corporate raider bent on making money by breaking up the airline.

The newspapers reported that although TWA passengers arriving at airports were mostly ignoring picket lines, a well known singer—Joan Baez—had switched to another airline when she learned that she had been booked on a TWA flight. It was also reported that the airline was losing over a million dollars a day.

Passengers confirmed union claims that on-board service was poor and that flight attendants were slow and inexperienced. Said one traveler after a transcontinental flight:

> It was just amateur hour on board! They took forever to serve the drinks and then forgot to come back and collect money from those who had had alcoholic drinks. The meal service was a shambles.

Many travelers also complained of delayed flights.

Both the union leadership and the rank and file continued to allege that flying on TWA was unsafe, since the new attendants lacked both experience and adequate training. TWA refuted the charge, stating that the FAA's stringent criteria had been fully met. Noting that "several hundred" IFFA members had defied their union and returned to work, TWA argued that the rank and file were not behind the strike and demanded that the leadership take a strike vote. Union leaders, however, scoffed at the claim and stated that the membership was "overwhelmingly" behind the strike.

The union's claim of safety problems received a significant boost a few days later when smoke filled the cabin of a TWA airliner descending for landing at Boston's Logan International Airport. Although the aircraft landed safely and there were no injuries, the shaken passengers told reporters that the flight attendants had panicked and that the situation in the cabin had been chaotic. The incident received wide publicity and the authorities announced that there would be an investigation.

On March 25, TWA and the union announced that they would resume negotiations the next day in New York.

PART VIII
Strategy and Integration

The Search for Synergy: What Marketers Need To Know About Service Operations

CHRISTOPHER H. LOVELOCK

Operational efficiency and customer satisfaction sometimes seem like conflicting goals. How can operations and marketing managers work together? Both parties must learn to appreciate the other's perspective. Marketers need to understand eleven key operational concepts that may be critical to achieving a productive and smoothly running service operation. Armed with this understanding, they will be better placed to work jointly with operations and human resource managers to create viable strategies.

Customers often complain that service organizations are unresponsive and bureaucratic. They describe confusing facilities in which they had to run from pillar to post in order to complete a transaction, lengthy lines, personnel who decline to serve them on the grounds that "that's not my job" or "I'm not allowed to do that," inconvenient service locations and hours, replacement of service people by machines that customers are expected to operate themselves, and seemingly unnecessary rules and regulations concerning the terms under which service will be provided.

These experiences are but a few of the many tedious impacts of operations on customers. However, an operations manager would be entirely justified in claiming that each of these situations also reflects a businesslike tradeoff of customer satisfaction against efficient management of operations.

CONFLICT AND COMPROMISE IN SERVICE BUSINESSES

Managing any type of organization entails conflict between differing goals and agendas.

This reading has been adapted from "The Interaction of Operations and Marketing: Their Impact on Customers" in David E. Bowen, Richard B. Chase, Thomas G. Cummings and Associates, *Service Management Effectiveness* (San Francisco: Jossey-Bass, Inc., 1990, pp. 343–368). Copyright © 1989, 1992 by Christopher H. Lovelock.

FIGURE 1
The Search for Compatibility

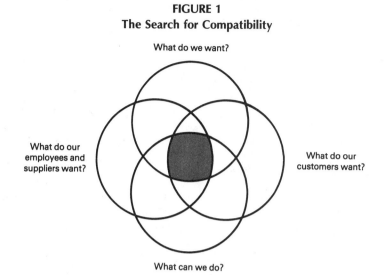

This is particularly true in services where there is a high degree of customer contact, since customers get far closer to those service operations than they do when dealing with a service firm at arm's length.[1] The challenge for service managers is to search for compatibility among four basic forces in a service business:

1. What the organization's management wants
2. What its employees and suppliers want
3. What customers want
4. What the organization is actually capable of doing.

These forces are represented as four circles in Figure 1.[2] To the extent that the four circles overlap, representing six specific communities of interest, a compatibility exists which bodes well for all parties. Hence, top management needs to consider the intersection of each of the six pairs of circles:

---

[1]Richard B. Chase, "The Customer Contact Approach to Services: Theoretical Bases and Practical Extensions," *Operations Research* 29 (4), 1981, 698–706 (reproduced on pages 43–49 of this book).

[2]This diagram extends an earlier, three-part framework, created by Robert Longman, "The W3 Diagram," unpublished, 1987.

- *Is what we (management) want also something that we (the firm) can do?* If not, then our goals are meaningless.
- *Is what we want also what our employees and suppliers want?* If not, many prospective employees may choose not to work for our organization, and neither employees nor suppliers will try very hard to help us achieve our corporate goals.
- *Is what we want also what our customers want?* If not, we may gain a reputation as a tightfisted, uncaring, even unethical organization unwilling to emphasize responsiveness to customers and interested only in our own goals and agenda.
- *Is what employees and suppliers want what customers want?* If not, customers will quickly detect a lack of interest among service personnel in meeting users' priorities and perhaps a lack of enthusiasm for providing customers with a quality service experience.
- *Is what employees and suppliers want what we can do?* If not, the firm may not be able to pay competitive wages and fees for services rendered, provide satisfactory working conditions, and offer either the training or the technological leverage that many service workers require to perform well and at top efficiency.
- *Is what we can do what our customers want?* If not, then both parties are barking up the wrong tree. Either we must look for different market segments which value what our firm has to offer, or we must change what we can do to bring it into line with what our customers want.

The goal of effective management, of course, is to bring all four spheres of interest into the closest possible convergence, so as to maximize the shaded area in the middle — the win–win area where all parties enjoy a mutually rewarding relationship. The concern of this chapter will be on enhancing the convergence between what the firm can do — which is largely determined by its operational capabilities — and providing what the customers want — which it's marketing's responsibility to determine and shape. But our discussion will touch on human resource issues, too, since execution of the operational concepts often takes place through service personnel.

Operations and Marketing

No management function is unimportant in service businesses, but two functions, operations and marketing, drive management strategy in today's marketplace. Unfortunately, managers responsible for these two functions are often at odds with one another in terms of their conceptions of how to meet the organization's goals. One result is that "boundary-spanning" employees find themselves caught in the middle, unsure whether their priorities should emphasize operational efficiency or service to customers.[3]

The operations function is at the core of the business, since it creates and assembles the service product, often working under real time conditions. Historically, operations concerns — to be discussed later in depth — have dominated service management.

With increasing competition in service industries, many service firms have sought to develop an effective marketing function to act as a bridge between the organization and the environment within which it operates. Marketing is concerned with identifying needs and trends within the marketplace and crafting a strategy for targeting specific market segments to serve. Marketers see their responsibilities as including creating new product concepts, distribution and pricing strategies; developing communication programs; and monitoring the activities of the competition.

But the introduction of a marketing orientation into service businesses has sometimes met with resistance from operations executives, who often see marketing as just an add-on function that should be confined to consumer research and communication efforts. Consequently, when marketers seek to get involved in product design and service delivery, their efforts may be resented by operations managers as an intrusion into the operating domain.

The issue is not merely a matter of turf — it reflects the operations focus on delivering a smooth-running and cost efficient service. Langeard *et al.* note how a seemingly attractive product innovation, championed by marketing management in a quick service restaurant chain, led to serious operational difficulties. The product in question was a new menu item. As recalled by a senior operations executive:

> It was a big mistake. Our stores are small. They didn't have space for the new equipment that was needed. It [the menu item] was really popular with our customers, but started to mess up the rest of our operation.... Marketing people are often very creative but should concentrate more on being total businessmen. Operations people tend to rate the marketing folks on how well they understand the operation.[4]

Key Operational Issues and Concepts

Despite interfirm and interindustry differences, there are a number of key operations issues and concepts with which all marketers of high contact services ought to be familiar. We will discuss eleven operational issues that are as relevant to marketers as to operations personnel. Several of them also impact human resource management. All are concepts commonly discussed in operations management textbooks. The eleven issues are:

[3]See David E. Bowen and Benjamin Schneider, "Boundary-Spanning-Role Employees and the Service Encounter: Some Guidelines for Management and Research." In J. A. Czepiel, M. R. Solomon, and C. F. Surprenant, *The Service Encounter* (Lexington, Mass.: D. C. Heath & Co., 1985), 127–48.

[4]Langeard, E., J. E. G. Bateson, C. H. Lovelock, and P. Eiglier, *Services Marketing: New Insights from Consumers and Managers.* (Cambridge, Mass.: Marketing Science Institute, 1981), page 89.

1. Productivity improvement
2. Make versus buy
3. Facilities location
4. Standardization versus customization
5. Batch versus unit processing
6. Facilities layout and design
7. Job design
8. Learning curve
9. Management of capacity
10. Quality control
11. Management of queues

Marketers need to understand why these issues are of concern to operations managers, how they impact both operations and marketing strategy, and why several of them have important implications for human resource management. But learning is not a one-way street: it's most important that operations and human resource managers recognize the implications of their strategies for the customers served by their firm.

Interrelationships Between Issues

Many operational issues are, of course, interrelated. For instance, effective management of capacity is very important for improving productivity. Establishing appropriate queuing systems helps to ensure that capacity is used to the best advantage. The actual design of facilities should reflect the need to handle any queues that might be anticipated. And consideration should be given to processing customers (or other objects requiring servicing) in batches rather than one by one.

Certainly, most of the previously noted issues also apply to low-contact services, such as mail-order, credit cards, insurance, and telecommunications — especially to their back office operations. However, when customers are virtually excluded from the factory and deal with service suppliers at arms' length, then the type of operation has less impact on the customer (and vice versa).

Issues such as facilities location, layout and design, or batch versus unit processing have little bearing on customers who only interact with the organization by mail, voice telephone, facsimile, or interactive computer. Hence our focus on those service industries — such as

passenger transportation, hospitality, health care, professional services, traditional forms of retail banking, participatory entertainment, education, and personal care — where service personnel tend to have a high degree of contact with their customers.

MARKETING AND HUMAN RESOURCE IMPLICATIONS OF OPERATIONAL CONCEPTS AND STRATEGIES

The eleven operational issues listed above start with what might be termed "macro" issues, involving decisions that reflect the broad operational strategy of the organization, and move gradually down to more "micro" issues involving day-to-day operational activities. We'll review each of them in the same order below, looking at how operational decisions impact customers (and sometimes service personnel themselves) and considering what might be an appropriate role for marketing to play in each instance.

Improving Productivity

At the heart of most operational strategies is the search for productivity improvements, which occur when the volume/value of output improves relative to the volume/value of inputs.[5] Operational approaches to achieving this goal include working employees harder; recruiting and training more productive employees; reducing employee turnover; investing in more efficient equipment; automating labor tasks; eliminating bottlenecks that lead to unproductive downtime in the operational processes; and standardizing both the process itself and the resulting service output. At issue for marketers is whether these approaches are positively or negatively received by customers. Among the potential marketing problems are that overworked employees may deliver lower quality service, customers may perceive automated service delivery as inferior to hu-

---

[5]Curtis R. McClaughlin and Sydney Coffey, Measuring "Productivity in Services," *International Journal of Service Industry Management* (reproduced on p 103–117 of this book).

man interaction, and they may also be turned off by too much standardization. Certainly, such approaches are likely to fail if not planned and managed with customer needs and preferences in mind.

In a high contact service, where customers are involved in the production process, there may be opportunities to make customers themselves more productive. Mills emphasizes the importance of socializing the customer to behave as a "partial employee."[6] Similarly, Bowen argues for managing customers as human resources in service organizations.[7]

Lovelock and Young suggest three broad strategies for changing customer behavior in ways that will increase the productivity of the operation:[8]

- Change the timing of customer demand to encourage use of the service during periods when demand is low and productive capacity is underutilized.
- Involve customers more in the production process, encouraging them through self-service or interactions with machines instead of people to take over tasks formerly performed by service personnel.
- Get customers to use intermediaries for the delivery of certain service elements.

What we see here is the use of marketing to help solve operational problems. However, incentives such as time and cost savings may be needed to motivate customers, especially when they are being asked to change established habits.

Make Versus Buy

Make or buy choices by a service company are simply vertical integration decisions, and usually reflect such criteria as costs, quality control, and availability of capacity. Ex-

amples of common "buy" decisions in services include: subcontracting recruitment and training of employees to temporary help firms; using contract food services; and entering into agreements with intermediaries such as travel agencies, 800-number operators, and brokers to suppy information, accept reservations, and make sales.

In some instances, the firm lacks the capability to do the work itself. But often management may conclude that outside suppliers can perform the task more cheaply or better (or both). Another reason for subcontracting tasks is that this decision frees up scarce capital and labor resources which can be better deployed on the core business.

From a marketing perspective, using outside suppliers results in loss of control to a third party who may place a higher priority on serving other clients. It may be harder for the firm to be responsive to customers and to resolve complaints. Further, customers will tend to blame the supplier of the core service — rather than the subcontractor — for any shortcomings.

But there may be important benefits, too, from buying rather than making. Subcontractors who specialize in delivering a particular service can generally do it better. Tapping into national networks and employing agency representation allows a firm to increase its geographic coverage and thus enhance its sales potential. Finally, the use of subcontractors at peak periods allows the firm to be responsive to surges in demand.

Work can also be delegated to customers through the medium of self service. Gas stations, for instance, often provide a choice of full-service versus self-service pumps, offering a substantial discount on the price per gallon delivered through the latter to compensate customers for their efforts.

At a broader level, do-it-yourself decisions by customers may actually represent competition for service businesses. Current or prospective customers may decide to employ their own labor and expertise rather than going to a service firm, purchase their own equipment instead of retaining a service supplier, or self-insure rather than buying insurance. Understanding customers' needs, motivations, and

---

[6]Mills, Peter, *Managing Service Industries: Organizational Practices in a Postindustrial Economy.* Cambridge, Mass.: Ballinger Publishing Co., 1985.

[7]Bowen, David E., "Managing Customers as Human Resources in Service Organizations," *Human Resource Management 25,* 1986, 371–84.

[8]Lovelock, Christopher H., and Robert F. Young, "Look to Consumers to Increase Productivity," *Harvard Business Review 50* (May–June) 1979. 168–78.

resources on the "make versus buy" dimension is central to the development of effective marketing strategies.

Facilities Location

Operations and marketing personnel are often at odds on where service facilities should be located. Operations concerns usually revolve around issues such as least-cost-per-square-foot, good access for delivery trucks and other suppliers, simplified maintenance, good security, and easy access for employees. Marketers, by contrast, seek a pleasant and safe location that will help to define the image of the service organization, often arguing for proximity to other services that the customer may need — especially when their own service is not normally a destination trip in its own right. They tend to want a site that customers will find easy to reach by car, public transportation, or on foot from their homes or workplaces.

In situations where marketers are concerned that the present site location is suboptimal, there are various opportunities for action. One approach is to make the most of the present site by promoting access to that location through such means such as better maps and signing, creating new parking areas, or offering shuttle bus service from more distant lots. Perhaps the appeal of the location can be enhanced by landscaping, decorative banners and structures, and developing cooperative efforts with complementary service providers. If the present location is negatively impacting sales, and there seems to be little chance of turning the situation around, then marketing's best course of action may be to conduct studies documenting the incremental net revenue potential of alternative sites.

Standardization Versus Customization in Delivery System Design

Standardization involves limiting service options and achieving consistency of output by adopting a production line approach to service creation and delivery — "manufacturing in the field" as Levitt described it.[9] This approach entails division of labor, limited discretion for workers, substitution of technology for people, and managing customer behavior to achieve conformance with the operating system. In search of greater productivity and the ability to compete on price, many service firms are moving away from customization and high client contact towards a "service factory" environment involving lower labor intensity.[10]

Led by franchisors, more and more service firms are standardizing their operating procedures. Costs are reduced as a result of economies of scale, and bottlenecks become easier to identify and eliminate. Quality control is aided by increased conformance to clear specifications. And standardization of job tasks allows the organization to recruit relatively unskilled, inexpensive workers who require only limited training to perform highly routinized tasks.

However, standardization has its disadvantages when seen from a marketing perspective: variations in needs tend to be ignored and customers may tire of a uniform, homogenized service output. Further, service may start to deteriorate as employees performing highly repetitive tasks become bored and robot-like in their dealings with customers.

Marketers should understand the forces that drive the search for standardization. Instead of resisting the concept as it relates to the core product, they should look for opportunities to customize peripheral service elements — such as letting customers choose garnishes, dressings and salad bar items in a fast food restaurant — or try to personalize service by using the customer's name in conversation or in print. Marketers should work with operations personnel to identify the relative appeal of alternative service formulations to different market segments, and should promote such advantages as consistency of quality and the sense that "you know what you're getting."

---

[9]Levitt, Theodore (1972), "Production Line Approach to Service," *Harvard Business Review* 50, (November–December 1972), 41–52.

[10]See, for example, David H. Maister and Christopher H. Lovelock, "Managing Facilitator Services," *Sloan Management Review,* Summer 1982, 19–31 (reproduced on pages 64–76) Roger W. Schmenner, "How Can Service Businesses Survive and Prosper?" *Sloan Management Review,* Spring 1986, 21–32 (reproduced on pages 31–42).

Batch vs. Unit Processing

Batch processing involves servicing multiple customers or items simultaneously instead of singly. This may yield economies of scale as well as making the most efficient use of capacity. Examples include transporting a group of people in a bus rather than sending each individual separately by taxi, teaching a large class of students rather than giving individual tutorials, or waiting for a sufficiently large group to form before giving a tour of a museum or historic site; another example comes from the restaurant chain Benihana of Tokyo, which seats and serves customers in groups of eight.[11]

Among the marketing drawbacks of batch processing are that customers feel they are just one of a crowd. Further, the behavior and demeanor of other customers becomes part of the service experience, service scheduling tends to be less flexible, and sometimes customers have to wait until a large enough group has been assembled to constitute an economically viable batch.

Marketing benefits can include lower prices and the fact that other customers may contribute positively to the experience ("meet interesting people"). Not all batch processing requires customers to interact directly with one another (airline flights, movies, sports events). But when people are thrust together in ways that require interaction, it's often a good idea for the marketer to facilitate introductions, such as holding a "Get Acquainted" cocktail party at the beginning of a vacation tour.

Facilities Layout and Design

A fundamental choice facing all service providers is how to arrange the layout of the workflow with an eye to both efficiency and customer satisfaction. Operations experts identify several alternatives for laying out departments within a service facility.[12] These alternatives include:

1. *A process or job-shop layout* in which similar equipment or functions are grouped together in one area, requiring customers to travel from area to area according to the established (or desired) sequence of operations. Hotels are a case in point, as are colleges and many hospital facilities. Such facilities are not always laid out with customer convenience in mind, requiring users to travel extensively around the facility and even to double back in their tracks.

2. *A flow-shop or assembly-line layout* is one in which equipment or work processes are arranged linearly according to the progressive steps by which the service is created or assembled. Examples include cafeteria service in a restaurant, or registration lines in colleges and motor vehicle license bureaus. One marketing challenge is to ensure that operations provides sufficient capacity at each step in the process to keep the line moving and also allows customers to skip steps in the process which they may not need — otherwise they may waste time waiting at several points in the process and become frustrated. Another problem emerges in self-service situations when a customer inadvertently forgets to take a particular step (such as picking up a dessert in the cafeteria line) and has to go through the entire process again in order to attend to just one item. Advance instructions for the entire process, proper signing of each step in the process, sequencing that reflects customers' logic (desserts after main dishes), and using roving service personnel to assist customers will help to minimize difficulties.

3. *A fixed position layout* is one in which customers remain at one location and service comes to them. Table service in a restaurant is one example, home shopping services another, and the in-flight portion of airline services (excepting use of the toilets) a third. But this approach is not always feasible. Many service organizations offer a bundle of services, comprising a combination of different processes which take place at different locations. Taking a flight, for instance, involves reservations, arrival at the airport, check-in, boarding, inflight service, disembarking, baggage retrieval, and departure from the airport. Switching from one location (and one process) to another can be confusing and dis-

---

[11]W. Earl Sasser and John Klug, "Benihana of Tokyo." Boston, Mass.: Harvard Business School, case no. 9-673-057, 1972.

[12]See, for example, R. B. Chase and N. J. Aquilano, *Production and Operations Management: A Life Cycle Approach,* 5th edition. Homewood, Ill.: Richard D. Irwin, Inc. 1989.

orienting for customers. The problem is likely to be compounded by poor signing, absence of instructions, and lack of assistance from service personnel.

Another issue in facilities design has to do with physical appearance and imagery. Kotler has argued that retailers (and by inference other service delivery sites) should be designed with "atmospherics" in mind, in order to create a desired mood, image, and ambience for the service organization.[13]

Many hotels, for instance, make elaborate attempts to create a dramatic atmosphere in their lobbies and atriums. The operational mindset may see such efforts as poor space utilization, requiring extra expenditures on climate control, and wasteful investment of scarce capital resources in unproductive assets such as sculptures and artwork. But marketers have their eyes focused on the revenue side of the ledger. They will argue for a landscaped exterior with ample parking, and for an attractive interior design geared to customer comfort, convenience and even excitement. They want their customers to feel that they are being *served*, rather than being *processed* like some inanimate object in a factory. They want customers to return in the future and to spread the word to friends and acquaintances. To the extent possible, marketers seek to disguise the factory.

Job Design

Although progress has been made in automation, many service delivery systems still involve interactions between customers and service personnel. Even automated services usually have to be backed up by customer service agents who can intervene — in person or by phone — to help customers who have run into problems. The goal of job design is to study the requirements of the operation, the nature of customer desires, the needs and capabilities of employees, and the characteristics of operational equipment in order to develop job descriptions that strike the best balance between these sometimes conflicting demands.

Marketers often worry that operations-oriented employees may be unresponsive to customer needs. They may argue that customer satisfaction should be paramount in designing and filling customer contact positions, but operations managers are likely to have other agenda. The latter want to develop the most efficient combination of labor and technology, to reduce the potential for human error, to minimize the risk of fraud and waste, and — in certain situations — to create teams of employees working on complementary tasks who will collectively be more productive than if they worked independently (even assuming that they possessed the full array of necessary skills).

As noted by Tansik, human resource programs need to structure the recruitment, selection, training, control, evaluation, compensation, and development activities in ways designed to ensure that the proper mix of technical and behavioral knowledge, skills, and abilities is maintained.[14]

Employees' careers should be managed in ways that provide stepping-stones to positions offering variety and opportunities for further advancement. As competition in service industries has increased, there is more pressure to design customer contact jobs with reference to customer needs. This has sometimes forced a change in recruitment criteria to include emphasis on personality characteristics as well as on technical skills. Increasingly, training has been revamped to reflect marketing considerations, and performance evaluations redesigned to include marketing-related criteria as well as operational ones.

In a number of instances, customer contact personnel may need to be given greater discretion and authority to deal with customer requests or emergencies, since there may not be time to pass the request "through channels."

Learning Curve

Formally defined, a learning curve is a line (usually sloping downwards from left to

---

[13]Philip Kotler, "Atmospherics as a Marketing Tool," *Journal of Retailing*, Winter 1974, 48–64.

[14]David A. Tansik, "Managing Human Resource Issues for High-Contact Service Personnel." In D. E. Bowen, R. B. Chase, T. G. Cummings and Associates, *Service Management Effectiveness* San Francisco: Jossey-Bass, 1990, 152–76.

right) which displays the relationship between the time or financial costs per unit of production and the number of consecutive units produced. As noted by Chase and Aquilano, such curves can be applied to both individual and organizational learning:

> Individual learning is improvement that results from a person repeating a process and gaining skill and efficiency....That is, "practice makes perfect." Organizational learning is improvement that results from practice as well but also comes from changes in administration, equipment and product design.[15]

An operational strategy predicted on driving the service production process down the learning curve poses both problems and opportunities for marketers. The most important challenge for marketing is to increase demand for the service, since without increased volume, it will take longer for the firm to move down the learning curve. Advertising, sales and promotional efforts, and lower prices may all have a role to play in demand stimulation. If service delivery speeds up as a function of greater experience, customers can expect to be served faster and the cost savings may be passed along to them in the form of lower prices, thus stimulating further demand (unless the firm decides to keep the benefits for itself in the form of higher profits).

Faster service with fewer errors may yield a competitive advantage, especially for time-sensitive consumers. On the other hand, if the service firm uses faster service as an excuse to cut the number of service delivery channels, customers are likely to find the wait for service just as long, even though transaction time itself is now shorter. Moreover, faster service may not be what customers want: they may feel that the quality of personal interactions with service providers has declined. Another risk when service providers focus on speed is that they may not take the time to determine customers' needs and problems carefully, thereby losing opportunities for cross-selling other services as well as failing to solve problems effectively.

When customers are actively involved in the production process, through self-service or working in cooperation with service personnel, learning curve theory may apply to the customers themselves. As customers get more proficient with machines such as ticket dispensers or automated teller machines, they can complete transactions more quickly: they save themselves time and hassle, make the machines more productive and reduce waiting time for others. Marketers can contribute to efficiency by pointing out to operations managers that when new services are being introduced (or new customers are being attracted to existing services), there is a learning curve for consumers, too. Providing education and assistance when customers first make use of the service may lead to faster and smoother interactions later — to the benefit of all parties.

Management of Capacity

The capacity of a specific service organization can be defined as the highest quantity of output possible in a given time period with a predefined level of staffing, facilities, and equipment. In short, there's an upper limit to the number of customers the operation can handle. Capacity planning is vital in capacity-constrained service organizations which need to match productive resources to fluctuating demand levels. It helps to keep costs down by avoiding wasteful underutilization of people, buildings and machines when demand is low, while also minimizing loss of revenues from customers seeking service during peak periods. Finally, it reduces the risks that staff and employees will become bored and sloppy as a result of having too little to do or burn out as a result of being overworked and under excessive pressure.

Possible approaches to managing capacity include using part-time employees, sharing capacity with other firms, and focusing employee efforts on key tasks during peak hours. Although such procedures may enable the firm to increase its capacity to serve more customers (which is a marketing plus), the downside is that regular customers may perceive service quality as compromised by such measures.

---

[15]Chase and Aquilano, *op cit.*, page 516.

Creative marketing solutions to resolving imbalances between demand and capacity include managing demand through pricing and promotional strategies, searching for countercyclical services in periods of low demand for the original service, and identifying countercyclical locations where movable assets (such as rental cars or certain employees) can be more profitably redeployed.[16]

Quality Control

"QC" is basically concerned with ensuring that service execution conforms consistently to predefined standards. The marketer's task is to ensure that these standards reflect the needs and expectations of target market segments.[17]

Budgetary pressures on operations may lead to nonconformance with specifications, reflecting problems such as understaffing, use of inferior labor or materials, inadequate supervision, lack of inspections, failure to invest in needed improvements, or skimping on maintenance and training. Poor execution often happens when employees feel overworked, underpaid, frustrated by unsatisfactory working conditions, or badly treated by management.

Quality problems are often perceptual: what an operator may consider to be quality work may not be so perceived by the customer. Sometimes this results from unrealistic customer expectations (perhaps stimulated by salespeople who promise too much or by overly optimistic advertising claims). On other occasions, customers may not realize just how good service execution really is, unless operations personnel actually draw their attention to the quality of work performed.

Marketing opportunities in quality start with continual monitoring of customer needs, expectations, and feedback. The findings may help operations personnel redesign the service, set new quality control standards, or improve execution against existing standards. One useful way for marketers to work with customer contact personnel is to get employee feedback on customer reactions to service. Research shows that such employees tend to have perceptions of service quality that are similar to those of the customers they serve.[18] Second, employees should be encouraged to draw customers' attention to features of performance execution that are not immediately obvious, in order to emphasize the quality of service delivered.

Management of Queues

Waiting for service is an almost universal phenomenon: virtually every organization faces the problem of queuing somewhere in its operation. People line up for tickets, they wait for seats in a theater, they wait for their bills after a restaurant meal. Physical and inanimate objects also wait for processing, of course: letters pile up on an executive's desk, shoes sit on racks waiting to be repaired at the shoemaker's, checks wait to be cleared at a bank, an incoming phone call waits to be switched to a customer service rep by the automatic call distributor. In each instance, a customer may be waiting for the outcome of that work — an answer to a letter, a pair of shoes ready to be picked up, a check credited to the customer's balance, or useful contact with the service representative (instead of listening to recorded Muzak while being kept on hold).

Waiting lines occur whenever the number of arrivals at a facility exceeds the capability of the system to process them. The first task in queue management is to determine the rate of arrivals over time, so that serving capacity may be planned accordingly. A typical operational strategy is to optimize the use of labor and equipment by planning for average throughput. So long as the people or things to be processed continue to arrive at the average rate, there will be no delays. However, fluctuations in arrivals (sometimes random, some-

[16]See Christopher H. Lovelock, "Strategies for Managing Demand and Capacity," on pages 154–168 of this book.

[17]The readings in Part V of this book provide a good background on generic quality criteria. See also A. Parasuraman, Leonard L. Berry, and Valarie A. Zeithaml, "Understanding Customer Perceptions of Service," *Sloan Management Review* 32, (Spring 1991), 39–48.

[18]See B. Schneider, J. J. Parkington, and V. M. Buxton, "Employee and Customer Perceptions of Service in Banks," *Administrative Science Quarterly* 25, June 1980, 252–67.

times predictable) will lead to delays at certain times as the line backs up following a "clump" of arrivals.

Managers can select from a variety of queuing systems to suit the nature of the operation. Options include single or multistage systems (in the latter instance, the customer goes through several sequential queues, receiving a different service element at each stage). Multiple channels may be offered to increase processing capacity, but managers need to decide whether each channel should have its own line (as in supermarket check-outs) or whether new arrivals should form a single line (like the "snakes" in bank lobbies and airport terminals) before being directed to the next available channel when they reach the head of the queue.

Another issue is whether to segregate customer lines according to the nature of the transaction — such as separate check-ins for first class, business class and economy class in an airline terminal; or express lines in supermarkets and banks for customers with simple transactions that can be made quickly.

An operational mindset might be swayed by considerations of space utilization, allocation of work between servers, and pressures on servers to process customers quickly. Marketers, however, should focus on choosing systems that customers find fair and simple to understand. Insights from segmentation research can help marketers decide whether or not to establish priority lines for certain types of customers — such as those who are valued and frequent users, or whose business is either more profitable (first class passengers) or faster to process (eight grocery items or less at a supermarket checkout).

Customers especially dislike being kept waiting for service, especially when it involves uncertainty or when the waiting process seems inequitable. Effective marketers try to anticipate the degree of *patience* in new arrivals: for any given size of line (or length of wait), how many prospective customers will simply balk at the apparent delay and walk away? Similarly, what proportion of those waiting for service would give up (or "renege") after a certain amount of time and leave the line?

Marketers should look for ways to make waiting more palatable.[19] There may be opportunities to take information, cross-sell other services, and entertain the customers while they wait. Theme park operators like the Disney Corporation cleverly design their waiting areas to make the wait look shorter than it is, find ways to give customers in line the impression of constant progress, and make time seem to pass more quickly by keeping customers amused or diverted while they wait.

STRATEGIC IMPLICATIONS

Coming to terms with the differing and sometimes conflicting perspectives of marketing and operations personnel poses a challenge for managers in both of these functional areas. Marketers need to understand operational concepts and strategies, both in general terms and as they apply to specific situations. They must recognize how pursuit of a particular operational strategy will contribute to the efficiency of the organization and result in cost savings, faster service, or other benefits. In addition to determining how a given operational strategy may affect customers and thereby impact marketing strategy, marketing managers should also ask themselves how a proposed marketing activity may impact operations.

Operations managers should recognize that an operational strategy designed to reduce costs may be equally — or even more — effective in turning off customers and thereby eroding revenues and net profits. Above all, when working in high-contact service environments, operations personnel should recognize that processing human beings is much more complex than processing inanimate objects.

Human resource managers need to understand both marketing and operational perspectives. They should try to act as facilitators to achieve consensus in the event of disagreement. Their goal should be to design jobs or

---

[19]For further insights, see K. L. Katz, B. M. Larson, and R. C. Larson, "Prescription for the Waiting-in-Line Blues: Entertain, Enlighten, and Engage" *Sloan Management Review,* reproduced on pages 176–187 of this book.

TABLE 1

Operations and Marketing Perspectives on Operational Issues

Operational Issues	Typical Operations Goals	Common Marketing Concerns
Productivity improvement	Reduce unit cost of production	Strategies may cause decline in service quality
Make-versus-buy decisions	Trade off control against comparative advantage and cost savings	"Make" decisions may result in lower quality and lack of market coverage; "buy" decisions may transfer control to unresponsive suppliers and hurt the firm's image
Facilities location	Reduce costs; provide convenient access for suppliers and employees	Customers may find location unattractive and inaccessible
Standardization	Keep costs low and quality consistent; simplify operations tasks; recruit low-cost employees	Consumers may seek variety, prefer customization to match segmented needs.
Batch versus unit processing	Seek economies of scale, consistency, efficient use of capacity	Customers may be forced to wait, feel "one of a crowd," be turned off by other customers
Facilities layout and design	Control costs; improve efficiency by ensuring proximity of operationally related tasks; enhance safety and security	Customers may be confused, shunted around unnecessarily, find facility unattractive and inconvenient
Job design	Minimize error, waste, and fraud; make efficient use of technology; simplify tasks for standardization	Operationally oriented employees with narrow roles may be unresponsive to customer needs
Learning curves	Apply experience to reduce time and costs per unit of output	Faster service is not necessarily better service; cost saving may not be passed on as lower prices
Management of capacity	Keep costs down by avoiding wasteful underutilization of resources	Service may be unavailable when needed; quality may be compromised during high-demand periods
Quality control	Ensure that service execution conforms to predefined standards	Operational definitions of quality may not reflect customer needs, preferences
Management of queues	Optimize use of available capacity by planning for average throughput; maintain customer order, discipline	Customers may be bored and frustrated during wait, see firm as unresponsive

positions that will achieve the mutual goals of both functions, and to fill them with employees who can achieve the desired synergy. Everybody loses when service personnel are placed in the impossible position of trying to serve two masters with conflicting objectives.

Table 1 summarizes the eleven concepts presented and the prototypical orientation of marketing and operations managers in each instance.

The challenge, of course, lies in finding the optimal balance between these sometimes conflicting concerns in the context of the firm's current business strategy. One possible starting point in evaluating these concerns can be found in the three generic competitive strategies developed by Michael Porter: overall cost leadership, differentiation, and focus.[20] Let's briefly consider their implications.

Cost Leadership Strategies

Achieving industry-wide cost leadership requires that all functional policies be oriented toward this objective. In operations, this means emphasizing efficient facilities, aggressively pursuing cost reductions, avoiding marginal customer accounts, and minimizing

---

[20]Michael E. Porter, *Competitive Advantage: Creating and Sustaining Superior Performance.* New York: The Free Press, 1985.

costs in such functional areas as customer service, personal selling, and advertising.

These policies will tend to favor the operations perspective in each of the eleven operational issues. Marketing's most effective role here will be to assist operations in achieving its objectives by (1) targeting communication efforts at those types of customers who will be most likely to accept a somewhat stripped-down level of service; (2) encouraging customers to use the service in ways that will contribute to increased productivity; (3) educating customers to use the service effectively without much assistance from sales or customer service staff; and (4) insisting on the lowest possible price consistent with profitability objectives, in order to compensate customers for the no-frills nature of the service and for such inconveniences as low-rent locations, bare-bones facilities, lack of personal assistance, and increased risk of queuing or crowding.

Differentiation Strategies

The generic strategy of differentiation involves creating an offering that is perceived industry-wide as unique. Distinctive service will usually support a higher price and tend to generate significant brand loyalty from customers willing to pay more in return for benefits unavailable elsewhere. Firms adopting this posture should evaluate each of the eleven operational issues with reference to their implications for customer satisfaction. Marketers will need sufficient clout to deal with operations on equal terms. Where disputes occur, top management may need to mediate. Here, the objective can be described as employing those operational concepts that will provide meaningful competitive differentiation, without allowing costs to balloon out of control or the operation to grind to a halt for lack of needed resources.

Focus Strategies

A focus strategy differs from the previous two in that it rests on selection of a narrow competitive thrust within an industry. It represents an intelligent choice for a smaller player, and begins with selection of a particular buyer group or geographic area, or the decision to offer only a limited product line. Some focus strategies seek to combine each of these elements, targeting a certain type of customer in a particular geographic area with a specific service. Within the target segment, focus strategies can be divided into cost focus and differentiation focus. In both instances, marketing input is critical in selecting the nature of the focus and ensuring that operations can deliver an appropriate configuration for the target segment. (If not, another segment must be sought.)

If the target segment is highly price-sensitive, operational strategies must emphasize cost control. But if marketers have researched segment needs, they will be able to argue against cost cutting measures that are insensitive to the needs of the chosen customers. For instance, the elderly are a growing market segment. The great majority of older consumers have limited resources and so are quite price sensitive. However, various infirmities, a reluctance to travel too far, and concerns over personal safety may make many of them unwilling to use self-service options, patronize distant facilities, or learn to use new high-tech delivery systems. On the other hand, being retired, they may be less time constrained and thus willing to wait longer for service and to patronize service facilities at off-peak times during daylight hours.

In instances where the target segment is willing to pay a premium for service features unavailable elsewhere — such as customized service where attention to customer preferences and convenience is a key objective — marketers should be in the driver's seat, much as they are in a differentiation strategy. A key task here is to discourage operations from seeking false efficiencies that will reduce customer satisfaction.

CONCLUSION

Historically, operations has been the dominant management function in most service businesses, reflecting its central role in creating and delivering the service. In today's highly competitive service markets, good marketing management is also becoming essential to success. Unfortunately, marketers and operations personnel may tend to pull in different directions, the former advocating improved service features that will appeal to customers, the latter emphasizing efficiency and cost control.

In practice, both groups of managers should be looking for ways to work together: marketers may be able to develop customer-oriented strategies designed to make the operation run more efficiently, while operations concepts can be employed to provide better service to customers. Human resource managers may be able to play a pivotal role in designing and filling jobs that serve both objectives without conflict.

Since the marketing function is still relatively new to many service firms, it is incumbent upon marketing managers to develop a good understanding of key operational concepts so that they can learn how the business works and then develop marketing strategies that mesh with those of operations.

Don't Change Corporate Culture — Use It!

PETER F. DRUCKER

Many service organizations need to change deeply ingrained habits to compete more effectively in a world where customers demand better quality and faster delivery and where employees are more conscious of their rights. However, attempting to change corporate culture may not be the best way to bring about needed changes in behavior. Instead, focus on changing habits.

Changing the corporate culture has become the latest management fad. Every business magazine carries articles about it. And not a week goes by without my being asked to run a seminar on the subject.

There is indeed a need to change deeply ingrained habits in a good many organizations. Electric-power and telephone companies always had their profits guaranteed by public regulation. Now they find themselves up against cut-throat competition. Customers demand just-in-time delivery. Consumers are increasingly picky about quality and service. Employees sue at the drop of a hat alleging discrimination and sexual harassment. And with product lives shrinking, there is an urgent need in most mechanical industries in the U.S. (and even more in those of Europe) to change drastically the way new products and new models are conceived, designed, made and marketed, with the process eventually being telescoped into months from years.

Form and Content

What these needs require are changes in behavior. But "changing culture" is not going to produce them. Culture — no matter how defined — is singularly persistent. Nearly 50 years ago, Japan and Germany suffered the worst defeats in recorded history, with their values, their institutions and their cultures discredited. But today's Japan and today's Ger-

---

many are unmistakably Japanese and German in culture, no matter how different this or that behavior. In fact, changing behavior works only if it can be based on the existing "culture."

Japan is the best example. Alone of all non-Western countries it has become a modern society, because her reformers, a hundred years ago, consciously based the new "Westernized" behavior on traditional Japanese values and on traditional Japanese culture. The modern Japanese corporation and university are thoroughly "Western" in their form. But they were used as containers, so to speak, for the traditional and thoroughly un-Western culture of the mutual obligations and loyalties of a clan society — e.g., in the lifetime commitment of company to employee and employee to company, or in organizing industry in *keiretsu,* groups of autonomous firms held together as "vassals" by mutual dependence and mutual loyalty.

The reformers of India and China, by contrast, felt that they had to change their countries' cultures. The only results have been frustration, friction, confusion — and no changes in behavior.

Another example: Konrad Adenauer in the 1920s was a vocal critic of Weimar Germany, for its "bourgeois" values, its greed, its materialism, its worship of money and business. When he became chancellor of a defeated Germany after World War II he deliberately and uncompromisingly strove to restore the pre-Hitler "bourgeois" Germany he so thoroughly detested. When criticized — and he was harshly attacked by well-meaning "progressives" both in Germany and in the West — he answered: "Pre-Hitler Germany, no matter how deficient, is the only culture Germans alive today know that still worked; we have no choice but to use it to build the new, the post-Hitler Germany."

But there is also a good — and American — business example: the railroads. In the late 1940s, the American railroads were losing money hand over fist. Worse still, they were losing market share to trucks and airplanes even faster. Yet they were clearly needed — and so Uncle Sam, everybody agreed, would

have to take them over. And most of the passenger business did indeed have to be taken over by government agencies. But passenger business was never more than one-tenth of railroad traffic.

The railroads' real business, freight traffic, remained totally private in the U.S. — the only country in the world where this is the case. Moreover, the American railroads are the only ones that make money. Every other railroad system is virtually bankrupt. And the railroads in the U.S. carry a significant share of the country's freight — a little more than one-third of long distance traffic — with no other system carrying more than 5% to 8% (and neither the British nor the Japanese railroads carry even that much). The American railroads based this turnaround on the existing values of their managers, their clerks, their train crews — on the railroaders' dedication to technical standards, for instance.

If you have to change habits, don't change culture. Change habits. And we know how to do that.

The first thing is to define what results are needed. In the hospital emergency room, for instance, each patient should be seen within one minute after arrival by a competent person — e.g., an emergency room nurse. The new model of the washing machine or of the laptop computer has to be ready for market testing within 15 months of its predecessor's introduction. Every customer inquiry, including every complaint, has to be settled by telephone within 24 hours (the standard of a well-run mutual-funds firm).

The next — and most important — step is *not* a "training session" or a management conference, let alone a lecture by the big boss. It is to ask: "Where within our own system do we *do* this already?"

The American railroads began their turnaround around 1948 or 1949 when executives at the Union Pacific, the Chesapeake & Ohio and the Norfolk & Western first asked: "What is the most important result we need?" They all answered: "To get back on the railroad the shipment of finished automobiles from factory to dealer." Then they asked, "Is anyone on any railroad actually doing this?"

The moment the question was asked, they all realized that one subsidiary of the Chesapeake & Ohio — the one serving Flint, Michigan, home of the Buick Division of General Motors — was actually increasing its share of finished-automobile shipments while every other railroad in the country was losing automobile business. Yet all these people in Flint had done was to find out what traditional railroad services Buick needed and was willing to pay for — and then to provide the service with true excellence.

Marshall Field in Chicago was one of the first of the high-class big-city department stores to get into trouble, in the 1970s — and one of the first ones to get out of trouble too. Three or four successive CEOs tried to change the culture — to no avail. Then a new CEO came in who asked, "What do we have to produce by way of results?" Every one of his store managers knew the answer, "We have to increase the amount each shopper spends per visit." Then he asked, "Do any of our stores actually do this?" Three or four — out of 30 or so — did it. "Will you then tell us," the new CEO asked, "what you people do that gives you the desired results?"

In every single case these results were achieved not by doing something different but by systematically doing something everyone had known all along should be done, had in the policy manuals, and had been preaching — but only the few exceptions had been practicing.

The next step, therefore, is for top management to make sure that the effective behavior as it develops out of the organization's own culture is actually being practiced. This means, above all, that senior management systematically asks, again and again: "What do we in senior management, and in this company as a whole, do that helps you to produce the results that all of us are agreed are the necessary ones?" And: "What do we do that hampers you concentrating on these necessary results?" People who successfully managed to get old and entrenched organizations to do the needed new things ask these questions at every single meeting with their associates — and take immediate action on what they hear.

Iraq vs. Grenada

Finally, changing habits and behavior requires changing recognitions and rewards. People in organizations, we have known for a century, tend to act in response to being recognized and rewarded — everything else is preaching. The moment people in an organization are recognized — for instance by being asked to present to their peers what made them successful in obtaining the desired results — they will act to get the recognition. The moment they realize that the organization rewards for the right behavior they will accept it.

The best example: the way the American military services worked together in the recent Iraq campaign. In the invasion of Grenada in 1983 there was no cooperation at all between the services — if there had been the slightest opposition, the invasion would have ended in disaster. The military immediately organized all kinds of conferences, pep sessions, lectures and so on, to preach cooperation. Still, less than a year and a half ago, the Panama invasion almost foundered because the services still did not cooperate.

Only a year later, in Iraq, cooperation worked as no service cooperation ever worked before. The reason: Word got around, I am told, that henceforth the appraisal of an officer's cooperation with other services — as judged by those other services — would be a material factor in promotion decisions.

Services Under Siege — The Restructuring Imperative

STEPHEN S. ROACH

Foreign competition and deregulation are exposing the U.S. service sector's hidden vulnerabilities: overinvestment in information technology and chronic inefficiency.

America's next wave of restructuring is at hand — but this time it is crashing down on the vast service sector. Once sacrosanct, services are undergoing in the 1990s the same difficult and painful shrinkage that manufacturing suffered in the 1980s. The enormous white-collar job losses in service companies over the past year — led by some of America's foremost banks, insurance companies, retailers, and airlines — are not simply a reflection of a temporary recession. Those jobs are gone for good, a harbinger of the even deeper changes that are in store for the service sector in the years ahead.

The explanation for this restructuring is quite simple. Until recently, services have been sheltered from competition and have had little incentive to drive out inefficiency. Shielded by regulation and confronted by few foreign competitors, service companies have allowed their white-collar payrolls to become bloated, their investments in information technology to outstrip the paybacks, and their productivity to stagnate.

Now competition, the great equalizer, is heating up and exposing these inefficiencies. Deregulation and foreign direct investment are introducing new players that are challenging the practices and philosophies of individual companies, whole industries, indeed the entire U.S. service sector. Just as intense competition forced the restructuring of Smokestack America in the 1980s, the quest for a new efficiency is causing major dislocations in many service markets. Mergers are taking the banking industry by storm, affecting such key players as Chemical Bank, Manufacturers Hanover, NCNB, and C&S/Sovran. The airline industry is carving up the remains of one of its former giants, Pan Am. And many big accounting firms — including Peat Marwick, Ernst & Young, and Deloitte & Touche — are downsizing.

U.S. service companies must prepare for radical change, a fact that may come as a great shock. As the United States mourned the decline of its manufacturing sector, there was consolation in the unbridled promise of a burgeoning service sector. The vision was renewed economic prosperity driven by service industries of great scope and diversity that could more than compensate for the slippage in manufacturing. The hope was for a virtually seamless transition to the postindustrial era.

But there is a painful irony at work: job creation, the very attribute proponents point to as proof that the service sector can propel the United States back to economic preeminence, is in fact a symptom of the sector's chronic neglect of economic efficiency. So too is the sector's inability to exploit the potential of new technologies. These shortcomings will make it hard for U.S. service companies to respond to the ever-shifting terms of global competition and the attendant risks to market share.

It's not too late for service companies to overcome their inefficiencies — but they must be careful. Although they may identify with the threats their manufacturing counterparts faced, they should not make the same mistake: cutting costs at the expense of securing enduring competitive strength. Over-zealous cost cutting could hollow the sector, leaving companies more efficient over the short haul but unable to innovate, respond to customers, or provide quality services over the long haul. A better response will balance the need for financial discipline with equally important considerations of quality and flexibility. The U.S. service sector must mount a full-blown and immediate reexamination of its strategy to meet the imperatives of a new competition.

THE PROMISED LAND

During the 1980s, when the United States lost nearly two million manufacturing jobs and its world economic standing, the fast-emerging service sector was a great frontier. If the United States saw steel, autos, tires, and machine tools go by the boards, there was consolation in the growth of retail, finance, health care, and professional services into not only successful U.S. enterprises but also, presumably, world-class operations. "Services" became the mantra of national progress as economists charted ever-impressive job growth figures. The United States was a powerful job machine, far more so than Europe or Japan.

On the surface, services appear to have met America's high hopes. Over the past decade, the sector has created nearly 20 million new jobs, more than enough to compensate for the losses in manufacturing. The result has been a stunning transformation of the U.S. work force. In the 1970s, the service sector accounted for 55% of all jobs in the private economy; in 1990, it accounted for 75%. Meanwhile, manufacturing's share of employment has been halved in the post-World War II era and currently accounts for only about one-quarter the number of jobs that services provide.

Contrary to conventional wisdom, service sector workers are not a vast cadre of hamburger flippers. The composition of the work force is quite varied. About two-thirds of its job holders can be classified as white-collar workers. Of those, about 43% are "knowledge workers" — managers, executives, and a variety of professionals ranging from scientists to lawyers to entertainers. Needless to say, these workers are generally well-educated and have career tracks and earning potential that compare favorably with any occupational group in manufacturing.

At the lower end of the job pyramid in services is an enormous support staff — fully 57% of the white-collar sector's work force — that toils on the new assembly line of the information economy. Occupations in this category range from sales workers and secretaries to bank tellers and computer operators. In general, their educational records are not particularly impressive, nor are their earning power and career opportunities. In the 1980s, no one seemed to care about the vast disparities of job opportunities in services. The proliferation of employment was itself something to celebrate.

In fact, however, these celebrations were unwarranted. Far from representing a national triumph, the sheer number of jobs and the pattern of job creation in services demonstrate a fundamental weakness in U.S. services. That hasn't always been the case. Indeed, since the industrial revolution, job creation in manufacturing and a strengthened economy have gone hand in hand. As the economy gains strength, the demand for goods rises, and companies increase their hiring and production — doing so with the improved efficiency of new techniques and more modern equipment. For Smokestack America, increased productivity has been synonymous with labor saving, and that translates into improved competitiveness. Only in recent history did U.S. manufacturing get lax about labor productivity. But after a tough period in the 1980s, manufacturing renewed its progress. By the end of the decade, American goods were again selling well overseas, and the mounting surge of imports had been stemmed at home. While hardly an industrial renaissance, the worst appeared to be over.

In services, the dynamics have been the opposite. While some jobs in the service sector have arisen to meet a growing demand for services, much of the job creation has been excessive. That is, it has been an unmistakable by-product of inefficiencies in existing operations. Productivity figures attest to this: nonmanufacturing productivity (a good proxy for productivity in the service sector) came to a virtual standstill in the mid-1970s, and the service sector has eked out only paltry gains in productivity ever since. Consequently, employment growth no longer reflects vitality and strength in the U.S. economy. Instead, it reflects the inherent weakness of an economy that is unable to make its workers more productive. (See the graph "Services Employ Lots of People...But Not Very Productively.")

With service workers now holding nearly four out of every five jobs in private industry, the service sector's inability to make those workers more productive is a serious problem for the United States. A rising standard of living depends on productivity improvement. If services aren't achieving this, the task falls to manufacturing. But manufacturing is losing its ability to shoulder this burden. The factory sector represents a quickly narrowing slice of the U.S. work force. And with the U.S. share of manufacturing output stagnating at best, productivity enhancement could mean further dramatic shrinkage of factory jobs.

The United States has become more dependent on services, which is precisely why it is important to address the sector's fundamental weaknesses. Those weaknesses put the entire U.S. service sector at risk. The excesses of the past simply won't be tolerated in the competitive climate of the 1990s. Even service companies that dominate their markets must face up to their productivity problems now or risk being overtaken by sleeker players.

TECHNOLOGY OVERDOSE

The service sector's lagging efficiencies may seem surprising in light of the costly bet that has been wagered on the promise of computers, telecommunications, and other forms of information technology to enhance productivity. While economists have long recognized the relationship between rising capital endowment and productivity enhancement, that relationship has not been borne out in services. The massive investments in technology simply have not improved productivity; on the contrary, they have made service organizations less profitable and less prepared to compete on other fronts.

Technology is expensive. In the aggregate, U.S. service companies are currently spending more than $100 billion annually to equip their growing cadre of white-collar workers with the hottest new technologies. Hardware is, of course, only the tip of the iceberg. Networks and their trappings add to the bill, as do the associated costs of R&D expenses for the development of control and analytical systems; in addition, there are expenses associated with extensive professional support and

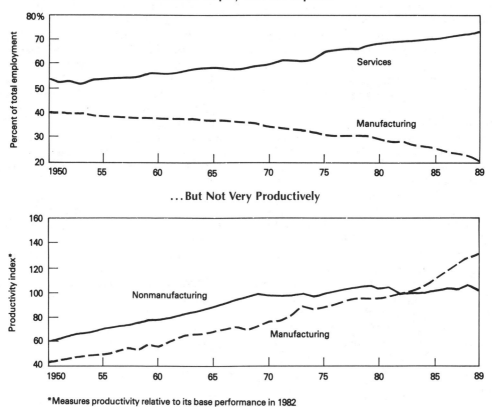

Services Employ Lots of People...

Percent of total employment

Services

Manufacturing

...But Not Very Productively

Productivity index*

Nonmanufacturing

Manufacturing

*Measures productivity relative to its base performance in 1982

SOURCE: U.S. Bureau of Labor Statistics

the demanding requirements of an increasingly short product-replacement cycle.

Over the past eight years, the service sector has put nearly all of its incremental capital endowment into information technology. In fact, the service sector now owns more than 85% of America's installed base of information technology. Not surprisingly, the service sector has a far greater proportion of its total capital committed to information technology than manufacturing does. In 1982, services invested $6,000 in information technology for each white-collar worker. Since then, the capital per white-collar worker has essentially doubled. (See the graph "Investment in Technology Outpaces White-Collar Productivity.")

But the fact is, information technology has not improved the productivity of the white-collar workers who use it. When a factory buys

equipment, that equipment typically includes state-of-the-art technologies that make workers more efficient. Individual workers produce more and unit labor costs go down. When a service company buys information technology, however, it tends to employ just as many workers as before, and labor costs stay the same.

What's more, evidence suggests that technology investments in back-office operations, long considered an area that lends itself well to automation, have done little to improve productivity. Some 30 million U.S. white-collar workers do things like process records and deliver messages in the back office. They support some 23 million managers, engineers, and other front-office knowledge workers. If information technology were truly automating the back office of the service sector, the

Investment in Technology Outpaces White-Collar Productivity

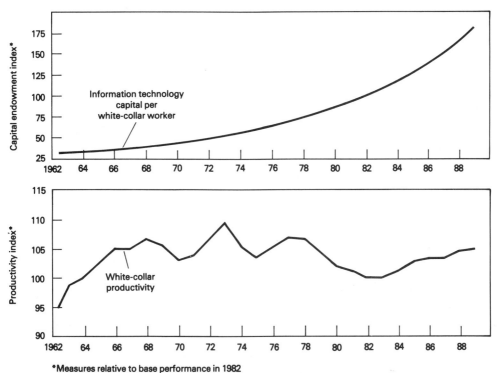

*Measures relative to base performance in 1982

SOURCE: Morgan Stanley estimates based on U.S. Department of Commerce and U.S. Bureau of Labor Statistics data

ratio of workers in the back office to those in the front office would fall over time. But that ratio has changed little over the past eight years, and it exceeds the ratio for manufacturing. In other words, the service sector's back office is less efficient than that of the manufacturing sector, and even worse, its efficiency is improving at a much slower rate — a clear testament to services' complacency. (See the graph "Manufacturing Uses Technology More Efficiently Than Services Do.")

Productivity benefits from information technology in open-ended office applications have been especially elusive. For example, the seemingly attractive and very expensive concept of the fully networked office environment rings increasingly hollow. Technology connects machines, but so far it has done little to instill productive synergy among people. An interconnected office environment may facilitate the flow of electronic messages, but the creative, high-value-added applications are still lacking. And yet it is precisely those types of innovative, idea-driven breakthroughs that lie at the heart of America's long history of productivity enhancement.

This is not to say that every application of information technology is a flop. There are numerous examples of successful transaction-specific uses of information technology: check clearing, securities trading, point-of-sale inventory control, and automated shipping and tracking systems. Also, when technology is embedded in the service, significant paybacks on the investment have often materialized. Examples include American Airlines' SABRE, a yield-management reservation system, and Morgan Stanley's TAPS, a transactions processing and reporting system. Unfortunately, these applications have been the exceptions and not the rule.

Manufacturing Uses Technology More Efficiently Than Services Do

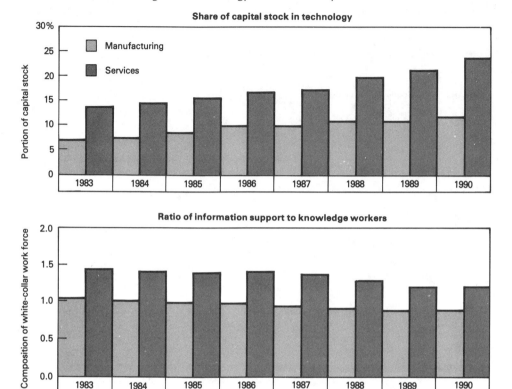

SOURCE: Morgan Stanley estimates based on U.S. Department of Commerce and U.S. Bureau of Labor Statistics data

As a result of heavy ongoing investments in technology, the service sector's cost structure has been ominously transformed. While workers can still be hired and fired, service companies are now strapped with a steady stream of expenses to support a flourishing technology infrastructure that has taken deep root. The bottom line is that service companies have moved from a variable-cost to a fixed-cost regime, thereby sacrificing flexibility without gaining any concomitant productivity benefits. That's the real price of the service sector's addiction to technology.

SUDDEN THREATS

A sizable fixed investment in information technology, bloated payrolls of white-collar workers, and stagnant productivity leave the service sector extremely vulnerable. Foreign competition and deregulation now threaten to expose those vulnerabilities. Until recently, Americans thought services were immune to foreign competition. The conventional wisdom held that while cars and VCRs could flow freely across U.S. borders, banking and retailing could not.

But that line of thinking is flawed. Competition is driven by opportunity, and there can be no mistaking the rewards available to those who capture market share in services, especially in the United States. The United States dominates the service outlays of the world's major industrialized countries. It accounts for about 48% of all service transactions in the G-7 grouping of industrialized countries. (The "Group of Seven" comprises the United States, Japan, Germany, the United

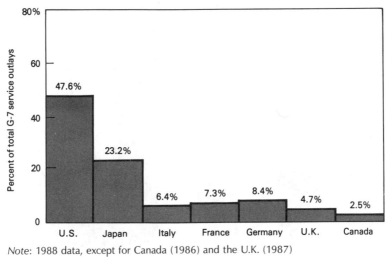

Kingdom, Canada, France, and Italy.) That figure represents approximately $2.9 trillion spent on services annually—twice as much as the runner-up, Japan. (See the graph "The U.S. Outspends Other Countries in Services.")

America's dominance in services partly reflects the sheer size of the U.S. economy. But there is also a basic structural difference between the United States and its major competitors. Where the private service sector accounts for 60% of the U.S. economy, it accounts for only 40% to 50% of other G-7 economies. Education and medical care cost more in the United States, but more important, the high degree of sophistication in the U.S. economy's demand for services like entertainment, travel, recreation, and personal grooming is lacking elsewhere.

America easily has the world's richest and deepest markets in services, and to multinational companies looking to expand, these are enticing prospects. Indeed, lost in all the clamor over foreign purchases of U.S. manufacturing facilities has been a dramatic acceleration of foreign direct investment in U.S. service industries. In the late 1980s, the average yearly inflow of foreign acquisitions in services amounted to some $22 billion—nearly three times the yearly amount in the first half of the decade and a rate comparable with the more visible investments in goods-producing industries, primarily manufacturing. (See the graph "U.S. Service Companies Attract Foreign Direct Investment.")

Most of the investment from overseas has gone into the nonfinancial segment of the service sector, into industries like retail and wholesale trade, business services, and hotels. The companies involved are hardly small players in America's service sector; they range from Columbia Pictures and J. Walter Thompson to Saks Fifth Avenue and Holiday Inns. (See the table "Notable Foreign Acquisitions of U.S. Service Companies, 1986 to 1991.") For nonfinancial companies, such foreign investment averaged $15.5 billion annually from 1986 to 1989. That's three times as much as in the preceding five years.

The rest of the foreign direct investment in services was in the financial sector. Purchases were largest in the insurance industry and in the "other" financial services grouping, which includes securities firms. Foreign direct investment in U.S. banks also accelerated slightly. (See the graph "Foreign Direct Investment in Services Is Accelerating.")

U.S. Service Companies Attract Foreign Direct Investment

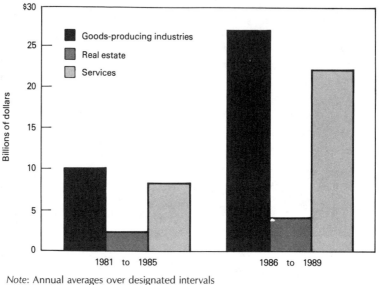

Note: Annual averages over designated intervals
SOURCE: U.S. Department of Commerce

This foreign direct investment is a bigger threat than it might appear. Certainly, overseas buyers are not about to run off with the assets of U.S. service companies. But their growing presence in U.S. markets will force U.S. service companies to meet the competitive challenge head on. Foreign players will be engaged directly in terms of capitalization, flexibility, and scale.

Strong capitalization is necessary to withstand the intensifying battle for market share. Foreign players will buy into U.S. service mar-

Notable Foreign Acquisitions of U.S. Service Companies, 1986 to 1991

Target	Purchaser	Amount in Millions
Entertainment		
MCA	Matsushita Electric (Japan)	$ 7,907
Columbia Pictures	Sony Corp. (Japan)	4,714
MGM/UA Communications	Pathe Communications (U.S. parent, Italian controlled)	1,670
Technicolor Holdings	Carlton Communications (Great Britain)	780
MTM Entertainment	Television South (Great Britain)	320
RKO Theaters	Cineplex Odeon (Canada)	169
Hotels		
Intercontinental (Grand Met)	Saison Group (Japan)	2,270
Motel 6	Accor (France)	2,262
Holiday Inn	Bass PLC (Great Britain)	2,225
Hilton International (UAL)	Ladbroke Group (Great Britain)	1,070
Ramada Inc.	New World Development (Hong Kong)	540
Advertising		
Ogilvy Group	WPP Group (Great Britain)	798
J. Walter Thompson	WPP Group (Great Britain)	541
Ted Bates Worldwide	Saatchi & Saatchi (Great Britain)	450

Notable Foreign Acquisitions of U.S. Service Companies, 1986 to 1991 (cont.)

Target	Purchaser	Amount in Millions
Miscellaneous Business Services		
Manpower Inc.	Blue Arrow PLC (Great Britain)	1,345
Rent-A-Center Inc.	Thorn EMI (Great Britain)	570
Honeywell Information Systems	NEC Corp & Compagnie des Machines Bull (France)	527
UAL Apollo Reservation System (50% share)	Covia Partnership (Great Britain)	500
Network Security Corp.	Inspectorate International (Switzerland)	390
Retail Trade		
Federated and Allied Department Stores	Campeau Corp. (Canada)	11,264
Saks Fifth Avenue (B.A.T.)	Investcorp Bank (Bahrain)	1,500
Brooks Brothers (Campeau)	Marks & Spencer (Great Britain)	750
Zale Corp.	People's Jewelers (Canada)	607
Key Jewelers	Ratners Group (Great Britain)	450
Transportation and Communications		
McCaw Cellular (22% interest)	British Telecom (Great Britain)	1,500
Soo Line	Canadian Pacific (Canada)	390
Sitmar Cruises	Peninsular & Oriental Steam (Great Britain)	210
Delta Air Lines (5% interest)	Swissair (Switzerland)	193
Delta Air Lines (5% interest)	Singapore Airlines (Singapore)	181
Majestic Shipping (Loews)	Hellesport Shipping (Great Britain)	154
Insurance		
Farmers Group	B.A.T. Industries (Great Britain)	5,158
Fireman's Fund Insurance	Allianz AG (Germany)	3,100
Equitable Life Assurance Society (share)	Groupe Axa S.A. (France)	1,000
Home Insurance (Ambase)	TVH Acquisition (Sweden)	970
Maryland Casualty Co.	Zurich Insurance (Switzerland)	740
Reliance Group	Winterthur Swiss Insurance (Switzerland)	630
Banking		
First Maryland Bancorp	Allied Irish Banks (Ireland)	1,101
First Jersey National	National Westminster Bank (Great Britain)	820
Citizens Financial Group	Royal Bank of Scotland (Great Britain)	790
First NH Banks	Bank of Ireland (Ireland)	776
Marine Midland	Hong Kong & Shanghai Banking (Hong Kong)	758
Securities and Other Financial Services		
CIT Group (Manufacturers Hanover)	Dai-Ichi Kangyo (Japan)	1,280
First Boston	Credit Suisse-First Boston (Switzerland)	1,100
Shearson Lehman Bros. (American Express, share)	Nippon Life (Japan)	538
Goldman Sachs (share)	Sumitomo Bank (Japan)	500
Aubrey Lanston	Industrial Bank of Japan (Japan)	234

SOURCE: Morgan Stanley & Co., Inc.

kets only if their pockets are deep enough to set up a viable subsidiary in this country. And foreign pockets are starting to look deeper than their U.S. counterparts are, many of which have had to write off assets of dubious quality in recent years. Needless to say, this threat to the capitalization of domestically owned companies has been particularly acute in the financial services sector. Well-capitalized foreign entrants that have not had to wrestle with financial adversity are better positioned to redeploy assets — which will undoubtedly be necessary as competition heats up.

Flexibility goes beyond the ability to move financial capital around quickly. Foreign companies that buy into U.S. service markets will have easy access to state-of-the-art technology and operating systems. They can avoid the expensive development and experimental stage and pick and choose only those applications and technologies proven most effective. They will not, however, be encumbered with the trappings of the massive technology infrastructure that has so altered the cost structure of U.S. service companies.

Foreign companies also may have certain advantages regarding scale. Economies of scale are just as important in services as they are in manufacturing. They allow a company to spread the fixed costs of a productive technology over a larger market base. The cost savings can then be transformed into market share through lower prices or expansion. A company with a multinational reach may have a clear advantage in scale over those companies that restrict their presence to a single market. In that light, the extent to which foreign companies are rushing into the deep U.S. markets — well ahead of America's push overseas — is disconcerting. This suggests that the balance of globalization is tipping in favor of foreign service companies, putting U.S. companies at a distinct disadvantage in reaping the scale benefits of an increasingly globalized market for services.

Foreign direct investment is not the only trend exposing services to new competitive pressures. Deregulation too is challenging many service industries by allowing new competitors to enter markets and squeeze margins. The current wave of deregulation began in

Foreign Direct Investment in Services Is Accelerating

	1981 to 1985	1986 to 1989
All Industries	$20.3	$54.1
Goods-Producing	9.8	27.8
Service Providing	10.5	26.2
Financial	3.1	6.6
Banking	1.4	2.1
Insurance	1.1	2.7
Other	0.6	1.8
Real Estate	2.7	4.1
Nonfinancial	4.7	15.5
Transportation	0.2	0.6
Communication, Public Utilities	0.1	0.0
Wholesale Trade	3.5	6.4
Retail Trade	0.6	2.5
Services	0.4	6.0
Hotels	0.1	1.8
Business Services	0.2	2.3
Other	0.1	1.9

Note: Annual averages in billions

SOURCE: U.S. Department of Commerce

the 1970s with airlines and trucking, and it spread quickly. It includes the breakup of the telephone industry's long-standing monopoly and the more recent birth of a largely unregulated cable television business. Regulatory shackles were also removed from the world's capital markets, initially by lifting ceilings on interest-yielding deposits, then by allowing a profusion of new instruments and nonbank institutions to facilitate the process of financial intermediation. And many services that were once the exclusive province of government — such as postal delivery, waste disposal, and water service — have been privatized, which is yet another form of deregulation.

BANKING: A CASE IN POINT

The combination of long-neglected inefficiencies and a sudden unleashing of competition should be vaguely reminiscent of the staging that led to manufacturing's traumatic decade. There is little chance that service companies will escape the kind of massive restructuring that manufacturing experienced.

Massive dislocations are already apparent in industries where the lack of competition has allowed inefficiencies to persist. Banking is one of the more visible industries in turmoil. Rules prohibiting interstate banking and separating banks from securities firms have prevented financial institutions from achieving the benefits of scale and have provided little incentive for discipline. The result has been a great deal of redundant and underproductive capacity. There were, for instance, 14,500 commercial banks in the United States in 1985, and each one had its own information systems, its own branch offices, and its own payrolls.

As regulation has eased, competitive pressures have spurred banks to merge and consolidate in an effort to achieve scale and to eliminate redundant capacity. The most prominent example of this trend is the recent announcement of the intent to merge by Chemical Bank and Manufacturers Hanover — two of the country's largest money-center banks. The trend is also spreading to the "superregional" banks, where NCNB and C&S/Sovran have agreed to join forces. By 1990, the number of banks nationwide had already been reduced by 14% from the high in the mid-1980s. Challenges came first from other domestic banks and then from the presence of foreign direct investment in the United States. Foreign money began pouring into U.S. banks in the early 1980s and accelerated by about 18% a year throughout the 1980s. Foreigners now have roughly a $20 billion ownership stake in U.S. banks — just over 20% of the industry's capital stock. By the end of the 1980s, four of California's ten largest banks, Union Bank, Bank of California, Sanwa, and Sumitomo, were in foreign hands.

Most U.S. banks have struggled to improve productivity, but the results are unimpressive. Banks continue to spend heavily, especially on information systems. Expenditures on such technology rose 20% a year during the 1980s; by 1989, such outlays totaled 45% of the banking industry's capital stock. Meanwhile, labor costs have changed little. Employment growth slowed only slightly, from 1% a year to .3%. In general, technology has not made banking operations more efficient, and the cost structure remains bloated. Add the crisis of nonperforming loans, and the U.S. banking system finds itself in a state of vulnerability not seen since the 1930s.

THE SERVICE AGENDA

The United States doesn't have to watch the service sector slip into deep decline. So far, services are following the script written by manufacturing. Fixated on the same cost-cutting mentality, they are slashing payrolls, eliminating business units, and consolidating operations. Much of this pruning is long overdue, but now the challenge facing services is to mount a comprehensive strategic response that will not hollow the remainder of corporate America. Services can learn from manufacturing's experience.

One lesson from the 1980s is that cost cutting must be judicious. While financial discipline is necessary, cuts cannot be made in a panic or without considering long-term risk. The factory sector opted to sell short its future by trading its long-term capacity requirements for the sake of near-term financial gain. The growth in manufacturing's capital stock averaged only .7% a year in the long expansion that ended in 1990 — a huge shortfall from the 3.7% longer term pace of capital formation. Moreover, the industrial-plant slice of this capital stock actually has been shrinking by close to 1% a year since 1983 — a dramatic break from the historical pattern of greenfield expansion. Thus the recent turnaround in manufacturing has occurred against a backdrop of virtual stagnation in capital formation, which some construe as a hollowing of Smokestack America. (See the graph "U.S. Manufacturing Has Hollowed Its Capital Stock.")

Capacity shrinkage is a steep price to pay for cost control. It puts U.S. companies far behind their ever-growing foreign counterparts and threatens their longer term ability to achieve sustainable gains in productivity. The risk is clear: enhancing short-term productivity objectives solely through reductions in the scale of operations is a recipe for the eventual capitulation of market share.

The fixation on slashing is damaging in another way: it deflects attention from other strategic considerations. As soon as U.S. manufacturers matched competitors on the cost front, they began to lose ground in quality enhancement and production flexibility. They failed to realize that the competitive challenge is a moving target.

The challenge facing services is primarily managerial. Although the specifics will depend on each industry's competitive environment, several guidelines seem appropriate in shaping the service agenda for the 1990s. To begin with, service companies will have to develop a new accounting metric. Traditional accounting standards are oriented toward the needs of factories and are woefully inadequate in measuring white-collar productivity. Since a service is more amorphous than a product, it would be a mistake to use the quantity-driven metrics of the factory.

Services need an accounting framework that can identify which activities add the most value, enabling organizations to distinguish between routine and creative tasks. Only then

can the costs of technology acquisition and white-collar hiring be evaluated accurately in the context of an organization's strategic objectives and competitive realities. In banking, for example, such criteria could imply a reallocation of information technology away from low-value-added activities like transaction processing and administration to more analytical applications like interest-rate swaps. Activity-based managerial accounting is a step in the right direction, but much more work in this area remains to be done.

It should go without saying that a metric for quality is equally important. Admittedly, quality in the service sector is hard to define. For transaction-driven activities, some form of error-count analysis might be helpful. In more analytic endeavors, customer feedback might be useful.

Only with the proper measurement tools in hand can services assess restructuring options. Streamlining should be a first consideration. Companies are likely to find excesses of information technology and white-collar employment once they look for them. In doing so, they may find it necessary to unbundle in-house service functions. Such shedding could help shift the business back to a variable-cost environment, essential if services are to regain flexibility.

The consolidation of back-office operations in the financial services industry is a clear example of cost-effective unbundling. Securities firms are already pursuing the option of relinquishing to outside vendors or to newly created strategic alliances certain transactional capacities that are a drag on efficiency. The same principles have great potential in insurance and commercial banking. Even health and education could benefit by sharing certain high-cost activities and facilities. Managers may resist the idea of joint ownership, but such arrangements may provide exactly the cost relief they need.

Streamlining operations is not an end in itself. As an intrinsically cost-intensive sector, services must also expand. The objective is to exploit economies of scale to support whatever fixed costs cannot be unbundled. Services must also expand if they are to maintain

U.S. Manufacturing Has Hollowed Its Capital Stock

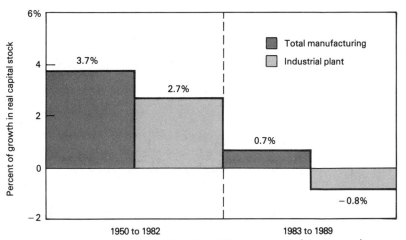

SOURCE: Morgan Stanley estimates based on U.S. Department of Commerce data

market share in a growing world economy. Multinational alliances and cross-ownership arrangements are ways to achieve strategic expansion, as are mergers and acquisitions.

The service company that responds to heightened competition will look very different from its predecessors. Strategically focused, it will have an efficient delivery system, a high-quality product, and a flexible cost structure. This configuration will allow for continued growth and broader reach in the global marketplace. Such a transformation may seem daunting, but the consequences of inaction will be even more alarming. Nothing short of America's future economic prosperity is at stake.

Singapore Airlines

SANDRA VANDERMERWE
CHRISTOPHER H. LOVELOCK

How can a successful international airline continue to increase its passenger volumes against stiff competition? Singapore Airlines is looking at ways to enhance the already high level of inflight service and is evaluating certain technologically-based improvements.

As Robert Ang[1] left the marketing executives' meeting and walked through the open air gallery back to his office in Airline House, he remembered what J. Y. Pillay, Singapore Airlines' Chairman, had said four years earlier at the company's 40th anniversary celebrations in 1987. "At 40 the symptoms of middle age begin and that's when complacency sets in," he had warned. Ang thought to himself, "And now that we are 44, this risk is even greater if we don't do something to hold onto our customer-oriented image." The discussion at the meeting on this fine May morning had centered on the role of technology in achieving this goal.

Ang paused to watch a Boeing 747-400 coming in to land. Dubbed the "Megatop" because of its extended upper deck, the aircraft was the most recent addition to the company's ultra-modern fleet. Singapore Airlines' blue, white, and yellow colors shone brightly in the steamy midday heat.

As Ang entered the office complex that housed his marketing systems team, he imagined the passengers starting to disembark after a 12- to 13-hour nonstop trip from Europe. What sort of flight had they had? Had the long journey gone well, reinforcing Singapore Airlines' reputation as one of the world's best airlines? The cabin crew would now be saying

[1]Disguised name

goodbye, and the passengers would soon be welcomed into the spacious elegance of Terminal 2 at Changi Airport, one of the largest and most modern in the world.

Ang knew that the company's achievements were already considerable; it had become one of the world's 10 biggest international airlines. But now, on the threshold of a new decade, the question was: could Singapore Airlines continue to attract increasing numbers of international customers?

"We are leaders in service, in comfort and luxury. Our customers tell us they fall in love when they fly with us. Where do we go from here?" were some of the remarks voiced at the meeting. For Robert Ang, there was only one logical answer: they had to satisfy the needs of contemporary travelers, which meant being able to bring the sophisticated technology found in people's homes and offices into the air. "Very little attention has been given to adapting technology strategically for our business," he had declared to his colleagues that morning. "For instance, home audio systems are fantastic. But in the air, they're terrible. We have to close this technology gap and provide modern customers with interesting and useful technology-based services."

Ang's views had been received with interest. His boss, the director of marketing planning, had closed the meeting by asking him to come up with some specific suggestions. "But," he had cautioned, "don't suggest anything that might conflict with the romance and superb personal service we're rightly famous for!"

BACKGROUND

"How did it all begin?" was a question that people encountering Singapore Airlines for the first time often asked. Many were surprised that a small island republic, measuring only 38 km long by 22 km wide (16×24 miles), and with a population of 2.7 million, could have one of the world's largest and most profitable airlines. Even more remarkable were the accolades bestowed by air travel organizations. In 1990, *Air Transport World* magazine named SIA "airline of the year"; *Conde Nast's*

Traveler termed it the "world's best airline"; and *Business Traveler International* called SIA the "best international airline."

Republic of Singapore

Just north of the equator, with a command of the straits between Malaysia and Indonesia, Singapore was ideally located for both shipping and airline routes. Being at the intersection of East and West, it saw itself at the heart of trade and business between the two.

In the 26 years since its independence in 1965, the nation had made what most observers considered to be astonishing economic progress. Per capita national income had reached US$10,450, representing 37% that of Switzerland, which Singaporean planners often cited as their economic model. It boasted not only one of the world's largest and most modern port facilities, but an airport, opened in 1981 and expanded in 1990, of equal caliber. Other accomplishments included a state-of-the-art telecommunications system, well-engineered highways, and the new Mass Rapid Transit rail system. Heavy investments in education and a strong work ethic had created a well-trained and motivated workforce. By 1991, Singapore was one of the world's largest shipbuilding and ship-repairing centers, the third largest oil refining and distribution complex, and had also become an important banking and financial center.

Singapore had made a particular effort to attract high technology firms, and many international companies had set up offices and plants on the island. Government planners saw technology as a driving force in the economy. As advances in telecommunications proceeded, and Singapore Telecom continued to push towards a fully digitalized system, planners spoke about creating an "intelligent island."

History of Singapore Airlines

Who would have believed that a country only one-quarter the size of Rhode Island, the smallest state in the US, would produce one of the most profitable airlines in the world? The story of Singapore Airlines officially started on May 1, 1947, when the first scheduled flight of Malaysian Airlines from Singapore landed in Penang. When both Malaysia and Singapore became independent in the mid-1960s, the name of the carrier was changed to Malaysia-Singapore Airlines. However it soon became obvious that the two nations had different priorities. Malaysia's main interest was having a flag carrier that would provide domestic and regional routes. But, being a small island, Singapore did not need domestic services; instead, its goal was to have long-distance international routes. It was agreed that the assets should be divided and two separate airlines created.

Singapore Airlines first flew under its own colors in October 1972. When it was announced that Malaysia and Singapore had agreed to establish two separate flag carriers, optimism was tempered by uncertainty and disbelief. Could an airline from such a small country compete in the international big league? Nevertheless, the 1970s seemed to be a good time for an airline to take off and succeed. Not only did the remarkable passenger growth of the 1960s — when traffic was doubling every five years — promise to continue, but ever increasing numbers of people worldwide were traveling to more places. In addition, exciting new high performance jets were being introduced.

Although Singapore Airlines (SIA) was state owned, the government's role in policy making and day to day management was minimal; senior executives were told not to expect any subsidy or preferential treatment. What the government did do, however, was to offer foreign carriers the opportunity to operate out of Singapore, under the condition that SIA would receive similar rights, even if they were not exercised immediately. The new airline pushed relentlessly for growth and innovation. Three months before operations began, it signed a contract with Boeing for the delivery of two B747-200s, with an option on two more. It was the first airline in Southeast Asia to order jumbo jets.

Singapore Airlines also concentrated on marketing: the airline's name and its logo — a stylized yellow bird — decorating the aircraft's dark blue tail fin soon became well known on the routes it operated. The goal

was to create a distinctly different airline that would be international but retain its Asian personality. Most importantly, top management insisted that it emphasize service to passengers who, they constantly reminded staff, were the unique reason for the airline's existence. In a world where one carrier resembled another, they realized that the cabin crew was the prime link between the passenger and the airline. The idea was to use the island's only real resource — the natural hospitality of its people — as a competitive advantage. In this way, it seemed certain that Singapore's national carrier would be remembered — and remembered favorably.

Research had shown that, when all other things were equal, passengers responded most to the appeal of high quality in-flight services. SIA was the first airline to put "snoozers" (fully reclining seats) in its aircraft. Since the company did not belong to IATA (International Air Transport Association), SIA's management went against the rules by serving free drinks, offering free movie headsets and other extras. The intent was to firmly establish an image of SIA in customers' minds as *the* airline for fine service.

The "Singapore Girl"— the personification of charm and friendliness — became a reality after painstaking recruiting, training and retraining. The best-looking and most helpful young women were selected as stewardesses. They were given a maximum of three contract terms of five years each, above average wages, and high status in the company. Better staff were given the possibility of promotion to senior jobs within SIA after the 15 year period. An extensive and distinctive advertising campaign promoted these stewardesses who dressed in sarong-sebayas, multicolored, ankle-length dresses made from traditional batik fabric designed by the Paris couturier Balmain. Male flight attendants were more conventionally dressed in light blue blazers and black trousers.

These distinctively uniformed women became the symbol of the airline's mission to deliver high quality personalized service. Research showed that they had the most lasting impact on passengers. Travelers reported that their beautiful uniform and charm were, in reality, all that the advertising had promised, and that in-flight service was better than anything they had experienced in a long time.

Top management was equally concerned with services on the ground. In 1973 a subsidiary company, Singapore Airport Terminal Services (SATS), was formed to perform ground handling, catering, and related tasks. Later, it started offering its services on a contract basis to other carriers that had operations in Singapore. In 1985, SATS was restructured into a holding company with four subsidiaries — SATS Passenger Services, SATS Catering, SATS Cargo, and SATS Apron Services.

Singapore Airlines survived the two oil shocks of the 1970s and continued to grow, creating headlines with such innovations as supersonic Concorde service between London and Singapore, operated jointly with British Airways, featuring BA colors on one side of the aircraft and SIA colors on the other. It also expanded its route structure. Huge aircraft orders, including what was then the largest in civil aviation history, were made. Thanks to strong profits, the airline was able to invest in new equipment without incurring significant debt. These enormous purchases were not all incremental additions to the fleet, for the company resold used aircraft after only a few years. Because they had been so well maintained, the "old" aircraft found ready buyers at good prices in the second-hand market.

THE SITUATION IN 1991

As one industry observer remarked, "1990 was a year that most airlines would sooner forget!" Battered by recession, a hike in oil prices, high interest rates on heavy debt loads, and the tensions arising from the Iraqi invasion of Kuwait, most major airlines suffered heavy financial losses. The outbreak of hostilities in the Gulf intensified problems — fear of terrorist attacks sharply reduced passenger loads on most international routes. But, at a time when many other airlines were retrenching, Singapore Airlines actually increased its advertising budget.

SIA's consolidated financial results for the fiscal year ending 31 March 1991 showed only a slight decline in revenues, from S\$5.09 billion to S\$4.95 billion.[2] The number of passengers carried climbed from 6.8 million to 7.1 million, even though the load factor dropped from 78.3% to 75.1% as a result of a jump in fleet size. In 1990, SIA had the highest operating profit of any airline in the world: US\$775 million. Apart from its marketing appeal, Singapore Airlines had another point in its favor — the higher margins obtained on airline services in Asia. The Asian carriers did not compete on price among themselves. They preferred nonprice forms of competition such as better service, more destinations, more frequent schedules, and newer fleets. With the entry of American players into the region, however, price became a more important feature.

The airline's fleet of 29 Boeing 747s and 14 Airbus 310s was the youngest fleet of all international carriers, with an average age of 4.75 years, compared to an industry average of around 10 years. The company had 36 new aircraft on order (of which 28 were the new B747-400s) and another 34 on option. Management was convinced that newer planes were not only more attractive to passengers and helped staff provide better service, but also offered other advantages such as greater reliability and lower fuel consumption. *Exhibit 1* compares Singapore Airlines' performance measures with those of other major international airlines.

By 1991 Singapore Airlines was among the ten biggest airlines in the world, as measured in terms of international tonne-kilometers of load carried. Its network linked 63 cities in 37 countries, and soon it would fulfill a long-held ambition to serve the east coast of the United States with transatlantic service from Frankfurt to New York. Singapore Changi Airport had become one of the world's largest and busiest terminals.

Government holdings had been reduced through stock sales to 54% of the company's

---

[2]Representative exchange rates for the Singapore dollar in mid-1991 were: S\$1.00 = US\$0.60 = £0.33.

EXHIBIT 1

Key Performance Measures 1990

1990 SCHEDULED PASSENGERS CARRIED (INTERNATIONAL)		1990 SCHEDULED PASSENGER-KILOMETERS PERFORMED (INTERNATIONAL)		1990 OPERATING PROFITS OF THE TOP TEN OF THESE AIRLINES	
Rank:	Numbers (in thousands)	Rank:	Numbers (in millions)	Rank:	US Dollars (millions)
1 British Airways	19,684	1 British Airways	62,834	1 Singapore Airlines	774
2 Lufthansa	13,326	2 Japan Airlines	42,690	2 Cathay Pacific	468
3 Air France	12,417	3 Lufthansa	38,744	3 Japan Airlines	464
4 Pan American	10,096	4 Pan American	38,241	4 British Airways	345
5 Japan Airlines	8,354	5 United	35,334	5 SAS	264
6 American Airlines	8,343	6 Singapore Airlines	31,544	6 American Airlines	67.9
7 SAS	8,335	7 Air France	29,023	7 Lufthansa	0
8 Cathay Pacific	7,378	8 Qantas	27,687	8 KLM	(19.3)
9 Alitalia	7,105	9 KLM	26,382	9 Alitalia	(75.7)
10 Singapore Airlines	7,093	10 American Airlines	24,086	10 Air France	(286)

assets. The airline had joined in a trilateral alliance with Swissair and the American carrier, Delta Airlines, to cooperate on customer servicing, interchangeable tour packages, through check-in, joint baggage handling, sharing of airport lounges, and joint promotions. It had also become a member of IATA in order to give the airline a voice in key industry forums, and greater access to their technical expertise and accredited sales agents. However, SIA did not want to participate in deliberations on tariff coordination where fare issues were discussed.

Despite the airline's achievements, there were some disquieting signs on the horizon. Competition was intensifying and service quality improving among a number of both Western and Asian airlines, including Hong Kong-based Cathay Pacific, Japan Airlines, a new strongly financed Taiwanese start-up called Eva Air, and Thai International and Malaysia Airlines. The latter two both featured stewardesses in eye-catching uniforms based on traditional costumes.

With rising living standards in Singapore came higher expectations among SIA's more than 13,000 employees, of whom some 4,200 were cabin crew. The company was finding it increasingly difficult to attract younger people, motivate existing employees and maintain its policy of employing the best staff for customer contact roles.

MAINTAINING THE CUSTOMER SERVICE PHILOSOPHY

Recognizing that the most exciting years were now over, top management continued to stress the importance of SIA's customer philosophy and service culture. The underlying principle that the customer came first was carried through at all levels of the organization. How customers were handled at each point of contact was considered of paramount importance. Company policy stated that if a trade-off had to be made, it should be made in favor of the customer. For example, contrary to the practice at other airlines, no customer was allowed to be downgraded for a Singapore Airlines senior executive who wanted a special seat.

Ground had recently been broken for a new US$50 million training center, designed to drill all employees in the fine art of serving customers. As reported in the *Straits Times,* Singapore's leading newspaper, everyone — from the floor sweeper to the deputy managing director — would receive this training. The underlying philosophy was to enable staff to place themselves in the customer's position. A lot of the training time was thus experientially based. Key people were sent on special missions to see what other airlines were doing and how customers were handled. Special delay simulation games groomed staff on ways to cope with delay situations, one of the major complaints received from passengers.

One principle remained constant: staff had to be as flexible as possible in their dealings with customers, even if it took more time and effort. Management constantly reiterated that customers could not be told what to do simply because it suited the company. Some passengers wanted to eat as soon as they boarded, others preferred to wait. Customers could not be pigeonholed, they often changed their minds. They might come on board intending to sleep and then decide to watch a movie after all. On long hauls, flexibility was especially important. Most passengers had individual habits that corresponded to their travel agendas, which could include sleeping at the beginning and working later, or vice versa.

Staff had learned that customers were happier when given a choice. Offering more meal variations automatically reduced the number of unhappy people. Menus, typically changed by other airlines no more than four times a year, were altered every week on SIA's high frequency flights. Information technology enabled the chefs to fine-tune meals and immediately withdraw any dishes that were poorly received. Although there were marginal costs associated with such tactics, management firmly believed that these efforts distinguished Singapore Airlines from its competitors. Staff were instructed to find other ways to save money. For instance, the chefs prepared meals only from ingredients in season. Crew members were briefed by the kitchen on how to prepare and serve anything new.

Complaints were encouraged as they provided insight about problems. Once they were received, something could be done to rectify the situation; all complaints were tracked down and followed up. Travelers were invited to submit these complaints in writing. While some customers — typically Americans, Germans and Australians — readily complied, others were less willing to do so in writing. These customers were specifically questioned in follow-up surveys.

A Service Productivity Index (SPI) was computed each quarter in order to assess service quality standards. Multilingual in-flight surveys were used to itemize customers' impressions on key issues; then this information was compiled along with data on punctuality, baggage mishandled/recovered per 1000 passengers, and the ratio of complaints to compliments addressed to management.

As soon as a complaint relating directly to a specific in-flight experience was received, crew members could be temporarily taken out of the system and given training. Cabin crew members were released from their flight schedules three or four times a year to meet with training experts. Senior cabin crew members met every Monday morning for feedback and exchange sessions with service support personnel. One "ritual" practiced was to address the crew from the control center just before takeoff about topical issues, special promotions and other issues relevant to services.

At the airport in Singapore, staff were encouraged to do everything possible to deal with legitimate customer problems. One story — now part of company folklore — was about a supervisor who found a tailor at midnight and paid a deposit from his own funds to have a suit made for a customer whose luggage had been lost so that the customer could attend an important meeting at noon the next day.

CUSTOMER PROFILE AND THE PRODUCT LINE

The product line was divided into three classes of travel — First, Raffles (business), and Economy. First Class accounted for 5% of passengers, Raffles Class for 10%, and Economy Class for 85%. About one million of the seven million seats sold annually were to Singaporeans. Revenues from non-Singaporeans were proportionately higher since they tended to fly longer distances. Of the airline's passengers, 75% were from outside the country and 25% were from home base.

Flights varied in length — from less than one hour to over 13 hours for nonstop flights to Europe. Flights under four hours were all non-smoking, reflecting Singapore's strong national commitment to curtailing tobacco use. *Exhibit 2* shows the percentage breakdown of the airline's daily flights by number

EXHIBIT 2
Details on Duration of Flights

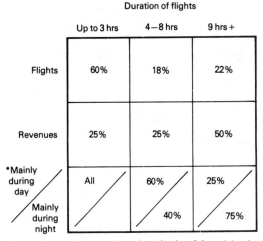

Duration of flights

	Up to 3 hrs	4–8 hrs	9 hrs +
Flights	60%	18%	22%
Revenues	25%	25%	50%
*Mainly during day / Mainly during night	All	60% / 40%	25% / 75%

*depending on if it goes through midnight of the originating point

of hours and amount of overnight travel.

On average, the load factor was somewhat higher in Economy Class (close to 80%) than in Raffles or First. Passengers who flew Raffles Class on a daytime flight might travel First Class on an overnight flight for the extra comfort.

Top management believed that the business passenger market held the future for the airline — both in numbers and yield. At the marketing executives' meeting Robert Ang had just attended, everyone had concurred that technology was the key to improving service to this segment of the market. The expectations of these particular customers, SIA executives knew, were constantly rising and their needs had changed greatly since the previous decade. Research revealed that business travelers:

- preferred to eat small amounts and less often;
- wanted more nutrition in their diet;
- tended to be impatient and resented having to wait;
- wanted to have the facilities found in airport lounges — such as showers and fax machines — also available in the sky;

- disliked wasting time on board and wanted to be occupied throughout the flight.

Technological Innovation

At the start of the meeting, Robert Ang had pointed out that the only way for the company to genuinely cater to travelers' increasingly sophisticated needs was to use technology more strategically for enhancing the quality of service. It was not enough to simply pick easily replicated innovations on an *ad hoc* basis. He had declared:

> Just going out and looking for technology-based solutions will give the market the impression that we are gimmicky and arbitrary in our approach. If we want to protect our competitive position, we've got to find ways to move faster than our competitors and create an enduring advantage for the company. There will be a million problems but, once we agree on the principle of "technology in the sky" as a competitive tool, we can solve the technical hassles. We have to use technology in the future as we used people in the past to serve customers. If we can match our high-tech services with our soft services, we will be irresistible to customers and will be distinguished from the rest.

Several technological innovations were already planned for introduction later that year. One was the installation of small TV screens at each First and Business Class seat, offering passengers video entertainment. Since other airlines were also doing this, ensuring variety would be pivotal. Another was satellite-linked air-to-ground telephone service which, unlike previously, allowed passengers to make calls even when the aircraft was above the ocean. Although these innovations were important, Ang felt they were not enough. He knew that there would be innumerable possibilities for adding value to the customers' total flying experience — but only if the know-how and technology could be applied correctly.

Almost 80,000 travelers were registered in the Priority Passenger Service (PPS) program. To become a member, a passenger had to fly at least 60,000km (37,500 miles) a year in First or Raffle Class. Benefits included extra baggage allowance, automatic flight reconfirmation, priority wait listing, a complimentary magazine subscription, and discounts on car rentals, hotels, and shopping. Information about each PPS member — such as seat and meal preferences — was stored in a computer and could be automatically implemented when reservations were made. Ang considered this kind of service to be only the beginning; there was no end to what information technology could do to improve customer service. There was also no compelling technological reason to confine the system to only 80,000 people.

ADVERTISING CAMPAIGNS

Around 2% of Singapore Airlines' gross income was devoted to advertising and promotion. All expenditures were carefully controlled by the head office, and strategic advertising decisions were all centralized. Tactical advertising that focused on specific routes, schedules, or promotions was handled locally, but was strictly monitored in Singapore to guarantee consistency.

The "Singapore Girl" theme had remained a key element in the company's advertising strategy since day one. Initially, the aim of this strategy was to impart a feeling of romance and luxury service, and so it was dominated by images of sarong-clad women against exotically romantic backdrops. The modern fleet campaign which followed featured aircraft exteriors or interiors with just a small cameo inset of a stewardess at one side.

The purpose of the fleet modernization campaign was to give another strong message to the market: that Singapore Airlines was a leader in aircraft technology. The object was to show that the "steel" did not overpower the "silk." The photographs gave the advertising a deliberately dream-like quality, a theme carried through in the 1990 Raffles campaign — SIA's first attempt to aim specifically at business class travelers.

Research revealed that two out of every three Europeans, Americans and Australians preferred the romantic ads to the technical ones. These passengers were spellbound by the beauty of the stewardesses and impressed by their competence and caring. Japanese and other Asian clients, on the other hand, seemed to prefer the high-tech ads which denoted modernity, reliability, and new experiences. The Singapore Girl did not seem so exotic, unusual or appealing to this group.

SALES AND DISTRIBUTION SYSTEM

Like most carriers, Singapore Airlines depended heavily on independent agents to sell its service. In 1973, the airline initiated its own computer reservation and check-in system, KRISCOM. By 1991 this had been replaced by Abacus, a computer reservation system which provided travel agents with an extended array of services including airline and hotel reservations, ground arrangements, and regional travel news. Originally created by Singapore Airlines and two other Asian carriers, Abacus was now owned and operated by SIA and nine other carriers, including three American firms. More than 100 carriers, 80 hotel chains, and many other travel services had signed up with Abacus to distribute their services through the system.

When reservations were made on Singapore Airlines by travel agents, the recorded preferences of Priority Passenger Service (PPS) travelers would automatically be retrieved from the computer. A wide variety of special meal options, reflecting the travelers' many different health and religious needs, were offered. Special meal requests were forwarded to the catering department which received a print-out of all such requests for each flight. The special meal request was linked to the seat allocated to the passenger. *Exhibit 3* shows a simplified flow chart of the linkages between the different databases and the departure control system.

TECHNOLOGY AND ON-THE-GROUND SERVICES

The Ground Services Department was responsible for the ground handling of passengers, baggage, cargo, and mail at all 63 airports in the Singapore Airlines network. At Changi, SATS were in charge, but at other airports the airline had to rely on subcontractors. Even

EXHIBIT 3
Flow Chart of Data Bases

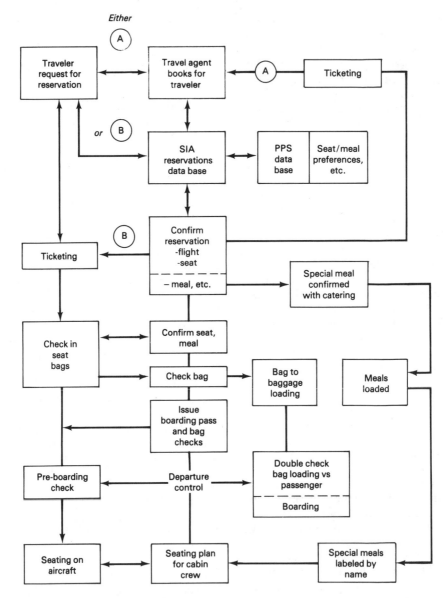

though some Singapore Airlines employees were allocated to these stations, most staff members were host country nationals and frequently had a different way of thinking.

Since what people really wanted was to get in and out of airports as quickly and easily as possible, Ang believed that interventions with staff should be kept to a minimum. Specific problems had to be dealt with and overcome:

It's easier to control the quality of service in the air than on the ground. Key decisions are made at the head office and implemented on board. Airports, on the other hand, are difficult to control. Technology is the key. The airports themselves are too crowded, with too few gates, too few counters and long lines. While in-flight service staff typically *give* customers something — free headsets, free newspapers, free drinks, free meals, free movies — ground service staff *take* — tickets, excess baggage fees, or they say you can't have the seat you want. Thirty percent of all complaints relate to seat assignments, another 20% to aircraft delays. How these delays are handled has a big impact on customer opinion. Passengers become really unhappy when staff can't provide information, find them seats on alternative airlines, or obtain hotel rooms when they are delayed overnight. Lost baggage also accounts for about 20% of total complaints. With better technology and information, not only can we give the same kind of service on the ground as in the air, but we can minimize our risk by providing everyone around the world with a system we know works.

An Outstanding Service On the Ground Program (OSG) had been started for all passengers and complemented the lounges, equipped with every possible luxury and convenience, instituted earlier for First and Business Class travelers. When Terminal 2 opened at Changi, a new Departure Control System (DCS90) was phased in. A key component was an improved simplified format for the screens used at check-in. It had become increasingly difficult to recruit and retain staff for check-in positions, and the complex software led to delays for passengers. A new user-friendly program, with menu-driven, on-screen commands was introduced, which simplified both the task and the training.

The benefits for passengers included a simplified and speedier check-in process, with boarding passes and baggage tags being automatically encoded and printed at the check-in. The boarding pass included seat allocation and gate information, and confirmed special requests such as vegetarian meals. At the boarding gate, passengers would simply slip their boarding passes through a reader at the gate and the DCS90 software would verify check-in details against boarding passengers. An important security benefit was the automatic matching up of checked baggage with passengers going on board. (Refer to *Exhibit 3*.)

A Telecar system was introduced to take baggage from one terminal to another within three minutes. It was then manually sorted and handled. If an urgent flight connection had to be made, this fact was communicated to the staff in advance so that baggage could be taken by trolley to the waiting aircraft. Unlike the situation at most other airports, the Skytrain not only took passengers to and from terminals, but staff directed and accompanied passengers to flights with short connecting times, thus minimizing confusion and delays.

TECHNOLOGY AND IN-FLIGHT SERVICES

By realizing such innovations as video screens at each seat and better air-to-ground telecommunications, Ang wanted to transform the cabin into an "office and leisure center in the sky" which would enhance entertainment as well as business services. Surely almost anything could be possible in the future thanks to technology. But what did customers value? What was feasible? What would distinguish Singapore Airlines from the competition? What were the real issues? At the meeting, he had told the others:

> We have to be able to provide passengers with as much distraction — be it entertainment or professional — as possible during their flight. It's just the opposite from the situation on the ground. Customers must be able to do whatever they need to do throughout their time with us. And, the choice must be theirs, not ours. They shouldn't have to encounter any problems in dealing with our staff and should, in fact, be encouraged to interact with them as much as possible, since we're very good at that. If technology is used properly and creatively, we can personalize our services still more and make people feel that we really care. For instance, hand-held computers can tell on-board crews everything they need to know about each customer so that services can be customized.

After the meeting, Ang's boss, the director of marketing planning, commented on the suggestions Ang had made. Although the ideas were interesting, he said, there should be

EXHIBIT 4
Customer Experience Preflight, Inflight, and Postflight

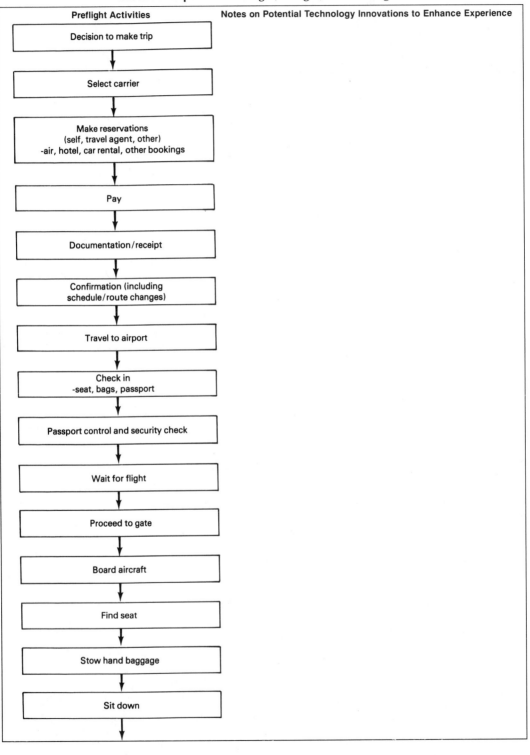

Preflight Activities	Notes on Potential Technology Innovations to Enhance Experience

Decision to make trip

Select carrier

Make reservations
(self, travel agent, other)
-air, hotel, car rental, other bookings

Pay

Documentation/receipt

Confirmation (including
schedule/route changes)

Travel to airport

Check in
-seat, bags, passport

Passport control and security check

Wait for flight

Proceed to gate

Board aircraft

Find seat

Stow hand baggage

Sit down

EXHIBIT 4
(continued)

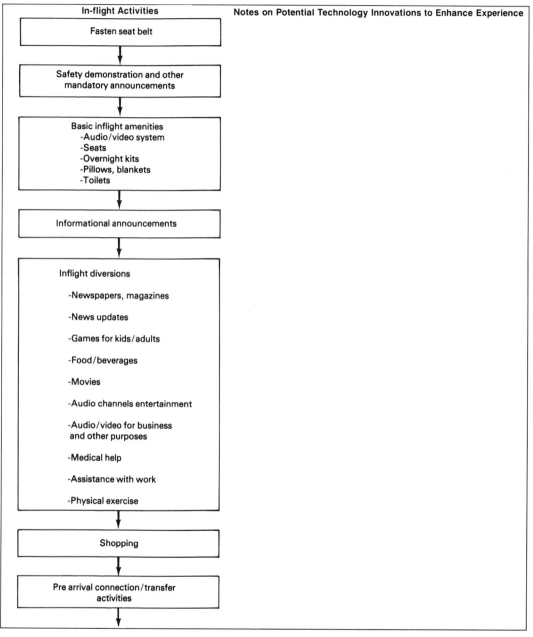

In-flight Activities	Notes on Potential Technology Innovations to Enhance Experience
Fasten seat belt	
Safety demonstration and other mandatory announcements	
Basic inflight amenities -Audio/video system -Seats -Overnight kits -Pillows, blankets -Toilets	
Informational announcements	
Inflight diversions -Newspapers, magazines -News updates -Games for kids/adults -Food/beverages -Movies -Audio channels entertainment -Audio/video for business and other purposes -Medical help -Assistance with work -Physical exercise	
Shopping	
Pre arrival connection/transfer activities	

nothing to disturb other passengers, reduce valuable seating space, or adversely affect the company's high level of personal service. Ang, who had anticipated this reaction, responded by saying that the location of the technology on board would be the determining factor. He could think of several options: centering the technology at each passenger's seat; demarcating work and leisure centers at a given spot inside the aircraft; or, alternatively, using crew members to handle the bulk of passenger requests, for instance sending faxes.

EXHIBIT 4
(continued)

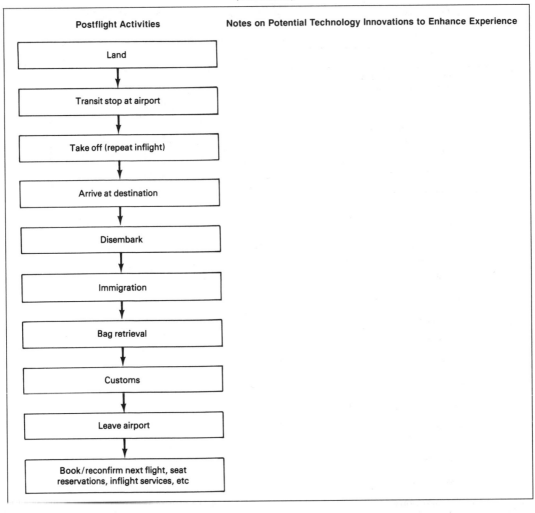

| Postflight Activities | Notes on Potential Technology Innovations to Enhance Experience |

Land

Transit stop at airport

Take off (repeat inflight)

Arrive at destination

Disembark

Immigration

Bag retrieval

Customs

Leave airport

Book/reconfirm next flight, seat reservations, inflight services, etc

ANG SETS TO WORK

Back in his office, with a good feeling about the meeting that morning, Robert Ang thought about the three pillars that provided the quality experience the company insisted on for its customers. First was modern aircraft, where Singapore Airlines was already ahead. Second was on-the-ground services, where much remained to be done, despite the accomplishments at Changi Airport. In particular, technology had to be developed so that the company's worldwide network of sales and air staff, agents, and subcontractors could function in unison.

Third was the question of in-flight services. What technology-based services should be developed to improve the customers' experience in the air? Could an "office in the air" actually work? To what extent could more comfort and entertainment be provided, and how could the first and business class facilities be differentiated from the ones in economy? Most importantly, how could all these ideas be consolidated and effected so that Singapore Airlines would be the technological leader in civil aviation?

Ang knew that the *how* questions needed a lot of thought before a formal presentation could be made to his boss. But it was even more crucial to find a cohesive concept that would be appreciated and bought company-wide. Perhaps it would be best to set out the various customer activities in a framework. He began to sketch out a rough flow chart showing the sequence of a typical journey.

Before long, he had segmented the chart into three sections: preflight activities, in-flight activities, and postflight activities. (Refer to *Exhibit 4*.) He began to fill in his ideas for using technology at each key point.

When he finally stopped for a coffee break, the sun had already begun to touch the horizon, creating a pale pink haze in the tropical sky. As he rose and stretched, he heard the soft hum of a plane above. "Must be the flight leaving for Frankfurt," he said aloud.

Museum of Fine Arts

CHRISTOPHER H. LOVELOCK

A large art museum has enjoyed great success. Attendance is up and the museum has had an annual operating surplus for several years. Can this momentum be maintained? Marketing, operational, and human resource issues are all under discussion as management evaluates lessons learned from a recent "blockbuster" show and seeks to apply them to planning and implementing a major new exhibition.

The *Boston Globe* was running a story about the Museum of Fine Arts. But instead of being featured in the Arts and Entertainment section, the June 16, 1987 article appeared on the front page of the paper's Business supplement. Titled "The Fine Art of Marketing," the story began:

> Eighteen months after the epochal Pierre-Auguste Renoir exhibition, the Boston Museum of Fine Arts resembles a large wharf cat sated with a discovered fish. He feels full, but he wonders where his next meal is coming from.
>
> The Renoir show helped give the museum a record surplus of $1.3 million in fiscal year 1986. Figures for fiscal year 1987 are not in, but [deputy] director Ross Farrar says, "It will be a good solid year." The surplus is expected to be about $200,000, the third-highest in the museum's history, with expenses of about $25 million.
>
> Farrar and retiring director Jan Fontein are pleased with the museum's financial condition, but say they are not complacent.
>
> "In a year with Renoir," said Fontein, you don't wake up in the night wondering where the money is going to come from. But we understand the fragility of our success. All you need is a couple of things to go wrong and you're in trouble again."

Ross W. Farrar read through the rest of the article, which described some of the changes that had taken place during Jan Fontein's eleven-year tenure as director, and looked ahead to possible developments in the future

This case was developed with support from the J. Paul Getty Trust. Copyright © 1987 by The J. Paul Getty Trust and the American Federation of Arts.

under Fontein's successor, Alan Shestack, who would take office in September.

Putting down the paper, Farrar reflected that it was nice to read a story about the museum that was fair, positive, and even reasonably accurate. "Jan's right, though," he said to himself. "It would be easy to get into trouble again. We need to take care of the details as well as keeping our eye on the big picture as we plan our next major exhibition."

BACKGROUND

The Museum of Fine Arts (MFA) was founded in 1870 at the initiative of the Boston Athenaeum. The Massachusetts Legislature passed an act establishing a "body corporate by the name of the Trustees of the Museum of Fine Arts for the purpose of erecting a museum for the preservation and exhibition of works of art, of making, maintaining and establishing collections of such works, and of affording instruction in the Fine Arts."

The first section of the new museum opened on July 4, 1876. It was expanded three years later by a new wing that also housed a School of Drawings and Paintings. In 1899, foreseeing the need to move to a larger facility, the Trustees purchased a twelve acre site on Huntington Avenue about a mile west of Boston's fashionable Back Bay area, and two miles from downtown. The imposing new granite building opened in 1910 and was expanded several times over the next sixty years in line with the growth of the collections. From 1918 to 1966, admission to the museum was free, seven days a week, but charges had to be imposed in the latter year to defray rising operational costs.

The MFA's collections were substantial, but not as large as those at some of the top-ranked American museums. Although most art experts considered the MFA to rank just below the leading art museums in New York (the Metropolitan and the Museum of Modern Art) and the National Gallery in Washington, many elements of its collections were seen as world class. Knowledgeable observers viewed the MFA as having superb collections in classical Greek art, American paintings and decorative arts, and the French Impressionists.

The MFA of the late 60s and early 70s was seen by many as elitist and poorly managed, resulting in substantial deficits. To many, the neoclassical building appeared oppressive rather than impressive, jealously hoarding its remarkable collections rather than inviting passers-by to come in and enjoy them. But during the second half of the seventies the museum began to change.

Jan Fontein, previously curator of the Asiatic Department, was named director of the Museum in 1976. That same year, the new position of associate director was created to manage the business affairs of the institution. When the first incumbent resigned after three years due to illness, Ross W. Farrar took over as associate director.

Farrar's background included an MBA from the Wharton School at the University of Pennsylvania, prior work experience with Arthur Andersen & Co. as a manager in the Administrative Services Group, and operating his own consulting practice.

Fontein's eleven-year tenure was described by the *Boston Globe* as "a huge success." Said the *Globe*,

> The sleepy, dusty mausoleum of the 1960s today is like a thriving city center, bursting with special exhibitions, lectures, and concerts. The shop and restaurants are packed and the line of cars waiting to get in stretches around the block.

The most visible changes at the MFA centered around the new West Wing, designed by I. M. Pei and completed in 1981. This included the Gund Gallery designed to house large exhibitions. More than $60 million was raised to finance both the new construction and the renovation and climate control of many of the existing galleries. The nearby Museum School was also expanded.

Financially, the MFA's situation improved steadily during the ten-year period 1975–76 to 1985–86. A deficit of $0.5 million on total revenues of $4.7 million was transformed into a surplus of $2.5 million on revenues of $28.9 million (Exhibit 1). Revenues benefited from increased gifts and grants (up from $451,000 to almost $2 million), a rise in membership from 14,296 to 41,049, and rapid growth in retail and catalog sales from $0.9

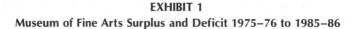

EXHIBIT 1

Museum of Fine Arts Surplus and Deficit 1975–76 to 1985–86

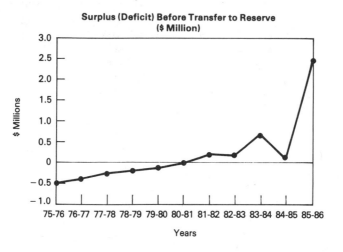

Surplus (Deficit) Before Transfer to Reserve
($ Million)

Years

million in 1975–76 to $11.4 million ten years later.

Underlying the growth of admissions were several blockbuster exhibitions, including "Pompeii: A.D. 79" (1978), "The Search for Alexander" (1981), and "Renoir" (1985–86). Exhibit 2 summarizes the growth in admissions between 1974–75 and 1985–86. Admissions revenues rose at a much faster rate as a result of increased prices.

Although enlarged facilities and exhibitions generated increased expenses, and inflation took its toll, Farrar was able to gain tighter control over costs as a result of improved budgetary and financial reporting procedures. He also emphasized the need for strategic planning and a stronger marketing orientation. In 1987, his title was changed from associate director to deputy director.

ORGANIZATIONAL STRUCTURE

Governance of the Museum of Fine Arts was entrusted to a board of between 25 and 39 elected, *ex officio,* and appointed trustees. In carrying out their responsibilities, the trustees oversaw all aspects of MFA operations, including raising and investing funds, maintaining and improving facilities, appointing senior staff, and improving the permanent collection. A subgroup of the trustees, known

as the executive committee, was intimately involved in the policy affairs of the museum and met regularly with staff members.

Responsibility for day-to-day management of the institution lay with the director and the deputy director. The former was primarily concerned with the nine curatorial departments, the library, research and educational programs, and the Museum School.

As deputy director, Ross Farrar focused on managing the business side of the institution, including membership services, development, finance, and operations. His job was complicated by the absence of a director of operations to oversee such functions as buildings and grounds, security, construction and food service. He hoped to fill this key position soon.

Managing the organization was a complex task, since it involved coordinating the activities of professional curatorial staff with those of administrative and support staff. The four floors of the museum building had an area of over half-a-million square feet, housing a priceless collection that had to be maintained under carefully controlled climatic conditions. The nearby Museum School had a floor area of 100,000 feet and an enrollment of 500 students.

There were more than 700 full-time, part-time, and temporary paid staff, who were assisted in their work by over 1700 volunteers.

EXHIBIT 2
Museum of Fine Arts Attendance Figures (Fiscal years ending June 30)

	1974–75	1975–76	1976–77	1977–78	1978–79	1979–80	1980–81	1981–82	1982–83	1983–84	1984–85	1985–86
July	42,960	32,607	24,248	30,253	125,636	31,657	29,545[4]	139,627[5]	5,725	50,869	52,157	42,120
August	48,571	34,595	30,821	41,394	38,096	41,810	34,249	142,674	56,286[6]	48,854	52,466	50,682
September	31,774	28,025	32,322	50,713	36,059	46,856	30,675	92,611	45,168	95,466[7]	46,959	36,299
October	42,613	43,425	73,722	104,284	55,039	85,313	45,012	81,202	86,979	150,487	61,472	196,438
November	55,101	44,385	56,310	54,942	78,945	75,449	46,449	111,944	120,804	136,349	75,331	213,716
December	46,692	45,777	48,624	61,530	68,897	36,211	32,915	90,699	71,674	64,115	72,647	199,328
January	48,929	33,596	34,039	63,694	75,459	38,317	32,254	83,449	66,608	49,468	55,823	61,659
February	59,481	39,548	43,686	237,445[3]	39,929	36,501	35,015	92,449	65,845	67,276	54,193	65,959
March	65,460	238,176[2]	43,440	45,876	47,877	42,982	38,222	96,481	71,235	60,884	62,442	68,057
April	50,061	27,594	52,008	116,164	59,686	36,273	33,548	68,954	68,719	74,722	55,385	75,295
May	235,945[1]	24,243	34,706	139,988	64,986	36,958	49,038	65,854	63,392	63,133	58,842	58,140
June	34,828	23,338	32,078	146,141	34,615	27,296	78,533	57,294	46,192	64,272	43,748	50,167
Totals	562,405	415,344	505,044	892,424	726,224	533,477	485,029	1,123,238	816,628	925,895	691,465	1,117,560

General Admission Fee History

Date Implemented	Fee	Date Implemented	Fee	Date Implemented	Fee
July 5, 1966 (instituted fee)	$ .50	[1]May 1, 1975 (increase)	$2.50	[5]July 22, 1981 (increase)	$2.50
February 1, 1969 (increase)	.75	[2]March 23, 1976 (decrease)	1.50	[6]August 31, 1982 (increase)	3.50
September 1, 1969 (increase)	1.00	[3]February 1, 1978 (increase)	1.75	[7]September 1, 1983 (increase)	4.00
July 1, 1973 (increase)	1.50	[4]July 1, 1980 (increase)	2.00	Renoir Exhibition only (increase) 10/1/85–1/5/86	5.00

More than 100 temporary staff members were hired between July and January to work at the mail-order business, which was housed separately in a 40,000 square foot warehouse. The 1987 retail catalog ran to 32 pages and listed some 800 different stock-keeping units (SKUs), including jewelry, scarves, books, and reproductions of paintings and sculpture. The retail store offered an even larger selection of items, including more than 2,000 book titles, for a total of some 5,000 SKUs.

The entire museum was normally open Tuesday through Sunday from 10 A.M. to 5 P.M., with hours extended to 10 P.M. on Wednesday evenings. In addition, the West Wing (which contained restaurants and the museum store, as well as exhibition galleries) remained open until 10:00 P.M. on Thursdays and Fridays.

THE RENOIR EXHIBITION OF 1985–86

No exhibition in the museum's history had so taxed the planning and management skills of both staff and volunteers as the "Renoir" show. Pierre-Auguste Renoir (1841–1919) was one of the most famous impressionist painters. The MFA was the only American museum to host this exhibition, which was also shown in Paris and London. As recalled by John Higgins, the MFA's financial director:

> The "Renoir" show required the most extensive planning exercise we had ever undertaken at the museum. It was a new pair of shoes for us — we learned a lot. Our planning was very participative and the lines of communication really opened up. Rather than having a single person orchestrating the entire thing, everyone got involved and pulled together their individual pieces.

Kathy Duane, director of exhibition projects, was assigned the task of coordinating the planning activities. She reported directly to Ross Farrar. Committees were set up to plan and implement the work of different departments.

Early in the planning stage, management concluded that crowd control would be a major problem. Duane remembered living through the experience of "A New World," an exhibition of American paintings held at the MFA in 1982. This show proved something of a sleeper, becoming extremely popular by word of mouth. Towards the end of its run, the galleries were packed and the newspapers ran photographs of lines outside stretching around the block.

Seeking to prevent such a recurrence, MFA staff members sought insights from other major museums in New York, Los Angeles, and Chicago. The decision was then taken to sell tickets in advance, entitling the purchaser to view the exhibit at a specific time on a given date. Tickets would be sold by the museum box office, by Ticketron outlets, and by phone through Teletron.

The upper limit to the number of tickets available in a given time slot was set by climate control considerations, since excessive heat or humidity could damage the paintings as well as proving uncomfortable for visitors. Although a ticket would entitle visitors to enter only within a half-hour time slot, they would be allowed to spend as long as they wished viewing the exhibit. So in calculating maximum loads, an average stay of one hour per visitor was predicted.

Financial planning for "Renoir" was based on modeling revenues and costs under different assumptions of (1) number of attendees; (2) mix of adults, children, seniors, and members (each of whom paid a different rate); and (3) admission fees for each category. Reducing ticket availability to achieve a less crowded hall would result in reduced revenues unless prices were raised.

For cost purposes, Higgins broke down the components of the show into seven cost centers: planning and administration; shared costs; installation and operations; ticketing and box office; educational programs; museum-hosted special events; and publicity/public relations. Projected costs were predicated on specific attendance levels.

By analyzing alternative levels of crowding, it was possible to predict where lines might build up. These insights were used to help design the exhibition facilities. The objective was to create the impression of a free form approach while channeling the crowd and keeping visitors moving. Guards and other security staff members were carefully trained

in how to move the crowd along discreetly. Extra staff were added to the cloakroom.

Anticipating serious parking problems, the museum contracted for a double decker bus to run continuously between the MFA and the huge parking garage at the Prudential Center, just under a mile away. Since the museum was about two miles from downtown Boston, frequent connections to the region's extensive rapid transit network were also needed, and the transit authority agreed to assign seven extra rail vehicles to the Huntington Avenue line for the duration of the exhibition.

Extensive advertising and publicity efforts were targeted at the general public. The principal motif was a detail of two dancers, wearing bright red and yellow hats, from Renoir's painting "Dance at Bougival," in the MFA's own collection. The museum also targeted corporate groups and intermediaries such as hotels that might wish to create packaged arrangements for out-of-town visitors.

A new telephone number was installed to help people obtain information on the exhibition. All they had to do was to dial 9-RENOIR. Special arrangements were made to provide private viewings for members, VIP guests, and certain groups. "Renoir" was not open to the public for the first eight days of showing, and on all subsequent Mondays attendance was restricted to members between 2 P.M. and 10 P.M. (Normally the museum was closed on Mondays). The public was admitted Tuesday through Friday from 10 A.M. to 10 P.M. and on weekends from 10 A.M. to 5 P.M.

To minimize lines for retail purchases and food service, a satellite shop was set up near the Huntington Avenue entrance, extra registers were installed in the main store, and a sandwich service was offered in the rotunda (some distance away from the "Renoir" exhibit and the main food services in the West Wing). Guards were instructed to redirect people to these satellite locations when the lines became too long in the West Wing.

RESULTS AND INSIGHTS

During the period October 1, 1985 through January 5, 1986, attendance at the MFA totalled 565,805, of whom 479,205 visited Renoir (the balance visited other parts of the museum). More than 92% of all available tickets for "Renoir" were sold.

After the exhibit closed, feedback was sought from the managers and department heads who had been most closely involved in the show. Excerpts from some of their evaluations are reproduced in the *Appendix* to the case.

Almost everyone agreed that admitting 400 persons per half-hour ticketing block was too much. Part of the problem was caused by many visitors staying longer than expected. There was also a tendency for people to arrive late, perhaps as a result of parking or transportation problems. Part-way through the show, ticket sales were reduced for certain half-hour blocks in order to reduce the press of new arrivals. This approach proved effective in reducing excessive crowding.

Although the 9-RENOIR number had generally worked well, some people misspelled the artist's name, resulting in numerous calls to 9-RENIOR being received by an office of the Bank of New England. One day a woman called the director in person, telling Jan Fontein angrily that she had been dialing 9-MONET for three days and couldn't even get a ringing tone. (Claude Monet was another much admired French Impressionist, whose paintings were well represented in the MFA collection.)

John Higgins, the finance director, had collected detailed statistics for attendance, parking, and store revenues on a day-by-day basis, making it possible to relate attendance revenues to retail sales and parking receipts. (See, for example, the October data in Exhibit 3). Said Higgins:

> One of the biggest problems in museum administration is that people quickly fall back into a mindset that says if you can't plan, you can't project. " They look at predicting as crystal-balling rather than as a way to manage the outcome. We now have an experience base and performance measures that enable us to take a lot of concepts out of the area of speculation into the world of reality. The Renoir show also taught me a bit about the elasticity of our operation — its ability to stretch to serve a given function without breaking. We couldn't do it all the time, of course.

Based on extensive market research among "Renoir" attendees, it was projected that the show had generated substantial incremental revenues not only for the MFA, but also for the Boston area in general. The average local visitor attended 1.55 times, the average out-of-towner made 1.05 visits to "Renoir." Additional findings on the show's impact are summarized in Exhibit 4.

A VISIT TO THE MUSEUM

On a cool, overcast June afternoon, 18 months later, the MFA was having a relatively slow day. Parking was available in the museum lot and at the meters along Museum Road. There were no lines at either the West Wing or Huntington Avenue entrances, although people were lining up for lunch at the Galleria Cafe and the cafeteria. There was room to browse comfortably in the museum shop, but it was far from deserted.

"We'll probably get between 1500 and 2000 visitors today," said Ross Farrar as he led his visitor up the escalator to the West Wing's second floor, which was lit by a dramatic curved skylight that ran the full length of the wing. To the right, the Fine Arts Restaurant was full and a short line waited outside (there were also a cafe and cafeteria on the two floors below). "All our food service is contracted out to a company called DAKA," remarked Farrar. "They hire their own staff."

The deputy director turned left to enter the Gund Gallery, pausing to chat with a security supervisor outside the doors. Inside, a new exhibition was being installed. A designer watched as two workers adjusted the height of a small, framed print. Other exhibition staff members were poring over a diagram of the gallery. The partitions had been rearranged and repainted to provide for an appropriate display of works by the French artist, Jean Arp (1886–1966).

This retrospective exhibit, "The Universe of Jean Arp," was scheduled to run from July 1 to September 13. It had previously toured Europe and been shown at the Minneapolis Institute of Arts. After Boston, the tour would conclude at the San Francisco Museum of Modern Art.

Most of the drawings, collages, prints, and textiles were already in place, but many sculptures and reliefs remained to be installed.

EXHIBIT 3
Attendance, Parking, and Retail Statistics at the Museum of Fine Arts October 1985*

OCTOBER		ATTENDANCE			ADMISSIONS INCOME			PARKING		Shop	PER CAPITA INCOME		
Date	Day	Renoir	General	Total	Renoir[1]	General	Total	Cars	Income	Sales	Attend	Sales	Park
1	Tuesday	1,477	1,346	2,823	$ —	$ 1,581	$ 1,581	302	$ 569	$ 17,144	$ .56	$6.97	$.20
2	Wednesday	4,551	1,589	6,140	—	1,444	1,444	724	2,041	45,307	.24	7.38	.33
3	Thursday	3,522	1,646	5,168	—	2,138	2,138	674	1,125	39,181	.41	7.58	.22
4	Friday	3,918	1,418	5,336	—	2,554	2,554	637	1,816	38,635	.48	7.24	.34
5	Saturday	5,140	3,342	8,482	—	2,771	2,771	418	1,388	43,856	.33	5.17	.16
6	Sunday	5,245	1,738	6,983	—	3,812	3,812	549	1,505	39,768	.55	5.69	.21
8	Tuesday	4,817	941	5,758	—	1,604	1,604	509	1,352	43,066	.28	7.48	.23
9	Wednesday	4,838	1,303	6,141	22,182	899	23,081	728	2,418	46,266	3.76	7.53	.39
10	Thursday	5,070	1,728	6,798	23,116	878	23,994	713	2,394	47,162	3.53	6.94	.35
11	Friday	6,658	1,377	8,035	30,682	975	31,657	802	2,764	61,765	3.94	7.69	.34
12	Saturday	4,417	2,180	6,597	21,484	2,018	23,565	539	1,761	49,906	3.57	7.56	.27
13	Sunday	4,588	2,855	7,443	21,484	7,428	28,912	539	1,781	46,659	3.88	6.27	.24
15	Tuesday	6,120	994	7,114	19,605	1,250	20,855	475	1,607	46,998	2.93	6.61	.23
16	Wednesday	6,557	1,398	7,995	32,924	1,234	34,158	817	2,737	62,541	4.29	7.86	.34
17	Thursday	5,574	1,198	6,772	28,799	1,017	29,816	751	2,628	54,659	4.40	8.07	.39
18	Friday	8,147	1,467	9,614	37,996	1,103	39,099	841	2,942	68,747	4.07	7.15	.31
19	Saturday	5,633	2,898	8,531	21,484	3,284	24,768	504	1,680	49,402	2.90	5.79	.20
20	Sunday	5,849	1,365	7,214	21,484	3,136	24,620	488	3,136	45,020	3.41	6.24	.43
21	Monday	2,043	—	2,043	5,745	—	5,745	441	988	13,193[2]	2.81	6.46	.49
22	Tuesday	4,694	1,227	5,921	20,448	1,146	21,594	566	1,518	48,847	3.65	8.25	.26
23	Wednesday	7,818	1,588	9,406	32,346	895	33,241	786	2,783	56,340	3.53	5.99	.29
24	Thursday	7,051	1,347	8,398	31,033	504	31,537	733	2,440	57,524	3.76	6.85	.29
25	Friday	8,308	1,236	9,544	36,513	1,482	37,995	814	3,013	68,313	3.98	7.16	.31
26	Saturday	5,969	2,614	8,583	21,484	1,651	23,135	592	1,556	56,375	2.70	6.57	.18
27	Sunday	5,347	1,322	6,669	21,484	3,064	24,548	553	1,769	41,409	3.68	6.21	.26
28	Monday	1,956	—	1,956	4,001	—	4,001	355	755	9,997[2]	2.05	5.11	.39
29	Tuesday	4,936	1,237	6,173	18,668	1,130	19,798	446	1,428	41,418	3.21	6.71	.23
30	Wednesday	7,089	1,653	8,742	31,103	1,060	32,163	781	2,703	62,577	3.68	7.16	.31
31	Thursday	4,830	1,269	6,099	21,460	719	22,179	602	2,068	44,684	3.64	7.33	.34
		152,162	44,276	196,438	$525,525	$47,868	$573,393	17,679	56,675	$1,346,760	$2.92	$6.39	$.29

*Note: Private showings were held for members and other guests from October 1–8, and thereafter every Monday.

[1]Actual for month — prorated daily.

[2]Exhibition shop only.

The designer noted that the arrangement of the partitions in the gallery had to be done with an eye both to enhancing the artist's work and generating a natural flow of visitor traffic. The total time allowed for installing this exhibit was four weeks.

From the Gund Gallery, which was reserved for special exhibits, Farrar strode briskly to the Asiatic Wing, where another exhibition was also in the process of being installed. "Stories from China's Past" was described as a unique exhibition of recent discoveries from the province of Sichuan in Southwest China, dating from the Han dynasty which had ruled China 1,700 to 2,100 years ago. The artifacts to be displayed included pottery, architectural models, and tomb reliefs depicting images of daily life. Three years had elapsed since the MFA was first contacted about hosting this exhibition.

Although part of this show would be housed in the Special Exhibition Gallery, it would also extend into galleries currently displaying items from the museum's extensive permanent collection of Asiatic art. "We prefer not to install two exhibitions simultaneously," remarked Farrar. He elaborated:

It means that more gallery space is out of commission at a single point in time, and it puts

EXHIBIT 4
Conclusions and Implications from Market Research Study of "The Renoir Influence"

Projecting survey data to the full attendance of the exhibition, we arrive at the following estimates (rounded off) of "The Renoir Influence":

Drawing Power

- 83,000 people exposed to the MFA for the first time
- 170,000 visits to the MFA *only* because of the Renoir Exhibit
- 3,600 new members directly traceable to the impact of Renoir
- 10,000 with strong potential as future members due to Renoir
- 70,000 out-of-towners more likely to return to MFA due to Renoir
- Outreach to a much wider spectrum of demographic segments than the more consistently older and more affluent MFA member base
- The 515,695 visits to Renoir were generated by roughly 408,000 people (average of approximately 1.26 visits per individual)

Revenues

- Expenditures at the MFA of $8,300,000, including $5,200,000 for books, posters, etc., and $1,600,000 on food and beverages
- 170,000 additional exposures to MFA permanent collections and 144,000 to other special exhibits
- 237,000 restaurant visits and 140,000 shopping trips which might not have occurred without the initial lure of Renoir
- 60,000 hotel nights (including 10,000 weekend packages) and 2,200 car rental days
- 33,000 air trips, 7,700 bus trips, and 6,700 train trips
- $29,800,000 in "found money" for the Boston area, including:

  $ 700,000 on local transportation
  5,100,000 on hotel/motel accommodations
  7,900,000 on food and beverages
  8,000,000 on retail merchandise

more pressure on our painters, carpenters, and electricians. And when you run two shows simultaneously, it removes an incentive for people to return, since they can see both at once. But we have to take traveling shows like these when they're available.

One of the Chinese galleries was a hive of activity. The floor was covered with huge wooden crates bearing the insignia of CAAC, the Chinese national airline. Several crates were in the process of being unpacked and their contents carefully checked and validated. An assistant curator explained that they were working to a tight schedule, since the exhibits had only arrived by truck from the Chinese Culture Center of San Francisco the previous day, June 22. The show would open on July 1 and run through August 16.

The Museum School's show had occupied the Exhibition Gallery until June 7, and two more days had been required to remove it. Since then, carpenters had been busy con-

structing a lifesize replica of a Chinese tomb; the interior dimensions were about 12 feet by 12 feet by 20 feet. Newly painted black, the "tomb" was now being wired by an electrician for a fiber optic lighting system that would highlight the tomb tiles while maintaining an otherwise sepulchral environment.

Walking through one of the Chinese galleries on the way back to his office, Farrar was approached by a young guard who asked him hesitantly where the Himalayan gallery was located. Farrar pointed her in the right direction, then informed his visitor:

We've got over 60 guards here and hire additional ones at busy times. Many of them are either artists like the one who just came up to us — she's new here — or older people who have retired from other jobs but don't want to quit working. Each guard reports to a supervisor, who in turn reports to our director of security. Most of the guards are in uniform, but we do have some plain-clothes security staff too;

there's usually one in the vicinity of the retail store. We've equipped a number of the guards and supervisors with walkie-talkies; these make it easier for them to summon help, as well as for the supervisors to relocate guards where they are most needed.

THE PERSONNEL DEPARTMENT

"People are attracted to us because we *are* the Museum of Fine Arts," observed Gail Mallard, director of personnel. Mallard supervised a staff of six, located in a suite of offices close to the staff cafeteria in the basement. Her responsibilities embraced some 600–700 paid employees of the museum; the number varied according to the time of year and the nature of the exhibitions being displayed. At times, there were more than 200 temporary workers on the payroll.

Every two months, there was an orientation for all newly hired personnel. Each senior administrator was invited to give a brief presentation and a tour of the museum facilities was provided. The department was putting together a slide show to make the orientation session more interesting and more useful.

Specific job-related training was usually done in the departments where the individuals worked. "Museums have a lot of catching up to do in supervisory training," remarked Mallard. "And the department heads have to learn to be accountable for the quality of service their employees provide."

Twice a week, Mallard made rounds of the museum to talk with the guards and other staffers. She expressed dissatisfaction with quality problems in several areas:

The switchboard area is one of my little thorns; the operators need to be monitored more closely. Smoking is another problem. There's a handful of people who have been here for ever and the department heads are reluctant to correct them. The new operations director is going to have to deal with most of this, shaking up the departments that need it.

Our managers are experts in their fields, but they haven't had enough experience in the people side of things. We're spending more money on training — our managers and supervisors must learn how to manage. We've got to have people at the department level who are made accountable.

Getting better performance starts with the job description. Then you must set standards, such as "must answer phone within three rings" and must answer in a certain manner. Not only do you have to get the departments to write these standards, but managers and supervisors need to be able to interpret them in making evaluations and awarding merit increases. It's very time consuming.

The previous month had seen the inauguration of the MFA's first annual employee service recognition program. There had been a ceremony in the auditorium, followed by a buffet supper. Over half of the staff had been with the museum for more than five years. "Two years is a long commitment for people in a job nowadays," Mallard noted.

Salary and wage rates at the museum were not high. There were no unions and no fixed term contracts. "Contrary to popular belief, there's no tenure here, not even for the curatorial staff," said Farrar. He admitted that the museum ran on a lean basis from both an administrative and support staff point of view.

My style has been to run lean [declared Farrar]. In getting control of the budget I have watched staff growth and wage and salary levels very carefully. Once you hire people here, its very difficult to cut back. As the museum has grown, I haven't allowed the staff to grow as fast.

That approach puts a lot of pressure on morale and staff effectiveness. I'm dealing with some of those issues now. We've had some agitation about levels of pay. We lose some people to better offers. You can't continue the song that the museum is in a deficit situation and we all have to sacrifice. And you can't hold back on staffing levels for ever, either — you can't let people burn themselves out.

Our growth curve is flattening out now, and one of the challenges we face is dealing with some of these issues as we move into this phase.

In addition to its paid staff, the museum was served by some 1700 volunteers, many of whom worked closely with staffers on a wide variety of jobs. The Ladies Committee ran the membership office and the information center, arranged flowers, and coordinated numerous other activities and events. The large Education Department was assisted by numerous volunteers; some of them led school groups while others went through a formal three-year training program to become gallery instructors who delivered lectures to visitors.

Finally, there was a large group of walk-in volunteers who were placed by the Personnel Department. Most of them were attracted by the possibility of working with the art, but their placements were more likely to be in clerical positions, the membership office, or the slide library. Quite often, such volunteers ended up applying for full-time positions at the MFA.

"My biggest concern with volunteers," said Mallard, "is the need to formalize our different volunteer programs under a single umbrella." She elaborated:

> A lot could be done if we joined forces. We need to hire a paid coordinator of volunteers, like they have at the Museum of Science. It's a shame not to groom and develop that group of people. I see that as a separate function from managing paid employees. We need a department in its own right.

However, Farrar and Fontein disagreed with this idea. They believed that the political problems of consolidating such important volunteer groups as the Ladies Committee (which was currently under the Membership Department) and the gallery instructors (who were under the Education Department) would make such a consolidation counterproductive. In any event, they felt that both groups functioned very effectively under the current organizational structure.

THE WYETH AND SHEELER EXHIBITIONS

One of Ross Farrar's current concerns was planning for two exhibitions in the fall. On October 14, 1987, the MFA was scheduled to open "Charles Sheeler," an exhibition of some 90 paintings and drawings and 100 photographs by the American modernist Charles Sheeler. At the request of the sponsors, the exhibition would be mounted in the Gund Gallery, where it would remain on view until January 3, 1988. All visitors to the museum would be able to view this exhibit at regular prices.

Two weeks later, the MFA was scheduled to present "Andrew Wyeth: the Helga Pictures," following its premiere at the National Gallery of Art in Washington. This highly publicized exhibition (which would subsequently be shown in several other cities) would be housed in the Special Exhibition Gallery and surrounding galleries in the Asiatic Wing and would run through January 3.

MFA administrators and professional staff were optimistic that the "Helga" exhibition would prove to be another blockbuster. Wyeth was one of America's best known and most popular living artists. Reproductions of many of his works were widely available and hung in thousands of homes. The "Helga" pictures consisted of some 240 drawings, watercolors, and paintings of Helga Testorf, a neighbor of Andrew Wyeth, who had depicted this subject in a variety of poses and contexts over a 15-year period. About 125 of these works were included in the exhibition which, after visiting Boston, would travel to four other cities.

Wyeth had allegedly kept the existence of his "Helga" pictures secret until he completed the series in 1985. When they were discovered — or rather information about them was released to the press in 1986 — they created a journalistic sensation. Contributing to the sensation was the news that the entire series had already been purchased by the collector Leonard E. B. Andrews, for "multimillions of dollars." Soon it was announced that a "Helga" book would be published, and then that the pictures would be exhibited, starting with the National Gallery.

Although the deputy director of the National Gallery declared that "Such close attention by a painter to one model over so long a period of time is a remarkable, if not singular, circumstance in the history of American art," others critics were less enthusiastic. Many decried Wyeth and Andrews for blatant commercialism. Others questioned the caliber of Wyeth's talent.

The MFA anticipated that "Helga" would be a major attraction, although not as dramatic as "Renoir." Managers believed that if the show was properly organized and promoted, they might be able to draw 60–70% of the attendance achieved by the earlier show. They decided to price the show at $6 (versus $5 for "Renoir"), to use advance ticketing, to promote "Helga" heavily, and to employ many of the same operational procedures, suitably modified in the light of both past experience and projected future attendance.

Since Kathy Duane had left the museum to start a family, the task of coordinating "Helga" was assigned to Chuck Thomas, director of membership, annual appeal and tours. Thomas declared that his pet peeves were likely to be parking, coat checking in winter, and poor signage ("people can't find the restrooms at the MFA and the information staff get frustrated with having to answer the same questions over and over again"). He saw a particular need to build up the morale of ticket sellers, coat checkers, and parking lot attendants:

They don't make much money. If I could run it the way I wanted to, I'd run it like Disneyland. Their people are so nice and so efficient.

Farrar agreed that Thomas's concerns about parking were well founded, since in the fall the MFA planned to start construction of a new 500-car parking garage. He conceded that construction activity would certainly aggravate the parking situation, but declared that the museum could not afford to delay the project until after "Helga."

Thomas and Farrar believed that planning for "Helga" would be simpler and less time-consuming, since much had been learned from the "Renoir" experience. However, both recognized that there was room for improvement.

APPENDIX

SELECTED POSTMORTEM COMMENTS ON "RENOIR" EXHIBITION

All staff members associated with the "Renoir" exhibition were asked to write up their observations on the show after it concluded. Selected comments from several individuals follow.

From the Curator of Paintings

Parking: I wouldn't be surprised if many of the no-shows were people who simply couldn't find parking spaces. However, the surprising fact is that, although parking was very difficult and very time-consuming, I at least had very few complaints about it. People are kind enough or smart enough, I guess, to realize that there was nothing that we could do about it.

Gallery Conditions: The biggest problem, however, and the one where I received many, many complaints concerned the delays in entering the gallery ("if I paid for a ticket and it says 10:30 on it, I should be able to get into the gallery at 10:30), and even more seriously, the constant and persistent overcrowding of the galleries. This is something we very clearly warned about in the beginning and we pleaded for a maximum of 700 people per hour. Most of the time we were putting in 800 an hour, and that was simply an error, and one which damaged the experience of

the show for a great many people. It was almost always too crowded.

In addition, the overcrowding led to climate problems in the Gund Galleries and the temperature there rose to over 80 degrees almost every day. The engineers were *superb* in trying to monitor and control the situation. We did receive several complaints from lenders with regard to the conditions, and the paintings suffered accordingly with the changes in climate. On the whole, the paintings survived the exhibition pretty well.

We did have a number of instances of damage and minor vandalism (or accident) in Founders Gallery and elsewhere in the building. We pleaded and pleaded for additional guarding around the building at the time of the exhibition, but generally to little avail.

From the Publicity Department

9-RENOIR Phone Number: Having the 9-RENOIR telephone line was a well-conceived public relations tool. Should a special telephone line be needed in the future I recommend taking a much more formal approach to staffing and training the operators — especially for weekend shifts.

Ticketing and Box Office: Instituting the pre-ticketing system proved absolutely vital in controlling the number of visitors to "Renoir" at any one time. For any future exhibitions with the suspected appeal of "Renoir" I would be in favor of using a pre-tickeing/Ticketron system again without reservation. While there are problems with the staffing of Ticketron outlets in some remote locations, it is the only way to ensure that tickets are available to everyone across the country.

Box Office: It bears comment that the attitude and disposition of the box office staff—manager and ticket sellers alike — was not at all reflective of the image of this institution. I found their manner rude and condescending to staff and visitors alike. While many Museum staff members go beyond the call of duty to service our customers, I think the box office staff presented a most improper negative first impression.

Shuttle Bus: The shuttle bus was a wonderful rolling exhibition billboard. As intended, the bus served its purpose in building awareness of the exhibition and in helping us cope with criticism of the parking situation.

Duty Officer: While the security staff did a phenomenal job with our visitors, I think having a duty officer present was helpful in alleviating some of the burden of special requests which seemed especially acute on the weekends.

From the Operations Manager

Coat Checking: In preparation for "Renoir," the coat rooms were fitted with new heavy duty hangers and color-coded tags. Lockers were overhauled and all machinery put in good working order. Two to four attendants were assigned, depending on the weather. On rainy days, umbrellas presented a serious problem and another storage rack is planned. Although the attendants were able to process the work well at most times, the arrival of several busloads simultaneously, or the exodus from a lecture, could overwhelm them for a period.

First Aid: In planning for "Renoir," the staff's two Emergency Medical Technicians were recertified. New first-aid kits were purchased for the gallery and entrances. Contact was made with the Police Department to review ambulance response procedures and ensure prompt action. There were two to six incidents in the typical day, most of them being fainting spells, but including several possible heart attacks in which the person was sent to the hospital.

From the Membership Director

Membership Operation: "Renoir's" tremendously increased workload was felt in every part of the membership operation both because of the volume of membership duties and the many tasks added specifically for "Renoir." The Ladies Committee and the Ladies Committee Associates contributed countless hours of work without which we could not have kept our operation going. Our challenge now is to retain the many members obtained through the spectacular "Renoir" exhibition and recruit new members.

Dunfey Hotels Corporation

ROBERT J. KOPP
CHRISTOPHER H. LOVELOCK

The president of a chain of 22 rather dissimilar hotels has developed procedures for standardizing the strategic planning process employed by each hotel. A concerted internal training and educational effort is employed to get managers to understand and use this process.

"THE DUNFEY CHAIN: A SAVIOR OF DYING HOTELS" ran the headline above a half-page story in the financial section of the Sunday *New York Times* for June 22, 1980. The story began:

> Suburban motor hotels. Sprawling convention hotels. Small and elegant city hotels. Foreign hotels. At first glance, the collection of properties under the Dunfey name seems an unmanageable mishmash.

> Yet the Dunfey Hotels Corporation, which within the last year and a half has put together such a chain of unlikely properties, is getting to be known as a comer in the lodging indus-

try, with a knack for taking over aging hotels and returning them to profitability. In fact, Dunfey is a success story on top of a success story.

Success Story No. 1 goes back to the 1950s and features the Dunfeys, an Irish-American family of eight brothers from Hampton, N.H. The Dunfey boys, who started with a hot dog stand at Hampton Beach, built a multimillion-dollar New England hotel and restaurant chain.

Success Story No. 2 stars Jon Canas, brought in by the Dunfeys as chief operating officer and executive vice president in 1975. Mr. Canas . . . is a marketing man who is not afraid to step in to operate a hotel where others have faltered. With Mr. Canas on board, Dunfey has become one of the nation's fastest growing hotel chains.

COMPANY HISTORY

After being discharged from military service shortly after World War II, John and William Dunfey opened a clam and hot dog stand on the boardwalk at Hampton Beach, New Hampshire. Soon John and William were joined in the business by four younger brothers. In 1954, the six brothers formed a partnership with their mother, and purchased Lamie's Tavern in Hampton, N.H., 3 miles from the original business in Hampton Beach.

In 1958, the family business headed in a new direction when a 32-room motor inn was constructed adjacent to Lamie's Tavern. Further acquisitions followed. By 1968, Dunfey Family Corporation, as the firm was then known, either owned or managed 18 hotels in the eastern U.S. Many of these properties, including the original Lamie's Motor Inn, were operated as franchises of Sheraton Hotels, the nation's largest hotel corporation.

In 1969, Dunfey Family Corporation made two new moves. First, Dunfey's Tavern Restaurants were opened in four of the company's New England properties. Second, the company acquired its first downtown hotel by purchasing the historic Parker House in Boston. The experience gained in succeeding years in renovating and repositioning the Parker House was to play an important role in shaping the future growth strategy for the Dunfey hotel business.

Injection of New Capital and Management

To finance further expansion following the purchase of the Parker House, the Dunfey family sold the company to the Aetna Life Insurance Co. in 1970. Six years later it was acquired from Aetna by Aer Lingus, the national airline of Ireland. But throughout these changes in ownership, the Dunfey

family maintained managerial control over the business, with Jack Dunfey continuing on as the chief executive officer.

During the early 1970s, a number of professional managers were hired. They included Jon Canas, who joined the company in 1975 as vice president of sales and marketing. Canas, a Frenchman by birth, had been educated at the Cornell School for Hotel Administration and also held an MBA from Northeastern University; he had worked for six years with the Hotel Corporation of America and, subsequently, four years with the Sheraton Corporation, where his most recent position had been vice president of sales and marketing for Sheraton's two international divisions—Europe/Africa/Middle East and Hawaii/Far East/Pacific.

A New Approach to Planning

Canas recalled how his experience with Sheraton had led him to develop a planning approach based on market segmentation for marketing widely diverse hotels:

About four years before coming to Dunfey, I was assigned the position of sales director of Sheraton's Hawaii Division, consisting at that time of seven hotels. Since I had no previous experience in the day-to-day operation of the selling function as such, I decided to approach the job from a planning point of view. I began immediately to ask those questions, the answers to which would result in a better understanding of the market: Why do people come to Hawaii? What kind of hotel experience are they looking for? What does competition currently offer? Are there segments of consumers who differ in their needs for the level and quality of service? The more I worked on it, the more I could see practical solutions evolving out of this approach.

In Hawaii, at that time, virtually the only thing standardized about the Sheraton properties was the Sheraton name. The individual hotels varied widely in terms of size, age, location, rates, and types of customers. Faced with marketing such a diverse portfolio of properties, I was forced into understanding market segmentation. In the hotel business, this translates into offering different types of hotels for different types of customers . . . the idea really isn't revolutionary but you must remember that it ran against the tide of an industrywide move toward standardization of the "product"—a move which was clearly at the heart of the corporate strategies of most chains. . . . We were very successful in Hawaii. Not only did current properties perform well, but two years later our territory was expanded to include several new and existing hotels in the Far East and the Pacific.

When the Dunfey opportunity came up, a friend of mine in the industry told me that, as a group, the Dunfey properties were "a mixed bag" of hotels, widely diverse in location and service level. Several had generally reached the end of their life cycle. I could see some similarities with the Hawaii situation. I took the job partially to see whether the planning approach I had developed was really successful or whether I had just been lucky in Hawaii.

Dunfey Hotel Properties

Since purchasing the Parker House, the Dunfeys had continued to acquire additional properties and management contracts as the opportunities presented themselves.[1] In 1972, for instance, when Aetna Life Insurance acquired Royal Coach Motor Inns, Dunfey was hired to manage four units of this chain, each located on a major suburban highway in Atlanta, Dallas, Houston, and San Mateo, California, respectively. Each was built in an exterior style reminiscent of sixteenth century English Tudor, set off against a round, stonefaced, castelled tower, while the hotel interiors were decorated in a Scottish clan theme. The previous owners had gone bankrupt.

By mid-1980, Dunfey Hotels fully or partially owned, leased, or managed 22 properties in the United States and Europe, containing a total of 8,950 rooms (*Exhibit 1*). Fourteen of these properties had been part of the Dunfey organization for six years or more. Each hotel was managed by a general

manager who headed an executive operating committee (EOC) of department heads.

The Dunfey inns and hotels were divided into four groups, each directed by a group director of operations (*Exhibit 2* shows a corporate organization chart). These groups were as follows:

1. Dunfey Classic & Luxury Hotels (four properties: the Parker House, Boston: the Ambassador East, Chicago; the Berkshire Place, New York; and The Marquette, Minneapolis).
2. Dunfey Major Meeting & Convention Hotels (seven properties, located in Atlanta, Dallas, Houston, Cape Cod, San Mateo, New York, and Washington).
3. Dunfey Inns and Airport Hotels (nine properties; located in New England and Pennsylvania).
4. International Hotels (two properties, located in London and Paris).

Some of the airport hotels and motor inns were affiliated, for marketing purposes only, with another chain (Sheraton or Howard Johnson). Although this affiliation had the advantage of linking the inns to national advertising campaigns and toll-free telephone reservation numbers, it did nothing for the visibility of the Dunfey organization.

Between 1974 and 1979, average occupancy, systemwide, increased from 56 percent to 72 percent. A financial summary, showing total revenues and operating profits for all U.S. units in the Dunfey organization, both owned and managed, appears below:

Dunfey Hotels Corporation Financial Summary
(U.S. units only)

Year	Total Revenues	Operating Profit
1976	$ 58 million	$ 7 million
1977	72 million	9 million
1978	88 million	16 million
1979	120 million	21 million
1980 (est.)	165 million	34 million

Jon Canas and the Dunfey "System"

When Canas joined Dunfey in May 1975, the company had a marketing staff, but not

---

[1]Between 1975 and 1980, the company had discontinued its relationship with twelve units. This turnover included properties that no longer fitted in with the Dunfey product line, either because of product, market, or owners' objectives. The properties replacing them tended to be larger and more important hotels.

EXHIBIT 1

Properties Owned or Managed by Dunfey Hotels, October 1980

Group	Type	Property	Location	Year Acquired	Status*	No. of Rooms
1	Classic Hotels	Ambassador East	Chicago, IL	1977	P	300
		Berkshire Place	New York, NY	1978	P	500
		Marquette	Minneapolis, MN	1979	M	270
		Parker House	Boston, MA	1969	F	550
2	Meeting and Convention Hotels	Dunfey Atlanta Hotel	Atlanta, GA	1971	F	400
		Dunfey Dallas Hotel	Dallas, TX	1971	F	650
		Dunfey Houston Hotel	Houston, TX	1971	L	450
		Dunfey San Mateo Hotel	San Mateo, CA	1971	F	300
		Dunfey Hyannis Resort & Conference Center	Cape Cod, MA	1972	F	250
	Other Metropolitan Hotels	New York Statler	New York, NY	1979	P	1,800
		The Shoreham	Washington, D.C.	1979	P	900
3	Inns	Howard Johnson's Motor Inn	Newton, MA	1970	L	275
		Sheraton Inn and Lamie's Tavern	Hampton, NH	1958	F	30
		Sheraton Lexington	Lexington, MA	1967	F	120
		Sheraton N.E. Philadelphia	Philadelphia, PA	1973	F	200
		Sheraton, Tobacco Valley	Windsor, CT	1968	F	130
		Sheraton Wayfarer	Manchester, NH	1962	F	200
	Airport Hotels	Sheraton Airport Inn	Philadelphia, PA	1974	M	350
		Sheraton Inn	South Portland, ME	1973	F	130
		Sheraton Airport Inn	Warwick, RI	1973	F	125
4	International Hotels	London Tara Hotel	London, England	1976	F	850
		Hotel Commodore	Paris, France	1979	L	170
	TOTAL: 22 Hotels					8,950 Rooms

*Key: F = Fully owned by Dunfey Hotels
P = Partially owned by Dunfey Hotels (joint venture with management contract)
L = Leased by Dunfey Hotels
M = Strictly management contract

SOURCE: Company records.

451

EXHIBIT 2
Corporate Organization Chart, December 1980

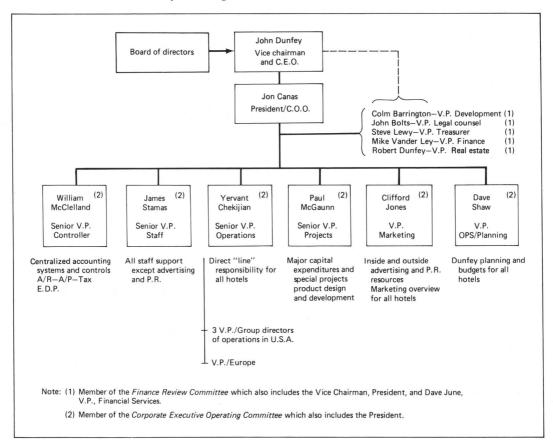

Board of directors → John Dunfey, Vice chairman and C.E.O.

Jon Canas, President/C.O.O.

Colm Barrington—V.P. Development (1)
John Bolts—V.P. Legal counsel (1)
Steve Lewy—V.P. Treasurer (1)
Mike Vander Ley—V.P. Finance (1)
Robert Dunfey—V.P. Real estate (1)

William McClelland (2) — Senior V.P. Controller
Centralized accounting systems and controls A/R—A/P—Tax E.D.P.

James Stamas (2) — Senior V.P. Staff
All staff support except advertising and P.R.

Yervant Chekijian (2) — Senior V.P. Operations
Direct "line" responsibility for all hotels
3 V.P./Group directors of operations in U.S.A.
V.P./Europe

Paul McGaunn (2) — Senior V.P. Projects
Major capital expenditures and special projects product design and development

Clifford Jones (2) — V.P. Marketing
Inside and outside advertising and P.R. resources Marketing overview for all hotels

Dave Shaw (2) — V.P. OPS/Planning
Dunfey planning and budgets for all hotels

Note: (1) Member of the *Finance Review Committee* which also includes the Vice Chairman, President, and Dave June, V.P., Financial Services.

(2) Member of the *Corporate Executive Operating Committee* which also includes the President.

an organized marketing effort. Recalled Canas:

> The operation was characterized by extremely tight cost control, declining occupancy, and declining market share. Internally, many units were perceived to be at the end of their life cycle. We moved quickly to take some specific actions which paid off, and we were helped along by an improving economy beginning in 1976. Group sales doubled in three years and occupancy went from below the industry average to above.

In reviewing the specific areas of the business that the company had concentrated on, Canas divided the years 1975–80 into three distinct periods:

> Our greatest need during 1975 and 1976 was to build occupancy. I don't have to tell you that profit in the hotel business comes from selling rooms, and we did everything possible to "keep the lights on," as they say in the industry. This meant going after any and all types of business, including lower rated (in terms of revenue-per-room night) market segments. As an example, we found early success in attracting what we call "training and destiny" business. This is primarily in-residence programs centered around training sessions, often lasting five to eight weeks. One example would be a flight attendant training program by an airline. Such programs are typically repeated many times over the course of a year by the same company, and effectively amount to an extended rental of space in the hotel. The meetings are planned far in advance and

don't require elaborate arrangements such as banquet facilities; demand is fairly price sensitive. Of course, as occupancy began to improve, we instituted a policy of actively pursuing higher rated segments and gradually substituting this new business for the lower rated segments.

During 1977 and 1978, we embarked on a major program to improve the overall appearance of our properties. In most cases this involved renovating, restoring, repositioning, and remarketing individual properties. Basically, we made the decision to *reject* the life cycle assumptions which prevailed in the firm at the time. The Parker House in Boston is a good example of this philosophy. The Parker House was an old property which had a deteriorating and outdated physical plant, declining occupancy, and had been given up on by the previous management. We saw an opportunity in the hotel's heritage—and the fact that it occupied an excellent location in a metropolitan area where quality lodging was in short supply. The result of this renovation was dramatic increases in occupancy and profitability.

Now as room occupancy rates topped-out on a companywide basis, we sought revenue in other departments. We went into a very creative period where new restaurants and lounges were created. We didn't just open a room, we created a *concept*. A key product of our "creative period" is the Tingles lounge and discotheques located in several of our hotels; these discos were unique in that the sound, loud over the dance floor, but softer at surrounding tables, allowed people to sit, relax, and converse. As an example of the impact on revenue, the conversion of the lounge in the Atlanta Hotel to a Tingles took food and beverage revenue from $8–9,000 per week to over $25,000 weekly in that room.

In 1979 we entered a new phase. With both room and food and beverage (F&B) revenues peaking, we turned our attention to better cost management to maintain profit growth. We brought in an outside consulting firm to help us develop a rather sophisticated cost management/payroll efficiency system. The system was tested at the Parker House in 1977–78 and was expanded to our other units in 1978–79. In addition, we sought cost savings in centralized purchasing and in better heat, light, and power management.

So in looking back, I suppose you could say

we concentrated our efforts on different areas of the business at different times. We were consciously trying to improve the "state of the art" in all areas of the hotel business, and I think the results show that we succeeded.

The situation facing Dunfey in 1975 was surprisingly similar to that of the Sheraton situation in Hawaii when I became sales manager: the mixed bag of food and lodging businesses grouped under the Dunfey corporate name ran the gamut from small, outlying motels to larger urban hotels. In fact, unlike Sheraton, the Dunfey group lacked a common name and identity—there were Sheratons, a Howard Johnson's, a group of four hotels purchased from Royal Coach renamed Dunfey Hotels, as well as several properties which stood alone in terms of identification. Thus, it was out of a need to simplify the management task that the Dunfey Planning Process and the Dunfey Management Approach evolved.

In essence, our approach to marketing planning is based on the belief that there exists a unique strategy or market position for each property which will maximize revenues in the long term. While other hoteliers were focusing on product efficiency and standardization, at Dunfey our commonality became the planning process. Of course, we've come a long way since 1975. In particular, we have grouped our hotels in a way where we can take advantage of some economies of scale in marketing. However, our basic approach is still at the individual hotel marketing level.

THE DUNFEY PLANNING PROCESS

As a first step toward development of a management system for all the Dunfey properties, Canas had drafted a series of internal documents. "The Dunfey Management Approach" and "The Way We Work" enunciated a management philosophy based on the conviction that each hotel had to recognize and satisfy certain needs from its customers, owners, and employees. The third document, titled "The Dunfey Planning Process," laid out a clearly defined system of annual and quadrimester (four-month) planning, dealing with objectives and strategies relating to customers, owners, and employees.

Canas believed that the planning system

for any given unit must begin with the needs of one or more clearly identified customer segments which, when related to the nature and extent of competition, served to determine the positioning the hotel would have in the marketplace. Time and again, remarked Canas, he had seen chains, which had standardized their offerings against certain market segments, expand unsuccessfully into geographic areas that already had an excess of hotel rooms serving those same segments.

He emphasized that profitability in the hotel business was primarily based on the revenue side and stressed the importance of good rooms merchandising through a specific planning process which was evaluated with the help of a performance measure he called Room Sales Efficiency (RSE).[2]

The key to good rooms merchandising and to good cost control, he said, was accurate forecasting of demand at all times of the week and all seasons of the year.

Every year, the management of each Dunfey hotel had to prepare both an annual plan and a series of three quadrimester (four-month) plans, referred to as Q-Plans. The planning process for each hotel proceeded through four basic steps, supported by appropriate documentation.

1. Assess supply-demand relationship—by examining the type (e.g., conventions, tourists, business travelers, etc.) and quantity of customers available in a given geographic market. A careful evaluation was made of the positioning of competitive hotels against each segment.
2. Determine where Dunfey *should be* in terms of the market position of the hotel as a whole, and of each food and beverage outlet within that hotel.
3. Identify the gap between the hotel's current position and the desired position.
4. Structure the measures required to move the hotel and F&B outlets toward the desired market position. Requests for capital expendi-

tures—to add to or improve facilities—were a key element of Step 4.

The outcome of Steps 2, 3, and 4 was a "Mission Statement" for each hotel which had as its input the supply/demand relationship, and as its output a set of specific operating objectives for all members of the field operations team.

Exhibit 3 summarizes the planning process. In essence, broad strategic goals embodied in the Mission Statement were "stepped down" into key result areas (KRAs)—specific actions to be undertaken in support of unit or departmental objectives—via a series of annual planning forms referred to as Y1s (unit objectives and strategies), Y2s (departmental objectives and strategies), and Y3s (specific goals for each unit and department objective). These goals formed the basis for the employees' incentive plan. Similar planning efforts, with a shorter-term focus, were undertaken each quadrimester; these were referred to as "Q-Plans."

The planning process for each unit (hotel) was carried out by that unit's executive operating committee (EOC) with the participation of the corporate planning committee (CPC). The unit EOC usually consisted of the general manager (GM), assistant general manager or resident manager, sales director, rooms manager, food and beverage (F&B) manager, and personnel director. The CPC comprised Jon Canas, the controller and five vice presidents in charge of operations, staff support, product design, profit planning, and marketing. The CPC was assisted in its review of individual unit plans by the vice president-sales, the corporate F&B director, and the relevant group director of operations.

Each group director of operations was responsible for coordinating the preparation of key planning documents by each of the unit EOCs in his group of hotels. The various documents were submitted to the corporate planning committee for approval in a succession of steps carried out from July 1 to November 1 of each year. Units were required to submit an outline of their pre-

---

[2]RSE equals the total room sales revenue received during a period divided by the total revenues that could have been obtained if all available rooms had been sold at the maximum price.

EXHIBIT 3

Dunfey Hotels Unit Planning Process

OBJECTIVE: Corporate Planning Committee (CPC) to provide corporate input and direction for each unit's 1981 Mission and Annual Plan; the CPC includes the Corporate Executive Operating Committee (see *Exhibit 2*) plus, as appropriate, Vice President—Sales, Corporate Food and Beverage Director, and the relevant Group Director of Operations (GDO).

    A. *For the CPC to do this, it needs:*

        1. *Marketing Assessment, which includes:*

            a. 1–3 page summary of supply/demand analysis.

            b. 1–page report to indicate if S/D calls for a significant change in strategies or product.

            c. Historical and Proposed (1981) Market Segmentation and F&B and total revenues.

        2. *Financial Assessment, which includes:*

            a. 1 page, outlining:

                1. Corporate Objectives for the Unit.

                2. Are we meeting Corporate objectives (if not, why)?

            b. Historical Financial Summary for 3–5 years showing financial results and key statistics.

        3. *Outside Owners' Assessment:*[*]

            a. Page outlining outside owners' Objectives.

            b. Assessment of current results.

    B. The CPC will review the above material resulting in a memorandum to the GDO and Unit EOC outlining:

        1. Unit is on track and should not change direction.

O.K. TO PROCEED
TO ITEMS C AND D

        2. Unit is on track except for certain items (outlined) which should be corrected (no major direction change).

NOT O.K. TO PROCEED
TO C AND D

        3. Unit is off track seriously—people will be assigned to assist in making major direction changes.

    C. The Director of Marketing and GDO will then write the Unit Mission Statement and send it to the units (after CPC has approved the wording).

    D. Unit EOC will then prepare Y-1, Y-2, and Y-3 (GDO and Corporate Staff must review and approve).

    E. CPC will have final approval on Item D.

[*]For properties managed by Dunfey Hotels for outside owners.

liminary thinking in July in order that the CPC could provide early feedback on the appropriateness of tentative plans.

Based on these early submissions, the CPC had, by early August, classified individual hotel plans as:

- "green," signifying that the unit was on track and should not change direction;
- "yellow," signifying that the unit was on track except for certain items (outlined) which should be corrected (no major direction change);
- "red," indicating that the unit was seriously off

EXHIBIT 3 (continued)

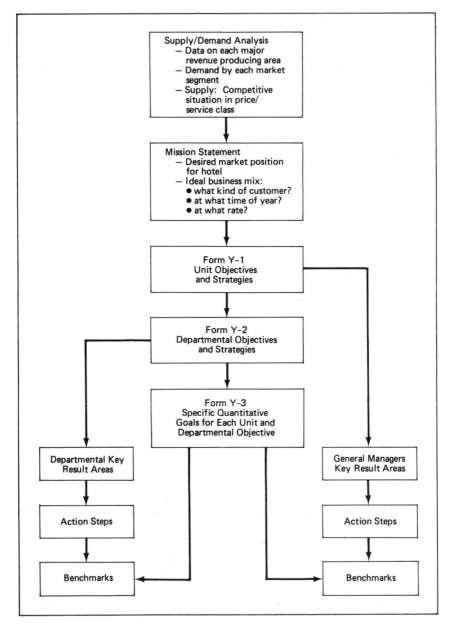

track—corporate staff would be assigned to assist in making major direction changes.

Each unit EOC, working with their group director, was required to prepare a Mission Statement addressing the following questions:

- What type of customer are we aiming for?
- Where do we stand versus the competition?
- What are we trying to be?
- Where should we focus our efforts to satisfy targeted customers, as well as dealing with owners/corporate needs and also employees' needs?

The hotel business, noted Canas, was operations oriented, involving a multitude of basic activities that were repeated again and again, yet could be done in a number of different ways. He continued:

We believe that people carry out functions in different ways depending on the purpose they have in mind. The GM may have one purpose, the F&B manager another—and neither may be in concert with the corporation. So, as simplistic as it sounds, the Mission Statement integrates the activity of unit and corporate management. Any management team that has succeeded in crystallizing and communicating the mission of the hotel will find the various departments pulling together, in the same direction, to create the sought-after hotel experience for the customer. It provides more fulfillment for the employees and better results for the owners and the corporation. Also, the process helps achieve agreement between corporate and unit management.

The Ideal Business Mix

"The most important part of the mission," Canas noted, "deals with what we call the IBM—ideal business mix. This defines the customer segments we will direct our sales efforts toward at various times of the year." He elaborated:

There are many ways to segment the market. The first, of course, is the way we categorize business on our control reports: for instance, pure transient, regular corporate group, bus tours, and so forth. In addition, we segment our marketing effort by geography and by industry, and we assign sales coverage to whatever groupings seem to make sense for a particular area.

The point is that, once we identify our desired segments, it becomes a simpler task to set objectives for the operating departments—such as sales, rooms, and food and beverage. We've found that certain segments of the market tend to have common needs—or "reason to buy." Very often the marketing challenge is to define these needs: is the customer primarily interested in price, in location, in facilities, in social status—or is he just looking for a hotel consistent with his personal tastes in furnishings and food?

The ideal business mix also carries implications for our capital spending and renovation and maintenance decisions. We often say, "We could reach this segment *if* we had certain facilities." The *if* here is important: we may have an intended market position, but we must have programs and facilities to reach it. The restoration and revitalization of the Parker House taught us a lot about repositioning—a lesson we have been able to apply to other properties in the chain.

After we have outlined our goals by type of customer, amount of room nights, period of year and rates, then we ask two further questions: (1) How do we market—how do we reach these customers? And (2) How do we deliver? (And deliver at a *profit?*)

Our Rooms Merchandising Plan and the supporting Account Coverage Program guide our sales efforts. As part of the Rooms Merchandising Plan, you have your ideal business mix prioritized by segments and by lead time in their respective buy decisions. If, for example, a convention cancels 9 months ahead of time, then you go after alternative segments. It's like starting all over again. But, at least you will have identified in advance where you are going to go to make up that business.

Most hotels hire a sales manager and tell him or her to "fill the rooms." This usually works in the short term, but is not a good business approach in the long term. Customers contribute to the atmosphere or hotel experience; you should choose your clientele selectively to match your market position. In our system we specify: (1) a certain kind of customer at (2) a certain time of year at (3) a certain rate.

With the Rooms Merchandising Plan you know what to ask sales and reservations people to do. In general, in the industry, salespeople often don't know who to see, they don't know how many rooms are available, and they don't know what rate to charge. At Dunfey we provide these guidelines as closely as possible in order to maximize our profitability and productivity.

In general, we find there is an inverse relationship in the lead time between the buy decision and consumption by various market segments and the rate we can get. In other words, the farther in advance groups book, the cheaper the rate usually is. So, most hotels used to book business way in advance, without consideration of more desirable business which could be booked later on.

So, the moral for the periods of time where we anticipate strong demand—and since we have a limited supply of rooms—is that we shouldn't sell on a first-come, first-served basis. For better profits, we plan the IBM proportion which is set aside for long lead time groups and for shorter lead time groups, and then save some capacity for higher rated walk-in business.

When business for the future begins to pick up, we try to monitor whether we're attracting our target customers. We want to build our business with the correct market segments—not just fill rooms—because we're building an image for the future and the profile of customers we take in has a tremendous impact on the position of the hotel. Of course, when occupancy is very low, oftentimes we will sell rooms to less desirable segments, but as we build occupancy, we can become more selective in our marketing.

Now, talking about the Account Coverage Program, in a lot of cases we find that 20 percent of the accounts give us 80 percent of our business. Therefore, it is important to identify, qualify, and quantify all our accounts to set proper sales priorities. It also allows us to know what accounts we'll have to approach to get what business. Moreover, we identify what "buy decisions" exist for each individual account. For instance, for corporate groups it's usually either a "price buy," a "location buy," or a "facilities buy."

Also, our sales department provides a significant amount of information and feedback on our supply-demand studies. Through the direct salespeople we know what to sell, to whom, and at what rates. We truly use "need satisfaction" as a sales approach to sell and get repeat sales.

A MANAGEMENT ISOLATION MEETING

An isolation meeting—so designated because the participants were isolated from the interruptions of the home office—was held in the early fall of 1979 to discuss the status of the 1980 planning process and to reinforce understanding of Dunfey management philosophies among the top 15 corporate operations and marketing executives.

Jon Canas opened the meeting by reiterating some of the basic precepts of the Dunfey Management Approach:

The Dunfey Management Approach is companywide. It includes not only the concepts inherent in the way we look at our business, but also includes the process and the systems through which we operate. We must have agreement at top on our philosophies. That means amongst all of us. And then we must attempt to achieve concurrence at lower levels.

What we're saying is that the traditional "get results and we don't care how you do it" doesn't work at Dunfey. We *do care* how you do it! We're concerned with the manner in which results are obtained.

The mission becomes the point of reference for the selection of unit objectives and strategies. The process to be followed by the EOC is to ask: "If we were totally successful in reaching our mission, what are the desirable things that would happen, or desirable conditions that would prevail (positive indicators of success), and what are the undesirable conditions that should be eliminated (negative indicators of success)?"

It's here that we should use the scenario approach: That is, take any aspect of the operations—such as the guest experience at the front desk—and talk through what would happen if we were successful. Each department and facet of the business should be able to visualize what the operation would look like if fully successful. Out of this come the specific action steps that we can focus on as our key result areas—KRAs.

Each department must understand what was expected of it, continued Canas, and how it contributed to the whole. "Sometimes," he observed, "we move too fast from the mission to our planning structure without understanding the implications of what we're doing."

Pushing the Dunfey Approach Down the Organization

Following a brief discussion of the basic approach, Canas turned to his area of principal concern.

Overall, I think you will agree we have been successful in establishing the Dunfey business philosophy among members of the organization down through the level of the EOCs of each hotel. The challenge I want to discuss with you today is in modifying the behavior of people farther down in the organization. In order to convey our philosophy and our approach to the customer, we must push a commitment to our management style down to the very lowest levels of the organization. This is a particular problem when, like us, you take on many new people during the year.

Also, we have had some areas of confusion, such as in defining KRAs. When we talk about key result areas, we're talking about the 20 percent of items against which we can devote effort which will account for 80 percent of the success in reaching our goals. A good selection of KRAs requires a narrow focus and clear delineation of those few key areas which will make the biggest difference in our results at the end of the year.

Now, for instance, if the food and beverage manager gives us 36 things he wants to do, these are *not* KRAs. Most of these are just doing his job; after we get through those, there are probably one or two KRAs which we can identify which will really make a quantum improvement in his operations. If he works 14 hours a day and doesn't accomplish his KRAs, he has failed. But if a manager has a list of 17 KRAs, he just doesn't understand our planning process!

Yervant Chekijian, at the time group director of operations for the three Dunfey Classic Hotels, caught Canas's eye and offered an illustration:

I can point to an example of that at the Ambassador East. The engineers had many KRAs but I noticed the stoppers in the sinks weren't working. I asked them to get to the basic problems like stoppers in the sink before they submitted a bunch of lofty KRAs. And I mentioned to them that they shouldn't just say they're going to fix the stoppers, they should propose an action plan as follows:

1. Inspection.
2. Locate the problems.
3. Define the scope of work.
4. Allocate man-hours.

5. Commit to having the job completed by a specific date.

Canas nodded agreement and added:

What we need is a scenario documented for each member of the operating team. We need to describe a certain level of service, start setting some standards of guest expectations, and relate the scenarios to these. Otherwise, the people we are dealing with at the lower levels easily forget the basics that we are expecting from them.

Canas turned towards the group directors of operations. "I guess you could say that our planning process and programs have given Dunfey people a common language. It also means we can transfer people from property to property and they will know the system." He went on to say, "One of the things I need to know is how well this planning process is actually being implemented by the EOC in each of our hotels."

Yervant Chekijian answered:

At the Parker House, the EOC meets on a weekly basis to go through the Q-Plan and review benchmarks. At the Ambassador East, on the other hand, they work with it, but they have a tendency to be overwhelmed by what happens during the day—putting out fires, if you will. They usually "intend" to use the plan when things are "normal." One general manager did the plan three times—over and over again—threw up his hands, and asked me if he should get back to work. My answer was, "How can you work without a plan?"

A regional director of sales observed that in some ways the plan was "sophisticated—even scary—but it's very natural when you get into it." Chekijian responded that the plan would not get used if its content wasn't real. The group directors, he said, must be responsible for ensuring that individual hotels not only understood the plan but had also proposed realistic goals and action steps.

Canas then turned the discussion towards the question of contingency planning:

We didn't predict the slowdown in business resulting from the 1979 gasoline shortages until nine months into the year. Very frankly, the oil crisis just wasn't predicted, so we didn't have a "Plan B" in marketing. However, we had one in cost control, which is a lot easier to implement. Another question is, how do you build in sales flexibility when rooms merchandising calls for such advance bookings?

Jurgen Demisch, group director of operations for Dunfey's Inns division, offered a solution: "If sales aren't coming in, we can go to the sales force and ask them to use their account coverage program and get more business from the segments lower down the list."

"So, what you're saying," responded Canas, "is that we already have a system. We have sales action plans, pricing flexibility, ability to cut costs over a 30-day period, and an account coverage program. What we need now is to fully learn to use these things."

"Overall, I see our planning as an evolutionary process," remarked Demisch. "As people learn to work with the plan, they become Dunfeyized, and then when these people are promoted, they can get into the plan from day 1 at any new property."

"We must get the planning process down to the third level: to restaurant managers, engineers, etc.—down the organization," Canas emphasized. "What I think we need for your division, Jurgen, is a simplification of The Way We Work. All the ingredients must be there and we don't want to short-circuit it—but Jurgen, we must find a way to have a simplified planning process for a division like yours where you take in so many new people in a short period of time. After all, the basic objective is to be professional innkeepers."

Chuck Barren, group director of operations for several medium-sized hotels, entered the discussion:

At Hyannis we have a very structured, Dunfeyized team. They are using the planning process and they're moving on without looking back to where they were. We've had a new sales manager in there for 10 days and he already has an excellent plan for the first quarter. The planning system was readily applied here and worked very well.

Baltimore was initially a distress property, and we said, "Do we really want to work from a checklist?" After three months, we went into the planning process. The owners sat in at our planning meetings and it really helped *them* understand our side of the business and to set mutual objectives.

It's clear that the planning process tends to break down where we don't have Dunfeyized people. And where this occurs, we should have a checklist or a simplified version of the plan to use in situations like takeovers.

Conclusion of Meeting

In answer to a question from one participant, Canas conceded that Dunfey had indeed developed its own management language, which made it hard to acculturate new people, and especially to bring in top management people at the operations level. On the other hand, he felt that the Dunfey process still allowed individual styles to come through, and in fact, called on the creativity of each manager. "The process provides no solutions," he stated, "only managers do!"

Before the meeting adjourned Canas reiterated the essence of the corporate operating mission, which he read to participants:

To create and/or maintain the structure that provides for the appropriate satisfaction of specifically defined needs of targeted customers, owners, and employees.

He added:

The key here is that we're talking about a structure—and a structure has strength. It has durability. It's an entity which must be full and self-supporting. The structure is our management philosophy and our planning process which, when implemented properly, will provide for the needs of owners, employees, and customers.

Index

B

C

M

N